Praise for *A Reader for College Writers*

A Reader for College Writers *is a well-planned, organized, student-and-teacher-friendly text. The models
make sense and the writing prompts are helpful transitions for writing.*

—John Isaacs, Waynesburg College

*Buscemi's reader is a good one. The essays he offers
work well and address a rich diversity of both ideas and
peoples; in addition, the various sections of the anthol-
ogy reinforce one another in effective ways. The sections
on the writing process add to the text's worth, for they
address writing concerns from the word to the essay,
helping the writer see necessary connections.*

—Bill Clemente, Peru State College

A Reader for College Writers *guides students through
the writing process, offers excellent exercises for getting started, and provides essays for critical reading and
modeling.*

—Diane Abdo, University of Texas at San Antonio

*It is complete, it has a variety of reading selections, and
it is organized well.*

—Robert Bailey, South Suburban College

SEVENTH EDITION

A Reader for College Writers

Santi V. Buscemi

Middlesex County College

McGraw-Hill
Higher Education

Boston   Burr Ridge, IL   Dubuque, IA   New York   San Francisco   St. Louis
Bangkok   Bogotá   Caracas   Kuala Lumpur   Lisbon   London   Madrid   Mexico City
Milan   Montreal   New Delhi   Santiago   Seoul   Singapore   Sydney   Taipei   Toronto

McGraw-Hill
Higher Education

A Division of The McGraw-Hill Companies

Published by McGraw-Hill, an imprint of The McGraw-Hill Companies, Inc., 1221 Avenue of the Americas, New York, NY 10020. Copyright © 2008. All rights reserved. No part of this publication may be reproduced or distributed in any form or by any means, or stored in a database or retrieval system, without the prior written consent of The McGraw-Hill Companies, Inc., including, but not limited to, in any network or other electronic storage or transmission, or broadcast for distance learning.

This book is printed on acid-free paper.

1 2 3 4 5 6 7 8 9 0 DOC/DOC 0 9 8 7

ISBN: 978-0-07-353309-4
MHID: 0-07-353309-2

Editor in Chief: *Emily Barrosse*
Publisher: *Emily Barrosse*
Sponsoring Editor: *Christopher Bennem*
Marketing Manager: *Tami Wederbrand*
Developmental Editor: *Laura Olsen*
Project Manager: *Amanda Peabody*
Manuscript Editor: *Patterson Lamb*
Design Manager: *Andrei Pasternak*
Photo Research: *Natalia Peschiera*
Production Supervisor: *Rich Devitto*
Composition: *10/12 Berkeley Old Style Book by Laserwords Private Limited*
Printing: *45# New Era Matte Plus, R..R..Donnelley & Sons/Crawfordsville, IN*

Library of Congress Cataloging-in-Publication Data

Buscemi, Santi V.
    A reader for college writers / Santi V. Buscemi. — 7th ed.
        p. cm.
    Includes index.
    ISBN-13: 978-0-07-353309-4 (acid-free paper)
    ISBN-10: 0-07-353309-2 (acid-free paper)
    1. College readers.   2. English language—Rhetoric—Problems, exercises etc. 3. Report writing—Problems, exercises, etc.   I. Title.
PE1417.B853 2008
808'.0427—dc22

                                                                    2007011114

The Internet addresses listed in the text were accurate at the time of publication. The inclusion of a Web site does not indicate an endorsement by the authors or McGraw-Hill, and McGraw-Hill does not guarantee the accuracy of the information presented at these sites.

www.mhhe.com

*For **Joseph** and **Theresa Buscemi** and for all the other Sicilian heroes who came to this country to make a better life for their children*

About the Author

Santi V. Buscemi teaches reading and writing at Middlesex County College in Edison, NJ. He is the author of AllWrite! 2.0 with Online Handbook, *McGraw-Hill's interactive electronic writing program, and co-author of* The Basics, Writing Today, *and* 75 Readings Plus. *He has lectured on developmental education at national conferences in the United States and South Africa.*

CONTENTS

CHAPTER 3

Special Paragraphs: Writing Introductions and Conclusions   125

SECTION TWO

Word Choice and Sentence Patterns   161

CHAPTER 4

Word Choice: Using Literal and Figurative Language Effectively   163

CHAPTER 5

Sentence Structure: Creating Emphasis and Variety   193

SECTION THREE

Description and Narration 229

CHAPTER 6

Description 233

CHAPTER 7

Narration   275

SECTION FOUR

Exposition   311

CHAPTER 8

Illustration   315

CHAPTER 9

Comparison and Contrast   349

CHAPTER 10

Process Analysis   385

CHAPTER 11

Definition   421

SECTION FIVE

Argumentation and Persuasion   463

CHAPTER 12

Argumentation 475

CHAPTER 13

Persuasion 515

THEMATIC TABLE OF CONTENTS

A Reader for College Writers is a brief, yet comprehensive rhetoric and reader for students in first-year composition courses. Trimmed down so the instruction can be managed in one semester, the text retains its original purpose: to help students read carefully, respond thoughtfully, and use those responses as creative springboards for writing. More than ever, research continues to affirm the close relationship between analytical reading and effective writing. *A Reader for College Writers* insists on this connection.

New to the Seventh Edition

A CHAPTER ON DEFINITION

This new chapter contains complete coverage of the many uses and forms of extended definition in college and professional writing with essays on varied subjects from the nature of evil to the Northern Lights. Challenging but very teachable essays by Joseph Epstein, Peggy Noonan, and David Blankenhorn appear here, as does a wonderful student research paper entitled "The Ordinariness of Evil."

PAIRED READINGS ON IMMIGRATION IN THE PERSUASION CHAPTER

This edition contains an exciting set of three new readings in the chapter on persuasion—including a piece that originally appeared in the University of Virginia's student newspaper—that debate offering in-state college tuition to undocumented immigrants.

OVER 20 NEW READING SELECTIONS

The essays and poems in the collection represent a range of cultural and academic interests and are enhanced in this edition by 20 new selections. New to this edition are essays by Amy Tan, Matt Welch, Peggy Noonan, Bailey White, and Richard Lederer. Several other new pieces, such as the one by the editors of *The Onion*, increase the presence of comic and satiric material in the text, and they show students that writing about even serious subjects can be fun.

A NEW, TRIM FORMAT

The author has streamlined the book considerably, keeping only the information that will be most helpful to students in composition courses, and retaining only the most interesting readings to spur classroom discussion and serve as models.

Proven Features of *A Reader for College Writers*

FOCUS ON CRITICAL READING AND WRITING

The introductory section "Getting Started" covers techniques important to developing critical reading and college writing skills. It stresses the fact that both reading and writing are processes and that there is a natural connection between the two. Moreover, the pedagogy appearing in each chapter introduction and after each selection shows students how to exploit this connection. Several sample student essays, which illustrate techniques for analysis, annotation, summary, and synthesis, appear in Getting Started. Yet another student piece illustrates the writing process. The creation of this essay is followed step-by-step from initial reading and note-taking through outlining and drafting to revision, editing, and proofreading.

ROBUST SUPPORT FOR READING SELECTIONS

Each reading selection is preceded by headnotes; an author biography, questions and comments under *Preparing to Read,* and a vocabulary section provide a context for reading and reinforce the notion that critical reading—like writing—is a process. Each reading selection is followed by Questions for Discussion, items for Thinking Critically, and Suggestions for Journal Entries, which help students to understand the reading and to draw inspiration from it for their own writing. In addition, the informal responses students make to the Suggestions for Journal Entries can double as prewriting for the formal essays they create in response to the Suggestions for Sustained Writing, which appear at the end of each chapter.

EXTENSIVE COVERAGE OF ARGUMENT AND PERSUASION

In addition to complete coverage of traditional methods of argumentation and persuasion, the two chapters in Section Five discuss both Toulmin and Rogerian argument. Paired readings appear in both chapters. As well, the introduction to this section includes coverage of visual argumentation, with examples of commercial ads and political cartoons.

INCLUSION OF STUDENT WRITING

Every chapter contains *at least* one student essay, with excerpts of the student's rough and final drafts compared in the chapter introductions. Many students welcome this side-by-side analysis; it clearly demonstrates that they can improve if only they approach writing as a meticulous process that includes careful revision and editing. These selections also serve as inspiration by encouraging current users of the text to produce the best writing they can. Indeed, some even express the hope that their work might appear in future editions of the text.

COLLABORATIVE ASSIGNMENTS

Writing to Learn assignments at the end of each chapter offer a step-by-step guide to the process of discussion, research, writing, and revision in groups.

ONLINE LEARNING CENTER, FEATURING RESEARCH PAPER INSTRUCTION

The *Reader for College Writers* Online Learning Center (http://www.mhhe. com/rcw) provides full coverage of the research paper and MLA, featuring an annotated student research paper on the rights of victims of violent crimes. Also important are the very thorough discussions of how to document online sources and to avoid plagiarism—both intended and unintended. The site also includes a variety of links related to the authors and themes of the reading selections.

ACKNOWLEDGMENTS

I sincerely appreciate the comments and suggestions from my colleagues across the country who reviewed the project at various stages: Diane Abdo, University of Texas—San Antonio; Brent Adrian, Central Community College—Grand Island; Charlotte Ash, Walla Walla Community College; Robert Bailey, South Suburban College; Gwen Ball, Golden Gate University; Pam Bell, Gordon College; Bill Clemente, Peru State College; Mark Coley, Tarrant County College; Joyce Goldenstern; Loyola University; John Isaacs; Mark Johnson, Winona State University; Jesse Kavadlo, Maryville University; Terri Long, Boston College; Robert Mayer, College of Southern Idaho; Eric Mein, Northwest Iowa Community College; Joyce Stoffers, Southwestern Oklahoma State University; and Lucette Wood, Linn-Benton Community College.

Among my friends and colleagues at Middlesex County College, I would like to thank Lucille Alfieri, Betty Altruda, Sallie Del Vecchio, Barry Glazer, James Keller, Jack Moskowitz, Georgianna Planko, Renee Price, Yvonne Sisko, Mathew Spano, Helena Swanicke, and Shirley Wachtel for their support and loyalty. I also want to express gratitude to my editors: Laura Olson and Lisa Moore, Victoria Fullard, and Jesse Hassenger at McGraw-Hill. Finally, I must express my love and gratitude to my family: Elaine, Pamela, Michael, and Matthew for supporting and encouraging their "Paka" throughout this revision.

Getting Started

A Reader for College Writers contains short readings by professional and student authors. Each paragraph, essay, and poem is accompanied by discussion questions, suggestions for writing, and other instructional aids.

The reading selections act as springboards to your own writing. Some supply facts and ideas you can include in our own work. Others inspire you to write about similar subjects by drawing details from your own experiences, observations, and readings. In short this book helps you make connections between reading and writing, and it shows you ways to improve both. The rest of the introduction, Getting Started, discusses

1. How to Use This Book
2. Becoming an Active College Reader
3. Using the Writing Process: A Tool for Discovery
4. The Making of a Student Essay: From Prewriting to Proofreading

How to Use This Book

The paragraphs, essays, and poems you will read are accompanied by instructional aids: (1) a note on the author and on the text's origins, (2) material that prepares you to read, (3) a vocabulary list, (4) discussion questions, (5) critical-thinking questions, and (6) suggestions for journal entries (short writings). Also, at the end of each chapter, you will find Suggestions for Sustained Writing (essay writing) as well as one suggestion for a group project. These materials help you make the most of your reading and get started on your own writing. Here's one way to use *A Reader for College Writers;* your instructor might ask you to use another:

1. The book is divided into five sections; each has at least two chapters. Begin each section by reading its introduction, for it contains important information (the introduction to Section I begins on page 00).
2. Next, read the chapter introduction, which explains principles and strategies of writing illustrated by the reading selections in that chapter. The introduction to Chapter 1 begins on page 51.
3. When you get to the individual reading selections, notice that each is preceded by an author biography, a section called Preparing to Read, and a vocabulary list. These help you review the selection. The first selection starts on page 63.

4. Now, read the selection itself; make notes in the margins, underline important ideas, and mark unfamiliar words or ideas, which you can look up before you reread the selection.

5. After you have reread the selection, answer the Questions for Discussion and the Thinking Critically items, which follow it. Try recording your answers on paper, in a computer file, or in the margins of the text.

6. Now, respond to at least one of the Suggestions for Journal Entries. Put your responses in a journal (notebook)—paper or electronic. Making regular journal entries is important. First, writing is mastered only through regular practice, and making journal entries provides this practice. Second, your journal contains responses to the readings, so it helps you make what you have read your own. Most important, keeping a journal helps you gather information for longer projects. Almost all the Suggestions for Sustained Writing (at the end of each chapter) refer to journal entries, so keeping a journal means that you will already have taken the first step in completing a major writing assignment.

7. Choose one of the Suggestions for Sustained Writing at the chapter's end as a prompt for a formal essay. Read each Suggestion carefully; then choose the one that interests you most. Almost all refer to earlier journal suggestions. If you haven't made a journal entry like the one referred to in the Suggestions for Sustained Writing, go back and do so.

8. If your teacher asks you to use library or Internet research in a paper, you might want to review Modern Language Association style, which is explained on this book's website (www.mhhe.com/rcw). If you are unsure about certain writing terms in this book, look them up in the glossary, which appears at the end.

Becoming an Active College Reader

- Preparing to read: Survey
- Reading and taking notes: Engage the text
- Writing an informal outline: Strengthen your grasp of the text
- Conversing with the text: Read it again
- Summarizing: Make what you have read your own
- Responding and Critiquing: Evaluate what you have read
- Synthesizing: Bring ideas together in a new statement

The more you read, the better you will write. Like writing, reading is an active process. Effective readers don't just sit back and absorb words. They *digest, interpret,* and *evaluate* what they read. They interact with the text by considering both *stated* and *unstated* (*implied*) messages. They question *facts* and *assumptions,* evaluate *evidence,* ask *questions,* and apply their own *insights* and *experiences* to what they read.

In college, you will read textbooks; essays in newspapers, journals, and anthologies; scientific materials; poetry, fiction, and other literature; and information on academic, professional, and government websites. Many people read such materials without fully understanding them the first time. If this happens to you, don't worry. Read them a second and third time, discuss them with classmates, or put them aside for a while to allow ideas to develop. (Doing so is like writing multiple drafts of an essay, getting feedback from others, and putting the paper aside before rewriting it.) Most important, don't be afraid to ask your instructor for help both in class and in tutorials.

SPECIAL TIPS ON READING SELECTIONS IN THIS BOOK

1. Prepare for a selection by first reading the author's biography, the vocabulary words, and the Preparing to Read section, which come before it.

2. Take notes while you read. You can do this in many ways, such as listing or outlining ideas on your computer or on a notepad. Two especially good methods are to make notes in the margins of the text and to keep a double-entry notebook. Both are explained below.

3. Answer the Questions for Discussion that appear after each selection in this textbook. Then, complete at least one of the Suggestions for Journal Entries and the Thinking Critically exercise.

PREPARING TO READ: SURVEY

Surveying, also called *previewing,* is an essential first step; it reveals much that will help you read more effectively and easily.

- Begin by looking for clues in the title, especially in essays or scholarly article. Titles often contain hints about content, purpose, and thesis.

- If a *biographical or introductory note* precedes the essay or article—as with the selections in this book—read this first. It should help you understand the cultural, historical, or political context in which the text was written, and it might provide clues to the author's *main idea (thesis).* If the note indicates the publication date or the title of the publication in which the text first appeared, you might be able to conclude something about the author's purpose and intended audience.

- Sometimes, essay writers state their theses (main ideas) in their *introductions or conclusions,* so read the first and last paragraphs carefully. The introductory paragraph(s) can also provide clues about the organization, purpose, and supporting ideas of the essay.

- Read *subheadings or subtitles.* They provide additional insight into the essay's organization. Then *skim* every paragraph for ideas that support the thesis. Often supporting ideas are expressed as conclusions—statements drawn from evidence. Look for words and phrases such as "therefore," "thus," and "as a result," which often introduce such statements.

EXERCISE 1: *Practice what you have learned*   Survey a chapter in a textbook or an article in a newspaper or magazine such as *US News & World Report* or *National Geographic,* or an article assigned by your instructor. You can read articles from such popular magazines online.

READING AND TAKING NOTES: ENGAGE THE TEXT

Some texts can be understood on the literal level. They mean exactly what they say. Others require you to draw inferences (conclusions) for yourself. In such cases, different readers may come up with different, but equally valid, interpretations. Generally, the richer and more complex the text, the more subject it is to interpretation. As you read something *for the first time,* keep the following in mind.

- This time around, focus on the literal meaning alone.
- Use a pencil to underline words and phrases and make notes in the margins. When you read the text a second time, you might want to change, delete, or clarify notes by erasing old material and adding new.
- If you come upon unfamiliar words or references, don't worry. Reading, like writing, involves discovery. But don't break your focus and look up these items immediately. Underline and circle them, but look them up in a dictionary or encyclopedia later.
- Mark the thesis and important ideas that support the thesis.
- In the margins, write comments about points you don't fully understand, find interesting, or want to question.

Study the notes and comments a student made when she first read a *USA Today* editorial entitled "Overreaction to Cloning Claim Poses Other Risks." Published in 2003, it is a statement of that newspaper's position on possible action by Congress to ban all cloning, including the cloning of human embryos, which is used to gather stem cells for medical research. An opposing view, by Kansas Senator Sam Brownback, accompanied that editorial. It appears later in Getting Started.

Overreaction to Cloning Claim Poses Other Risks

A *USA Today* Editorial

M uch of the world is now holding its breath, wonder- 1
ing whether Eve, the supposed first-ever human
clone, born Dec. 26 [2002] is real or a twisted publicity ← *Interesting phrase.*
stunt. Her existence certainly sounds like something out
Meaning? of science fiction: announced by the Raelians, a bizarre
sect that believes the human race was cloned from aliens
25,000 years ago.

The Raelians Clonaid organization promises to pro- 2
vide scientific proof of Eve's authenticity through genetics *Meaning?*
Yea, right! experts, though it refuses to produce Eve or her 31-year-
probably a old American mother. It also claims that four more clones
hoax! are due to be born by February [2003]—a statistic that
Meaning? stretches credulity given that the cloning of mammals
since Dolly the sheep in 1997 has usually taken hundreds *Check out*
of tries and produced Frankenstein-leaning deformities. *on Internet.*

Whether or not Eve proves to be genuine, any clone 3
Why? would catch Americans spectacularly unprepared. That's
because conservative Republicans and the Bush admin-
istration have insisted on pursuing a ban on all cloning.
Their overreach overlooks a more sensible alternative:
Meaning? outlawing the morally reprehensible cloning of humans
Meaning? but permitting cellular cloning that could cure ailments
from Alzheimer's to spinal injuries.

True to form, within day's of Eve's birth announce- 4
ment, conservatives promised a push for Senate legislation to ban all human cloning. . . . Yet such a knee-jerk *Which*
reaction ignores critical differences between cloning of the *ones?*
Meaning? human and therapeutic variety: *Thesis?*

- **Human cloning aims to replicate humans.** It
  requires implanting a cloned embryo into a
  woman's uterus. The Raelians' claims aside, the
  practice holds moral, technical and practical risks.
  Attempts to clone humans are certain to follow the
  path of animal cloning. That means hundreds of

failures and the death within days of most clones that do not reach birth. Survivors, even if they seem healthy, could be time bombs with unknown genetic abnormalities. Besides such vexing moral questions as who has the right to clone another person, family relationships and rights would become a minefield of ambiguity. Eve's mother, for example, would really be her twin.

Meaning?

- **Therapeutic cloning aims to develop medical therapies.** Cloned embryos are grown only up to 14 days, long enough to harvest their stem cells, which may eventually prove useful in treating diseases including Parkinson's, leukemia and diabetes. Embryos aren't implanted in a woman's uterus, the step required to clone a human.

Strong argument!

Supporters of a total ban would shut off this promising avenue of U.S. research. Yet investigations would continue overseas.

Is this point really valid? So what?

5

A far more sensible approach was proposed last year when the National Academy of Sciences called for a five-year renewable ban on the cloning of human beings while allowing research on therapeutic cloning.

Appeal to experts! Seems reasonable.

6

Regardless whether Eve is a clone, her announced arrival delivers a call for responsible action. Like it or not, we already are in a brave new world of medical advances.

Why brave?

7

EXERCISE 2: *Practice what you have learned*   Use a pencil to take notes on an editorial in a newspaper or other periodical. Issues of many newspapers and magazines are available online See, for example the *New York Times* at www.nyt.com. Underline the thesis and supporting ideas, and ask questions or make comments by writing brief notes in the margins.

WRITING AN INFORMAL OUTLINE: STRENGTHEN YOUR GRASP OF THE TEXT

After your first reading, look over the words, phrases, and sentences you have underlined or marked, and read your notes in the margins. This review alone can provide enough information to create an informal outline, which will strengthen your understanding of what you have read. (Such an outline is just like the informal outline you make before writing an essay, as explained later in Getting Started, page 32.)

1. Start by stating the essay's thesis.
2. List each of the major ideas the author uses to support that thesis.
3. Under each of these major ideas, list or summarize important details that illustrate, develop, or otherwise support each of these supporting ideas.

An Alternative: Keep a Double-Entry (Summary/Response) Notebook

Keeping a double-entry notebook is another way to summarize and respond to a text. In the long run, it will help you become a more efficient reader. In the short run, keeping it will help you respond to the Suggestions for Journal Entries, which appear after each reading selection in this textbook.

1. Before reading, draw a line from top to bottom down the middle of the notebook page.
2. Label the left column *Summary,* the right column *Response.*
3. As you read the essay, poem, or other kind of text, *summarize* the major ideas in each paragraph or section in the left column. (A summary condenses—puts in a briefer form—what you have read and expresses it in your own words.)
4. Next, in the right column, write brief responses to the summary statements you made. They can take various forms but will probably be similar to notes you could have written in the text. You might (1) ask a question, (2) disagree with an opinion, (3) identify the central idea (thesis), (4) mark a phrase you especially like, (5) note a word or reference you will need to look up later, (6) explain how the reading relates to you.

Here is Tennyson's "The Eagle," followed by a notebook entry summarizing and responding to the poem:

The Eagle
He clasps the crag with crooked hands;
Close to the sun in lonely lands,
Ring'd with the azure world, he stands.

The wrinkled sea beneath him crawls;
He watches from his mountain walls,
And like a thunderbolt he falls.

Summary	**Response**
Stanza 1—Grasping a large rock, an eagle stands on high and lonely cliff.	The eagle is "close to the sun." He's higher than we are, but also alone. Why are his feet called "hands"?
Stanza 2—The eagle looks down at the sea from on top of a high mountain. He drops down quickly, furiously.	Why is the sea "wrinkled"? Because he's so high up? When he falls, what is he going after? Food? An enemy? "Thunderbolt" is a great word. He's an incredibly majestic, powerful animal—and dangerous, maybe?

CONVERSING WITH THE TEXT: READ IT AGAIN

As you read the text again, pretend to have a conversation with the author. The text is the author's part of the conversation; yours is making marginal notes that do the following:

- Add information that helps you understand a point, state agreement or disagreement, or express your own point of view.
- Draw conclusions from the material, and add insights and facts from your own observations or reading.
- Challenge facts, opinions, statistics, "expert" testimony, or other evidence.
- Challenge illogical conclusions. For example, if a writer claimed that because your college president has a doctorate in English she will not support programs in the technologies, you would challenge that statement as illogical.
- Question the author's use of undocumented sources. If you read that "A recent study proves that listening to rap music makes children aggressive," you might ask questions such as "Which study?" "Who conducted it?" "Where was it published?"

- Comment on the author's tone and language.
  1. Is his or her language fair and objective or is it "loaded"; that is, do the words call up emotions that might interfere with a reader's reasoned response to the material?
  2. Does the author express a legitimate concern, complaint, or purpose, or is his or her position compromised by self-interest, personal feelings, or even ignorance?
  3. If the essay's purpose is to persuade, does the writer remain fair while appealing to the reader's emotions or self-interest, or is his approach biased; that is, does the author tell the reader everything, or does she withhold critical information or present it in a misleading way?
- Make appropriate changes to the notes you made during your first reading.
- Be skeptical; don't believe everything you read. After all, even villains and liars have had their works published. Questioning, challenging, and demanding proof are signs of an enlightened reader.

Here are notes and comments a student made on her second reading of "Overreaction to Cloning Claim Poses Other Risks."

Interesting language draws reader into editorial

Much of the world is now holding its breath, wondering whether Eve, the supposed first-ever human clone, born Dec. 26 [2002] is real or a <u>twisted publicity</u> stunt. Her existence certainly sounds like something out of science fiction: announced by the Raelians, a (bizarre) sect that believes the human race was cloned from aliens 25,000 years ago.

interesting phrase.

meaning? = strange, odd.

meaning? = science of heredity.

meaning? = believability.

good image!

Why? We've known about Dolly since 1997.

The Raelians Clonaid organization promises to provide scientific proof of Eve's authenticity through (genetics) experts, though it refuses t<u>o produce Eve or her 31-year-old American mother</u>. It also claims that four more clones are due to be born by February[2003]—a statistic that stretches (credulity) given that the cloning of mammals since <u>Dolly the sheep in 1997</u> has usually taken hundreds of tries and produced <u>Frankenstein-leaning deformities</u>.

Yea, right! Probably a hoax!

Check out on Internet—British scientists produced first cloned mammal.

Whether or not Eve proves to be genuine, any clone would <u>catch Americans spectacularly unprepared</u>. That's because <u>conservative Republicans</u> and the Bush administration have insisted on pursuing a ban on all cloning.

Why conservatives? Generalization.

1

2

3

Thesis!

meaning? = embryonic

Tone sarcastic why?

Which ones?

Their overreach overlooks a more sensible alternative: outlawing the morally (reprehensible) cloning of humans but permitting (cellular) cloning that could cure ailments from Alzheimer's to spinal injuries.

meaning? = evil

True to form, within day's of Eve's birth announcement, conservatives promised a push for Senate legislation to ban all human cloning. . . . Yet such a knee-jerk reaction ignores critical differences between cloning of the human and (therapeutic) variety:

4

Thesis? - No

meaning? = relating to medical treatment

- **Human cloning aims to replicate humans.** It requires implanting a cloned embryo into a woman's uterus. The Raelians' claims aside, the practice holds moral, technical and practical risks. Attempts to clone humans are certain to follow the path of animal cloning. That means hundreds of failures and the death within days of most clones that do not reach birth. Survivors, even if they seem healthy, could be time bombs with unknown genetic abnormalities. Besides such vexing moral questions as who has the right to clone another person, family relationships and rights would become a minefield of (ambiguity.) Eve's mother, for example, would really be her twin.

supporting idea

good detail!

meaning? = lack of clarity

good example!

- **Therapeutic cloning aims to develop medical therapies.** Cloned embryos are grown only up to 14 days, long enough to harvest their stem cells, which may eventually prove useful in treating diseases including Parkinson's, leukemia and diabetes. Embryos aren't implanted in a woman's uterus, the step required to clone a human.

supporting idea

5

strong argument!

Should we do this because others will?

Supporters of a total ban would shut off this promising avenue of U.S. research. Yet investigations would continue overseas.

Is this point really valid? So what?

6

A far more sensible approach was proposed last year when the National Academy of Sciences called for a five-year renewable ban on the cloning of

Appeals to experts! Seems reasonable.

*Why brave? =
Reference to
Huxley's Brave
New World,
a novel about
cloning.*

human beings while allowing research on therapeutic cloning.

Regardless whether Eve is a clone, her announced arrival delivers a call for responsible action. Like it or not, we already are in <u>a brave</u> new world of medical advances.

*A reasonable
compromise!*

7

EXERCISE 3: Practice what you have learned   Reread the editorial from a newspaper or other periodical that you read earlier. Converse with the author: underline words and sentences and make additional marginal notes. You might also revise or remove notes you made during your first reading. Then, review and, if appropriate, revise the informal outline you made after your first reading.

SUMMARIZING: MAKE WHAT YOU HAVE READ YOUR OWN

Summarizing restates the text's main and supporting ideas in your own words. It requires you to wrestle with the author's language and transform it into your own. Thus, it forces you to put into concrete form ideas and insights that otherwise would have remained vague. Summarizing improves comprehension; if you can summarize accurately, you can be sure that you've understood a selection.

Be Original: Avoid Plagiarism

You can find out more about summarizing, paraphrasing, and quoting in *Writing a Research Paper Using Modern Language Association Style,* which appears on this textbook's website at www.mhhe.com/rcw. For now make sure your summary is your original restatement of the text and that it contains no traces of *plagiarism*—that is, passing off words or ideas of another person as your own.

The two items below summarize the first paragraph of the *USA Today* editorial you read earlier (page 5). The first contains unintentional plagiarism; the second does not.

Unintentional plagiarism: Many people are now <u>wondering whether</u> the claim that a cloned baby girl has actually been born is <u>real</u> or whether the whole thing is just a <u>stunt</u> to get <u>publicity.</u> The claim was made at the end of December 2002 by the Raelians, a

(continued)

cult that <u>believes</u> that humans were <u>cloned from</u>
<u>aliens 25,000 years ago.</u>

More original summary: In late December 2002, a
group called the Raelians claimed that the world's
first cloned human had been born. The Raelians
also claim that visitors from outer space cloned the
human race into existence thousands of years ago.
However, some people believe that the Raelians' news
may be a hoax to get media attention.

The underlined words in the first example come directly from the editorial. Also, this version follows the original's organization too closely. The second example is completely new, in both language and organization. It shows that the student has understood the content of the editorial.

USING THE SPLIT-SCREEN FUNCTION TO PARAPHRASE AND CHECK FOR PLAGIARISM

Most word processors offer a split-screen function, which can aid you in checking for plagiarism and in summarizing material. The split-screen function allows you to scan the original version of a text on the top half of the screen. (This works best for original material in electronic form. Otherwise, you will have to type it in yourself, which you might want to do anyway, especially when taking notes for research.) You can then independently summarize that text on the bottom half of the screen. Each half can be scrolled separately, allowing you to compare specific sentences carefully so as to make your summary more accurate and to eliminate unintentional plagiarism.

Unlike a paraphrase, which only restates the original in new words, a summary also *condenses* the original. Depending on length, a chapter in a textbook or an article in a journal might be summarized in a few paragraphs. A summary of an essay of 1,500–2,000 words might span about 150 words. Read the following tips on writing summaries. Then, read the summary of the *USA Today* editorial, which follows these tips:

• After rereading the text again, review the marginal notes and ideas you have marked.

- As a general rule, begin your summary by stating the essay's thesis (explicit or implied), its purpose, and its intended audience.
- Next, state each of the supporting ideas used to develop the thesis.
- Depending on the thoroughness required, include one or two examples of the details used to develop each supporting idea.
- If you need to use some of the author's own words, introduce them appropriately, and place quotation marks around them (see www.mhhe.com/rcw.)
- Don't summarize each paragraph one by one. Authors often develop supporting ideas with details spread over a few paragraphs, so summarizing every paragraph is often unnecessary. (A summary is a condensation, not the restating of every detail.) Including too much detail can be misleading because it places emphasis on minor aspects of the essay, and it shows that the reader's grasp of the text is weak.

Student Summary of USA Editorial

A USA Today editorial of January 3, 2003, argues that, while US lawmakers should prohibit human cloning, they should encourage cellular cloning, which will help medical researchers find cures to many illnesses. The editorial appeared shortly after the announcement by a group called the Raelians that "the supposed first-ever human clone" was born late last year. According to USA Today, legislation proposed by conservatives in Congress that would prevent human cloning will go too far by also banning research into cellular or "therapeutic" cloning, which produces human embryos from which stem cells can be gotten. Such stem cells can be used in the fight against diseases "including Parkinson's, Alzheimer's, leukemia, and diabetes." Therapeutic cloning poses none of the scientific or ethical problems of cloning human beings. Unlike attempts to clone another individual, it does not involve the placement of a cloned embryo in a host mother, a practice that, in the case of experimentation with animals, has often resulted in the death of the embryo before birth. Even if therapeutic cloning is banned in the United States, it is sure to continue in other parts of the world.

EXERCISE 4: *Practice what you have learned* Write a summary of a newspaper or periodical article. Try using your word processor's split-screen function to do this.

RESPONDING AND CRITIQUING: EVALUATE WHAT YOU HAVE READ

You can respond to the ideas in a text, you can critique (evaluate) its message and presentation, or you can do both. In a *response,* you comment on the author's ideas by agreeing, disagreeing, drawing comparisons, adding new evidence, presenting another point of view, raising questions, applying these ideas to other things you have read or observed, or doing all of the above. You engage the text just as you do when making notes in the margins, but now your part of the conversation is more formal. You are creating your own text, which might complement, add to, or reject the original text. In fact it might do a combination of all of these things.

In a *critique,* you evaluate the text's message and its presentation. Although the words "critique" and "criticism" are related, a critique is not just "critical"; it can mention both strengths and weaknesses. Begin by reviewing your marginal notes and your summary. If necessary, go back to the text itself and reread it. Revise the notes you have already made in light of criteria (measuring sticks) you are using to evaluate what you have read.

Criteria used to evaluate a text can differ from reader to reader. Below are only a few questions you might ask as you critique a text. Perhaps they will help you create some of your own criteria. After you have read all of these questions, read the student critique of the *USA Today* editorial, which follows them.

CRITIQUING: SUGGESTED CRITERIA FOR EVALUATION

- What are the author's credentials? Is the publication in which the essay was first published reputable?
- Are the essay's thesis and purpose clear and reasonable?
- Are supporting ideas logical and well developed?
- Does the author make unsubstantiated claims?

- Does the author use evidence from studies or experts to support the thesis without naming these authorities?
- Is the author impartial, or does he or she use language that appeals to the reader's emotions and self-interest? If the latter, is this language simply strong and moving, or is it unfair or biased?
- Does the author use information that is incomplete or incorrect?
- Does the essay lack important information that you know might contradict one of its supporting ideas or even its thesis?
- Does the author raise important questions and answer them adequately? Does he or she address opposing arguments fairly?
- Is the language of the essay appropriate to the intended audience? Does it contain jargon or other language that is unnecessarily complicated?

Note: When critiquing and responding, feel free to include some of the author's own words if you believe doing so is necessary, but remember to *use quotation marks.*

Matthew Roberts

Professor Spano

ENG 101-33

19 November, 2004

Critique of **USA Today** Editorial:

"Overreaction to Cloning Claim Poses Other Risks"

In arguing for the continuation of research into cellular

or therapeutic cloning, USA Today's editorial "Overreaction to

Cloning Claim Poses Other Risks" (January 3, 2003) takes a

reasonable approach to an issue that, in the last several months,

has been hotly debated in a less-than-productive manner. Citing

a recommendation from the National Academy of Sciences, the

editors argue that, while the cloning of people may be morally

wrong, the cloning of embryos to gather stem cells, which are

1

important to medical research, should be encouraged. The editorial makes a clear distinction between the dangers of human cloning and the benefits of cellular or "therapeutic" cloning. Especially important are the technical and moral arguments against cloning that "aims to replicate humans."

At first glance, then, the editorial's argument against the Bush 2 administration's proposed ban on all human cloning, including that of embryos, is convincing. Its recommendation to continue cloning "to harvest stem cells" for medical research seems like a middle path we should follow. Still, one has to ask why the editorial gives so much coverage to the bizarre claim by the Raelians that a human child has been successfully cloned? Shouldn't this claim have been given no more than passing notice in so serious an article? It is interesting that mention of the Raelians is used to introduce a proposal by "conservative Republicans" to ban cloning of any sort, a proposal that the editorial describes with loaded words such as "overreaction," "knee-jerk reaction," and "overreach." Aren't there people other than conservative Republicans who are against all cloning?

In addition, the claim that "any clone would catch Americans 3 spectacularly unprepared" seems hard to believe. The media has covered cloning and stem-cell research extensively in the recent past. Most Americans know that sheep can be cloned ever since hearing about Dolly in 1997.

In fact, Americans may have "vexing moral questions" about 4 both kinds of cloning, questions that the article never addresses. For example, the article skirts the issue that many Americans

believe that human embryos—whether grown in a test tube or
implanted in a uterus—are human beings. What about the fact
that destroying embryos to harvest stem cells devalues human
life, even if it is important to research that may save lives? And if
we say therapeutic cloning is unethical, should we allow it simply
because others countries will do it?

There are compelling arguments on both sides of the issue   5
of therapeutic cloning, but such questions must be addressed
if we are to understand this issue and make informed choices.
Nonetheless, the editorial is correct: the announcement of a cloned
human—true or false—"is a call for responsible action." We are in
fact "in a brave new world of medical advances."

EXERCISE 5: *Practice what you have learned* Write a critique of an
essay, article, or textbook chapter you have been reading. Begin by reviewing
the suggested criteria for evaluation on p. 14.

SYNTHESIZING: BRING IDEAS TOGETHER IN A NEW STATEMENT

Learning to synthesize or to bring ideas together from different sources is a
logical step in developing critical reading skills. Synthesizing requires the
coherent *restating, combining, and reconciling* of information from different
sources.

In various college courses, you may be asked to evaluate one writer's position against another's, compare/contrast ideas on the same issue, and even
create an entirely new perspective after reading several different discussions
on an issue. However, this new product should be more than a collection of
borrowed elements. It should also reflect your own thinking, perspectives, and
experiences. Just as important, it should be developed and organized in a way
that suits your purpose.

Read "All Human Cloning Is Wrong" by U.S. Senator Sam Brownback. This
guest editorial appeared in *USA Today* as an opposing view to "Overreaction
to Cloning Claim Poses Risks." Then, read Matthew Roberts' "Adult Stem-Cell
Research: An Alternative to Cloning," a student essay that synthesizes materials
from both editorials as well as from a third source.

All Human Cloning Is Wrong

Senator Sam Brownback

The announcement of the possible first live-born human clone came as a   1
shock to many. And it should.

However, what the Raelians claim to have done is at its most basic level no   2
different from what numerous biotech companies in this country and elsewhere
are attempting to do. As observers of this issue know, there are several biotech
companies and university research labs engaged—or soon will be—in the mass
production of human embryos for research purposes. The human embryos will
be harvested for their material, then destroyed.

This grisly prospect—creating human life merely to conduct research on   3
it—must be outlawed.

Some proponents of human cloning would have society believe that there   4
are two different types of cloning: so-called reproductive and so-called therapeutic. Science, however, tells us that there are not two types of cloning—there
is only one, and it always results in the creation of a new human embryo.

The essential point: cloning is cloning is cloning, and all cloning is the   5
same.

Whether the embryo created through the process of somatic-cell transfer   6
(the technical name for cloning) is destined for implantation or for destructive research that ultimately kills him or her—it is the same, and it should be
banned.

Some Congress members who favor cloning in certain circumstances are   7
offering a bill that bans the implantation of clonal human embryos while at
the same time authorizing biotech companies to create thousands of human
embryos.

Let us be clear: this proposal is not in any way a ban on human cloning. It   8
is an endorsement of human cloning that attempts to restrict some of the ways
the human clones may be used.

If we do not ban the cloning of human embryos now, we will quickly find   9
ourselves unable to put the genie back in the bottle.

The only solution to the problem now facing humanity is to act quickly   10
and to ban all human cloning now.

Along with Sen. Mary Landrieu, D–La., I have authored a bipartisan bill   11
that bans all human cloning. The House has passed such a bill, and the president had indicated his strong support for this measure. Congress and the country can afford to wait no longer.

Student Synthesis

Matthew Roberts

Professor Spano

ENG 101-33

November 29, 2003

Adult Stem-Cell Research: An Alternative to Cloning   1

The controversy over human cloning, which began in earnest in
1997, after British scientists announced the cloning of a sheep, is
coming to a head. The Bush administration supports legislation to
prohibit all human cloning. However, many medical researchers,
such as those in the National Academy of Sciences, oppose the ban
because it would outlaw therapeutic cloning, which creates
embryos from which stem cells used in medical research
can be taken ("Overreaction . . ." A8). In short, what the Bush
administration considers unethical, many researchers believe is
important to the advancement of medicine and ultimately to the
saving of lives. However, there is an alternative that accommodates
both of these positions: the use of adult stem cells.

The Bush administration's opposition to all human cloning   2
"ignores critical differences between cloning of the human and the
therapeutic variety," claim the editors of USA Today. ("Overreaction
. . ." A8). The editors forthrightly condemn the implanting of a
cloned embryo into a uterus, the process by which a human being
might be duplicated. However, they support therapeutic cloning,
which provides stem cells used in research to combat leukemia,
diabetes and other terrible diseases. It is difficult, then, to argue

with the "end" to which the cloning of human embryos is aimed. But what about the "means"?

It can be argued that cloning human embryos in order to grow   3
stem cells—therapeutic cloning—is as morally offensive as cloning human beings (Brownback A8). Senator Sam Brownback (R-Kansas), who, with Senator Mary Landrieu (D-Louisiana), is cosponsoring a ban on all cloning, objects to therapeutic cloning because it destroys human life. It is a "grisly prospect," says Brownback, "creating human life merely to conduct research on it." Researchers clone human embryos only to harvest stem-cells, and then they dispose of them. "If we do not ban the cloning of human embryos now," says Brownback, "we will quickly find ourselves unable to put the genie back in the bottle" (Brownback A8). For Senators Brownback and Landrieu, the end does not justify the means.

However, there is a middle ground that should be explored   4
to meet the needs of medical researchers and to address the objections of those opposed to embryonic cloning. It is the harvesting of a patient's own stem cells for use in treating his or her disease. "Adult stem cells are now beginning to ameliorate suffering in human beings," claims Wesley J. Smith, a senior fellow at the Discovery Institute (2).

After culturing stem cells taken from a Parkinson's sufferer,   5
Smith reports, doctors were able to inject the cells into the patient's brain, resulting in a 37% increase in his motor skills. "One year after the procedure, the patient's overall Unified Parkinson's Disease Rating Scale had improved by 83%—this at a time when he was not taking any other Parkinson's medications!" (Smith 2).

Adult stem cells have also been used to treat patients with
multiple sclerosis at Seattle's Washington Medical Center.
Twenty-six patients were involved; of these, twenty showed marked
improvement after receiving treatment using their own stem cells.
As reported in the Globe and Mail, Canadian researchers have
treated four other MS patients using therapies involving adult
stem cells (Smith 3).

Stem-cell research offers far too many promises for advances
in medical research not to be pursued vigorously. Fortunately,
there is some evidence that we can avoid the ethical problem of
cloning embryos to harvest the stem cells we need to save lives.
But more needs to be done. Medical researchers must be willing
to consider new avenues and to pursue the use of adult stem cells
as a realistic alternative to cloning. And government must be
willing not simply to ban all cloning, but to provide the money that
researchers will need to continue and accelerate adult stem-cell
research.

6

7

Works Cited

Brownback, Sam. "All Human Cloning Is Wrong. Opposing Opinion."
USA Today 3 Jan. 2003: A8.

"Overreaction to Cloning Claim Poses Other Risks." Editorial, USA
Today 3 Jan. 2003: A8.

Smith, Wesley. "Spinning Stem Cells." National Review Online 23
Apr. 2002. 5pp. 30 Dec. 2002.
<http://www.nationalreview.com/comment/
comment-smith042302.asp>.

CREDITING YOUR SOURCES

When you use other authors' materials in a synthesis, you must provide parenthetical citations, thereby informing your reader that the material is not your own. *You must do this whether you paraphrase, summarize, or quote directly.* Follow standard guidelines such as those published by the Modern Language Association (see this textbook's website www.mhhe.com/rcw) or by the American Psychological Association (see http://owl.english.purdue.edu/handouts/research/r_apa.html) or by another professional group as required by your instructor.

EXERCISE 6: Practice what you have learned   Find another essay or editorial that relates directly to the topic or issue addressed in an essay or editorial you have read recently. Synthesize ideas from what you have read with your own ideas.

Using the Writing Process: A Tool for Discovery

Part 3 of Getting Started (GS) explains steps in the writing of an essay:
- The Writing Process: An Overview
- Prewriting
- Outlining
- Drafting and Revising
- Editing and Proofreading

THE WRITING PROCESS: AN OVERVIEW

Both writing and reading are processes. The writing process can be explained in four steps: *prewriting, outlining, drafting/revising,* and *editing/proofreading.*

Prewriting, also called invention, consists of two activities:
- Deciding upon your intended audience (your readers), purpose, and style.
- Gathering information.

Professors Gilbert Muller and Harvey Weiner explain the importance of this first step:

> Few writers begin without some warm-up activity. Generally called prewriting, the steps they take before producing a draft almost always start with thinking about their topic. They talk to friends and colleagues; they browse in libraries . . . ; they read newspaper and magazine articles. Sometimes they jot down notes and lists in order

to put on paper some of their thoughts in very rough form. Some
writers use free-association; they record as thoroughly as possible
their random, unedited ideas. . . . Using the raw, often disorganized
materials produced in this preliminary stage, many writers try to
group related thoughts with a scratch outline. ("On Writing")

In addition to helping you answer important questions about your writing
project, prewriting provides insights about how your ideas might be organized
and leads to the second step in the process: outlining.

Outlining provides a blueprint or framework through which to present information in an easy-to-follow manner. As you will see later in Getting
Started, you can use two types of outlines: formal and informal.

Drafting and revising are the heart of the process. In general, you should
begin drafting after deciding on purpose and audience, gathering information,
and making an outline. Remember that first drafts are also called "rough drafts."
So, spend time revising—completely rewriting and restructuring—your first,
second, and third drafts until you are sure that your paper says what you want
it to say clearly and completely.

Editing and proofreading may come last, but they are extremely important. Neglect them, and you risk embarrassing yourself or confusing and frustrating the reader.

These steps are neatly defined, but they are not always separate. For example, while editing, you might realize that you need to add more information or
correct a serious organizational problem. If this happens, don't worry. Go back
and make the changes. That's how the process should work.

PREWRITING

This section explains (1) how to determine purpose, audience, and style and
(2) how to gather information.

Determining Purpose, Audience, and Style

Determine Your Purpose. Writing is practical; it always serves a purpose,
whether it be to produce a technical report, to explain a scientific process, to
argue about a social issue, or simply to make an entry in a diary. Purpose determines the major approach or method a writer uses and the form the document
will take. In order to explain the workings of a cell phone, you might use a technique called *process analysis* to list the steps in the transmission of sound over
a wireless system. If you are trying to convince the state legislature to increase
funding of school athletic programs, you would probably use *persuasion*. If you
are simply making a diary entry, you might use *narration* to record events in
the order they occurred.

However, pieces of writing rarely use only one method or approach. For example, a *process analysis* paper that explains how cell phones work might also use *definition* to explain what a transmission tower is. It might contrast land-line and wireless phones. In short, even though a piece of writing relies on one major approach, it can also use other approaches, depending of course on the writer's purpose.

In first-year college writing courses, instructors sometimes specify the purpose of an assignment and even require the student to take a specific approach. At times, however, professors ask students to choose their own purposes and then decide for themselves on how best to achieve them. This is part of maturing as a writer. Although we often think of writing as a matter of sticking to the rules of grammar and mastering the techniques of rhetoric, good writing also requires the ability to make judgments. For example, you must decide on a topic's particular focus, identify relevant information, and determine ways to fulfill your purpose.

A writer develops judgment only through experience—trial and error. So, don't get discouraged if you suddenly discover that you have chosen the wrong approach or that you have to redefine your purpose. Go back and rethink things. Then, start again. Of course, this might require doing more information gathering by using one of the prewriting techniques explained in the next few pages. It might also require you to get rid of some information gathered earlier simply because it is irrelevant to your new purpose. However, this is normal—writing is a process of discovery and revision.

The best time to think about your purpose for an academic essay is before you begin gathering information. After carefully considering the assignment, write a statement of purpose (a sentence or two) on an index card or scrap of paper. Keep in mind that you might revise this statement later—after you have gathered information, made an outline, or even written a first draft. You will learn more about purpose in Chapter 1.

Consider the Audience. The audience for any piece of writing is its readers. You should consider your audience even before you begin gathering information. Let's say your purpose is to convince your classmates to use the library's online periodical database to find information on their majors. You might first have to define "periodical" and "database." You might have to explain that "periodicals" come in various types: magazines, professional journals, and newspapers. You might also have to convince your readers of the ease with which "databases" can be used.

On the other hand, what if you are trying to convince college librarians to subscribe to a particular online database? You certainly would not explain terms like "periodical" and "database." Doing so would bore and insult them.

The primary audience for any college paper is the instructor. However, you might be asked to discuss your work in a small writing group or with the entire class. In such cases you must consider your whole audience—both instructor and students—and you might need to include explanatory information and definitions of special terms that you would not have included had you been writing for your instructor alone.

Even if you are writing only for your instructor, evaluating the needs of a reader can get tricky. Most college composition instructors have advanced degrees in English or related disciplines. Thus, you can assume that they are well trained in their field. But can they be expected to be knowledgeable in other specialized areas? Would they know the process by which atoms are split or be familiar with the latest theories relating to prison reform? If you choose to write about popular music, can you assume that your instructor knows the difference between "hip-hop" and "gangsta rap"? Again, try to determine your audience's needs before you begin gathering information, but remember that you can revise your evaluation of your readers any time in the writing process. You will learn more about evaluating an audience in Section Five of this book.

Use Formal Style in Academic Writing. Style refers to the level of language you use. Essentially there are three levels. But *formal style* is preferable in academic writing.

Informal style is used when writing to a limited audience—a close friend, a classmate—in emails, short notes, or personal letters. Such writing may contain colloquialisms, or conversational expressions used only in certain locales. Informal style also allows for slang and private language, which have special meanings within a limited group and change rapidly. It can also contain clichés, common phrases heard over and over again. Consider this passage from a student's email to a friend:

> Most guys in my frat are pretty brainy, and they hit
> the books hard. But they aren't that stuck up, not like
> the Geek Patrol we knew at Jefferson High. In fact,
> they're cool! They even tutor kids whose grades are
> tanking.

Terms like "guys," "brainy," "stuck up," "Geek Patrol," "kids," and "tanking" are examples of informal language.

Familiar style is used in short business memos, in letters to the editor of newspapers, and in emails or letters to older relatives or acquaintances. Here is a version of the above paragraph as it appeared in the student's letter to his former boss.

> You would like the students in my fraternity. They
> are fairly smart, and they really put their noses to
> the grindstone when they want to ace a big exam.
> However, they're not snobs. In fact, they often tutor
> other kids who are having trouble with their studies.

This version is somewhat more formal. It does not include slang or private language, but it does use colloquialisms such as "ace a big exam," and a cliché—"noses to the grindstone." In the familiar style, it also addresses the reader directly by using the word "you."

Formal style belongs in academic papers, in answers to essay questions, and in business letters and reports. Notice that the writer now replaces all colloquialisms, slang, and clichés and that he no longer addresses the reader directly by using "you." The vocabulary is more sophisticated than the relaxed choice of words in the two previous versions.

> Students in my fraternity are quite likable. They are
> intelligent, and they are also diligent, studying hard
> especially when it comes to major examinations.
> However, they are not snobs. In fact, they often tutor
> other students who are having difficulty with their
> studies.

Try to use formal style from the moment you begin drafting your paper. However, you can always eliminate slang, colloquialisms, and nonformal elements when you edit.

Gathering Information for Writing You can use seven techniques to gather facts, ideas, and opinions for any assignment, especially for journal entries, like those responding to the Suggestions for Journal Entries after each reading selection in this book. A good way to start a journal entry is to read the notes you took in the margins of a reading selection. (You learned more about note-taking in the first part of Getting Started, page 4.) Then, just follow the Suggestions for Journal Entries, which often recommend using one of the information-gathering techniques explained below.

Listing involves putting down details that you believe are most important, startling, or obvious about your chosen topic. At times, you can compile a list simply by writing down whatever comes to mind. Here's a list that student Aggie Canino made when asked to describe the effects of a storm:

Clogged rain sewrs

Giant trees down, across lawns, roads

Wires down, no telephone, no lights

Flooding

50-mile per hour winds, thunder, lightening

Ligtening destroys old oak on neighbors lawn

Dog hides under bed

Terrifying sounds

Flooded basements

Lasts one hour

Howling wind, crash of thunder—frightened

Complete darkness at 2 pm

Crack utility poles

Flooded streets

Bridge washed away, road closed—trafic detured

This is repetitious and has spelling errors, but don't worry about such problems now; you can correct them later. Just concentrate on your topic and record details.

After you run out of things to say, stop writing and read your list. Cross out information that is repetitious and correct spelling. As you do this, new details will pop into your head. You will also make some items more specific. For example, Aggie expanded "crack utility poles" to include "white sparks flying from downed power lines," and she expressed the terror she felt as she heard the "splintering of a sixty-foot oak struck by lightning" and the "breaking of windows into which tree limbs flew."

Focused freewriting is a common technique to help overcome writer's block, a problem that results in staring at a blank paper while trying to come up with something to say. Freewriting involves writing nonstop for 5 or 10 minutes and recording ideas that come to mind at random. Focused freewriting is similar, but it involves concentrating on one topic. Let's say you want to freewrite by focusing on a storm. Your results might look like this:

The clogged rain sewers were overflowing, and there was a

lot of flooding with strong winds knocking down power lines.

> Thunder crashed, and lightning flashed. Giant tree limbs fell across the road and a birch was bent double, and there were lots of flooded basements. Even so, the storm lasted only one hour. Several downed power lines threw threatening sparks and flashes across the road. My street was blocked; a large oak had fallen across it. We lost our electricity. The crash of thunder shook me to my bones. My dog hid under the bed. We were terrified.

Again, don't worry about grammar and other errors at this time. Just focus on your topic and record ideas quickly. As always, read your journal notes immediately after you've recorded your ideas. Doing so helps cut out repetition, rework parts that require clarification, and add details that come to mind in the process.

Clustering can turn a broad subject into a limited and manageable topic. Also called *mapping* and *webbing*, it is another effective way to gather information. Like focused freewriting, clustering uses free association. Here's what to do:

1. In the center of a blank piece of paper, write and circle the word or phrase that stands for the broad topic you want to write about. Let's say it's *dance*. Then, think of subtopics such as ballet, ballroom dancing, folk dancing, or modern dance. Arranging these subtopics in circles around a general subject might result in a diagram that looks like this:

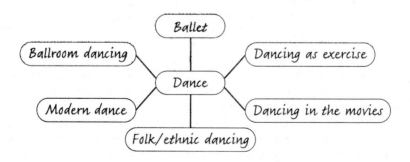

2. Write down details related to these subtopics; continue until you run out of things to say. Circle each word or phrase, and draw lines between each

of your subtopics and the ideas and details that relate to them. Here's what your paper might look like when you have finished.

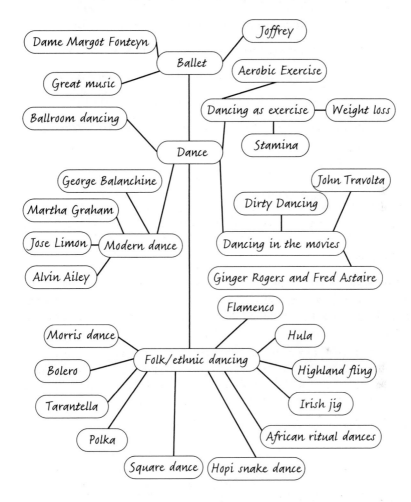

Notice that some subtopics have been given more attention than others. That just means that you might know more about folk/ethnic dancing than ballroom dancing. In fact, clustering has helped you focus on the topic that you know most about or are most interested in.

Of course, you might stop at this stage, review your notes, and even write a working thesis statement for a paper on ethnic dancing. Or, you might focus your topic even more by getting more specific. Let's say you are particularly interested in African ritual dancing and want to learn more about it through Internet or library research. You can extend your cluster by focusing on that subtopic. Here's what that cluster might look like:

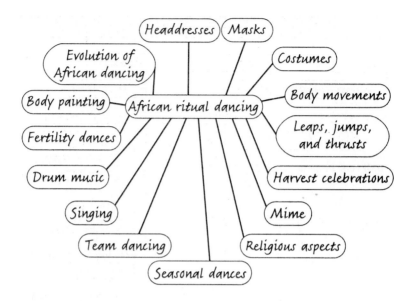

Drawing a subject tree is another way to settle on a manageable topic and gather information. As with clustering, start with a broad topic. Then, divide it into two or three subtopics or branches. Next, subdivide each branch until you have limited your topic sufficiently and have gathered enough information to write a working thesis statement and an outline.

As you draw a subject tree, you will naturally put down more details under subtopics with which you are most familiar or in which you have the greatest interest. For example, the writer who created the subject tree for "uses of computers" would probably choose to write an essay on the ways computers help students and teachers.

Brainstorming is a tool used to gather information in a small group and results in a random collection of words and phrases written across a page. Often, people working together can gather far more information than people working independently. One of the most effective ways to begin brainstorming is to ask the journalists' questions. Reporters ask these when they plan their stories: *What happened? When did it happen? Who did it? Where did it happen? Why did it happen?* and *How did it happen?* An easy way to remember questions journalists use is to think of them as the five Ws and the H.

Journalists' questions work best if you want to tell a story or explain how or why something happens or should happen. However, you might have to think of different questions if you have other purposes in mind. Say you want to describe Uncle Charlie; you might ask: *What does he look like? Who are his friends? What kind of job does he have?* In any case, remember that prewriting is also called invention, so invent as many kinds of questions as you like.

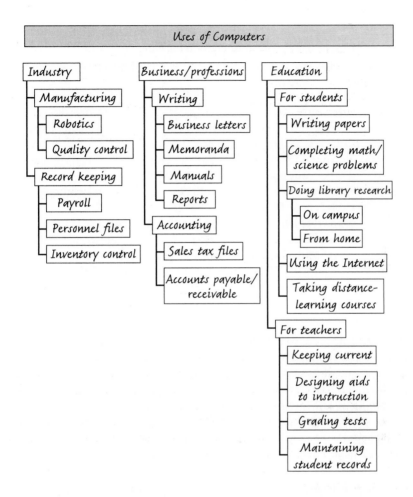

Not all questions yield useful information. However, the answers to only one or two might suggest ideas and details to other members of your brainstorming group. In a little while, a mental chain reaction will occur, and you will find yourself discussing ideas, facts, and opinions that seem to pop up naturally.

EXERCISE 7: *Practice what you have learned*   Pick a topic related to your academic major or to a long-time interest. If you are majoring in nursing, you might focus on pediatric nursing or emergency-room nursing. If you are a psychology major, consider the causes of anorexia nervosa. Or focus on a hobby or sport such as model railroading, camping, or basketball. Begin gathering what you already know about this topic through listing. Then, using the same topic, try clustering or drawing a subject tree.

Interviewing requires you to ask appropriate questions of people who know about your topic. Like brainstorming, interviewing gives you other perspectives from which to view your topic, and it often yields new and valuable information.

The kinds of questions you ask should be determined by your purpose. If you want to learn why something happened, what someone did, or how something works, you might begin your interview with questions like those journalists ask: *Who, When, What, Where, Why, and How.* Just make sure that the person you interview is knowledgeable and is willing to spend enough time with you to make your interview worthwhile. When you arrange to meet with this person, discuss your purpose and the kinds of questions you might ask. This will enable him or her to prepare thoughtful responses.

Finally, come to the interview prepared. Write down a few important questions ahead of time. You can use these in the interview to encourage your subject to begin talking. If your questions are clear and interesting, you should gather more information than you bargained for. On the other hand, don't be upset if the interview doesn't go as planned. Your subject might not answer any of your questions but simply discuss ideas as they come to mind. Such interviews can be very successful—just take good notes!

Summarizing is an information-gathering technique that condenses another writer's ideas and puts them into your own words. It can be used to combine information you have read with details gathered from your own experiences. Just be sure to use your own words throughout the summary. Also, if you use this information in an essay, give the source of the material credit by mentioning the author's name or the title of the work. For example, if you decide to summarize a paragraph from Richard Marius's "Writing and Its Rewards" (an essay in Chapter 1), you might begin: *As Marius argues . . .*

EXERCISE 8: Practice what you have learned   Read Richard Marius's "Writing and Its Rewards" in Chapter 1. Then summarize this essay paragraph by paragraph. Try to capture the content of each paragraph in one sentence.

OUTLINING

After gathering information and deciding on a working thesis statement, many writers construct an outline, which makes the writing of a rough draft easier. Think of an outline as a blueprint, which guides you through the drafting process.

For most short essays, an informal or scratch outline is sufficient. However, if you are writing a lengthy essay, such as a library research paper, you might want to use a formal outline, which can also serve as a table of contents. Ask your instructor if you should have an outline and, if so, what type. In any event, spend a few minutes on a working thesis statement, your essay's central idea. Then, jot down at least a scratch outline of the essay's main points. (You will learn more about writing thesis statements and developing paragraphs in Chapters 1 and 2.)

Writing an Informal Scratch Outline   Let's say you review the notes you took when you completed a clustering exercise about African ritual dancing (page 30). Realizing that the most important aspect of what you know about such dancing is that it is energetic and fascinating, you decide to write an essay whose working thesis might be: *African ritual dances, which I observed in Zimbabwe, are the most dramatic, colorful, and exciting folk dances I have ever seen.*

As you review your notes a second time, you realize that several of the ideas you have down in your clusters do not relate to your working thesis. For example, the fact that certain dances are seasonal does not support or develop your thesis, so you decide not to mention it. Instead, you focus on aspects of the dances that are dramatic, colorful, and exciting. Here's a sample scratch outline for such a paper:

> Working Thesis: African ritual dances, which I observed in
> Zimbabwe, are the most dramatic, colorful, and exciting folk
> dances I have ever seen.
>
> 1. Colorful masks.
>
> 2. Frightening costumes.
>
> 3. Bodies painted in bright colors, eye-catching patterns.
>
> 4. Joyful music.
>
> 5. Vivid body movements.

This outline is no more than a brief list of details pulled from the clustering exercise completed earlier. However it provides a pattern the writer can follow to construct a first, or working, draft.

Writing a Formal Outline   A formal outline differs from a scratch outline in that it is more complete and more consistent in structure. A formal outline for an essay on African ritual dancing might look like this:

I. Introduction.

    A. Folk dances differ in form and purpose from culture to culture.

    B. Many European and American folk dances reveal much about the cultures in which they originated.

    C. Thesis: African ritual dances, which I observed in Zimbabwe, are the most dramatic, colorful, and exciting folk dances I have ever seen.

II. Many dancers wear bizarre masks intended to startle and even frighten the audience.

   A. Patterns painted on these masks are varied and vivid.

   B. They take odd shapes and are often very large.

      1. Many are triangular or pointed; others resemble shields used in warfare.

      2. Some triple the size of the wearer's face so as to make him appear monstrous.

      3. Some look like the faces of animals; others suggest that the dancer has come from another planet.

III. The costumes are rich, complex, and colorful.

   A. Some are made of animal skins; others are woven from native vegetable fibers.

   B. All are extremely colorful.

   C. The costumes make great use of fascinating geometric patterns.

   D. Huge headdresses are worn, some resembling the heads of animals.

IV. Drum music gets the heart pounding; the air is sometimes filled with song.

   A. The musicians keep the pace energetic, often adding to the dramatic effect.

   B. A chorus of women singing sweetly often accompanies the dancers.

V. The real spectacle comes in the dancers' acrobatics.

   A. Each dancer conveys a message or vivid story through movement.

   B. Performers run, stomp, and leap high into the air.

   C. Some prance around on huge stilts, standing 15 feet tall.

    D.   They even approach members of the audience,

         pretending to threaten them with lunges and howls.

This formal outline is very different from the scratch outline:

1. It contains more detail. Each of its major sections is subdivided into more specific subheadings.
2. Each heading is a complete sentence. In fact, the writer might use each of these as the topic sentence of a paragraph. A topic sentence expresses a paragraph's main or central idea. (You will learn more about topic sentences in Chapters 1 and 2.)
3. Sections of the formal outline are identified by number or letter. The major headings have Roman numerals (I, II, III). These are subdivided into items with capital letters (A, B, C), and these are followed by Arabic numerals (1, 2, 3). It isn't necessary to divide each major heading into an equal number of subheadings. For example, IV is divided into two subheadings, but V is subdivided into four. Actually, the pattern to follow is straightforward:
   - **I.** (Roman numeral)
     - **A.** (Capital letter)
       - **1.** (Arabic numeral)
         - **a.** (Lowercase letter)
4. Each unit is divided into at least two subunits. Never place only one subheading below a more important heading. If you can't divide a heading into two or more subdivisions, leave it alone.

Not	But	Or
I.	I.	I.
A.	A.	A.
1.	1.	B.
B.	2.	
	B.	

Whether you make a scratch or formal outline, remember that an outline is only a guide to drafting an essay. As you begin your first draft, stick to your outline closely, but don't be afraid to add new information, make changes in organization, replace or delete parts, or revise your working thesis. Of course, if you are writing a long paper and want your outline to serve as a table of contents, you will have to revise it to reflect changes you have made. But this can be done later. Just remember that writing is a process of discovery; the deeper you get into it, the better you will understand what you have to say.

Writing Other Types of Outlines for Special Purposes   Here are some other kinds of outlines you might use depending upon the purpose of your paper.

I. AN ESSAY THAT MAKES MORE
THAN ONE POINT IN ITS THESIS

If your thesis makes more than one point, you might expand upon each of those points in a separate body paragraph or group of paragraphs. Here's a blueprint based upon student Siu Chan's essay, "Suffering," which appears in Chapter 1.

(Paragraph 1): Introduces Essay and States Following Thesis:

[Living] in Cambodia from 1975 to 1979 was the worst time in

Point A	**Point B**

my life: I was allowed little personal freedom, I witnessed the

Point C

death of my family, and I nearly died of starvation.

(Paragraph 2): Develops Point A: . . . When the communists took over, the government destroyed nearly all my personal freedom.

(Paragraph 3): Develops Point B: During those years, I lost six members of my family.

(Paragraph 4): Develops Point C: I can still remember a three-month period during which I nearly starved to death.

(Paragraph 5): States Essay's Conclusion: Having gone through [that suffering], I can appreciate the life I have now.

II. AN ESSAY THAT COMPARES OR CONTRASTS

As you will see in Chapter 9, there are two methods to outline an essay that compares subjects (i.e., explains their similarities) or contrasts them (i.e., explains their differences). These are the point-by-point method and the subject-by-subject method.

Point-by-Point: This method compares or contrasts various aspects of the two subjects you are discussing, one-by-one, in a separate paragraph or group of paragraphs. Let's say you want to point out differences between (contrast) attending a small college and going to a large university.

(Paragraph 1): Introduces Essay and States Following Thesis: The advantages of attending a small college, as opposed to a university, outweigh the disadvantages.

(Paragraph 2): First Point—Class Size: In small colleges, class sizes tend to be smaller than at large universities, making it easier to ask questions and to enter into discussion with faculty and other students.

(Paragraph 3): Second Point—Access to Faculty: Some students attending small colleges say they have easy access to their teachers, who are often available for tutoring. Friends attending large universities have greater access to a professor's teaching assistants than to the professor.

(Paragraph 4): Third Point—Campus Life: Most large universities offer a fuller and more diverse exposure to the arts, lectures, and other cultural activities than smaller colleges do. On the other hand, small campuses are more intimate and more welcoming to new students.

(Paragraph 5): Fourth Point: Life after Graduation: Thanks to name recognition, graduating from a large and prestigious university may increase one's career opportunities. On the other hand, students who learn better in intimate settings will probably exit a small college with a higher GPA, which will make them better candidates for jobs or professional training.

(continued)

(Paragraph 6): States Conclusion: Although large universities offer students a great deal, attending a small college is a smarter choice for many. Students who learn better in more intimate environments should choose a smaller school.

Subject-by-Subject: This method compares or contrasts two subjects one at a time, in separate sections of the paper. It is best used for shorter papers.

(Paragraph 1): Introduces Essay and States Following Thesis: The advantages of attending a small college, as opposed to a university, outweigh the disadvantages.

(Paragraph 2): Attending a Large University

· Class Size

· Access to Faculty

· Campus Life

· Life after Graduation

(Paragraph 3): Attending a Small College

· Class Size

· Access to Faculty

· Campus Life

· Life after Graduation

(Paragraph 4): Conclusion

III. AN ESSAY THAT SUPPORTS AN OPINION

As you will see in Chapter 12, one of the best ways to argue an opinion is through the conclusion-and-support method. Start by stating a general idea (your thesis, also known as a "conclusion" in argumentation).

Then, in the essay's body paragraphs, discuss in detail ideas that support the thesis. In other words, explain the reasons you hold this opinion. Of course, some supporting ideas may need more than one paragraph to be developed adequately. (Note that authors of argument papers often find it effective to anticipate and answer the opposition's arguments, in addition to supporting their own. In the sample outline following, the writer does this in paragraph 5.)

(Paragraph 1): Introduces Essay and States Following Thesis: Term limits should be established for all elected officials, local, state, and national.

(Paragraph 2): Develops Supporting Idea A: Limiting the time politicians can serve prevents them from becoming too powerful.

(Paragraph 3): Develops Supporting Idea B: Term limits create an opportunity for a greater number of people to serve, thereby making government more representative.

(Paragraph 4): Develops Supporting Idea C: Term limits would remove the incumbents' advantage over lesser-known opponents at election time. This would make it easier to infuse government with the new ideas new people will bring.

(Paragraph 5): Anticipates and Answers Opposing Argument: Opponents of term limits argue that politicians with seniority can do more for the people back home than newcomers. However, this just supports the notion that long-time office holders have too much power.

(Paragraph 6): Concludes the Essay by Summing Up and Restating Thesis

EXERCISE 9: Practice what you have learned   Review the notes you made for Exercise 7 on page 31. Then write a formal or informal outline for an essay that might use this information.

DRAFTING AND REVISING
Start the first draft several days before the paper is due. This will give you time to revise, edit, and proofread it without rushing.

Drafting
1. Begin drafting by reviewing decisions you made about purpose, audience, and style. With these in the back of your mind, reread the notes you took when gathering information through listing, researching, or other method discussed earlier. Check your working thesis and your outline, and make last minute changes if necessary. For example, when rereading your notes, you might discover that you left out an important point when you wrote the outline.
2. Keep your working thesis and your outline in front of you as you begin to draft. Following your outline, put down important ideas and concrete details paragraph by paragraph. Include as much information as you can. If you repeat yourself or write more than you need to, no matter. You can remove words, sentences, and even whole paragraphs when you revise. And don't worry about grammar or spelling errors; you can correct them when you edit.
3. If you get tired before completing this draft, take a break. However, finish it before beginning another project. Once you have done so, put the rough draft aside for 24 hours if possible. When you get back to it, you will approach it with a clearer head.

Revising
1. Read your rough draft two or three times. Revise your working thesis if you believe that what you wrote in your paper no longer matches what is in the thesis. As you will see, the final draft will often reveal exactly what you meant to say in the first place. This is only one reason writing is called a "process of discovery."
2. At this point, you might decide to add details that will make your paper more convincing. If so, return to prewriting and gather this information. Then, in your second draft, add it to an existing paragraph or give it a paragraph of its own.
3. Now read your second draft. Do you need still more information? If so find and add it. Next, rewrite paragraphs that are too long or that contain information irrelevant to the thesis. Combine short paragraphs that relate to the same point. Change the positions of paragraphs if doing so will make your paper easier to follow or more logical. Do the same with

sentences: add to, combine, separate, and reposition them as needed. (Chapters 2 and 5 discuss paragraph and sentence structure.)

3. Don't be afraid to cut information you don't need. Perhaps you have repeated ideas. There is no sin in that; eliminate one version. Perhaps you have offered three examples when two will do. Remove the third. Just remember that "all writing is rewriting."

EDITING AND PROOFREADING

Editing means reading the best of your drafts to correct errors in grammar, punctuation, sentence structure, and mechanics. It also means cutting out wordiness and eliminating diction problems. **Proofreading** is a final check for spelling and typographical errors.

There are many ways to edit and proofread. Some writers read their papers backward, sentence by sentence. Others read aloud to friends to make sure that they haven't left out words and that their sentences make sense. Some read their final drafts several times, concentrating on one major editing problem each time. For example, they read once to correct sentence-structure errors such as fragments and comma splices. They read a second time for grammar, a third for punctuation, and so on. However you proceed, take your time. A paper might be organized and well developed, but if it is not edited and proofread carefully, it can suffer from errors that distract and confuse readers.

For more on editing and proofreading try these websites:

• Purdue University Online Writing Lab: http://owl.english.purdue.edu/
• List of writing labs collected by McGraw-Hill Higher Education: http://www.mhhe.com/socscience/english/compde/wlsub1.html

EXERCISE 10: Practice what you have learned   In Exercise 7 (page 31), you were asked to gather information on a particular topic. In Exercise 9 (page 40) you were asked to write an outline using this material. Following your outline, draft a short essay that uses information you have collected. Revise this essay at least once. Then edit and proofread it.

The Making of a Student Essay: From Prewriting to Proofreading

This part of Getting Started traces the writing of a full-length essay by first-year nursing student Deborah Diglio. As her essay proves, she sees writing as a process of steps that need to be followed carefully.

• Prewriting to gather information
• Making a scratch outline
• Writing a working draft

- Revising the working draft
- Editing and proofreading

PREWRITING TO GATHER INFORMATION

The process began when Diglio was inspired by Carl Sandburg's "Child of the Romans," a poem about the difficult job of an Italian immigrant who maintains the stone bed on which railroad tracks lie.

Child of the Romans

Carl Sandburg

The dago shovelman sits by the railroad track
Eating a noon meal of bread and bologna.
A train whirls by, and men and women at tables
Alive with red roses and yellow jonquils,
Eat steaks running with brown gravy,
Strawberries and cream, éclairs and coffee.
The dago shovelman finishes the dry bread and bologna,
Washes it down with a dipper from the water-boy,
And goes back to the second half of a ten-hour day's work
Keeping the road-bed so the roses and jonquils
Shake hardly at all in the cut glass vases
Standing slender on the tables in the dining cars.

Responding to a journal assignment from her instructor, Diglio used focused freewriting to gather information about a job she once held. Here's what she wrote in her journal about waitressing.

> People ordering food. The night was going by fast.
> Nervous. First nights can be scary. Keep a pleasant
> attitude. I could do the job easily. Training period
> over, I was on my own. I needed this job. We needed
> the money. I felt confident, too confident. I can
> now laugh at it. Not then. Society may not place
> waitressing high on the social ladder, but you have
> got to be surefooted, organized, you have to have a
> sense of humor, and a pleasant personality. You have
> to be able to learn from your mistakes. Eventually,
> I did learn but then I thought I would die. This old

woman left her walker in the corner. How did I know

it wasn't a tray stand? Still I should have! Why didn't

I just look more closely. Why didn't my brain take

over. And the old folks didn't mind. We should look

back at ourselves and laugh sometimes.

As you can see, there is no particular order to Diglio's notes, and like most freewriting, it uses quick phrases as much as full sentences. Nonetheless, an event that might make interesting reading is coming through. So is the idea that Diglio learned something from the experience and can now look back at it with a smile.

MAKING A SCRATCH OUTLINE

After discussing her journal entry with her instructor, Diglio decided to tell her story in full-length essay. She reviewed her journal entry and thought about a working thesis. After adding notes to her original entry, she made this scratch outline:

Working thesis: Sometimes, we need to look back at ourselves and laugh.

1. *Describe the restaurant, set the stage.*

2. *State the thesis.*

3. *Describe the job.*

4. *Tell what happened that first night:*

   How well it went first—thought I was a "born natural."

   The old couple and their walker.

   I wanted to crawl into a hole.

5. *What I learned from my mistake.*

WRITING A WORKING (FIRST) DRAFT

Diglio's outline served as a blueprint for her first draft. Each paragraph in that draft corresponds roughly to the five major headings in her outline. However, the act of writing inspired her and, as she wrote, more details and ideas came to mind.

This proves an important point: an outline—especially a scratch outline—can be used only to get started. Don't be a slave to your outline; if the act of writing adds new details or takes you in a new direction, so be it. Again, writing is a process of discovery, and good writers change their minds at many points.

When Diglio finished her first draft, she read it over, a process that helped her recall even more details, which she squeezed in between paragraphs and sentences and in the margins of her paper. The result was messy, so she retyped the working draft as shown below. This early draft of her paper contains more detail and is better written than her journal entry or outline, but it is only a start. Note that this draft contains many errors. No one would suggest that these are acceptable, merely that early drafts often contain such errors.

Waitressing

It was a typical Saturday night. I was standing there, paying no attention to the usual racket of the dinner crowd. The restaurant was crowded. I was waiting for my next table. I try to listen to the sounds around me. I hear the stereo.

In come my eight oclock reservation, fifteen minutes late. There is an elderly woman with them. She reminded me of something that happened when I started working there many years before. Recalling that story taught me to look back and laugh at myself.

When my second child was born. It became clear that I needed to find a part-time job to help make ends meet. A friend said I should waitress at the restaurant where she worked. I thought about it for a few days. I decided to give it a try. I bluffed my way thru the interview. A new chapter in my life began. Since then, I have learned from many mistakes like the one I am going to describe. My friends told me that, someday, I would look back and laugh at that night. I guess after fifteen years that day has come!

I followed another waitress for a few days and then I was released on my own. All went well that first week. When Saturday night came, I had butterflies in my stomache. I was given four tables not far from the kitchen. It was an easy station. Oh, God, was I happy, however I still felt awkward carrying those heavy trays. Before I new it, the restaurant was packed resembling mid-day on wall street. I moved slowly organising every move. I remember the tray stand in my station. It looked a little different than the one I was trained on. It had nice grips for handles of which made it easier to move around. I was amazed at how well things were going. I was too confident. I remember thinking that I was a born natural. Than, this jovial looking old man came over, and taped me on the shoulder, and said "Excuse me, dear, my wife and I loved watching you work. It seems your tray stand has been very handy for you, but we are getting ready to leave now, and my wife needs her walker back." I wanted to crawl into a hole and hide. What a fool I had made of myself. I was so glad when that night ended.

Since then, I have learned from many mistakes such as the one I just described.

REVISING THE WORKING DRAFT

The essay above makes for entertaining reading, but Diglio knew it could be improved. She revised it several times to get to the last draft (but not the final version) of her paper, which appears below. This draft is not perfect, but it is more complete and polished than the one you just read. Again, it contains unacceptable errors, which were corrected in editing.

Lessons Learned

It was a typical Saturday night at Carpaccio's Restaurant. I was standing there, paying no attention to the usual merrymaking of the dinner crowd. Just two of the restaurant's twenty-five tables were vacant. As I waited for my next table, I absorbed a few of the sounds around me: clanging trays, the ringing of the cash register. I could even hear Dean Martin belting out a familiar Italian song in the background.

Finally, in come my eight o'clock party. As they were seated, my attention was drawn to an elderly woman with a walker slowly shuffling behind the others. She brought back a memory I had locked away for fifteen years.

After the birth of my second child, I needed a part-time job to help make ends meet. A friend suggested I apply for a waitressing job at a new restaurant where she worked. I decided to give it a shot. I bluffed my way through the interview and was hired. A new chapter in my life began the next evening.

After trailing an experience waitress for a few days, I was allowed to wait tables on my own. All went well that first week. When Saturday night came, the butterflies in my stomach were set free. I was given the apprentice station that night, four tables not far from the kitchen. Oh, God, was I relieved, however I still felt awkward carrying the heavy trays.

Before I new it, the restaurant was packed; it resembled mid-day on wall street. I moved slowly, organising every step. I remember how impressed I was with the tray stand in my station, it looked different than the one I was trained on. It had nice grip-like handles, of which made it easier to manuver. I was amazed at how well things were going. I began to believe I was a natural at this job.

Then, a jovial, old man approached, tapped me on the shoulder, and said, "Excuse me, dear, my wife and I loved watching you work. It seems your tray stand has been very handy for you, but we are getting ready to leave now, and my wife needs her walker back."

At first his message did not register. "What was he talking about!" Then, it sank in. I had set my trays on his wife's orthopedic walker. I stood there frozen as ice, but my face was on fire. I wanted to crawl into a hole; I wanted to hibernate.

Since then; I have learned from many mistakes such as the one I just described. I have learned to be more observant and more careful. I have learned to guard against overconfidence, for no matter how well things are going, something will come along eventually to gum up the works. Most of all, I have learned that the best way to get over honest embarrassment is to look back and laugh at yourself.

As this draft shows, Diglio made important revisions. She

1. Changed the title to clarify purpose; "Waitressing" didn't reveal her main point.

2. Moved the central idea—the point she wanted to make—to the end. This allowed her to tell the story first and then explain its importance clearly.

3. Added details to make her writing exact and vivid. In the later version, she names the restaurant and explains that just two of its "twenty-five tables were vacant," not simply that it was "crowded." She even mentions that "Dean Martin [was] belting out a familiar Italian song."

4. Divided paragraph 4 into several new paragraphs, each of which focuses on a different idea, makes a new point, or tells another part of the story.

5. Removed unnecessary words to eliminate repetition.

6. Replaced some words with more exact and interesting substitutes. For example, in paragraph 1, the dinner crowd's "racket" is changed to "merrymaking."

7. Combined short sentences to create longer, smoother ones and to increase variety.

8. Corrected some—not all—problems with spelling, verb tense, sentence structure, punctuation, and mechanics.

EDITING AND PROOFREADING

Although Diglio's last draft is better than her first, she wanted to remove annoying errors that could interfere with the reader's appreciation of her work. Using a pencil, a dictionary, and a handbook of college writing, she corrected problems in grammar, spelling, style, and other areas. Here's what two paragraphs from that draft looked like after she edited them.

After trailing an experience$_\wedge^d$ waitress for a few

days, I was allowed to wait tables on my own. All went

well that first week. When Saturday night came, the

butterflies in my stomach were set free. I was given

the apprentice station that night, four tables not far

from the kitchen. Oh, God, was I relieved/$_\wedge^;$ however, I

still felt awkward carrying the heavy trays.

Before I $_\wedge^k$new it, the restaurant was packed; it

resembled mid-day on $\overset{W}{W}$all $\overset{S}{S}$treet. I moved slowly,

organi$\overset{z}{s}$ing every step. I remember how impressed

I was with the tray stand in my station,/∧ it looked

different ~~than~~ *from* ∧ the one I was trained on. It had nice

grip-like handles, ∅f which made it easier to maneuver.

I was amazed at how well things were going. I began

to believe I was a natural at this job.

Of course, a paper full of such corrections is too sloppy to submit in a college class. So, after correcting her final draft in pencil, Diglio typed one last, clean copy for her instructor.

The methods you use to write a paper may be different from those Deborah Diglio used. They also may be different from ways your classmates write. And no one says that any of the steps explained above has to be done separately from the others. In fact, some folks edit while they revise. Some continue to gather information as they write their third and fourth drafts. Nevertheless, writing is a serious business, and completing only one or two drafts will never enable you to produce quality work.

Organization and Development

"Getting Started" taught you to gather information about your chosen subjects. Collecting sufficient information—making sure you know as much about your subject as you need to—is an important first step in the writing process.

Next, you must determine what it is about your subject that you wish to communicate and how to use your information to get your point across clearly and effectively. Making such decisions is what the three chapters in Section One discuss.

Chapter 1 explains that two crucial steps early in the writing process are focusing and limiting the information you've collected so that you can decide on a central idea. Sometimes referred to as the *main* or *controlling idea*, the central idea of a paragraph or essay expresses the main point its writer will develop. Begin deciding on a central idea by reviewing the information you collected in your journal through focused freewriting, clustering, or other prewriting technique explained in "Getting Started." Then evaluate these details to determine what they tell you about your subject and what specifically you want to say about it in your paper. The more information you collect about your subject, the easier it will be to find an interesting central idea. Once you have a central idea, you will find it easier to decide which of the details you first gathered should be included in your writing project and which should be left out.

Chapter 2 explains how to make the paragraphs in the body of your essay unified, coherent, and well developed. If an essay is unified, all of its paragraphs relate directly to its thesis, a statement of its central idea. If a paragraph is unified, each piece of information relates directly to its topic sentence, the paragraph's central idea. If an essay or paragraph is coherent, it is easy to follow, for the writer has included logical connections between paragraphs and sentences. If a piece of writing is well developed, it contains enough detail to support or prove its central idea.

Chapter 3, "Introductions and Conclusions," offers suggestions for creating other types of paragraphs—those that make effective openings and closings for essays.

The reading selections in Section One contain examples of the important principles of organization and development explained in the chapter introductions. They are also a rich source of subjects for your own writing. However, like other sections in this book, each has a value of its own. Whether written by professionals or college students like you, they are interesting, informative, and even touching. Here's hoping they will inspire you to read and write about a variety of subjects, especially those you care about most.

CHAPTER 1

The Central Idea

A writer needs to know how to organize information in a form that is easy to follow. The best way to do this is to arrange, or focus, the details you have collected around a central idea.

Identifying the Central Idea

The central idea is often called the *main idea* because it conveys the writer's main point. It is also called the controlling idea, for it controls the kinds and amounts of detail a paragraph or essay contains.

Think of the central idea as the focal point to which all the information in an essay or paragraph points. Just as you focus a camera by aiming at a fixed point, you focus your writing by making all the details in it relate directly to the central idea. Everything you include should help prove, illustrate, or support that idea.

You can also think of a central idea as an umbrella. It is the broadest or most general statement; all other information is more specific and fits under it. (See the illustrations on page 54.)

Read these two paragraphs; all the information in them focuses on or points to their central ideas (in italics). Notice that the central ideas are broader than the details that support them.

> *Talk about bad days: today is a classic.* First, I woke up to hear my parents screaming in my ear about a bill I have to pay. Then I went to school to find out I had failed my art project. After that, I called home to learn that I might have my license revoked, and the accident wasn't even my fault. Finally, while walking out of the cafeteria, I tripped over somebody's book bag and made myself look like an ass. And it's only two in the afternoon! (Donna Amiano, "Bad Days")

> *My life is full of risks.* As a stair builder who works with heavy machinery, I risk cutting off a finger or a limb every day. Each Monday and Thursday, I risk four or five dollars on the state lottery. Every time I take my beat-up, 1981 Chevy Caprice Classic for a drive, I risk breaking down. However, the biggest risk I've ever taken was my decision to attend DeVry Institute this year. (Kenneth Dwyer, "Risks")

In most cases, the central idea of a paragraph is expressed in a *topic sentence*; the central idea of an essay is expressed in a *thesis statement*. Sometimes, however,

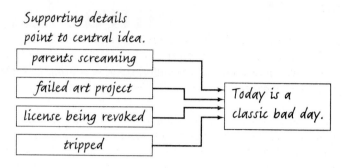

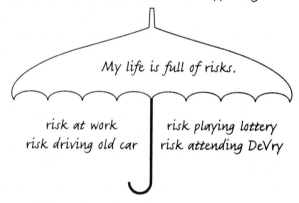

the central idea is so obvious that the author does not need to express it formally. In such cases, the central idea is *implied*. This is often true of narration and description, the kinds of writing that appear in Section Three. However, it can apply to any type of writing. (Note that in "A Typical Morning," the paragraph on page 64, the central idea is implied.)

Nonetheless, as a college writer, you should always try to state your central idea outright, in either a topic sentence (paragraph) or thesis statement (essay). Doing so will help you organize your work effectively. Often, the central idea can be expressed at the beginning of an essay or paragraph. But this is not always the best place for it. For example, if you need to give readers some explanatory detail first, you might state your central idea in the middle or even at the end of your writing. Delaying the central idea can create suspense; it can also avoid turning away readers who, at first, might be opposed to an opinion you are presenting.

Writing a Preliminary Topic Sentence or Thesis Statement

Creating an effective central idea for your writing is a process. Begin by jotting down a preliminary (working) version of your central idea on scratch paper or in your journal. This is a *working* version because you can and often should make significant changes to it after you have begun writing your paragraph or essay.

Of course, before you draft the working version of a topic sentence or thesis statement, you need to choose a subject to write about. By its very nature, a subject is general, abstract, and incomplete. A central idea, on the other hand, is specific, concrete, and complete. Notice how much more meaningful the subject "Skydiving" becomes when turned into a central idea: "*Skydiving* can be dangerous."

To turn any subject into a working topic sentence (paragraph) or thesis statement (essay), you must first *focus* your discussion of that subject by saying something concrete and specific about it. You can then **limit** your topic sentence or thesis in such as way as to keep the length of the paragraph or essay manageable.

FOCUS YOUR DISCUSSION

A good time to draft a working topic sentence or thesis is after reviewing the notes you made in your journal through listing, focused freewriting, or other information-gathering (prewriting) technique. While this information is fresh in your mind, ask yourself:

1. What is my **purpose?** What do I want my writing to accomplish?
2. What is the **main point** I wish to make about my subject?
3. What **details** can I use to develop this main point?

Purpose   Your purpose may be to entertain your readers with a colorful story or description, to explain a process, to contrast two types of popular music, or to convince the reader to adopt an opinion on a controversial issue. Once you have determined your purpose, you can decide which of the details and ideas you have gathered through prewriting will help you achieve that purpose.

Let's say your purpose is to describe the state forest you hiked through on a fall weekend. After reviewing your notes, you decide to talk about the brilliant oranges, yellows, and reds of the falling leaves. You also think about describing the family of deer that scampered by you. You even plan to include the tire that was dumped on the side of the trail. Finally, you want to explain that you felt more calm and relaxed at the end of the hike than at the beginning.

However, you decide not to write about your three-hour trip to the park in a pickup truck or about the friend you met as you were leaving. They have nothing to do with the forest.

Main Point   Now, ask yourself what is the most important or interesting aspect of your subject. Perhaps your hike helped you relax after a long week of studying. This will be your main point, the point you will make about your subject: "Hiking through Sandburg State Park helped me relax after a tough week at school."

Focusing turns an abstract, general idea into a central idea for a paragraph or essay. Notice how much clearer ideas on the right are as compared to subjects on the left.

Subject	Central Idea
Rock music	Rock music can damage one's hearing.
Alternative fuels	Alternative fuels can reduce our need for foreign oil.
Cell phones	Cell phones can be expensive, annoying, even dangerous.
Majoring in biology	Majoring in biology can prepare a student for a career in medicine, dentistry, or laboratory research.
Types of Chinese food	Szechwan, Hunan, and Cantonese cooking differ in several ways.

Details   Focusing also provides a starting point for the first draft of an essay because it helps you decide which details in your prewriting to include and which to discard. Let's say your working thesis is "Hiking through Sandburg State Park helped me relax after a tough week at school." You might discuss the vibrant colors of the leaves and describe the deer you encountered. But would you also include a description of the old tire you saw? No. You would certainly discard this information.

LIMIT YOUR DISCUSSION TO A MANAGEABLE LENGTH

Typically, students are asked to write short essays, usually ranging between 350 and 750 words. That's why it's important to limit your central idea. Otherwise, you won't be able to discuss it in enough detail to make your point effectively.

Let's say you choose to contrast two popular makes of automobiles. In a short essay, it would be foolish to discuss cost, performance, handling, comfort, reliability, safety features, and sound systems. A far more reasonable approach is to cover only two or three of these items. In fact, you might even limit yourself to cost; then you can divide your topic into more specific subsections like purchase price, yearly maintenance costs, and gas mileage. Here's what the thesis for your paper might look like: "The 2008 Mountain Marauder is far more economical than the 2008 Cross-Country Bandit."

SOME TIPS ON WRITING TOPIC SENTENCES AND THESIS STATEMENTS

1. Make sure your topic sentence or thesis is a complete sentence. A complete sentence contains a subject and a verb, and it expresses a complete thought.

   Not: Computers and being a successful college student.

   Or: Using computers to succeed in college.

   Or: How computers can help students succeed in college.

   But: Computers can help students succeed in college.

2. State your main point directly; don't announce it.

   Not: I am going to write about how computers can help students succeed in college.

   Or: This paper will discuss the fact that computers can help students succeed in college.

   But: Computers can help students succeed in college.

3. In most cases, readers will naturally assume that what you are writing about is your own opinion or is what you believe. There is no need to explain that.

   Not: I believe that computers can help students succeed in college.

   Or: It is my opinion that computers can help students succeed in college.

   But: Computers can help students succeed in college.

4. Make sure your topic sentence or thesis clearly states the point you want to make about your subject.

   Not: Computers affect student performance in college.

   But: Computers can help students succeed in college.

Controlling Unity and Development

The central idea is sometimes called the controlling idea, for it helps determine the kind and amount of information a paragraph or essays contains. This is explained further in Chapter 2. For now, remember that a piece of writing is unified if all the information relates to its central (controlling) idea. It is well developed if it contains all of the information it needs to prove, illustrate, or support that idea.

Revising the Central Idea

Always revise the working or preliminary version of your thesis statement or topic sentence as you go through the writing process. Like taking notes or writing a rough draft, writing a working thesis statement or topic sentence is intended only to give you a starting point and a direction. There is no rule that prevents you from stopping at any point in the process, looking back at what you have done, and changing it as often as you like. So don't be afraid to revise or change it at any time. Writing always involves discovery. The more you write and revise, the more likely you are to understand your subject and to revise what you *thought* you had wanted to say about it.

Study the three drafts of the introductory paragraphs from "Echoes," an essay by student Maria Cirilli. Each time Cirilli revised her work, she came to a clearer understanding of her subject and of what she wanted to say about it. This can be seen best in the last sentence, Cirilli's thesis. Her complete essay appears later in this chapter.

Cirilli—Draft 1

I hardly remember my grandmother except for the fact that she used to bounce me on her knees by the old-fashioned brick fireplace and sing old songs. I was only four years old when she died. Her face is a faded image in the back of my mind.

In contrast, I remember my grandfather very well. He was 6'4" tall. He possessed a deep voice, which distinguished him from others whether he was in the streets of our

small picture-perfect town in southern Italy
or in the graciously sculptured seventeenth-
century church. He appeared to be strong and
powerful. In fact he used to scare all my
girlfriends away when they came to play or
do homework. Yet, I knew that there was
nothing to be afraid of.

Is this thesis clear? Does it tell what the essay will say about Cirilli 's grandfather?

Cirilli—Draft 2

I hardly remember my grandmother except for
the fact that she used to bounce me on her
knees by the old-fashioned brick fireplace
and sing old songs. I was only four years
old when she died.

The last sentence of draft 1 has been removed.

In contrast, I remember my grandfather
very well. He was 6'4" tall, a towering man

Detail added to describe him better.

with broad shoulders and a pair of mustaches
that I watched turn from black to grey over
the years. He possessed a deep voice, which
distinguished him from others whether he was
in the streets of our small picture-perfect
town in southern Italy or in the graciously
sculptured seventeenth-century church. He
appeared to be strong and powerful. In fact,
he used to scare all my girlfriends away
when they came to play or do homework, yet
he was the most gentle man I have ever
known.

The thesis is clearer. But, will essay also discuss fear?

Cirilli—Draft 3

I hardly remember my grandmother except for the fact that she used to bounce me on her knees by the old-fashioned brick fireplace and sing old songs. I was only four years old when she died. Her face is a faded image in the back of my mind.

Cirilli reuses this sentence from draft 1.

In contrast, I remember my grandfather very well. He was 6'4" tall, a towering man with broad shoulders and a mustache that I watched turn from black to grey. His voice was deep, distinguishing him from others in

Detail about church removed; not needed.

our small picture-perfect town in southern Italy. To some, my grandfather appeared very powerful, and he used to scare my girlfriends away when they came to play or do homework. In fact, he was strong, but he was the gentlest and most understanding man I have ever known.

Thesis is expanded; now includes "most understanding."

Thesis stands alone in its own sentence; much clearer.

Practicing Writing Central Ideas

To turn a subject into a central idea, you must make a main point about the subject. In the left column are subjects that might be discussed in a paragraph or essay. Turn them into central ideas. Start by asking yourself what is most interesting or important about your subject. Express your central idea in a complete sentence, which has a subject and a verb and which expresses a complete idea. The first item is done for you.

┌─────────── **Central Idea** ───────────┐

Subject	**Main Point**
1. A successful diet	requires much will power.
2. College textbooks	
3. Computers	
4. My family	
5. Noise pollution	
6. Listening to music	
7. Buying a used car	
8. AIDS (or another disease)	
9. Learning to drive (swim, play tennis, use a computer, cook, fix cars, etc.)	
10. Studying mathematics (science, accounting, a foreign language, etc.)	

The principles just discussed are illustrated in the following reading selections. Read them carefully, take notes, and respond to the Questions for Discussion and Suggestions for Journal Entries that accompany them.

Four Paragraphs for Analysis

The four paragraphs that follow show the importance of focusing on a central idea. Written by various authors, they discuss four different ideas, but each focuses clearly on a main point developed through detail.

Barbara Dafoe Whitehead is a noted social historian and author. Her writing has appeared in several American magazines and professional journals. Gen X is an abbreviation for Generation X, a term that, roughly speaking, includes people in their late teens to late twenties. "The Girls of Gen X" first appeared in The American Enterprise *magazine (1998).*

Stephen Fox is the author of "The Education of Branch Rickey," one of many essays published in 1995 to mark the fiftieth anniversary of Jackie Robinson's breaking of professional baseball's color barrier. Branch Rickey was the owner of the Brooklyn Dodgers at the time. The paragraph included here is from that essay.

Ernest Albrecht is a professor of English, a drama critic, and the author of three books on the circus.

Denise Kormondy was a college freshman when she wrote "A Typical Morning," which discusses her early morning tugs-of-war with her father.

Preparing to Read

1. As the following four paragraphs show, a writer who wants to express a central idea in a topic sentence need not start with that sentence. Depending on the paragraph's purpose, he or she might provide a few sentences of background or explanation first. To create emphasis, a writer might even wait until the end of a paragraph before stating the central idea. In fact, as you will see in Denise Kormondy's paragraph from "A Typical Morning," writers sometimes choose not to express central ideas at all. Instead, they make readers draw their own conclusions. In such cases, the central idea is said to be implied.

2. As you read the first sentence of paragraph 1, try to identify Whitehead's main point. Keep this in mind as you read the details in the rest of the paragraph, which relate to that point.

3. Paragraphs 2, 3, and 4 contain several personal and place names, such as Branch Rickey, Brooklyn Dodgers, Jackie Robinson, and Madison Square Garden. Be on the lookout for them. If you are unsure about what they contribute to the meaning of the paragraph, look them up in an encyclopedia or on the Internet. In fact, if you have never heard of these people or places, look them up now.

Vocabulary

adolescence (noun)	The stage of growth between childhood and maturity, roughly from 10 to 18 years.
binge (adjective)	Excessive, uncontrolled.
controversial (adjective)	Causing disagreement; disputable, arguable.
debris (noun)	Waste, litter.
depression (noun)	A psychological disorder in which the patient feels sad, hopeless.
enigmatic (adjective)	Puzzling, mysterious.
harbinger (noun)	Sign of things to come, forerunner.
hippodrome (noun)	Arena for horses.
lathe (noun)	Machine for shaping wood.
roustabouts (noun)	Workers, laborers.
venereal (adjective)	Relating to sexual indulgence, most commonly as in a disease resulting from sexual contact.
wary (adjective)	Careful, cautious.

The Girls of Gen X

Barbara Dafoe Whitehead

ALL IS NOT well with the women of Generation X. Consider the evidence: Close to 40 percent of college women are frequent binge drinkers, a behavior related to date rapes and venereal disease. Young women suffer higher levels of depression, suicidal thoughts and attempts than young men from early adolescence on. Between 1980 and '92, the rate of completed suicides more than tripled among white girls and doubled among black girls. For white women between 15 and 24, suicide is the third leading cause of death.

The Example of Jackie Robinson*

Stephen Fox

FIFTY YEARS ago this fall, Branch Rickey announced that Jackie Robinson had signed a contract to play with the Brooklyn Dodgers organization, thus breaking the "color line" that had kept African-Americans out of white organized baseball in the 20th century. With that single stroke, the crafty, enigmatic

---

*Editor's title.

63-year-old white man and the wary, explosive 26-year-old black man helped spark a social revolution. Intensely controversial at the time, the signing of Robinson now seems a harbinger of the postwar civil-rights movement: three years before the integration of the armed forces, nine years before the Supreme Court's *Brown* decision, ten years before the Montgomery, Alabama, bus boycott.

Sawdust

Ernest Albrecht

A S A TEN year old, I watched as miniature mountains of the magical debris took shape around my father's lathe or his table saw, and with hardly any effort at all I imagined three rings and a hippodrome track sprinkled with the stuff in various colors. Having once conjured that, it didn't take much more effort to envision the ropes and cables that the circus roustabouts spun into a fantastic web transforming the old Madison Square Garden on Eighth Avenue and 49th Street (New York) into an exotic world of wonder and fantasy. That is why, of all the changes that progress has wrought upon the circus, I lament the loss of the sawdust the most. Rubber mats may be practical, but they have no magic.

A Typical Morning

Denise Kormondy

W HEN I HEARD the alarm, I turned it off, put the light on, and rolled over. I convinced myself that I was going to get out of bed, but I knew I wouldn't—I never do. Before I could fall back to sleep, I heard my father asking if I was awake. I assured him that I was and pulled the covers over my head. As I lay there, I noticed that the light at the top of the stairs was going on and off. That's one of my father's favorite tricks. I yelled down to him and insisted that I was up. I even turned on the television, but that didn't seem to fool him either. As I was falling back to sleep, he announced that it was snowing and, being half asleep, I believed him. Never mind that this happened in the middle of September. I looked out the window, but it was too dark to see anything, so I ran downstairs. Needless to say, there was no snow, but at least I was out of bed.

Read More on the Web*

St. Cloud State University's Literacy Education Online:
   http://leo.stcloudstate.edu/acadwrite/thesistatement.html

University of North Carolina Writing Center: http://www.unc.edu/depts/
   wcweb/handouts/thesis.html

Generation X Sources on the Web: http://membres.lycos.fr/coupland/
   coupgx.html

Site of the Jackie Robinson Foundation: http://www.jackierobinson.org/

Site of the Jackie Robinson Society: http://www.utexas.edu/students/
   jackie/

Site of the Circus World Museum: http://www.circusworldmuseum.com/

Questions for Discussion

1. What are the topic sentences in the first three paragraphs?
2. In your own words, what is the central idea of Kormondy's paragraph
    from "A Typical Morning"?
3. Would "The Girls of Gen X" have been as effective and easy to read
    had the topic sentence appeared in the middle of the paragraph? At
    the end of the paragraph?
4. What important information does Fox provide before the topic
    sentence in "The Example of Jackie Robinson"?
5. What is the main point of "Sawdust"? Why does Albrecht wait until
    the end of the paragraph to reveal it?

Thinking Critically

Remember that a central idea acts as an umbrella under which all the details and other, more limited, ideas in a paragraph or essay fit. The central
idea for the following paragraph is unstated. Read the paragraph; then, in
your journal, write your own central idea for it in a complete topic sentence. Remember, the idea in a topic sentence is broader than any other
idea in a paragraph.

> The planet Mars takes its name from the Roman god of war.
> Mercury is the Roman god of commerce; and Venus, the
> goddess of love. Pluto is named for the Greek god of the

---

*Note that URLs change frequently. If a site in which you're interested doesn't appear at the URL
listed, try typing the *name* of the site into a search engine such as Google. If the site still exists,
you're likely to find it.

underworld, Neptune rules the sea, and Jupiter reigns as king of the gods. Even the planets Saturn and Uranus borrow their names from ancient deities.

Suggestion for a Journal Entry

This journal entry is in three parts:

First, pick a limited subject you know a lot about. Here are some examples: waiting on tables, last year's Fourth of July picnic, your bedroom at home, feeding a baby, your car, studying math, your Uncle Mort, going to a concert, watching baseball on television.

Second, decide what are the most interesting or important points you can make about that subject. Choose *one* of these as the main point of a central idea. Write that central idea down in the form of a topic sentence for a paragraph you might want to write later.

Third, do the same with three or four other limited subjects you know about. Here's what your journal entry might look like when you have finished:

1. **Limited subject:** Feeding a baby

    Main points: Sometimes messy, always fun

    Topic sentence: Feeding a baby can be messy.

2. **Limited subject:** Uncle Mort

    Main points: Old, handsome, outgoing, considerate

    Topic sentence: My Uncle Mort was one of the most considerate people in my family.

3. **Limited subject:** Last year's Fourth of July picnic

    Main points: Much food, many people, lots of rain

    Topic sentence: Last year's Fourth of July picnic was a washout.

Echoes

Maria Cirilli

Born in a small town in southern Italy, Maria Cirilli immigrated to the United States in 1971. She earned her associate's degree in nursing from a community college and is now an assistant head nurse at the Robert Wood Johnson University Hospital in New Brunswick, New Jersey. Cirilli has completed her bachelor's in nursing at the University of Medicine and Dentistry of New Jersey. Since writing "Echoes" for a college composition class, she has revised it several times to add detail and make it more powerful.

Preparing to Read

1. Cirilli chose not to reveal the central idea of this essay—her thesis statement—in paragraph 1. However, the first paragraph is important because it contains information that we can contrast with what we read in paragraph 2.
2. The two main points in the thesis (paragraph 2) are important because they give us clues about the topic sentences in the body paragraphs, which follow.

Vocabulary

distinguishing (adjective)	Making different from.
exuberance (noun)	Joy, enthusiasm.
manicured (adjective)	Neat, well cared for.
mediator (noun)	Referee, someone who helps settle disputes.
negotiating (adjective)	Bargaining, dealing.
placate (verb)	Pacify, make calm.
siblings (noun)	Sisters and brothers.
solemnly (adverb)	Seriously.
tribulation (noun)	Trouble, distress.
vulnerable (adjective)	Open, without defenses.
with a vengeance (adverb)	Skillfully, earnestly.

Echoes

Maria Cirilli

I HARDLY REMEMBER my grandmother except for the fact that she used to bounce   1
me on her knees by the old-fashioned brick fireplace and sing old songs.
I was only four when she died. Her face is a faded image in the back of my
mind.

In contrast, I remember my grandfather very well. He was 6'4" tall, a   2
towering man with broad shoulders and a mustache that I watched turn from
black to grey. His voice was deep, distinguishing him from others in our small
picture-perfect town in southern Italy. To some, my grandfather appeared very
powerful, and he used to scare my girlfriends away when they came to play or
do homework. In fact, he was strong, but he was the gentlest and most understanding man I have ever known.

I still see him weeping softly as he read a romantic novel in which his   3
favorite character died after many trials and much tribulation. And I will never
forget how carefully he set the tiny leg of our pet bird, Iario, who had become
entangled in a fight with frisky Maurizio, our cat. Once, my brother and I accompanied him to our grandmother's grave at a nearby cemetery that was small
but manicured. As we approached the cemetery, my tall grandfather bent down
from time to time to pick wild flowers along the road. By the end of the journey,
he had a dandy little bouquet, which he placed solemnly at my grandmother's
grave while bountiful tears streamed down his husky, vulnerable face.

My grandfather was always available to people. Mostly, he helped se-   4
nior citizens apply for disability or pension benefits or file medical-insurance
claims. Several times, however, he was asked to placate siblings who had quar-
reled over a family inheritance. Many angry faces stormed into our home dissatisfied with what they had received, but they usually left smiling, convinced
by my grandfather that their parents had, after all, distributed their possessions
fairly.

At times, he could even play Cupid by resolving disputes between couples   5
engaged to be married. Whether the problem concerned which family would
pay for the wedding or who would buy the furniture, he would find a solution.
As a result, our family attended many weddings in which my proud grandfather
sat at the table of honor.

On Sundays, there was always a tray of fresh, homemade cookies and a pot   6
of coffee on our oversized kitchen table for visitors who stopped by after Mass.
Seeking advice about purchasing land or a house, they asked my grandfather if
he thought the price was fair, the property valuable, the land productive. After
a time, he took on the role of mediator, negotiating with a vengeance to obtain
the fairest deal for both buyer and seller.

I remember most vividly the hours we children spent listening to our   7
grandfather's stories. He sat by the fireplace in his wooden rocking chair and
told us about the time he had spent in America. Each one of us kids would aim

for the chair closest to him. We didn't want to miss anything he said. He told us about a huge tunnel, the Lincoln Tunnel, that was built under water. He also described the legendary Statue of Liberty. We were fascinated by his stories of that big, industrialized land called America.

As I grew up and became a teenager, I dreamt of immigrating to America   8 and seeing all the places that my grandfather had talked about. His exuberance about this land had a strong influence on my decision to come here.

A few months before I arrived in America my grandfather died. I still miss   9 him very much, but each time I visit a place that he knew I feel his presence close to me. The sound of his voice echoes in my mind.

Read More on the Web

University of Wisconsin site on parenting and grandparenting: http:// www1.uwex.edu/topics/Parenting_and_grandparenting.cfm

Extensive annotated bibliography on the relationship between grandchildren and grandparents: http://www.nnfr.org/igen/stressc. html

Questions for Discussion

1. What important information does Cirilli give us in paragraph 1?
2. What is her thesis? Why does she wait until paragraph 2 to reveal it?
3. Pick out the topic sentences in paragraphs 3 through 7, and explain what each tells us about Cirilli's grandfather.
4. What evidence does the author give to show that her grandfather was "gentle"? How does she prove he was "understanding"?
5. What about the fact that Cirilli's grandfather scared her girlfriends? Why does the author give us this information?
6. Why is "Echoes" a good title for this essay?

Thinking Critically

1. Reread the three drafts of Cirilli's introduction, which appear earlier in this chapter (pages 58). Then, in your journal, write a paragraph that explains the major differences you see among the versions. Use the notes in the margins as guides, but write the paragraph in your own words. If you read carefully, you will find even more differences than those described in the margins.
2. Cirilli tells us that her grandmother's "face is a faded image in the back of [her] mind." Why did she put this line back into the third version after taking it out of the second (page 60)? Explain in two or three sentences why keeping this line is important to Cirilli's essay.

Suggestions for Journal Entries

1. Use focused freewriting to gather information that shows that someone you know practices a particular virtue. Like Cirilli's grandfather, your subject might be gentle or understanding. Then again, he or she might be charitable, hardworking, generous, or considerate of others. Reread paragraph 3 or 4 in "Echoes" to get an idea of the kinds of details you might put in your journal. After completing your entry, read it carefully and add details if you can. Finally, write a sentence that expresses the main point you have made and that might serve as a topic sentence for a paragraph using this information.

2. Think of someone special in your life and write down a wealth of details about this person. Use brainstorming, interviewing, or any other information-gathering techniques discussed in "Getting Started." Then, discuss this special person in three or four well-written sentences. Like the topic sentences in "Echoes," each of yours should focus on only one main point you want to make about your subject or about your relationship with this person.

Suffering

Siu Chan

Siu Chan was born in Cambodia of Chinese parents. Her father owned a small business in Phnom Penh, the capital, where Siu lived with her parents and her five brothers and sisters. In 1975 her life changed drastically. That was the year that the Khmer Rouge, the movement headed by communist leader Pol Pot, took control of the country. The atrocities committed by this group resulted in the extermination of millions of native Cambodians and other people with millions more displaced from their homes and sent to live in work camps. In fact, the communists nearly evacuated the city of Phnom Penh and redistributed the people in rural areas.

This essay tells of Siu Chan's experience during the four years she lived under the tyranny of the Khmer Rouge. In 1979, she and three younger brothers and sisters escaped from Cambodia into Vietnam traveling by bus, boat, bicycle, and on foot. They spent five years in Vietnam before immigrating to the United States, where an uncle who sponsored them was waiting. Today, Siu works two jobs to help support her family and attends college part-time, majoring in accounting. As she explained to her writing instructor, she works seven days a week and has not had a day off in over three years.

Preparing to Read

1. Chan states a thesis in her first paragraph. It contains three main points. Make sure you understand each before going on to the rest of the essay.

2. This is a five-paragraph essay. Paragraph 1 is the introduction, with the essay's thesis statement. Each of the three main points in Chan's thesis is the basis for the topic sentence you will find in each body paragraph—2, 3, and 4. Paragraph 5 is the essay's conclusion.

3. Think about the significance of Chan's title. Doing so makes reading her essay easier.

4. The horrors that the Khmer Rouge created in Cambodia are documented in *The Killing Fields*, a film that you can find on videotape.

Vocabulary

authorities (noun)	People in charge.
craved (verb)	Desired.
malnutrition (noun)	Lack of proper food, inadequate diet.
nourishment (noun)	Proper food, sustenance.
tyranny (noun)	Oppression, dictatorship.

Suffering

Siu Chan

WHENEVER I THINK about the word "suffering," the first thought that comes 1
to mind is the time I lived under the dictatorship of the Khmer Rouge
from 1975 though 1979 in my homeland of Cambodia. It was the worst time
in my life: I was allowed very little personal freedom, I witnessed the death of
my family, and I nearly died of starvation.

Starting in 1975, when the communists under Pol Pot took over, the gov- 2
ernment destroyed nearly all personal freedom. Families were split apart, with
each member being forced to live separately. Even my two-year-old brother was
taken away to live with a group of children the same age. We were never able
to visit each other, and when my parents passed away I wasn't even able to see
them for a final goodbye. In addition, the communists forced me into slave labor. I got up at 3:00 AM every day, sometimes to work on a roadbuilding project
for which I carried water and earth and sometimes to dig a hole for an artificial
pond. Our work day sometimes ended at 11:00 PM. Moreover, I was allowed to
speak only one language: Cambodian. At home, we had spoken Chinese. The
authorities would not allow any criticism of the government, and I had to be
very careful about what I said and did. Otherwise, they would kill me.

During those four years, I lost six members of my family. First my grand- 3
parents passed away about two months apart. They were old and ill. Because
my country had experienced war and tyranny for many years, they could not
get the medicines they needed. Approximately four months later, my uncle
died; he was overworked and did not have enough food to eat, so he became
ill. There was no medicine to help him either. One year later, my little brother
died after suffering from a fever for one full week. Again, no medication was
available. After another six months, my parents also died one month apart.
They starved to death.

I had to eat food that the communist government gave me whether it was 4
good or not. Usually it was just plain white rice, sometimes with a few wild
vegetables mixed in, but it was never enough to fill me up. I can still remember
a three-month period during which I nearly starved to death. The rice crop
had failed because of flooding, so I had to go into the woods to search for tree
roots and other wild foods. But they satisfied me only temporarily, and they
did not have enough nourishment to keep me healthy. I began to suffer from
malnutrition, and my body became swollen. In fact, I was so hungry for real
food that I sometimes burst into tears. I craved food all the time. I even dreamt
about it. I would have been very satisfied with only a bowl of plain rice or a
slice of bread.

Throughout those four years, I suffered a great deal. I cannot find the ap- 5
propriate words to describe that horror. However, having gone through it, I can
appreciate the life I have now. My spirit and my mind get stronger each day.

I learned not to waste anything—especially food—when I was in Cambodia, and I am doing well in the United States. I work hard and I have even started going to college. What's more I feel confident about the future. My suffering has prepared me to face any obstacle.

Read More on the Web

The Cambodian Genocide Project Website: http://www.yale.edu/cgp/

Questions for Discussion

1. What is Chan's thesis? What are the three main points found in that thesis?
2. Identify each of the topic sentences Chan uses in paragraphs 2, 3, and 4.
3. Explain how the details in paragraphs 2, 3, and 4 relate to their topic sentences.

Thinking Critically

1. Why do you think the authorities allowed people to speak only Cambodian?
2. What questions might you ask Chan if you had the opportunity? Write those questions in the margins.

Suggestions for Journal Entries

1. Recall a personal experience in which your freedom was limited and/ or your well-being was threatened because of the power someone had over you. Use clustering, a subject tree, or listing to record details.
2. Recall a battle with serious illness from which you or someone you know well suffered. What caused it? What were its symptoms? What kind of suffering did it cause? Was the illness ever overcome? How?

Writing and Its Rewards

Richard Marius

Richard Marius directed the expository writing program at Harvard University. He began his career as a historian and has authored biographies of Thomas More and Martin Luther. He also wrote four novels and several books on writing, including The McGraw-Hill College Handbook, *which he co-authored with Harvey Wiener. "Writing and Its Rewards" is from* A Writer's Companion, *Marius's splendid guide for both experienced and developing writers. Richard Marius died in 1999.*

Preparing to Read

1. Writing is a process of drafting and revising, Marius tells us. As you probably learned in "Getting Started," *drafting* means putting down facts and ideas in rough form, no matter how disorganized your paragraph or essay might seem at first. *Revising* involves rewriting, reorganizing, adding to, deleting from, and correcting earlier drafts to make them more effective and easier to read.

2. In paragraph 5, Marius mentions three writers whose work you may want to read: Geoffrey Chaucer, Leo Tolstoy, and W. H. Auden. To learn more about them, look up their names in an encyclopedia or reference book recommended by your college librarian.

Vocabulary

eighteenth century (adjective and noun)	The 1700s.
embodied (adjective)	Contained.
enduring (adjective)	Lasting.
lexicographer (noun)	Writer of a dictionary.
parable (noun)	Story with a lesson or moral.
profound (adjective)	Deep, extreme.
weighing (adjective)	Carefully considering.

Writing and Its Rewards

Richard Marius

WRITING IS hard work, and although it may become easier with practice it   1
is seldom easy. Most of us have to write and rewrite to write anything well. We try to write well so people will read our work. Readers nowadays will

[handwritten margin notes: hard to understand / difficult writing]

seldom struggle to understand difficult writing unless someone—a teacher perhaps—forces them to do so. Samuel Johnson, the great eighteenth-century English writer, conversationalist, and lexicographer, said, "What is written without effort is in general read without pleasure." Today what is written without effort is seldom read at all.

[handwritten margin notes: investments of / requires time / planing / serious / must]

Writing takes time—lots of time. Good writers do not dash off a piece in an hour and get on to other things. They do not wait until the night before a deadline to begin to write. Instead they plan. They write a first draft. They revise it. They may then think through that second draft and write it once again. Even small writing tasks may require enormous investments of time. If you want to become a writer, you must be serious about the job, willing to spend hours dedicated to your work.

[handwritten margin notes: A good writer is / able to put their full / attention to / their work / allow their full / and is able to give 100% into their work]

Most writers require some kind of solitude. That does not mean the extreme of the cork-lined room where the great French writer Marcel Proust composed his huge works in profound silence. It does mean mental isolation—shutting yourself off from the distractions around you even if you happen to be pounding a computer keyboard in a noisy newspaper office. You choose to write rather than do other things, and you must concentrate on what you are doing.

[handwritten margin notes: be able to handle / failure & move / forward / pay attention 2 / details]

In a busy world like ours, we take a risk when we isolate ourselves and give up other pursuits to write. We don't know how our writing will come out. All writers fail sometimes. Successful writers pick themselves up after failure and try again. As you write, you must read your work again and again, thinking of your purpose, weighing your words, testing your organization, examining your evidence, checking for clarity. You must pay attention to the thousands and thousands of details embodied in words and experience. You must trust your intuitions; if something does not sound right, do it again. And again. And again.

[handwritten margin notes: have confidence / in what you / have written]

Finally you present your work to readers as the best you can do. After you submit a final draft, it is too late to make excuses, and you should not do so. Not everybody will like your final version. You may feel insecure about it even when you have done your best. You may like your work at first and hate it later. Writers wobble back and forth in their judgments. Chaucer, Tolstoy and Auden are all on record for rejecting some of their works others have found enduring and grand. Writing is a parable of life itself.

Read More on the Web

University of North Carolina Writing Center: http://www.unc.edu/depts/wcweb/handouts/thesis.html

St. Cloud State University's Literacy Education Online: http://leo.stcloudstate.edu/acadwrite/thesistatement.html

Questions for Discussion

1. Reread Marius's introduction. What is his thesis? What is the main point of that thesis?
2. Identify the topic sentences in paragraphs 2–5.
3. Explain how the topic sentences in paragraphs 2–5 relate to Marius's thesis.
4. What does Marius mean by "writing is a parable of life itself"? What is a parable, and why might writing be one?

Thinking Critically

One assumption Marius makes is that all educated people need to be competent writers. Is that true of you? Will you need strong writing skills for the job you take after college? Contact someone practicing in that field or profession. Ask her or him about the need for good writing skills. Then write a short report of your interview.

Suggestions for Journal Entries

1. Marius says "Most writers require some kind of solitude." Do you? Use your journal to describe the place in which you write or study most often. Is it comfortable? Can you concentrate there? Should you find another place to work?
2. "Writing and Its Rewards" contains advice to make us better writers. Use your journal to list three or more specific pieces of advice to help you or a classmate become better at an important activity you know a lot about. Here are examples of such an activity: studying or doing homework; dressing for school or work; driving in heavy traffic or bad weather; communicating with parents, children, teachers, or classmates; maintaining a car; losing weight; sticking to a nutritious diet; or treating members of a different race, age group, religion, or sex with respect.

   Express each piece of advice in a complete sentence, the kind that can serve as the topic sentence to a paragraph you might write later on to explain that piece of advice more fully.

Suggestions for Sustained Writing

1. Recall what you have read about writing central ideas at the beginning of this chapter: a central idea contains a subject and makes a point about that subject, a point that is focused and specific. Think about a subject you

know a great deal about. Then write four or five sentences that express different points about that subject. Let's say your subject is Thanksgiving dinner. You might write the following central ideas:

Subject	Main Point
Thanksgiving dinner at my house	is always very noisy.
In my family, Thanksgiving dinner	means eating a lot and watching football.
Our Thanksgiving dinners	are not very traditional.
A typical Thanksgiving dinner	can kill a diet.
Preparing a Thanksgiving dinner	takes a lot of work.

Next, use each of these sentences as the topic sentence for a different paragraph. When you write each paragraph, remember to include details that support or explain the paragraph's central idea as expressed in its topic sentence. Here's what one of the paragraphs you are going to write might look like:

> <u>Preparing a Thanksgiving dinner takes a lot of work</u>. First you'll have to prepare the stuffing. This means peeling and cutting up the apples, chopping up and soaking the bread, mixing in the raisins and the spices. After you're done, you'll have to stuff the turkey with this gooey mixture. While you're waiting for the bird to roast, you should peel, boil, and mash the potatoes, and cook any other vegetables you will serve. You'll also have to bake the biscuits, set the table, pour the cider, and put the finishing touches on the pumpkin and apple pies you spent three hours preparing the night before.

As you learned in "Getting Started," don't be satisfied with the first draft of your work; rewrite it several times. Then, correct spelling, grammar, punctuation, and other distracting problems.

2. If you haven't done so already, complete the Suggestion for a Journal Entry after "Four Paragraphs for Analysis." Use *each* of the topic sentences you were asked to write as the beginning of a paragraph in which you explain the main point you are making in that topic sentence. You should wind up with the rough drafts of four or five paragraphs, each of which is several sentences long.

    Rewrite these rough drafts until you are satisfied that your topic sentences are clear and that you have included enough information to help your readers understand the main point in each paragraph easily. Complete the writing process by editing your work just as student writer Deborah Diglio did with her paper in "Getting Started."

3. In item 2 of the Suggestions for Journal Entries after Maria Cirilli's "Echoes," you were asked to write three or four sentences, each of which was to focus on a single aspect or characteristic of someone special in your life. Make each of these the topic sentence of a paragraph that describes or explains that aspect or characteristic. If necessary, reread "Echoes." Many of the paragraphs in the body of this essay will serve as models for your writing.

    Next, write an appropriate thesis statement for an essay containing the three or four paragraphs you've just written. Make sure that your thesis statement somehow reflects the main points found in the topic sentences of the three or four paragraphs in your essay. Make this thesis part of your essay's first or introductory paragraph.

    Again, approach this writing assignment as a process. Complete several drafts of your paper, and don't submit your final product until you are satisfied that you have dealt with problems in grammar, spelling, punctuation, and the like.

4. Have you ever lived under the tyranny of a government, organization, or person? If so, explain how this experience affected you in two or three ways. Like Siu Chan ("Suffering," page 72), begin your essay with an introductory paragraph that contains a thesis statement. Make sure that the two or three main points in this thesis statement express the effects that living under this oppression caused you. Then, make these main points the basis of the topic sentences you use in your essay's body paragraphs. Again, use Chan's essay as your model.

    Begin by reviewing the notes you made in your journal after reading Chan's essay. They might provide you with materials with which you can get started. Then, do some more prewriting to gather even more information. Next, write a preliminary thesis statement, which might appear in your introductory paragraph. Also write a preliminary or working topic sentence for each of your essay's body paragraphs. Again, base each topic sentence on one of the main points stated in your thesis. Next, make a rough outline of your essay.

Write a rough draft and several revisions of your essay. Don't be afraid to revise your working thesis and topic sentences if you need to. End your essay with a conclusion, such as the one Chan used. Finally, edit and proofread the whole paper carefully.

5. If you responded to item 2 in the Suggestions for Journal Entries after Marius's "Writing and Its Rewards," you have probably listed three or four sentences that give advice on a particular activity you know a lot about. Use *each* of these sentences as the topic sentence of a paragraph that explains the advice you are giving in detail. For example, if you are trying to help a friend lose weight, one thing you might suggest is that he or she get a lot of exercise. That would make a good topic sentence of a paragraph that goes like this:

> *Get a lot of exercise.* Wake up early and jog two or three miles. Use the weight room in the college gymnasium several times a week or ride one of the stationary bicycles you will find there. If all else fails, walk the three miles to school every day, do sit-ups in your room, or jump rope in your backyard.

After you have written three or four such paragraphs, decide on a thesis statement that might express the central idea of the essay in which these paragraphs will appear. Make your thesis broad enough to include the main points you made in all three or four of your topic sentences. Use the thesis statement as the basis of a paragraph that comes before and introduces the three or four body paragraphs you have just completed.

Now, rewrite your paper several times. Make sure it is clear and well organized.

6. Write a short essay in which you explain three reasons that you are doing something important in your life. Include these three reasons in a central idea that you will use as your thesis statement. Let's say that you decide to explain three of your reasons for going to college. You might write: "I decided to attend Metropolitan College to prepare for a rewarding career, to meet interesting people, and to learn more about music and literature." Put this thesis somewhere in your introductory paragraph.

Next, use *each* of the reasons in your thesis as the main point in the topic sentences of the three paragraphs that follow. In keeping with the example on the previous page, you might use the following as topic sentences for paragraphs 2, 3, and 4. The main point in each topic sentence is in italics:

Paragraph 2: The most important reason I decided to attend Metropolitan College was *to prepare myself for a rewarding career.*

Paragraph 3: *The opportunity to meet interesting people* was another reason I thought that going to college would be a good idea.

Paragraph 4: My decision to continue my schooling also had a lot to do with my desire to *learn more about literature and music.*

Try to develop each of these in a paragraph of three or four sentences that will help you explain the main point of your topic sentence completely and effectively. Finally, as with other assignments in this chapter, revise and edit your work thoroughly.

Writing to Learn: A Group Activity

THE FIRST MEETING

Meeting in a group of three or four classmates, reread Stephen Fox's paragraph, "The Example of Jackie Robinson" on page 63. Ask each member of the group to research a person, place, event, or thing that played an important role in the struggle to secure civil rights for African-Americans. Here are some examples.

Martin Luther King, Jr.'s "I Have a Dream" Speech

Rosa Parks

Medgar Evers

Malcolm X

Jesse Jackson

The Montgomery, Alabama, bus boycott

The U.S. Supreme Court's *Brown v. Board of Education* decision

The 1965 Civil Rights Law

The Ku Klux Klan

RESEARCH

You can learn about the subject you choose by looking it up in a current encyclopedia or on the World Wide Web or by interviewing someone, such as a history, political science, law, or other professor, who knows a great deal about the civil rights movement.

Find out why your subject is important to the struggle for civil rights for African-Americans. After completing your research, summarize what you have learned in a paragraph of about 100 of your own words. A good way to start is with a topic sentence that explains your subject's importance to the civil rights movement. Then, fill your paragraph with details that prove, support, or explain that idea. Finally, in another, shorter paragraph, explain the steps you took to gather information.

THE SECOND MEETING

When you meet with your group again, give each member a copy of your paragraph. As you discuss each other's work, make suggestions that will help each student revise and edit his or her writing.

CHAPTER 2

Paragraphs: Mastering Unity, Coherence, and Development

Chapter 1 explained how to focus your writing through a central idea. Deciding on the kinds of information to include in a piece of writing and organizing that information in a logical way are governed by the principles of *unity* and *coherence*. Deciding how much information to include has to do with *development*.

Creating Unity

Writing is unified if it contains only those details that help support or explain—develop—the central idea. The central idea contains a subject and the main point the writer wants to make about that subject. In the following paragraph, Dorian Friedman expresses his central idea in the first sentence, his topic sentence. Its subject is "the child"; its main point is "appears unusually cranky." Note that all of the details in the paragraph relate directly to this idea.

> It was South American fishermen who first dubbed [named] the December arrival of warm coastal currents "El Niño"—for the baby Christ—and this year, the child *appears unusually cranky.* Scientists tracking a mass of warm water building along the equatorial Pacific say it may signal the most pronounced El Niño of the century. The cyclical phenomenon—El Niño visits every two to seven years—occurs when trade winds and ocean currents change course for reasons still not understood. Already this year's system is scrambling climatic conditions worldwide, causing droughts in Asia and Brazil and torrential rains in Peru. Meanwhile, Californians are bracing [preparing] for rains and flooding this winter [1997–1998] that could match the 1982–83 El Niño.

It is not hard to lose focus on the main point and include irrelevant information—information that doesn't explain or support a central idea. Including such information will sidetrack your readers by drawing their attention to ideas that don't serve your purpose. It may even make your writing difficult to follow. So make sure to check for unity when you revise your rough drafts.

The following paragraph is based on one by Geoffrey Ward, who wrote an article about the fiftieth anniversary of India's independence for *National Geographic* magazine. However, Ward's original paragraph has been rewritten and now contains information irrelevant to its central idea. This information was added to show that such information can destroy paragraph unity.

> [1] Indian civilization has an astonishingly long history, and Delhi has witnessed a good deal of it. [2] There have been at least eight cities here in the past 3,000 years, beginning with Indraprastha, the capital mentioned in the Hindu epic [heroic poem], the *Mahabharata.* [3] Some scholars believe that if all the smaller settlements and fortifications and military outposts whose remnants are scattered across the landscape were taken into account, the actual number would be closer to 15. [4] Today, remnants of several old civilizations can also be found in Rome, Italy. [5] Monuments, ruins, and relics of the rich past are everywhere. [6] The high-rise office buildings that have gone up near Connaught Place in recent years cast their reflections into the green waters of a 14th-century steppe well. [7] In fact, as one of the world's fastest growing countries, India is experiencing a great deal of urban construction. [8] Traffic on one of New Delhi's busiest thoroughfares has to swerve around the masonry slab that marks a Muslim saint's grave. [9] Under the Independence Act of 1947 the Muslim state of Pakistan emerged as a separate country. [10] Even on the fairways on the New Delhi Golf Club . . . royal tombs offer unique hazards.

Ward establishes his focus in the first sentence; his subject is "Delhi"; his main point is that it "has witnessed a good deal" of Indian civilization's "long history." Each detail that follows this sentence should relate directly to the main point. However, this is not the case with the irrelevant information added, as the following explanation shows.

> **Sentence 1,** the topic sentence, expresses the central idea.
> **Sentence 2** tells us about cities that existed on this site as far back as 3,000 years ago, so it helps explain the "long history" mentioned in the topic sentence.
> **Sentence 3** continues the idea begun in sentence 2, so it too is relevant to the topic sentence.
> **Sentence 4** makes an interesting comparison between Rome and Delhi. However, it does not help convince the reader that Delhi has witnessed a great deal of Indian history. It should be removed.
> **Sentence 5** mentions the city's "rich past." Therefore, it belongs in the paragraph.

Sentence 6 tells us about a 600-year-old well, another sign of Delhi's "long history." It too belongs.

Sentence 7 makes no reference to the past; it is entirely about the present. It is irrelevant and should be removed.

Sentence 8 is relevant; it explains that a modern highway has been designed in such a way as to preserve a historical site, in this case the grave of a Muslim saint.

Sentence 9 is irrelevant. It has nothing to do with Delhi, the paragraph's subject, or about the long history that the city has witnessed. It doesn't belong.

Sentence 10 is relevant to the topic sentence. The royal tombs are more evidence that Delhi has seen much of the country's history.

Maintaining Coherence

A paragraph is coherent if the sentences it contains are connected clearly and logically in an order that is easy to follow. An essay is coherent if there are logical connections between paragraphs. The thought in one sentence or paragraph should lead directly—without a break—to the thought in the next sentence or paragraph.

You can create these logical connections in two ways: (1) using transitional devices and (2) referring to what you have mentioned earlier.

USE TRANSITIONAL DEVICES

Transitional devices, also called transitions or connectives, are words, phrases, and even whole sentences that create clear relationships in and between sentences and paragraphs. They can be used for different purposes.

To Indicate Time   You would be indicating the passing of time if you wrote: "Arturo left before dawn. *In a while,* sunlight burst over the green hills." Other transitions indicating time include these:

After a while	In the meantime
Afterward	Meanwhile
At that time	Now
Back then	Soon
Before long	Suddenly
Before that time	Then
In a few minutes (hours, days, etc.)	While

To Indicate Similarities or Differences   You can use transitions to show that things are similar or different: "Philip is following in his sister's footsteps. *Like her,* he is majoring in engineering. *Unlike her,* however, he hates math." Here are other examples:

Similarities		Differences
In addition	Although	On the other hand
In the same way	However	Still
Likewise	In contrast	Though
Similarly	Nevertheless	Yet

To Introduce Examples, Repeat Information, or Emphasize a Point   You would be introducing an example if you wrote: "Mozart displayed his genius early. *For example,* he wrote his first symphony when only a boy."

You would be repeating information if you wrote: "At age 21, he was appointed court composer in Vienna. This was *another* early indication of his genius."

You would be emphasizing a point if you wrote: "The end of Mozart's career was hardly spectacular. *In fact,* he died in poverty at age 35." Here are some more examples:

Introducing Examples	Repeating Information	Emphasizing a Point
As an example	Again	As a matter of fact
For instance	Once again	Indeed
Specifically	Once more	More important
Such as		To be sure

To Add Information   If you wanted to add information by using a transition, you might write: "When Grant and Lee met at Appomattox Courthouse in 1865, they brought the Civil War to an end. *What's more*, they opened a new chapter in U.S. history." Here are other such transitions:

Also	Furthermore
And	In addition
As well	Likewise
Besides	Moreover
Further	Too

To Show Cause and Effect   If you wanted to explain that one action caused another, you might write: "During the early days of the Revolution General Washington was unable to defend New York City. *Consequently,* he retreated to Pennsylvania." Other cause-effect transitions include these:

As a result	So that
Because	Then
Hence	Therefore
Since	Thus

To Show Condition   If you needed to explain that one action or fact depends on another, you might create a relationship based on condition by using words like *if*, as in this sentence: "Jones should arrive soon. *If she doesn't*, we will have to go on alone." Here are other transitions that show condition:

As long as	In case	Unless
As soon as	In order to	When
Even if	Provided that	Whenever

REFER TO MATERIAL YOU MENTIONED EARLIER

You can refer to material mentioned earlier by (1) using pronouns that link details and ideas and (2) restating important words or ideas.

Using Linking Pronouns   Linking pronouns point directly to specific names or words you have mentioned earlier. Such pronouns direct the reader to nouns in earlier sentences or paragraphs; these nouns are called *antecedents*. Relying on pronouns to maintain coherence also helps you avoid repeating the same nouns over and over.

In this paragraph by Mother Teresa, the Roman Catholic nun who dedicated herself to the poor, linking pronouns appear in italics.

> Here in Calcutta, we have a number of non-Christians and Christians *who* work together in the house of the dying and other places. There are also *some who* offer *their* care to the lepers. One day an Australian man came and made a substantial donation. But as *he* did *this he* said, "*This* is something external. Now I want to give something of *myself*." *He* now comes regularly to the house of the dying to shave the sick men and to converse with *them*. *This* man gives not only *his* money but also *his* time. *He* could have spent it on *himself*, but what *he* wants is to give *himself*.

Here are other pronouns you might want to use to create coherence:

Personal pronouns refer to people and things:

I (me, my, mine)	We (us, our, ours)
He, she, it (him, his; her, hers; its)	You (your, yours)
	They (them, their, theirs)

Relative pronouns help describe nouns by connecting them with clauses, groups of words with subjects and verbs:

Who (whose, whom)	Whatever
That	Which
What	Whichever

Demonstrative pronouns precede and stand for the nouns to which they refer: "*This* is my book" or "*These* are the best seats in the house." The most common demonstrative pronouns are *this, that, these,* and *those.*

Indefinite pronouns make general rather than specific reference. You can use them as long as you are sure the reader can identify their antecedents easily. For example: "*Both* Sylvia and Andy were in an accident. *Neither* was seriously injured." Here are other indefinite pronouns:

All	Neither	None	Some
Another	Either	No one	Somebody
Anyone	Everybody	Others	Someone
Each	Nobody	Several	

Restating Important Details and Ideas   The second way to refer to material that has come before is by repeating words and phrases or by using *synonyms,* terms that have the same or nearly the same meanings. Read this paragraph by Shen C. Y. Fu, a curator of Chinese art for the Smithsonian Institute. Fu uses the word *calligraphy* four times, but he also uses synonyms.

> *Calligraphy* is generally defined as beautiful *writing.* In the West the *term* applies to *decorative writing* or may simply mean *good pen-manship.* In China, however, *calligraphy* is regarded as the ultimate artistic expression, requiring years of training, discipline, and dedication before mastery can be achieved. Like music and dance, *calligraphy* is an art of performance. But unlike music and dance, each performance of *calligraphy* results in a tangible [material] creation that both captures the artist's technical skills at the time and provides concrete evidence of his or her immediate mood and innate [inborn] personality.

Developing Effective Paragraphs

A paragraph or essay is well developed if it contains all the details it needs to prove, support, or illustrate its central idea. You should include enough detail to make your point clearly and convincingly. You should also arrange details in a way that fits your purpose.

DETERMINING HOW MUCH INFORMATION IS ENOUGH

In some paragraphs, you will have to supply many concrete details, examples, and other information important to your topic sentence. In others, you might be able to make your point with only one or two supportive details. And in a few, one sentence is all you might need to achieve your purpose. (However, remember that using too many one-sentence paragraphs can make your writing choppy.)

Rely on your central idea to guide you. After all, it contains the main point you want to make, and it can help you determine the kind and amount of detail to include. Let's say you begin with this topic sentence: "Majoring in biology is a good foundation for several careers." You might discuss careers in medicine or dentistry. But since your thesis mentions several reasons—three or more—you would also have to mention other careers, like those in teaching, environmental management, or forestry.

In short, think of a central idea as a promise you make to your reader to discuss your main point in as much detail as appropriate. If you start by saying that "there are three ways to reduce the risk of heart attack," then discuss all three, not just two, as fully as you can. If you want to prove that your brother is a slob, don't just describe the mess in his closet; talk about the jumble of old food containers in his car; the torn, dirty jeans he wears; the pile of papers and books he often leaves on the kitchen table.

Deciding how much information to include isn't always easy. For now, remember that it is always better to provide too much information than not enough. Too much information might bore readers, but too little might leave them confused or unconvinced.

Just how much to include was what the writer of the following email had to decide as she wrote to her children about her trip to Australia. Her topic sentence is in italics:

Dear Tess and Mike,

Hope things are well with you. *I'm having a great time.* Yesterday we went "canyoning" And, believe it or not, your mother rappelled off the face of a sixty-foot cliff (I have pictures to prove it!) into the dark tunnel entrance of a beautiful canyon filled with what looked like prehistoric plants. All that was missing was the T Rex stalking around the corner! It scared the heck out me the first time, but after the third and last descent it was great and about the best time I've had! We had to climb out of the canyon along the ice cold stream bed and actually had to swim for about 50 ft in frigid water (remember the water in the Oregon caves? It was almost as cold.) The stream had bright red lobster-like creatures (yabbies) and big snakes. (I learned that little bit of news after we were half way through and past the point of no return!) However, I've met a lot of nice people—including some from Eugene [the author's hometown]. I hope you enjoy your vacation. I miss you guys and wish you were here—maybe next year!

See you soon, Mom. ("An Awesome Time," Dr. Marie Sorrentino)

Obviously the author could have used even more examples, but the ones included here convince us that she is surely "having a great time."

CHOOSING THE BEST METHOD OF DEVELOPMENT

You can develop an idea in many ways. The one you choose depends on your purpose—the effect you want your writing to have on your readers—and your main point. Your purpose might be to narrate, to describe, to explain, to persuade, or any combination of these.

Description and Narration   If your purpose is to introduce your readers to a person, place, or thing, you might describe it in concrete detail. The easiest way to gather such detail is by using the five senses: sight, hearing, smell, taste, and touch. Chapter 6 covers description in detail. If you want to tell a story—explain what happened—you can narrate events as they occurred in time, discussing each event as it happened. Chapter 7 covers narration in detail.

Explanation and Argument   If your purpose is to explain an idea (exposition) or to argue an opinion (argumentation), you can use several methods. Among these are, of course, narration and description. But there are others:

- Conclusion/support: Use concrete details and facts to support or clarify an idea.
- Illustration: Develop an idea with examples.
- Definition: Explain a new, complicated, or sophisticated term or concept.
- Classification: Distinguish between types or classes.
- Comparison/contrast: Point out similarities or differences.
- Analogy: Compare an abstract idea to something that is concrete and familiar. The subjects being compared may seem unrelated at first.
- Cause/effect: Explain why something happens.
- Process analysis: Explain how something happens or how to do something.

Deciding which method of development to use depends upon your purpose. Let's say you want to persuade readers that the best way to clean up the rivers in your town is to find polluters. The cause/effect method might work well. If you want to explain how a recent high school graduate should prepare for college, you might use process analysis. In some cases, you might want to use a variety of methods. For example, if your purpose is to convince people that hybrid vehicles are one answer to the energy crisis, you might first have to define "hybrid," contrast such cars to traditional models, and explain the effects on oil consumption that these cars might help us achieve. Chapters on process analysis, comparison/contrast, illustration, argumentation, and persuasion appear later in this book.

DECIDING HOW TO ARRANGE THE IDEAS AND DETAILS IN A PARAGRAPH

Narration and Description   Often, the best way to organize narration or description is to recall details just as you saw or experienced them. In *narration,* you can arrange details just as they happened, in chronological (time) order. In the following narrative paragraph, John Steinbeck writes of a young man being chased by the police. Words that relate to narration are in italics.

> Pepé *stumbled* down the hill. His throat was almost closed with thirst. *At first* he *tried to run,* but immediately he *fell* and *rolled. After that* he *went* more carefully. The moon *was just disappearing* behind the mountains *when* he *came* to the bottom. He *crawled* into the heavy brush *feeling* with his fingers for water. There was no water in the bed of the stream, only damp earth. Pepé *laid* his gun *down* and *scooped up* a handful of mud and put it in his mouth, and *then* he *spluttered* and *scraped* the earth from his tongue with his finger, for the mud *drew* at his mouth like a poultice [plaster dressing]. He *dug* a hole in the stream bed with his fingers, *dug* a little basin to catch water; but *before* it was very deep his head *fell forward* on the damp ground and he *slept.* ("Flight")

When *describing* you can put details into a spatial pattern, in any arrangement you think best. You might describe a place from east to west or left to right; an object from top to bottom; a person from head to toe. In the following paragraphs, South African novelist Alan Paton uses sight and hearing to show us a view from a hilltop near the town of Ixopo. Note the italicized words, which direct us to various parts of the scene as the author describes them. Also note the place names that he includes; they are in bold.

> There is a lovely road that runs from **Ixopo** into the hills. These hills are grass-covered and rolling, and they are lovely beyond any singing of it. The road climbs seven miles into them, to **Carisbrooke,** and *from there,* if there is no mist, you look *down* on one of the fairest valleys of Africa. *About you* there is grass and bracken [large fern] and you may hear the forlorn [sad] crying of the titihoya, one of the birds of the veld [grassland]. *Below you* is the valley of the Umzimkuhu [river], on its journey from **Drakensberg** to the sea; and *beyond and behind* the river, great hill after great hill.

Expository and Argumentative Writing   Again, several choices are available when trying your hand at exposition— writing that explains—and at argument—writing that proves a point or defends an opinion. Here are a few patterns of arrangement you can use.

From General to Specific   Starting with a general statement and supporting it with specific details or ideas is a common way to organize a paragraph. Each of the following paragraphs has a different purpose and uses a different method of development. However, all begin with a general statement (the topic sentence) that is followed and developed by specific information.

Comparison and Contrast: Point Out Similarities and Differences

Grant and Lee were in complete contrast, representing two diametrically opposed elements in American life. Grant was the modern man emerging: behind him, ready to come on the stage, was the great age of steel and machinery, of crowded cities and a restless, burgeoning [blossoming] vitality. Lee might have ridden down from the old age of chivalry, lance in hand, silken banner fluttering over his head. Each man was the perfect champion of his cause, drawing both his strengths and his weaknesses from the people he led. (Bruce Catton, "Grant and Lee: A Study in Contrasts")

Classification: Distinguish between Types or Classes

Many religions have definite beliefs regarding hell. Some Christians see it as a fiery pit—much like what Dante described in the *Inferno*—where sinners suffer eternal damnation. Islamic texts describe it as a lake of fire spanned by a bridge over which souls must travel to get to heaven. Evil doers, who fall off the bridge, are cast into the lake, there to spend eternity. Buddhism and Hinduism describe many hells through which a soul must pass in order to be cleansed of any evil so as to be reincarnated and eventually to reach a state of perfection. For the ancient Greeks and Romans, Hades, or the underworld, was populated by the shades or shadows of people who had once walked the earth. Few ever escaped this miserable place. In Judaic theology, hell was once a real place, but for most modern Jews, hell is merely an idea discussed in the scriptures so as to help people understand evil. (Karen Staples, "Deep Down Under")

Analogy: Compare an Abstract Idea to Something That Is Concrete and That the Reader Knows

The American political system is like a gigantic Mexican Christmas fiesta. Each political party is a huge piñata—a papier-maché donkey, for example. The donkey is filled with full employment, low interest rates, affordable housing, comprehensive medical benefits, a balanced budget and other goodies. The American voter is blindfolded and given a stick. The voter then swings the stick wildly in every direction, trying to hit a political candidate on the head and knock some sense into the silly bastard. (P. J. O'Rourke, *Parliament of Whores*)

From Specific to General   Beginning with specific details and moving toward a general conclusion (the topic sentence) that relates to these details is another way to arrange information. Although the following paragraphs use different methods of development, all move from specific to general.

Illustration: Develop Ideas with Examples

The ancient Chinese thought they were celestial brooms wielded [operated] by the gods to sweep the heavens free of evil. In the West they were believed to presage [foretell] the fall of Jerusalem, the death of monarchs and such anomalies as two-headed calves. The Norman Conquest of England was attributed to the 1066 flyby of Halley's, history's most famous comet, which has been linked to everything from Julius Caesar's assassination to the defeat of Attila the Hun. Told that Earth would pass through Halley's tail during its 1910 visit, many Americans panicked and bought gas masks and "comet pills." Alan Hale calls these waves of fear and mysticism "comet madness," and as co-discoverer of Comet Hale-Bopp, he's seen more than his share. (Leon Jaroff, "Crazy about Comets")

Comparison and Contrast: Point Out Similarities and Differences

In *The Expression of the Emotions in Man and Animals,* Darwin made a systematic study of how animals look when they are afraid. In both humans and animals, he found, some or all of the following may occur: the eyes and mouth open, the eyes roll, the heart beats rapidly, hairs stand on end, muscles tremble, teeth chatter, and the sphincter loosens. The frightened creature may freeze in its place or cower. These rules hold true across a remarkable array of species. Somehow it is surprising to learn that when dolphins are terrified, their teeth chatter and the whites of their eyes show, or that a frightened gorilla's legs shake. Such familiar behavior in a wild animal is a reminder of our ultimate kinship. Melvin Konner has written, "We are—not metaphorically, but precisely, biologically— like the doe nibbling moist grass in the predawn misty light; chewing, nuzzling a dewy fawn, breathing the foggy air, feeling so much at peace; and suddenly, for no reason, looking about wildly." (Jeffrey M. Masson and Susan McCarthy, *When Elephants Weep*)

You learned earlier that various methods of development can be used together. The paragraph above uses both comparison and description.

From Question to Answer   A good way to begin a paragraph is with an interesting question. You can then devote the rest of your paragraph to details that develop an effective answer to that question.

Definition: Explain a Term or Concept

What does it mean to be poor in America? We can offer no single description of American poverty. But for many, perhaps most, it means homes with peeling paint, inadequate heating, uncertain plumbing. It means that only the very lucky among the children receive a decent education. It often means a home where some go to bed hungry and malnutrition is a frequent visitor. It means that the most elementary components of the good life in America—a vacation with kids, an evening out, a comfortable home—are but distant and unreachable dreams, more likely to be seen on the television screen than in the neighborhood. And for almost all the poor it means that life is a constant struggle to obtain the merest necessities of existence, those things most of us take for granted. We can do better. (Late U.S. Senator Paul Wellstone, "If Poverty Is the Question . . .")

From Problem to Solution   Organizing a paragraph by stating a problem and explaining how to solve it in the sentences that follow is much like asking a question and answering it. It is especially effective when you are explaining a process or analyzing causes and effects. But it can be used with other methods of development as well.

Process Analysis: Explain How to Do Something

For most people, being overweight is not simply a matter of vanity. Excess weight is a threat to health and longevity. You should start losing weight by getting a thorough physical examination, then begin following a regular exercise program prescribed by your doctor. Next, start counting calories; read labels or look up the caloric content of your favorite foods in diet guides available at most super markets and drugstores. Finally, stay away from high-fat animal products and rich desserts. Fill up on fruits, vegetables, natural grains and other high-fiber foods. (Diana Dempsey, "Tightening Our Belts")

By Order of Importance   Writers of fiction often place the most important bit of information last. If arranged in this pattern, an expository or argumentative paragraph can help you create emphasis by guiding your readers to the details and ideas you believe are most important.

Cause and Effect: Explain Why Something Happens

Despite high-profile death sentences like Scott Peterson's in California, public support for the death penalty is falling. The reasons lie partly in mounting evidence that innocent people have been condemned and—in some cases—put to death. Supreme Court Justice Sandra Day O'Connor said that "the system may well be allowing some innocent defendants to be executed." And a recent report by the nonprofit Death Penalty Information Center, *Innocence and the Crisis in the American Death Penalty*, describes how a shift in public perceptions of capital punishment has indeed been taking place. The report notes, for example, that death sentences have dropped by 50 percent over the past five years and that the numbers on death row have also fallen. ("Innocence and the Death Penalty," an editorial in *America: The National Catholic Weekly*)

Analogy: Compare an Abstract Idea to Something Concrete or Something the Reader Knows

"Call waiting" is . . . like an electronic 8-year-old who is simply incapable of shutting up while you are conversing with somebody else. The differences are that 1) an 8-year-old does not have the gall to charge you a monthly fee for this service; and 2) an 8-year-old can interrupt you only if he's in the same room, whereas with the incredible capabilities of "call waiting," your conversations can be interrupted by everybody in the entire world who has access to a telephone. It doesn't even have to be a person. A computer can interrupt you. In fact, through a combination of "call waiting" and "auto-dialing," it is now technically possible for your telephone conversations to be interrupted by a trained chicken. (Dave Barry, "We Interrupt this Column . . .")

Around a Pivot   The pivoting pattern begins with one idea, then changes direction—pivots—by presenting a different or contrasting idea. The topic sentence normally appears in the middle of the paragraph and announces the shift. Often, but not always, the topic sentence is introduced by a transition such as *but, however,* and *nonetheless.*

Illustration: Develop an Idea with Examples

I sometimes hear people who should know better saying that we would be healthier if we depended solely on herbal remedies and refused to take the synthetic drugs purveyed [supplied] by modern scientific medicine. Browse through a pharmacopoeia [list of medicines] and see how many of the medicines prescribed by doctors and sold by druggists are prepared from plants. Quinine for malaria, ephedrine for asthma, cascara for constipation, digitalis for heart conditions, atropine for eye examinations and a great host of other valuable medicines in constant use came directly from folk herbal medicines, and are still prepared from wild plants or those recently brought under cultivation. (Euell Gibbons, *Stalking the Wild Asparagus*)

Visualizing Unity, Coherence, and Development

The following paragraphs are from Rudy Chelminsky's "The Curse of Count Dracula," an essay published in *Smithsonian* magazine in 2003. Notes in the margins and highlighting in the text explain how the author developed his ideas and maintained unity and coherence.

Unity/Coherence   *Development*

Establishes context/setting.

> Over the past year and a half, a furious controversy surrounding a proposal [to build a Dracula theme park] has focused attention on an area so obscure that many people today

Paragraph moves from general to specific.

Uses transition.

> still assume it's fictitious: Transylvania. But located high within the curling grip of the rugged Carpathian Mountains in central

States central idea.

Repeats "Transylvania."

> Romania, Transylvania is as real as real can be—rich in mineral resources, blessed with fertile soil and filled with picturesque scenery.

Contrasts.

Uses transition/ linking pronouns.

Uses synonyms for "area."

> Although its name means "land beyond the forest," this historical province of more than seven million souls was not known as a particularly spooky place until 1897, when the

Adds information to show place is "as real as real can be."

Repeats "Dracula." "Backdrop" connects to topic sentence.

> Irish writer and critic Bram Stoker published his sensational gothic novel *Dracula*: Casting about for a suitable backdrop for his eerie

Defines by telling us about the "eerie yarn."

Uses "yarn" as synonym.

> yarn about a nobleman who happened to be a bloodsucking vampire, Stoker hit upon

Another mention of Transylvania's environment.

> Transylvania, which he described as "one of the wildest and least known portions of Europe."

Describes.

Refers to Dracula.

Uses repetition to connect with preceding paragraph.

⌐ *Dracula* proved to be one of those rare tales that

tap a vein [touch something] deep within

the human psyche. The book has never been

out of print, and Transylvania, through no

└ fault of its own, is doomed to be forever

⌐ *Cause/effect paragraph moves from specific to general.*

"This" refers to idea earlier in paragraph. "Outrage" refers to idea in first paragraph.

"Region" is a synonym for "Transylvania."

⌐ associated with the sanguinary [bloody] count.

This [fact] explains . . . outrage that [the

└ proposed theme park has] provoked.

⌐ It was Romania's own minister of tourism who

came up with the idea of building a Dracula

└ theme park in the heart of Transylvania. For the

"It" refers to "idea" earlier in paragraph.

⌐ region as a whole . . . it's only the latest chapter

in a long history of unwelcome intrusions from

└ the outside.

⌐ *Cause/effect paragraph arranged around a pivot.*

"It" refers to "long history" in previous paragraph.

⌐ It all began with the Romans, who arrived

└ late in the first century to impose their harsh

discipline and Latin tongue on the ancient

"Area" refers to "Transylvania."

"Next" and "then" create transition between sentences.

"They" refers to intruders mentioned above.

⌐ Dacian people native to the area. Next came

the Magyars from what is now Hungary,

followed by various barbarians and Mongols,

└ then the Turks of the Ottoman Empire. Back

⌐ and forth they all went in true Balkan style,

└ and the dust never settled.

⌐ *Conclusion/ support paragraph arranged from specific to general.*

Revising to Improve Unity, Coherence, and Development

Read the following sets of paragraphs, which are taken from the rough draft and the final draft of "Oma," an essay written by student Maria Scamacca. The final draft appears in its entirety later in this chapter. Pay particular attention to the notes in the margins. They explain how the essay was revised to improve unity, coherence, and development.

Maria Scamacca—Rough Draft

Paragraphs 1-3

Use transition to explain when this occurred.

Oma looked old. She wore a flowered house dress a starched white apron, and old, scuffed leather loafers.

Add detail about how old she looked.

Oma was deaf in one ear from a neglected childhood

Combine sentences for smoothness.

ear infection. Symptoms of Bell's palsy were present. She shuffled her feet and held on to the furniture

Add detail about symptoms.

with swollen, scarred hands as she walked. She lived alone the house looked neat. There were small

Add transitions and combine sentences for smoothness.

crumbs and stains on the tables, and particles of food were stuck to some of the dishes.

She led me to a back door to a garden that she boasted of planning and maintaining alone. It was like no garden I had ever seen, an acre of food and beauty. I sensed immediately that this paradise was

Add detail to prove this.

Paragraph not unified. This information does not relate to the garden. Put it elsewhere.

the creation of a unique energy, courage, and beauty I came to see in Oma. She had married a widower with a young daughter; the couple eventually had three other children. They lived on a farm near the Rumanian border on which they grew and raised all their food, even the grapes from which they made their own wine.

Combine with material about garden in preceding paragraph.

> Ready to be picked in the garden were neat and orderly rows of potatoes, carrots, asparagus, onion, peppers, lettuce, lima beans, and string beans as well as many other vegetables I had never heard of.

Add examples of "fruits" and "flowers."

Add transition.

> There were fruits and flowers everywhere.

Paragraphs 7–10

Add transitions and combine sentences for smoothness.

> Farm life was hard. Oma took it well. She cooked and kept house. The horses and other farm animals had to be looked after. She baked bread, made sausage, and salted the meats the family would eat year round.

> Oma is fond of telling me how she force-fed geese by stuffing balls of bread down their long necks with her fingers. Her geese got so fat they couldn't fly, but they brought the best prices at the market, she often reminds me.

Combine with preceding paragraph.

Add transitions and combine sentences for smoothness.

> Her family ∧raised their own pigs. It came time to kill them. ∧Her husband, Opa, asked his neighbor to slaughter the animals. ∧Opa slaughtered the

Seems contradictory; use transition to make clearer.

> neighbor's pigs. "He felt bad, you know, killing his own pig," Oma said. Oma and Opa hired outside help, whom they paid with bread and salted meat. They did most of the work themselves, and they prospered.

Add transitions to bridge sentences and paragraphs.

> ∧The war came. ∧The horses were stolen by Russian soldiers. ∧The family was removed from their farm, and Oma found herself in a Russian concentration camp. The stories are confusing. I

Provide a general statement as a topic sentence.

Strengthen coherence between sentences. have heard bits and pieces repeatedly over the past

six years and I have had to reconstruct them myself. *Explain what these stories relate to.*

Once in a while I ask Oma to clarify the order of

events, but she doesn't get very far until she starts

an entirely new story.

Maria Scamacca—Final Draft

Paragraphs 1–2

Adds transition to explain when this meeting occurred. When I first met Oma six years ago, she looked about

eighty-years old, was a few pounds over-weight for *Includes new detail about how old she looked.*

her medium frame, and was slightly hunched over.

She wore a flowered house dress a starched white

Combines sentences for smoothness. apron, and old, scuffed leather loafers. She was deaf

in one ear from a neglected childhood ear infection,

and half of her face drooped from Bell's palsy. She *Adds detail about symptom of Bell's palsy.*

shuffled her feet and held on to the furniture with

Adds transitions and combines sentences for smoothness. swollen, scarred hands as she walked. Despite Oma's

disability and the fact that she lived alone, her house

looked neat, but there were small crumbs and stains

on the tables, and particles of food were stuck to

some of the dishes, unnoticed by eyes weakened

with age.

Adds transition to bridge paragraphs. That's why I was shocked when she led me to a

back door to a garden that she boasted of planting

and maintaining alone. It was like no garden I had

Rewrites entire paragraph to create unity. ever seen, an acre of food and beauty. Ready to be

picked in the garden were neat and orderly rows of

potatoes, carrots, asparagus, onion, peppers, lettuce., lima beans, and string beans. Her garden also boasted strawberries, blueberries, gooseberries, currant, peaches, watermelons, and many other fruits. And there were flowers everywhere: zinnias, day lilies, marigolds, irises, and petunias. I sensed immediately that this paradise was the creation of a unique energy, courage, and beauty I came to see in Oma.

Names fruits and flowers to prove that garden is "acre of food and beauty."

Note that paragraph is arranged from specific to general—topic sentence is the last.

Paragraphs 7–9

Adds transitions and combines sentences for smoothness.

Farm life was hard. However, Oma took it well. In addition to cooking and housekeeping, she had to tend the horses and other farm animals, bake bread, make sausage, and salt the meats the family would eat year round. Oma is fond of telling me how she force-fed geese by stuffing balls of bread down their long necks with her fingers. Her geese got so fat they couldn't fly, but they brought the best prices at the market, she often reminds me.

Combines two paragraphs into one.

Adds transitions and combines sentences for smoothness.

Her family also raised their own pigs. But when it came time to slaughter the animals, her husband, Opa, asked his neighbor to slaughter the animals. In return Opa slaughtered the neighbor's pigs. "He felt bad, you know, killing his own pig," Oma said. At times, Oma and Opa hired outside help, whom they paid with bread and salted meat. However, they did most of the work themselves, and they prospered.

Adds transitions to clarify idea.

Adds transitions to bridge paragraphs and improve coherence between sentences.

> Then the war came, and Oma's family suffered. First the horses were stolen by Russian soldiers. Then the family was removed from their farm, and Oma found herself in a Russian concentration camp.

Provides a general statement as a topic sentence.

> The stories from this period of her life are confusing. I have heard bits and pieces repeatedly over the past six years, and I have had to reconstruct them myself. Once in a while, I ask Oma to clarify the order of events, but she doesn't get very far until she starts an entirely new story.

Adds detail; explains when stories took place.

Practicing Unity and Coherence

Read this paragraph—written by Stacy Zolnowski for a first-year writing class—to learn more about paragraph unity. Then, using complete sentences, answer the questions that follow in the spaces provided:

> [1] Throughout history, left-handedness has been deemed a nasty habit, a social infraction, a symptom of neurosis, or even a sign of mental retardation. [2] More recently, however, its social, educational, and psychological implications have acquired a more enlightened appreciation. [3] Nonetheless, left-handers continue to be discriminated against in an environment that conforms to the needs and prejudices of a right-handed society. ("The Left-Handed Minority")

1. Assume that the paragraph's topic sentence is the third sentence. What, in your own words, is the paragraph's central idea?

_____

_____

_____

_____

2. How do sentences 1 and 2 relate to the central idea?

_____

_____

_____

3. What transitional devices does the writer use to maintain coherence?

   _____

   _____

   _____

4. In what other ways does the writer maintain coherence?

   _____

   _____

   _____

Practicing Methods of Development

Complete the paragraphs begun below. Include information based on your own observations and experiences. Use whatever method of development you think the topic sentence, which begins each paragraph, calls for.

1. My family provides me with a great deal of emotional support. For example,

   _____

   _____

   _____

   _____

   _____

   _____

   _____

   _____

2. There are three types of students at my college. The first _____

   _____

   _____

   _____

   _____

   _____

   _____

3. If you want to flunk a test, do the following:

_____

_____

_____

_____

_____

4. Most people gain weight because _____

_____

_____

_____

_____

_____

5. My sister (brother, best friend) is a _____ type of person. I, on the other hand, am

_____

_____

_____

_____

_____

_____

_____

Oma: Portrait of a Heroine

Maria Scamacca

Maria Scamacca graduated from college with a degree in nursing and is now a critical-care registered nurse at a large hospital. "Oma: Portrait of a Heroine" was written in a freshman composition class in response to an assignment that asked students to describe people they found inspiring. After reading Scamacca's essay, it is easy to understand why she chose to write about Oma.

Preparing to Read

1. Look for various kinds of connectives—transitions, linking pronouns, repeated words and synonyms—that form bridges between this essay's paragraphs.

2. Look for various methods of developing paragraphs in this essay. In particular, try to identify one that uses narration, another that uses conclusion/support, and one that uses cause/effect.

3. Look for at least one paragraph that is arranged from specific to general, one that is arranged by order of importance, and one that is arranged around a pivot.

Vocabulary

black market (noun)	Underground commercial system in which banned or stolen goods are sold or traded.
compensation (noun)	Payment.
displaced (adjective)	Forced to move.
equivalent (noun)	The equal of.
humane (adjective)	Kind, charitable, benevolent.
implores (verb)	Begs.
palsy (noun)	Paralysis.
provisions (noun)	Necessities, supplies.

Oma: Portrait of a Heroine

Maria Scamacca

WHEN I FIRST met Oma six years ago, she looked about eighty years old, 1 was a few pounds over-weight for her medium frame, and was slightly hunched over. She wore a flowered house dress, a starched white apron, and old, scuffed leather loafers. Oma was deaf in one ear from a neglected childhood ear infection, and half of her face drooped from Bell's palsy. She shuffled her feet and held on to the furniture with swollen, scarred hands as she walked. Despite Oma's disability and the fact that she lived alone, her house looked neat, but there were small crumbs and stains on the tables, and particles of food were stuck to some of the dishes, unnoticed by eyes weakened with age.

That's why I was shocked when she led me through the back door to a gar-   2
den that she boasted of planting and maintaining alone. It was like no garden I had ever seen, an acre of food and beauty. Ready to be picked and eaten were neat and orderly rows of potatoes, carrots, asparagus, onions, peppers, lettuce, lima beans, and string beans. Her garden also boasted strawberries, blueberries, gooseberries, currants, peaches, watermelons, and many other fruits. And there were flowers everywhere: zinnias, day lilies, marigolds, irises, and petunias. I sensed immediately that this paradise was the creation of a unique energy, courage, and beauty I came to see in Oma.

Each year the impossible garden yields bushels of fruits and berries for   3
the jams and jellies that Oma cooks and jars herself. She also cans fruit and vegetables, and she uses the fruit in the fillings of luscious pastries that, as I was to learn, have made her famous among friends, family, and neighbors. She still does all of her own cooking and had been known, until only recently, to throw holiday dinners for more than twenty people.

From the day I met Oma, I grew to admire her and have looked forward to   4
visiting. Almost every Sunday after church, my husband's family and I gather around her dining room table for fresh coffee, homemade Prinz Regent Torte (a seven-layer cake), Schwarzwälder Kirschtorte (Black Forest cherry cake), warm cookies, and good talk.

Oma dominates the conversation, filling us with stories of her childhood   5
and of World War II; she hardly stops to take a breath unless one of us asks a question or implores her to translate the frequent German or Hungarian phrases that pop out of her mouth. At such times, we play guessing games as Oma tries to explain in broken English a word or expression for which she knows no English equivalent.

Oma was born in Hungary. She was an only child—rare in the early days   6
of this century—the only surviving baby of four pregnancies. Her mother died when Oma was in her teens, and she was left alone to keep house for her father. At eighteen, she married a widower with a young daughter; the couple eventually had three other children. They lived on a farm near the Romanian border on which they grew and raised all their food, even the grapes from which they made their own wine.

Farm life was hard. However, Oma took to it well. In addition to cooking   7
and housekeeping, she had to tend to the horses and other farm animals, bake bread, make sausage, and salt the meats the family would eat year round. Oma is fond of telling me how she force-fed geese by stuffing balls of bread down

their long necks with her fingers. Her geese got so fat they couldn't fly, but they brought the best prices at the market, she often reminds me.

Her family also raised their own pigs. But when it came time to slaughter 8 the animals, her husband, Opa, asked his neighbor to do it. In return, Opa slaughtered the neighbor's pigs. "He felt bad, you know, killing his own pig," Oma said. At times, Oma and Opa hired outside help, whom they paid with bread and salted meat. However, they did most of the work themselves, and they prospered.

Then the war came. First her horses were stolen by Russian soldiers. Then 9 the family was removed from their farm, and Oma found herself in a Russian concentration camp. The stories from this period of her life are confusing. I have heard bits and pieces of them repeatedly over the past six years, and I have had to reconstruct them myself. Once in a while I ask Oma to clarify the order of events, but she doesn't get very far until she starts an entirely new story.

After the war, the borders of countries were redrawn, and Oma's family 10 was displaced with only a few hours' notice. Allowed to take only the clothes on their backs and whatever they could carry, they were put into a cattle car on a long freight train. The new government provided no compensation for their land and told them to leave all of their possessions behind. The only explanation was that their family had originally come from Germany and that they were required to leave Hungary and return to the land of their ancestors. This was not punishment, the authorities explained; it was "humane displacement."

Before they boarded the train, the family had to collect enough grain and 11 other provisions to feed themselves during the long trip. But they saw little of their food; Oma thinks it was stolen and sold on the black market. "There were no bathrooms on the train," Oma explained. "If someone had to defecate or urinate, they were held by others out of the open doors over the side of the moving train. And they call that humane!"

When they arrived in Germany, Oma and her family were placed in a room 12 in a run-down building that had holes in the walls and was full of rats. Her husband developed pneumonia. Sick for months, he almost lost the will to live and just lay in bed. When he finally recovered, they moved to America, but they had to leave their daughter behind because she had tuberculosis. Oma still weeps openly whenever she recalls being forced to abandon her child. Luckily, however, things turned out well for "Tante Vicki," who still lives in Germany and now has a family of her own.

In time, the family settled in Millstone, New Jersey, and began to build a 13 new life in what was then a small rural community. In the early 1950s, however, Oma and Opa lost their oldest son in the Korean War, so when the other two boys married and moved out of the house, the two old people were on their own.

Several years ago, Opa died of lung cancer contracted from many years of   14
working in an asbestos factory. Oma continues to receive a good pension and
health benefits from his employer. They come in handy, for over the past few
years she has been hospitalized several times. Last summer she got so sick she
couldn't even plant her garden, so all of her grandchildren got together to plant
it for her. That is the only request she has ever made of them.

It is hard to see a woman who was once so strong grow old and weak. At   15
times, Oma feels quite useless, but she can still tell wonderful stories, and we
listen avidly. I wonder if there will be a garden this year.

Read More on the Web

Holocaust Learning Center site with links to other information:
    http://www.ushmm.org/wlc/article.jsp?ModuleId=10005186
Library of Congress country study site on Hungary:
    http://memory.loc.gov/frd/cs/hutoc.html

Questions for Discussion

1. What is Scamacca's thesis?
2. Where does the topic sentence in paragraph 2 appear? Identify the
    topic sentence in at least one other paragraph.
3. The central idea in paragraph 6 is implied. State it into your own
    words.
4. Pick out elements that the author uses to maintain coherence
    between paragraphs throughout this essay.
5. Reread paragraphs 9–12, and circle words and phrases the author
    uses to maintain coherence in them.
6. Identify a paragraph that uses the conclusion/support method,
    another that uses cause/effect, and still another that uses narration.
7. Identify one paragraph that is arranged by order of importance,
    one that moves from specific to general, and one that is organized
    around a pivot.

Thinking Critically

1. If you were able to meet Oma, what would you ask her about her
    life? As you reread this essay, write questions to her in the margins
    of the text when they occur to you. Then do some creative guessing.
    On the basis of what you know about Oma, answer your questions
    in a paragraph or two.

2. Reread Maria Cirilli's "Echoes" in Chapter 1. In what ways is this essay similar to Scamacca's? In what ways are these essays different?

3. Pretend that the government has decided to take almost everything you own and send you to another country. Would you resist? If so, how? If not, how would you prepare for this drastic change? Put your answer in two or three paragraphs that are unified and coherent. Make sure to include transitions between paragraphs as well.

Suggestions for Journal Entries

1. Do you have an older relative, friend, or neighbor whose attitude toward life you consider heroic? Choose your own definition of the word *heroic*. Freewrite for about five minutes about an event from this person's life that might show his or her heroism.

2. Interview the person mentioned above. Try to find out more about his or her attitude toward life. A good way to do this is to ask your subject to tell you about a difficult or depressing time and to explain how he or she dealt with it.

3. Brainstorm with one or two others who know the person mentioned above. Try to gather facts, direct quotations, and opinions that you could use in a paper that describes your subject as heroic.

Study Calculus!

William J. Bennett

*Secretary of education and chairman of the National Endowment for the
Humanities in the Reagan administration, William J. Bennett holds a doctorate
in political philosophy from the University of Texas and a law degree from
Harvard University. Under the first President Bush, Bennett directed the war on
drugs as head of the Office of National Drug Control Policy. This essay, which
reveals much about Bennett's thinking when he was secretary of education, is
taken from* The De-Valuing of America: The Fight for Our Children. *Bennett
is also the author of the best-selling* Book of Virtues: A Treasury of Great Moral
Stories *as well as several other books.*

Preparing to Read

1. The title provides a clue to the essay's thesis. Why didn't Bennett use
   "Math" instead of "Calculus"?
2. Look for the linking pronouns and other connective devices Bennett
   uses to create coherence in and between paragraphs.
3. This essay ends with several one-sentence paragraphs. Although not
   common in college writing, such paragraphs are useful here because
   they convey dialogue, conversation between people.
4. Some teachers in the high school in which this essay takes place
   claimed that teaching calculus to inner-city students was a "quixotic
   fantasy." Don Quixote, the title character of a seventeenth-century
   Spanish novel, was a dreamer who often found himself in trouble by
   attempting the impossible. Therefore, "quixotic" has come to mean
   "foolish" or "impractical."
5. Bennett uses a variety of methods to develop and arrange his
   paragraphs. Find at least one paragraph using narration, one
   using cause/effect, and one using illustration. Also find at least one
   paragraph that is arranged according to order of importance.

Vocabulary

calculus (noun)	A branch of mathematics important to science, engineering, and other disciplines.
canard (noun)	False belief, principle, rule, or story.
ethic (noun)	Principle, belief in.
pedagogy (noun)	Education, schooling, teaching.
skepticism (noun)	Doubt, distrust, disbelief.

Study Calculus!

William J. Bennett

PRINCIPAL HENRY Gradillas at Garfield High School in East Los Angeles let 1
Jaime Escalante teach. And did the students ever learn. Escalante, a Bolivian
immigrant, arrived at the school in 1974 to teach math. Now perhaps America's
most famous teacher, he wanted to return something to the country that had
taken him in and given him opportunity.

His plan to teach calculus to disadvantaged Hispanic youngsters was 2
greeted with skepticism and laughter by his colleagues, and he encountered
resistance from his students. But he told me that the greatest resistance came
not from the students but from others in the profession, other teachers and
counselors who urged him not to push so hard. They told him that his
plan to teach calculus was a quixotic fantasy. "If you try," some told him,
"the students will fail. They can't do it. They will be embarrassed, and their
self-esteem will suffer. What you want to do—teach calculus—will be
dangerous."

Escalante told me what he told his critics: "If you are fifteen or sixteen years 3
old, in the barrio of East Los Angeles, there are a lot of things that are dangerous. But calculus isn't one of them." His principal, Henry Gradillas, encouraged
him to proceed.

Escalante persisted, and in 1982 eighteen of his students took the 4
Advanced Placement (AP) calculus test. By 1991, 160 students from Garfield
took the test. According to Jay Mathews, author of *Escalante: The Best Teacher
in America,* Escalante has given Garfield the most successful inner-city
mathematics program in the United States. In recent years only four or five
secondary schools in the country have prepared more students for the AP
calculus examination (tests so difficult that fewer than 2 percent of American
students even attempt them). Because of Escalante's efforts, about a fourth of
all the Mexican-American students in the country who pass AP calculus come
from Garfield.

Escalante's methods and approach (celebrated in the movie *Stand and* 5
Deliver) are in marked contrast to the theory and practice of pedagogy as taught
in most American schools of education. He consistently violates the canard that
a teacher shouldn't "impose his values on students." Indeed, he seeks every
opportunity to impose his ethic of achievement, success, and hard work on
them. His reason, as expressed to me, is simple: "My values are better than
theirs." His way of doing this is direct, manly, no nonsense. In the early days of
his career at Garfield, he asked a student whether he wanted to study calculus.
"No," said the student, "I want to see my girlfriend."

"Well, then," responded Escalante, "go over to woodworking class on your 6
way out."

"Why," the student asked. 7

"So you can learn how to make shoeshine boxes so you can have a career   8
shining the shoes for Anglos as they pass through Los Angeles International
Airport on their business trips."

"I don't want to shine Anglos' shoes," protested the student.   9

"Then study calculus," was Escalante's reply.   10

Read More on the Web

Website of the Bolivia Hall of Fame containing more information on
    Escalante: http://www.boliviaweb.com/hallfame/escalante.htm

The Math Forum at Drexel University: http://mathforum.org/library/
    drmath/drmath.college.html

Questions for Discussion

1. What is the essay's thesis?
2. Explain how Bennett uses linking pronouns to maintain coherence in
    paragraph 2.
3. Find two transitional words or phrases in paragraph 1. Then, find
    three more in the rest of the essay.
4. What use does Bennett make of repetition to maintain coherence
    between paragraphs?
5. Which paragraph uses narration? Which uses illustration? Which
    uses the cause/effect method?
6. Which paragraph is arranged by order of importance?
7. Why didn't Bennett combine paragraphs 6–10 into one paragraph?

Thinking Critically

1. Do you agree with the way in which Escalante challenged his
    students? Think of another way that you might motivate students
    to study a difficult subject if you were a teacher. Explain this in a
    paragraph or two.
2. What kinds of values is Escalante talking about in paragraph 5?
    Should teachers be allowed to impose other values—social, political,
    or moral, for example—on students? On a separate sheet of paper list
    the advantages and disadvantages of allowing them to do so.
3. Why do you think some teachers had a low opinion of the abilities
    of students whom Escalante helped? What connection, if any, is there
    between a teacher's attitude and student success?

Suggestions for Journal Entries

1. Use clustering or listing to come up with several characteristics or qualities of a good teacher. You might begin by thinking about the best teacher or teachers you have had. Consider those qualities that caused you to admire them or that made them effective instructors.

    For example you might write that

    Ms. Jones challenged students.

    Mr. Mendoza graded homework and tests carefully.

    Dr. Patel inspired confidence in you.

    Ms. Fernandez made geometry interesting and easy to understand.

    By the way, you don't need to limit yourself to teachers you have had in school. Family members, employers, neighbors, coaches, and members of the clergy often teach us a lot as well.

2. Freewrite for about 10 minutes to gather information about the teacher who has influenced you most. Again, don't limit yourself to teachers you have had in school.

Burger Queen

Erin Sharp

Erin Sharp was a sophomore at Cornell University when she wrote this essay. It first appeared in The American Enterprise *magazine.*

Preparing to Read

1. The information in this essay comes from Sharp's employment at a McDonald's restaurant. Before you begin reading, think about the variety of people who work and eat at a fast-food restaurant.
2. What is Sharp hinting at in the title?
3. If you were writing about your place of employment, what subjects and details would you discuss to help your readers understand what it means to work there?
4. You might find unfamiliar words in this essay that are not listed in the vocabulary. Try to get at their meanings by using context clues. For example, the author says that some customers "bickered" with her "over a measly ten-cent increase in the price of an Egg McMuffin." What might "bickered" and "measly" mean in this sentence?

Vocabulary

coveted (adjective)	Desired.
forfeited (verb)	Gave up.
freelance (adjective)	Self-employed, temporary, hired for a one-time job.
hoard (verb)	Save, hide away.
quipped (verb)	Answered in a joking or sarcastic way.
pathologist (noun)	Doctor who diagnoses physical changes caused by disease.
perspective (noun)	Point of view.
reimbursement (noun)	Refund.
scam (verb)	To cheat.
stereotypes (noun)	Labels, types.
tackiness (noun)	Bad taste.
tempered (adjective)	Moderated, lessened, toned down.

Burger Queue

Erin Sharp

WHEN I ANNOUNCED the change of my major from biology with pre-med 1
aspirations to English, my advisor simply raised an eyebrow and asked
if I planned to work at McDonald's for the rest of my life. "Actually," I quipped,
"I've been working at McDonald's for two and a half years, and it's sort of fun."
His surprise was evident, a typical reaction to my shocking side occupation. I
spoke the truth, though; I have held a dozen jobs ranging from camp counselor
to pathologist's assistant (now including, I suppose, freelance journalism), yet
none have been as entertaining as my stints at the Golden Arches.

My double life as Erin Sharp, Ivy League McDonald's Worker, has revealed 2
twin stereotypes to me. People told I go to Cornell view me as bright and
ambitious. Put me behind the counter at McDonald's, however, and I am
usually assumed to be a high school dropout with fifteen unseen piercings.

When I was six years old, McDonald's was my favorite place to eat, and 3
kids have not changed much in the last dozen years. I am often asked whether
I have actually met "The Ronald" McDonald, and have been given letters to pass
along to him, like one of Santa Claus's elves. Among kids, McDonald's workers
rank right up there with policemen and firefighters.

Yet this perspective rarely survives adolescence. Respect for the workers 4
of the fast food industry is lost among most adults, with absurd results. Many
adults seem to assume that McWorkers are stupid, attempting to scam us out of
free food and coupons. The depths of tackiness to which some human beings
will stoop in order to save a few pennies at a drive-thru window are worthy
of "Candid Camera." Grown men driving Lincoln Town Cars have bickered
with me for five minutes over a measly ten-cent increase in the price of an Egg
McMuffin. Perhaps they imagine that I overcharge each patron and hoard mis-
begotten dimes in a piggy bank behind the shake machine?

Once, my store even received a phone call at noon from a furious woman 5
demanding reimbursement for the breakfast she had bought that morning via
drive-thru; apparently, it was cold when she arrived at work over an hour later.
Our most famous TIC (Truculent, Irate Customer) lost her temper when we
could not (in her eyes, would not) provide the grilled chicken sandwich she
craved in the middle of breakfast rush hour. An entirely new traffic pattern
was created in drive-thru for the 25 minutes spent in fruitless argument and
accommodation attempts by our managers as the grill team thawed frozen
meat, heated a grill to cook on and produced the coveted sandwich for her.
When at last presented with it, she lofted the bag triumphantly and accused
us of withholding it from her for the entire time, then zoomed off with the last
words: "I'm never coming back here again!" The effectiveness of this condemnation was tempered by her license plate, which proclaimed her to be from
Delaware—over an hour away.

A small portion of our patrons are so confused that there is really nothing   6
to do but wait for them to leave. My most prominent example of this sort of
"guest" is the infamous Snack Attack Lady, who ordered hotcakes and sausage
during our 90-second-guaranteed-service hour and then ate her breakfast right
outside the drive-thru window. Heedless of the frenzied honking behind her,
she carefully opened the platter, poured a puddle of syrup, rolled the sausage
in a hotcake and dipped both daintily into the syrup. My co-workers and
I watched in speechless amazement. When asked what she was doing, she
rolled her eyes and snapped, "What does it look like I'm doing? I'm eating my
breakfast!" That woman has permanently forfeited all rights to complain about
slow drive-thru service.

And yet, there are some great customers out there, like the Morning Crew: 7
the seven retired men and one active police officer who wait for our doors to
open every day so that they can enjoy their dawn coffee and conversation.
If I missed a day of work, I would return to inquiries about my health and
concern that all was well. The greatest customers ever to grace our store were
two deliverymen who drove up to the window one spring afternoon two years
ago with armfuls of roses for my co-worker and me. They were moving their
business out of state, they explained, and wanted to thank us for making their
afternoons brighter.

Well, boys, if you are reading this article, thank you again for that fabulous   8
surprise. I still have the ribbon which bound them.

Read More on the Web

HRZone.com article on image of fast-food restaurant workers:
http://www.hrzone.com/articles/applicant_attract2.html

US Department of Labor Occupational Outlook Handbook:
http://www.bls.gov/oco/ocos024.htm

Questions for Discussion

1. What is Sharp's central idea?
2. Why does Sharp tell us that her advisor was surprised when she told him she worked at McDonald's? How does doing so help introduce her central idea?
3. What is the topic sentence in paragraph 4? How does that sentence also serve as the topic sentence in paragraph 5?
4. Explain the ways in which Sharp maintains coherence between paragraphs 4, 5, 6, 7, and 8.
5. In which paragraphs does Sharp use illustration?
6. What method of development is seen in paragraph 1?
7. Identify the patterns of organization in paragraphs 1 through 7.

Thinking Critically

1. In Preparing to Read, you were asked to use context clues to determine the meaning of some of Sharp's vocabulary. What does she mean by "pre-med," "aspirations," and "stints" in paragraph 1; "truculent," "irate," "fruitless," and "lofted" in paragraph 5; "heedless" and "frenzied" in paragraph 6?

2. What are the Ivy League, "Candid Camera," and McWorkers? You might find more about the first two terms on the Internet or in your college library, but you will have to figure out the third term on your own.

3. What is the pun (play on words) Sharp uses in the title?

Suggestions for Journal Entries

1. Use focused freewriting, listing, or clustering to gather information that describes customers or employees or both at a place at which you work or have worked. Focus on people with the most interesting or distinctive personalities.

2. Sharp's essay is more than a listing of complaints about annoying customers. It is a statement—and a positive one at that—about her role and image as a worker in a fast-food restaurant. Use clustering or any other prewriting method to explain your feelings—be they positive, negative, or mixed—about a job you hold or once held.

A Brother's Dreams

Paul Aronowitz

Paul Aronowitz was a medical student at Case Western Reserve University when he wrote this very sensitive essay comparing his dreams, hopes, and ambitions with those of his schizophrenic brother. Schizophrenia is a mental illness characterized by withdrawal from reality.

Aronowitz's love, compassion, and understanding come across clearly as he unfolds the story of how he learned to deal with the fact that his brother's strange, sometimes violent behavior was the symptom of an illness and not a defect in character. This essay is also Aronowitz's admission and unselfish affirmation that, however "elusive" and "trivial," his brother's dreams might be even more meaningful than his own.

"A Brother's Dreams" first appeared in "About Men," a weekly column in the New York Times Magazine.

Preparing to Read

1. Aronowitz's central idea concerns how he came to understand his brother's illness and to accept the fact that his brother's dreams were important. However, he does not reveal his central idea until near the end of the essay, and he never puts it into a formal thesis statement.

2. Many paragraphs in this essay are developed through narration and description, but it also uses cause and effect, comparison and contrast, illustration, and conclusion and support.

3. Josef Mengele, mentioned in paragraph 5, was a Nazi doctor who conducted unspeakable experiments in which he tortured, maimed, and killed thousands of human beings.

Vocabulary

acrid (adjective)	Bitter, harsh, sharp.
aimlessly (adverb)	Without purpose.
alienate (verb)	Make enemies of, isolate oneself from.
delusions (noun)	Misconceptions, fantasies.
depravity (noun)	Immorality, corruption.
elusive (adjective)	Hard to grasp, intangible.
niche (noun)	Position, role, slot.
paranoid (adjective)	Showing unreasonable or unwarranted suspicion.

prognosis (noun)	Prediction about the course or outcome of an illness.
resilient (adjective)	Able to bounce back.
siblings (noun)	Sisters and brothers.

A Brother's Dreams

Paul Aronowitz

EACH TIME I go home to see my parents at their house near Poughkeepsie, 1
N.Y., my brother, a schizophrenic for almost nine years now, comes to visit
from the halfway house where he lives nearby. He owns a car that my parents
help him to maintain, and his food and washing are taken care of by the halfway
house. Somewhere, somehow along the way, with the support of a good physician, a social worker and my ever-resilient parents, he has managed to carve a
niche for himself, to bite off some independence and, with it, elusive dreams
that, to any healthy person, might seem trivial.

My brother sits in a chair across from me, chain-smoking cigarettes, trying 2
to take the edge off the medications he'll be on for the rest of his life. Sometimes
his tongue hangs loosely from his mouth when he's listening or pops out of his
mouth as he speaks—a sign of tardive dyskinesia, an often-irreversible side
effect of his medication.

He draws deeply on his cigarette and tells me he can feel his mind healing— 3
cells being replaced, tissue being restored, thought processes returning. He
knows this is happening because he dreams of snakes, and hot, acrid places in
which he suffocates if he moves too fast. When he wakes, the birds are singing
in the trees outside his bedroom window. They imitate people in his halfway
house, mocking them and calling their names. The birds are so smart, he tells
me, so much smarter than we are.

His face, still handsome despite its puffiness (another side effect of the 4
medications that allow him to function outside the hospital), and warm brown
eyes are serious. When I look into his eyes I imagine I can see some of the
suffering he has been through. I think of crossed wires, of receptors and neu-
rotransmitters, deficits and surpluses, progress and relapse, and I wonder, once
again, what has happened to my brother.

My compassion for him is recent. For many years, holidays, once happy 5
occasions for our family of seven to gather together, were emotional torture
sessions. My brother would pace back and forth in the dining room, lecturing
us, his voice loud, dominating, crushing all sound but his own, about the end
of the world, the depravity of our existences. His speeches were salted with
paranoid delusions: our house was bugged by the F.B.I.; my father was Josef
Mengele; my mother was selling government secrets to the Russians.

His life was decaying before my eyes, and I couldn't stand to listen to   6
him. My resentment of him grew as his behavior became more disruptive and
aggressive. I saw him as being ultimately responsible for his behavior. As my
anger increased, I withdrew from him, avoiding him when I came home to visit
from college, refusing to discuss the bizarre ideas he brought up over the dinner table. When I talked with my sister or other two brothers about him, our
voices always shadowed in whispers, I talked of him as of a young man who
had chosen to spend six months of every year in a pleasant, private hospital
on the banks of the Hudson River, chosen to alienate his family with threats,
chosen to withdraw from the stresses of the world. I hated what he had become.
In all those years, I never asked what his diagnosis was.

Around the fifth year of his illness, things finally changed. One hot sum-   7
mer night, he attacked my father. When I came to my father's aid, my brother
broke three of my ribs and nearly strangled me. The State Police came and took
him away. My father's insurance coverage had run out on my brother, so this
time he was taken to a locked ward at the state hospital where heavily sedated
patients wandered aimlessly in stockinged feet up and down long hallways.
Like awakening from a bad dream, we gradually began talking about his illness.
Slowly and painfully, I realized that he wasn't responsible for his disease any
more than a cancer patient is for his pain.

As much as I've learned to confront my brother's illness, it frightens me to think   8
that one day, my parents gone from the scene, my siblings and I will be responsible
for portions of my brother's emotional and financial support. This element of the
future is one we still avoid discussing, much the way we avoided thinking about the
nature of his disease and his prognosis. I'm still not capable of thinking about it.

Now I come home and listen to him, trying not to react, trying not to show   9
disapproval. His delusions are harmless and he is, at the very least, communicating. When he asks me about medical school, I answer with a sentence or
two—no elaboration, no revelations about the dreams I cradle in my heart.

He talks of his own dreams. He hopes to finish his associate's degree—the   10
same one he has been working on between hospitalizations for almost eight
years now—at the local community college. Next spring, with luck, he'll get a
job. His boss will be understanding, he tells me, cutting him a little slack when
he has his "bad days," letting him have a day off here or there when things aren't
going well. He puts out his cigarette and lights another one.

Time stands still. This could be last year, or the year before, or the year   11
before that. I'm within range of becoming a physician, of realizing something
I've been working toward for almost five years, while my brother still dreams
of having a small job, living in his own apartment and of being well. As the
smoke flows from his nose and mouth, I recall an evening some time ago when
I drove upstate from Manhattan to tell my parents and my brother that I was
getting married (an engagement later severed). My brother's eyes lit up at the
news, and then a darkness fell over them.

"What's wrong?" I asked him.   12

"It's funny," he answered matter-of-factly. "You're getting married, and I've 13
never even had a girlfriend." My mother's eyes filled with tears, and she turned
away. She was trying her best to be happy for me, for the dreams I had—for the
dreams so many of us take for granted.

"You still have us," I stammered, reaching toward him and touching his 14
arm. All of a sudden my dreams meant nothing; I didn't deserve them and they
weren't worth talking about. My brother shrugged his shoulders, smiled and
shook my hand, his large, tobacco-stained fingers wrapping around my hand,
dwarfing my hand.

Read More on the Web

Schizophrenia Home Page: http://www.schizophrenia.com/

National Institute of Mental Health Page on Schizophrenia:
  http://www.nimh.nih.gov/publicat/schizoph.cfm

Questions for Discussion

1. Write a formal thesis statement for this essay in your own words.
2. Explain the ways in which Aronowitz maintains coherence between
   paragraphs 1 through 10.
3. Identify one of the two paragraphs that use description. What
   important idea does this paragraph communicate?
4. The purpose of paragraph 6 is to explain a cause and an effect.
   Identify the cause in the topic sentence; then identify the details
   (effect) that develop the paragraph.
5. In paragraph 10, the author uses the conclusion and support method.
   What is his conclusion and how does he support it?
6. Paragraph 11 contrasts the author's dreams to some of his brother's.
   In what other paragraphs is contrast used?
7. Most paragraphs in this essay proceed from the general to the
   specific. However, paragraphs 11 and 13 are organized by order of
   importance. What is the most important idea in these paragraphs?

Thinking Critically

Explaining how he came to terms with his brother's illness, Aronowitz
says his compassion for his brother is only "recent." Pretend you are
interviewing Aronowitz. What would he say is the reason for not feeling
compassion earlier? What caused his change in attitude?

Suggestions for Journal Entries

1. Aronowitz writes about a person whose lifestyle and dreams are very different from those of most other people. Do you know someone like this? If so, write a paragraph showing how this person's lifestyle or dreams differ from those of most others. Use one major method of development; for instance, you might *describe* what this individual looks like (much in the way Aronowitz describes his brother in paragraphs 2 and 4), or you might use *narration* to tell a story about the kind of behavior you have come to expect from the person (as Aronowitz does in paragraphs 3, 5, and 7). You might even want to try your hand at the cause-and-effect method by telling your reader how you normally react to or deal with this person and then explaining what causes you to react in this way.

2. Aronowitz's essay contrasts his brother's dreams to his own. Write a paragraph in which you show how different you are from your brother, sister, or other close relative by contrasting a major goal in your life to one of his or hers.

    Clearly identify the two different goals in your topic sentence, and fill the rest of your paragraph with details showing how different they are; that is, develop the paragraph by contrast. Your topic sentence might go something like this: "My sister Janet intends to move to the city and find a high-paying job, even if she hates every minute of it; I'll be happy earning the modest income that comes with managing our family farm."

Suggestions for Sustained Writing

1. Review the journal entry(ies) you made after reading Maria Scamacca's "Oma: Portrait of a Heroine." Use this information in a short essay that explains why a certain person you know is heroic. Provide at least three reasons to support that idea.

    Paragraph 1: Captures the readers' interest and states the thesis. Your thesis statement might resemble this: *My neighbor Mrs. Rozowski faces life with a smile even though she has experienced suffering and heartache.* In the rest of this paragraph you might explain that *Mrs. Rozowski suffers from arthritis, lives on a very small pension, and has just lost her husband of 50 years.*

    Paragraph 2: Mentions Mrs. Rozowski's arthritis and its painful symptoms. But it also discusses the many things she does to keep active despite that pain. This paragraph might use illustration—giving examples—as its major method of development. It might be arranged from general-to-specific, by order of importance, or through questions/answer.

Paragraph 3: Explains that, living on a small pension, Mrs. Rozowski, has learned several ways to save money such as growing much of her own food, making her own clothes, and even doing simple house repairs. This paragraph might employ the cause/effect method as well as examples. It might be arranged from problem-to-solution or around a pivot.

Paragraph 4: Discusses her devotion to her husband and her willingness to care for him during his battle with Alzheimer's disease. This paragraph might use process analysis, narration, description, or a combination of all three. It might be arranged by order of importance or from specific-to-general.

Paragraph 5: Restates your admiration for your subject and explains what you have learned about facing life's problems from this woman. It also expresses your hope that you will have the same courage when you are elderly.

As you revise the first draft of your essay, make sure that you have included enough detail to make every paragraph convincing. If you haven't, do some more information gathering as explained in Getting Started. Also, check to see that your paragraphs are both unified and coherent and that you have maintained coherence between paragraphs.

2. Review the notes you made for the first journal entry following Bennett's "Study Calculus!" If you have not responded to that journal prompt yet, do so now. Use this information to write the thesis statement for an essay that might be entitled "The Ideal Teacher." In that thesis, mention at least three qualities that make for excellent teaching. Here's how such a thesis might read:

> The best teachers challenge their students, inspire confidence in them, and work harder than anyone else in class.

Place this thesis statement in your first paragraph, your introduction. Now use each of the three or four characteristics of good teaching in your thesis as the basis for the topic sentences of your essay's body paragraphs. Here's how each of the topic sentences for paragraphs 2, 3, and 4 of your essay might read:

Paragraph 2: The best teachers challenge their students.

Paragraph 3: Inspiring confidence in students is another sign of good teaching.

Paragraph 4: Good teachers work harder than their students.

Develop each of these body paragraphs with examples relating to a teacher or teachers you have known. You need not discuss the same teacher in each paragraph. If you completed the second journal suggestion after Bennett's essay, you might have already gathered some information you can use.

After writing several drafts of your paper, check that you have maintained coherence in and between paragraphs by using techniques explained in this chapter. Finally, remember that the best essays are those that are reviewed and edited carefully.

3. Read the journal notes you made after reading Sharp's "Burger Queen." Use this material in an essay that explains your general impression or opinion of a place in which you have worked or are now working. Your opinion might be positive, negative, or mixed, but make sure to state it clearly in a thesis statement, which should appear in your first paragraph.

   To practice the writing of several different paragraph types, try to include one of each of the following:

   • A paragraph defining the type of business conducted or work performed.

   • A paragraph providing examples of your usual duties or tasks.

   • A paragraph describing the physical environment of the workplace— the store, factory, office building, or other setting. If it's an outdoor job, describe the kinds of locations in which you have worked.

   • A paragraph that contrasts this job with another you have held.

   • A paragraph that narrates incidents with customers, employees, and/or bosses to explain the social atmosphere of your workplace.

   You might want to begin by making an outline of your paper based on the model provided above. After writing a first draft, make sure that each paragraph supports and relates directly to your thesis. Remember that your thesis states your opinion, so provide enough detail to support it, and make sure you are not including extraneous information. As you revise again, check to see that you have maintained coherence in and between paragraphs.

4. After completing Paul Aronowitz's "A Brother's Dreams," you might have written a paragraph in your journal explaining how different your goal in life is from that of your brother, sister, or other close relative. If so, the method by which you developed this paragraph was contrast.

   Reread this paragraph. What does it tell you about your subject's character? What kind of person is he or she? Turn your answer into the central idea (thesis statement) of an essay in which you continue to discuss this relative. In fact, make the paragraph you've already written the introduction to your essay.

   As you plan this essay, consider writing a paragraph or two in which you describe this individual—the way he walks, the way she dresses, and so on. You might also want to include a narrative paragraph, one in which you tell a story that helps support what you say about him or her in your thesis. Finally, think about using additional methods of development—illustration, and conclusion and support, for example—in other paragraphs to develop your thesis further.

Once again, remember that writing is a process. You owe it to yourself and your readers to produce the most effective paper you can through painstaking rewriting and editing.

5. Are you a creature of habit? If so, write an essay in which you explain why you do three or four things routinely. You might begin by explaining why you are always or seldom on time for work, for a date, or for class. You might go on to discuss why you study in the same place every night, why you wear the same color of clothes every day, why you use the same route to school or work, or why you frequent the same club, bar, or restaurant.

Of course, this assignment lends itself to the cause-effect method. (Examples of cause-effect paragraphs appear in "A Brother's Dreams.") But you might also have a chance to use narration, description, and process analysis among other methods of development.

You can begin this essay by using a startling remark such as: *I have never taken a shower!* Or you might say that *you spend five full hours a day on the telephone.* These kinds of statements will surely draw your readers into your essay. Of course, later in the paragraph, you can explain that you take a bath every day, or that you work as a receptionist in a busy medical practice. After discussing each of your habits fully in the body paragraphs, you can conclude the essay by explaining which of the habits you discussed will continue and which might be broken.

As you revise drafts of your paper, add or remove detail as necessary, and insert details that will make your writing easier to follow. In addition, use what you have learned in this chapter to improve coherence in and between paragraphs.

Writing to Learn: A Group Activity

THE FIRST MEETING

Pretend you and several others have been asked to contribute to a brochure that will help students choose an academic major. (For inspiration, reread Bennett's "Study Calculus!") Meet in a group of three or four

(continued)

students and ask each to research one (only one) major, perhaps from the list below or from a list that the group makes for itself:

Accounting	Dental hygiene	Nursing
Anthropology	Economics	Pharmacy
Architecture	History	Physical education
Biology	Journalism	Political science
Business	Literature	Psychology
administration	Mathematics	Rehabilitation science
Chemistry	Mechanical	Sociology
Computer science	engineering	Speech therapy
Civil engineering	Modern languages	Theater
Criminal justice		

RESEARCH

Make sure each member covers a different major. Search the Internet, do some research in your college's career placement center, or interview professors who teach courses in the assigned areas of study. Find out

• What courses are required of students who major in this area.
• What careers are open to students who graduate with this major.
• What rewards (monetary and other) these careers offer.
• What some of the negative aspects of these careers are.

WRITING

Then, write an essay that discusses most or all of these points for the major each of you chose. In your second group meeting, share early drafts (not first drafts) of each other's papers and suggest revisions. Be especially concerned with changes that will help the writer improve unity and coherence as explained in this chapter. In your third group meeting, distribute final versions of your papers. Finally, ask everyone to write a paragraph that explains whether the reading of these essays has influenced his or her choice of a major.

from an editorial in *America* magazine on the current situation in Sudan, a country in northern Africa:

> *The disaster unfolding in the Darfur region of Sudan shines a spotlight once again on the plight of refugees and internally displaced persons.* The Sudanese government has stood by as . . . militias [armed bands] engaged in the systematic destruction of . . . villages and water sources. Thirty thousand people have been killed, and rape has been widespread. A hundred and fifty thousand have fled westward to refugee camps in Chad, and one million are internally displaced. ("Refugees: Darfur and Beyond")

A startling statement is often followed by explanatory details. In *Victims of Vanity*, Lynda Dickinson spreads startling remarks and statistics over three short paragraphs:

> Lipstick, face cream, anti-perspirant, laundry detergent . . . these products and hundreds of other personal care and household items have one common ingredient: the suffering and death of millions of animals.
>
> An average of 25 million animals die every year in North America for the testing of everything from new cosmetics to new methods of warfare. Five hundred thousand to one million of these animals are sacrificed each year to test new cosmetics alone.
>
> *Of all the pain and suffering caused by animal research, cosmetic and household product testing is among the least justifiable, as it cannot even be argued that tests are done to improve the quality of human life.*

ASK A QUESTION OR PRESENT A PROBLEM

If you begin with a question or statement of a problem, you can devote the rest of your essay to answering that question or discussing that problem. "Old, Ailing, and Abandoned," an editorial appearing in the Philadelphia Inquirer, begins with three thought-provoking questions about the care of the elderly.

> How would you punish the people responsible for letting 18 hours pass before getting emergency medical help to an epileptic with second- and third-degree burns, while large sections of her skin were peeling off? What justice is there for a man whose amputated foot is allowed to become infested with maggots while he's paying for care in a specialized rooming house? And what's the proper penalty for someone who leaves a mentally ill woman alone for three days with little food and no medication?

In the first paragraph of "The Ambivalence of Abortion," Linda Bird Francke introduces the problem she and her husband faced over an unplanned pregnancy, thus preparing us for her discussion of abortion later in the essay:

> We were sitting in a bar on Lexington Avenue when I told my hus-
> band I was pregnant. It is not a memory I like to dwell on. Instead
> of the champagne and hope which had heralded [announced] the
> impending [coming] births of the first, second and third child, the
> news of this one was greeted with shocked silence and Scotch.
> "Jesus," my husband kept saying to himself, stirring the ice cubes
> around and around, "Oh Jesus."

CHALLENGE A WIDELY HELD OPINION

This method acts much like the use of a startling statement. Take this opening
paragraph from an essay by Hall of Fame pitcher Robin Roberts; it questions
the benefits of an activity commonly seen as wholesome.

> In 1939, Little League baseball was organized by Bert and George
> Bebble and Carl Stotz of Williamsport, PA. What they had in mind in
> organizing this kids' baseball program, I'll never know. *But I 'm sure
> they never visualized the monster it would grow in to.* ("Strike Out
> Little League")

In "Gen X Is OK," Professor Edward E. Ericson, Jr., writes an introduction
that both challenges an opinion and offers a surprise ending.

> Today's young adults read little. They're poorly prepared for col-
> lege. They're suckers for the instant gratification of booze and
> drugs. They're enormously confused about sex and scared to death
> of marriage. They're all for a woman's right to choose an abortion,
> especially the men. They force metal rings through the most unwel-
> coming of facial orifices [openings]. They're so light on civic duty
> that few vote and fewer still can imagine why one would die for
> one's country. *And I like them.*

The last line of the paragraph is Ericson's thesis. It makes us wonder why
the author likes people whom he has just described so negatively. So, we read
on!

USE COMPARISON, CONTRAST, OR ANALOGY

Comparison points out similarities; **contrast** points out differences. Both
methods can help you provide important information about your subject,
clarify or emphasize a point, and catch the reader's attention.

Donald M. Murray offers students good advice by contrasting the way they
sometimes complete writing assignments with the more thorough and careful
process used by professionals:

> When students complete a first draft, they consider the job of writ-
> ing done—and their teachers too often agree. *When professional
> writers complete a first draft, they usually feel that they are at the*

start of the writing process. When a draft is completed, the job of writing can begin. ("The Maker's Eye")

In the following paragraph, student Dan Roland uses both **comparison** and **contrast**. He begins by likening Kingston, Jamaica, to any city the reader might recognize, only to follow with a stark contrast between the extremes of wealth and poverty found there. The effect is startling and convincing. Roland has prepared his readers well for the thesis at the end of the paragraph.

> From my seat on an American Airlines 727, Kingston, Jamaica, looks like any other large urban center to me: tall buildings dominate the skyline, traffic weaves its way through roadways laid out like long arteries from the heart of the city. But Kingston is not like other cities, for it is here that some of the most extreme poverty in the world exists. The island of Jamaica was founded as a slave colony to help satisfy Europe's great demand for sugar cane, and its inhabitants are the descendants of slaves. Despair and poverty are part of everyday life and have been for centuries. The leading industry is tourism; every year thousands of well-to-do vacationers, mostly Americans and Canadians, come to stay in the multitudes of luxurious hotels and resorts. *Jamaica is one of the most beautiful places on Earth; it is also one of the most destitute [poorest].* ("Which Side of the Fence?")

Analogy helps explain ideas that are sometimes hard to grasp by comparing them with things readers can understand easily. On the surface, however, these things might seem unrelated. In a *U.S. News & World Report* article published in January 2005, Dr. Bernadine Healy uses analogy to teach us a lesson about nature.

> There is a sameness to brutal natural disasters. It's the final body count that chillingly distinguishes one from another. [The] tsunami in Southern Asia, which rose up from an earthquake in the Indian Ocean, swamping 11 countries and quickly claiming more than 120,000 lives, is . . . one of the worst floods in history. With our minds focused on war and political terrorism, Mother Nature proves to be the worst of all terrorists in the horror of her sudden assault on vulnerable innocents. ("Mother Nature, Terrorist")

TELL AN ANECDOTE OR DESCRIBE A SCENE

Anecdotes are brief, interesting stories that illustrate or support a point. An anecdote can help you prepare readers for the issues or problems you will be discussing without having to state the thesis directly. For example, this anecdote, which begins a *Wall Street Journal* editorial, makes the essay's central idea clear even though it does not express it in a thesis statement:

> We don't know if Janice Camarena had ever heard of *Brown v. Board of Education* when she enrolled in San Bernadino Valley College in California, but she knows all about it now. Mrs. Camarena was thrown out of a class at her public community college because of the color of her skin. When she sat down at her desk on the first day of the semester in January 1994, the instructor asked her to leave. That section of English 101 was reserved for black students only, she was told; Mrs. Camarena is white. ("Affirmative Reaction")

Another way to prepare readers for what follows is to **describe a scene** in a way that lets them know your feelings about a subject. Take the introduction to "A Hanging," an essay in which George Orwell reveals his view on capital punishment. Orwell does not express his opinions in a thesis statement; the essay's gloomy setting—its time and place—does that for him:

> It was Burma, a sodden [soggy] morning of the rains. A sickly light, like yellow tinfoil, was slanting over the high walls into the jail yard. We were waiting outside the condemned cells, a row of sheds fronted with double bars, like small animal cages. Each cell measured about ten feet by ten and was quite bare within except for a plank bed and a pot for drinking water. In some of them brown silent men were squatting at the inner bars, with their blankets draped around them. These were the condemned men, due to be hanged within the next week or two.

Use a Quotation

Quoting an expert or simply using an interesting, informative statement from another writer or from someone you've interviewed can lend interest and authority to your introduction. Just remember to quote your source accurately and make sure that the quotation relates directly to other ideas in your paragraph.

In the following example, Philip Shabecoff uses a quotation from world-famous scientist Rachel Carson to lead us to his thesis in the introduction to his essay on pesticides.

> "The most alarming of all man's assaults upon the environment is the contamination of air, earth, rivers, and sea with dangerous and even lethal materials," Rachel Carson wrote a quarter of a century ago in her celebrated book *Silent Spring*. Today there is little disagreement with her warnings in regard to such broad-spectrum pesticides as DDT, then widely used, now banned. *But there is still hot debate over how to apply modern pesticides—which are designed to kill specific types of weeds or insects—in ways that do not harm people and their environment.* ("Congress Again Confronts Hazards of Killer Chemicals")

DEFINE AN IMPORTANT TERM OR CONCEPT

Defining a term can explain aspects of your subject that will make it easier for readers to understand your central idea. But don't use dictionary definitions. Because they are often limited and rigid, they will make the beginning of an essay uninteresting. Instead, rely on your own ingenuity to create definitions that are interesting and appropriate to your purpose. This is what student Elena Santayana has done in the introduction to a paper about alcohol addiction:

> Alcoholism is a disease whose horrible consequences go beyond the patient. Families of alcoholics often become dysfunctional; spouses and children are abandoned or endure physical and emotional abuse. Co-workers suffer too. Alcoholics have high rates of absenteeism, and their work is often unreliable, thereby decreasing office or factory productivity. Indeed, alcoholics endanger the whole community. One in every two automobile fatalities is alcohol-related, and alcoholism is a major cause of violent crime. ("Everybody's Problem")

ADDRESS YOUR READERS DIRECTLY

In "What Is Poverty," Jo Goodwin Parker uses this method, combined with a question. The result is an opening that is both urgent and emphatic.

> You ask me what is poverty? Listen to me. Here I am, dirty, smelly, and with no "proper" underwear on and with the stench of my rotting teeth near you. I will tell you. Listen to me. Listen without pity. I cannot use your pity. Listen with understanding. Put yourself in my dirty, worn out, ill-fitting shoes, and hear me.

OPEN WITH A PARADOX

A paradox is a statement that, while true, seems to contradict itself. Because such statements are interesting in themselves, they make effective beginnings for essays. Take this introduction to James Herbert's "Tourist Trap":

> It's difficult to contemplate the concept of time travel without getting into some serious weirdness.
>
> An example: If you hitch a ride into the past on a time machine and prevent your parents from meeting, does that mean you won't be born?
>
> And if you weren't born, how could you have gone back in time in the first place?
>
> Those who study the ideas of time travel have a word for these little hang-ups: paradoxes.

Writing Conclusions

Sometimes, it is on the basis of the conclusion alone that readers respond to an essay. The conclusion's length depends on the essay's length and purpose. For very short essays, you might simply end the last paragraph with a concluding sentence, as does Kenneth Jon Rose in "2001 Space Shuttle." Rose's last sentence is his essay's conclusion.

> [T]he sky turns lighter and layers of clouds pass you like cars on a highway. Minutes later, still sitting upright, you will see the gray runway in the distance. Then the shuttle slows to 300 mph and drops its landing gear. Finally, with its nose slightly up like the Concorde SST and at a speed of about 225 mph, the shuttle will land on the asphalt runway and slowly come to a halt. *The trip into space will be over.*

Although one-sentence conclusions are fine for short essays, you will often need to close with at least one full paragraph. Either way, a conclusion should bring your discussion of the thesis to a timely and logical end. Try not to conclude abruptly; always give a signal that you are about to wrap things up. And never use your conclusion to introduce new ideas—ideas for which you did not prepare your readers earlier in the essay.

There are many ways to write conclusions. Here are seven:

1. Make reference to your thesis.
2. Summarize or rephrase your main points.
3. Offer advice; make a call to action.
4. Look to the future.
5. Explain how a problem was resolved.
6. Ask a question or series of questions.
7. Close with a statement or quotation readers will remember.

MAKE REFERENCE TO YOUR THESIS

Referring to your thesis in your conclusion is a good way to emphasize your central idea. This is what Professor Edward E. Ericson does in the three-part conclusion to "Gen X Is OK," the introduction to which appears on page 128.

> I didn't plan to develop a special fondness for today's young. My students made me do it. Of course I haven't stopped worrying. This generation does not seem headed for greatness. They have suffered too much cultural despoliation [loss], too much distortion of personhood, for that. It would take a global cataclysm [catastrophe] for them to have any chance of rising to the heights of human valor.

> But will they be basically sensible, productive adults? Were I a betting man, I'd put my money on them. And the more intergeneration friendships they form, the better their odds will be.
>
> All in all, I think Gen X is OK.

Ericson rephrases his thesis when he says, "Gen X Is OK." But he also restates four important points he made in the body of his essay:

1. His students caused him "to develop a special fondness for today's young."
2. Members of Gen X don't seem "headed for greatness."
3. They will become "sensible, productive adults."
4. Friendships between members of different generations will help improve their chances for success.

SUMMARIZE OR REPHRASE YOUR MAIN POINTS

For long essays, restating your thesis can be combined with summarizing or rephrasing each of the main points you have made in the body paragraphs. Doing so will help you write an effective summary of the entire essay and emphasize important ideas. This is exactly what Robin Roberts has done in his two concluding paragraphs of "Strike Out Little League" (see his introduction on page 128):

> I still don't know what those three gentlemen in Williamsport had in mind when they organized Little League baseball. I'm sure they didn't want parents arguing with their children about kids' games. I'm sure they didn't want young athletes hurting their arms pitching under pressure. . . . I'm sure they didn't want young boys . . . made to feel that something is wrong with them because they can't play baseball. I'm sure they didn't want a group of coaches drafting the players each year for different teams. I'm sure they didn't want un-qualified men working with the young players. I'm sure they didn't realize how normal it is for an 8-year-old boy to be scared of a thrown or batted baseball.
>
> For the life of me, I can't figure out what they had in mind.

OFFER ADVICE: MAKE A CALL TO ACTION

An example of a conclusion that offers advice appears in Elena Santayana's "Everybody's Problem," the introduction to which appears on page 131:

> If you have alcoholic friends, relatives, or co-workers, the worst thing you can do is to look the other way. This disease and its effects are simply not theirs to deal with alone. Try persuading them

to seek counseling. Describe the extent to which their illness is hurting their families, co-workers, and neighbors. Explain that their alcoholism endangers the entire community. Above all, don't pretend not to notice! Alcoholism is everybody's problem.

LOOK TO THE FUTURE

This method allows you to wonder what might occur in the future as a result of current situations you have just discussed. This kind of conclusion appears at the end of "Refugees: Darfur and Beyond," an editorial about the plight of Sudanese refugees. Note that it presents two very different outcomes. The introduction to this paragraph appears on page 127.

> Resettlement [of displaced persons] offers a solution to only part of the war-driven refugee crisis, whether in Sudan or elsewhere, but it does present an opportunity for the rich countries to show a greater measure of generosity than has so far been the case. In the meantime, without stronger peace making pressure from the U.N. Security Council and the powerful nations of the North, humanitarian disasters like the one in Sudan may burst forth in other parts of the world as well in years to come.

EXPLAIN HOW A PROBLEM WAS RESOLVED

In "The Ambivalence of Abortion" (see page 128 for the introduction to this essay), Linda Bird Francke writes about the difficulty she and her husband had in deciding whether to have or abort their fourth child. Francke's conclusion tells us how they resolved the question:

> My husband and I are back to planning our summer vacation and his career switch. And it certainly does make sense not to be having a baby right now—we say to each other all the time. But I have this ghost now. A very little ghost that only appears when I'm seeing something beautiful, like the full moon on the ocean last weekend. And the baby waves to me. And I wave at the baby. "Of course, we have room," I cry to the ghost. "Of course, we do."

ASK A QUESTION OR SERIES OF QUESTIONS

Ending with questions can keep your readers thinking long after they have read your essay. In "Old, Ailing, and Abandoned," the introduction to which appears on page 127, the conclusion is especially thought-provoking:

> Communities, stretched though they may be, need to remember [the] forgotten elderly living in our midst. What if every church in the

region agreed to regularly visit residents at just one [nursing] home? How about local government, or advocate agencies, linking the owners of small facilities more closely with existing services, such as rehab grants that could improve conditions?

This paragraph ends with rhetorical questions (whose answers are obvious). Such questions invite readers to participate in the essay's conclusion by answering in their own words. If your essay has made the answer so obvious that readers will respond as you want them to, ending with such a question can help make your essay memorable.

CLOSE WITH A STATEMENT OR QUOTATION READERS WILL REMEMBER

Deciding whether a statement will stick in readers' minds isn't easy. Trust your instincts. If you find a particular remark memorable, so might your readers. In any case, make sure that the statement relates directly to what you have discussed in your essay. That's what Dr. Bernadine Healy does in her conclusion to "Mother Nature, Terrorist," the introduction to which appears on page 129:

> Serving with the American Red Cross, I witnessed the washed-out roads, collapsed buildings, and far-flung rubble of Princeville, a small North Carolina town founded by slaves after the Civil War. It was completely destroyed by a massive flood in 1999. In a nearby rescue center, I met an elderly woman who told of standing alone in her house there, as water gushed in. . . . Struggling out to her porch, she grabbed a chair underwater and shimmied up on her roof, where she clung to its shingles for more than seven hours. . . . Though still shaky, she told me how happy she was to have painted her house that summer, and looked at me as if I were a dunce when I reassured her that someone else would redo her paint job. "You don't get it, Dr. Healy—how do you think I learned to get up on my roof?" I have not forgotten her wisdom. If we choose to live in health with Mother Nature, we still have lots to learn about preparing for her fury.

Visualizing Ways to Write Introductions and Conclusions

Read the introduction and conclusion to Michael Ryan's "They Track the Deadliest Viruses," which appear below. Comments in the margins identify effective techniques you might use in your own introductions and conclusions.

Ryan—Introduction

Makes a startling statement and challenges an assumption. "A disease that's in a faraway place today may be in our own backyard tomorrow," said Dr. James Hughes [of] the Centers for Disease Control and Prevention (CDC) in Atlanta. "We're certainly not immune."

Creates a contrast. A few years ago, this statement would have surprised many Americans. The advent [coming] of "miracle drugs and vaccines that conquered such plagues as polio, smallpox and even measles led many of us—including some scientists—to believe that the age of killer diseases was coming to an end.

The AIDS epidemic changed that . . . *States essay's thesis.*

Ryan—Conclusion

On my visit to Atlanta I . . . met with the associate director of the CDC, Dr. James Curran. He has been involved in the fight against AIDS since 1981. "The first five years, through 1985, was the age of discovery. . . . We discovered the global extent of the epidemic, the virus, antibody tests, AZT. *Refers to thesis.* It was an exciting time, but when it ended, half a million people in the U.S. already were infected.

Today, Dr. Curran said, the Centers for Disease Control and Prevention's response to *Looks to the future.* the AIDS epidemic has changed. "We're trying

Uses a quotation readers will remember.

to help the country evaluate the blood supply, develop test kits and work on prevention and counselling strategies. . . .

Information alone isn't sufficient, we have to find ways to change behaviour— especially in young people, who sometimes think they're invulnerable".

Makes a call to action.

Revising Introductions and Conclusions

Later in this chapter, you will read Ryan Paul Kessler's "An Unusual Affliction." Kessler knew that the first version of his essay was not the best he could do, so he rewrote the paper several times. Compare the rough and final drafts of the introduction and conclusion to his essay.

Kessler's Introduction—Rough Draft

Introduction is bland. Use one or more of the techniques explained in this chapter to draw the readers' interest.

My stuttering has been an endless source of embarrassment ever since I can remember. The ability to express oneself through speech is something I think most people take for granted. A lot of people don't realize how difficult even simple tasks are to a person

Provide examples of some simple tasks.

This thesis announces what the essay will do. It does not make a main point. Rewrite to improve focus.

who cannot communicate clearly. Throughout this essay I will share an experience or two to help the reader get a better understanding of what exactly a speech impediment does to one's confidence and psyche.

Kessler's Introduction—Final Draft

Begins with a question and addresses reader directly.

Have you ever been deep in a conversation with someone, and, all of a sudden, some jerk walks up and starts interrupting? It happens to me every time I start to engage in a conversation. For me, that jerk is not a friend or a classmate. It's not even a person. It's my speech impediment—stuttering to be more precise.

Uses startling language.

Builds suspense to surprise the reader.

This unusual affliction has been an an endless source of embarrassment ever since I can remember. The ability to express oneself through speech is something I think most people take for granted. A lot of people don't realize how difficult and frustrating even

Adds examples of "simple tasks" to make introduction more believable.

simple tasks such as ordering food in a restaurant, asking for directions, or answering a question in class are to a person who cannot communicate clearly. If you have never had a

Includes startling image in thesis.

speech impediment, you really can't imagine how brutally it can attack your psyche and destroy your self-confidence.

Rewrites thesis to focus on a main point.

Kessler's Conclusion—Rough Draft

Conclusion is rather short and is not memorable.

In the years past I have come up with my own ways of dealing with stuttering, one of which is to use synonyms for words that cause a speech "block." So naturally, I

Use one or more techniques for concluding discussed in this chapter. Try looking to future?

spend most of my free time looking for synonyms of words I commonly use on websites like www.dictionary.com. While this is not a solution to my problem, I am hoping new technological devices such as Fluency Master™ that are currently under development will provide a positive result that does not involve time consuming and embarrassing therapy.

Provide examples of such words.

Kessler's Conclusion—Final Draft

Over the years, I have come up with my own ways of dealing with this demon, one of which is to use synonyms for words that cause a speech "block." So naturally, I spend most of my free time looking for synonyms of words I commonly use on websites like www.dictionary.com. For example, instead of saying "ingenious" or "intelligent," I might use "smart."

Provides examples.

Looks to the future.

This is not a solution to my problem, but it has improved my confidence. I am hoping that, someday, new technological devices such as Fluency Master,™ which is currently under development, will provide positive results that do not involve time-consuming and

Closes with a memorable statement.

embarrassing therapy. Until then, I can take comfort in and gain confidence from knowing that I can write well. Armed with

References his introduction and his thesis.

⌈these weapons, I will continuing fighting off

that jerk who seems intent upon interrupting

⌊my life and my dreams.

Practicing Writing Introductions

Write a one-paragraph introduction for an essay you might compose on one of the following topics. Try using one of the methods for writing introductions suggested with each topic.

1. **Topic:** A terrifying, tragic, or emotionally charged experience.

   Method: Use a startling remark or statistic.

   _____

   _____

   _____

   _____

   _____

2. **Topic:** Dealing with an allergy or other common health problem.

   Method: Ask a question or present a problem.

   _____

   _____

   _____

   _____

   _____

3. **Topic:** The benefits (or dangers) of physical exercise.

   Method: Tell an anecdote or use contrast.

   _____

   _____

   _____

   _____

   _____

4. **Topic:** Ways to overcome pain other than using drugs.

   Method: Challenge a widely held opinion, use contrast, or present a problem.

   _____

   _____

   _____

   _____

   _____

5. **Topic:** What your clothes (car, home, or room) say about you.

   Method: Describe a scene, use a quotation, or address your readers directly.

   _____

   _____

   _____

   _____

   _____

6. **Topic:** The role of a father or mother in a young family.

   Method: Ask a question or challenge a widely held opinion.

   _____

   _____

   _____

   _____

   _____

7. **Topic:** Overcoming a fear of math (heights, closed-in places, water, etc.).

   Method: Address your readers directly, ask a question, or define a term.

   _____

   _____

   _____

   _____

8. **Topic:** Practicing safe sex.

   Method: Present a problem, define a term, or address your readers directly.

   _____

   _____

   _____

   _____

   _____

An Unusual Affliction

Ryan Paul Kessler

Ryan Paul Kessler was a student in a developmental writing class when he wrote the first draft of this very personal essay. Subsequent to completing the course, he revised and expanded it. The problem described in this essay, which the author has suffered from since he learned to speak, afflicts millions of people. However, Kessler refuses to allow this affliction to limit his dreams. A fighter, he has devised ways to compensate for and address the problem. While his career plans are still uncertain, Kessler is continuing his college studies and has decided to major in English for the present.

Preparing to Read

1. Identify one or more methods for writing introductions—as explained earlier in this chapter—in Kessler's first two paragraphs. As you get near the end of the essay, identify one or more methods for writing conclusions that you read about earlier.
2. Look for Kessler's thesis in his second paragraph and express it in your own words.
3. Once you get to the body of the essay, pick out ways in which the author maintains coherence in and between paragraphs. You probably read about such methods in Chapter 2.

Vocabulary

affliction (noun)	Suffering, trouble, illness.
belittlement (noun)	Disparagement, contempt.
chasm (noun)	Gap, gulf.
futile (adjective)	Useless.
pathologist (noun)	Medical specialist.
prepubescent (adjective)	Juvenile, before the age of puberty.
psyche (noun)	Mind, personality, consciousness.
schmuck (noun)	Slang term for fool, dope.
wanes (verb)	Decreases.

An Unusual Affliction

Ryan Paul Kessler

Have you ever been deep in a conversation with someone, and, all of a sud-   1
den, some jerk walks up and starts interrupting? It happens to me every
time I start to engage in a conversation. For me, that jerk is not a friend or a
classmate. It's not even a person. It's my speech impediment—stuttering to be
more precise.

This unusual affliction has been an endless source of embarrassment ever   2
since I can remember. The ability to express oneself through speech is something I think most people take for granted. A lot of people don't realize how
difficult and frustrating even simple tasks such as ordering food in a restaurant,
asking for directions, or answering a question in class are to a person who
cannot communicate clearly. If you have never had a speech impediment, you
really can't imagine how brutally it can attack your psyche and destroy your
self-confidence.

The first such experience I can remember when stuttering reared its ugly   3
head was during a grade school presentation on the solar system. I was assigned
to do a report on the planet Pluto. Upon completion of the project, I was told to
present it to the class, roughly 30 people. After my name was called, I shuffled
down the row of desks to the front of the classroom. The second I hit the word
"Pluto," the "P" sound kept repeating, over and over for what seemed like an
eternity. Not knowing how to react, I continued to try to say the word but,
alas, my attempts were futile. The other children broke out into uncontrollable
laughter, and I sat down feeling defeated. Incidents like this have occurred
over and over as I have gotten older, and the result has always been the same:
complete and utter embarrassment.

I am usually fine when I feel no pressure to perform. However, when I   4
am in situations in which I want to do my best, my emotions get the better of
me, and my confidence wanes. Job interviews, for example, have been hellish.
Some interviewers have been polite and patient, but it's almost impossible to
land a job that requires interacting with the public. This limits my opportunities, for most part-time jobs today involve talking with customers or clients.
Stuttering has also become a barrier to socializing and making new friends. And
it has made asking girls out on dates almost impossible.

After I left grade school, the laughter and teasing of prepubescent schmucks   5
were replaced by just facial expressions of pity or discomfort—reactions that
were almost as depressing to me. So, I decided to seek some help from a
speech pathologist. Upon walking into the office for my first appointment, I
tripped over what appeared to be a toy. Lo and behold, the office was set up
for children under twelve. After waiting about twenty minutes, a middle-aged
woman walked in and started going over speech exercises with me. Apparently,
the therapy was designed for children too because after five minutes I felt as if

I had sunk into a chasm of belittlement after repeating the words "the dog in dungarees has his day" thirty times. It figures that such an embarrassing affliction has a cure that is also embarrassing.

People react to my stuttering in different ways. When I start to stutter, 6 some people try to help me finish the word or sentence. This often turns into a bizarre game of charades that can lead to miscommunication and more embarrassment. Others try to ignore it and let me try to finish the word. However, they soon regret their decision after becoming exposed to what sounds like a broken record. This often leaves me and the person I am talking to feeling ridiculous. A few people even try to assist me by advising me to "slow down," "take a breath," or "relax," but that does not help. It is hard to say how I want someone to react, for it really does not matter. Above all, I just want people to be patient, understanding, and respectful, just like they would be with a person having any other disorder—and to try to hold back the laughter, at least until I leave the room.

Over the years, I have come up with my own ways of dealing with this 7 demon, one of which is to use synonyms for words that cause a speech "block." So naturally, I spend most of my free time looking for synonyms of words I commonly use on websites like www.dictionary.com. For example, instead of saying "ingenious" or "intelligent," I might use "smart."

This is not a solution to my problem, but it has improved my confidence. 8 I am hoping that, someday, new technological devices such as Fluency Master, which is currently under development, will provide positive results that do not involve time consuming and embarrassing therapy. Until then, I can take comfort in and gain confidence from knowing that I can write well. Armed with these weapons, I will continue fighting off that jerk who seems intent upon interrupting my life and my dreams.

Read More on the Web

National Institute on Deafness and Other Communication Disorders site: http://www.nidcd.nih.gov/health/voice/stutter.asp

Stuttering Foundation of America site: http://www.stutteringhelp.org/

"What Causes Stuttering," article in PLOS Biology, a peer-reviewed open-access journal: http://biology.plosjournals.org/perlserv?request=get-document&doi=10.1371/journal.pbio.0020046

Questions for Discussion

1. To capture the readers' attention, Kessler begins with a question and a startling remark. However, his introduction is two paragraphs long. What other techniques for writing effective introductions does he use?

2. Identify techniques for writing conclusions seen in paragraphs 8 and 9.
3. Where does Kessler state his thesis?
4. Where does he use examples?
5. What does the anecdote in paragraph 5 tell us about Kessler's problem?
6. Explain how the author maintains coherence in and between paragraphs. Focus on paragraphs 7 and 8.

Thinking Critically

1. In what way does Kessler's title—especially the word "unusual"—shed light on the emotions that he expresses in this essay?
2. Kessler mentions several ways in which people react to his stuttering. Explain how you react to and interact with people who have an "affliction."

Suggestions for Journal Entries

1. Have you found yourself in an extremely embarrassing situation? If so, use listing or focused freewriting to explain what happened and how you reacted. Note that the situation need not be as serious as what Kessler discusses. In fact, you might want to write about a situation that you can now laugh about.
2. Kessler tells us that a speech impediment can "attack your psyche" and "destroy your self-confidence." Has your psyche ever been attacked or your self-esteem weakened because of a particular incident, problem, situation, or person? Ask the journalists' questions to develop your response: Who was involved? What happened? Where and when did this occur? How did you overcome or attempt to deal with the emotional effects that resulted?

How to Keep Air Clean

Sydney Harris

Sydney Harrris (1917–1986) was born in London and raised in Chicago. He began writing for the Chicago Daily News *in 1941 and later wrote for the Chicago Sun-Times. Harris's column "Strictly Personal," which he began in 1944, became so popular that it was soon syndicated in many U.S. and Canadian newspapers. Models of interesting and effective process, Harris's columns, such as "How to Keep Air Clean," proved him to be an important American essayist and earned him thousands of devoted readers over the years. In 1953, Harris gathered his "Strictly Personal" columns in a book by the same name, publishing seven more such anthologies in subsequent years.*

Preparing to Read

1. Although this essay was first published 1969, it is still relevant. As you read "How to Keep Air Clean," take notes in which you point out facts and ideas that are still important to us.
2. The essay's introduction consists of the first three paragraphs. Read these carefully and determine which technique Harris relies on most to open this piece.
3. Harris uses terms from meteorology, the study of the earth's atmosphere. The *troposphere* (paragraph 4) is the bottom layer of the atmosphere, where our weather occurs. The *stratosphere* (paragraph 2), directly above the *troposphere,* extends to about 30 miles up.
4. In his conclusion, Harris mentions the Industrial Revolution, which occurred in the eighteenth and nineteenth centuries in Europe and North America. Not an armed conflict, the Industrial Revolution was a series of technological developments that led to the modern factory system, mass production, and automation.

Vocabulary

infinitely (adverb)	Without end.
irreversible (adjectives)	Permanent, not repairable.
noxious (adjectives)	Toxic, dangerous, harmful.
particulates (noun)	Small particles.

How to Keep Air Clean

Sydney Harris

Some months ago, while doing research on the general subject of pollution, I   1
learned how dumb I had been all my life about something as common and
familiar—and essential—as air.

In my ignorance, I had always thought that "fresh air" was infinitely avail-   2
able to us. I had imagined that the dirty air around us somehow escaped into
the stratosphere, and that new air kept coming in—much as it does when we
open a window after a party.

This, of course, is not true, and you would imagine that a grown man with   3
a decent education would know this as a matter of course. What is true is that
we live in a kind of spaceship called the earth, and only a limited amount of air
is *forever* available to us.

The "walls" of our spaceship enclose what is called the "troposphere,"   4
which extends about seven miles up. This is all the air that is available to us.
We must use it over and over again for infinity, just as if we were in a sealed
room for the lifetime of the earth.

No fresh air comes in, and no polluted air escapes. Moreover, no dirt or   5
poisons are ever "destroyed"—they remain in the air, in different forms, or
settle on the earth as "particulates." And the more we burn, the more we replace
good air with bad.

Once contaminated, this thin layer of air surrounding the earth cannot   6
be cleansed again. We can clean materials, we can even clean water, but we
cannot clean the air. There is nowhere else for the dirt and poisons to go—we
cannot open a window in the troposphere and clear out the stale and noxious
atmosphere we are creating.

Perhaps every child in sixth grade and above knows this, but I doubt that   7
one adult in a hundred is aware of this basic physical fact. Most of us imagine,
as I did, that winds sweep away the gases and debris in the air, taking them far
out into the solar system and replacing them with new air.

The United States alone is discharging *130 million tons of pollutants a year* into   8
the atmosphere, from factories, heating systems, incinerators, automobiles and
airplanes, power plants and public buildings. What is frightening is not so much
the death and illness, corrosion and decay they are responsible for—as the fact
that this is an *irreversible process*. The air will never be cleaner than it is now.

And this is why *prevention*—immediate, drastic and far-reaching—is our   9
only hope for the future. We cannot undo what we have done. We cannot restore the atmosphere to the purity it had before the Industrial Revolution. But
we can, and must, halt the contamination before our spaceship suffocates from
its own foul discharges.

Read More on the Web

"Our Spaceship Earth"—Buckminster Fuller Institute site:
  http://www.bfi.org/taxonomy/term/37
"Spaceship Earth"—Science Netlinks site:
  http://www.sciencenetlinks.com/lessons.cfm?DocID=295

Questions for Discussion

1. Reread paragraph 3. What is Harris's thesis statement?
2. What techniques discussed earlier in this chapter does Harris use in his introduction?
3. What is the analogy that Harris uses in paragraph 3? In what other paragraphs does he refer to this analogy?
4. What techniques does he use to close this essay?
5. The essay is well developed and organized. What techniques does the author use to create coherence in and between paragraphs? (For ways to maintain coherence, see Chapter 2.)

Thinking Critically

1. As you have learned, Harris uses an analogy when he compares earth to a spaceship. Write a short paragraph in which you develop three or four specific comparisons between earth and a spaceship.
2. List some ways in which you might help in the fight to prevent further pollution of the atmosphere.

Suggestions for Journal Entries

1. Summarize in a paragraph of your own the three paragraphs Harris uses to introduce his essay. Make sure to use your own words throughout.
2. Think of a widely held opinion or assumption that you believe is incorrect. In a sentence or two, write this idea in your journal. Then, in preparation for writing a full-length essay, use one of the prewriting techniques discussed in "Getting Started" to write down your major reasons for disagreeing. Here are a few examples of the kinds of opinions or assumptions you might want to correct:

- Someone who had had only one or two drinks shouldn't be prevented from driving a car.
- Breaking an alcohol, smoking, or drug addiction is relatively easy.
- Being exposed to secondhand smoke while dining in a restaurant isn't harmful.
- Women have no aptitude for math.
- Reading poetry, listening to opera, and going to the ballet aren't things that "real" men do.
- Cats are not as bright as dogs.
- Global warming is a real threat to the environment.
- There is no such thing as global warming.

Fish Cheeks

Amy Tan

Amy Tan was born in Oakland, California (1952). Earlier, her parents had escaped from Communist China and settled in America. At the heart of this essay is the clash between new and old cultural values and its effect on the maturation of the young Amy. Tan received a B.A. and an M.A. from San Jose State University. In 1989, her first novel, The Joy Luck Club, *became an overnight best seller. Among her other novels are* The Hundred Secret Senses *(1995) and* The Bonesetter's Daughter *(2001). She has written essays for a number of widely read magazines including the* Atlantic Monthly *and* McCall's. *Written in 1987, "Fish Cheeks" was first published in* Seventeen Magazine.

Preparing to Read

1. The essay's introduction spans two paragraphs, which use three of the techniques for writing introductions discussed in the beginning of this chapter.

2. The essay's conclusion also spans two paragraphs. Make sure to identify at least two of the techniques for writing conclusions discussed earlier.

3. "Mary," mentioned in the first paragraph, is the mother of Jesus Christ.

Vocabulary

appalling (adjective)	Embarrassing.
clamor (noun)	Loud noise, uproar.
grimaced (verb)	Scowled, frowned.
muster (verb)	Bring up.
prawns (noun)	Large shrimp.

Fish Cheeks

Amy Tan

I fell in love with the minister's son the winter I turned fourteen. He was not   1
Chinese, but as white as Mary in the manger. For Christmas I prayed for this
blond-haired boy, Robert, and a slim new American nose.

When I found out that my parents had invited the minister's family over for   2
Christmas Eve dinner, I cried. What would Robert think of our shabby Chinese
Christmas? What would he think of our noisy Chinese relatives who lacked
proper American manners? What terrible disappointment would he feel upon
seeing not a roasted turkey and sweet potatoes but Chinese food?

On Christmas Eve I saw that my mother had outdone herself in creating a   3
strange menu. She was pulling black veins out of the backs of fleshy prawns.
The kitchen was littered with appalling mounds of raw food: A slimy rock cod
with bulging eyes that pleaded not to be thrown into a pan of hot oil. Tofu,
which looked like stacked wedges of rubbery white sponges. A bowl soaking
dried fungus back to life. A plate of squid, their backs crisscrossed with knife
markings so they resembled bicycle tires.

And then they arrived—the minister's family and all my relatives in a   4
clamor of doorbells and rumpled Christmas packages. Robert grunted hello,
and I pretended he was not worthy of existence.

Dinner threw me deeper into despair. My relatives licked the ends of their   5
chopsticks and reached across the table, dipping them into the dozen or so
plates of food. Robert and his family waited patiently for platters to be passed
to them. My relatives murmured with pleasure when my mother brought out
the whole steamed fish. Robert grimaced. Then my father poked his chopsticks
just below the fish eye and plucked out the soft meat. "Amy, your favorite," he
said, offering me the tender fish cheek. I wanted to disappear.

At the end of the meal my father leaned back and belched loudly, thanking   6
my mother for her fine cooking. "It's a polite Chinese custom to show you are
satisfied," explained my father to our astonished guests. Robert was looking
down at his plate with a reddened face. The minister managed to muster up a
quiet burp. I was stunned into silence for the rest of the night.

After everyone had gone, my mother said to me, "You want to be the   7
same as American girls on the outside." She handed me an early gift. It was a
miniskirt in beige tweed. "But inside you must always be Chinese. You must be
proud you are different. Your only shame is to have shame."

And even though I didn't agree with her then, I knew that she understood   8
how much I had suffered during the evening's dinner. It wasn't until many years
later—long after I had gotten over my crush on Robert—that I was able to fully
appreciate her lesson and the true purpose behind our particular menu. For
Christmas Eve that year, she had chosen all my favorite foods.

Read More on the Web

Salon interview with Amy Tan: **http://www.salon.com/12nov1995/ feature/tan.html**

Chinese-American Museum site containing stories of Chinese-American families: **www.eskimo.com/ camla/voices**

Dissertation abstract on Chinese-American Parent-Child Conflict resolution: **http://www.sfsu.edu/ multsowk/title/337.htm**

Questions for Discussion

1. Does Tan express a formal thesis in this essay? Where might it be found?
2. Where in the introduction does the author use a startling remark?
3. Explain how contrast is used in Tan's introduction.
4. What is the problem that Tan explains in her introduction?
5. How does the conclusion serve to resolve that problem?
6. What other method does Tan use to conclude this essay?
7. What is the significance of the title?

Thinking Critically

1. This essay narrates a Christmas feast. Is this the only reason Tan tells us that Robert was "as white as Mary in the manager"? Or is there another reason? What light does this statement cast on her central idea? Explain this in a short paragraph.
2. What does Tan's mother mean when she says "your only shame is to have shame"? Write a short paragraph in which you explain this idea.

Suggestions for Journal Entries

1. Think of a time when your parents, siblings, or other close relatives put you into a social situation that made you feel very uncomfortable or embarrassed. Gather details about this incident through clustering, focused freewriting, or listing.
2. This essay explains differences in the eating habits of two groups of people. What are family feasts like at your house? Begin gathering details about the way people in your family behave at a holiday dinner or other celebration.

A Prayer for the Days of Awe

Elie Wiesel

Elie Wiesel was born in Romania in 1928. In 1944, he was imprisoned in Aus-chwitz and Buchenwald, two of the many infamous Nazi death camps where six million Jews and millions of other people were murdered. This horror is now called the Holocaust, a word derived from the fact that the bodies of many victims of this mass murder were burned in ovens after having been gassed or killed in other ways. Wiesel's autobiographical novel Night *recalls his experience in the camps, and his many other novels, plays, and stories are aimed at making sure the Holocaust is never forgotten. Wiesel was awarded the Nobel Peace Prize in 1986. He now teaches at Boston University.*

Preparing to Read

1. This essay appeared in the *New York Times* shortly before Rosh Hashanah, the Jewish New Year Holiday, which is observed in prayer and begins the Ten Days of Penitence, ending with Yom Kippur, the Day of Atonement. These Days of Awe conclude with the faithful's praying for forgiveness for the previous year's sins.

2. As Wiesel's title indicates, this is not just an essay; it is a prayer. Keep this in mind as you read this selection, for Wiesel is addressing two—and perhaps three—different audiences.

3. How might Wiesel be using the word "awe"? Look this word up in a dictionary.

Vocabulary

annihilate (verb)	Destroy completely, exterminate.
culpability (noun)	Guilt, responsibility.
fervor (noun)	Enthusiasm, eagerness, passion.
Sabbath (noun)	Day of worship.
testimony (noun)	Written or spoken statement that something is true.
theological (adjective)	Having to do with the study of God.
Treblinka (noun)	Another Nazi concentration camp.
tribunal (noun)	Council, court.
Zionism (noun)	A movement that attempted to reestablish the Jewish state in Palestine.

A Prayer for the Days of Awe

Elie Wiesel

Master of the Universe, let us make up. It is time. How long can we go on 1
being angry?

More than 50 years have passed since the nightmare was lifted. Many 2
things, good and less good, have since happened to those who survived it.
They learned to build on ruins. Family life was recreated. Children were born,
friendships struck. They learned to have faith in their surroundings, even in
their fellow men and women. Gratitude has replaced bitterness in their hearts.
No one is as capable of thankfulness as they are. Thankful to anyone willing to
hear their tales and become their ally in the battle against apathy and forgetful-
ness. For them every moment is grace.

Oh, they do not forgive the killers and their accomplices, nor should 3
they. Nor should you, Master of the Universe. But they no longer look at every
passer-by with suspicion. Nor do they see a dagger in every hand.

Does this mean that the wounds in their soul have healed? They will never 4
heal. As long as a spark of the flames of Auschwitz and Treblinka glows in their
memory, so long will my joy be incomplete.

What about my faith in you, Master of the Universe?   5

I now realize I never lost it, not even over there, during the darkest hours 6
of my life. I don't know why I kept on whispering my daily prayers, and those
one reserves for the Sabbath, and for the holidays, but I did recite them, often with my father and, on Rosh Hashanah eve, with hundreds of inmates at
Auschwitz. Was it because the prayers remained a link to the vanished world
of my childhood?

But my faith was no longer pure. How could it be? It was filled with 7
anguish rather than fervor, with perplexity more than piety. In the kingdom
of eternal night, on the Days of Awe, which are the Days of Judgment, my
traditional prayers were directed to you as well as against you, Master of the
Universe. What hurt me more: your absence or your silence?

In my testimony I have written harsh words, burning words about your 8
role in our tragedy. I would not repeat them today. But I felt them then. I felt
them in every cell of my being. Why did you allow if not enable the killer day
after day, night after night to torment, kill and annihilate tens of thousands of
Jewish children? Why were they abandoned by your Creation? These thoughts
were in no way destined to diminish the guilt of the guilty. Their established
culpability is irrelevant to my "problem" with you, Master of the Universe. In
my childhood I did not expect much from human beings. But I expected everything from you.

Where were you, God of kindness, in Auschwitz? What was going on in 9
heaven, at the celestial tribunal, while your children were marked for humilia-
tion, isolation and death only because they were Jewish?

These questions have been haunting me for more than five decades. You 10 have vocal defenders, you know. Many theological answers were given me, such as "God is God. He alone knows what He is doing. One has no right to question Him or His ways." Or: "Auschwitz was a punishment for European Jewry's sins of assimilation and/or Zionism." And: "Isn't Israel the solution? Without Auschwitz, there would have been no Israel."

I reject all these answers. Auschwitz must and will forever remain a ques- 11 tion mark only: it can be conceived neither with God nor without God. At one point, I began wondering whether I was not unfair with you. After all, Auschwitz was not something that came down ready-made from heaven. It was conceived by men, implemented by men, staffed by men. And their aim was to destroy not only us but you as well. Ought we not to think of your pain, too? Watching your children suffer at the hands of your other children, haven't you also suffered?

As we Jews now enter the High Holidays again, preparing ourselves to pray 12 for a year of peace and happiness for our people and all people, let us make up, Master of the Universe. In spite of everything that happened? Yes, in spite. Let us make up: for the child in me, it is unbearable to be divorced from you so long.

Read More on the Web

Biography of Elie Wiesel with links to bibliography of his works and to Report to the President on the President's Commission on the Holocaust: http://xroads.virginia.edu/~CAP/HOLO/ELIEBIO.HTM

Home page of the United States Holocaust Memorial Museum: http://www.ushmm.org/

Nobel Prize Internet Archive on Elie Wiesel: http://almaz.com/nobel/peace/1986a.html

Questions for Discussion

1. What method or methods for writing introductions does Wiesel use?
2. What method does he use to close the essay?
3. Why does the author refer to God as "Master of the Universe" rather than use a more personal form of address?
4. This selection is addressed to at least two audiences: God and the readers of the *New York Times*. Why did Wiesel choose to address both? Why didn't he write it solely for human readers?
5. Is Wiesel also writing to himself? Explain.

6. In paragraph 10, Wiesel tells us that many questions have been "haunting [him] for more than five decades." What are those questions?

7. Reread paragraphs 11 and 12. What do they reveal about the reason or reasons Wiesel wants to make peace with God?

Thinking Critically

1. In a 1998 interview with George Plimpton, Wiesel said: "I rarely speak about God. To God, yes. I protest against Him. I shout at Him. But to open a discourse [discussion] about the qualities of God, about the problems that God imposes . . . , no. And yet He is there, in silence." What light does this quotation shed on "A Prayer for the Days of Awe"? What is Wiesel's purpose in writing this prayer? Has his attitude toward God changed from what it was when he spoke with Plimpton?

2. Do you have a favorite prayer, poem, or hymn? Read it carefully; then, summarize it in your journal. In the process explain why this particular piece is meaningful to you.

Suggestions for Journal Entries

1. Sometimes life seems illogical, and tragedies strike for no apparent reason and with no warning. If such an incident has occurred in your life or in the life of someone you know, write down everything you know about this event.

2. Have you ever been angry with God or with the universe for allowing some difficulty or horror to visit you or others? Record the particulars of this situation. Make sure to explain why you are or were angry.

Suggestions for Sustained Writing

1. If you responded to the first Suggestion for Journal Entries after Ryan Kessler's "An Unusual Affliction," you have probably begun gathering information about an embarrassing experience. Continue adding notes in your journal; then use this information in a fully developed essay that discusses what happened, why you were embarrassed, and how you dealt with or attempted to deal with the embarrassment.

If this doesn't interest you, write an essay that recalls a situation or incident in which your self-esteem came under attack. Explain what or who caused this to happen, how you reacted, and whether you have recovered from this assault on your psyche. Like Kessler, be brave! Express your emotional reaction to this situation openly and freely. Once again, check your journal. You might have gathered relevant information for this assignment if you responded to the second journal suggestion after Kessler's essay.

Whichever option you choose, make sure to write an effective introduction and memorable conclusion by using one or more of the techniques for beginning and ending an essay, which are explained earlier in this chapter.

2. In the second of the Suggestions for Journal Entries after Sydney Harris's "How to Keep Air Clean," you were asked to write a number of reasons that have led you to disagree with a widely held assumption or opinion. If you responded to this item, read over what you wrote in your journal. Then, do the following:

   a. Write an introductory paragraph—complete with a formal thesis statement—that challenges this assumption and briefly explains your reasons for disagreeing.

   b. Make each of your reasons for disagreeing the topic of a well-developed paragraph. Use these paragraphs as the body of your essay.

   c. Write a concluding paragraph that
      • Rephrases your thesis or summarizes your major points.
      • Makes a call to action, as Harris does at the end of his essay.
      • Looks to the future.
      • Asks a question or series of questions.

   Note that you need not complete these steps in the order they are presented. For example, writing the body paragraphs and the conclusion before you write the introduction might be an easier way to proceed. In any event, remember that writing is a process of discovery. Often you might have to revise one part of the essay in light of what you said in another. Therefore, if you begin the assignment by drafting your introduction, don't be afraid to rewrite it later if what you put into the body of the paper demands a change in your thesis or in other parts of the introduction. Finally, no matter how many times you rewrite your paper, make sure to edit and proofread the final draft carefully.

3. Read over the notes you made after the first of the Suggestions for Journal Entries following Amy Tan's "Fish Cheeks." You have probably gathered information relating to a time when your parents or other close relative put you into a situation in which you felt embarrassed or uncomfortable. Now, add information to this journal entry. Make sure to include details about

your emotional reaction at the time this occurred. Finally, explain whether, like Tan, your embarrassment was of your own making, or whether, in fact, it was an appropriate reaction to the situation. In other words, was this really a problem or not?

Narrate the story by drafting three or more paragraphs that will form the body of your essay. After revising these for development, unity, and coherence, think about the introduction and conclusion. You can certainly begin by stating a problem or perceived problem. But make the introduction even more inviting by using at least one of the other methods for writing openings discussed in this chapter. You can end by looking back at what happened and explaining what it all means to you now. To make your conclusion even more memorable, however, try including another method for writing conclusions as well.

4. The second journal suggestion after "Fish Cheeks" asks you to describe the eating habits of your family during a particular holiday feast or some other celebration. In addition to mentioning the kinds of food served and the table setting, focus on the people and their behavior or conversation before, during, and after the meal. What are their table manners like? Is food passed around in an orderly manner, or do people just grab? Do they speak loudly and laugh heartily? How do they treat each other?

Once you have drafted the body paragraphs of the essay, think about your introduction. You might begin with a description of the scene, a question or startling remark, a contrast, or a statement of a problem. To conclude, try looking to the future or asking a question.

5. If you responded to either of the suggestions for journal writing after Wiesel's "A Prayer for the Days of Awe," read the notes you made in preparation for the writing of a letter to God or to the Master of the Universe (in other words, a prayer). You might write about your concerns and frustrations over an incident in which someone has been harmed, or you might express your anger to the Creator for allowing evil, sorrow, and injustice to exist either in general or in a particular situation you have observed. Or you might simply discuss some questions that have been bothering you about yourself, about your relationship with God, or about life in general.

Whichever path you choose, remember that your letter/prayer will be read by a human audience, so provide enough details to ensure that your readers will understand the situations, concepts, and emotions you are discussing. In addition, use one or more of the methods for writing introductions and conclusions that you have learned in this chapter. Whether human or divine, your audience deserves interesting and effective openings and closings.

Finally, write several drafts of your paper. Revise and edit it carefully. God may forgive sloppy writing, but other readers won't.

Writing to Learn: A Group Activity

THE FIRST MEETING

For inspiration, reread and discuss Elie Wiesel's "A Prayer for the Days of Awe" as well as the following short prayer from the Koran, the Islamic holy book:

> *In the Name of God, the Compassionate, the Merciful*
>
> Praise be to God, Lord of the worlds!
> The compassionate, the merciful!
> King on the Day of reckoning!
> Thee *only* do we worship, and to Thee do we cry for help.
> Guide Thou us on the straight path,
> The path of those to whom Thou has been gracious;—with
> whom Thou art not angry, and who go not astray. (Sura I)

Now pretend that you have been asked to write a group letter to the Master of the Universe. Brainstorm for at least 20 minutes to come up with three or four questions that you might ask about the nature of life, of the universe, of the afterlife, of God Himself, or of any other relevant issues important to you. Write out each question in a clear and complete sentence. Assign each student of the group—except one—to discuss this question in a fully developed paragraph that he or she will complete for homework. Assign the remaining student the task of writing the introduction and conclusion for an essay that will include the three or four paragraphs written by the other group members. Everyone should bring several copies of his or her work to the next meeting.

THE SECOND MEETING

Distribute the materials everyone has brought. Now decide which paragraphs need to be expanded or revised in any way. Make suggestions as needed. Then decide on the order in which each paragraph should appear in the paper. Rewrite your paragraphs for homework, making enough copies to distribute at the next meeting.

THE THIRD MEETING

Distribute the materials everyone has brought. Arrange all the paragraphs in the order they are to appear in the essay's final version. Collectively, make sure that there are transitions in and between paragraphs, that the paper begins and ends in interesting and logical ways, and that it makes sense over all. Next, edit the paper for grammar, spelling, sentence structure, and other errors. Finally, assign one person the job of typing the paper as a whole and of making enough copies for each member of the group and for the instructor.

Word Choice and Sentence Patterns

In Section One you learned how to approach a subject, to focus on a purpose and central idea, and to organize and develop the information you collected. The two chapters in Section Two explain how to use language and sentence structure to make your writing clearer, more interesting, and more emphatic.

What you will learn in Section Two is just as important as what you learned earlier. In most cases, however, the techniques discussed in this section—refining word choice, creating figures of speech, and reworking sentence structure for emphasis and variety—are things you will turn your attention to after having written at least one version of a paper, not while you are focusing on a central idea, organizing details, or writing your first rough draft.

Keep this in mind as you read the next two chapters. Chapter 4 explains how to choose vocabulary that is concrete, specific, and vivid as well as how to use figurative language: metaphor, simile, and personification. Finally, Chapter 5 will increase your ability to create variety and emphasis through sentence structure.

Enjoy the selections that follow. Reading them carefully and completing the Questions for Discussion, the Suggestions for Journal Entries, and the Suggestions for Sustained Writing will not only help you learn more about the writing process but should also inspire you to continue developing as a writer.

CHAPTER 4

Word Choice: Using Literal and Figurative Language Effectively

This chapter explains ways to enhance your ability to choose just the right words for a variety of writing purposes and situations. Language can work in many different ways. Most often, writers use a straightforward approach by relying on language that is literal—that means exactly what it says. As you will see, the most effective words of this type are concrete, specific, and vivid.

At times, however, writers may also need to explain complex ideas or to make their writing more colorful. In such cases, they can also turn to language that is figurative. The most well-known figures of speech are simile, metaphor, and personification. Figurative language does not explain or represent a subject directly, as does literal language. Instead, it creates a comparison or other relationship between an idea you want to explain and something concrete that readers can recognize easily.

Showing Readers What You Mean

A writer has three ways to communicate a message: (1) by implying, (2) by telling, and (3) by showing. Of course, all three types of writing serve specific and important purposes. Usually, however, writing that is the clearest and has the greatest impact uses language that shows. Words that show are more concrete, specific, and usually more interesting than those that simply tell or imply a message.

Although the following two paragraphs discuss the same subject, they contain very different kinds of language. Which of the two will have the greatest impact on readers?

Writing That Tells

Michael's old car is the joke of the neighborhood. He should have gotten rid of it years ago, but he insists on keeping this "antique" despite protests from his family and friends. The car is noisy and unsafe. What's more, it pollutes the environment, causes a real disturbance whenever he drives by, and is a real eyesore.

Writing That Shows

Whenever Michael drives down our street, dogs howl, children scream, and the elderly shut their doors and windows as if to prepare for a hurricane. His 1975 Chevrolet Nova has been through the traffic wars, and, fatally wounded, it is now suffering a prolonged and painful death. Originally painted emerald green, the exterior is so covered with scrapes, dents, and patches of rust that it is hard to tell what it looked like when new. His wife and children have pleaded with him to junk this corroded patchwork of steel, rubber, and chewing gum, but Michael insists that he can restore his "baby" to its former glory. It does no good for them to argue that its cracked windshield and bald tires make this old crate a road hazard. Nor is Michael moved by their complaints about the roar and rattle of its cracked muffler, the screech of its well-worn brakes, and the stench of the cloud of black smoke billowing from its rusty tail pipe.

As you will learn in the chapters on narration and description, language that shows makes for effective and interesting writing, especially when your purpose is to describe a person or place or to tell a story. The next few pages explain how to improve your writing by

1. Choosing **concrete** nouns and adjectives over those that are abstract.
2. Including words that are **specific** rather than those that are general.
3. Adding **vivid** verbs, adjectives, and adverbs.
4. Using **figurative** language: simile, metaphor, personification.

Making Your Writing Concrete

Concrete language points to or identifies things readers can experience for themselves. Things that are concrete are material; they can be seen, touched, heard, smelled, or tasted. The opposite of concrete is *abstract*, a term that refers to ideas, emotions, or other intangibles. While very real, these things exist in our minds and hearts. That's why readers find it harder to grasp the abstract than the concrete.

Compare the nouns in these two lists. Words on the right are physical signs of emotions on the left.

Abstract	Concrete
Joy	Laughter
Hatred	Sneering, cursing
Anger	Shouting
Sadness	Weeping
Fear	Screaming, gasping

Here are three ways to make your writing more concrete.

Use Your Five Senses to Recall an Experience

Providing a realistic account of how things look, sound, smell, taste, and feel can make your writing concrete. In "Once More to the Lake," E. B. White recalls concrete, sensory details about arriving at the camp in Maine where he once spent his summers. The only sense White does not refer to is taste.

> The arriving . . . had been so big a business in itself, at the railway station the farm wagon drawn up, the first smell of the pine-laden air, the first glimpse of the smiling farmer . . . and the feel of the wagon under you for the long ten-mile haul, and at the top of the last long hill catching the first view of the lake after eleven months of not seeing this cherished body of water. The shouts and cries of the other campers when they saw you, and the trunks to be unpacked, to give up their rich burden.

Create a Concrete Image

An image is a mental picture that expresses an abstract concept in concrete terms. You can create images by packing your writing with concrete nouns and adjectives. The word *image* is related to the word *imagine*, so a good time to use an image is when writing about something your readers have never experienced and can only imagine from the information that you provide. In "Searching for El Dorado," Marc Herman creates an image to help us experience "a natural paradise."

> The Guiana Shield region of South America is a natural paradise. The moisture from its waterfalls sifts over lush forests, producing daily rainbows that span hundreds of miles at their base and widen into double spectra across cliff faces. Tourists come here to see Angel Falls, the world's highest, or Canaima National Park, a plateau with Wyoming's sky, Yosemite's waterfalls, and New Mexico's mesas. The tallest of these mesas, Mount Roraima, creates its own weather, as clouds slip off the top and twist beside the cliffs like dropped scarves, catching the sunlight and staining the brush below a dense, woven brown the color of a monk's robe. The landscape is studded with Pemon Indian houses shaped like rockets—wood and mud cylinders with conical roofs made of dried leaves.

Use Examples

If you want to explain that your Uncle Wendell is eccentric, you can write that "he is odd" or "strange." But such synonyms are as abstract and hard to grasp as "eccentric." Instead, you might provide examples that readers can understand. You can show them what "eccentric" means by explaining that Uncle Wendell never wears two socks of the same color, that he cuts his own hair, and that his favorite dessert is chocolate-covered seaweed.

In "The Human Cost of an Illiterate Society," Jonathan Kozol uses examples to portray the frustration, loss, and risks faced by people who cannot read and write:

> Illiterates cannot read the menu in a restaurant.
>
> They cannot read the cost of items on the menu in the window of the restaurant before they enter.
>
> Illiterates cannot read the letters that their children bring home from their teachers. They cannot study school department circulars that tell them of the courses that their children must be taking if they hope to pass the SAT exams. They cannot help with homework. They cannot write a letter to the teacher. They are afraid to visit the classroom. They do not want to humiliate their child or themselves.

Making Your Writing Specific

Writing that lacks specificity often contains language that is general, making it difficult to communicate clearly and completely. A good way to make your writing specific is to choose nouns and adjectives carefully. Nouns name persons, places, or things; adjectives describe nouns, thereby making them more distinct and exact. Compare the words and phrases in each column:

General	More Specific	Most Specific
leader	president	Abraham Lincoln
automobile	sports utility vehicle	Ford Explorer
school	college	University of Tennessee
television show	reality series	Survivor
lunch	sandwich special	California burger on a whole wheat roll
beverage	soft drink	diet ginger ale

You probably noticed that several of the "Most Specific" items contain capitalized words. These are proper nouns, which name specific persons, places, and things. Use proper nouns that your readers will recognize when you can. Doing so will show how much you know about your subject and increase your readers' confidence in your writing. More important, it will make your ideas easier to grasp.

Notice the difference between the following two paragraphs. The first uses vague, general language; the second uses specifics—nouns and adjectives—that make its meaning clearer and that hold the readers' interest better.

General

The island prison is covered with flowers now. A large sign that is visible from a long way off warns visitors away. But since the early 1960s, when they took the last prisoners to other institutions, the sign has really served no purpose, for the prison has been abandoned. The place is not unpleasant; in fact, one might enjoy the romance and solitude out there.

Specific

Alcatraz Island is covered with flowers now: orange and yellow nasturtiums, geraniums, sweet grass, blue iris, black-eyed Susans. Candytuft springs up through the cracked concrete in the exercise yard. Ice plant carpets the rusting catwalks. "WARNING! KEEP OFF! U.S. PROPERTY," the sign still reads, big and yellow and visible for perhaps a quarter of a mile, but since March 21, 1963, the day they took the last thirty or so men off the island . . . the warning has been only *pro forma* [serving no real purpose]. It is not an unpleasant place to be, out there on Alcatraz with only the flowers and the wind and the bell buoy moaning and the tide surging through the Golden Gate. (Joan Didion, "Rock of Ages")

The differences between these two paragraphs can be summed up as follows:

- The first calls the place an "island prison." The second gives it a name, "Alcatraz."

- The first claims that the prison is covered with flowers. The second shows us that this is true by naming them: "nasturtiums, geraniums," and so on. It also explains exactly where they grow: "through the cracked concrete" and on "rusting catwalks."

- The first tells us about a sign that can be seen "from a long way off." The second explains that the sign is "visible for perhaps a quarter of a mile" and shows us exactly what it says.

- The first mentions that the last prisoners were removed from Alcatraz in the 1960s. The second explains that they numbered "thirty or so" and that the exact date of their departure was March 21, 1963.

- The first tells us that we might find "romance and solitude" on Alcatraz Island. The second describes the romance and solitude by calling our attention to "the flowers and the wind and the bell buoy moaning and the tide surging through the Golden Gate."

Making Your Writing Vivid

Besides using figurative language (the subject of the next part of this chapter), you can make your writing vivid by choosing verbs, adjectives, and adverbs carefully.

1. Verbs express action, condition, or state of being. If you wrote that "Jan *leaped* over the hurdles," you would be using an action verb. If you explained that "Roberta *did not feel* well" or that "Mario *was* delirious," you would be describing a condition or a state of being.

2. Adjectives describe nouns. You would be using adjectives if you wrote that "the *large, two-story white* house that the *young Canadian* couple bought was *old* and *weather-beaten.*"

3. Adverbs modify (tell the reader something about) verbs, adjectives, or other adverbs. You would be using adverbs if you wrote: "The *easily* frightened child sobbed *softly* and hugged his mother *very tightly* as she *gently* wiped away his tears and *tenderly* explained that the knee he had *just* scraped would stop hurting *soon.*"

Choosing effective verbs, adjectives, and adverbs can turn dull writing into writing that keeps the reader's interest and communicates ideas with greater emphasis and clarity. Notice how much more effective the rewritten version of each of the following sentences becomes when the right verbs, adjectives, and adverbs are used:

1. The old church needed repair.

    The pre–Civil War Baptist church cried out for repairs to its tottering steeple, its crumbling stone foundation, and its cracked stained-glass windows.

2. The kitchen table was a mess. It was covered with the remains of peanut butter and jelly sandwiches.

    The kitchen table was littered with the half-eaten remains of very stale peanut-butter sandwiches and thickly smeared with the crusty residue of strawberry jelly.

3. A pathetic old homeless person was in an alley among some garbage.

    The body of a homeless man, his face wrinkled and blistered, lay in a pile of oil-covered rags and filthy cardboard boxes piled in the corner of a long alley devoid of life and light.

Using Figurative Language

Earlier you learned that figurative language is called *figurative* because it does not explain something directly. Instead it conveys meaning by comparing the thing you are explaining to something else. Figures of speech can help you explain an idea more clearly and emphatically than if you used literal language alone. In fact, they can create images, mental pictures that allow readers to *see* what you mean.

So, instead of saying that your cousin Mort dresses shabbily, you might say that he "looks like a caveman." Comparing Mort to a caveman brings up images of a scruffy, bug-infested beard, of hair that is rarely combed, and of clothes that are beyond cleaning and mending. Once again, the most common types of figurative language are simile, metaphor, and personification.

Simile

A simile creates a comparison between two things by using the words *like* or *as*. For example, say that you're writing your sweetheart a letter in which you want to explain how much you need him or her. You can express your feelings literally and directly by writing "I need you very much." Then again, you can *show* how strongly you feel by writing that you need him or her "as an oak needs sunlight," "as an eagle needs the open sky," or "as the dry earth needs spring rain."

Read the following list carefully. Notice how much more concrete, exciting, and rich the ideas on the left become when they are expressed in similes:

Literal Expression	Simile
She arrived on time.	She arrived as promptly as the sunrise.
Snerdly's face was sunburned.	Snerdly's face was as red as the inside of a watermelon.
Eugene is a fancy dresser.	Eugene dresses like a peacock.
The tires made a loud noise.	The tires screeched like a wounded animal.
The dog moved slowly.	The dog moved like corn syrup on a cold day.

Finally, have a look at "Harlem" by Langston Hughes, an important twentieth-century American poet, who was one of the lights of the Harlem Renaissance, an artistic and cultural flowering of the 1920s. Hughes uses five similes in eleven lines.

What happens to a dream deferred?

Does it dry up
like a raisin in the sun?
Or fester like a sore—
And then run?
Does it stink like rotten meat?
Or crust and sugar over—
like a syrupy sweet?

Maybe it just sags
like a heavy load.

Or does it explode?

Metaphor

A metaphor also uses comparison to show the relationship between things in order to make the explanation of one of these things clearer and livelier. In fact, a metaphor works just like a simile except that it does not make use of *like* or *as*. For instance, you can turn the simile "Eugene dresses like a peacock" into a metaphor by writing "Eugene is a peacock." In neither case, of course, do you actually mean that Eugene is a bird; you're simply pointing out similarities between the way he dresses and the showiness we associate with a peacock.

Remember that, like all figures of speech, similes and metaphors turn abstract ideas (such as "Eugene is a fancy dresser") into vivid, concrete images. In other words, they communicate more emphatically and clearly than if the writer had used literal language alone. Study the following list of similes and metaphors. What effect do they have on you, especially when compared with the literal expressions on the left?

Literal Expression	Simile	Metaphor
My old car is hard to drive.	My old car drives like a tank.	My old car is a tank!
She works too hard for her family.	She works like a slave for her family.	She is a slave to her family.
During holidays, shopping malls are crowded and noisy.	During holidays, shopping malls are so crowded and noisy that they seem like madhouses.	During holidays, shopping malls are so crowded and noisy that they become madhouses.
The hayloft was hot.	The hayloft was as hot as a blast furnace.	The hayloft was a blast furnace.

Read the following excerpt from Martin Luther King's "I Have a Dream," a speech he delivered at the Lincoln Memorial during the 1963 march on Washington. Identify the metaphors and similes that Dr. King used to captivate the thousands in his audience and to make his message more concrete, vivid, and effective:

> Five score years ago, a great American, in whose symbolic shadow we stand today, signed the Emancipation Proclamation. This momentous decree came as a great beacon light of hope to millions of Negro slaves who had been seared in the flames of withering injustice. It came as a joyous daybreak to end the long night of their captivity.

But one hundred years later, the Negro still is not free. One
hundred years later, the life of the Negro is still sadly crippled by
the manacles of segregation and the chains of discrimination.

Personification

Personification is the description of animals, plants, or inanimate objects by
using terms ordinarily associated with human beings. Like metaphor and
simile, personification is an effective way to turn abstract ideas into vivid and
concrete realities that readers will grasp easily and quickly.

One common example of personification is Father Time, the figure of an
old man trailing a white beard and carrying a scythe and hourglass. Another
is the Grim Reaper, the representation of death pictured as a skeleton holding
a scythe. Shakespeare often used personification to enrich the language of his
poems and plays. In "Sonnet 18," for example, he described the sun as "the eye
of heaven." William Least Heat Moon does something similar when, in *Blue
Highways*, he describes the saguaro cactus of the southwestern United States:

Standing on the friable slopes . . . saguaros mimic men as they
salute, bow, dance, raise arms to wave, and grin with faces carved
in by woodpeckers. Older plants, having survived odds against their
reaching maturity of sixty million to one, have every right to smile.

Visualizing Effective Word Choice

In the following paragraphs from "Where the World Began," Margaret Laurence
describes her small hometown on the Canadian prairie. Comments in the margins point to effective use of both literal and figurative language. After studying
the first paragraph, find and circle examples of effective language—both literal
and figurative—in the other three.

*Adjectives
appeal to
senses.*

Summers were scorching and when no rain

came and the wheat became bleached and dried

before it headed, the faces of farmers and

townsfolk would not smile much, and you took

for granted, because it never seemed to have

*Startling
image.*

been any different, the frequent knocking at the

back door and the young men standing there,

mumbling or thrusting defiantly their requests

*Farming
metaphor
("headed").*

Proper nouns used to name specific historical events.

for a drink of water and a sandwich. . . . They were riding the freights, and you never knew where they had come from, or where they might end up. . . . The Drought and the Depression were like evil deities [gods] which had been there always. You understood and did not understand.

Specific type of train.

Simile.

Yet the outside world had its continuing marvels. The poplar bluffs and the small river were filled and surrounded with a zillion different grasses, stones, and weed flowers. The meadowlarks sang undaunted [courageously] from the twanging telephone wires along the gravel highway.

Once we found an old flat-bottomed scow [small boat] and launched her, poling along the shallow brown waters, mending her with wodges [chunks] of hastily chewed Spearmint, grounding her among the tangles of yellow marsh marigolds that grew succulently along the banks of the shrunken river, while the sun made our skins smell dusty-warm.

In winter, we used to hitch rides on the back of the milk sleigh, our moccasins squeaking and slithering on the hard rutted snow . . . our hands in ice-bubbled mitts hanging onto the box edge of the sleigh for dear life. . . . Those mornings, rising, there would be the perpetual fascination of the frost feathers on windows, the ferns and flowers and eerie faces traced there during the

night by unseen artists of the wind. Evenings,
coming back from skating, the sky would be
black but not dark, for you could see a cold
glitter of stars from one side of the earth's
rim to the other. And then the sometime
astonishment when you saw the Northern
Lights fanning across the sky, like the scrawled
signature of God.

Revising for Word Choice

Read these two excerpts from the rough and final drafts of Louis Gonzalez's "Music," a student essay that appears in this chapter. As you will see, the revision process has enabled Gonzalez to make his writing stronger, livelier, and more interesting.

Gonzalez—Rough Draft

With my record player and some old 45s from
my dad's collection, I locked myself into the
garage. As the music played, tools became musical
instruments, and I played 'em all man! I wore
those old 45s down until there was almost
nothing left. I spent most of my childhood in that
garage listening to to my favorite jazz musicians
while other kids played football and video games.
Even though my parents said I was wasting
my time there, the experience made me want to
become a musician.

   As I became a little older and entered high
school, my interests shifted toward learning to
play a musical instrument. After a little experimentation, the bass guitar became my love. It

produced warm, confident tones. They danced around my head. The guitar became the implement of my creativity. It soon became the center of my existence. I felt naked and insecure without it. Its weight was a lover's hand upon my shoulder.

Gonzalez—Final Draft

Adds effective adjective and verb.

Armed with my record player and some old 45s I liberated from my dad's collection, I locked

Adds metaphor.

Creates an effective image; uses a proper noun.

myself into the garage and entered another world. Instead of remaining surrounded by tools and half-empty paint cans, I lowered the lid of that cheap Fisher-Price [record player] and transported myself to a smoky club somewhere

Names the tools used as instruments.

in the city. As the music played, wrenches became saxophones, boxes became a set of drums, and the workbench became a sleek black piano. I played 'em, all man! I wore those old 45s

Creates metaphors.

Adds details that appeal to senses.

down until there was nothing left but pops, cracks and the occasional high note. I spent most of my childhood in that smelly garage

Mentions specific musician.

listening to Miles Davis and my other patron saints, while other kids played football and video

Creates another metaphor.

Adds vivid verb, adjective, and noun.

games. Even though my parents said I was wasting my time there, the experience instilled in me a burning desire to become a musician.

When I entered high school, my interests
shifted toward playing a musical instrument.
After a little experimentation, I fell in love with
the bass guitar. It covered me with warm,
confident tones—blankets of pure ecstasy. They
were poised ballroom dancers waltzing elegantly
around my head. The guitar became the implement of my creativity, the brush with which
painted portraits of candid love and dark
emotion. I was naked and insecure without it.
Its weight was a lover's hand upon my shoulder,
and its smooth hourglass body was a pleasure
to hold. It whispered sweet kisses in my ear.

Includes vivid adjectives and adverb.

Adds personification by comparing "guitar" to a lover and "tones" to "dancers."

Uses a metaphor to compare guitar to painter's "brush."

Adds detail to continue personifying guitar as lover.

Practicing the Use of Effective Language—Literal and Figurative

In the spaces provided, rewrite each sentence using language that is more effective than in the original. Use language that is concrete, specific, and vivid. In addition, try your hand at creating similes, metaphors, and personification, as discussed earlier. The first item is done for you.

1. The desk in the corner of the office was cluttered.

   The large, unused desk in the corner was the office garbage dump,
   overflowing with yellowing newspapers and torn magazines, used coffee
   cups, and even an old computer monitor.

2. A construction worker hung from a beam above the street.

   _____

   _____

   _____

3. The exterior of the house needed painting.

    _____

    _____

    _____

4. The bus was crowded.

    _____

    _____

    _____

5. Eating at the Greasy Spoon Restaurant is dangerous.

    _____

    _____

    _____

6. Cheryl treats her mother well.

    _____

    _____

    _____

7. He ran to the end of the street and jumped over the barricade.

    _____

    _____

    _____

8. The village was flooded.

    _____

    _____

    _____

9. The wind was strong.

    _____

    _____

    _____

10. The newspaper photograph contained a warning about drunk driving.

    _____

    _____

    _____

Music

Louis Gonzalez

When asked by his professor to define a concept, idea, or activity that was important to him, Louis Gonzalez knew immediately what he would write about. The challenging part came in making this abstraction real to his readers. He did this by choosing concrete, specific, and vivid vocabulary and by filling his writing with powerful figures of speech. In other words, he showed the reader what he meant.

Gonzalez writes musical reviews for a local magazine and is considering a career as a writer. He was a first-year liberal arts student when he wrote this essay.

Preparing to Read

1. Pay special attention to paragraphs 3 and 4. The rough draft of these paragraphs appears with the author's revisions earlier in the chapter. It shows the care with which Gonzalez approaches the process of writing.

2. In addition to using all three figures of speech, Gonzalez introduces us to hyperbole, or exaggeration. Look for an example of this other figure of speech at the end of paragraph 7.

Vocabulary

cathartic (adjective)	Cleansing, purifying.
chaotic (adjective)	Confusing, disorderly.
licks (noun)	Musical phrases created when improvising.
mesmerizing (adjective)	Absorbing, hypnotizing.
obsession (noun)	Passion, fixation.
orgasms (noun)	Sexual climaxes.
oscillating (adjective)	Moving from side to side.
poised (adjective)	Balanced.
preoccupied (adjective)	Absorbed in, wrapped up in.
reverberates (verb)	Echoes.
tangible (adjective)	Able to be touched, felt.
tenacity (noun)	Determination, persistence.
venues (noun)	Places where events take place.
yoke (noun)	Shackle, chain.

Music

Louis Gonzalez

MUSIC IS MY obsession. It reverberates across every fiber of my being. I have 1
spent endless hours of my life creating music, performing it, or even just
dreaming about it. My thoughts are filled with the angelic sigh of a bow kissing
the string of a violin, or the hellish crash of batons torturing the skin of a kettle
drum. But my favorite instrument is the vociferous world around us. The scuff
of a penny loafer against a wood floor, the clinking of Crayolas across a child's
desk, or the mesmerizing hum of an oscillating fan are all part of this chaotic
symphony. It is within this sonic spectrum that I exist.

I have long been preoccupied with the audible world. When I was younger, 2
anything and everything that made a sound became a musical instrument. My
mother's pots, empty soda bottles, even the railing on my front porch became
part of my private symphony orchestra. Then, for my ninth birthday, I received
a Fisher-Price record player. A single tin speaker was built into the base, and
the needle was attached to a wooden lid, which I had to shut in order to make
the thing work. More often than not, the lid would fall accidentally and cut
deep scratches into the record. But to my young ears, it made the sounds of
heaven.

Armed with my record player and some old jazz 45s I liberated from my 3
dad's collection, I locked myself in the garage and entered another world.
Instead of remaining surrounded by tools and half-empty paint cans, I lowered
the lid of that cheap Fisher-Price and transported myself to a smokey club
somewhere in the city. As the music played, wrenches became saxophones,
boxes became a set of drums, and the workbench became a sleek black piano.
I played 'em all, man! I wore those old 45s down until there was nothing left
but pops, cracks, and the occasional high note. I spent most of my childhood
in that smelly garage listening to Miles Davis and my other patron saints, while
other kids played football and video games. Even though my parents said I
wasted my time there, the experience instilled in me a burning desire to become a musician.

When I entered high school, my interests shifted towards learning to 4
play a musical instrument. After a little experimentation, I fell in love with
the bass guitar. It covered me with warm, confident tones—blankets of pure
ecstasy. They were poised ballroom dancers waltzing elegantly around my
head. The guitar became the implement of my creativity, the brush with
which I painted portraits of candid love and dark emotion. I was naked and
insecure without it. Its weight was a lover's hand upon my shoulder, and its
smooth hourglass body was a pleasure to hold. It whispered sweet kisses in
my ear.

As my skills increased, so did my yearning to play those old jazz songs of 5
my youth. But the harder I tried, the less I succeeded. It seemed as though I was

simply incapable of playing those songs. All those wild bass licks that poured out of that Fisher-Price record player were ripped from my dreams.

My lust for jazz was then replaced by the desire to perform in a live rock band. So, I joined a local college group and began to play small venues. The shows were like cathartic orgasms of sweaty bodies undulating as the sensation of music overwhelmed them. While I was on stage, the power of the music pierced through the air like a volley of arrows falling upon the flannel-clad flesh whirling below me. But I felt as though the music was in control and I was just letting it happen. That feeling began to consume my spirit and destroy my sense of oneness with the music.   6

There was definitely something missing. Even though what I played was structurally powerful, it lacked a soul. I also realized that my style of playing lacked a human quality. So when I came upon my old jazz records, I listened to them with new ears. I dropped all of my preconceived notions of song structure. As the records popped and scratched their way around the turntable, the secrets of the universe were finally revealed to me.   7

I realized that my approach had been all wrong. All my songs were suffocated under the weight of formality. Harnessed to the yoke of "proper" song structure and arrangement, they were never allowed to grow fully. So, I picked up my bass with a fresh tenacity and dropped all my inhibitions. Not, surprisingly, those old jazz songs started to pour out. I played them as if I had known them all of my life.   8

I look back on that day and realize that I did know how to play those songs all along. It wasn't a tangible lack of something—like talent or effort—that held me back. I just needed to *feel* the music—to feel the sweet life a musician blows into, to feel it the way that innocent child felt in the garage all those years ago.   9

Read More on the Web

National Association for Music Education site: http://www.menc.org/information/infoserv/careersinmusic.htm

University of Illinois at Urbana site on the value of teaching music in the schools: www.ed.uiuc.edu/ups/curriculum2002/music/phase3narr.shtml

Questions for Discussion

1. What is Gonzalez's thesis? Has he proved it?
2. How would you describe the introduction to this essay? Does it use one or more of the techniques explained in Chapter 3? Which one or ones?
3. Paragraphs 1, 2, and 3 show that Gonzalez uses concrete and specific nouns. Find examples of such nouns.

4. Vivid verbs make paragraph 7 especially interesting. Identify a few of them.

5. Find examples of metaphor in paragraphs 3 and 4. Explain each of them.

6. Where does the author use simile?

7. Find two paragraphs in which personification is used. Explain these figures of speech.

Thinking Critically

1. Gonzalez uses hyperbole, another figure of speech, in paragraph 7. Explain what he means. Is his use of exaggeration effective?

2. If you could speak to Gonzalez, what would you ask him about his experiences with music? Write these questions in the margins of the essay.

Suggestions for Journal Entries

1. What is your obsession? Use freewriting or brainstorming to record facts about your love for an activity or idea that will show how much you are committed to it. Then read over your notes, and add nouns, verbs, adjectives, and adverbs that will make your work more concrete, specific, and vivid.

2. Create a list of metaphors, similes, or personifications, that might describe how you feel when you are doing a particular activity you really enjoy. For inspiration, reread paragraphs 1, 3, 4, and 6 of "Music."

Those Winter Sundays

Robert Hayden

Robert Hayden (1913–1980) taught English at Fisk University and at the University of Michigan. For years, the work of this talented African-American writer received far less recognition than it deserved. Recently, however, his reputation has grown, especially since the publication of his complete poems in 1985.

"Those Winter Sundays" uses the author's vivid memories of his father to show us the depth and quality of love that the man had for his family. Unlike much of Hayden's other work, this poem does not deal with the black experience as such, but it demonstrates the same care and skill in choosing effective language that Hayden used in all his poetry.

If you want to read more by Hayden, look for these poetry collections in your college library: A Ballad of Remembrance, Words in Mourning Time, Angle of Ascent, *and* American Journal.

Preparing to Read

1. Hayden's primary purpose is to explain his father's love for his family. Look for details that are physical signs of that love.
2. The author says his father "made/banked fires blaze." Wood and coal fires were "banked" by covering them with ashes to make them burn slowly through the night and continue giving off heat.
3. The word *offices* isn't used in its usual sense in this poem. Here, it means important services or ceremonies.

Vocabulary

austere (adjective)	Severe, harsh, difficult, without comfort.
chronic (adjective)	Persistent, unending, constant.
indifferently (adverb)	Insensitively, without care or concern.

Those Winter Sundays

Robert Hayden

Sundays too my father got up early
and put his clothes on in the blueblack cold,
then with cracked hands that ached
from labor in the weekday weather made
banked fires blaze. No one ever thanked him.   5

I'd wake and hear the cold splintering, breaking.
When the rooms were warm, he'd call,
and slowly I would rise and dress,
fearing the chronic angers of that house,

Speaking indifferently to him,   10
who had driven out the cold
and polished my good shoes as well.
What did I know, what did I know
of love's austere and lonely offices?

Read More on the Web

Academy of American Poets site on Hayden: http://www.poets.org/poets/
poets.cfm?prmID=200

Modern American Poetry site on Hayden: http://www.english.uiuc.edu/
maps/poets/g_l/hayden/life.htm

Questions for Discussion

1. Does this poem communicate a central idea? In a few words, state the author's opinion of his father.
2. In line 2, "blueblack" is used to describe the cold inside the house. What other effective adjectives do you find in the poem?
3. Hayden shows his father in action. What are some of the things this man did to show his love for his family?
4. What does Hayden mean by the metaphor "love's austere and lonely offices?"
5. Explain why "chronic angers of that house" is personification.
6. What was Hayden's reaction to these offices when he was a boy? What does this reaction tell us about the reason he wrote this poem?

Thinking Critically

Hayden mentions that he feared "the chronic angers of that house." What might he mean by that? Do you associate any "chronic angers" with your home?

Suggestions for Journal Entries

1. In Preparing to Read, you learned that Hayden describes his father's love by using language that is concrete, specific, and vivid. In your own words, discuss the kind of love that Hayden's father showed his family.

2. Do you know someone who demonstrates love for other people day in and day out, as Hayden's father did? In your journal, list the offices (services, tasks, or activities) that he or she performs to show this love. Include as many concrete and specific terms as you can. Then expand each item in your list to a few short sentences, showing that these activities are clearly signs of love.

Jeffrey Dahmer, Cannibal

Angie Cannon

Angie Cannon is a writer for US News & World Report, *a weekly news magazine. In December 1999, the magazine ran a multipart feature entitled "Crimes of the Century." This essay was one of the many that made up that feature.*

Preparing to Read

1. Consider Cannon's title. Is the author trying to shock us, or is she warning sensitive readers about the gory nature of her subject? What other purposes might this title serve?
2. Given the length of the essay, its introduction is fairly long, but it clearly states the central idea. The thesis is repeated later in the essay. Look for it in both places.

Vocabulary

barbell (noun)	Used in body building, a metal bar with weights at both ends that can be added or removed.
biceps (noun)	Muscle that has two points of origin.
depraved (adjective)	Degenerate, mentally and spiritually twisted.
fetish (noun)	Mania, compulsion, obsession.
forensic (adjective)	Having to do with legal proceedings including criminal investigations and trials.
putrid (adjective)	Disgusting, rotten, rank.
repulsive (adjective)	Horrible, disgusting.
revolting (adjective)	Offensive, disgusting, nauseating.
torso (noun)	Trunk of the body.
zombies (noun)	In folklore, dead bodies that have been taken over by a spirit or outside power.

Jeffrey Dahmer, Cannibal

Angie Cannon

HE WAS A former chocolate factory worker with a fetish for flesh. In his pu-   1
trid, one-bedroom apartment in Milwaukee, he saved painted skulls and severed heads, including one stashed in the fridge next to a box of baking soda.

He had a kettle and a freezer of body parts. He stored torsos in a vat of acid. He drilled holes in his victims' heads and had sex with dead bodies. He chewed on body parts, once using Crisco and meat tenderizer on a biceps. Over 13 years, mostly through the excessive 1980s, Jeffrey Dahmer, alone in his poisoned world, was monstrous, repulsive, depraved. But the most frightening thing about Dahmer is what he was not: insane. He was objectively judged to be sane. He did what he did with his wits intact. "He was a man who made a decision that he would satisfy himself," says E. Michael McCann, the Milwaukee district attorney who put Dahmer away in 1992. "He liked sex with dead bodies. It was the ultimate in self-indulgence."

In an interview with NBC's *Dateline* in March 1994, Dahmer said lust drove   2
him to lure his victims, most of them black and gay, from bars, bus stops, and shopping malls, to his apartment, where he drugged, strangled, and dismembered them. "Once it happened the first time, it just seemed like it had control of my life from there on in," he said. "The killing was just a means to an end. That was the least satisfactory part. I didn't enjoy doing that. That's why I tried to create living zombies with ... acid and the drill."

His killing spree started in 1978 with an 18-year-old hitchhiker whom   3
Dahmer met and brought home for a few beers. Dahmer, who had just graduated from high school, battered him with a barbell, cut up the body, and scattered the crushed bones behind his parents' house. By the time he was arrested on July 22, 1991, after a man he had handcuffed escaped from his apartment and flagged down a police car, Dahmer had killed 17 men and boys. He confessed, saying simply, "I carried it too far, that's for sure."

The only issue at his 1992 trial was whether to accept his plea that he   4
was criminally insane—and therefore not responsible for his revolting actions. Dr. Park Dietz, a respected California forensic psychiatrist, determined that he was not insane. "Dahmer was quiet, introverted, and performed his job pretty well until he finally fell asleep and couldn't do his work because he couldn't keep up with his nighttime dastardly deeds," says prosecutor McCann.

Dahmer was serving 16 consecutive life terms when inmates beat him to   5
death in a prison bathroom in November 1994. Two years later, a businessman offered more than $400,000 to buy his implements—the refrigerator, the vats, the drills, the saws—to prevent a public auction. They were secretly buried.

Read More on the Web

Case study of Dahmer: http://www.extentia.net/thrillers/case_study.htm

Links to sites about mass murderers and serial killing: http://crime.about.com/cs/massmurderers/

Questions for Discussion

1. Reread paragraph 1, and identify verbs and adjectives that are particularly vivid. Where else in this essay does Cannon use vivid details?

2. What examples of concrete language appear in paragraph 1? What about paragraph 3?

3. Why didn't Cannon say that Dahmer "put vegetable shortening on body parts" rather than that he spread "Crisco . . . on a biceps"?

4. This essay relies heavily on language that is literal. However, Cannon does use figures of speech. Identify them.

5. The journalist who wrote this was careful about researching specific facts and statistics. What evidence do you find of such research?

6. Why does Cannon use direct quotations in this essay? Who are the sources for such quotations?

7. What method or methods explained in Chapter 3 does the author use to introduce this essay? To conclude it?

Thinking Critically

1. "The most frightening thing about Dahmer," claims the author, "is what he was not: insane." Consider this statement. Then explain why it was necessary for Cannon to include so many gruesome details in paragraph 1.

2. What does Cannon's concluding paragraph say about our society?

Suggestions for Journal Entries

1. This essay is the portrait of a serial killer, but concrete, specific, and vivid language can be used to discuss anyone's life—unknown or famous, good or evil. Think about an individual you admire or dislike. Your subject can be someone you know personally or someone you have only read or heard about such as an entertainer, a politician, or even a historical figure. Make a list of as many concrete, specific, and vivid details as you can to describe this individual's personality or character.

2. Cannon quotes Dahmer directly so as to help us understand his motives and his character. Freewrite for at least 10 minutes about having done something or having made a decision that you now deeply regret. Explain what it was, why you did it, and why you regret it.

What the Gossips Saw

Leo Romero

A native of New Mexico, Leo Romero is among a growing number of contemporary Southwestern writers whose poetry and fiction are becoming popular across the country. Romero studied at the University of New Mexico, where he took a degree in English. His poems have appeared in several recent collections of poetry and prose. "What the Gossips Saw" was first published in 1981 in a collection of his poetry called Agua Negra.

Preparing to Read

1. This is the story of the community's response to a woman who had her leg amputated. It says a great deal about the way society sometimes reacts to those of us who are different, and it can be compared with other selections such as Schwartz's "The Colossus in the Kitchen" (Chapter 7).

2. Romero chooses to leave out periods and other end marks. Doing so can help a poet create dramatic effects. Nonetheless, college writers should always use such punctuation in essays and other academic writing.

Vocabulary

alluring (adjective)	Appealing, tempting.
conjecture (noun)	Guessing, speculation.
hobble (verb)	Limp.
in cohorts (adjective)	In league with, cooperating with.
murmur (verb)	Mumble discontentedly.

What the Gossips Saw

Leo Romero

Everyone pitied Escolastica, her leg
had swollen like a watermelon in the summer
It had practically happened over night
She was seventeen, beautiful and soon
to be married to Guillermo who was working   5
in the mines at Terreros, eighty miles away
far up in the mountains, in the wilderness
Poor Escolastica, the old women would say
on seeing her hobble to the well with a bucket
carrying her leg as if it were the weight   10

of the devil, surely it was a curse from heaven
for some misdeed, the young women who were
jealous would murmur, yet they were grieved too
having heard that the doctor might cut
her leg, one of a pair of the most perfect legs   15
in the valley, and it was a topic of great
interest and conjecture among the villagers
whether Guillermo would still marry her
if she were crippled, a one-legged woman—
as if life weren't hard enough for a woman   20
with two legs—how could she manage
Guillermo returned and married Escolastica
even though she had but one leg, the sound
of her wooden leg pounding down the wooden aisle
stayed in everyone's memory for as long   25
as they lived, women cried at the sight
of her beauty, black hair so dark
that the night could get lost in it, a face
more alluring than a full moon

Escolastica went to the dances with her husband   30
and watched and laughed but never danced
though once she had been the best dancer
and could wear holes in a pair of shoes
in a matter of a night, and her waist had been
as light to the touch as a hummingbird's flight   35
And Escolastica bore five children, only half
what most women bore, yet they were healthy
In Escolastica's presence, no one would mention
the absence of her leg, though she walked heavily
And it was not long before the gossips   40
spread their poison, that she must be in cohorts
with the devil, had given him her leg
for the power to bewitch Guillermo's heart
and cloud his eyes so that he could not see
what was so clear to them all   45

Read More on the Web

Twelve poems online by Leo Romero: http://sfpoetry.org/romero.html
Notes on Leo Romero: sfpoetry.org/bionote2.html

Questions for Discussion

1. What is Romero trying to tell us about gossip? In other words, what
    is his central idea?

2. Identify examples of concrete language. Then find examples of vivid verbs and adjectives.

3. The author creates two images (pictures in words) in the second stanza (verse paragraph) of this poem. What are these images, and why does Romero include them?

4. Where in this poem does he use simile? What other figures of speech does Romero use?

5. The poem takes place in a village where life is hard. Why is it important for us to know that?

6. How do the gossips explain Guillermo's marrying Escolastica even after she loses her leg? What does this say about them?

7. The gossips believe Guillermo "could not see/what was so clear to them all." What does Guillermo see that they don't?

8. What can we conclude about the gossips' opinion of men in general?

Thinking Critically

1. Many of us know people like the gossips. Do such people deserve blame or pity? Are they malicious or just ignorant? Make a list of similes or metaphors that might help describe such people.

2. Schwartz's "Colossus in the Kitchen," an essay in Chapter 7, shows that bad luck can be mistaken by small-minded people as a sign of God's punishment for sinning. Where does this theme appear in Romero's poem? Make notes in the margins to identify this theme.

Suggestions for Journal Entries

1. Think of a person or an event that was the subject of gossip in your school or community. Use listing or another method for gathering details discussed in "Getting Started" to explain how much the gossips exaggerated, twisted, or lied about the facts. Try to show how they changed the truth to make the story seem more sensational, startling, racy, or horrible than it was.

2. Not all communities react badly to people who are different. Do you agree? If so, provide evidence from personal experience, from newspapers, or from other sources to support this idea. For example, talk about how quickly people in your city responded when they heard a neighbor needed expensive medical care, or explain how well students at your school accept newcomers from other cultures.

Suggestions for Sustained Writing

1. Read the journal notes you made after completing Louis Gonzalez's "Music." If you responded to either or both of the Suggestions for Journal Entries, you have a good start on an essay that will discuss an obsession of your own.

   Begin with an introduction that, like Gonzalez's, explains the extent to which you are committed to a particular pursuit, idea, study, activity, hobby, art form, or sport. Then go on to explain how this obsession developed in you. End your essay by looking to the future or by using any of the other types of conclusions discussed in Chapter 3.

   As always, remember that one draft is never enough. When you write your second draft, include concrete and specific nouns and adjectives. Add vivid verbs, adjectives, and adverbs as well. When you revise this draft, try to add figures of speech like those discussed in this chapter. Then, revise your third draft to improve organization, sentence structure, and grammar. The final step is, of course, to edit and proofread your work carefully.

2. Hayden's "Those Winter Sundays" praises a man who demonstrates his love for others. If you responded to the second journal suggestions after this poem, you made a list of the "offices" (activities, tasks, or services) that someone you know performs to show his or her love.

   Focus on at least three "offices" that mean the most to you, and expand your discussion into an essay that proves how much this person does for others. Begin with a preliminary thesis that expresses your feelings about your subject, but remember that you can revise this statement after you write your first draft.

   Limit each of the body paragraphs to only one of the offices in your list. Develop these paragraphs by using methods explained in Chapter 2; narration, process analysis, conclusion and support, and illustration might work well. Whatever you decide, follow Hayden's lead, and use language that is concrete, specific, and vivid. Take the opportunity to improve word choice when you revise the first and second drafts of your paper. This is also a good time to create figures of speech that will help you make your writing even more powerful.

   And don't skimp on the introduction and conclusion of your essay. Try using the techniques you read about in Chapter 3. As always, edit and proofread your revised essay carefully before you submit it to your instructor.

3. Read the notes you made in response to either of the Suggestions for Journal Entries after Angie Cannon's "Jeffrey Dahmer, Cannibal." Do more listing or freewriting to add concrete and specific nouns and vivid verbs, adjectives, and adverbs to this information. You might also want to include some figures of speech that will add interest to your writing. Then, use this prewriting to develop an essay that either describes a person's character (journal entry #1) or explains the motivations behind your once doing something or making a decision that you now regret (journal entry #2).

If you are describing someone's personality, interview people who know your subject. (If your subject is well known, find out what others have said about him or her in newspapers or other sources.)

If you are writing about yourself, interview people who witnessed or heard about the action or decision you now regret. Quote these people directly; they will help make your writing believable and interesting.

Revise your first draft—as often as you need to—by adding details, refining your thesis statement, and sharpening your introduction and conclusion. Then, edit and proofread your final revision carefully.

4. In "What the Gossips Saw," Romero shows that gossips can exaggerate or twist a story so badly that, in their mouths, the truth becomes unrecognizable. If you responded to the first of the journal prompts after Romero's poem, read your notes. Then, draft an essay that tells what happened when gossips spread rumors about a person or event in your school or community.

As with other assignments, you can organize your thoughts in several different ways. For example, you might start by revealing the truth of a story and then explaining—step-by-step—how the gossips distorted it. Or, you might recall how false rumors began, how they spread, and how they affected people. A good way to end this story is to tell the truth as you know it.

Whichever approach you choose, rewrite the paper several times. In your second and subsequent drafts, try hard to include figures of speech—simile, metaphor, and/or personification—to describe people, motives, places, and events and to give your writing greater variety and interest. Doing so will also make your writing more convincing.

Finally, explain what observing or experiencing the effects of gossip taught you about it and about the people who spread it. The best place to do this is in the paper's introduction or conclusion.

Writing to Learn: A Group Activity

Robert Hayden does not reveal what his father does for a living, but we can be sure, from obvious hints in "Those Winter Sundays," that his work is hard and his hours long. Choosing an occupation is an important decision for most young people no matter what their level of education. Yet, some of them know relatively little about the kinds of occupations that await them in the world of work.

FIRST MEETING

Choose a research question from the list below (or make up one of your own) which might serve as a prompt for a paper that focuses on the world of work.

- Which occupations will be in greatest demand during the next two decades?
- Which occupations promise to pay the highest salaries during the next two decades?

- Which occupations offer the greatest opportunities for company-sponsored travel?
- Which occupations offer the greatest personal satisfaction to employees?
- Which occupations will undergo the greatest changes in technology demanding employee flexibility, during the next two decades?
- In which occupations will the demand for employees rise most in the next two decades?
- In which occupations will the demand for employees drop most in the next two decades?
- Which occupations pose the greatest physical dangers to employees?
- Which occupations exert the greatest emotional stress on employees?

Before the meeting ends, ask each member of the group to complete preliminary Internet or library research so as to collect a short list of occupations appropriate to the chosen research question. Bring this list to the next meeting. For example, if the group has decided to discuss occupations that pose the greatest physical danger, the list might include firefighting, coal mining, farming, logging, and heavy construction.

SECOND MEETING

Review the lists of occupations submitted by students and ask each group member to focus on one of the occupations mentioned. Ask him or her to research that occupation as it relates to the research question the group has chosen. If a student were researching coal mining, for example, he or she might find out how many coal miners are injured or killed each year, why mining is so dangerous, and what causes mining accidents. Ask students to make copies of their notes in order to distribute them at the next meeting.

THIRD MEETING

Evaluate the notes each student has distributed to the group. Ask him or her to add to, edit, or condense these notes if necessary. Then, with the chosen research question in mind, ask every student to write several paragraphs based on his or her notes and to present copies of this work at the final meeting.

FINAL MEETING

Review the written paragraphs prepared by each group member. Recommend revision and editing as needed, and ask the students to submit final drafts of their work in a few days to a student who has been assigned to combine all of this material in a coherent paper, complete with an introduction and conclusion. After the final draft has been written, ask still another student to complete final editing and proofreading before submitting the finished product to the instructor.

CHAPTER 5

Sentence Structure: Creating Emphasis and Variety

Emphasis

Communicating ideas clearly often demands the ability to emphasize or stress one idea over another. By arranging words in a sentence carefully, you can emphasize certain ideas and direct your readers' attention to the heart of your message.

A good way to emphasize an idea is to express it in a short, simple sentence of its own. But you will never develop your writing skills if you use such sentences all the time. Even the shortest writing projects require sentences containing two or more ideas. In some cases, these ideas will be equally important; in others, one idea will need to be emphasized over the other or others.

CREATE EMPHASIS THROUGH COORDINATION

Ideas of equal importance can be expressed in the same sentence by using coordination. Take this sentence, which coordinates (makes equal) three words in a series: *fed, cured,* and *sheltered.*

> Mother Teresa *fed* the hungry, *cured* the sick, and *sheltered* the homeless.

You can also use coordination to join two or more main clauses if you want to give them equal emphasis. A main clause contains a subject and verb, and it expresses a complete idea, even when it stands alone. You can join main clauses with a comma and a coordinating conjunction: *and, but, for, nor, or, so,* and *yet.* What results from this combination is a *compound sentence.* (One way to remember the coordinating conjunctions is to use the acronym *FANBOYS.* F = *for,* A = *and,* etc.)

The following compound sentences contain a comma followed by a coordinating conjunction:

> *Asteroids are smaller than planets,* **and** *meteorites are smaller than asteroids.*

193

> Robert Frost wrote poetry set in New England, **but** he was born in California.

> I floss my teeth daily, **for** I want to avoid gum disease.

> Switzerland did not fight in World War II, **nor** did Spain.

> Modern drugs can perform miracles, **or** they can destroy lives.

> The area was contaminated, **so** the medical examiners wore protective clothing.

Another way to coordinate (make equal) main clauses is to join them with a semicolon:

> Methane is hard to detect; it is an odorless, colorless gas.

> Neptune is the eighth planet from the sun; Pluto is the ninth.

CREATE EMPHASIS THROUGH SUBORDINATION

The sentences above contain main ideas that are equal in importance. But what if you decide that one idea in a sentence is more important than the other? You can put that other idea into a phrase or a subordinate clause, thereby making it less important than the first. A phrase is a group of words without a subject and verb; a subordinate clause contains a subject and verb but, unlike a main clause, it does not express a complete idea. Say you wrote these sentences:

> Some dinosaurs were over 80 feet long, and they weighed almost 75 tons.

> Most dinosaurs were cold-blooded, but a few were warm-blooded.

You might revise them by subordinating one idea to the other in each sentence:

> Weighing almost 75 tons, some dinosaurs were over 80 feet long.
> (The first idea has been put into a phrase.)

> Although most dinosaurs were cold-blooded, a few were warm-blooded.
> (The first idea has been put into a subordinate clause.)

Three ways to create phrases and subordinate clauses are to use (1) participles, (2) relative pronouns, and (3) subordinating conjunctions.

1. **Participles** are adjectives formed from verbs; like other adjectives, they describe nouns and pronouns. Participles can end in *-ing, -ed, -d, -n,* or *-t.* Each of the following sentences has been revised by turning one if its main clauses into a phrase that begins with a participle:

Original: Mario loved everything about Brazil, and he even started to learn Portuguese.
(*Sentence contains two ideas of equal importance.*)
Revised: Loving everything about Brazil, Mario even started to learn Portuguese.
(*One idea is expressed in a phrase beginning with the participle "loving." It is less important than the other idea, which remains in a main clause.*)

Original: Many Midwest farmers were ruined by the long drought of the 1930s, so they gave up their land and moved to California.
(*Sentence contains two ideas of equal importance.*)
Revised: Ruined by the long drought of the 1930s, many Midwest farmers moved to California.
(*One idea is expressed in a phrase beginning with the participle "ruined." It is less important than the other idea, which remains in a main clause.*)

2. **Subordinating conjunctions** are words like *after, as, because, even though, if, since, unless, until,* and *while.* They can be used to turn a main clause into a subordinate clause.

    Original: The French military leader Joan of Arc was condemned as a witch, so she was burned at the stake.
    (*The ideas are equally important.*)
    Revised: Because she had been condemned as a witch, the French military leader Joan of Arc was burned at the stake.
    (*The second idea, expressed in a main clause, is emphasized. The first idea is now in a subordinate clause, which begins with "Because."*)

3. **Relative pronouns**—*who, whom, whose, that,* and *which*—can also be used to subordinate one idea to another. Subordinate clauses beginning with relative pronouns describe nouns in the sentence's main clause.

    Original: We visited Scotland's famous Loch Ness; this lake is said to be home to an ancient dragon-like monster.
    (*Sentence has two main clauses.*)
    Revised: We visited Scotland's famous Loch Ness, *which* is said to be home to an ancient dragon-like monster.
    (*Sentence begins with a main clause, followed by a subordinate clause beginning with "which."*)

    Original: James Madison was the fourth president of the United States, but he is also remembered as the "master builder" of the U.S. Constitution.
    (*Sentence has two main clauses.*)

Revised: James Madison, *who* was the fourth president of the United States, is also remembered as the "master builder" of the U.S. Constitution.
(*Note that the subordinate clause, introduced by* who, *comes in the middle of the sentence.*)

CREATE EMPHASIS BY USING PERIODIC SENTENCES

You can create emphasis by putting the strongest or most important word or idea at the end of the sentence. Such sentences are called periodic because the emphasis comes just before the period. Here are three examples:

The Bible claims Methuselah lived 969 years.

India, where over half a billion people have the right to vote, is the world's largest democracy.

Zora Neale Hurston is remembered not for her work in anthropology, the field in which she was trained, but for her novels.

CREATE EMPHASIS BY USING A COLON

A colon can be used in place of a semicolon in a compound sentence when the second main clause explains the first. The effect is similar to the one created by a periodic sentence.

Nitrous oxide is called "laughing gas" for good reason: when used as an anesthesia for dental patients, it creates in them a sense of happiness and well-being.

CREATE EMPHASIS BY USING THE ACTIVE OR PASSIVE VOICE

Sentences that use the *active voice* contain subjects—persons, places, or things—that perform an action. Sentences that use the *passive voice* contain subjects that are acted upon. Notice how the structure of a sentence changes when it is put into the passive voice.

Active: Gabriel Maria Marquez won the Nobel Prize for literature in 1982.
Passive: The Nobel Prize for literature was won by Gabriel Maria Marquez in 1982.

Generally, using the active voice makes it easier to stress the subject of a sentence. For instance, if you wanted to report that the president of your college announced her decision to resign, you wouldn't use the passive voice by writing, "Her decision to resign was announced by President Green." The active voice works better: "President Green announced her decision to resign."

However, there are times when using the passive voice can create emphasis. In some cases, you might decide that the receiver of an action is more important than the person, place, or thing completing the action. For example:

> Arnold Schwarzenegger was elected governor of California in 2003.

is more emphatic than

> The citizens of California elected Arnold Schwarzenegger governor in 2003.

Sometimes, in fact, you might not know who is responsible for an action, and you will have to use the passive voice:

> Windows were smashed, books were scattered across the room, and furniture was torn to shreds.

CREATE EMPHASIS BY REPEATING KEY WORDS AND PHRASES

Repeating important words and phrases, carefully and sparingly, can help stress important ideas over those that need less emphasis. In his inaugural address (1961), President John F. Kennedy gave special meaning to his plans for the nation when he said:

> All this will not be *finished* in the first one hundred days. *Nor* will it be *finished* in the first one thousand days, *nor* in the life of this administration, *nor* even perhaps in our lifetime on this planet. But let us begin.

Dr. Martin Luther King, Jr., used repetition to communicate a sense of urgency about civil rights in "I Have a Dream," a speech delivered to a massive audience at the Lincoln Memorial in 1963.

> Now is the time to make real the promises of democracy. Now is the time to rise from the dark and desolate valley of segregation to the sunlit path of racial justice. Now is the time to lift our nation from the quicksands of racial injustice to the solid rock of brotherhood. Now is the time to make justice a reality for all of God's children.

CREATE EMPHASIS THROUGH PARALLELISM

> We the people of the United States, in Order to *form* a more perfect union, *establish* Justice, *insure* domestic Tranquility, *provide for* the common defence, *promote* the general Welfare, and *secure* the Blessings of Liberty to ourselves and our Posterity, do ordain and establish this Constitution for the United States of America.

What you have just read begins the United States Constitution; it is one of the best-known sentences in American history. One reason it is so powerful and memorable is that it uses six phrases (the reasons for establishing the Constitution) that follow the same pattern—a verb followed by a direct object. Repeating patterns is known as *parallelism*.

Parallelism is a way to connect a series of facts and ideas of equal importance, thereby giving them added emphasis. Sentences that are parallel list items in the same grammatical form. This paragraph from Adlai Stevenson's eulogy of Winston Churchill, the great British prime minister, does just that:

> The voice that led nations, raised armies, inspired victories and blew fresh courage into the hearts of men is silenced. We shall hear no longer the remembered eloquence and wit, the old courage and defiance, the robust serenity of indomitable faith. Our world is thus poorer, our political dialogue is diminished, and the sources of public inspiration run more thinly in all of us. There is a lonesome place against the sky.

In the first sentence, Stevenson placed equal emphasis on Churchill's accomplishments by expressing each through a verb followed by a direct object: "led nations," "raised armies," "inspired victories," and "blew fresh courage into the hearts of men." He created parallelism in the second sentence in a series of adjectives and nouns that describe Churchill's best qualities: "the remembered eloquence and wit," "the old courage and defiance," "the robust serenity of indomitable faith." In the third sentence, he explained the effects of Churchill's death in a series of main clauses: "Our world is thus poorer," "our political dialogue is diminished," and "the sources of public inspiration run more thinly in all of us."

Consistency is the key to making sentences parallel. Express every idea in a list in the same grammatical form. Without a doubt, the eulogy you just read would have sounded awkward and been less emphatic had Stevenson written that Churchill's voice "led nations, raised armies, inspired victories, and it blew fresh courage into the hearts of men." The first three items are verbs followed by objects; the fourth is a main clause.

Here are three other examples of how parallelism creates emphasis:

> The president enjoys *reading* mystery novels, *fishing* in Maine, and *speaking* with young people.
> (*The sentence contains gerunds, nouns formed from verbs by adding "ing"; gerunds show activity.*)

> *To master* the piano, *to compose* beautiful music, and *to lead* a symphony orchestra seemed to be her destiny.
> (*The sentence contains infinitives, which are formed by placing* to *before the present tense of the verb. Infinitives act as nouns, adjectives, or adverbs.*)

They vowed to battle the invaders *on the land, on the sea,* and *in the air.*
(*The sentence contains* prepositional phrases; a preposition *is a short word—such as* at, in, *or* on—*that shows the relationship of a noun or pronoun to the rest of the sentence.*)

Variety

One sure way to make your readers lose interest in what you have to say—no matter how important—is to ignore the need for variety. Good writers try not to repeat vocabulary monotonously, and they vary the length and structure of their sentences whenever possible.

CREATE VARIETY BY CHANGING SENTENCE LENGTH

A steady diet of long, complicated sentences is sure to put your readers to sleep. On the other hand, relying solely on short, choppy sentences can make your writing seem disconnected and even childish. Therefore, one of the most important things to remember about the sentences you write is to vary their length. You can do this by combining some of them into longer, more complex units and by leaving others short and to the point.

Reread the passage from President Kennedy's Inaugural Address on page 197. One reason it holds our interest is that it contains sentences of different lengths. The last of these leaves a lasting impression, not simply because it comes at the end but because it is so much shorter than the others and carries a special punch.

You can combine two or three short sentences into a longer unit in three ways: coordination, subordination, or compounding.

Coordination   This method is useful if you want to write a longer sentence in which all the main ideas receive equal emphasis. The easiest way to do this is to combine sentences with a comma and the appropriate coordinating conjunction or to use a semicolon, as explained on pages 193–194.

Subordination   As you know, subordination lets you combine two or more sentences to emphasize one idea over another. It also helps you vary sentence length and make your writing more interesting. Say you've just written:

I had been waiting at the bus stop for 20 minutes. The afternoon air was hot, thick, and humid. I became uncomfortable and soon began to perspire. I wished I were home. I thought about getting under the shower, cooling off, and relaxing. My day at work had been long and hard. I looked up from the newspaper I was reading.

> I saw a huge truck. It sped by, and it covered me with filthy exhaust.
> I prayed the bus would come soon.

As you read this paragraph, you realize that you haven't emphasized your most important ideas and that your style is choppy and monotonous. Therefore, you decide to rewrite by combining sentences through subordination (you can review ways to do this by rereading pages 194–196):

> I had been waiting at the bus stop for 20 minutes. Because the afternoon air was hot, thick, and humid, I became uncomfortable and soon began to perspire. Wishing I were home, I thought about getting under the shower, cooling off, and relaxing. My day at work had been long and hard. As I looked up from the newspaper I was reading, I saw a huge truck, which sped by and covered me with exhaust. I prayed the bus would come soon.

In combining some sentences, you've made your writing smoother and more interesting because you've created sentences of different lengths. What's more, some ideas have gained emphasis.

Compounding   This method involves putting subjects, verbs, adjectives, and adverbs together in the same sentence as long as they relate to one another logically.

Sometimes, ideas that are very similar seem awkward and boring if expressed in separate sentences. For example: "Egbert has been transferred to Minneapolis. Rowena has also been transferred to that city." Notice how much more interesting these short sentences become when you combine their subjects: "Egbert and Rowena have been transferred to Minneapolis." Here are a few more examples:

> **Original:** The doctor rushed into the emergency room. She went immediately to a patient who had been stung by wasps.
> **Compound verb:** The doctor rushed into the emergency room and went immediately to a patient who had been stung by wasps.

> **Original:** Grieving over the loss of her child, the woman wept openly. She wept uncontrollably.
> **Compound adverb:** Grieving over the loss of her child, the woman wept openly and uncontrollably.

CREATE VARIETY BY CHANGING SENTENCE PATTERNS

Complete sentences contain a subject and verb, and they express a complete idea. Most also contain modifiers, such as adjectives, adverbs, and prepositional phrases, as well as other elements. However, there is no rule that a sentence must begin with a subject followed immediately by a verb. Depending upon your purpose, you can create as many patterns as you need to make your writing interesting and effective.

Begin with an Adverb   Adverbs modify verbs, adjectives, or other adverbs. They help explain *how, how much, when, where, what kind of,* or *why.* Most, but not all, adverbs end in *-ly.* The following sentences begin with adverbs or groups of words that act as adverbs:

> *Near ancient Thebes,* monuments to the pharaohs glisten in the sun.

> *Seldom* was the old mansion visited by tourists.

> *Brightly* blazed the signal fires across the harbor.

Note that you could also have written "The signal fires blazed brightly across the harbor," but putting adverbs at the beginning of a sentence once in a while makes for variety.

Begin with an Infinitive or a Gerund   An **infinitive** is the present tense of a verb with the word *to* in front of it. Infinitives acting as nouns can make good sentence openers.

> *To study* archaeology was her childhood dream.

> *To defend* unpopular ideas takes courage.

> *To call* him a coward is unfair.

You could have written that "It is unfair to call him a coward," but beginning with the infinitive works just as well.

A **gerund** is a noun that is made from a verb by adding *-ing.* Gerunds name activities.

> *Reading* the works of Mark Twain is his favorite way to relax.

> *Measuring* the height of a heavenly body is the purpose of a sextant.

> *Preventing* global warming is the goal of many environmentalists.

Begin with a Preposition or Prepositional Phrase   Prepositions connect or show relationships between nouns or pronouns and the rest of a sentence. Prepositional phrases contain a preposition, a noun or pronoun, and any words that modify the noun or pronoun.

> *Among* the best and oldest rock groups is the Rolling Stones.

> *With* malice toward none, *with* charity for all, *with* firmness in the right as God gives us to see the right, let us strive on to finish the work we are in. (Abraham Lincoln)

> *Before* the line of worshippers walked a Mayan priest.

Note that you could also have written "A Mayan priest walked before the line of worshippers."

Begin or End with a Participle or Participial Phrase   A participle is a verb turned into an adjective. Many end in -*ed*, -*en*, -*ing*, or -*t*. A participial phrase is a group of words containing a participle.

> *Exhausted*, the soldiers fell asleep without bothering to eat.

> *Swollen* because of torrential rains, the Mississippi River overflowed its banks.

> *Directing* the fortunes of Florence for over three centuries, the Medici were once the most powerful family in Europe.

> *Bent* nearly double, the birch trees were covered with snow and ice.

> *In* A.D. 79, Mt. Vesuvius erupted violently, *spewing* lava and ash over the Bay of Naples and *destroying* the cities of Pompeii and Herculaneum.

> The earthquake victims wept openly, their lives *destroyed*.

Use an Appositive   An appositive is a word or phrase that renames or describes a noun that comes before it.

> Greenland, *a semi-independent region of Denmark*, lies northeast of Canada.
> Insisting that the company not sell contaminated food earned the supervisor a written reprimand, *her badge of honor*.

Ask a Rhetorical Question   You learned in Chapters 2 and 3 that asking a question is a good way to begin a paragraph or essay. A rhetorical question —one to which the answer is obvious—can also create emphasis and variety. Take this example from a 2005 end-of-the-year column by humorist Dave Barry:

> [In] November, Americans find themselves heatedly debating a difficult question: Is it truly in the nation's best interests for its citizens to be fighting, and suffering heavy casualties, to achieve the elusive goal of buying a laptop computer marked down to $300 at Wal-Mart the day after Thanksgiving?

On a more serious note, President Ronald Reagan used a series of rhetorical questions in a 1983 speech to emphasize his point that sexuality must be seen as something "sacred," to be governed by deep moral convictions:

> No one seems to mention morality as playing a part in the subject of sex. Is all of Judeo-Christian tradition wrong? Are we to believe that something so sacred can be looked upon as a purely physical thing with no potential for emotional and psychological harm? And isn't it the parents' right to give counsel and advice to keep their children from making mistakes that may affect their entire lives?

CREATE VARIETY BY USING A COLON

Use a Colon after an Independent Clause to Introduce Information That Names or Explains Something in That Clause   Such information can be expressed in a word or phrase, a list of words, or even a sentence.

> **Word:** Cardiology treats an essential organ: the heart!
> (*Heart names the organ.*)

> **List:** During 13 years in the White House, Franklin D. Roosevelt had three vice-presidents: Garner, Wallace, and Truman.
> (*Garner, Wallace, and Truman name the vice-presidents.*)

> **Sentence:** Princeton, New Jersey, is a hub of intellectual activity: it is home to Princeton University, the Institute for Advanced Study, and numerous research centers.
> (*The sentence after the colon explains intellectual activity.*)

Use a Colon to Introduce a Quotation   Using a colon is a good way to introduce someone else's words and at the same time use a different sentence pattern. Let's say you wanted to quote from President Kennedy's inaugural address. You might write:

> Today we would do well to remember JFK's exhortations to his fellow Americans: "Ask not what your country can do for you—ask what you can do for your country."

CREATE VARIETY BY USING PARENTHESES

There are three major uses for parentheses when creating variety:

1. **To set off an explanatory sentence within or immediately following another sentence. Ordinarily, material within the parentheses is less important than material not in parentheses.**

   > Mary Queen of Scots (she was the daughter of King James V of Scotland) became queen upon the death of her father, only six days after her birth.

   > The university just opened a modern art museum. (It houses only 10 paintings, but the trustees are trying to raise money to buy more.)

2. **To enclose a brief definition**

   > The children learned to construct an anemometer (instrument for measuring wind speed) from the Franklin Institute's website.

3. **To set off words that clarify or specify.**

   > The leaders of Nazi Germany and the Soviet Union (Hitler and Stalin) made a pact with the devil.

CREATE VARIETY BY USING A DASH

Create a dash by typing two hyphens, but do not include a space between the dash and the words that come before and after it. A dash can be used to emphasize, expand upon, or explain information earlier in the sentence and to signal a shift in meaning or tone.

Emphasis: Every employee of the company—from the president to the janitor—must now pay his or her own health insurance premiums.

Expansion: Three Supreme Court justices—Scalia, O'Connor, and Kennedy—were nominated by President Reagan.

Explanation: Paying your $1,000 in parking fines beats the alternative—spending a week in the work house.

Shift: He made his fortune in less than two years—and lost it in less than two days.

Visualizing Sentence Structure

To see how some of the principles you have just learned work in professional writing, read these paragraphs from Pete Hamill's autobiography, *A Drinking Life*. Comments in the left margin explain how Hamill created emphasis. Those on the right discuss variety. Hamill is writing about World War II.

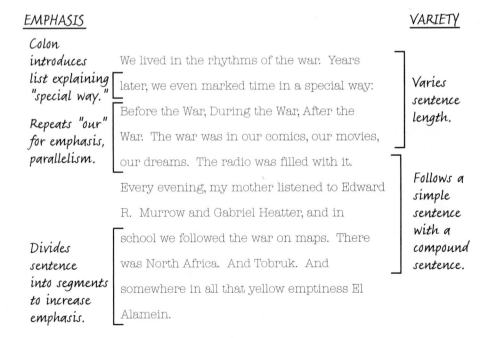

EMPHASIS   *VARIETY*

Colon introduces list explaining "special way."

We lived in the rhythms of the war. Years later, we even marked time in a special way:

Varies sentence length.

Repeats "our" for emphasis, parallelism.

Before the War, During the War, After the War. The war was in our comics, our movies, our dreams. The radio was filled with it.

Every evening, my mother listened to Edward R. Murrow and Gabriel Heatter, and in

Follows a simple sentence with a compound sentence.

Divides sentence into segments to increase emphasis.

school we followed the war on maps. There was North Africa. And Tobruk. And somewhere in all that yellow emptiness El Alamein.

At Holy Name, I heard about the war from new teachers every year, each of them rolling down the maps and showing us the places that were in the newspapers and on the radio.

Ends sentence with participial phrases.

Subordinates one idea to another.

There was so much excitement when the Allies landed in Sicily because the parents of most of the Italian kids were from that island.

Follows long sentence with short one.

They wanted the Americans to win.

Coordinates two equally important ideas.

They had brothers in our army, and some of the brothers died in those first battles.

Follows simple sentence with compound sentence.

All of them said their parents were worried.

Creates emphasis through repetition.

I got an aunt there, said Vito Pinto. My grandmother is there, said Michael Tempesta. I got an uncle over there, said George Poli. The war went on and on.

Revising to Create Variety and Emphasis

Read these two versions of paragraphs from Alice Wnorowski's "A Longing," which appears in this chapter. Although the rough draft is correct, Wnorowski knew that revising it would allow her to give important ideas the appropriate emphasis and to bring variety to her writing style.

Wnorowski—Rough Draft, Paragraphs 3 and 4

Vary length?

The morning dew chilled my naked feet. I stopped on the sandy lane. From out of the corner of my eye, I suddenly caught a movement. Something was moving in the wide, open hay field that lay before me. Five deer, three does and two fawns, were grazing

Vary structure?

in the mist-filled dips of the roller-coaster landscape. I sat down in the damp earth to watch them. I got my white nightdress all brown and wet.

What is being emphasized in this one-sentence paragraph?

The deer casually strolled through the thigh-high grass, stopping every other step to dip their heads into the growth and pop them back up again with long, tender timothy stems dangling from the sides of their mouths.

Too long?

Wnorowski—Final Draft, Paragraphs 3 and 4

Combines sentences through coordination, subordination, and compounding.

The morning dew chilled my naked feet, and I stopped on the sandy lane. From out of the corner of my eye, I suddenly caught a movement in the wide, open hay field that lay before me. In the mist-filled dips of the roller-coaster landscape grazed five deer: three does and two fawns. I sat down in the damp earth to watch them and got my white nightdress all brown and wet.

Creates variety by reversing subject and verb. Uses colon to introduce a list.

Divides paragraph into two sentences; emphasizes both ideas.

The deer casually strolled along through the thigh-high grass, stopping every other step to dip their heads into the growth and pop them back up again. Long, tender timothy stems dangled from the sides of their mouths.

Practicing Combining Sentences

The two paragraphs below lack emphasis and variety because the sentences they contain are similar in length and structure. Use techniques explained in this chapter to rewrite the paragraphs in the spaces that follow them. Combine sentences, remove words, add details, choose new vocabulary, or make any other changes you wish to create more interesting and effective paragraphs.

Ramses II

Ramses II was a pharaoh [ruler] of Egypt. He lived approximately 3,300 years ago. He took the throne when he was only 24. He ruled for 66 years. He died at about age 90. He had a huge family. He had more than 100 children. He is thought to be the pharaoh when Moses led the Hebrews from bondage in Egypt. He is also remembered for his many important building projects. He was an industrious and resourceful king. He left his mark on the Egyptian landscape. He built temples and other magnificent monuments in every major city of his kingdom. His projects included expanding the famous temples at Karnak and at Luxor. He is buried in the Valley of the Kings. This place is near Luxor. Luxor used to be called Thebes.

_____

_____

_____

_____

_____

_____

_____

_____

_____

_____

_____

Trinity

The prefix "tri" means three. Traditional Christianity
teaches that God exists in a trinity, three persons.
These are the Father, the Son, and the Holy Spirit.
Christianity is not the only religion that has a trinity.
Hinduism also has a trinity. It is called the Trimurti.
"Murti" means shape in Sanskrit. Sanskrit is the
ancient language of India. Many classical religious
and literary works are written in this language. The
Hindu trinity has three members. They are Brahma,
Vishnu, and Shiva. Brahma is the creator. Vishnu is
the preserver. Shiva is the destroyer.

_____

_____

_____

_____

_____

_____

_____

_____

A Longing

Alice Wnorowski

"A Longing" is a tender, almost dreamlike recollection of a beautiful childhood experience that continues to haunt the author. Wnorowski wrote this short essay in response to a freshman English assignment designed to help students learn to use concrete detail. However, it also illustrates several important principles about sentence structure discussed earlier in this chapter. Wnorowski began her studies at a community college. She has since earned a B.S. with honors in engineering.

Preparing to Read

1. You've learned that coordination can be used to create sentences in which two or more ideas receive equal emphasis and that subordination can be used to create sentences in which one idea is stressed over others. Look for examples of coordination and subordination in this essay.

2. The author puts variety into her writing by using techniques discussed earlier in this chapter. They include beginning sentences with an adverb and a prepositional phrase and using participles to vary sentence structure and length.

3. Remember what you learned about using details in Chapter 4, especially those that appeal to the five senses. Identify such details in "A Longing."

Vocabulary

acknowledge (verb)   Recognize.
conceived (verb)   Understood.
yearn (verb)   Desire, long for.

A Longing

Alice Wnorowski

A N EASY BREEZE pushed through the screen door, blowing into my open face   1
and filling my nostrils with the first breath of morning. The sun beamed warm rays of white light onto my lids, demanding they lift and acknowledge the day's arrival.

Perched in the nearby woods, a bobwhite proudly shrieked to the world   2
that he knew who he was. His song stirred deep feelings within me, and I

was overcome by an urge to run barefoot through his woods. I jumped up so abruptly I startled the dog lying peacefully beside me. His sleepy eyes looked into mine questioningly, but I could give him no answer. I only left him bewildered, pushing through the front door and trotting down the grassy decline of the front lawn.

The morning dew chilled my naked feet, and I stopped on the sandy lane. From out of the corner of my eye, I suddenly caught a movement in the wide, open hay field that lay before me. In the mist-filled dips of the roller-coaster landscape grazed five deer: three does and two fawns. I sat down in the damp earth to watch them and got my white nightdress all brown and wet. 3

The deer casually strolled along through the thigh-high grass, stopping every other step to dip their heads into the growth and pop them back up again. Long, tender timothy stems dangled from the sides of their mouths. 4

The fawns were never more than two or three yards behind their mothers, and I knew a buck must not be far off in the woods, keeping lookout for enemies. Suddenly, a car sped along the adjacent road, disrupting the peace of the moment. The deer jumped up in terror and darted toward the trees. They took leaps, clearing eight to ten feet in a single bound. I watched their erect, white puffs of tails bounce up and down, until the darkness of the woods swallowed them up and I could see them no more. 5

I don't think that at the simple age of eleven I quite conceived what a rare and beautiful sight I had witnessed. Now, eight years later, I yearn to awaken to the call of a bobwhite and to run barefoot through wet grass in search of him. 6

Read More on the Web

Nature Writing for Readers and Writers: http://www.naturewriting:com/
Virginia Commonwealth University site on nature writing with several useful links: http://www.vcu.edu/engweb/eng385/natweb.htm

Questions for Discussion

1. Find a few examples of both coordination and subordination in this essay.
2. Identify some adverbs, prepositional phrases, and participles Wnorowski uses to create variety.
3. In which sentence are the normal positions of the subject and verb reversed?
4. In paragraph 5, the author varies the length and structure of her sentences to make her writing more interesting. What methods discussed in this chapter does she use?
5. To which of our five senses do the details in this essay appeal?

6. What is the meaning of Wnorowski's title? Why is it appropriate?
7. What techniques does the writer use to maintain coherence in and between paragraphs?

Thinking Critically

1. This selection reveals as much about the writer as about the experience she recalls. From what you have just read, what can you say about Wnorowski's personality?
2. For anyone living in or near a rural area, seeing a family of wild animals is not an unusual event. Why, then, is this event so special to the writer?

Suggestions for Journal Entries

1. Think back to an experience you would like to relive. Make a list of the things that made this experience memorable and that will explain why you have such "a longing" to relive it.
2. Use the brainstorming technique discussed in "Getting Started" to list details about a natural setting (for example, a meadow, mountain, seashore) that you experienced recently or remember vividly.

Why Does Everybody Hate Me?

Satan

This selection is a humor column published in the November 23, 2005, issue of the Onion, *a satirical weekly newspaper. In this essay, an* Onion *staff writer makes Satan the speaker. In other words, he or she pretends to allow Satan to speak for himself. Doing so allows the author to explore the "soul" of a character thought by many to be the source of world evil. It also allows him or her to use irony. Irony is a literary technique in which the speaker's meaning or beliefs are not what he or she says they are. Here, for example, Satan claims that he's "not that bad a guy!"*

Preparing to Read

1. While this piece is predominantly humorous, there is also something serious about it. Look for this aspect of the author's message in the last paragraph.
2. Paragraph 3 makes reference to characters in the film *The Exorcist* (1973), based on the novel by William Peter Blatty. In this film, the devil has possessed a young girl. Her mother calls on a Roman Catholic priest who drives the devil out through a religious ritual known as an exorcism.

Vocabulary

acolytes (noun)	Followers, servants.
despoiler (noun)	Robber, pillager.
defiler (noun)	Polluter, fouler, someone who makes things unclean.
corporeal (adjective)	Material, physical.
embodiment (noun)	Physical representation.
entity (noun)	Thing, unit.
fallibility (noun)	Weakness, imperfection.
firmament (noun)	Heavens, sky.
inherent (adjective)	Inborn.
levitate (verb)	Raise.
mewling (adjective)	Whimpering, crying.
receptacle (noun)	Container, vessel.
reviled (adjective)	Hated, detested.
spawn (noun)	Offspring, seed.
suppurating (adjective)	Erupting, discharging pus.
visage (noun)	Face.
visceral (adjective)	Instinctive, emotional, from the gut.

Why Does Everybody Hate Me?

Satan

I'VE TRIED, I really have, but nothing ever goes right for me. Everywhere I go,   1
it's the same thing: people talking about me like I'm not even there, saying
how terrible I am. Telling other people not to walk in my path. Urging that I
be shunned and reviled, and commanding me in the name of all that is holy to
get myself behind them. I swear, sometimes it seems like everybody thinks I'm
the worst entity in creation.

I'm not that bad a guy, okay? I have my flaws, but I'll have you know I used   2
to be considered quite the golden boy back in my day. Do you even know what
the name Lucifer means? Depending on how it's translated, it can be "Bright and
Shining One" or "Bringer of Light," or all kinds of pretty names. I'm telling you,
I was the fairest star in the firmament once. The only reason I even got kicked
out of Heaven in the first place is because I was more beautiful than God.

Yeah, well, now look at me. I can't even possess a lousy 10-year-old girl   3
without some geezer in a white collar screaming "The power of Christ compels
you!" in my face and insisting that I leave immediately. Look, I just want to
connect with a human being for a little while! Levitate a few beds, spin a couple
necks around, have some deep, throaty laughs. Is that so wrong? Everybody
treats me like some kind of lowlife just because I'm the symbolic embodiment
of all the evil in the universe.

Have you heard the things they call me? I can take a good-natured ribbing   4
as much as the next guy, but some of these names are just so *mean*. Do you
have any idea how it feels to be called the "Lord of Lies"? Ouch. Look, I may
be mankind's greatest fears and weaknesses made flesh, but my feelings can
get hurt just like anybody else's. "Prince of Darkness"? How would you feel if
everybody called you "The Defiler," or "The Despoiler," or "The Unclean One"?
It's not my fault that my terrifying visage erupts into suppurating boils when
exposed to the holy light of truth and righteousness. It's hideous enough without people always needing to rub it in.

I'll bet I'm the most despised and hated being in the whole wide world. I   5
even wrote a poem about it once in my creative-writing class, but when I read it
out loud, everybody just laughed at me. I only took that class to make friends,
but even the biggest dorks there reacted to my very presence with visceral re-
pulsion. I'm telling you, I felt like the lowest of the low. The only way I could
get anyone to talk to me was by promising this one guy I'd make his stupid legal
thrillers into bestsellers in exchange for his immortal soul. Now he's had a string
of hit movie adaptations and I'll bet I don't even hear word one from him until
he shows up mewling and begging at the gateway to the underworld.

Oh sure, there are the occasional few who want to be my acolytes, but come   6
on. I mean, have you *seen* these people? They're plain *weird*. Sure, they say that
the reason they're into me is because they're rejecting society's small-minded

notions of petty morality and embracing a world where "do as thou wilt" shall be the whole of the law, but it's pretty obvious that they're really just mad that nobody else in the corporeal realm wants anything to do with them.

. . .

And while we're on the subject of my mortal followers, don't believe a   7
word you hear about all these so-called "spawn of Satan"—that phrase gets thrown around quite a bit, but believe you me, most women won't even come *near* me. I guess I've never really known how to show affection. But I have needs too, you know! I just wish I could meet a nice virgin half-goat woman who totally gets me. But every time I get involved with a receptacle for my seed, it always ends badly.

The only person who understands me is my friend Gene. Sure, he knows   8
I'm a mythical representation of all the tragic and self-defeating fallibility inherent in the human condition, but he doesn't judge me for it. Lately though, I hardly ever get to see him. Ever since he settled down, he's spending more and more time with his wife and kid. I know he's busy, but I miss him. He was an okay enough guy . . . not quite evil enough for my tastes, maybe, but an okay guy all the same.

Read More on the Web

Devil. Entry in *Catholic Encyclopedia:* http://www.newadvent.
    org/cathen/04764a.htm *The Problem of Evil in World Religions:*
    http://www.comparativereligion.com/evil.html

Satan. Wikipedia (online encyclopedia) site on Satan with links for
    further study: http://en.wikipedia.org/wiki/Satan

Questions for Discussion

1. In addition to making us laugh, what is the purpose of this essay?
2. Where and for what purpose does the author use a colon?
3. Find examples of parallel structure in this essay.
4. Identify one or two periodic sentences in this piece.
5. The essay makes ample use of rhetorical questions. Find at least three examples and explain why the author has included them.
6. Find examples of sentences that begin and end with participial phrases.
7. Where does the author use a dash? For what purpose?
8. Explain what techniques the author has used to create variety in paragraphs 5 and 6.

Thinking Critically

1. In the last paragraph, the author may be arguing that the devil is in all of us. Write a short paragraph that points to specific words and phrases to explain that idea.

2. Explain why the rhetorical question in paragraph 3 is ironic.

Suggestions for Journal Entries

1. Think about a historical figure who is seen as the representation of evil. Then, read more about him or her in the library or on the Internet. Here are some people you might look up:

Idi Amin	Pol Pot
John Wilkes Booth	Jack the Ripper
Caligula (Roman emperor)	Kim-Jong Il
Adolph Hitler	Charles Manson
Attila the Hun	Mao Zedong
Saddam Hussein	Benito Mussolini
Heinrich Himmler	Vald III (Dracula)

   Write a paragraph or two that, using what you have learned, summarizes the evil deeds of these villains.

2. The author of "Why Does Everybody Hate Me?" implies that the potential for evil exists in all of us. While few of us are truly evil, none of us is perfect. Reflect on yourself, make a list of things that you need to do or to stop doing to make yourself more considerate, tolerant, caring, or morally responsible.

Gettysburg Address

Abraham Lincoln

Perhaps the best-loved American president, Abraham Lincoln was a model of what a leader should be: decisive, principled, hard working, and compassionate. He was also among the most eloquent of public speakers. His Second Inaugural Address and Gettysburg Address are landmarks of American oratory. In November 1863, Lincoln came to Gettysburg, Pennsylvania, to dedicate a cemetery at the site of the Civil War's bloodiest battle. The turning point of the war, the Battle of Gettysburg had raged for four days and killed 50,000 Americans, both Union and Confederate, before Southern forces under General Robert E. Lee withdrew. Lincoln's Gettysburg Address is an eloquent and powerful statement of his belief that "all men are created equal"; of his grief over the death of his countrymen on both sides; and of his faith that "government of the people, by the people, for the people, shall not perish from the earth." Incidentally, Lincoln did not rely on a speech writer; he composed the Gettysburg Address himself.

Preparing to Read

1. Note that Lincoln makes excellent use of repetition. One word in particular is used seven times in this short speech. Look for and underline it each time.

2. Lincoln begins with a reference to the past, moves to the present, and ends with the future. Such references help organize the speech. Read the speech once; then, reread it to spot these references.

3. Another technique used to hold this speech together and give it greater emphasis is parallelism. Look for examples of this technique throughout the Gettysburg Address.

4. In the last sentence, Lincoln describes a "great task remaining before us." Read this important sentence several times to make sure you understand it fully.

Vocabulary

conceived (adjective)	Created.
consecrate (verb)	Bless.
dedicate(d) (verb/adjective)	Set aside for a purpose, sometimes to honor or worship.
detract (verb)	Take away from, lessen, decrease.
hallow (verb)	Make holy or sacred, sanctify.

in vain (adjective)	For no reason or purpose.
measure (noun)	Amount.
proposition (noun)	Idea, principle.
resolve (verb)	Decide, determine.

Gettysburg Address

Abraham Lincoln

FOUR SCORE AND SEVEN years ago our fathers brought forth on this continent 1
a new nation, conceived in Liberty, and dedicated to the proposition that
all men are created equal.

Now we are engaged in a great civil war, testing whether that nation, or 2
any nation so conceived and so dedicated, can long endure. We are met on a
great battlefield of that war. We have come to dedicate a portion of that field,
as a final resting place for those who here gave their lives that that nation might
live. It is altogether fitting and proper that we should do this.

But in a larger sense, we can not dedicate—we can not consecrate—we can 3
not hallow—this ground. The brave men, living and dead, who struggled here,
have consecrated it, far above our poor power to add or detract. The world will
little note, nor long remember what we say here, but it can never forget what
they did here. It is for us the living, rather, to be dedicated here to the unfinished
work which they who fought here have thus far so nobly advanced. It is rather
for us to be here dedicated to the great task remaining before us—that from
these honored dead we take increased devotion to that cause for which they
gave the last full measure of devotion—that we here highly resolve that these
dead shall not have died in vain—that this nation, under God, shall have a new
birth of freedom—and that government of the people, by the people, for the
people, shall not perish from the earth.

Read More on the Web

Online biography of Lincoln: http://gi.grolier.com/presidents/ea/bios/
    16plinc.html

Links to the first and second inaugural addresses and the Emancipation
    Proclamation: http://libertyonline.hypermall.com/Lincoln/Default.
    htm

Links to historical documents: http://www.law.ou.edu/hist/

Military History Online's history of the Battle of Gettysburg:
    http://www.militaryhistoryonline.com/gettysburg/getty1.aspx

Questions for Discussion

1. What examples of repetition appear in this speech?

2. The most obvious example of parallelism in the Gettysburg Address appears at the very end: "government of the people, by the people, for the people, shall not perish from the earth." What other examples of parallelism do you find?

3. Most sentences in this speech are long, but Lincoln does vary sentence length. Where does he do this?

4. What two participial phrases does Lincoln use at the end of the first sentence? Would it have made better sense to put the information they convey into another sentence? Why or why not?

5. Where in paragraph 2 does Lincoln use a participial phrase?

6. What effect does repeating the word "dedicate" or "dedicated" have? Does the word have any religious significance?

7. Where else does Lincoln use words that have a religious significance? What is he trying to tell us by using such vocabulary?

8. What is Lincoln's central idea? What devices does he use to maintain coherence?

Thinking Critically

1. In Preparing to Read, you learned that Lincoln makes reference to the past, to the present, and to the future. Find places in which he does this. What is he trying to accomplish by setting up this pattern other than helping to organize the speech? What does he accomplish each time he references a specific time?

2. Reread the last sentence. Is there a pattern in Lincoln's resolving that "these dead shall not have died in vain," that "this nation, under God, shall have a new birth of freedom," and that democracy "shall not perish from the earth"? What is that pattern, and why would such a pattern be so effective in a speech?

Suggestions for Journal Entries

1. In what ways do you think the government should be "for the people"? What rights, and/or services, should it guarantee us? Use clustering, draw a subject tree, or freewrite for about 10 minutes on this question. After you have completed your journal entry, read it to classmates or friends. Together, brainstorm for a few minutes to collect more ideas.

2. Many speeches in American history have served as sources of inspiration from decade to decade, from generation to generation. With the help of your instructor or your college librarian, locate a speech that you'd like to read or reread. Then analyze this speech. Pick out examples of parallelism, repetition, and other techniques the writer has used to create emphasis. Here are a few speeches you might choose from:

> Abraham Lincoln, Second Inaugural Address
>
> Franklin Delano Roosevelt, First Inaugural Address
>
> Adlai Stevenson, Eulogy for Eleanor Roosevelt
>
> Dwight D. Eisenhower, Farewell Address
>
> John F. Kennedy, Speech at the Berlin Wall
>
> Martin Luther King, Jr., Speech at the Lincoln Memorial ("I Have a Dream")
>
> Ronald Reagan, Speech at Moscow State University
>
> George W. Bush, State of the Union Address (January 29, 2002)

3. Using as many paragraphs as you like, rewrite Lincoln's speech in your own words. Make sure that you express his central idea clearly and that you emphasize his other important ideas through parallelism, repetition, or any of the other techniques you've learned for creating emphasis.

Skinwalkers

Richard Louv

Richard Louv (b. 1949) has been a columnist for the San Diego Union Tribune *and has written for the* Christian Science Monitor, *the* Washington Post, *and* Orion *magazine. He has been described as a futurist who is concerned about nature, the family, and the fate of our children. Among his books are* 101 Things You Can Do for Your Children's Future *(1993), and* Last Child in the Woods: Saving Our Children from Nature-Deficit Disorder *(2005).*

This essay is from The Web of Life: Weaving Values That Sustain Us *(1996). Throughout this book, Louv argues that our happiness depends on our abilities to strengthen our connections with other people—family, friends, co-workers—and the community as a whole. For him, the quality of life depends on a fragile web of connections that we make between ourselves and others.*

Preparing to Read

1. Look up the word "skinwalker" using an Internet search engine. Read a little bit about this figure in Native American lore on the Web before you start reading Louv's essay.

2. As you read, make notes in the margins to record the beliefs about skinwalkers that Louv includes in this essay.

3. This essay contains a good bit of dialogue—conversation—between the narrator (Louv) and the other characters. Pay special attention to what they talk about and what they say.

Vocabulary

hexes (noun)	Spells, curses.
hogan (noun)	Navajo dwelling, house.
pinon (adjective)	Kind of pine.
retribution (noun)	Revenge, payback.
velveteen (adjective)	Made of a cotton pile fabric.
warp (noun)	The weave in a rug.

Skinwalkers

Richard Louv

THE SKINWALKERS had been bothering Mary Begay. She stepped out of the   1
mobile home into the morning glare. She wore a little white shell in her hair. Beneath her velveteen blouse, her body was still covered with paint. The

medicine man had been here the night before and his blessing was still on her. He had made a sand painting in the ceremonial hogan next to the mobile home. He had laid Mary Begay (this is not her real name) down on the design and had painted her. He had built a fire next to her, and he and his assistants had sung in the smoke all night. This was done to make the skinwalkers go away.

The strands of our spirit are fragile and so easily warped.   2

"She is very tired," said her son, in his twenties. He spoke for his mother 3 because she only speaks the Navajo language. He was sitting on a big piece of petrified wood in front of the mobile home. The Begay place is down a mud road far out in the pinon forest; this forest stretches across northern Arizona and New Mexico and a long way into the past. "We can't keep her away from her weaving. She won't eat right. She has lost a lot of weight." He said the skinwalkers were stealing her health.

Before I had gone out to Mary Begay's place, Jackson Clark had explained her 4 situation to me. Clark, a respected and level-headed trader from Durango, Colorado, markets Begay's rugs. He told me that skinwalkers are a problem for some of his weavers, particularly the best ones. And Mary Begay is one of the best.

Night after night, he said, the shapes flit along the ridge in the moonlight. 5 Covered with the skins of coyotes, the people build fires and howl and holler until they turn into things. They circle and circle and beat on the windows and the doors, and they cry: "Mary Begay, don't you weave no more, you're takin' money from the people."

Sometimes, the next morning, coyote tracks are found around the trailer. 6 The Navajos follow the tracks for a few hundred feet, and the tracks, they say, turn into human tracks.

Clark once asked Begay's daughter, "What do you do when the skinwalkers 7 come?" She had replied, "We blow out the lantern and huddle in the corner." Then Clark had asked, "Why don't you get a gun and shoot 'em?" And she had answered: "We can't do that! They might be friends of ours."

So, standing there in the morning light, with Mary Begay and her son, 8 I looked at the ground. I cleared my throat. The ground was too hard for tracks.

"The sing cost us $300," said her son. The son stood up. He and his mother 9 walked past two piles of fresh wool, draped over a pine pole fence. The wool seemed to glow in the light. They entered a tall shed next to the hogan, and I followed and stepped inside. It took a while for my eyes to adjust. Back where the light was weak you could see something incredible.

It went clear to the high ceiling, fifteen or twenty feet up and just as wide. 10 The design came into focus, bars of red and brown, patterns with the geometric intricacy of a silicon chip. The rug was a huge one, hanging unfinished on the loom. Mary Begay sat down in front of the rug, on an old Coca Cola crate, feet tucked under her skirt.

She smiled and the gold showed in her teeth. Her face was beautiful. She 11 could not demonstrate the weaving for me, for she could not weave for four days, until the blessing ended, until she washed off the body paint. I asked what thoughts came into her mind as she wove.

"Only the weaving," she said, through her son. "I must concentrate."   12

The whole rug, all of its intricacy, springs entirely from her mind, said her 13 son. No pattern is put on paper. She and her family clip and card the wool by hand and twist it into yarn on the ends of primitive spindles, a technology that pre-dates the spinning wheel. Sage is boiled to dye the yarn a mustard color; crushed walnuts are used for black. She comes out here at dawn and works through lunch until midafternoon, until the shed is too hot. Then she breaks until dinner time, and then returns to the shed and works until nine o'clock.

Sometimes at the loom she hears steps behind her and feels a skinwalker's 14 hot breath on her neck, but when she turns around nothing is there. If the skin-walkers leave her alone, this big rug will take her a year and a half to complete. Near the end of the process, the warp of the rug will be so close and tight that her fingers will blister and bleed.

Does this rug have a special meaning for her?   15

Her son translated and she looked confused and said nothing. He said, "A 16 long time ago the designs did symbolize things; now it's more of an abstrac-tion." Then his mother said something soft to him.

"She says the rug has a meaning but she keeps it to herself."   17

Creating this rug must be more like creating a book than a painting. A 18 painting is finished relatively quickly, but a book is a solitary work that goes on and on. I mentioned this and she smiled again and nodded.

In the past, she wove large rugs with her sister, but when the two of them 19 worked together there were too many mistakes. So now she weaves alone. Three times she made errors on this rug that meant pulling out several feet of yarn and losing weeks of labor. This rug may be her last large one.

Is there such a thing as a perfect rug?   20

The question seemed to make her uneasy.   21

Her son answered: "The weaver places a spirit line in the rug, an imperfec- 22 tion through which all labor and concentration can escape."

If Mary Begay finishes this rug, it will sell for $25,000 to $30,000, and 23 she will get $15,000 to $20,000 of that—which seems like a lot of money, until one realizes how much the world's top painters or writers would get for a comparable project. Still, among her relatives and neighbors—always at work on their own little rugs—her success creates intense jealousy.

So the skinwalkers come.   24

In recent months, Begay's vision has begun to fade. She must lean up close 25 to the weave. She fears that the skinwalkers have come to take her sight.

In her culture, sharing is everything. To excel, to rise above your relatives 26 and neighbors, is among the greatest of sins, and retribution must be paid for this. Yet Navajos (Dineh) are surrounded by the world's most competitive, capitalistic culture. And so they are trapped in this terrible contradiction; no wonder the Dineh die so cheaply from alcohol and suicide and other things.

"Navajo witchcraft thrives on envy," the trader had told me. "Hexes are 27 placed on people here, and they die. They do die."

Driving down the mud road away from Mary Begay's place, I kept thinking 28 about what he had said, and the strangeness of it.

Then it occurred to me that skinwalkers are not quite so foreign or so alien. 29 They come in every culture; they just walk in different skins.

I'll bet you even know a few.   30

Read More on the Web

A Conversation with Richard Louv. *Online Newshour's* interview with Louv conducted by Margaret Warner on July 4, 2000: http://www. pbs.org/newshour/gergen/july-dec00/louv_7-4.html

"Richard Louv." Louv's professional history as well as links to many of his columns: http://www.citistates.com/assocspeakers/r_louv.html.

"Navajo Witches: Skinwalkers": http://www.geocities.com/asdzani/ navajo/skinwalk.html

Questions for Discussion

1. What is Louv's purpose in this essay? In your own words, state his central idea.
2. In paragraph 5, Louv makes effective use of repetition. Explain why he uses this technique in this paragraph, and find other examples of repetition in this essay.
3. An appositive is used in paragraph 4. Where else does the author use an appositive?
4. Find a sentence that begins with a gerund and one that begins with an infinitive.
5. Does the author use a rhetorical question? Does he use periodic sentences? Where?
6. In paragraph 13, we are told that "no pattern is put on paper." Where else in this paragraph is the passive voice used? For what reason?
7. Paragraph 9 mentions a "sing." What is a sing?

Thinking Critically

1. Write a short paragraph in which you explain why this essay is similar in purpose and message to Romero's poem "What the Gossips Saw" (Chapter 4).
2. What are the skinwalkers? Make a list of various beliefs about the skinwalkers as explained in this essay. (If you want to read more about skinwalkers, visit the third site listed under Read More on the Web.)

3. In paragraph 26, the author tells us that in the Navajo culture "sharing is everything." Is this true of the culture in which you live? Or is your culture "more competitive"?

Suggestions for Journal Entries

1. Do you know someone, perhaps yourself, who has experienced the effects of envy over some accomplishment that he, she, or you are justly proud of? Use freewriting or listing to gather details that you might later put into a story about the ill-effects of such envy.

2. Make a list or use clustering to gather information about various cultural, spiritual, or personal beliefs that you hold and that others outside your family, your community, or your culture might find new or strange. If this doesn't interest you, recall what Louv says in his very memorable conclusion (paragraphs 27–30). Are there any skinwalkers in our midst? Briefly state who these people are and then explain why they fit the definition of a skinwalker.

Suggestions for Sustained Writing

1. One of the Suggestions for Journal Entries after Alice Wnorowski's "A Longing" asks you to think about an experience you would like to relive. If you responded to this suggestion, you've made a list of effective details that will help explain why you have such a longing to repeat this experience.

    Add to your notes, and expand them into an essay that shows what made the experience so memorable. Develop your thesis in concrete detail, and make your writing unified and coherent by using techniques discussed in Chapter 2.

    After you've written your first draft, read your essay carefully. Should you do more to emphasize important ideas or to maintain your reader's interest? If so, revise your paper by using techniques for creating emphasis and variety explained in the introduction to this chapter. As usual, edit and proofread the final draft of your paper.

2. The second item in Suggestions for Journal Entries after "A Longing" invites you to begin listing details about a natural setting—a forest, meadow, seashore, mountain, river—that you visited recently or remember vividly.

    Follow the advice in item 1 of Suggestions for Sustained Writing above, and turn these notes into a short essay.

3. If you responded to the first of the journal prompts after "Why Does Everybody Hate Me?" write an essay in which you explain why the

villain you chose to research is really a villain. Use as much of your own knowledge as you can in this paper, but also use information from Internet and print sources. If you are summarizing, paraphrasing, or quoting from what you have read, make sure to give your sources credit by providing internal citations and a Works Cited list. You can learn more about how to do this by going to www.mhhe.com/rcw.

If this assignment doesn't interest you, write an essay that outlines ways in which you can make yourself into a more considerate, tolerant, caring, or morally responsible person. If you responded to the second journal assignment after "Why Does Everybody Hate Me?" you probably have gathered some information to get you started. Add to this information now and write a scratch outline that will guide you through your rough draft.

Whether you chose the first or second option in this assignment, try to create emphasis and variety in your paper by incorporating some of the techniques explained in this chapter. The best time to do so is during the revision process.

4. Read the notes you made in response to the first of the Suggestions for Journal Entries following Lincoln's "Gettysburg Address." (If you haven't completed this short assignment, do so now.)

Next, focus on three or four of the rights and/or services that democratic governments should guarantee their people. Choose those you believe are essential. Define each of these items in one or two sentences; then arrange them in a list that ends with the one item you consider most important of all.

Use this list as a blueprint or outline for an essay that explains, develops, and supports each of these ideas (rights/services) in a separate paragraph or group of paragraphs. When you begin revising your rough draft, write an introductory paragraph that contains a thesis and captures the reader's attention. Also, write a concluding paragraph based on one of the techniques explained in Chapter 3. As you rewrite this and subsequent drafts, create variety and emphasis by using the advice in this chapter. The next step, of course, is to edit and proofread your work.

5. If you have completed a journal entry in response to item 1 in the Suggestions for Journal Entries after "Skinwalkers," turn these notes into an essay that narrates a story in which you explain the ill effects of envy on you or on someone you know over an accomplishment one might be proud of. In addition, be sure to explain how you or your subject faced or overcame these effects, if in fact they were overcome.

As you revise the early drafts of your paper, make sure to include items for creating emphasis and variety as discussed in this chapter. For example, can you emphasize certain ideas by writing periodic sentences, by using parallel structure, or by repeating key words and phrases? For variety, can you begin a few sentences with infinitives or gerunds? Can you add participial phrases, use appositives, and vary sentence length and patterns? After you are satisfied with your revisions, make sure to edit and proofread.

6. Are there skinwalkers in your midst? Perhaps you started writing about them in response to the second journal prompt after Louv's essay. Expand your notes into a full-length essay by providing three or four examples of people you think qualify as skinwalkers. Make sure to include enough detail to prove to your readers that the people you are describing truly fit the definition of a skinwalker. If you believe that you have enough information to limit yourself to only one "skinwalker," then discuss him or her alone. Make sure not to identify your subject or subjects by their real names.

   If this doesn't interest you, write an essay in which you explain that the social environment you live in seems to be just too competitive, too greedy, too selfish, or too uncaring for its own good. To prove your point, narrate two or three different personal experiences in which you or others you know have demonstrated one or more of these traits. Discuss each incident in as much detail as you can. Then, when it comes time to revise your draft, try making your sentences more emphatic and more varied, as explained earlier. For example, use parallelism and repetition to emphasize certain points. And don't begin every sentence with its subject; instead start with a participle, an adverb, or a prepositional phrase now and again. As always, edit and proofread before handing your work in.

Writing to Learn: A Group Activity

Abraham Lincoln's Gettysburg Address is perhaps the best piece of oratory in world history. However, other great speeches need to be studied, not simply for their rhetorical values but also for what they tell us about the times in which they were delivered.

FIRST MEETING
Lincoln spoke at Gettysburg during a time of national emergency. Though eternal in its message, his address was aimed at the particular needs of his time. Ask each member of your group to find, read, and analyze one speech on a major issue(s) that the nation was facing during the time the speech was delivered. You might want to limit yourselves to presidential addresses such as

• Abraham Lincoln's Second Inaugural Address
• Franklin Roosevelt's Four Freedoms Address to Congress or his First Inaugural Address

• Ronald Reagan's address at Berlin's Brandenburg Gate
• George W. Bush's speech to the UN General Assembly in November 2001

On the other hand, you might limit yourselves to speeches made by famous women, such as

• Anna Howard Shaw's The Fundamental Principle of a Republic (1915)
• Margaret Chase Smith's Declaration of Conscience (1950)
• Mary Church Terrell's What It Means to Be Colored in the Capital of the United States (1906)
• Eleanor Roosevelt's The Struggle for Human Rights (1948)
• Barbara Bush's Commencement Address at Wellesley College (1990)
• Mary Fisher's Whisper of AIDS speech to the Republican National Convention (1992)

Or, you might also choose from the speeches of civil rights leaders such as

• Booker T. Washington's Atlanta Compromise Speech (1895)
• W. E. B. Du Bois's Men of Niagara speech (1906)
• Dr. Martin Luther King's "I Have a Dream" speech (1963), his Nobel Prize Acceptance speech (1964), or his "I've Been to the Mountain" speech (1968)
• Malcolm X's Message to the Grass Roots (1963) or his speech at the Audubon Ball Room (1964)

Whatever speeches your group decides to research, try to select from a group of addresses that have something in common, as illustrated in the previous examples.

RESEARCH AND WRITING

You can find the speeches just mentioned as well as many more on the Internet. Make sure to locate and research at least two commentaries on the speech you are studying. Commentaries on these addresses are plentiful both on the Web and in print. Then, write the first draft of a short research essay (250–500 words) that explains the purpose of the speech and the social or political environment in which it was delivered. Make sure to quote and/or paraphrase from your primary source (the speech) and from secondary sources (commentaries on the speech). Use a citation format approved by your instructor. Make photocopies of your work.

MARGINAL NOTE

Learn how to use MLA format at www.mhhe.com/rcw

SECOND MEETING

Distribute and discuss copies of each student's first draft. Evaluate content, development, and the inclusion of researched material. Make suggestions for revision. In addition, evaluate the paper on the basis of sentence structure. Has the student made his or her writing varied, interesting, and emphatic? Ask students to rewrite their papers based upon the group's evaluation and to resubmit them at the third meeting.

THIRD MEETING

Distribute and review the second drafts of each student's paper. If necessary, recommend additional revision. Also, offer suggestions toward editing and/or proofreading. Once again, pay special attention to what you have learned in this chapter about improving sentence variety and emphasis.

Description and Narration

The two chapters in this section explain how to create vivid verbal portraits of people, places, and things and to narrate stories about meaningful events. As you read Chapters 6 and 7, remember that the more details you put into any piece of writing the more believable, interesting, and effective it will be.

Knowing Your Subject

The more you know about your subject or event, the easier it is to choose effective details that communicate its significance to your readers. If you need to learn more about what you are describing, you can always observe it more closely and even use your other four senses—hearing, touch, taste, and smell—to gather information. If you are narrating an event you experienced or observed, you might recall additional details about it through focused free-writing, listing, or another of the pre-writing techniques explained in Getting Started. You can also interview other people involved to get their recollections. In fact, interviewing is also a good way to gather information about an incident you did not observe firsthand. This is what journalists and historians often do. Finally, you might also gather narrative details through library or Internet research, but be sure to credit your sources through appropriate citations (see the Appendix to this textbook for information on the Modern Language Association citation format: www.mhhe.com/rcw).

Using Language That Shows

As you learned in Chapter 4, using language that shows makes your writing more concrete, specific, and vivid than using language that simply tells. For example, it's one thing to say: "The firefighters risked their lives to save two people." It is another to say: "Their faces and protective clothing blackened from the suffocating smoke that had filled the hallways, the firefighters ran out of the tenement carrying a mother and infant whose apartment was now engulfed in flame." The first version is vague and unconvincing—a statement we soon forget. The second paints a memorable picture. It doesn't tell us that the firefighters were in danger, but the details it includes make that conclusion unavoidable. It also provides information about the building, the people who were saved, and the extent of the fire.

USE CONCRETE NOUNS AND ADJECTIVES

If you are describing a friend, don't just say that "He's not a neat dresser." Include nouns and adjectives that will enable readers to come to that conclusion on their own. Talk about "the red dirt along the sides of his scuffed, torn shoes; the large rips in the knees of his faded blue jeans; and the many jelly spots on his shirt." Concrete nouns and adjectives are also important to narration. For example, in "Mid-Term Break" (Chapter 7), Seamus Heaney creates a mood appropriate to a wake when he tells us that

> Whispers informed strangers I was the eldest
> Away at school, as my mother held my hand
>
> In hers and coughed out angry tearless sighs.
> At ten o'clock the ambulance arrived
> With the corpse stanched and bandaged by the nurses.

INCLUDE SPECIFIC DETAILS

After you have chosen important details that are concrete—that show rather than tell—make your writing more specific. For example, revise the description of your friend's attire to "The sides of his scuffed, torn loafers were caked with red clay. His knees bulged from the large rips in his faded Levis; and strawberry jam was smeared on the collar of his white Oxford shirt." Notice that "loafers" has replaced "shoes," "red clay" has replaced "red dirt," "Levis have replaced "blue jeans," and "shirt" has been revised to "white Oxford shirt."

CREATE FIGURES OF SPEECH

In Chapter 4, you learned that one of the best ways to make your writing clear and vivid is to use figures of speech, expressions that convey a meaning beyond their literal sense. The most common figures of speech are metaphor, simile, and personification. Writers often rely on such expressions to explain or clarify abstract, complex, or unfamiliar ideas. In "If at First You Do Not See . . ." (Chapter 6), Jesse Sullivan describes trees that seem "to bow their heads in sorrow," their branches "twisted and ill-formed, as if poisoned by the very soil in which they are rooted."

Figures of speech are also used extensively in narration. Take, for example, the metaphors Adrienne Shwartz uses in a passage from "The Colossus in the Kitchen," a story about her childhood home in South Africa (Chapter 7): "In those days . . . the adults were giants bestriding the world with surety and purpose. Tandi, the cook, reigned with the authoritarian discipline of a Caesar. She held audience in the kitchen. . . ."

RELY ON YOUR FIVE SENSES

Personal observation and experience often yield visual details. However, using your other four senses can provide even more important information, especially when you are describing. Of course, explaining what something sounds, tastes, smells, or feels like can be harder than showing what it looks like. But the extra effort is worthwhile. Whether you are describing or telling a story, the greater the variety of details you include, the more realistic and convincing your writing will be.

Next to sight, hearing is the sense writers rely on most. In "Flavio's Home" (Chapter 6), an essay that combines narration and description, Gordon Parks describes a boy holding a "bawling naked baby in his arms." He goes on to explain that the boy "whacked" the baby's bottom and that, later, two of the family's daughter's "burst into the shack, screaming and pounding on one another."

When writers describe rain-covered sidewalks as "slick," scraped elbows as "raw" or "tender," or the surfaces of bricks as "coarse" or "abrasive," they appeal to the sense of touch. Another example appears in "Watching the Reapers" by Po Chu-i (Chapter 6) when he writes that the reapers' "feet are burned by the hot earth."

Tastes and smells, though sometimes difficult to re-create, can also make your writing interesting and believable. Notice how well Mary Taylor Simeti uses them to recall an Easter picnic of take-out food from a hillside restaurant in Sicily:

> . . . [Our] obliging host produces [brings out] three foil-covered plates, a bottle of mineral water, and a round kilo loaf of fragrant, crusty bread. We drive back along the road a little way to a curve that offers space to park and some rocks to sit on. Our plates turn out to hold spicy olives, some slices of *prosciutto crudo* [cold ham] and of a peppery local salami, and two kinds of pecorino [sheep's milk] cheese, one fresh and mild, the other aged and sharper. With a bag of oranges from the car, the sun warm on our backs, the mountains rolling down at our feet to the southern coast and the sea beyond, where the heat haze clouds the horizon and hides Africa from view, we have as fine an Easter dinner as I have ever eaten. (*On Persephone's Island*)

Being Objective or Subjective

Objective writing requires you to report what you see, hear, or experience accurately and thoroughly—without revealing your feelings or opinions. Subjective writing allows you to convey your personal perspective on or reactions to a subject or experience. Both types of writing have their places in description and narration.

Most journalists and historians try to remain objective by communicating facts, not opinions about those facts. In other words, they try to give us the kind of information we'll need to make up our own minds about the subject. This is what Meg Potter does when she describes a woman living on the streets of a large American city:

> This particular [woman] had no shoes on, but her feet were bound in plastic bags that were tied with filthy rags. It was hard to tell exactly what she was wearing. She had on . . . a conglomeration of tattered material that I can only say . . . were rags. I couldn't say how old she was, but I'd guess in her late fifties. The woman's hair was grey and silver, and she was beginning to go bald.
>
> As I watched for a while, I realized she was sorting out her bags. She had six of them, each stuffed and overflowing. . . . I caught a glimpse of ancient magazines, empty bottles, filthy pieces of clothing, an inside-out umbrella, and several mismatched shoes. The lady seemed to be taking the things out of one bag and putting them into another. All the time she was muttering to herself. ("The Shopping Bag Ladies")

In some cases, however, authors find it important to make their feelings known. Take this short excerpt from Ichimaru's "Nagasaki. August 9, 1945," which appears in Chapter 7. Here the author speaks about his dying friends:

> I talked with them and they thought they would be O.K. but all of them would eventually die within weeks. I cannot forget the way their eyes looked at me and their voices spoke to me forever.

Watch for examples of objective and subjective writing in Section Three. At the same time, identify concrete and specific details and figures of speech to learn more about how they contribute to the making of effective description and narration.

CHAPTER 6

Description

This chapter presents selections that describe people, places, and things. It also discusses some techniques discussed in the introduction to Section Three, which are important to both description and narration. For example, you might recall the importance of using concrete nouns and adjectives, including specific details, relying on your five senses, and creating figures of speech (simile, metaphor, and personification). You might also remember the need to decide whether to remain objective or to take a more subjective approach when you write. Keeping this advice in mind will help you make your subjects as interesting and vivid to your readers as they are to you. In addition, however, you should learn several techniques especially important when you are describing, whether your subject is a place, a thing, or a person.

Techniques for Describing Places and Things

In addition to filling your writing with concrete details and figures of speech, try to include *proper nouns*, which name particular persons, places, and things. Here are some examples: Arizona, the University of Tennessee, Lake Michigan, the First Baptist Church, Microsoft Windows, Chinese, the *Chicago Tribune*, Rosedale Avenue, the San Francisco Opera House, and Fort Worth, Texas.

Including proper nouns that readers recognize or words made from such nouns can make your description more realistic and interesting. Take this paragraph from Mark Twain's *Life on the Mississippi*:

> The *Mississippi* is well worth reading about. . . . Considering the *Missouri* its main branch, it is the longest river in the world—four thousand three hundred miles. It seems safe to say that it is also the crookedest river in the world, since in one part of its journey it uses up one thousand three hundred miles to cover the same ground that the crow would fly over in six hundred and seventy-five. It discharges three times as much water as the *St. Lawrence*, twenty-five times as much as the *Rhine*, and three hundred and thirty-eight times as much as the *Thames*. No other river has so vast a drainage-basin: it draws its water supply from twenty-eight States and Territories; from *Delaware*, on the *Atlantic* seaboard, and from all the country between that and *Idaho* on the *Pacific* slope—a spread of forty-five degrees of longitude. The area of its drainage-basin is as great as the combined areas of *England, Wales, Scotland, Ireland, France, Spain, Portugal, Germany, Austria, Italy*, and *Turkey*;

and almost all this wide region is fertile; the *Mississippi* valley, proper, is exceptionally so.

USING EFFECTIVE VERBS

We know how important verbs are to narration, but effective verbs can also add much to a piece of description. Writers use verbs to make descriptions more specific, accurate, and interesting. For instance, "the wind had chiseled deep grooves into the sides of the cliffs" is more specific than "the wind had made deep grooves." The verb *chiseled* also gives the reader a more accurate picture of the wind's action than *made* does.

In the introduction to Section Three, you've just read about how to enrich the description of a friend's clothing by adding specific details. Returning to that sentence, notice that lively verbs (in italics) make as much of a difference as do concrete nouns and adjectives:

> Red clay *was caked* along the sides of his scuffed, torn loafers; his knees *bulged* from the large rips in his faded Levi's; and strawberry jelly *was smeared* on the collar of his white Oxford shirt.

Something similar can be said about the verbs and participles (adjectives made from verbs) that Alan Paton uses in his description of the mountains and valley near Ixopo in his native South Africa:

> The grass is rich and matted; you cannot see the soil. It *holds* the rain and mist, and they *seep* into the ground, *feeding* the streams in every kloof [ravine]. It is well *tended,* and not too many cattle *feed* upon it; not too many fires *burn* it, *laying* bare the soil. *Stand unshod* upon it, for the ground is holy, *being* even as it came from the Creator. *Keep* it, *guard* it, *care* for it, for it *keeps* men, *guards* men, *cares* for men. *Destroy* it and man *is destroyed* . . . .
>
> But the rich green hills *break down.* They *fall* to the valley below, and *falling* change their nature. For they grow red and bare; they *cannot hold* the rain and mist, and the steams are dry in the kloofs. Too many cattle *feed* upon the grass, and too many fires have *burned* it. *Stand shod* upon it, for it is coarse and sharp, and the stones *cut* under the feet. It is not *kept,* or *guarded,* or *cared for;* it no longer *keeps* men, *guards* men, *cares* for men. The tithoya *does not cry* here any more.

INCLUDING ACTION AND PEOPLE IN THE DESCRIPTION OF A PLACE

Narration and description are closely related, and they often appear together. Storytellers describe places where their narratives take place. Writers of description often reveal the character or atmosphere of a place by narrating events that occur in it or by describing people who appear in it.

A selection in this chapter that shows how actions and the people who perform them can help reveal the character of a place is Gordon Parks's "Flavio's Home." In the following passage, Parks reveals the hopelessness and poverty that fills the da Souza home when he tells us about the fear, sadness, and anger with which the family's children conduct themselves:

> Maria's eyes flashed anger. ". . . I'll beat you, you little bitch." Liza threw a stick at Maria and fled out the door. Zacarias dropped off to sleep. Mario . . . slouched in the corner and sucked his thumb. Isabel and Albia sat on the floor, clinging to each other with a strange tenderness. Isabel held on to Albia's hair and Albia clutched at Isabel's neck. They appeared frozen in an act of quiet violence.

Techniques for Describing People

You just learned that writers often go beyond physical appearance when describing a place or thing; they reveal its character as well. This is even more true when they describe people. Writers describe human beings because they are fascinated by their personalities, values, and motivations, as well as by their looks and the sound of their voices. Writers may start by describing physical appearance—what's on the outside. But they often end up talking about their subjects' characters—what's on the inside.

DESCRIBING A SUBJECT'S APPEARANCE AND SPEECH

Someone's appearance—height and weight, eye color, and so on—can be an end in itself. However, physical appearance and the clothes someone wears can also help you begin discussing his or her personality. The way people speak and what they say can provide additional information about their characters and internal makeups.

Take this example from John Cheever's essay about the New Jersey Pinelands. In one paragraph, he describes Fred Brown, a man who has lived in the wild all of his life and who is obviously plainspoken, down-to-earth, and comfortable with himself:

> He was dressed in a white sleeveless shirt, ankle top shoes, and undershorts. He gave me a cheerful greeting, and without asking what I wanted, he picked up a pair of khaki trousers that had been tossed on one of the . . . chairs and asked me to sit down. He set the trousers on another chair, and apologized for being in the middle of his breakfast, explaining that he seldom drank much but the night before he had had a few drinks and this had caused his day to start slowly. "I don't know what's the matter with me, but there's got to be something the matter with me because drink don't agree with

> me anymore," he said. He had a raw onion in one hand, and while he talked he shaved slices from the onion and ate them between bites of [a pork] chop. He was a muscular and well-built man, with short, bristly white hair, strong with large muscles in the calves. I guessed that he was about sixty and for a man of sixty he seemed to be in remarkably good shape. He was actually seventy-nine. "My rule is: Never eat except when you're hungry," he said, and he ate another slice of the onion.

Note that in addition to describing Brown's physical appearance and quoting him, this passage includes other clues about his character. Picturing him conversing with the author in his underwear and eating a raw onion and a pork chop for breakfast reveals a great deal.

REVEALING WHAT YOU KNOW ABOUT YOUR SUBJECT

In the paragraph above, Cheever makes a statement about Fred Brown through his behavior or actions. In this regard, you might also want to include anecdotes in your descriptions of people. Anecdotes are brief stories that highlight or illustrate an important aspect of a subject's personality. For example, Barry Shlachter in "Charisma Fortified by 'Chutzpah'" demonstrates Mother Teresa's ability to inspire others by telling a brief story about her directing relief efforts in a town devastated by a cyclone. Stories such as these help reveal how someone reacts to various people, places, and problems, thereby revealing a great deal about their attitude toward life.

REVEALING WHAT OTHERS SAY ABOUT YOUR SUBJECT

One of the quickest ways to learn about someone is to ask people who know this individual to tell you about his or her personality, lifestyle, morals, disposition, and so on. Often, authors use dialogue or quotations from other people to reveal something important about their subject's character. In "Crazy Mary," student Sharon Robertson combines physical description (concrete details) with information she learned from other people (dialogue) to create a memorable and disturbing portrait of an unfortunate woman she once knew:

> She was a middle-aged woman, short and slightly heavy, with jet-black hair and solemn blue eyes that were bloodshot and glassy. She always looked distant, as if her mind were in another place and time, and her face lonely and sad. We called her "Crazy Mary."
>
> Mary came to the diner that I worked in twice a week. She would sit at the counter with a scowl on her face and drink her coffee and smoke cigarettes. The only time she looked happy was when an old song would come on the radio. Then Mary would close her eyes, shine a big tobacco-stained smile, and sway back and forth to the music.

One day an elderly couple came in for dinner. They were watching Mary over their menus and whispering. I went over to their table and asked if they knew who she was. The old man replied, "Aw, dat's just old Mary. She's loonier than a June bug, but she ain't nutten to be afraid of. A few years back, her house caught fire and her old man and her kids got kilt. She ain't been right since."

After hearing this, it was easy to understand her odd behavior.

Other people can make good sources of information. We know from experience, however, that what others say about a person is often inaccurate. Sometimes, in fact, different people express very different—even contradictory— opinions about the same person. Consider how differently supporters and critics of a particular politician or entertainer view their subject. Today, President Abraham Lincoln enjoys the greatest respect among historians and the public alike. When he was alive, however, opinions about him differed; he was seen as a rustic frontiersman by some people, as a crafty tyrant by others, and as an embattled defender of human rights by still others.

Visualizing Details That Describe Places and Things

The following paragraphs from John Ciardi's "Dawn Watch" describe the sights, sounds, and smells of sunrise in his backyard.

The traffic has just started, not yet a roar *Appeals to senses.* and stink. One car at a time goes by, the tires humming almost like the sound of a *Uses simile.* brook a half mile down in the crease of a mountain I know—a sound that carries not because it is loud but because everything else is still.

The lawns shine with a dew not exactly dew. There is a rabbit bobbing about on the *Includes action.* lawn and then freezing. If it were truly a dew, his tracks would shine black on the grass, and he leaves no visible track. Yet, there is something on the grass that makes it glow a depth of green it will not show

Relies on concrete, specific nouns.

Uses metaphor.

Uses simile.

Appeals to senses.

again all day. Or is it something in the dawn air?

Our cardinals know what time it is. They drop pure tones from the hemlock tops. The black gang of grackles that makes a slum of the pin oak also knows the time but can only grate at it. They sound like a convention of broken universal joints grating up hill. The grackles creak and squeak, and the cardinals form tones that only occasionally sound through the noise.

Reveals subjective reaction to cardinals and grackles.

Visualizing Details That Describe People

The two short selections that follow use techniques important to describing people. The first, by Dr. Richard Selzer, describes the physical appearance of an AIDS patient in Haiti. The second, by Jade Snow Wong, describes the personality of a man who works in a factory that is run by the author's family and that doubles as their home.

"Miracle" by Richard Selzer

Uses specific details: nouns, adjectives.

Uses vivid adjectives

A twenty-seven-year-old man whose given name is Miracle enters. He is wobbly, panting, like a groggy boxer who has let down his arms and is waiting for the last punch. He is neatly dressed and wears, despite the heat, a heavy woolen cap. When he removes it, I see that his hair is thin, dull reddish and straight. It is one of the signs of AIDS in Haiti. . . .The man's skin is covered with a dry, itchy rash. Throughout

Uses simile to describe appearance.

the interview and examination he scratches
himself slowly, absentmindedly. The rash is
called prurigo. It is another symptom of
AIDS in Haiti. The telltale rattling of the
tuberculous moisture in his chest is audible
without a stethoscope. He is like a leaky
cistern [tank for liquid] that bubbles and
froths.

*Conveys
action.*

*Appeals to
hearing.*

*Uses a simile to
create an image.*

"Uncle Kwok" by Jade Snow Wong

After Uncle Kwok was settled in his chair,
he took off his black, slipperlike shoes.
Then taking a piece of stout cardboard from
a miscellaneous pile which he kept in a box
near his sewing machine, he traced the
outline of his shoes on the cardboard.
Having closely examined the blades of his
scissors and tested their sharpness, he
would cut out a pair of cardboard soles,
squinting critically through his inaccurate
glasses. Next he removed from both shoes the
cardboard soles he had made the day before
and inserted the new pair. Satisfied with
his inspection . . . he got up . . . disposed
of the old soles, and returned to his
machine. He had not yet said a word to
anyone.

*Recalls a
recurring
action that
tells us about
Kwok's
personality.*

*Uses vivid
adjectives/adverb
to create
an image.*

*Reveals an
important aspect
of his personality.*

Daily this process was repeated. . . .

Describes his clothing as a clue to his personality.

The next thing Uncle Kwok always did was to put on his own special apron, homemade from double thicknesses of heavy burlap and fastened at the waist by strong denim ties. This long apron covered his thin, patched trousers and protected him from dirt and draft. After a half hour had been consumed by these chores, Uncle Kwok was ready to wash his hands. He sauntered into the Wong kitchen, stationed himself at the one sink which served both family and factory, and with characteristic meticulousness [care], now proceeded to clean his hands and fingernails.

Uses vivid verbs.

It was Mama's custom to begin cooking the evening meal at this hour . . . but every day she had to delay her preparations at the sink until slow-moving Uncle Kwok's last clean fingernail passed his fastidious [close] inspection. One day, however, the inconvenience tried her patience to its final limit.

Recalls an action to describe Kwok.

Trying to sound pleasantly persuasive, she said, "Uncle Kwok, please don't be so slow and awkward. Why don't you wash your hands at a different time, or else wash them faster?"

Explains what someone else thinks of Kwok.

Uncle Kwok loudly protested . . . "Mama,
I am not awkward. The only awkward thing
about my life is that it has not yet
prospered!" And he strode off, too hurt even
to dry his hands, finger by finger, as was
his custom.

Allows Kwok to reveal himself in his own words.

Revising Descriptive Essays

Read these two versions of three paragraphs from Jessie Sullivan's "If at First
You Do Not See . . .," a student essay that appears later in this chapter in its
entirety. Though the rough draft is powerful, Sullivan's revision smooths out
rough spots, improves wording, and provides additional detail that makes her
writing even more vivid and effective.

Sullivan—Rough Draft

I live in an apartment on the outskirts of
New Brunswick, New Jersey. To the right of
my building is Robeson Village, a large low-
income housing project with about two-
hundred apartments facing each other on
opposite sides of a wide, asphalt driveway
that runs the length of the complex. In this
driveway, drug dealers and buyers congregate

Wordy?

daily, doing business in front of anyone who
cares to watch. Sometimes, children who have
witnessed these transactions look over
paraphernalia the dealers and their
customers have left in their wake.

What kind of paraphernalia?

   To the left of my building is Henry
Street, a street that has grown to be

synonymous with illegal drugs over the
years. It is truly a pathetic sight. The
block consists of a half dozen vacant and
condemned buildings, all of which are still
inhabited by addicts and dealers who have
set up store there in much the same way a
legitimate business owner decides on a
particular location where business will be
most profitable.

*If "vacant,"
how can
they be
"inhabited"?*

Wordy?

. . .

Whose eye?

To the eye, the community appears to be
in a state of depression. Even trees, which
traditionally symbolize life and vitality
reflect this. Pungent odors are made worse
by the stench of rotting food, spilled from
overturned garbage cans onto the sidewalk
and cooking in the heat of the sun.

*Make this
more vivid?*

*What kinds
of "pungent
odors"?*

*Make this
image more
active, lively?*

Sullivan—Final Draft

I live in an apartment on the outskirts of
New Brunswick, New Jersey. To the right of
my building is Robeson Village, a large low-
income housing project with about two-
hundred apartments facing each other on
opposite sides of a wide, asphalt driveway
that runs the length of the complex. Here,
drug dealers and buyers congregate daily,
doing business in front of anyone who cares
to watch. Sometimes, children who have

*Substitutes one
word for three.*

witnessed these transactions look over the

crack vials, hypodermic needles, syringes,

and other paraphernalia the dealers and

their customers have left in their wake.

Adds specific detail to define "paraphernalia."

To the left of my building is Henry

Uses fewer words than original.

Street, which has become synonymous with

illegal drugs. It is a pathetic place. The

block consists of a half dozen condemned

buildings, all of which are lived in or

frequented by addicts and dealers. The

Changes wording to be more accurate.

latter have set up stores there in much the

Uses fewer words than original.

same way legitimate merchants choose

locations where they think business will be

profitable.

. . .

Adds effective adjective.

To the eye of the visitor, the community

appears to be in a chronic state of

Adds detail.

depression. Even trees, symbols of life and

vitality, seem to bow their heads in sorrow.

Rather than reaching up in praise, their

branches are twisted and ill-formed, as if

poisoned by the very soil in which they are

Uses personification to create a vivid image.

Uses specifics to explain what kinds of odors.

rooted. The pungent odors of urine, feces,

and dead, wet leaves are made worse by the

stench of rotting food, which spills from

overturned garbage cans onto the sidewalk

and cooks in the heat of the sun.

Uses verbs to make image active, lively.

Practicing Techniques That Describe

1. Write a paragraph that describes an eating area in your college's student center, a reading area in your college's library, or a coffee shop, a bar, a restaurant, or some other public place where people gather. Appeal to the senses, and include information about the appearance and behavior of people who frequent the place.

   _____

   _____

   _____

   _____

   _____

   _____

2. In a short paragraph or two, describe a specific animal (your pet frog "Meteor") or a type of animal (frogs, in general). Use simile, metaphor, or personification. Also appeal to the senses.

   _____

   _____

   _____

   _____

   _____

   _____

3. Describe the inside of your car, your bedroom, your family's kitchen, or any other room in which you spend a great deal of time. Appeal to the senses and use simile.

   _____

   _____

   _____

   _____

   _____

   _____

4. Write a paragraph that describes your physical appearance. Include details that appeal to the senses, and try to use figures of speech. Be specific about your height, weight, hair color, eye color, and so on.

_____

_____

_____

_____

_____

_____

_____

5. Write a paragraph that describes your best or worst quality. For example, discuss your patience or impatience, your tolerance or lack of tolerance for differences in people, your ambition or laziness, or your knack for making or losing friends. Show readers what you mean by using examples and by recalling what others have said about you.

_____

_____

_____

_____

_____

_____

_____

If at First You Do Not See . . .

Jessie Sullivan

When Jessie Sullivan began this essay for a college composition class, she wanted simply to tell her readers what her neighborhood looked like. As she revised and developed her work, however, she discovered that the place in which she lived had a vibrant character beyond what the eye can see. Slowly, she expanded and refined her purpose until description became a tool for exploring the sorrow and the promise of her world. Sullivan majors in liberal arts and business. She plans to study business administration in graduate school.

Preparing to Read

1. As you learned in Chapter 2, narration and description can sometimes be used to explain ideas. Sullivan uses description to explain what is wrong with her neighborhood but also to reveal her hope for the people and place she loves.
2. In creating the contrast explained above, Sullivan reveals much about herself: her courage, her vision, and her desire to make a difference.
3. You know that this essay uses both description and contrast. Look for examples as well.

Vocabulary

bewilderment (noun)	Astonishment, confusion.
condone (verb)	Make excuses for.
defaced (verb)	Made ugly, disfigured.
diversified (adjective)	Varied, different.
illicit (adjective)	Illegal, prohibited.
infamous (adjective)	Dishonorable, known for evil or wrongdoing.
obscenities (noun)	Words or drawings that are indecent and offensive.
oppressive (adjective)	Harsh, severe, hard to bear.
paraphernalia (noun)	Gear, equipment used in a particular activity.
pathetic (adjective)	Pitiful, wretched, miserable.
preconceived notions (noun)	Prejudices, opinions formed before having accurate information about something.
sober (adjective)	Reliable, serious, steady.
superficial (adjective)	Quick and careless, shallow, on the surface.

If at First You Do Not See . . .

Jessie Sullivan

A look of genuine surprise comes over some of my classmates when I mention where I live. My neighborhood has a reputation that goes before it. People who have never been there tend to hold preconceived notions about the place, most of which are negative and many of which are true. Those who actually visit my neighborhood usually notice only the filth, the deterioration of buildings and grounds, and the crime. What they fail to see isn't as apparent, but it is there also. It is hope for the future.

I live in an apartment on the outskirts of New Brunswick, New Jersey. To the right of my building is Robeson Village, a large low-income housing project with about two-hundred apartments facing each other on opposite sides of a wide, asphalt driveway that runs the length of the complex. Here, drug dealers and buyers congregate daily, doing business in front of anyone who cares to watch. Sometimes, children who have witnessed these transactions look over the crack vials, hypodermic needles, syringes, and other paraphernalia the dealers and their customers have left in their wake.

To the left of my building is Henry Street, which has become synonymous with illegal drugs. It is a pathetic place. The block consists of a half dozen condemned buildings, all of which are lived in or frequented by addicts and dealers. The latter have set up stores there in much the same way legitimate merchants choose particular locations where they think business will be profitable.

It is this area, three blocks in radius, that is infamous for illicit drugs, prostitution, and violence of every sort. Known as the "Vil," it is regarded as the city's hub of criminal activity and immorality.

With the growing popularity of crack, the appearance of the community has gotten worse and worse, as if it were on a collision course with destruction. Fences that once separated one property from another lie in tangled rusted masses on sidewalks, serving now only as eyesores. Almost all of the buildings are defaced with spray-painted obscenities and other foul messages. Every street is littered with candy wrappers, cardboard boxes, balled-up newspapers, and broken beer and soda bottles.

But Henry Street is undeniably the worst. The road is so covered with broken glass that the asphalt is barely visible. The way the glass catches the sunlight at every angle makes the street look almost magical, but there is nothing magical about it. Henry Street is a dead-end in more than the literal sense. In front of apartment buildings, the overgrown lawns, which more closely resemble hay than grass, are filled with old tires, cracked televisions, refrigerators and ovens with missing doors, rusted bikes, broken toys, and worn chairs and tables without legs. Dozens of abandoned cars, their windows shattered and their bodies stripped of anything of value, line the curbs. The entire block is so cluttered with refuse that strangers often mistake it for the junk yard, which is five blocks up.

To the eye of the visitor, the community appears to be in a chronic state of 7
depression. Even trees, symbols of life and vitality, seem to bow their heads in
sorrow. Rather than reaching up in praise, their branches are twisted and ill-
formed, as if poisoned by the very soil in which they are rooted. The pungent
odors of urine, feces, and dead, wet leaves are made worse by the stench of
rotting food, which spills from overturned garbage cans onto the sidewalk and
cooks in the heat of the sun.

Most people familiar with the neighborhood are aware that the majority of 8
us residents are virtual prisoners in our homes because of the alarming crime
rate. Muggings, rapes, and gang-related shootings, many of which do not get
reported in newspapers, are commonplace. Many residents live in such fear
that they hide in their apartments behind deadbolt locks and chains, daring to
peer out of their peepholes only when a frequent gunshot rings out.

Many of my neighbors have adopted an I-mind-my-own-business attitude, 9
preferring to remain silent and blind to the goings-on around them. This is the
case for so many of them that many nonresidents believe everyone feels this
way. Unfortunately, most outsiders learn about our community from people
who have been here only once or twice and who leave with unfair and dangerous misconceptions about us. They see the filth and immorality, and that is
all they see. They take one quick look and assume none of us cares about the
neighborhood or about the way we live.

I see my neighborhood from the inside, and I face all of the terrible things 10
I have mentioned on a day-to-day basis. I also see aspects of my community
that cannot be appreciated with a superficial first glance. If you look at the place
closely, you will find small strong family units, like my own, scattered amid the
degeneration and chaos. Working together, struggling to free themselves from
oppressive conditions, these families are worth noticing! We are sober, moral
people who continue to live our lives according to the laws of society and, more
important, according to the laws of God Himself.

Look closely and you will find those of us who pick up the trash when we 11
see it scattered on our small lawns, sidewalks, and doorsteps. We discourage
our children from disrespecting the area in which they live, and we see to it
that they don't litter or deface public property. We emphasize the importance
of schooling, and we teach them about the evils of drugs and crime, making
certain that they are educated at home as well.

Most important, we practice what we preach. We show the children with 12
our actions that we do not condone the immoral and illegal acts around us,
and we refuse to take part in any of them. We call the police whenever we hear
gunshots, see drug transactions, or learn of any other unlawful activity. The
children know that we care and that we are trying to create a brighter future
for them.

However, the most visible sign of hope is that young people from my 13
neighborhood—and from many neighborhoods like mine, for that matter—are
determined to put an end to the destruction of our communities. It angers

us that a minute yet very visible group of negative individuals has come to represent the whole. It saddens us that skills, talents, and aspirations, which are so abundant in our communities, should go untapped. Therefore, we have decided to take matters into our own hands; we will get the education we need and solve the problems of our neighborhoods ourselves.

Many of us attend the local county college, where we come together often 14 to share ideas for a better future for our community. We also give each other the moral support we need to achieve our educational goals. Our hope binds us together closely and is itself a sign that things will get better.

This May, I was proud to see a number of friends receive associate's degrees 15 and get admitted to four-year colleges and universities for advanced degrees. I hope to do the same soon. We are studying for different professions, but no matter how diversified our goals, we will use our knowledge for the benefit of all. This means returning to the community as doctors, lawyers, teachers, entrepreneurs. We will build programs to assist the people of our community directly: day care centers for children with working mothers; family mental and physical health clinics; job-training and placement facilities; legal service centers; youth centers; and drug/alcohol rehabilitation programs. Given the leadership of educated people like those we will become, such facilities can eventually be operated by community residents themselves. Most important, we intend to serve as visible and vocal role models for our children—for the leaders who will follow us and keep our hope alive. Eventually, we will bring about permanent change and make it impossible for a misguided few to represent a proud and productive community.

When friends visit me in my apartment for the first time, they frequently 16 ask in awe and bewilderment, "How can you live in such a bad place?" I always give the same reply: "It isn't where you live, but how you live and what you live for."

Read More on the Web

People's Weekly World site on the state of Black America:
  http://www.hartford-hwp.com/archives/45a/188.html
Urban Institute site with links to many other resources:
  http://www.urban.org/

Questions for Discussion

1. What does Sullivan mean in paragraph 1 when she says that her "neighborhood has a reputation that goes before it"? Does this statement help introduce what follows in the rest of the essay?
2. Where in this essay does Sullivan include proper nouns? How do they help her achieve her purpose?

3. One reason this essay is so powerful is that it uses specific details. Which paragraphs make the best use of such details? What do such details tell us about Sullivan's attitude toward her neighborhood?
4. What image does Sullivan create in paragraph 7? What figure of speech does she use to develop this image?
5. Does action play a role in this essay? What is it?
6. Sullivan mentions her neighbors. How do they help define the neighborhood?
7. What sense other than sight does Sullivan appeal to?
8. When does she make use of illustration (examples)?

Thinking Critically

1. Why do you think Sullivan bothers to tell us that many shootings never get reported in the newspapers?
2. Summarize Sullivan's central idea in your own words.
3. This is a thought-provoking essay. What questions might you ask Sullivan about herself or her neighborhood if you were able to interview her? (For example, who or what has been her greatest inspiration?) Write your questions in the right- and left-hand margins.

Suggestions for Journal Entries

1. Make a list of the qualities you admire most about the neighborhood in which you live or grew up. Then make another list of ways it might be improved.
2. Use any technique discussed in "Getting Started" to gather information about what your home, neighborhood, or town might look like to someone seeing it for the first time. Then, go beyond appearances and discuss the real character of the place. Like Sullivan, describe what's on the "inside."
3. Think of a community, a family, or any group of people struggling to grow, improve, or even survive. What makes their life a struggle? What hope do you see for this place or these people?

Watching the Reapers*

Po Chü-i

Perhaps one of the most productive of all Chinese poets, Po Chü-i lived between 772 and 846. Many of his works, though seemingly simple in content, reveal a profound concern for others. Some of them, aimed at the consciences of the ruling class, recall the social evils of his day. Others use description as a tool for exposing guilt, heartache, or other strong emotion in the poet. "Watching the Reapers" does all of these things.

Preparing to Read

1. In the introduction to this chapter, you learned that including action is a good way to capture the character of a place or scene. "Watching the Reapers" makes good use of this technique.
2. Description can have many uses. Here it becomes a tool for self-reflection as well as social commentary.
3. The "fifth month" in line 2 refers to midsummer. In lines 19 and 20, Po mentions that the reapers have paid a tax to the state equal to the amount of grain they had raised themselves. This statement is a clear indication that one of the purposes of this poem is to expose a political and economic evil. In line 23, Po tells us that, as a government official, he is paid in "stones," which are measures of grain.

Vocabulary

glean (verb)   Gather.
grudging (adjective) Resenting.
lingered (verb)   Remained, stayed around.

Watching the Reapers

Po Chü-i

Tillers of the earth have few idle months;
In the fifth month their toil is double-fold.
A south wind visits the field at night;
Suddenly the ridges are covered with yellow corn.
Wives and daughters shoulder baskets of rice,   5

---

*Translated by Arthur Waley.

Youths and boys carry flasks of wine,
In a long train, to feed the workers in the field—
The strong reapers toiling on the southern hill,
Whose feet are burned by the hot earth they tread,
Whose backs are scorched by the flames of the shining sky.   10
Tired they toil, caring nothing for the heat,
Grudging the shortness of the long summer day.
A poor woman with a young child at her side
Follows behind, to glean the unwanted grain.
In her right hand she holds the fallen ears,   15
On her left arm a broken basket hangs.
Listening to what they said as they worked together
I heard something that made me very sad:
They lost in grain-tax the whole of their own crop;
What they glean here is all they will have to eat.   20
And I today—in virtue of what desert
Have I never once tended field or tree?
My government pay is three hundred stones;
At the year's end I have still grain in hand.
Thinking of this, secretly I grew ashamed   25
And all day the thought lingered in my head.

Read More on the Web

Selected poems of Po Chu-I (AD 772–846) Translated by Howard
    S. Levy and Henry Wells: http://www.darsie.net/library/pochui.html
Links to Literature site including biography of the poet and several
    translated poems: http://www.linkstoliterature.com/po.htm

Questions for Discussion

1. What concrete nouns does Po use in this poem?
2. Where does he use effective verbs and adjectives?
3. Explain how Po's description of the reapers helps him describe the fields in which they toil.
4. One of Po's objectives is to make us aware of how hard a life the reapers have. How do his descriptions of the fields, the wind, and other natural objects help him do this?
5. Why does Po make sure to include action in this poem?
6. What does the conclusion of the poem reveal about Po's purpose?

Thinking Critically

1. If Po were writing in our day, what would he say about the way our society treats its workers? As you think about this topic, focus on a particular industry, business, or trade.

2. Reread line 12. What does Po mean by the "shortness of the long summer day"?

Suggestions for Journal Entries

1. Use listing, clustering, or freewriting to begin gathering concrete details about a place that you have worked in and that you have found interesting. You don't have to have liked this place; you need only have found it interesting. Try to remember the kinds of people and activities that one would normally find there, but keep your information factual and objective. Do not include details that would reveal your feelings about the place.

2. Read over your response to Suggestion 1. Now, be subjective. Through freewriting, explain your feelings about this workplace, the people in it, and the kind of work that goes on there. Finally, answer this question: Would you recommend this job to one of your friends?

Flavio's Home

Gordon Parks

Gordon Parks (1912) is a film director/producer, author, composer, and photographer. His feature films include Shaft *(1972),* The Super Cops *(1974),* Leadbelly *(1976), and* Moments without Proper Names *(1986). He also made the television documentary* The Diary of a Harlem Family *(1968), for which he won an Emmy Award. Perhaps his most memorable film is* The Learning Tree *(1969), a fictionalized account of his childhood in Kansas.*

Parks is the founder and was the editorial director (1970–73) of Essence *magazine, and he has written many works of nonfiction—including several memoirs and many books on the art of photography—as well as a novel,* Shannon *(1981). Today, however, his fame rests chiefly on his photography and on the writings that accompany his photography collections. In* Voices in the Mirror *(1990), a memoir in which "Flavio's Home" first appeared, Parks said that he used "photography as a weapon against poverty and racism." As a staff writer for* Life *magazine, he was once assigned to complete a photo-essay on poverty in one of the "favelas," or slums, of Rio de Janeiro, Brazil. The essay that follows is based on what he witnessed on that trip.*

Preparing to Read

1. Read Parks's first paragraph several times to determine his purpose.
2. Is the first line of this essay a warning of what is to come?
3. Look for images of and references to death starting with paragraph 2. What do you think "Catacumba," the name of the slum where Flavio lives, means in English? Look up words that begin with "cata" in the dictionary if necessary.
4. Read paragraph 3 carefully. Like other paragraphs, it uses effective language, but it also hints at something we will learn about at the essay's end.

Vocabulary

afflictions (noun)	Troubles, suffering, illnesses.
excrement (noun)	Bodily waste.
hemmed and hawed (verbs)	Hesitated before speaking.
jaundiced (adjective)	Yellowed because of illness or malnutrition.
maze (noun)	Confusing set of passageways in which one gets lost easily.
mobilize (verb)	Put into action.

plankings (noun)	Rough boards.
plush (adjective)	Rich, luxurious.
scurried (verb)	Ran around or hurried nervously.
skepticism (noun)	Lack of trust or faith.
wallowing (adjective)	Rolling around, as a pig does in the mud.

Flavio's Home

Gordon Parks

I'VE NEVER LOST my fierce grudge against poverty. It is the most savage of all 1
human afflictions, claiming victims who can't mobilize their efforts against it,
who often lack strength to digest what little food they scrounge up to survive. It
keeps growing, multiplying, spreading like a cancer. In my wanderings I attack
it wherever I can—in barrios, slums and favelas.

Catacumba was the name of the favela where I found Flavio da Silva. It was 2
wickedly hot. The noon sun baked the mud-rot of the mountainside. Garbage
and human excrement clogged the open sewers snaking down the slopes. José
Gallo, a *Life* reporter, and I rested in the shade of a jacaranda tree halfway up
Rio de Janeiro's most infamous deathtrap. Below and above us were a maze
of shacks, but in the distance alongside the beach stood the gleaming white
homes of the rich.

Breathing hard, balancing a tin of water on his head, a small boy climbed 3
toward us. He was miserably thin, naked but for filthy denim shorts. His legs
resembled sticks covered with skin and screwed into his feet. Death was all over
him, in his sunken eyes, cheeks and jaundiced coloring. He stopped for breath,
coughing, his chest heaving as water slopped over his bony shoulders. Then
jerking sideways like a mechanical toy, he smiled a smile I will never forget.
Turning, he went on up the mountainside.

The detailed *Life* assignment in my back pocket was to find an impover- 4
ished father with a family, to examine his earnings, political leanings, religion,
friends, dreams and frustrations. I had been sent to do an essay on poverty.
This frail boy bent under his load said more to me about poverty than a dozen
poor fathers. I touched Gallo, and we got up and followed the boy to where he
entered a shack near the top of the mountainside. It was a leaning crumpled
place of old plankings with a rusted tin roof. From inside we heard the bab-
blings of several children. José knocked. The door opened and the boy stood
smiling with a bawling naked baby in his arms.

Still smiling, he whacked the baby's rump, invited us in and offered us a 5
box to sit on. The only other recognizable furniture was a sagging bed and a
broken baby's crib. Flavio was twelve, and with Gallo acting as interpreter, he
introduced his younger brothers and sisters: "Mario, the bad one; Baptista, the
good one; Albia, Isabel and the baby Zacarias." Two other girls burst into the

shack, screaming and pounding on one another. Flavio jumped in and parted them. "Shut up, you two." He pointed at the older girl. "That's Maria, the nasty one." She spit in his face. He smacked her and pointed to the smaller sister. "That's Luzia. She thinks she's pretty."

Having finished the introductions, he went to build a fire under the stove—a rusted, bent top of an old gas range resting on several bricks. Beneath it was a piece of tin that caught the hot coals. The shack was about six by ten feet. Its grimy walls were a patchwork of misshapen boards with large gaps between them, revealing other shacks below stilted against the slopes. The floor, rotting under layers of grease and dirt, caught shafts of light slanting down through spaces in the roof. A large hole in the far corner served as a toilet. Beneath that hole was the sloping mountainside. Pockets of poverty in New York's Harlem, on Chicago's south side, in Puerto Rico's infamous El Fungito seemed pale by comparison. None of them had prepared me for this one in the favela of Catacumba. 6

Flavio washed rice in a large dishpan, then washed Zacarias's feet in the same water. But even that dirty water wasn't to be wasted. He tossed in a chunk of lye soap and ordered each child to wash up. When they were finished he splashed the water over the dirty floor, and, dropping to his knees, he scrubbed the planks until the black suds sank in. Just before sundown he put beans on the stove to warm, then left, saying he would be back shortly. "Don't let them burn," he cautioned Maria. "If they do and Poppa beats me, you'll get it later." Maria, happy to get at the licking spoon, switched over and began to stir the beans. Then slyly she dipped out a spoonful and swallowed them. Luzia eyed her. "I see you. I'm going to tell on you for stealing our supper." 7

Maria's eyes flashed anger. "You do and I'll beat you, you little bitch." Luzia threw a stick at Maria and fled out the door. Zacarias dropped off to sleep. Mario, the bad one, slouched in a corner and sucked his thumb. Isabel and Albia sat on the floor clinging to each other with a strange tenderness. Isabel held onto Albia's hair and Albia clutched at Isabel's neck. They appeared frozen in an act of quiet violence. 8

Flavio returned with wood, dumped it beside the stove and sat down to rest for a few minutes, then went down the mountain for more water. It was dark when he finally came back, his body sagging from exhaustion. No longer smiling, he suddenly had the look of an old man and by now we could see that he kept the family going. In the closed torment of that pitiful shack, he was waging a hopeless battle against starvation. The da Silva children were living in a coffin. 9

When at last the parents came in, Gallo and I seemed to be part of the family. Flavio had already told them we were there. "Gordunn Americano!" Luzia said, pointing at me. José, the father, viewed us with skepticism. Nair, his pregnant wife, seemed tired beyond speaking. Hardly acknowledging our presence, she picked up Zacarias, placed him on her shoulder and gently patted his behind. Flavio scurried about like a frightened rat, his silence plainly 10 expressing the fear he held of his father. Impatiently, José da Silva waited for Flavio to serve dinner. He sat in the center of the bed with his legs crossed beneath him, frowning, waiting. There were only three tin plates. Flavio filled them with black beans and rice, then placed them before his father. José da Silva tasted them, chewed for several moments, then nodded his approval for the others to start. Only he and Nair had spoons; the children ate with their fingers. Flavio ate off the top of a coffee can. Afraid to offer us food, he edged his rice and beans toward us, gesturing for us to take some. We refused. He smiled, knowing we understood.

Later, when we got down to the difficult business of obtaining permission 11 from José da Silva to photograph his family, he hemmed and hawed, wallowing in the pleasant authority of the decision maker. He finally gave in, but his manner told us that he expected something in return. As we were saying good night Flavio began to cough violently. For a few moments his lungs seemed to be tearing apart. I wanted to get away as quickly as possible. It was cowardly of me, but the bluish cast of his skin beneath the sweat, the choking and spitting were suddenly unbearable.

Gallo and I moved cautiously down through the darkness trying not to 12 appear as strangers. The Catacumba was no place for strangers after sundown. Desperate criminals hid out there. To hunt them out, the police came in packs, but only in daylight. Gallo cautioned me. "If you get caught up here after dark it's best to stay at the da Silvas' until morning." As we drove toward the city the large white buildings of the rich loomed up. The world behind us seemed like a bad dream. I had already decided to get the boy Flavio to a doctor, and as quickly as possible.

The plush lobby of my hotel on the Copacabana waterfront was crammed 13 with people in formal attire. With the stink of the favela in my clothes, I hurried to the elevator hoping no passengers would be aboard. But as the door was closing a beautiful girl in a white lace gown stepped in. I moved as far away as possible. Her escort entered behind her, swept her into his arms and they indulged in a kiss that lasted until they exited on the next floor. Neither of them seemed to realize that I was there. The room I returned to seemed to be oversized; the da Silva shack would have fitted into one corner of it. The steak dinner I had would have fed the da Silvas for three days.

Read More on the Web

Biography of Gordon Parks: http://www.galegroup.com/free_resources/ bhm/bio/parks_g.htm

Photo gallery and video clips including one in which Parks speaks about Flavio da Silva: http://www.pdnonline.com/legends/parks/ mainframeset.shtml

UNICEF site on how poverty affects children: http://athena.tbwt.com/ content/article.asp?articleid=2414

Questions for Discussion

1. In which parts of the essay does Parks remain objective? Where does he become subjective by reacting to and commenting upon what he witnesses?
2. What references to and images of death can be found in this essay?
3. What other examples of figurative language does Park use?
4. In what parts of the essay does the author appeal to the senses?
5. Analyze paragraphs 2, 3, and 6 carefully. What descriptive techniques discussed earlier in this chapter do they use?
6. How does using contrast help Parks establish tone? How would you describe his tone?
7. Why does the author describe Flavio in such detail? Isn't this supposed to be a description of a place?
8. What happens in a place helps reveal its character. What do the events Parks narrates tell us about Flavio's home? Start with paragraph 7.
9. Why does the author bother to include the names of all the da Silva children? What other proper nouns do you find?
10. Why does he include dialogue—what the people say—in this essay?
11. In what paragraph does Parks prepare us for Flavio's coughing, which we learn about in paragraph 11?
12. Why does the author describe his hotel room?

Thinking Critically

1. What do paragraphs 11 and 12 reveal about the author's character and his purpose for writing this essay?
2. Why does Parks bother to tell us about the lovers kissing in the elevator? How do you react to their ignoring his presence and carrying on with their love-making?
3. Compare this essay to Jessie Sullivan's "If at First You Do Not See . . .," which also appears in this chapter. In what ways are they different? Is Sullivan's purpose the same as Parks's?

Suggestions for Journal Entries

1. Parks has a talent for piling detail upon detail to paint a vivid and compact word picture of what he describes. In paragraph 6, for example, he tells us that the da Silvas' stove was the "rusted, bent top of an old gas range resting on several bricks." In fact, the entire

paragraph shows Parks's ability to accumulate concrete, specific, and vivid detail.

Try your hand at doing the same by writing a one-sentence description of a common object. For example you might start with an ordinary piece of furniture—perhaps the desk or table you are working on right now—and then add details until you have a list that looks something like this:

> The desk
>
> The wooden desk
>
> The large wooden desk
>
> The large brown wooden desk
>
> The large brown wooden desk covered with junk
>
> The large brown wooden desk covered with junk, which squats in the corner of my room
>
> The large brown wooden desk covered with junk, books, and papers, which squats in the corner of my room.

Repeat this process, adding as many items as you can, until you've exhausted your mind's supply of nouns and adjectives. Then review your list. Can you make your description even more specific and concrete? For instance, the above example might be revised to read:

> **The four-foot-long dark brown oak desk was covered with my math book, an old dictionary with the cover ripped off, two chemistry test papers, today's French notes, a half-eaten bologna sandwich, and a can of diet cola.**

2. This essay contains both objective and subjective descriptions of "Catacumba," a symbol for poverty and human misery if there ever was one. Have you ever seen such a place in your own country? If so, begin recording details that might describe it. If this topic doesn't appeal to you, gather details about any public place such as a bus station, amusement park, sports arena or stadium, airport, shopping mall, or waterfront—just to name a few examples.

Whatever topic you choose, approach this journal entry in two steps. Begin by gathering details that describe the place objectively. Then, record your subjective reaction. Use clustering or listing to gather information that might describe this location.

Fish Camp

Bailey White

A native of Georgia, Bailey White (b. 1950) earned a B.A. at Florida State University. She taught first grade in Thomasville, Georgia, for more than 20 years. In 1993, White published her first book, Mama Makes Up Her Mind and Other Dangers of Southern Living, *which became a best seller. She is also the author of* Quite a Year for Plums *(1998) and* Sleeping at the Starlite Motel *(1996), from which "Fish Camp" is taken. Much of her work is light-hearted, but it is also very thought-provoking. As this essay shows, White is concerned about the interaction of people and nature. Indeed, "Fish Camp" proves that description can be used to make serious statements about our values, our environment, and ourselves.*

Preparing to Read

1. Look for elements in this essay that reveal White's ideas (values) about the way human beings should relate to nature.

2. White uses a number of concrete nouns, both common and proper, to strengthen her description of the camp. Mark these as you read the essay.

3. Also, pay attention to the things that Annie, the woman who runs the camp, says and does.

4. This is the description not only of a person but also of a place. Look for techniques the author uses to describe both.

Vocabulary

contemplative (adjective)	Thoughtful.
garishly (adverb)	Tastelessly, flamboyantly.
ponderous (adjective)	Heavy, weighty.
raucous (adjective)	Noisy, grating, gruff.
saunters (verb)	Strolls, walks in a relaxed manner.
stagnant (adjective)	Still, sluggish.

Fish Camp

Bailey White

THERE'S A SMELL OF STAGNANT WATER AND roses and cigarette smoke in the open   1
air. There's the gurgling hum of the circulating pump and the flash of wild
shiners in the concrete bait tanks. Occasionally the high-pitched "*eeee*" of an

eagle can be heard overhead, and at night there are the thumps of armadillos under the floors of the shabby little cabins, and from the creek and swamp the raucous squawk of limpkins.

In the screened front room of the main building there are a Coke machine, 2 a cricket box, and a display of garishly colored rubber worms, and under a scratched-up pane of glass on the counter are photographs of filthy, happy people, mostly barefoot, holding the fish they have caught—warmouth perch, bluegills and shellcrackers, sunshine bass, largemouth bass, speckled perch, crappie. Below each picture, important information is printed carefully with a permanent marker:

> Sweet talker buzz bait
> October 27, 1987—7½ pounds

I came down here to central Florida with my brother, who likes to fish. But 3 on this afternoon I stay on the porch with Annie, and we watch my brother's little boat skim down the canal and out into the black water of Lake Lochloosa.

"Georgia," says Annie. "That's nothing new. They come from all over— 4 Connecticut, Kentucky, Tennessee, Michigan, Alabama, Louisiana, Illinois, Wisconsin. They come to fish, honey, and they keep on coming back every year, until they pass away."

Annie is a big woman. She has a slow and thorough way of moving, like an 5 old elephant who knows his business. Annie has been owner and operator of Twin Lakes Fish Camp since 1974, through the bad years when the water was low and boats couldn't get in and out of the slips, through the sad years after her first husband dropped down dead of a heart attack on a fishing expedition, and into this year—a good wet spring, plenty of water in the lakes and the creek, the wild roses in full bloom along the canal, and Ted, an industrious cousin retired from the military, repairing boat motors on weekends.

Annie takes a contemplative drag on her cigarette. "Oh yes," she says, 6 "they're old when they come. Only trouble is, they get to be like family, you see, and it tears you up when they pass away."

Inside, the house is dark and cool. On the walls are framed prints of her- 7 ons and egrets in cypress swamps and watery glades. But the pictures look dry and dull compared to the view out any of Annie's windows, where every green thing glistens, the water in the lakes and creek glows black, and even the air shimmers with light and moisture.

On the kitchen table are strewn the body parts of a dismantled wooden 8 Easter bunny. Annie carefully puts him together—his pair of pink-lined ears, back legs, and tail fit into sawed-out slots on his back—and sets him up on the Formica tabletop. She stands back and gives him a look.

"Harry made him," she says. "Harry's one of my boyfriends. That's why 9 I got so many china cabinets, honey, to put all this stuff they give me." Sure enough, the walls are lined with glass-fronted cabinets, and every shelf is filled with objects of art and craft, neatly arranged.

"Yep," says Annie, "Harry, he misdialed the telephone one day up in 10 Gainesville, drunk, got me by mistake, came out to fish, and been coming ever since. Nine, ten years, out of Michigan."

Annie peers down into the bait tank, scoops out a dead shiner, and flips it 11 over into a potted tomato plant.

"Most of them are nice," she says, "but you do get your funny ones, 12 weird—well, different. I shouldn't say 'weird.' In the spring of the year, honey, most of them come out of Ohio."

Twin Lakes Fish Camp provides trailer hookups, tent camping sites, and 13 several little cottages. In an effort to encourage good housekeeping Annie has put up neatly lettered signs in the kitchens:

Do not clean fish in the sink
Please wash up

The cottages are neat and clean, with stacks of mismatched towels and 14 washrags in the bathrooms, plastic dishes in the kitchen cupboards, and an assortment of fish-cleaning gadgets in the drawers. But the floors feel spongy with moisture, and the air is saturated with the smell of mildew and fried fish. Behind the cabins are a bait house and a vegetable garden, and across the path are the boat slip, with boats and canoes lined up under a tin-roofed shed, and a ramp where you can launch your own boat (one dollar).

"There goes Sam Martin," says Annie. A spidery looking old man climbs 15 carefully down into a boat and gently nudges it out into the slip. "He's an old bachelor, never been married. All he's got is high blood pressure. He's been coming since 1978, and still fishing. Now there's some of them don't fish. Thelma, she don't fish. She just comes down and stays in a travel trailer six months. Thelma's from New Hampshire. She's into the peace movement, picketing, all that. Went to Mississippi to help them two gay-lesbian women. Been coming down here six years."

Annie is the only woman fish camp owner in Alachua County. "They wanted 16 to see me go under," she says. "They wanted to see me fall on my face. I had to outlast 'em. Now I'm the only one still here—but one, Jimmy Easterbrook at North Bank Fish Camp. We're buddies now. I told him, 'Jimmy, if you give up, I'll give up.' See, honey, I'm one of them determinationed people."

Annie hauls herself out of her chair, nets a shiner from the tank, and throws 17 it out the screen door. A big white heron gallops out of the creek on his gawky orange legs and gobbles it up. Then he saunters delicately back down the bank where he poses gracefully, surrounded by shining black and green.

"That's Fred," says Annie. She continues, "Yep, in '89 the water was so low 18 there was grass growing in the boat slip. Had to mow it with a lawn mower. Weeds higher than your head in the canal—we cut 'em with a Weed Eater. Three years of drought. I had ulcers from the stress, honey. I was afraid to lose everything. But one Sunday in 1991 I went to church and I told Him, 'I can't do nothing about this, Lord, it's your problem. I'm trucking on with my life.' And I did."

Annie takes me on a tour of the fish camp. She shows me the fishy- 19
smelling bait house, with tanks of wild shiners, grass shrimp, and minnows.
She shows me the little pepper, cucumber, and tomato plants she has started
in plastic tubs, the boat slip, and the "couples cabin." It has a basket filled with
old *Woman's Day* magazines, ruffled curtains at the windows, and framed pictures of kittens and fawns on the walls. She shows me the metal shed up the
hill where she gives parties.

"My birthday one year they brought me two bushels of oysters. We 20
ate oysters every which way—raw, fried, stewed, and steamed. And, honey,
Thanksgiving and Christmas?" She lays a hand on my arm and says confiden-
tially, "I've got people, before they pass away, rather have Thanksgiving and
Christmas with me than home with the kids."

She shows me a giant turnip plant someone gave her. "It's my monster," 21
she says, and it is taller than she is, with thick deep green leaves. She digs up
a runner for me from another plant with flowers that look like red pinecones,
and wraps it up in wet newspaper.

"Dan Ross, why he's alive I don't know," Annie says. "Five bypasses. 22
Doctors in Fargo, North Dakota, told him to go home and die. He turned
around and drove down here, walked into the clinic in McIntosh having a heart
attack. Told me if he died, have him cremated. They told him, 'She can't do
that, she don't have power of attorney.' Dan's a sweetheart. He don't fish, now,
on account of his health."

We settle back down on Annie's screen porch. The sun is lower now, and 23
the sounds have changed from the bright midday chirps and whistles to the
settling-in sounds of late afternoon. Annie's cousin Ted and his wife come up on
the porch, and Harry comes in from cleaning fish. He's wearing short pants and
flip-flops. Annie gives him a hug and takes him in to show him how cute his
Easter bunny looks all put together on the kitchen table. Then they all sit in the
plastic sofas and chairs on the porch and smoke cigarettes and talk about fishing.
Annie says she and Dan Ross are going to go marlin fishing. Ted tells her she'll
get seasick. Harry tells her you have to pull four, five hours to land a marlin.

We look out at the canal, and they tell me about the developer who was 24
inspired by the movie version of *Cross Creek* to turn one of the uninhabited
islands in Lake Lochloosa into a town with stores, houses, and a golf course.
Local residents put a stop to it, and ospreys and bald eagles continue to build
their nests in the giant old cypress trees and long-leafed pines on the island.

"There's one eagle around here runs with a buzzard," says Annie. "They fly 25
around, eat roadkill together. I says to myself, Now that's different."

There is still light in the sky, but the sun has disappeared behind the trees
when my brother comes in. While he hauls up his boat, Annie gets her clip-
pers. I stand around and slap mosquitoes in her backyard while she picks me
an armload of Don Juan roses to take home.

"Listen, honey," she says to me, "don't pay any attention to them. I've got 26
my plans: there's one thing me and Dan Ross are going to do before he passes
away, and that's go marlin fishing."

Annie stands in the road and waves good-bye to my brother and me. Then   27
she turns and with that steady and ponderous gait she heads back up to the
porch.

Read More on the Web

New Georgia Encyclopedia article on Bailey White:
    http://www.georgiaencyclopedia.org/nge/Article.jsp?id=h-510
Links to several of her essays via RealAudio®:
    http://www.fsu.edu/~wfsu_fm/specials/bw/bwsound.html

Questions for Discussion

1. Where does White use proper nouns? Why is the word *Formica*
    (paragraph 8) capitalized?
2. Reread this essay and underline names of animals and plants that
    White mentions to make her writing more convincing.
3. To what senses does the author appeal in the beginning of the essay?
    Where else does she use sensory details?
4. What does White's description of the environment in which Annie
    has chosen to live tell us about Annie?
5. What simile is used to describe Annie in paragraph 5? What does it
    reveal about her?
6. Where else does White describe her physical appearance?
7. In several paragraphs, including 6, 9, 16, and 18, White allows Annie
    to speak for herself. How does what she says and how she says it
    reveal her character?
8. Why does Annie name the white heron that appears in paragraphs 17
    and 18?
9. Review some of the other things Annie does. What does her behavior
    tell us about her?

Thinking Critically

1. The camp and Annie seem perfectly suited to one another. Write a
    short paragraph in which you show that the camp is the perfect place
    for Annie to live and work. Make specific reference to the essay when
    you do this.
2. What is White telling us about the individual's relationship with
    nature? Again make specific reference to the essay when you explain
    this.

Suggestions for Journal Entries

1. In response to the first item of Thinking Critically, you might have explained why the fish camp is the perfect place for Annie to live. Now use freewriting, clustering, or listing to gather details about the kind of place that you believe would be perfect for you to live in.

2. Annie's personality makes her well suited to run the fish camp. Think about your personality, values, work ethic, talents, and interests. Then put down some details that might lead to a full-length discussion of the kind of job for which you think you are well suited.

Charisma Fortified by "Chutzpah"

Barry Shlachter

Barry Shlachter is a reporter for the Star Telegram *in Forth Worth, Texas. For more than a decade, he worked as a correspondent for the Associated Press, a service that provides news stories to papers around the world, in both Asia and Africa. Shlachter met, interviewed, and has written about Mother Teresa, the subject of this piece, on several occasions. Mother Teresa was born in Macedonia but left her homeland to join an Irish order of Roman Catholic nuns and eventually dedicated her life to serving the poor, the homeless, and the defenseless. She died at the age of 87 on September 5, 1997, in Calcutta, India.*

Preparing to Read

1. Indira Gandhi, mentioned in paragraph 3, was the prime minister of India until her assassination in 1984. Eva Peron was the wife of Argentine dictator Juan Peron. Eva enjoyed a great deal of political power until her death of cancer at age 33 in 1954.

2. *Charisma* means personal warmth, charm, allure, or appeal. The word is often associated with political leaders. *Chutzpah* is a Yiddish word meaning courage and determination. It too is rarely used when speaking of religious leaders, but both terms capture Shlachter's vision of Mother Teresa and play important roles in his title and central idea.

3. "Fortified" is also an important word in the title. Consider its meaning as you read on.

Vocabulary

aimlessly (adverb)	Without purpose or plan, disorganized.
bureaucrats (noun)	Government officials.
clerics (noun)	Priests, nuns, or other members of the clergy.
cynical (adjective)	Critical, skeptical.
epiphany (noun)	Awakening, realization.
fended off (verb)	Fought off, avoided.
habit (noun)	Nun's attire, clothing.
hospice (noun)	Place where terminally ill are cared for.
indifferent (adjective)	Unconcerned, apathetic.
sari (noun)	Indian dress.
understated (adjective)	Subtle.
unfazed (adjective)	Undisturbed.
vestige (noun)	Trace.

Charisma Fortified by "Chutzpah"

Barry Shlachter

S HE WAS A tiny woman who spoke remarkably simple words. Yet Mother 1
Teresa used that unadorned speech to bend the will of indifferent bureaucrats, cynical journalists and at least one of the world's most despised tyrants.

I know: I watched her. 2

If she had gone into politics instead of missionary work, I thought after 3
first meeting her after a 1977 cyclone in India, she would have put an Indira
Gandhi or an Eva Peron to shame. That thought was reinforced upon seeing
her again two years later when she won the Nobel Peace Prize and during the
1984 Ethiopian famine.

Few could resist this woman in the home-spun sari-like habit. Born in 4
what is now Macedonia of ethnic Albanian parents, she came to India with an
Irish order, became a naturalized Indian, and founded her own Missionaries of
Charity at a time when foreign clerics were seen as an unwanted vestige of the
colonial era. Ministering to the poorest of Calcutta's poor, she won national,
then world, fame for her selfless work.

On a stretch of coastal road in south India, she once came upon a group of 5
government doctors stranded when their vehicle broke down. After she spoke
to them briefly, they unanimously volunteered to join her cyclone relief effort,
abandoning their own assignments.

"It's hard to say 'no' to a living saint," explained a relief official who knew 6
her, a Hindu like the majority of Indians. "Few are left unaffected by her
charisma," a priest told me. It was that understated charisma, fortified with
well-intentioned chutzpah, that helped bring about what she invariably called
"God's miracles."

Her caravan of trucks and cars made its way to Mandapakala, once a pros- 7
perous farming community flattened by the storm. It was piled with corpses
that day Mother Teresa arrived to supervise relief operations. Methodically,
she issued instructions on the disposal of bodies, a health hazard to the
living.

"The best thing would be to build a single long trench and lay the bodies 8
in a file," she crisply told members of her order and a crowd of volunteers she
had attracted along the way. "That, we discovered, was the simplest method
when the floods took their toll in Jalpaiguri in Bengal last year."

Many of the survivors wandered aimlessly about the village or picked 9
through rubble in search of a pot to hold water or boil rice. A woman called to
Mother Teresa, pointing to her only surviving family member, a 6-year-old deaf
mute, and asked: "What will I do with him? Is he worth anything?" The boy
approached the nun and played with her wooden rosary. Mother Teresa gathered him in her arms and the child, unable to speak, gurgled with delight.

"See," she told the distraught mother. "The child is happy." 10

Turning to those accompanying her, the nun said: "Where there is tragedy, 11 there is salvation. Even when the mother cries, the child finds happiness. It is eternal."

In Ethiopia, I witnessed two small "miracles" during a visit by Mother 12 Teresa—and those were aside from all the life-saving efforts by her missionaries among the starving.

Toward the end of my second or third stint in Ethiopia, an Associated Press 13 colleague based in Zimbabwe flew up to relieve me. The late John Edlin was something of a legend in Africa press circles. A hard drinking New Zealander, he had lost count of the times his wife had thrown him out. Sent to cover Sen. Ted Kennedy's famine tour, Edlin was too pickled to dictate more than two paragraphs each night of what was a major story.

Then he met Mother Teresa.   14

It was an epiphany for Edlin. At first, he considered chucking his job to 15 handle her order's press relations in Ethiopia. (Mother Teresa did this all too well on her own.) In the end, the tough Kiwi became an overnight humanitarian who quietly set up and financed an orphanage for children who lost their parents in the famine. Then he returned to reporting.

If the 1984 drought was of biblical proportions, so was the raw cruelty of 16 the country's dictator, Col. Mengistu Haile Mariam. His Marxist regime killed an estimated 150,000 people, while Mengistu is widely believed to have personally strangled his predecessor, Emperor Haile Selassie.

It is well known that the country's Jews, known as Falasha, were perse- 17 cuted. But Mengistu was equally brutal toward a Lutheran-linked church and to practicing Roman Catholics, said my best source in Addis Ababa, the papal nuncio (the Vatican ambassador). Ordinary people were terrified of Mengistu and would not utter his name.

Unfazed, Mother Teresa requested a meeting with the dictator, telling 18 reporters she would ask him to hand over the late emperor's palace for use as a hospice. She didn't get the palace, but to the amazement of everyone I ran across, she received a piece of land smack in the middle of the capital.

For a journalist, interviewing Mother Teresa about herself was a task. Not 19 that she fended off such encounters; she just wouldn't say much about herself. Instead, she'd speak of miracles, large and small, that materialized, thanks to God, when they were needed most.

"It's His work, not mine," she told me at the Calcutta home for the desti- 20 tute and dying after winning the 1979 Nobel Peace Prize. "God is our banker, He always provides." She recalled a day at the home when "we found we had nothing, not a single piece of bread to give our people."

"You know what happened? For some mysterious reason, all the schools 21 suddenly closed that day and their bread was sent to us," she said.

"Now who else but God could have done that?"   22

Read More on the Web

Site features a short biography and several important links to other
   Internet sites: http://almaz.com/nobel/peace/1979a.html

Site includes links to writings and speeches of Mother Teresa: http://
   home.attbi.com/~motherteresasite/mother.html

Questions for Discussion

1.   Where in this essay does the author provide detail to show that
     Mother Teresa had charisma? Where does he provide evidence that
     she had chutzpah?

2.   Barry Shlachter tells us little about Mother Teresa's appearance
     in paragraphs 1 and 4. Yet, what he tells us is important to begin
     understanding her character. Explain what this information reveals.

3.   One of the ways to reveal character is to relate what others have said
     about your subject. Where does Shlachter do this, and how does it
     help him describe his subject?

4.   What a person does often tells us more about his or her character
     than what others say about him or her. Where in this essay does
     Shlachter use anecdotes (brief stories) to tell us about his subject?

5.   Shlachter includes his own insights into the character of Mother
     Teresa. What do these insights reveal?

6.   Why does the author bother to tell us about John Edlin's drinking
     problem (paragraph 13)? Why does he include so much about
     the brutal regime of Ethiopian dictator Mengistu Haile Mariam
     (paragraphs 16–18)?

7.   Reread paragraphs 8 through 11. Explain why leaving those
     paragraphs out would have made the essay far less effective.

Thinking Critically

1.   Recall what you know or have learned about Indira Gandhi and
     Eva Peron. If you need more information about these women, read
     about them in an encyclopedia. Then explain why Shlachter makes
     reference to them in paragraph 3.

2.   Reread the essay, paying special attention to the quotations Shlachter
     takes from Mother Teresa herself. Underline or highlight phrases
     or sentences that you think are especially telling of Mother Teresa's
     character and beliefs. Summarize these ideas by making notes in the

margins or on a separate piece of paper. Then turn your notes into a short paragraph.

Suggestions for Journal Entries

1. Many people believe that Mother Teresa will be sainted. Whether or not that ever comes to pass, Shlachter's essay paints the picture of a holy and charitable person who deserves to be held up as an example of human charity and unselfishness. If you know someone who you think might be an example to others, use interviewing, clustering, or freewriting to gather information that you might use to describe him or her. Focus on only one or two virtues that this person possesses.

2. In paragraph 15, we learn that journalist John Edlin experienced an epiphany when working with Mother Teresa. *Epiphany,* from the Greek word for "showing," means a revelation or an awakening. As was the case with Edlin, it usually results in a significant change. Do you know someone whose life has changed drastically because of an epiphany? Use focused freewriting or clustering to gather details that will help explain what brought on this realization and what changes it caused in his or her character or lifestyle.

Suggestions for Sustained Writing

1. If you read "If at First You Do Not See . . .," follow Sullivan's lead: describe a place you know well by presenting two views of it. For example, one view might be negative, the other positive. Another way to proceed is to describe what newcomers see when they visit this place as opposed to what you see in it. A good place to describe might be your neighborhood or other part of your hometown, your high school or college campus, a run-down but beautiful old building, or the home of an interesting relative or friend.

    Although your paper need not be as long as Sullivan's, it should use techniques like those found in hers. For example, appeal to the senses, include action, use figures of speech to create images, or describe the people who live in or frequent the place.

    Check the journal entries you made after reading Sullivan's essay. They might help you get started. Once you have finished several drafts, write an introduction that captures the readers' attention and expresses your central idea in a formal thesis statement. Put the finishing touches on your writing by correcting errors that will reduce its effectiveness or distract your readers. Be sure all your spelling is correct.

2. Read over the notes you made in response to both Suggestions for Journal Entries after Po's "Watching the Reapers." If you have not responded to both of these suggestions, do so now.

   Using description as your main method of development, write an essay in which you explain why you would or would not recommend that a good friend take a job at the place you have begun to describe in your journal. Before beginning your rough draft, try making an outline of your paper. For example, you might organize it in three sections, each of which covers a body paragraph or two. The first could describe the physical characteristics of the workplace itself. The second might focus on the kinds of activities—the work—that normally takes place there. The third might describe the people who work in or frequent the place.

   As you begin to draft your paper, remember that you are trying to answer a specific question: Would you recommend this job to a friend? If the answer is no, make sure you include sufficient negative details to support this view and vice versa. One way to introduce this essay is to address the reader directly, ask a question, or make a startling remark. A good way to end it is to restate or summarize some of the points you have made in the body of your essay or offer your reader advice.

   However you decide to proceed, make sure that you provide sufficient detail to make your argument convincing. Then, revise, edit, and proofread.

3. If you responded to the second Suggestion for Journal Entries after "Flavio's Home" by Gordon Parks, turn these notes into a full-length essay that describes a place about which you have already gathered information. Begin by recording even more details about your subject. If you can, brainstorm with a fellow student who is also familiar with this place.

   In the first draft, include details that paint an objective picture of your subject. Talk about the general layout, shape, or dimensions of the place, the colors of walls, ceilings, and floors, the kinds of furniture and other objects it contains. If you're writing about an outdoor place, mention trees, rocks, streams, bridges, park benches, walls, lampposts, and so on. In your next draft(s), add information about what the place looks, smells, and sounds like. If possible, make use of narration to re-create the kind of activity that normally occurs in this place and to introduce your readers to people who frequent it. In the process, begin revealing your subjective reactions. Use concrete details and vivid verbs, adjectives, and adverbs as well as figures of speech to let readers know what you think about this place and of the people you find there. Like Parks, do not be afraid to express your emotions.

After completing your second or third draft, write a thesis stating your overall opinion. Put this thesis in an introductory paragraph designed to capture the reader's attention. Close your essay with a memorable statement or summary of the reasons you are or are not planning to visit this place again. Finally, edit your work by checking grammar, spelling, and sentence structure.

4. Read over the journal notes you made after Bailey White's "Fish Camp." If you responded to the first journal prompt, you have probably already gathered a few details to describe a place that you believe would be perfect to live in. Make sure you have gathered the kinds of effective descriptive details that you have been reading about in this chapter. Now add even more details by engaging in some more freewriting or other type of information-gathering technique.

After making a brief outline of your paper, write a rough draft. As you revise this draft, remember that describing a place can involve appealing to the senses, using figures of speech, including concrete nouns—common and proper—talking about the kinds of people who frequent it, and even narrating events that take place in it.

If this assignment doesn't interest you, think about the kind of job that is ideal for you and that you might someday want to have. If you responded to the second journal item after White's "Fish Camp," you have probably gathered information about your personality, talents, and interests as well as the kind of job that is best suited to them. Turn these notes into a full-length essay that describes the environment in which you would like to work and which explains both the responsibilities and the rewards of the career you might someday pursue.

5. Reread the journal entries you made after reading Barry Shlachter's "Charisma Fortified by 'Chutzpah.' " Then, expand these notes into a full-length essay.

If you responded to the first suggestion you will be describing a person you consider an example for others to follow. To gather more information, discuss our subject with mutual friends, interview your subject directly, or recall anecdotes (brief stories) containing facts to support your belief that this person should be looked up to.

If this assignment doesn't interest you, use the notes you made in response to the second suggestion for journal writing to write an essay explaining how an epiphany (revelation) changed the life or character of someone you know. Like many good papers describing people, yours can rely on anecdotes as well as direct quotations. Begin by explaining what brought on this epiphany. In the rest of your paper, compare your subject's life or character after the epiphany to what it was before.

Whichever topic you choose, begin by making at least a rough outline. Then, go through the writing process carefully, making sure to revise several times and to edit carefully.

6. Most people send friends and relatives store-bought greeting cards on their birthdays. Try something different. Write a birthday letter to a friend or relative whom you love and admire. Begin with a standard birthday greeting if you like. But follow this with four or five well-developed paragraphs that explain the reasons for your love and admiration. Use your knowledge of your reader's past—what you have learned firsthand or heard from others—to recall anecdotes that support your opinion. In other words, show what in his or her character deserves love and admiration.

   Not everything you say in this letter has to be flattering. In fact, this is a good chance to do some mild kidding. So, don't hesitate to poke good-natured fun at your reader—and at yourself—as a way of bringing warmth and sincerity to your writing. Just remember that your overall purpose is positive.

   This assignment is different from most others. Nonetheless, it demands the same effort and care. In fact, the more you love or admire your reader, the harder you should work at revising and editing this tribute.

Writing to Learn: A Group Activity

You have read Shlachter's essay on Mother Teresa in this chapter. Some say that Mother Teresa should be declared a saint. Whether or not this occurs, few can dispute the fact that this tiny nun was an example of unselfishness worthy of imitation.

THE FIRST MEETING

Assign each student to research another great humanitarian. Here's a list of some figures some might want to learn more about:

Clara Barton	Martin Luther King, Jr.
Carlos Costa	Florence Nightingale
Father Flanagan	Albert Schweitzer
Mohandas Gandhi	Raoul Wallenberg
Dolores Hope	

Of course, you might choose your own subjects. As a matter of fact, one of you might find information on an organization such as the Red Cross, the Red Crescent, Save the Children, or Doctors without Borders. Just make sure that each student researches a different subject.

RESEARCH

Search for information on the Internet, in your library's book catalog, or in a CD or online database for periodicals and newspapers. If you are researching a person, summarize important events in his or her life and list significant contributions he or she has made. If you are researching an organization, define the group's objective and report on the work it is doing. As always, make photocopies of your notes for distribution at your group's next meeting.

THE SECOND MEETING

After distributing copies of everyone's notes, ask each student to explain what he or she discovered. Make recommendations for further research, especially to students whose notes need greater detail. Then ask everyone to turn his or her notes into one or two well-developed, well-organized paragraphs whose purpose it is to prove that his or her subject is an example of humanitarianism. Ask group members to bring photocopies of their work to the next meeting.

THE THIRD MEETING

Distribute and read the paragraphs each group member has brought. Then, ask one person to organize these paragraphs into a coherent essay that defines the term *humanitarianism* by using the subjects your group wrote about as examples. Assign a second person to write an introduction (complete with thesis statement) and a conclusion to this essay. Assign still another to revise and edit it. Finally, ask one other person to type and proofread the final version before submitting it to your instructor.

CHAPTER 7

Narration

Narration is the process of recalling events, usually in order of time (chronological order). In other words, it is storytelling. The arrangement of events is called the *plot*. Writers usually begin by relating the first event in a series, which usually sets the plot in motion. They usually end the story with the last event.

However, this is not always the case. Where a writer begins and ends depends upon the kind and purpose of the story being told. Some stories begin in the middle or even at the end and then recall what happened earlier. Others are preceded or followed by information that the author thinks important to fully understand the story.

More than 2,300 years ago, the Greek philosopher Aristotle taught that a narrative must have a beginning, middle, and end. In short, a successful story must be complete. It must contain all the information readers will need to understand what happened and to follow along easily. This is the most important idea to remember when writing narratives, but there are others.

Determining Purpose and Theme

There are two types of narration: nonfiction and fiction. Works of nonfiction record stories of actual events. Fiction, though sometimes based on real life, is born mainly of the author's imagination and does not re-create events as they happened.

Of course, the narrative method is used by both historians and journalists. Indeed, nonfiction can explain complex ideas or make important points about very real situations. Adrienne Schwartz's "The Colossus in the Kitchen," for example, exposes the evil and stupidity of apartheid, a political system once used in South Africa. In fact, many nonfiction narratives are written to explain an important (central) idea, often called a *theme*. They reveal something important about human nature, society, or life itself. At times, the theme is stated as a *moral*, as in Aesop's fables, the ancient Greek tales that teach lessons about living. More often, however, the theme of a narrative remains unstated or implied. It is revealed only as the plot unfolds; in such cases, the story speaks for itself.

Always ask yourself whether the story you have chosen to tell is important to you. This doesn't mean that you should limit yourself to events you have witnessed or experienced, although personal experience can provide information needed to spin a good yarn. It does mean that the more interested you are in

275

the people, places, and events you are writing about, the better able you will be to make your writing meaningful and appealing.

Finding the Meaning in Your Story

As explained earlier, you don't have to reveal the purpose or theme (central idea) of a narrative. You can allow the events to speak for themselves. At first, you may not clearly understand what the theme of your story is or why it is important. But that's fine. Writing is a voyage of discovery. It teaches you things about your subject (and yourself) that you would not have known had you not started the process in the first place. Just write about something you believe is interesting and important. You can always figure out why your story is important or what theme to demonstrate when you write your second or third draft.

Deciding What to Include

In most cases, you won't have trouble deciding which details to include, for you will be able to put down events as you remember them. In some cases, however—especially when trying to project a particular theme or idea—you will have to decide which events and people should be discussed in great detail, which should be mentioned only briefly, and which should be excluded from your story.

Showing the Passage of Time

The most important thing about a story is plot, a series of events occurring in time. Writers must make sure that their plots make sense, that they are easy to follow, and that each event or incident flows into the next logically.

A good way to indicate the passage of time is to use transitions or connectives, the kinds of words and expressions used to create coherence within and between paragraphs. (You can learn more about transitions in Chapter 2.) In an eyewitness account of the atomic bomb attack on Nagasaki, Japan, Michito Ichimaru uses such words and phrases to make logical connections and to indicate the passage of time.

> At 11 a.m., I was sitting in my room with a fellow student *when* I heard the sound of a B-29 passing overhead. *A few minutes later,* the air flashed a brilliant yellow and there was a huge blast of wind.

Describing Setting and Developing Characters

Establishing the setting of your story involves indicating the time and place in which it occurs. Describing characters allows you to make your story more believable and convincing. (You can find more about describing places and people in Chapter 6.) Remember that your chief purpose is to tell a story, but the people in that story and the time and place in which it occurs may be as interesting as the events themselves.

An important element in narrative is dialogue, the words a writer allows people in the story to speak. Dialogue can expose important aspects of a character's personality, describe setting, and even reveal events that help move the plot along. Writers often allow their characters to explain what happened or to comment on the action in their own words, complete with grammatical errors and slang expressions.

Making Your Stories Interesting and Believable

One of the best ways to keep your readers' interests is to use effective **verbs.** More than any other parts of speech, verbs convey action—they tell what happened. It's important to be accurate when reporting an event. You should recapture it exactly as you remember and without exaggeration. However, good writing can be both accurate and interesting, both believable and color-ful. You can achieve this balance by using verbs carefully. In Seamus Heaney's "Mid-Term Break," for instance, the speaker reports that his mother "*coughed out angry tearless sighs.*" He could have said that she was so angry she could not cry, but that would not have given us a sense of the emotional torture she suffered.

A good way to make your writing believable is to use proper nouns that create a realistic setting, that name real people, or that reveal other aspects of your story to make it more convincing. In "37 Who Saw Murder Didn't Call the Police," Martin Gansberg mentions easily recognizable place names such as Kennedy International Airport. He includes specific street addresses as well as the names of neighborhoods, and he identifies both the major and minor characters in this news story.

Writing about Ourselves and about Others: Point of View

The essays and poems in this chapter may be divided into two categories. The first, including Heaney's "Mid-Term Break" and student Diaz-Talty's "The Day I Was Fat," are autobiographical. They look inward to explain something impor-tant about the narrator (storyteller). They are told from the first-person point of view, using the pronouns *I* or *we*. In these selections, the narrator is involved in the action. Also included in this group is Schwartz's "The Colossus in the Kitchen," a student essay in which the young narrator is not the major charac-ter. Nonetheless, her voice is heard clearly as she comments upon institutional racism and tells us about one of its most innocent victims.

The second category includes Gansberg's "37 Who Saw Murder Didn't Call the Police," which reports on events involving others. Told from the third-person point of view, it uses pronouns such as *he, she, it,* and *they.*

Visualizing Narrative Elements

The paragraphs that follow are from "Padre Blaisdell and the Refugee Children," René Cutforth's true story of a Catholic priest's efforts to save abandoned children during the Korean War. The place is Seoul; the time, December 1950.

Describes setting and introduces the main character.

At dawn Padre Blaisdell dressed himself in the little icy room at the top of the orphanage at Seoul. He put on his parka and an extra sweater, for the Siberian wind was fluting in the corners of the big grey barrack of the school. . . . The water in his basin was solid ice. . . .

His boots clicked along the stone flags in the freezing passages which led to the main door. The truck was waiting on the snow-covered gravel in the yellow-grey light of sunrise. The two Korean nurses stood as

Describes other characters.

usual, ready for duty——pig-tailed adolescents, their moon faces as passive and kindly as cows.

Uses a transition to show passage of time.

By the time he reached Riverside Road the padre had passed through the normal first stage of reaction to the wind . . .; he was content now in his open vehicle to lie back and admire the effortless skill of the wind's razor as it slashed him to the bone.

Uses a metaphor, action verb.

Uses vivid adjectives and proper nouns to describe setting.

There's a dingy alley off Riverside Street, narrow, and strewn with trodden straw and refuse which would stink if the cold allowed it life enough. This alley leads to the arches of the railway bridge across the Han River. The truck's wheels crackled over the frozen . . . alley, passed from it down a sandy track and halted at the second arch of the bridge [in front of which] lay a pile of filthy rice sacks,

Uses vivid verbs and adjectives.

clotted with dirt and stiff as boards. It was a child, practically naked and covered with filth. It lay in a pile of its own excrement in a sort of nest it had scratched out among the rice sacks. Hardly able to raise itself on an elbow, it still had enough energy to draw back cracked lips from bleeding gums and snarl and spit at the padre like an angry kitten. Its neck was not

Uses a simile.

much thicker than a broom handle and it had the enormous pot-belly of starvation.

Uses a transition to show passage of time.

At eleven o'clock in the morning, when the padre returned to the orphanage, his truck was full. "They are the real victims of the war," the padre said in his careful . . . colorless voice. "Nine-tenths of them were lost or abandoned. . . . No one

Uses dialogue to provide information and explain story's purpose.

will take them in unless they are relations, and we have 800 of these children at the orphanage. Usually they recover in quite a short time, but the bad cases tend to become very silent. . . . I have a little boy who has said nothing for three months now but *Yes* and *No*."

TRACKING THE PASSAGE OF TIME: "PADRE BLAISDALE AND THE REFUGEE CHILDREN"

We can divide the story roughly into three major sections, each of which is introduced by transitions that relate to time.

"At dawn . . ."
Padre Blaisdale and the nurses leave the
orphanage in search of orphans.

↓

"By the time he reached Riverside Road . . ."
They find the child in the alley.

↓

"At eleven o'clock in the morning . . ."
They return with a truckload of children.

Revising Narrative Essays

The first selection in this chapter, "The Colossus in the Kitchen," was written by Adrienne Schwartz, a student who recalls the racial prejudice aimed at Tandi, a black woman who worked for the author's family in South Africa. Realizing narrative essays require as much care as any others, Schwartz made important changes to her rough draft and turned an already fine essay into a memorable experience for her readers.

Schwartz—Rough Draft

Our neighbors, in conformity with
established thinking, had long called my
mother, and therefore all of us, deviants,
agitators, and no less than second cousins
to Satan himself. The cause of this

Use a quotation to show this? ⌈dishonorable labeling was the fact that we
had been taught to believe in the equality
and dignity of humankind.⌋

 That was why I could not understand the
apoplectic reaction of the neighbors to my
excited news that Tandi was going to have a
baby. After all, this was not politics; this
was new life. Tandi's common-law husband
lived illegally with her in the quarters

Connect these ideas better? ⌈assigned to them; complying with the law on
this and many other petty issues was not
considered appropriate in our household. It
was the Group Areas Act that had been⌋
responsible for the breakup of Tandi's
marriage. Her lawful husband, who was not
born in the same area as she, had been
refused a permit to work in the Transvaal, a

Make smoother? ⌈province in northeastern South Africa, where
we lived. In the way of many others, he had ⌉ *Needed?*
been placed in such a burdensome situation
and found the degradation of being taken

More vivid? from his wife's bed in the middle of the
night and joblessness more often than he

Clarify? could tolerate. He simply went away, never to be seen or heard from again.

Find a better place for this idea? The paradox of South Africa is complex in the extreme. It is like a rare and precious stone set amid barren wastes, and yet it feeds off its own flesh.

The days passed, and Tandi's waist got

Slow down? Show passage of time? bigger and pride could be seen in her eyes.

The child died after only one day.

Schwartz—Final Draft

Our neighbors, in conformity with established thinking, had long called my mother, and therefore all of us, deviants, agitators, and no less than second cousins to Satan himself. The cause of this

Uses a direct quotation to prove an idea. dishonorable labeling was the fact that we had been taught to believe in the equality and dignity of humankind.

"Never take a person's dignity away from him," my mother had said, "no matter how angry or hurt you might be because in the end you only diminish your own worth."

That was why I could not understand the apoplectic reaction of the neighbors to my excited news that Tandi was going to have a

Moves this information to a more baby. After all, this was not politics; this was new life. But the paradox of South Africa is complex in the extreme. The

logical place.

country is like a rare and precious stone set amid barren wastes, and yet close up it

Adds vivid details in a metaphor.

is a gangrenous growth that feeds off its own flesh.

Tandi's common-law husband lived illegally with her in the quarters assigned to them; complying with the law on this and many other petty issues was not considered appropriate in our household. It was the Group Areas Act that had been responsible

Adds transition to connect ideas.

for the breakup of Tandi's marriage in the first place. Her lawful husband, who was not born in the same area as she, had been refused a permit to work in the Transvaal

Removes unnecessary information.

Adds vivid verbs; makes sentences smoother.

and, like others placed in such a burdensome situation, suffered the continuous degradation of being dragged from his wife's bed in the middle of the night and of being denied work more often than he could tolerate. Eventually he simply melted away,

Adds transitions to show time passing.

never to be seen or heard from again, making legal divorce impossible.

As the days passed, Tandi's waist swelled, and pride glowed in her dauntless eyes.

Uses vivid vocabulary.

And then the child was born, and he lived for a day, and then he died.

Expands this sentence for dramatic effect.

Practicing Narrative Skills

What follows is an eyewitness account of the last moments of the Titanic, which sank in 1912 after striking an iceberg. The writer views the scene from a lifeboat after having abandoned ship. Practice your skills by following the instructions for each section of this exercise.

1. Underline words and phrases that make this an effective narrative. Look especially for vivid verbs, adjectives, and adverbs. Also underline transitions.

> In a couple of hours . . . [the ship] began to go down . . . rapidly. Then the fearful sight began. The people in the ship were just beginning to realize how great their danger was. When the forward part of the ship dropped suddenly at a faster rate . . . there was a sudden rush of passengers on all the decks towards the stern. It was like a wave. We could see the great black mass of people in the steerage sweeping to the rear part of the boat and breaking through to the upper decks. At a distance of about a mile we could distinguish everything through the night, which was perfectly clear. We could make out the increasing excitement on board the boat as the people, rushing to and fro, caused the deck lights to disappear and reappear as they passed in front of them. [Mrs. D. H. Bishop]

2. Important words have been removed from the following paragraphs. Replace them with words of your own. Use only the kinds of words indicated. Avoid *is, are, was, were, have been, had been,* and other forms of the verb *to be.*

> This panic went on, it seemed, for an hour. _____ the ship
>   TRANSITION
>
> seemed to _____ out of the water and stand there perpendicu-
>   VERB
>
> larly. It seemed to us that it stood _____ in the water for four
>   ADVERB
>
> full minutes. _____ it began to _____ gently downwards.
>   TRANSITION   VERB
>
> Its speed increased as it went down head first, so that the stern
>
> _____ down with a rush.
>   VERB
>
>   The lights continued to burn till it sank. We could see the
>
> people _____ _____ in the stern till it was gone. . . .
>   VERB   ADVERB

_____ the ship sank we _____ the screaming a mile
ADVERB OF TIME   VERB

away. Gradually it became fainter and fainter and died away. Some

of the lifeboats that had room for more might have _____ to
VERB

their rescue, but it would have meant that those who were in the

water would have _____ aboard and sunk them.
VERB

The Colossus in the Kitchen

Adrienne Schwartz

Adrienne Schwartz was born in Johannesburg in the Republic of South Africa, where she now lives. "The Colossus in the Kitchen" is about the tragedy of apartheid, a political system that kept power and wealth in the hands of whites by denying civil and economic rights to nonwhites and by enforcing a policy of racial segregation. Tandi, the woman who is at the center of this story, was Schwartz's nursemaid for several years.

Schwartz wrote this essay in 1988. Since that time, South Africa has abolished apartheid and extended civil rights to all citizens. Nelson Mandela, a black political leader who had been imprisoned by the white minority government during the apartheid era, became South Africa's first freely elected president.

Preparing to Read

1. The Group Areas Act, which Schwartz refers to in paragraph 7, required blacks to seek work *only* in those areas of the country for which the government had granted them a permit. Unfortunately, Tandi's legal husband was not allowed to work in the same region as she.

2. The Colossus was the giant bronze statue of a male figure straddling the inlet to the ancient Greek city of Rhodes. It was known as one of the seven wonders of the ancient world. More generally, this term refers to anything that is very large, impressive, and powerful. As you read this essay, ask yourself what made Tandi a colossus in the eyes of young Schwartz.

Vocabulary

apoplectic (adjective)	Characterized by a sudden loss of muscle control or ability to move.
ashen (adjective)	Gray.
bestriding (adjective)	Straddling, standing with legs spread widely.
cavernous (adjective)	Like a cave or cavern.
confections (noun)	Sweets.
cowered (adjective)	Lowered in defeat.
dauntless (adjective)	Fearless.
deviants (noun)	Moral degenerates.
disenfranchised (adjective)	Without rights or power.
entailed (verb)	Involved.

flaying (noun)	Whipping.
gangrenous (adjective)	Characterized by decay of the flesh.
nebulous (adjective)	Without a definite shape or form.
prerogative (noun)	Privilege.
sage (adjective)	Wise.

The Colossus in the Kitchen

Adrienne Schwartz

I REMEMBER WHEN I first discovered the extraordinary harshness of daily life for   1
black South Africans. It was in the carefree, tumbling days of childhood that
I first sensed apartheid was not merely the impoverishing of the landless and
all that that entailed, but a flaying of the innermost spirit.

The house seemed so huge in those days, and the adults were giants be-   2
striding the world with surety and purpose. Tandi, the cook, reigned with the
authoritarian discipline of a Caesar. She held audience in the kitchen, an enormous room filled with half-lights and well-scrubbed tiles, cool stone floors and
a cavernous black stove. Its ceilings were high, and during the heat of midday
I would often drowse in the corner, listening to Tandi sing, in a lilting voice, of
the hardships of black women as aliens in their own country. From half-closed
eyes I would watch her broad hands coax, from a nebulous lump of dough, a
bounty of confections, filled with yellow cream and new-picked apricots.

She was a peasant woman and almost illiterate, yet she spoke five lan-   3
guages quite competently; moreover, she was always there, sturdy, domineering
and quick to laugh.

Our neighbors, in conformity with established thinking, had long called   4
my mother, and therefore all of us, deviants, agitators, and no less than second
cousins to Satan himself. The cause of this dishonorable labeling was the fact
that we had been taught to believe in the equality and dignity of humankind.

"Never take a person's dignity away from him," my mother had said, "no   5
matter how angry or hurt you might be because in the end you only diminish
your own worth."

That was why I could not understand the apoplectic reaction of the neigh-   6
bors to my excited news that Tandi was going to have a baby. After all, this was
not politics; this was new life. But the paradox of South Africa is complex in the
extreme. The country is like a rare and precious stone set amid barren wastes,
and yet close up it is a gangrenous growth that feeds off its own flesh.

Tandi's common-law husband lived illegally with her in the quarters   7
assigned to them; complying with the law on this and many other petty issues
was not considered appropriate in our household. It was the Group Areas
Act that had been responsible for the breakup of Tandi's marriage in the first
place. Her lawful husband, who was not born in the same area as she, had

been refused a permit to work in the Transvaal and, like others placed in such a burdensome situation, suffered the continuous degradation of being dragged from his wife's bed in the middle of the night and of being denied work more often than he could tolerate. Eventually he simply melted away, never to be seen or heard from again, making legal divorce impossible.

As the days passed, Tandi's waist swelled, and pride glowed in her daunt- 8 less eyes.

And then the child was born, and he lived for a day, and then he died.   9

I could not look at Tandi. I did not know that the young could die. I 10 thought death was the prerogative of the elderly. I could not bear to see her cowered shoulders or ashen face.

I fled to the farthest corner of the yard. One of the neighbors was out 11 picking off dead buds from the rose bushes. She looked over the hedge in concern.

"Why! You look terrible . . . are you ill, dear?" she said.   12

"It's Tandi, Mrs. Green. She lost her baby last night," I replied.   13

Mrs. Green sighed thoughtfully and pulled off her gardening gloves. "It's 14 really not surprising," she said, not unkindly, but as if she were imparting as sage a piece of advice as she could. "These people (a term reserved for the disenfranchised) have to learn that the punishment always fits the crime."

Read More on the Web

A history of apartheid in South Africa: http://www-cs-students.stanford.
    edu/~cale/cs201/apartheid.hist.html

South Africa's Apartheid Era and the Transition to Multiracial
    Democracy: http://www.facts.com/cd/o94317.htm

Questions for Discussion

1. Why does Schwartz spend so much time describing the kitchen in paragraph 2?

2. What details do we learn about Tandi, and what do they tell us about her character? Why does the author call her a "colossus"?

3. Why are we told so little about the story's characters other than Tandi?

4. Why does Schwartz recall events from Tandi's past (paragraph 7)?

5. The author makes especially good use of verbs in the last half of this essay. Find some examples.

6. Where does Schwartz use dialogue, and what does it reveal?

Thinking Critically

1. Apartheid was not "merely the impoverishing of the landless" but also "a flaying of the innermost spirit," says Schwartz. What does she mean by this? If necessary, use the encyclopedia to do a little research on apartheid.

2. Is Schwartz's message or central idea similar to Romero's in "What the Gossips Saw" (Chapter 4)? Write a paragraph in which you compare (point out similarities between) the central ideas of these selections.

Suggestions for Journal Entries

1. Have you or anyone you know well ever witnessed or been involved in a case of intolerance based on race, color, creed, or sex? List the important events that made up this incident and, if appropriate, use focused freewriting to write short descriptions of the characters involved.

2. Schwartz's essay is a startling account of her learning some new and very painful things about life. Using any of the prewriting methods discussed in "Getting Started," make notes about an incident from your childhood that opened your eyes to some new and perhaps unpleasant reality.

3. Were you ever as close to an older person as Schwartz was to Tandi? Examine your relationship with the individual by briefly narrating one or two experiences you shared with him or her.

Mid-Term Break

Seamus Heaney

Seamus Heaney (1939—) was born in County Derry in Northern Ireland. The son of a farmer, Heaney took a B.A. at Queen's University in Belfast and then began teaching in secondary school. He is now professor of poetry at Oxford University in England and has been a visiting lecturer at Harvard University and at the University of California. Called the greatest living Irish poet, Heaney has won many awards including the Nobel Prize for literature (1995), the most prestigious honor a writer can receive. His poems focus on the land, people, and history of Northern Ireland. Some of his works also discuss the political and religious turmoil that have plagued his country. Collections of Heaney's poetry include Field Work *(1979),* Station Island *(1984), and* The Hero Lantern *(1987).*

Preparing to Read

1. What does the title tell us about the speaker of this poem?
2. As you read the first stanza (verse paragraph), ask yourself why the speaker tells us about spending "all morning in the college sick bay [infirmary]."
3. At the beginning of the poem, the speaker mentions bells ringing. For what might this prepare us?

Vocabulary

gaudy (adjective)	Conspicuous, ugly, in bad taste.
knelling (adjective)	Ringing.
poppy (adjective)	Red or deep orange.
pram (noun)	Baby carriage.
snowdrops (noun)	White flowers that bloom in early spring.
stanched (adjective)	Wrapped so as to stop the flow of blood.

Mid-Term Break

Seamus Heaney

I sat all morning in the college sick bay
Counting bells knelling classes to a close.
At two o'clock our neighbours drove me home.

In the porch I met my father crying—
He had always taken funerals in his stride—   5
And Big Jim Evans saying it was a hard blow.

The baby cooed and laughed and rocked the pram
When I came in, and I was embarrassed
By old men standing up to shake my hand

And tell me they were "sorry for my trouble."   10
Whispers informed strangers I was the eldest,
Away at school, as my mother held my hand

In hers and coughed out angry tearless sighs.
At ten o'clock the ambulance arrived
With the corpse, stanched and bandaged by the nurses.   15

Next morning I went up into the room. Snowdrops
And candles soothed the bedside; I saw him
For the first time in six weeks. Paler now,

Wearing a poppy bruise on his left temple,
He lay in the four foot box as in his cot.   20
No gaudy scars, the bumper knocked him clear.

A four foot box, a foot for every year.

Read More on the Web

Biography of Heaney with links to recordings of his readings:
    http://www.ibiblio.org/ipa/heaney/
Biography of Heaney with a bibliography of and about his works:
    http://www.nobel.se/literature/laureates/1995/heaney-bio.html

Questions for Discussion

1. What transitions does Heaney use to move this brief story along?
2. What function does dialogue play in this poem?
3. What do the reactions of the speaker's mother and father reveal about them?
4. Comment upon the poet's choice of verbs in stanzas 5, 6, and 7. What use of adjectives, especially participles, does he make?
5. Explain how changes in setting help the speaker convey his reaction to the death of his brother?
6. Find examples of figurative language.

Thinking Critically

1. We are shocked to learn of the death of a child at the end of this poem, but Heaney has prepared us all along. Make notes in the margins where you find clues about the poem's ending.

2. What contrasts does Heaney draw in this poem?

3. Heaney attended St. Columb's College before entering Queens University. What might the word "college" mean as used in "Mid-Term Break"?

Suggestions for Journal Entries

1. In the Questions for Discussion, you were asked to consider the different ways in which Heaney's mother and father reacted to the loss of their child. Some people react differently to death than others. Use freewriting, clustering, or listing to gather details that might help explain how you or someone you know reacted to the death of a loved one. Try to use vivid language and be as detailed as you can as you gather this information.

2. In stanza 6, Heaney writes: "Snowdrops/And candles soothed the bedside." Find out more about "snowdrops" in an unabridged dictionary or concise encyclopedia. Then, using freewriting, compose a detailed picture of what you imagine this scene to be. Base your description on Heaney's words, but go beyond them by adding detail from your own imagination.

The Day I Was Fat

Lois Diaz-Talty

When she isn't waitressing part-time or taking care of her family of four, Lois Diaz-Talty studies nursing and writes interesting essays such as the one below. She credits her husband and children for encouraging her academic efforts. Nonetheless, as the essay shows, she is an energetic, determined, and intelligent woman, who is sure to succeed. When asked to write about a pivotal event or turning point in her life, Diaz-Talty recalled an incident that is burned into her memory and that has helped shape her life.

Preparing to Read

1. The significance of the event narrated in this essay is explained in its thesis, which appears near the end.
2. Diaz-Talty's style is conversational and often humorous, but her essay is always clear and focused. Pay attention to her use of dialogue, which captures the flavor of the moment.
3. Her title is unusual. What does it signal about what is to come?

Vocabulary

condiments (noun) Seasonings, flavorings.
committed (adjective) Determined.
ironically (adverb) Having an effect opposite the one expected.
limber (adjective) Able to bend easily, flexible.
notorious (adjective) Shameful, bad.

The Day I Was Fat

Lois Diaz-Talty

I WAS NEVER in great shape. As a child, I was always called "plump," and my friend "Skinny Sherri" was always, well, skinny. I could never sit Indian-style the way other kids did, and when I made the cheerleading squad in eighth grade it was because I had a big mouth and a great smile, not because I could execute limber splits or elegant cartwheels. Although I maintained a respectable weight throughout high school (after all, my "entire life" depended upon my looks and popularity), there was always a fat person inside of me just waiting to burst onto the scene.

Adulthood, marriage, and settling down had notorious effects on my   2
weight: I blew up! The fat lady had finally arrived, saw the welcome mat, and
moved right in. No one in my family could tell me I was fat. They knew that
I had gained weight, I knew that I had gained weight, and I knew that they
knew that I had gained weight. But to discuss the topic was out of the question.
Once, my mother said, "You're too pretty to be so heavy"; that was the closest
anyone had ever come to calling me fat. Later, my husband teased me because
we couldn't lie on the couch together anymore, and I just cried and cried. He
never dared to mention it again, but I didn't stop eating.

I had just given birth to my first child and was at least fifty pounds over-   3
weight. Nonetheless, I remember feeling that that was the greatest time in my
life. I had a beautiful new baby, new furniture, a great husband, a lovely house.
What more could anyone want? Well, I knew what else I wanted: I wanted to
be thin and healthy. I just didn't care enough about myself to stop my frequent
binging. I tried to lose weight every day, but I couldn't get started. Diets didn't
last through lunch, and I got bigger by the day.

One summer afternoon in 1988, as I was headed to the pool with my   4
sister-in-law Mary Gene and our children, I got into an argument with a
teenager who was driving fast and tail-gating our car. When he nearly ran us
off the road, I turned around and glared at him to show my disapproval and
my concern for our safety. Suddenly, we began yelling at each other. He was
about 18, with an ugly, red, swollen face. The few teeth he had were yellow and
rotten. He followed us to the pool and, as he pulled into the parking lot behind
us, our argument became heated.

"What's your problem, bitch?" he screamed.   5

"You drive like an idiot! That's my problem, okay?"   6

When I got out of the car and walked around to get the baby, he laughed   7
to his friend, "Ah, look at 'er. She's fat! Go to hell, fat bitch." And then they
drove away.

Once inside the gates to the pool, my sister-in-law advised me to forget   8
the whole incident.

"Come on," she said. "Don't worry about that jerk! Did you see his teeth?   9
He was gross."

But I couldn't get his words out of my mind. They stung like a whip. "I'm   10
fat," I thought to myself. "I haven't just put on a few pounds. I'm not bloated. I
don't have baby weight to lose. I'm just plain fat." Nobody had ever called me
fat before, and it hurt terribly. But it was true.

On that very day, as I sat at the pool praying that nobody would see me in   11
my bathing suit, I promised myself that no one would ever call me fat again.
That hideous, 18-year-old idiot had spoken the words that none of my loved
ones had had the heart to say even though they were true. Yes, I was fat.

From then on, I was committed to shedding the weight and getting into   12
shape. I started a rigorous program of running and dieting the very next day.

Within months, I joined a gym and managed to make some friends who are still my workout buddies. However, in the past seven years, I've done more than lose weight: I've reshaped my attitude, my lifestyle, and my self-image. Now, I read everything I can about nutrition and health. I'm even considering becoming an aerobics instructor. I cook low-fat foods—chicken, fish, lean meats, vegetables—and I serve my family healthy, protein-rich meals prepared with dietetic ingredients. The children and I often walk to school, ride bikes, rollerblade, and run. Health and fitness have become essential to our household and our lives. But what's really wonderful is that, some time between that pivotal day in 1988 and today, my self-image stopped being about how I look and began being about how I feel. I feel energetic, healthy, confident, strong, and pretty. Ironically, the abuse I endured in the parking lot has helped me regain my self-esteem, not just my figure. My body looks good, but my mind feels great!

I hope that the kid from the pool has had his teeth fixed because I'm sure   13
they were one source of his misery. If I ever see him again, I won't tell him that he changed my life in such a special way. I won't let him know that he gave me the greatest gift he could ever give me just by being honest. I won't give him the satisfaction of knowing that the day he called me fat was one of the best days of my life.

Read More on the Web

American Obesity Association site: http://www.obesity.org/

Surgeon General's site on being overweight and obese:
   http://www.surgeongeneral.gov/topics/obesity/default.htm

Questions for Discussion

1. Where does Diaz-Talty express the essay's central idea? In other words, which sentence is her thesis?
2. What purpose does the author's quoting herself serve in this essay? Why does she quote her mother?
3. Why did the author quote the exact words of the 18-year-old who harassed her? Would simply telling us what happened have been enough?
4. Why does Diaz-Talty bother to describe this person? Why does she make sure to reveal her attitude toward him?
5. Reread three or four paragraphs, and circle the transitions used to show the passage of time and to create coherence.
6. Find places in which the author uses particularly good verbs, adjectives, and adverbs.

Thinking Critically

1. Make notes in the margins next to details that reveal important aspects of the author's personality.

2. If you were in the author's place, how would you have reacted to the insult? Now think about an aspect of your personality or lifestyle that needs improvement. Write a paragraph that explains how you might improve it.

Suggestions for Journal Entries

1. Recall a painful experience that changed your life for the better. Answer the journalists' questions to collect details about this event and to explain how it helped you. For example, here is the journal entry Lois Diaz-Talty made in preparation for "The Day I Was Fat":

   When? In 1988, shortly after I gave birth to Tommy.

   What? An argument with a teenager who had been driving behind us. He called me fat.

   Who? I and a rude, 18-year-old stranger, who looked gross.

   Where? On the way to the pool.

   Why important? Because I *was* fat.

   How? His insult shamed me. Made me work harder to lose weight and helped restore self-esteem.

2. Use focused freewriting to gather details about how you reacted to an incident in which someone hurt, insulted, or cheated you, or did something else unpleasant to you. In the process, analyze your reaction to this event. What did it reveal about your character?

37 Who Saw Murder Didn't Call the Police

Martin Gansberg

Martin Gansberg was a reporter and editor at the New York Times *when he wrote "37 Who Saw Murder Didn't Call the Police" in 1964. This story about the murder of a young woman is doubly terrifying, for the witnesses to the crime might very well have saved her life if only they had had the courage to become involved.*

Preparing to Read

1. The setting is Kew Gardens, a well-to-do neighborhood in Queens, New York. One reason Gansberg describes it in great detail is to make his story realistic. Another is to show his readers that the neighbors had a clear view of the crime from their windows. But there are other reasons as well. Pay close attention to the details used to describe the setting.

2. Gansberg begins the story by using dialogue to report an interview he had with the police. He ends it similarly, including dialogue from interviews with several witnesses. Read these two parts of the narrative as carefully as the story of the murder itself. They contain important information about Gansberg's reaction to the incident and his purpose in writing this piece.

3. The story of Kitty Genovese is a comment about the fact that people sometimes ignore their responsibilities to neighbors and lose that important sense of community that binds us together. Identify this central idea, or theme, as you read "37 Who Saw Murder Didn't Call the Police."

Vocabulary

deliberation (noun)	Thinking.
distraught (adjective)	Very upset, nervous.
punctuated (adjective)	Were clearly heard (literally "made a mark in").
recitation (noun)	Speech, lecture.
Tudor (adjective)	Type of architecture in which the beams are exposed.

37 Who Saw Murder Didn't Call the Police

Martin Gansberg

For more than half an hour 38 respectable, law-abiding citizens in Queens 1
watched a killer stalk and stab a woman in three separate attacks in Kew
Gardens.

Twice their chatter and the sudden glow of their bedroom lights inter- 2
rupted him and frightened him off. Each time he returned, sought her out, and
stabbed her again. Not one person telephoned the police during the assault;
one witness called after the woman was dead.

That was two weeks ago today.   3

Still shocked is Assistant Chief Inspector Frederick M. Lussen, in charge of 4
the borough's detectives and a veteran of 25 years of homicide investigations.
He can give a matter-of-fact recitation on many murders. But the Kew Gardens
slaying baffles him—not because it is a murder, but because the "good people"
failed to call the police.

"As we have reconstructed the crime," he said, "the assailant had three 5
chances to kill this woman during a 35-minute period. He returned twice to
complete the job. If we had been called when he first attacked, the woman
might not be dead now."

This is what the police say happened beginning at 3:20 A.M. in the staid, 6
middle-class, tree-lined Austin Street area:

Twenty-eight-year-old Catherine Genovese, who was called Kitty by almost 7
everyone in the neighborhood, was returning home from her job as manager
of a bar in Hollis. She parked her red Fiat in a lot adjacent to the Kew Gardens
Long Island Railroad Station, facing Mowbray Place. Like many residents of
the neighborhood, she had parked there day after day since her arrival from
Connecticut a year ago, although the railroad frowns on the practice.

She turned off the lights of her car, locked the door, and started to walk the 8
100 feet to the entrance of her apartment at 82-70 Austin Street, which is in a
Tudor building, with stores in the first floor and apartments on the second.

The entrance to the apartment is in the rear of the building because the 9
front is rented to retail stores. At night the quiet neighborhood is shrouded in
the slumbering darkness that marks most residential areas.

Miss Genovese noticed a man at the far end of the lot, near a seven-story 10
apartment house at 82-40 Austin Street. She halted. Then, nervously, she
headed up Austin Street toward Lefferts Boulevard, where there is a call box to
the 102nd Police Precinct in nearby Richmond Hill.

She got as far as a street light in front of a bookstore before the man 11
grabbed her. She screamed. Lights went on in the 10-story apartment house at
82-67 Austin Street, which faces the bookstore. Windows slid open and voices
punctuated the early-morning stillness.

Miss Genovese screamed: "Oh, my God, he stabbed me! Please help me! 12
Please help me!"

From one of the upper windows in the apartment house, a man called 13
down: "Let that girl alone!"

The assailant looked up at him, shrugged and walked down Austin Street 14
toward a white sedan parked a short distance away. Miss Genovese struggled
to her feet.

Lights went out. The killer returned to Miss Genovese, now trying to make 15
her way around the side of the building by the parking lot to got to her apartment. The assailant stabbed her again.

"I'm dying!" She shrieked. "I'm dying!"   16

Windows were opened again, and lights went on in many apartments. The 17
assailant got into his car and drove away. Miss Genovese staggered to her feet.
A city bus, Q-10, the Lefferts Boulevard line to Kennedy International Airport,
passed. It was 3:35 A.M.

The assailant returned. By then, Miss Genovese had crawled to the back 18
of the building, where the freshly painted brown doors to the apartment house
held out hope for safety. The killer tried the first door; she wasn't there. At the
second door, 82-62 Austin Street, he saw her slumped on the floor at the foot
of the stairs. He stabbed her a third time—fatally.

It was 3:50 by the time the police received their first call, from a man who 19
was a neighbor of Miss Genovese. In two minutes they were at the scene. The
neighbor, a 70-year-old woman, and another woman were the only persons on
the street. Nobody else came forward.

The man explained that he had called the police after much deliberation. 20
He had phoned a friend in Nassau County for advice and then he had crossed
the roof of the building to the apartment of the elderly woman to get her to
make the call.

"I didn't want to get involved," he sheepishly told the police.   21

Six days later, the police arrested Winston Moseley, a 29-year-old business- 22
machine operator, and charged him with homicide. Moseley had no previous
record. He is married, has two children and owns a home at 133-19 Sutter
Avenue, South Ozone Park, Queens. On Wednesday, a court committed him to
Kings County Hospital for psychiatric observation.

When questioned by the police, Moseley also said that he had slain 23
Mrs. Annie May Johnson, 24, of 146-12 133rd Avenue, Jamaica, on Feb. 29
and Barbara Kralik, 15, of 174-17 140th Avenue, Springfield Gardens, last July.
In the Kralik case, the police are holding Alvin L. Mitchell, who is said to have
confessed to that slaying.

The police stressed how simple it would have been to have gotten in touch 24
with them. "A phone call," said one of the detectives, "would have done it." The
police may be reached by dialing "O" for operator or Spring 7-3100.

Today witnesses from the neighborhood, which is made up of one-family 25
homes in the $35,000 to $60,000 range with the exception of the two apartment

houses near the railroad station, find it difficult to explain why they didn't call the police.

A housewife, knowingly if quite casually, said, "We thought it was a 26 lover's quarrel." A husband and wife both said, "Frankly, we were afraid." They seemed aware of the fact that events might have been different. A distraught woman, wiping her hands on her apron, said, "I didn't want my husband to get involved."

One couple, now willing to talk about that night, said they heard the first 27 screams. The husband looked thoughtfully at the bookstore where the killer first grabbed Miss Genovese.

"We went to the window to see what was happening," he said, "but the 28 light from our bedroom made it difficult to see the street." The wife, still apprehensive, added: "I put out the light and we were able to see better."

Asked why they hadn't called the police, she shrugged and replied: "I don't 29 know."

A man peeked out from the slight opening in the doorway to his apart- 30 ment and rattled off an account of the killer's second attack. Why hadn't he called the police at the time? "I was tired," he said without emotion. "I went back to bed."

It was 4:25 A.M. when the ambulance arrived to take the body of Miss 31 Genovese. It drove off. "Then," a solemn police detective said, "the people came out."

Read More on the Web

De May, J. "Kitty Genovese: What You Think You Know about the Case Might Not Be True." *A Picture History of Kew Gardens*. 9 July 2005: http://www.oldkewgardens.com/ss-nytimes-3a.html

"Kitty Genovese": http://www.answers.com/topic/kitty-genovese

Questions for Discussion

1. Catherine Genovese "was called Kitty by almost everyone in the neighborhood" (paragraph 7). What does this fact reveal about her relationship with her neighbors?
2. In Preparing to Read, you learned that there are several reasons for Gansberg's including details to describe the setting of this story. In what kind of neighborhood does the murder take place? What kind of people live in it?
3. In reporting several interviews he had with the police and with witnesses, Gansberg frames the story with dialogue at the beginning and end. What do we learn from this dialogue?

4. The author keeps the story moving by mentioning the times at which various episodes in the attack took place. Where does he mention these times?
5. In addition, what transitional words or expressions does Gansberg use to show the passage of time?
6. The story's verbs demonstrate how brutal and terrifying the murder of Kitty Genovese actually was. Identify a few of these verbs.

Thinking Critically

1. Make a list of things you might have done to help Kitty Genovese had you witnessed the attack.
2. Gansberg quotes several witnesses. If you had had the opportunity to interview these people, what would you have asked or told them? Write your questions and comments in the margins alongside their remarks.
3. The title of this article is "37 Who Saw Murder Didn't Call the Police." Yet the first line mentions 38 witnesses. Explain this apparent discrepancy.

Suggestions for Journal Entries

1. This story illustrates what can happen when people lose their sense of community and refuse to "get involved." Use focused freewriting to make notes about one or two incidents from your own experiences that illustrate this idea too.
2. Recall a time when you thought you were in some danger. Briefly describe what it was like. What did you do to try to avoid or escape physical harm?

Nagasaki, August 9, 1945

Michito Ichimaru

Michito Ichimaru has taught at the Nagasaki University School of Medicine in Japan and is a leading medical researcher of the long-term effects of the nuclear weapons used against Japan at the end of World War II. His eyewitness account of the dropping of the atomic bomb on Nagasaki, though published about 40 years after the event, is vivid testimony to the unthinkable horror of modern warfare. On August 6, 1945, an American warplane dropped the first atomic bomb on Hiroshima, inflicting 130,000 casualties and destroying 90 percent of the city. After waiting three days for an offer of unconditional surrender from the Japanese, the United States dropped a second atomic weapon on Nagasaki, killing or wounding an additional 75,000 people.

Preparing to Read

1. This essay clearly shows narration as a tool for recording history. In addition, note that Ichimaru uses this piece to warn us that history can and often does repeat itself.

2. Earlier you learned that in addition to using concrete nouns, narration relies on vivid verbs to make it convincing. Look for both in this essay. Also look for other narrative elements such the use of dialogue and of proper nouns.

Vocabulary

hypocenter (noun)	Area directly beneath the bomb blast.
malaise (noun)	Sadness, depression.
necrosis (noun)	Death of a tissue or organ.
rads (noun)	Units of radiation absorption.
tram (noun)	Streetcar.

Nagasaki, August 9, 1945

Michito Ichimaru

IN AUGUST 1945, I was a freshman at Nagasaki Medical College. The ninth   1
of August was a clear, hot, beautiful, summer day. I left my lodging house, which was one and one half miles from the hypocenter, at eight in the morning, as usual, to catch a tram car. When I got to the tram stop, I found that it had been derailed in an accident. I decided to return home. I was lucky. I never made it to school that day.

At 11 A.M., I was sitting in my room with a fellow student when I heard 2 the sound of a B-29 passing overhead. A few minutes later, the air flashed a brilliant yellow and there was a huge blast of wind.

We were terrified and ran downstairs to the toilet to hide. Later, when I 3 came to my senses, I noticed a hole had been blown in the roof, all the glass had been shattered, and that the glass had cut my shoulder and I was bleeding. When I went outside, the sky had turned from blue to black and the black rain started to fall. The stone walls between the houses were reduced to rubble.

After a short time, I tried to go to my medical school in Urakami, which 4 was 500 meters from the hypocenter. The air dose of radiation was more than 7,000 rads at this distance but I could not complete my journey because there were fires everywhere. I met many people coming back from Urakami. Their clothes were in rags, and shreds of skin hung from their bodies. They looked like ghosts with vacant stares. The next day, I was able to enter Urakami on foot, and all that I knew had disappeared. Only the concrete and iron skeletons of the buildings remained. There were dead bodies everywhere. On each street corner we had tubs of water used for putting out fires after the air raids. In one of these small tubs, scarcely large enough for one person, was the body of a desperate man who sought cool water. There was foam coming from his mouth, but he was not alive.

I cannot get rid of the sounds of crying women in the destroyed fields. As 5 I got nearer to school, there were black charred bodies, with the white edges of bones showing in the arms and legs. A dead horse with a bloated belly lay by the side of the road. Only the skeleton of the medical hospital remained standing. Because the school building was wood, it was completely destroyed. My classmates were in that building attending their physiology lecture. When I arrived some were still alive. They were unable to move their bodies. The strongest were so weak that they were slumped over on the ground. I talked with them and they thought they would be O.K., but all of them would eventually die within weeks. I cannot forget the ways their eyes looked at me and their voices spoke to me forever. I went up to the small hill behind the medical school, where all of the leaves of the trees were lost. The green mountain had changed to a bald mountain. There were many medical students, doctors, nurses, and some patients who escaped from the school and hospital. They were very weak and wanted water badly, crying out, "Give me water, please." Their clothes were in rags, bloody and dirty. Their condition was very bad. I carried down several friends of mine on my back from this hill. I brought them to their houses using a cart hitched to my bicycle. All of them died in the next few days. Some friends died with high fever, talking deliriously. Some friends complained of general malaise and bloody diarrhea, caused by necrosis of the bowel mucous membrane by severe radiation.

One of my jobs was to contact the families of the survivors. In all the public 6 schools I visited, there were many many survivors brought there by the healthy people. It is impossible to describe the horrors I saw. I heard many voices in pain, crying out, and there was a terrible stench. I remember it as an inferno. All of these people also died within several weeks.

One of my friends who was living in the same lodging houses cycled back   7 from medical school by himself that day. He was a strong man doing Judo. That night he gradually became weak but he went back to his home in the country by himself the next day. I heard he died a few weeks later. I lost many friends. So many people died that disposing of the bodies was difficult. We burned the bodies of my friends in a pile of wood which we gathered in a small open place. I clearly remember the movement of the bowels in the fire. On August 15, 1945, I left Nagasaki by train to return to my home in the country. There were many survivors in the same car. Even now, I think of the grief of the parents of my friends who died. I cannot capture the magnitude of the misery and horror I saw. Never again should these terrible nuclear weapons be used, no matter what happens. Only when mankind renounces the use of these nuclear weapons will the souls of my friends rest in peace.

Read More on the Web

Remembering Nagasaki: www.exploratorium.edu/nagasaki/

The Avalon Project at Yale Law School Site on Hiroshima and Nagasaki: http://www.yale.edu/lawweb/avalon/abomb/mpmenu.htm

Questions for Discussion

1. What is Ichimaru's thesis? What is his purpose?
2. Pick out a few of the transitional devices for moving the plot along in this essay.
3. Identify a few examples of Ichimaru's use of verbs that make his writing style vivid and convincing.
4. Where in this essay does Ichimaru rely on his senses?
5. In paragraph 5, he writes that "the green mountain had changed to a bald mountain." Where else does he create imagery to convey the horror of the scene?
6. What is the effect of his including the laments of people who survived the destruction of the hospital?

Thinking Critically

1. Given the widespread destruction Ichimaru describes, why does he bother to mention the death of the man who practiced Judo? Why does he discuss the burning of his friends' bodies?
2. Ichimaru speaks both as an eyewitness—a reporter—and as a physician. Find evidence of both of these roles.

Suggestions for Journal Entries

1. If you have ever endured the loss of a loved one or actually witnessed the loss of life, use your journal to record what you experienced.

2. Near the end of this essay, the author tells us that one of "his jobs was to contact the families of the survivors." Have you ever been in a difficult situation in which other people needed your help. Use listing or focused freewriting to explain the circumstances that put them in need and to discuss what you did to help them.

Suggestions for Sustained Writing

1. Have you ever been treated unfairly, belittled, or held back because of your race, religion, nationality, physical handicap, personal belief, or any other reason? Tell your story vividly and completely. In the process, explain what the experience taught you about other people or society in general. Express this idea as your thesis statement somewhere in the essay.

   A good example of an essay that uses narration to develop a strong thesis statement is Schwartz's "The Colossus in the Kitchen." In her first paragraph, Schwartz defines apartheid as "a flaying of the innermost spirit," then uses the rest of her essay to support that idea.

   Begin working by reviewing journal notes you made after reading this essay. Then outline and draft your paper. Like Schwartz, you can focus on one event. On the other hand, you might narrate two or three events to support your thesis. Either way, include details about the people in your story as you draft or revise. Describe their personalities by revealing what they said or did. Then, as you edit for grammar, punctuation, and spelling, pay special attention to the vocabulary you have chosen. Include proper nouns as appropriate, and make sure your language is specific and vivid.

2. If you responded to the first Suggestion for Journal Entries after Heaney's "Mid-Term Break," write an essay in which you explain your reaction or the reaction of someone you know to the death of a loved one. Now, add information to the notes you have already taken on this topic in your journal. If possible, interview or brainstorm with another person who has shared this loss—perhaps another family member or a close friend. Delve into your subject's character by explaining how he or she reacted to the shock, grieved over the loss, and dealt with the grief, if at all. Your narrative might span a few days, a few weeks, or even a few years.

   As you revise your first draft, add concrete details, figures of speech, and vivid verbs and adjectives. When you revise your second draft, try adding dialogue, and make sure you have described the setting and the people in your story well. Finally, check to see if you have included transitional devices and effective verbs to move the story along and to make it easy to follow. Next, edit your work for grammar; sentence structure, length, and variety; word choice; and punctuation and spelling. As always, proofread. This will probably be a powerful story—you don't want to spoil it with silly mistakes in writing or typing.

3. Use narration to explain what someone did to influence you either positively or negatively. Show how this person encouraged or discouraged you to develop a particular interest or talent; explain what he or she taught you about yourself; or discuss ways he or she strengthened or weakened your self-esteem.

    You need not express yourself in an essay. Consider writing a letter instead. Address it to the person who influenced you, and explain your appreciation or resentment of that influence. Either way, put your thesis—a statement of just how positively or negatively he or she affected you—in the introduction to your essay or letter.

    Before you begin, check the journal entries you made after reading the essay by Diaz-Talty. Then, write one or two stories from personal experience that show how the person in question affected you. After completing your first draft, try adding dialogue to your stories. Reveal your subject's attitude toward you by recalling words he or she used when answering your questions, giving you advice or instructions, or commenting on your efforts.

    As you revise your work further, make sure you have explained the results of this person's influence on you thoroughly. Add details as you move from draft to draft. Then, edit for grammar, punctuation, spelling, and other problems that can make your writing less effective.

4. The first of the Suggestions for Journal Entries after Diaz-Talty's "The Day I Was Fat" asks you to gather information about a painful experience that changed your life for the better. Use this information to begin drafting a full-length essay that explains what happened.

    You might begin the first draft by stating in one sentence how this event changed you; this will be your working thesis. You can then tell your story, including only those materials that help explain or prove the thesis. For example, Diaz-Talty says that being called fat helped her regain her self-esteem and her figure; every detail in her story helps prove this statement.

    As you write later drafts, add dialogue and descriptive detail about people in your story, just as Diaz-Talty did. If you are unhappy with your introductory and concluding paragraphs, rewrite them by using techniques explained in Chapter 3.

    Before you get to your final draft, make certain your paper contains vivid verbs, adjectives, and adverbs, which will keep readers interested. If it doesn't, add them. Then, edit and proofread your work carefully.

5. Have you ever witnessed or experienced an automobile accident, a robbery, a mugging, a house fire, serious injury, sudden illness, or other violence or misfortune? Tell what happened during this terrible experience and describe the people involved. However, spend most of your time discussing the reactions of people who looked on as the event took place. Were you one of them? What did they do or say? What didn't they do that they should have done?

   You might find inspiration and information for this project in the journal entries you made after reading Schwartz and Gansberg. Before you write your first draft, however, think about what the event itself and the onlookers' reactions taught you about human nature. Were you encouraged or disappointed by what you learned? Express your answer in a preliminary thesis statement. Write at least two drafts of your story, and make sure to include details that will support this thesis.

   Then revise at least one more time by turning what you have just written into a letter to the editor of your college or community newspaper. Use your letter to explain your approval or disappointment about the way the onlookers reacted, but don't mention their names. If appropriate, offer suggestions about the way your readers might respond if faced with an experience like the one you have narrated. Whether or not you send your letter to a newspaper, edit it carefully, just as if it were going to be published!

6. Michito Ichimaru endured the trauma that results from witnessing the loss of life. If you have had the misfortune of witnessing an incident in which someone was badly hurt or killed, write an essay that both re-creates the experience and explains your emotional reactions. Read the response you made to the first journal suggestion following "Nagasaki, August 9, 1945," for details that might help you get started.

   If this assignment doesn't interest you, tell the story of an event in which you offered your help to one or more people during a time of great need. Explain why these individuals needed your help, and tell your readers what you did to assist them. If you responded to the second suggestion for journal writing after Ichimaru's essay, read your journal entry before you begin outlining or drafting your paper. It may provide valuable information with which to get started.

   Whichever option you choose, try writing an introduction that uses a startling statement or statistic or that describes a scene. When it comes to concluding, take your lead from Ichimaru and look to the future or make a comment on the human significance of what you have just reported. As with any other essay, write several drafts. When it comes to revising your essay, pay special attention to the use of transitions as well as to the inclusion of proper nouns and vivid verbs.

Writing to Learn: A Group Activity

Martin Gansberg's "37 Who Saw Murder Didn't Call the Police" tells the story of a gruesome murder. In the process, it also reveals a great deal about the question of civic responsibility. The Kitty Genovese murder was an extremely high-profile case, which prompted a great deal of discussion about the kind of society in which we live. However, this was not the first nor the last criminal case to do so. In fact, we can learn a great deal about our society by researching criminality and the public's reaction to it.

THE FIRST MEETING

Begin the process of deciding on another high-profile murder case to research and write about. Here are some examples:

• The murders of Nicole Brown Simpson and Ronald Goldman
• The Scarsdale Diet Doctor murder
• The Unabomber murders
• The Lindbergh baby kidnapping
• The Leopold and Loeb case
• The disappearance and presumed murder of Jimmy Hoffa
• The murder of Marilyn Shepherd
• The Charles Manson murders
• The Menendez brothers' murder of their parents.

Choosing from this list or a list of your own, assign each member of your group to research one particular murder case and to write a short (about 100 words) preliminary report on it for presentation at your next meeting.

SECOND MEETING AND RESEARCH

After hearing reports on the cases that were assigned, decide which *one* of these will make the most interesting topic for a group report. Then ask each member of your group to research and to prepare a short report on one of the various aspects of this particular case.

Here is a possible list of questions to be covered—one per student writer.

• The victims: Who were they? Why were they killed? What was their relationship to the killer?
• The killer(s): Who was the killer? What was his or her motive? How did he or she carry out the murder(s)?
• The police: How did they identify and arrest the murderer?

• The trial: What was the outcome: guilty or innocent? What evidence was presented? Was the trial televised? Was the trial fair? Was there anything unusual about the trial to make it noteworthy?

• The public: What was the public's initial reaction to the murder(s)? What was its reaction to the trial and to the verdict?

Ask each student to make copies of his or her report for distribution at the third meeting.

THE THIRD MEETING

Distribute copies of the reports students have brought. Critique each and, if necessary, ask students to continue researching to add more detail. When these reports are in their final form, have one member of the group collect them and write a longer report that combines information from the separate, shorter reports submitted. Ask this student to make copies of his or her work for distribution at the next meeting.

FOURTH MEETING

Review the completed combined report. Then ask another student to prepare a final copy by revising and editing. Note: if more information is needed, ask the group members to give this directly to the student who has been asked to prepare the final copy. He or she should add this information when revising. He or she should also meet with yet another member of the group to proofread the final draft before it is submitted to the instructor.

Exposition

Many new writers begin to develop their skills by practicing the kinds of writing found in Section Three: Description and Narration. As you learned in previous chapters, description and narration usually involve writing about subjects that are concrete and, often, very specific—people, places, events, or objects that the reader can picture or understand easily. The primary purpose of description, of course, is to explain what someone or something looked like, sounded like, and so forth. The primary purpose of narration is simply to tell what happened, although many short stories and narrative essays do a great deal more.

At times, however, new writers face the challenge of discussing abstract ideas that can't be explained through narration and description alone. In such cases, they must rely on a variety of methods of development and techniques associated with exposition. *Exposition* is writing that explains.

Each essay selection in Chapters 8, 9, 10, and 11 explains an idea by using illustration, comparison and contrast, process analysis, or definition as its *primary* method of development. However, these selections also rely on other methods explained earlier in this book (see Chapter 2). In fact, most writers of exposition combine methods to develop ideas clearly and convincingly. Comparison-and-contrast papers frequently contain definitions, anecdotes, and examples; process analyses include accurate, sometimes vivid descriptions; and illustration essays sometimes use comparisons, anecdotes, and descriptions.

Whatever your purpose and however you choose to develop ideas, you will have to know your subject well, include enough accurate information to make your writing convincing, and present that information in a way that is clear and easy to follow.

Explaining through Illustration

One of the most popular ways to explain an idea is illustration, a method of development you read about in Chapter 2. Illustration uses examples to turn an idea that is general, abstract, or hard to understand into something readers can recognize and, therefore, grasp more easily. As the word implies, an illustration is a concrete and specific picture of an idea that would otherwise have remained vague and undefined.

For instance, if you wanted a clearer and more definitive notion of what your friend meant when she claimed to have met several "interesting characters" since coming to school, you might ask her to describe a few of those characters specifically and to show you in what ways they were interesting. Each of the people she discussed would then serve as an illustration or picture of what she meant by the abstract word *interesting*.

Explaining through Comparison and Contrast

This method of development involves pointing out similarities or differences, or both, between two people, objects, places, experiences, ways of doing something, and the like. Writers compare (point out similarities between) and contrast (point out differences between) two things to make one or both more recognizable or understandable to their readers. Let's say you want to explain a computer monitor to someone who has never seen one. You might compare it with a television set. After all, both have glass screens on which electronic images appear. To make your explanation more complete and accurate, however, you might also need to contrast these two devices by pointing out that only on television can one watch a baseball game, a soap opera, or reruns of *I Love Lucy*. Contrast also comes in handy when you want to explain why you believe one thing is better than another. For example, "Watch the Cart!" an essay in the introduction to Chapter 9, points out differences to explain why the author thinks women are more adept at grocery shopping than men.

There are many reasons for comparing or contrasting the subjects you wish to write about. Whatever your purpose, you may find that comparing or contrasting will help you bring abstract ideas into sharper focus and make them more concrete than if you had discussed each of your subjects separately.

Explaining through Process Analysis

Process analysis is used in scientific writing to help readers understand both natural and technical processes such as the formation of rain clouds, the circulation of blood through the body, or the workings of a CD player, for example. However, it also has a place in nonscientific writing. For example, you might want to use process analysis to explain how U.S. presidents are elected, how money is transferred from one bank to another electronically, or even how your Aunt Millie manages to turn the most solemn occasion into a party.

Process analysis is useful when you need to provide the reader with directions or instructions to complete a specific task. Subjects for such essays might include "how to change the brakes on a Ford Mustang," "how to bake lasagna," or "how to get to school from the center of town."

In each of these examples, the writer is assigning him- or herself the task of explaining, as specifically and as clearly as possible, an idea that might be very new and unfamiliar to the reader. And, in each case, the essay will focus on how to do something or how something is done.

Though it may often seem deceptively simple, writing a process paper is often a painstaking task and must be approached carefully. Remember that your readers might be totally unfamiliar with what you're explaining and will need a great deal of information to follow the process easily and to understand it thoroughly.

As a matter of fact, the need to be clear and concrete often causes writers of process analysis to rely on other methods of development as well. Among them are narration, description, illustration, and comparison and contrast. Of these, writers of process analysis rely most heavily on narration. After all, a process is a story. Like narratives, process papers are often organized in chronological order and explain a series of events. Unlike narratives, however, process essays don't simply tell *what* happens; they also explain *how* something happens or *how* something should be done.

Explaining through Definition

Unlike some of the other types of exposition, definition relates more to purpose than it does to any specific type of method or technique. In fact, definition essays employ a variety of the other methods of development—most often description, illustration, comparison/contrast, and cause/effect—to make their points. The purpose of definition, as you learned in Chapter 2, is to introduce a term, concept, or idea that may be totally unfamiliar to the reader. In some ways, it is like description. However, while description works with the concrete—subjects that can be seen, heard, smelled, felt, or tasted—definition works with both the concrete and the abstract.

However, even when dealing with the concrete, definition goes beyond description by explaining the nature of a subject. For example, while a descriptive essay might focus on a particular father and tell us what he looks and acts like, a definition essay would focus on the notion of fatherhood. A descriptive paper might reveal the beauty of the Northern Lights, while a definition paper would tell us what they are by also explaining what causes them, how they occur, and how they affect our civilization. Finally, as you will see when you read the essays in Chapter 11, definition can be used to deal with subjects that are purely abstract and that do not lend themselves to explanation by description—or by any of the other methods—alone. Examples include *materialism, jealousy, poverty, conservatism, faith, perseverance, youth culture, fatherlessness,* and *evil.*

CHAPTER 8

Illustration

You have learned that the most interesting and effective writing uses specific and concrete details to *show* rather than to *tell* the reader something. This goes for all types of writing, including exposition. One of the best ways to show your readers what you mean is to fill your writing with clear, relevant examples. Examples are also referred to as *illustrations*. They act as pictures—concrete representations —of an abstract idea you are trying to explain, and they make your writing easier to understand and more convincing for your readers. Illustration can be used as the primary method to develop a thesis in your expository writing.

Effective illustrations make reference to specific people, places, and things—familiar realities that your readers will recognize or understand easily. Say that you want to convince them that your 2008 Wizbang hybrid is an economical car. Instead of being content to rely on their understanding of a vague word like *economical,* you decide to provide examples that show exactly what you think this term means. Therefore, you explain that the Wizbang gets about 65 miles per gallon around town, that its purchase price is $4,000 less than its least expensive competitor's, and that it needs only one $50 tune-up every 40,000 miles. Now that's economical!

Several types of examples are discussed below. The important thing to remember is that the examples you choose must relate to and be appropriate to the idea you're illustrating. For instance, you probably wouldn't cite statistics about the Wizbang's safety record if you wanted to impress your readers with how inexpensive the car is to own and operate.

Specific Facts, Instances, or Occurrences

A good way to get examples into your writing is to use specific facts, instances, or occurrences relating to the idea you are explaining. Let's say you want to prove that the Wizbang does not perform well in bad weather. You can say it stalled twice during a recent rainstorm or that it did not start when the temperature fell below freezing last week. If you want to show that people in your town are community-minded, you might mention that they recently opened a shelter for the homeless, that they have organized a meals-on-wheels program for the elderly, or that they have increased their contributions to the United Way campaign in each of the last five years. If you want to prove that the 1960s were years of turmoil, you can recall the assassinations of John and Robert Kennedy and Martin Luther King, Jr., the antiwar marches, and the urban riots.

The selections in this chapter use specific facts, instances, or occurrences to illustrate and develop ideas. Grace Lukawska's "Wolf" is full of revealing facts about this animal. Specific instances and occurrences can be found in Philip K. Howard's "The Death of Common Sense." The same can be said of Richard Lederer's essay, which is filled with examples of anomalies, contradictions, and peculiarities to prove that "English Is a Crazy Language."

Statistics

Mathematical figures, or statistics, can also be included to strengthen your reader's understanding of an abstract idea. If you want to prove that the cost of living in your hometown has increased dramatically over the last five years, you might explain that the price of a three-bedroom home has increased by about 30 percent, from $100,000 to $130,000, that real estate taxes have doubled from an average of $1,500 per family to $3,000 per family, and that the cost of utilities has nearly tripled, with each household now spending about $120 per month on heat and electricity. Philip K. Howard's "The Death of Common Sense" makes good use of statistics.

Specific People, Places, or Things

Mentioning specific people, places, and things familiar to the readers can also help you make abstract ideas easier to understand and more convincing. If you want to explain that the American South is famous for the presidents and statespeople it has produced, you might bring up George Washington, Thomas Jefferson, Henry Clay, Lyndon Johnson, Martin Luther King, and Jimmy Carter. If you need to convince readers that your city is a great place to have fun, you will probably mention its amusement park, professional football stadium, brand new children's zoo and aquarium, community swimming pool, campgrounds, and public golf courses. Specific people, places, and things are mentioned throughout Howard's "The Death of Common Sense."

Anecdotes

As you probably know, anecdotes are brief, informative stories that develop an idea or drive home a point. They are similar to and serve the same purpose as specific instances and occurrences, and they are sometimes used with such illustrations to develop an idea more fully. However, anecdotes often appear in greater detail than other types of examples. Look for anecdotes especially in Howard's "The Death of Common Sense" and Howe's "Covert Force," an essay about women who, disguised as men, fought in the Civil War.

Visualizing Examples

The following paragraphs are from Alleen Pace Nilsen's "Sexism in English: A 1990's Update." They explain interesting facts about etymology, the origins of words.

States her thesis.

... in American culture a woman is valued for the attractiveness and sexiness of her body, while a man is valued for his physical strength and accomplishments. A woman is sexy; a man is successful.

A persuasive piece of evidence supporting this view are the eponyms——words that have come from someone's name——found in English.

Creates an interesting contrast.

[After researching this subject] I had a two-and-a-half-inch stack of cards taken from men's names, but less than a half-inch stack from women's names, and most of those came from Greek mythology. In words that

Uses specific instances.

came into American English since we separated from Britain, there are many eponyms based on the names of famous American men: bartlett pear, boysenberry, diesel engine, franklin stove, ferris wheel, gatling gun, mason jar, sideburns, sousaphone, Schick test, and Winchester rifle. The only common eponyms taken from

Mentions specific people.

American women's names are *Alice blue* (after Alice Roosevelt Longworth), *bloomers* (after Amelia Jenks Bloomer) and *Mae West jacket* (after the buxom actress). Two out of the

three feminine eponyms relate closely to a
woman's physical anatomy, while the
masculine eponyms (except for sideburns
after General Burnsides) have nothing to do
with the namesake's body, but instead honor
the man for an accomplishment of some kind.

Although in Greek mythology women played
a bigger role than they did in the biblical
stories of the Judeo-Christian

*Mentions
specific
mythological
figures;
mentions
things
readers
will
recognize.*

cultures . . . the same tendency to think of
women in relation to sexuality is seen in
the eponyms *aphrodisiac* from Aphrodite, the
Greek name for the goddess of love and
beauty, and venereal disease, from Venus,
the Roman name for Aphrodite.

Another interesting word from Greek
mythology is Amazon. According to Greek
folk etymology, the *a* means "without" as in
atypical or *amoral* while *mazon* comes from
mazos, meaning breast as still seen in
mastectomy. In the Greek legend, Amazon
women cut off their right breasts so that

*Tells an
anecdote.*

they could better shoot their bows.
Apparently, the story tellers had a feeling
that for women to play the active,
"masculine" role that the Amazons adopted
for themselves, they had to trade in part of
their femininity.

Revising Illustration Essays

Before writing "Wolf," student Grace Lukawska had completed a great deal of prewriting in her journal to get started. When she finished her first draft, however, she realized she would have to add more detail, restructure her essay, and improve some of her word choices to make her point effectively. By the time she finished, she had written several drafts, but the final product shows that careful revision is always worth the effort. Read these paragraphs from two versions of the complete paper, which appears in this chapter. Information in parentheses refers to Candace Savage's *Wolves,* a book in which Lukawska researched facts about her subject.

Lukawska—Rough Draft

Make introduction more interesting?

There are still popular misconceptions of the wolf as predator. Many people think that wolves kill for pleasure or just to

Include vivid details and examples to explain misconceptions?

show their dominance over other animals. However, the truth is that wolves are very fascinating and intelligent.

Their intelligence manifests itself in their behavior. Wolves belong to a group of animals who live in hierarchical groups. According to Candace Savage, a large, well-organized pack consists of an upper class—parents, a middle class—uncles and aunts, a lower class—children, and finally "helpers"

For what? Explain?

who are inexperienced hunters and who depend on the pack (55). Their role is to baby-sit youngsters while the other wolves are hunting (62).

Another example of wolves' aptitude is clear communication. The leader of the

Does this relate to communication?

group, usually the male, establishes regulations so that each animal knows whom it can boss and to whom it must <u>submit</u>. For instance, a middle-class wolf must obey the leader's orders; children and helpers must <u>submit</u> to their relatives. These rules help to prevent fights or disagreements in packs.

Say more about their language? Use examples?

Furthermore, wolves have their own language which is based on different sound levels in their voices. For example, according to Savage, a whimper indicates a friendly attitude; snarls convey warnings and admonitions (58).

Lukawska—Final Draft

For centuries, popular misconceptions have pictured the wolf as a terrifying predator

Creates vivid images that serve as examples.

that kills for pleasure. The name itself calls up nasty images: the glutton who "wolfs" down his food; the werewolf, who, during a full moon, grows hair all over his body, howls into the night, and claws beautiful maidens to death. Even in fairy

Mentions specific story, which readers might recognize

tales, such as "Little Red Riding Hood," the wolf is pictured as shrewd and bloodthirsty.

Makes thesis clearer, stronger.

But is the wolf really a cold-blooded killer? Not at all; the wolf is a magnificent animal which displays many of the characteristics we value in human beings.

The intelligence of the wolf manifests
itself in its behavior. The wolf's society
is well organized and hierarchical.

Mentions title of Savage's book.

According to Candace Savage, author of
Wolves, a pack consists of an upper class——
parents, a middle class——uncles and aunts, a
lower class——children, and finally "helpers,"
who are inexperienced hunters and who depend
upon the pack for their food (55). Their
role is to baby-sit youngsters while the
other wolves are hunting (62). Like humans,
wolves practice adoption. If parents die,
their children are cared for by another
family.

Becomes more specific.

The leader of the group, usually a male,
establishes regulations so that each animal
knows whom it can boss and to whom it must
submit. For instance, a middle-class wolf
must obey the leader's orders; children and
helpers must submit to their relatives.
This rule helps prevent disagreements and
fights.

New paragraph explains behavior, not communication.

Another indication of the wolf's
intelligence is the ability to communicate.
Wolves have their own language, which is
based on the use of different intonations.
According to Savage, a whimper communicates
friendship, snarls convey warnings and
admonishments, and a "special chirplike tone

Creates a new paragraph to discuss communication. Expands her discussion.

Uses description to create examples.

expresses sexual interest" (58). Like
dogs, wolves also use gestures and facial
expressions to communicate. <u>By moving their
foreheads, mouths, ears, and eyes, they</u>
express their emotions and announce their
ranks. Frightened wolves keep their teeth
covered, "eyes slightly closed, ears flat to
the head" (Savage 55). They also bend their
legs and tuck in their tails. Wolves that
are self-confident, on the other hand, point
their ears forward and bare their teeth.

Includes concrete, specific vocabulary.

Wolves of the highest rank reveal their
positions by <u>keeping their tails and ears up</u>
and by <u>looking directly</u> into the eyes of
other animals. Members of the pack show
respect for them; like dogs, they keep their
ears tucked in, their heads down, and their
legs slightly bent.

Practicing Illustration

Examples can be defined as concrete signs of abstract ideas. Below are several topic sentences expressing abstract ideas. Use the spaces below each to write a paragraph relating to each sentence. Develop your paragraph by using at least three examples of the kinds you have just read about. First, however, make a quick list of the examples you will use on a sheet of scratch paper. You can discuss them in detail when it comes time to write the paragraph.

Feel free to reword these sentences any way you like.

1. Wherever you go these days, people seem to be recycling.

_____

_____

_____

_____

_____

_____

_____

_____

_____

2. Some people I know are very materialistic.

_____

_____

_____

_____

_____

_____

_____

_____

3. A friend of mine often engages in self-destructive behavior.

_____

_____

_____

_____

_____

_____

_____

4. _____ (name a person) succeeds at whatever sport (or other type of activity) he (or she) pursues.

_____

_____

_____

_____

_____

_____

_____

_____

_____

5. Electronic devices play important roles in the modern home.

_____

_____

_____

_____

_____

_____

_____

6. People in my town seem to be getting richer and richer (or poorer and poorer).

_____

_____

_____

_____

_____

_____

_____

Wolf

Grace Lukawska

Born in Boleslawiec, Poland, Grace Lukawska came to the United States in 1986. After studying English for speakers of other languages, she enrolled in a developmental writing course in which she wrote this paper. In Poland, Lukawska had seen many television specials on wild animals. When asked to write about a fascinating animal, she immediately thought of the wolf. Lukawska is now a medical assistant.

Preparing to Read

1. The author develops this essay with examples, but she also uses comparison and description.
2. Pay particular attention to the essay's good organization. Consider what Lukawska has done to keep her essay focused.
3. "Getting Started," the introductory chapter of this book, explains that summarizing written materials is a good way to gather information. Another is to quote directly from a source. Lukawska summarizes and quotes directly from Candace Savage's *Wolves*. She credits this book by indicating in parentheses the pages from which she took information. These entries are called parenthetical (internal) citations. She also provides full bibliographical information about the book at the end of her paper. You can learn more about crediting sources in the website for this textbook (www.mhhe.com/rcw).

Vocabulary

admonishments (noun)	Condemnations, rebukes.
attribute (verb)	Associate with, blame for.
glutton (noun)	Someone who eats too much.
hierarchical (adjective)	Arranged by rank or importance.
intonations (noun)	Levels of sound, pitches.
manifests (verb)	Shows.
misconceptions (noun)	Incorrect opinions.
solidarity (noun)	Unity, mutual support, togetherness.

Wolf

Grace Lukawska

FOR CENTURIES, POPULAR misconceptions have pictured the wolf as a terrifying 1
predator that kills for pleasure. The name itself calls up nasty images: the
glutton who "wolfs" down his food; the werewolf, who, during a full moon,
grows hair all over his body, howls into the night, and claws beautiful maidens to death. Even in fairy tales, such as "Little Red Riding Hood," the wolf
is pictured as shrewd and bloodthirsty. But is the wolf really a cold-blooded
killer? Not at all; the wolf is a magnificent animal which displays many of the
characteristics we value in human beings.

The intelligence of the wolf manifests itself in its behavior. The wolf's so- 2
ciety is well organized and hierarchical. According to Candace Savage, author
of *Wolves,* a pack consists of an upper class—parents, a middle class—uncles
and aunts, a lower class—children, and finally "helpers," who are inexperienced
hunters and who depend upon the pack for their food (55). Their role is to baby-
sit youngsters while the other wolves are hunting (62). Like humans, wolves
practice adoption. If parents die, their children are cared for by another family.

The leader of the group, usually a male, establishes regulations so that each 3
animal knows whom it can boss and to whom it must submit. For instance,
a middle-class wolf must obey the leader's orders; children and helpers must
submit to their relatives. This rule helps prevent disagreements and fights.

Another indication of the wolf's intelligence is the ability to communicate. 4
Wolves have their own language, which is based on the use of different intonations. According to Savage, a whimper communicates friendship, snarls convey
warnings and admonishments, and a "special chirplike tone expresses sexual
interest" (58). Like dogs, wolves also use gestures and facial expressions to communicate. By moving their foreheads, mouths, ears, and eyes, they express their
emotions and announce their ranks. Frightened wolves keep their teeth covered,
"eyes slightly closed, ears flat to the head" (Savage 55). They also bend their legs
and tuck in their tails. Wolves that are self-confident, on the other hand, point
their ears forward and bare their teeth. Wolves of the highest rank reveal their
positions by keeping their tails and ears up and by looking directly into the eyes
of other animals. Members of the pack show respect for them; like dogs, they
keep their ears tucked in, their heads down, and their legs slightly bent.

Like people, wolves are sociable. In a group, they constantly check one 5
another by sniffing. To show affection, they nuzzle each other as if to kiss. To
express hostility, they lick their cheeks, wag their tails, howl, and even stick
out their tongues. This kind of behavior serves not only to locate companions
outside the pack but also to mark their territory and tell enemies of the family's
solidarity (Savage 59).

Regardless of rank or age, wolves enjoy playing games with other members 6
of their pack. Even the leader, who may appear to be aggressive and ruthless,

takes an active part in these activities, which include chasing one another and rolling over. Another sign of intelligence, such exercises not only give them pleasure, but also help them keep physically fit.

Wolves are natural-born strategists and planners. Hunting a large animal 7 like a deer or moose is very dangerous for a single wolf. Therefore, they hunt in groups. After locating a herd, one might act as a decoy to draw males away from the herd while the rest single out and attack the victim. Wolves kill only weak or sick animals, and they never kill more than they need. In case there is any excess, leftovers are buried near their dens.

The reputation from which wolves suffer is undeserved and unfair. Wolves 8 can be violent, and they are terrifying hunters. But they kill only to feed and protect their families; they never commit distinctly "human" crimes such as murder, theft, and rape. Wolves are not bloodthirsty monsters that should be feared and eradicated. They are magnificent animals, and they deserve their place on earth.

Works Cited: Savage, Candace. *Wolves.* San Francisco: Sierra Club, 1980.

Read More on the Web

NOVA site on wolves in the wild: http://www.pbs.org/wgbh/nova/wolves/howl.html

International Wolf Center site: http://www.wolf.org/wolves/

Questions for Discussion

1. What is the essay's thesis? What techniques does the author use to maintain unity and coherence?
2. What kinds of examples does Lukawska rely on most in this essay? Does she ever refer to specific persons, places, or things?
3. Where in this essay does she use comparison?
4. Where does she create verbal images? Why are they so effective?
5. What techniques for writing introductions and conclusions has Lukawska used? (Check Chapter 3 if you need to review these techniques.)

Thinking Critically

1. Consider another animal that has a bad reputation: a rat, a snake, a bat, a pig, a spider, or some other unpopular beast. Then in a paragraph or two discuss the positive qualities of this creature.

For example, many people hate and fear rats, but laboratory rats play an important role in medical research.

2. Reread Lukawska's introduction. Then list other examples that would illustrate the popular misconception of wolves as bloodthirsty monsters.

3. The author suggests that human beings can sometimes be more beastly than the beasts. What does she mean? Do you agree? Can you provide some examples?

Suggestions for Journal Entries

1. Think of an animal or species of animal you know well—your Siamese cat or all domestic cats, the neighbor's German shepherd or all shepherds, a bird that often visits your backyard or all common birds. List important things you know about this creature—anything that would provide clues about its behavior, lifestyle, or personality.

   Then ask yourself what this information tells you. Draw three or more general conclusions about the animal from the details you have listed. Write these conclusions in the form of topic sentences for paragraphs that you might later develop in an essay.

2. Are human families as well organized and as close as the wolf family? Think of your own family. Then write a paragraph in which you use illustrations to evaluate the kind of family to which you belong. Perhaps the best types of illustrations to use are anecdotes taken from your own experiences.

Covert Force

Robert F. Howe

This article first appeared in the October 2002 issue of Smithsonian *magazine. Robert F. Howe is a freelance writer based in California, who has published an article on Doolittle's Raiders in* Smithsonian.

Preparing to Read

1. Women are taking an increasingly active role in warfare. However, consider the position of women in America about 150 years ago. They didn't have the vote or, in most cases, the right to own property. They were discouraged from entering professions, and they certainly weren't admitted to the military. Keep this in mind as you determine the purpose of this essay.

2. Howe's essay uses information from *They Fought Like Demons: Women Soldiers in the American Civil War,* a book by Lauren Cook and DeAnne Blanton, and he discusses these two contemporary women in addition to telling the stories of women Civil War soldiers. To fully appreciate his purpose, ask yourself how discussing Cook and Blanton fits into a discussion of women soldiers.

Vocabulary

a.k.a. (abbreviation)	"Also known as."
alluded (verb)	Suggested, implied.
avenge (verb)	Get revenge.
buffs (noun)	People with an avid interest in a particular subject.
compilation (noun)	Collection.
covert (adjective)	Hidden, secretive.
cursory (adjective)	Casual, superficial.
depraved (adjective)	Morally corrupt, evil.
deranged (adjective)	Mentally unbalanced, insane.
destitution (noun)	Poverty.
fending (adjective)	Fighting, defending against.
inebriated (adjective)	Drunk.
medic (noun)	Medical officer.
prevailing (adjective)	Accepted.
tilled (verb)	Worked the soil, cultivated.
unadulterated (adjective)	Pure.

Covert Force

Robert F. Howe

AUGUST 30, 1862, proved to be yet another bloody day. Henry Clark was in 1
the thick of things, fending off Federal troops in the Battle of Richmond,
Kentucky, when the Confederate private caught an enemy shell in the thigh.
Clark was swarmed by bluecoats and taken prisoner.

It was presumably when a Union medic treated Clark's wound that the 2
soldier's tightly held secret was unmasked. Henry's real name was Mary Ann.
Indeed, she was a divorced mother of two.

When Federal troops realized that they had a woman on their hands, they 3
moved quickly to release her—as long as she swore to return to the life of a
proper lady. They even gave her a dress to wear. She agreed and was freed, then
quickly cast off the frock and made her way back to the rebel army, where she
was promptly promoted. Not long after, a young Confederate soldier—having
joined a crowd gathered around Clark, then apparently serving openly as a
female officer—wrote home: "Pa among all the curiosities I have seen since I
left home one I must mention, a female Lieutenant."

A curiosity, yes, but to the surprise of many Civil War buffs even today, 4
Clark was by no means unique. She was one of an estimated 400 women who
took up arms in the war; they were not nurses, or laundresses or cooks, but actual female soldiers disguised as men, who marched, mastered their weapons,
entered into battle and even gave their lives.

Various histories have alluded to women's roles in combat during the War 5
Between the States, but none have made so detailed and convincing a case as
They Fought Like Demons: Women Soldiers in the American Civil War. Coauthors
Lauren Cook and DeAnne Blanton spent more than ten years combing through
letters, archives and news reports to document some 250 women warriors.

"No one has accumulated this much data," says Cook, 46, who first tilled 6
this turf in her 1994 *An Uncommon Soldier* (Oxford University Press), a compi-
lation of letters from a female Civil War soldier. The authors' mission was not
just to catalog the combatants. Their extensive research convinced them that
the prevailing notions about women's participation in the war—that they had
to be deranged or depraved—were way off the mark.

"We felt those women had not been given their due, that they were thor- 7
oughly misunderstood by military historians and the general public," says
Cook, a special assistant to the chancellor for communications at Fayetteville
State University–UNC in North Carolina. In fact, Cook contends, "they were
just as successful as their male comrades, and what enabled them to be so successful was that no one knew that they were women."

What would compel a woman to march into that terrible combat—and 8
how could she conceal her identity in what must have been uncomfortably
close quarters? Blanton and Cook offer a number of persuasive answers. In the

case of Clark, for example, a bad marriage and the death of a brother-in-law at the hands of a pro-Union mob took such an emotional toll that she sought refuge in the military, according to a letter from her mother uncovered by the authors. But Martha Parks Lindley joined up just two days after her husband left for the 6th U.S. Cavalry. "I was frightened half to death," she told a newspaper. "But I was so anxious to be with my husband that I resolved to see the thing through if it killed me." It did not, and fellow troopers simply assumed that Lindley and the "young man" known as Jim Smith were just good friends. Then there was Charlotte Hope, who signed up in the 1st Virginia Cavalry to avenge the death of her fiancé, killed in a raid in 1861. Her goal: to slay 21 Yankees, one for each year of her beau's life.

Some joined to escape the misery of prostitution or destitution—a com- 9 mon problem with so few jobs open to women. Finance clearly figured into the decision of Sarah Rosetta Wakeman, alias Pvt. Lyons Wakeman, to sign up for the Union army. "I got 100 and 52$ in money," she wrote proudly. "I can get all the money I want."

Loreta Velazquez, a.k.a. Lt. Harry T. Buford, was one of several women 10 who fought simply for the unadulterated thrill of it: "I plunged into adventure for the love of the thing," she said after writing a postwar memoir called *The Woman in Battle*. Many women felt the keen tug of patriotism. Union soldier Sarah Edmonds, an immigrant from Canada, expressed thanks that she was "permitted in this hour of my adopted country's need to express a tithe of the gratitude which I feel toward the people of the Northern States."

"What surprised me most was the realization that women soldiers enlisted 11 largely for the very same reasons as the men did," says Blanton, 38. "Some were rebelling against the strict roles that society confined them in, but then there were women who went because the pay was good, or because everybody else in the family was signing up, or because they wanted to defend their country. Some just signed up to run away from home, just like so many boys did."

To get to the front lines, each woman had to pass herself off as a man. 12 Many were detected immediately and given the boot. But physical exams of the time tended to be cursory, and both armies were often so desperate for recruits that virtually anyone could pass. Occasions for discovery were limited; troops routinely slept in uniform, baths were a novelty and latrines were so foul that many soldiers sought refuge in nearby woods. A high-pitched voice or a lack of facial hair could be attributed to youth. Several women attempted to blend in by learning to cuss like sailors, taking up gambling, or even dating local young ladies.

Some female combatants were given away by ladylike mannerisms and 13 others were undone by boastings while inebriated. But as with Clark, most were unveiled only when doctors stripped away their clothes to examine a war wound.

A native of Grand Rapids, Michigan, Cook had virtually no interest 14 in the Civil War until 1987, when she toured the battle site at Gettysburg,

Pennsylvania. She was so moved by the experience that she joined a fife and drum corps and began participating in battle reenactments. Then, in 1989, during a re-creation of a military hospital at the Antietam National Battlefield in Sharpsburg, Maryland, she dressed as a male soldier "because I felt that was historically accurate." But when she visited the ladies' room, she caused a stir—not only among the women inside but with a ranger, who brusquely informed her that park rules did not allow women to participate in reenactments. "Their attitude was that the women of that era must have been oddballs, eccentrics and crazy, and didn't merit any kind of recognition or respect," says Cook. Her lawsuit against the Department of the Interior ultimately changed the rules.

A decade after teaming up to work on *Demons,* Cook and Blanton are still 15 fitting pieces of the puzzle. They cite the case, as it unfolded in letters written by soldiers, of a New Jersey woman who participated in the Union army's June 1862 siege of Richmond, Virginia, was wounded at the Battle of Antietam in September, and fought in the Union defeat at Fredericksburg in December. Just a few weeks later, on January 19, an astonished colonel in the Army of the Potomac wrote home: "A corporal was promoted to sergeant for gallant conduct at the battle of Fredericksburg—since which time the sergeant has become the mother of a child."

And there the story stops. "When she and her baby went home, was she cel- 16 ebrated or shunned?" Blanton asks. "I hope that a descendant will read our book and call up and say, 'Hey, that lady was my great-great-great-grandmother.'"

Read More on the Web

Primary sources (letters, diaries, etc.) written by women during the Civil War: http://scriptorium.lib.duke.edu/women/cwdocs.html

Text of Loreta Velazquez's *The Woman in Battle:* http://docsouth.unc.edu/velazquez/menu.html

Questions for Discussion

1. What is the purpose of this essay? Was it simply to tell readers about the Civil War's women soldiers?
2. What is Howe's thesis? Can you tell if this thesis is similar to the thesis of Cook and Blanton's book?
3. In what ways were women's reasons for going to war the same as those of men?
4. In order to be effective, illustrations must be believable. Are the illustrations in this essay believable? What makes them so?
5. Why were so many women able to pass themselves off as men without being detected?

6. Why does the author mention *The Woman in Battle* by Loreta Velazquez, a.k.a Lt. Harry Buford?

7. Comment upon the fact that Howe quotes Cook and Blanton directly as well as including direct quotations from women Cook and Blanton quoted. What is the effect on the essay?

8. Why does the author introduce this essay with an illustration? Which other method for introducing essays, which you learned about in Chapter 3, does Howe use? Which method for concluding essays, as explained in Chapter 3, does he use?

Thinking Critically

1. Reread this essay carefully. As you do, make marginal notes that will point out similarities between the women who fought in the Civil War and today's American women.

2. What can you tell about Cook and Blanton that might explain why they might be so intent about telling the story of women combatants?

Suggestions for Journal Entries

1. It should not come as a surprise that today women can be found doing a variety of jobs once reserved for men. Women are fire fighters, police officers, doctors, mechanics, sanitation workers, etc. Make a list of women you know or have learned about who hold jobs that 30 years ago might have been reserved for men. Or, make a list of men you know who hold jobs that your parents or grandparents might have thought were suited only to women.

2. Use the Internet to find out more information about women combatants in the Civil War or on the role women played in other American wars. For example, you might research the contributions women made on the home front and overseas during World War II. Or you might try to find out more about the American women who died in Vietnam. Print out any articles you find online and make notes in the margins using the techniques you read about in "Getting Started," which is at the beginning of this book.

English Is a Crazy Language

Richard Lederer

Richard Lederer (1938–) is a retired English teacher who devotes much of his time to writing humorous and thought-provoking essays and books on the peculiarities of the English language. In addition to Crazy English *(1989), the book from which this essay is taken, his other books include* Anguished English *(1989),* More Anguished English *(1994),* Sleeping Dogs Don't Lay *(2001), and* The Bride of Anguished English *(2002). All of them contain examples of the many wonders of our "crazy language."*

Preparing to Read

1. As always, pay attention to the essay's title.
2. Lederer uses many words that may be new to you. Not all of these are listed in the vocabulary. To fully appreciate the author's humor, use a dictionary to look up those words that you are not familiar with.

Vocabulary

annals (noun)	History, historical records.
bizarre (adjective)	Strange, odd.
culinary (adjective)	Having to do with cooking.
indispensable (adjective)	Necessary.
mammaried (adjective)	Having breasts.
mess (noun)	Military dining hall.
paradoxes (noun)	A construction of words that seem to contradict themselves.
propagate (verb)	Reproduce.
vagaries (noun)	Uncertainties.

English Is a Crazy Language

Richard Lederer

ENGLISH IS THE most widely spoken language in the history of our planet, 1 used in some way by at least one out of every seven human beings around the globe. Half of the world's books are written in English, and the majority of international telephone calls are made in English. English is the language of over sixty percent of the world's radio programs, many of them beamed, ironically, by the Russians, who know that to win friends and influence nations, they're best off using English. More than seventy percent of international mail is written and addressed in English, and eighty percent of all computer text is stored in English. English has acquired the largest vocabulary of all the world's languages, perhaps as many as two million words, and has generated one of the noblest bodies of literature in the annals of the human race.

Nonetheless, it is now time to face the fact that English is a crazy language. 2

In the crazy English language, the blackbird hen is brown, blackboards 3 can be blue or green, and blackberries are green and then red before they are ripe. Even if blackberries were really black and blueberries really blue, what are strawberries, cranberries, elderberries, huckleberries, raspberries, boysenberries, mulberries, and gooseberries supposed to look like?

To add to the insanity, there is no butter in buttermilk, no egg in eggplant, 4 no grape in grapefruit, neither worms nor wood in wormwood, neither pine nor apple in pineapple, neither peas nor nuts in peanuts, and no ham in a hamburger. (In fact, if somebody invented a sandwich consisting of a ham patty in a bun, we would have a hard time finding a name for it.) To make matters worse, English muffins weren't invented in England, french fries in France, or danish pastries in Denmark. And we discover even more culinary madness in the revelations that sweetmeat is candy, while sweetbread, which isn't sweet, is made from meat.

In this unreliable English tongue, greyhounds aren't always grey (or gray); 5 panda bears and koala bears aren't bears (they're marsupials); a woodchuck is a groundhog, which is not a hog; a horned toad is a lizard; glowworms are fireflies, but fireflies are not flies (they're beetles); ladybugs and lightning bugs are also beetles (and to propagate, a significant proportion of ladybugs must be male); a guinea pig is neither a pig nor from Guinea (it's a South American rodent); and a titmouse is neither mammal nor mammaried.

Language is like the air we breathe. It's invisible, inescapable, indispens- 6 able, and we take it for granted. But when we take the time, step back, and listen to the sounds that escape from the holes in people's faces and explore the paradoxes and vagaries of English, we find that hot dogs can be cold, darkrooms can be lit, homework can be done in school, nightmares can take place in broad daylight, while morning sickness and daydreaming can take place at night, tomboys are girls, midwives can be men, hours—especially happy hours and rush hours—can last longer than sixty minutes, quicksand works *very* slowly, boxing rings are square, silverware can be made of plastic and tablecloths of paper, most telephones are dialed by being punched (or pushed?), and most bathrooms don't have any baths in them. In fact, a dog can go to the bathroom under a tree—no bath, no room; it's still going to the bathroom. And doesn't it seem at least a little bizarre that we go to the bathroom in order to go to the bathroom?

Why is it that a woman can man a station but a man can't woman one, 7 that a man can father a movement but a woman can't mother one, and that a king rules a kingdom but a queen doesn't rule a queendom? How did all those Renaissance men reproduce when there don't seem to have been any Renaissance women?

A writer is someone who writes, and a stinger is something that stings. But 8 fingers don't fing, grocers don't groce, hammers don't ham, and humdingers don't humding. If the plural of *tooth* is *teeth,* shouldn't the plural of *booth* be *beeth?* One goose, two geese—so one moose, two meese? One index, two indices—one Kleenex, two Kleenices? If people ring a bell today and rang a bell yesterday, why don't we say that they flang a ball? If they wrote a letter, perhaps they also bote their tongue. If the teacher taught, why isn't it also true that the preacher praught? Why is it that the sun shone yesterday while I shined my shoes, that I treaded water and then trod on soil, and that I flew out to see a World Series game in which my favorite player flied out?

If we conceive a conception and receive at a reception, why don't we grieve 9 a greption and believe a beleption? If a horsehair mat is made from the hair of horses and a camel's hair brush from the hair of camels, from what is a mohair coat made? If a vegetarian eats vegetables, what does a humanitarian eat? If a firefighter fights fire, what does a freedom fighter fight? If a weightlifter lifts weights, what does a shoplifter lift? If *pro* and *con* are opposites, is congress the opposite of progress?

Sometimes you have to believe that all English speakers should be com- 10 mitted to an asylum for the verbally insane. In what other language do people drive in a parkway and park in a driveway? In what other language do people recite at a play and play at a recital? In what other language do privates eat in the general mess and generals eat in the private mess? In what other language do men get hernias and women get hysterectomies? In what other language do people ship by truck and send cargo by ship? In what other language can your nose run and your feet smell?

How can a slim chance and a fat chance be the same, "what's going on?" 11 and "what's coming off?" be the same, and a bad licking and a good licking be the same, while a wise man and a wise guy are opposites? How can sharp speech and blunt speech be the same and *quite a lot* and *quite a few* the same, while *overlook* and *oversee* are opposites? How can the weather be hot as hell one day and cold as hell the next?

If *button* and *unbutton* and *tie* and *untie* are opposites, why are *loosen* and 12 *unloosen* and *ravel* and *unravel* the same? If *bad* is the opposite of *good,* *hard* the opposite of *soft,* and *up* the opposite of *down,* why are *badly* and *goodly,* *hardly* and *softly,* and *upright* and *downright* not opposing pairs? If harmless actions are the opposite of harmful actions, why are shameless and shameful behavior the same and pricey objects less expensive than priceless ones? If appropriate and inappropriate remarks and passable and impassable mountain trails are opposites, why are flammable and inflammable materials, heritable and inheritable property, and passive and impassive people the same and valuable objects less treasured than invaluable ones? If *uplift* is the same as *lift up,* why are *upset* and *set up* opposite in meaning? Why are *pertinent* and *impertinent, canny* and *uncanny,* and *famous* and *infamous* neither opposites nor the same? How can *raise* and *raze* and *reckless* and *wreckless* be opposites when each pair contains the same sound?

Why is it that when the sun or the moon or the stars are out, they are vis-   13 ible, but when the lights are out, they are invisible, and that when I wind up my watch, I start it, but when I wind up this essay, I shall end it?

English is a crazy language.   14

Read More on the Web

Verbivore, an Internet site authored by Lederer: http://www.verbivore.com/

National Public Radio site featuring Lederer's *Language Pet Peeves:*
    http://www.npr.org/programs/watc/lpp/lppindex.html

Questions for Discussion

1. Find the three places in which Lederer states the essay's thesis.
2. Reread the introductory paragraph. In what way do the examples found here differ from those in the rest of the essay?
3. Why does Lederer include the information in this first paragraph?
4. Discuss two or three of the paragraphs found in paragraph 6 and explain why they qualify as paradoxes.
5. What simile is used to define language in paragraph 6? What is the author saying about our perception of the words we use every day.
6. In paragraph 7, Lederer groups examples of phrases pertaining to men and women. Analyze paragraphs 3, 4, 5, and 6 and identify each of the principles the author uses to group examples in them.
7. Why does he use so many rhetorical questions? What is their effect on the reader?

Thinking Critically

1. Reread the first paragraph and write a summary that explains, in your own words, why English is an important language. Can you add to the reasons Lederer provides?
2. What other world languages do you think are important and worth studying? In each case list reasons that support your opinion.
3. Many of the paradoxes we find in English come in the form of oxymorons, phrases that seem self-contradictory but that convey

a legitimate meaning. "Student teacher," "jumbo shrimp," and the "sound of silence" are just a few examples. Make a list of some others. If this doesn't interest you, make a list of words or phrases you find illogical, paradoxical, or just odd.

Suggestions for Journal Entries

1. Our language is full of contradictions, absurdities, illogicalities, and inconsistencies. But so is life itself. In fact, life can be unfair. Look back on your own life or on the lives of people you know well. Using listing, focused freewriting, or brainstorming with a friend, develop at least one example that might illustrate the illogicality or unfairness of life.

2. In paragraph 7, Lederer includes phrases that are based upon gender. Recently many words such as "waiter/waitress" and "steward/stewardess" have been replaced by less sexist alternatives such as "server" and "flight attendant." Make a list of job titles that indicate the sex of the persons who hold them. Now, list alternative, gender-neutral titles for those jobs.

The Death of Common Sense

Philip K. Howard

This essay, which appeared in Reader's Digest, *was excerpted in 1995 from a book by the same title. The book's subtitle, which reveals much about its contents, is* How Law Is Suffocating America. *The author is an attorney who has done a great deal of research on the effect of the growing mass of government regulations on every segment of American society.*

Preparing to Read

1. This essay contains a variety of examples: specific instances and occurrences, statistics, and anecdotes. It also mentions familiar persons, places, and things. Look for such examples as you read it.

2. Find places where Howard uses dialogue. Ask yourself how this helps him make his point.

3. What clues about the essay's thesis and contents does the title provide?

Vocabulary

abode (noun)	Home, residence.
citing (adjective)	Criticizing, finding fault with, penalizing.
deplorable (adjective)	Terrible, distressing.
dictates (noun)	Rules, regulations.
edifice (noun)	Building.
explicitly (adverb)	Clearly, in an outspoken manner.
frailty (noun)	Weakness, fragility.
idiosyncrasy (noun)	Individuality, oddity, irregularity.
mammoth (adjective)	Huge.
pH (noun)	A measurement of acidity or alkalinity used in chemistry.
Providence (noun)	Heaven.
saris (noun)	A kind of dress worn by many women in India and Pakistan.
specific gravity (noun)	The mass of a volume of a substance as compared to the mass of an equal volume of water.

The Death of Common Sense

Philip K. Howard

IN THE WINTER of 1988, Mother Teresa's nuns of the Missionaries of Charity   1
walked through the snow in the South Bronx in their saris and sandals looking for abandoned buildings to convert into homeless shelters. They found two,
which New York City offered them at $1 each. The nuns set aside $500,000 for
the reconstruction. Then, for a year and a half, they went from hearing room to
hearing room seeking approval for the project.

Providence, however, was no match for law. New York's building code   2
requires an elevator in all new or renovated multiple-story buildings of this
type. Installing an elevator would add upward of $100,000 to the cost. Mother
Teresa didn't want to devote that much money to something that wouldn't really help the poor. But the nuns were told the law could not be waived even if
an elevator did not make sense.

The plan for the shelter was abandoned. In a polite letter to the city, the   3
nuns noted that the episode "served to educate us about the law and its many
complexities."

What the law required offends common sense. After all, there are probably   4
over 100,000 walk-up apartment buildings in New York. But the law, aspiring
to the perfect abode, dictates a model home or no home.

Today, laws control much of our lives: fixing potholes, running schools,   5
regulating day-care centers and the workplace, cleaning up the environment—
and deciding whether Mother Teresa gets a building permit.

Our regulatory system has become an instruction manual, telling us ex-   6
actly what to do and how to do it. The laws have expanded like floodwaters
breaking through a dike—drowning the society we intended to protect.

In 1993, at Long Island's John Marshall Elementary School, the local fire   7
chief appeared around Halloween dressed as Officer McGruff, the police dog
that promotes safety. He noticed all the student art tacked to the walls. Within
days, McGruff had done his duty: the art was gone.

Why? The New York State fire code addresses this public hazard explicitly: 8
"[S]tudent-prepared artwork . . . [must be] at least two feet from the ceilings
and ten feet from exit doors and . . . [must] not exceed 20 percent of the wall
area."

No one had ever heard of a fire caused by children's art. The school super-   9
intendent, accused of permitting a legal violation, suggested that he had used
a rule of thumb "on how much to decorate."

Liz Skinner, a first-grade teacher, was confused: "The *essence* of primary 10
education is that children show pride in their work." Now, said one observer,
the school looked "about as inviting as a bomb shelter."

Government has imposed fire codes for centuries. But only our age has 11
succeeded in barring children's art from school walls.

Safety also was the goal of Congress when in 1970 it created the 12 Occupational Safety and Health Administration. For 25 years OSHA has been hard at work, producing over 4,000 detailed rules that dictate everything from the ideal height of railings (42 inches) to how much a plank can stick out from a temporary scaffold (no more than 12 inches). American industry has spent several hundred billion dollars to comply with OSHA's rules. All this must have done some good.

It hasn't. The rate of workdays missed due to injury is about the same as in 13 1973. A tour through the Glen-Gery brick factory near Reading, PA, indicates why.

People have been making bricks more or less the same way for thousands 14 of years. No hidden hazards have ever been identified. But OSHA inspectors periodically visit the Glen-Gery factory and walk around with measuring tapes. They are especially interested in railings, citing Glen-Gery for having railings of the wrong height.

Glen-Gery has never had a mishap related to railings. But inspectors won't 15 discuss if a violation actually has anything to do with safety. They are just traffic cops looking for violations. "We've done basically everything they asked for the last 20 years," says Bob Hrasok, Glen-Gery's full-time manager in charge of regulatory compliance.

As a result, warnings are posted everywhere. For example, a large 16 "Hazardous Material" sign was placed on one side of a storage shed—holding sand. OSHA categorizes sand as a hazardous material because sand—identical to the beach sand you and I sunbathe on—contains a mineral called silica, which some scientists believe under some conditions might cause cancer.

In 1994, Glen-Gery was required to include with shipments of brick a 17 form describing, for the benefit of workers, how to identify a brick (a "granular solid, essentially odorless," in a "wide range of colors") and giving its specific gravity (approximately 2.6). In fact, OSHA issued 19,233 citations in 1994 for not keeping its forms correctly. According to one expert, filling out these forms takes Americans 54 million hours per year.

Solid, objective rules, like the precise height of railings, satisfy lawmakers' 18 longing for certainty. Human activity, however, cannot be so neatly categorized. And the more precise the rule, the less sensible the law.

Until recently, Dutch Noteboom, 73, owned a small meat-packing plant in 19 Springfield, OR. The U.S. Department of Agriculture (USDA) had one full-time inspector on the premises and one supervisor who visited regularly. This level of attention is somewhat surprising, since Noteboom had only four employees. But the rules required it. Every day the inspector sat there, "often talking on the phone," says Noteboom. But they always found time to cite him for a violation: one was for "loose paint located 20 feet from any animal."

"I was swimming in paper work," says Noteboom. "You should have seen 20 all the USDA manuals. The regulations drove me out of business."

The Soviets tried to run their country like a puppeteer pulling millions of 21 strings. In our country, government's laws have become like millions of trip-wires, preventing us from doing the sensible thing.

On the banks of the Mississippi River in Minneapolis, a mountain of 22 75,000 tons of lime sludge was built up over 60 years, the by-product of a nearby plant. By the early 1980s, it sat in the path of a proposed highway.

Government rules designate any material with a pH of over 12.5 as "haz- 23 ardous waste." That may generally make sense, but not for lime, which is used to improve the environment by lowering the acidity of land and water.

The mountain of lime, whose alkalinity was also raised by dampness, had 24 a pH of 12.7. The highway was stopped dead in its tracks for many months because Minnesota had no licensed hazardous-waste-disposal site for the lime. Eventually, it was pushed onto adjoining land, where, with the help of the sun, it dried its way into lawfulness.

People tend to have their own way of doing things. But law, trying to 25 make sure nothing ever goes wrong, doesn't respect the idiosyncrasy of human accomplishment. It sets forth the approved methods, in black and white, and that's that. When law notices people doing it differently, it mashes them flat.

Gary Crissey and a partner have run a tiny coffee shop in New York's Little 26 Italy for years. Recently, some customers were dismayed when served with disposable plates and forks. Crissey explained that restaurant inspectors had stopped by and told him the law would not let him operate if he continued to wash dishes by hand. The code requires an automatic dishwasher or a chemical process. But the idea of using chemicals was unappealing, and Crissey's coffee shop is so small that it has no room for a dishwasher. The only solution was disposables. Now everything is plastic.

Today we have a world in which people argue not about right and wrong, 27 but about whether something was done the right way. With enough proce-dures, it's argued, no bureaucrat will ever again put his hand in the till. And so, by 1994, the Defense Department was spending almost half as much on proce-dures for travel reimbursement ($1.5 billion) as on travel itself ($3.5 billion).

→   Plato argued that good people do not need laws to tell them to act responsi- 28 bly, while bad people will find a way around law. By pretending procedure will get rid of corruption, we have succeeded only in humiliating honest people and have provided a cover of darkness and complexity for the bad.

By the mid-1980s, Brooklyn's Carroll Street Bridge, built in 1889, was in 29 disrepair. The city budgeted $3.5 million for an overhaul. Under procurement procedures, the renovation was estimated to take seven years.

But with the bridge's 100th anniversary approaching, Sam Schwartz, the 30 chief engineer responsible for bridges, thought the bridge should be fixed in time for a centennial party. Eleven months later, at a cost of $2.5 million, the bridge had been fixed. Practically the entire neighborhood participated in the centennial party, by all accounts a wonderful affair.

For his leadership in completing the job in one-seventh of the time and at 31
70 percent of budget, Schwartz received a reprimand.

Our modern legal system has achieved the worst of all worlds: a system 32
of regulation that goes too far—while it also does too little. A number of years
ago, two workers were asphyxiated in a Liberal, KS, meat-packing plant while
checking on a giant vat of animal blood. OSHA did virtually nothing. Stretched
thin giving out citations for improper railing height, OSHA reinspected only
once in eight years a plant that had admittedly "deplorable" conditions.

Then three more workers died—at the same plant. The government re- 33
sponse? A nationwide rule requiring atmospheric testing devices in confined
work spaces, though many of them have had no previous problems.

Most such legal dictates are stacked on top of the prior year's laws and rules. 34
The result is a mammoth legal edifice: federal statutes and rules now total about
100 million words. The Federal Register, a daily report of new and proposed
regulations, increased from 15,000 pages in the final year of John F. Kennedy's
Presidency to over 68,000 pages in the second year of Bill Clinton's.

Whenever the rules are eased, however, America's energy and good sense 35
pour in like sunlight through opened blinds. After the 1994 earthquake in
Los Angeles toppled freeways, Gov. Pete Wilson suspended the thick book of
procedural guidelines and gave incentives for speedy work.

From law's perspective, the Los Angeles repair project was a nightmare of 36
potential abuse. The process wasn't completely objective; almost nothing was
spelled out to the last detail. When disagreements occurred, private contractors
and state bureaucrats had to work them out. Rather than specifying every iron
rod, state inspectors took responsibility for checking that the work complied
with general standards. The result? Instead of a 2½-year trudge through government process, the Santa Monica Freeway was rebuilt in 64 days to a higher
standard than the old one.

"I'm proud," said Dwayne Barth, a construction supervisor. "It feels good 37
having a stake in rebuilding L.A."

When the rule book got tossed, all that was left was responsibility. No one 38
decided to spite Mother Teresa. It was the law. No one wants to take down
children's art. It's the law.

"The idea of law," Yale professor Grant Gilmore cautioned in 1977, has 39
been "ridiculously oversold."

The rules, procedures and rights smothering us are aspects of a legal tech- 40
nique that promises a permanent fix for human frailty. This legal experiment,
we learn every time we encounter it, hasn't worked out. Modern law has not
protected us from stupidity and caprice, but has made stupidity and caprice
dominant features of society.

Energy and resourcefulness are what was great about America. Let judgment 41
and personal conviction be important again. Relying on ourselves— rather than
the law—to provide answers is not a new ideology. It's just common sense.

Read More on the Web

Site of Common Good, a coalition chaired by Philip K. Howard and "dedicated to overhauling America's lawsuit culture": http:// ourcommongood.com/

American Enterprise Institute—Brookings Joint Center site containing links to opinion papers on public policy, many of which are authored by Philip K. Howard: http://www.aei.brookings.org/ publications/index.php?menuid=3&tab=date

Questions for Discussion

1. What is Howard's purpose? What is his thesis? Why did he use illustration to develop it? Would explaining how various laws came into being (process analysis) have been a good way to proceed?

2. Where does Howard cite statistics? Where does he use anecdotes?

3. How does his quoting people affected by overregulation help him achieve his purpose?

4. You know that it is not uncommon to find several methods of development in one essay. Where in this essay do you find comparison?

5. Describe the author's tone. What kind of language does he use to convey this tone?

6. Howard's examples refer to a variety of regulations, occupations, people, and sections of the country. Explain how this variety contributes to the essay's success.

Thinking Critically

1. Read Glazer's "The Right to Be Let Alone" in Chapter 12. Explain the similarities between Glazer's ideas and Howard's in a short paragraph.

2. Is Howard against all government regulation? From what he has said, determine the kinds of regulations he might support to ensure workers' safety, to protect the environment, to maintain bridges, to keep schools safe, and so on. Reread the essay and make notes about such regulations in the margins. Then explain one of your examples in a well-developed paragraph.

3. Use the double-entry (summary/response) method you learned about at the beginning of this book in "Getting Started" to analyze and respond to three or four paragraphs in this essay. Don't be afraid to express your disagreement with anything Howard says. If you need to review how a double-entry notebook works, reread pages 7.

Suggestions for Journal Entries

1. List three laws or rules enforced by your college, community, or state that offend common sense. Then, brainstorm with a friend; gather details to show that these regulations should be changed to meet the needs for which they were intended. If you can't find a partner, do some freewriting or listing on your own.

2. Think of some rules enforced by your college, community, or state that make sense and that meet the needs for which they were intended. List them, and then explain briefly why you think they should not be changed.

3. Howard claims "people have their own way of doing things. But law, trying to make sure nothing ever goes wrong, doesn't respect the idiosyncrasy of human accomplishment." Freewrite for five minutes to explain what he means. Then list three examples to show that people who "break the rules"—who follow their own dreams instead of doing what they are told—sometimes accomplish a great deal. Take your examples from your own experiences, observations, or reading.

Suggestions for Sustained Writing

1. If you responded to the first of the Suggestions for Journal Entries after Lukawska's "Wolf," you have already written three topic sentences that express conclusions about the behavior or personality of a particular animal or species of animal.

   Use these topic sentences in the body paragraphs of an essay that, like "Wolf," expresses your views on the character of this animal. Develop these paragraphs with illustrations. Perhaps some of the information in your journal will serve this purpose. Then, summarize in one statement the ideas expressed in your topic sentences; make this your essay's thesis.

   After completing your first draft, return to your paper and insert additional details and examples that will make it more convincing and clear. In your third draft, work on creating an effective introduction; like Lukawska, try using a startling remark or challenging a widely held opinion. In your conclusion, rephrase your thesis or look to the future. Then, revise the entire paper once more to improve word usage and sentence structure. End this careful process by editing for grammar and by proofreading.

2. If you responded to the first of the journal prompts after Howe's "Covert Force," turn your notes into an illustration essay explaining the fact that jobs once filled by members of only one of the sexes are now open to both. On the other hand, if you researched the role of women in wars, as suggested

in item 2 of the Suggestions for Journal Entries after the essay by Howe, use this information to write an illustration essay that explains the role of women in a particular war. If you want, do some additional library or Internet research to gather more information. Make sure you cite any information taken from Internet or from print sources per the Modern Language Association style (or per any style sheet assigned by your instructor). MLA style is explained on the website for this textbook (www.mhhe.com/rcw).

For both types of papers, remember that you need to develop illustrations that are credible and detailed. After you write your first draft, read it over carefully. Refine your thesis if necessary to make it clear and more focused. Then, add details and even whole events or instances that will better convince your reader of the validity of that thesis.

3. In response to the first of the Suggestions for Journal Entries after Lederer's "English Is a Crazy Language," you probably wrote about an incident or problem that illustrates the illogicality, absurdity, or unfairness life sometimes throws at us. Use this example as the basis for an essay that develops this idea fully. Unlike Lederer, you don't have to include hundreds of brief examples. Just add two or three other longer, more fully developed examples to the one already in your journal.

On the other hand, like Lederer, make sure to organize your essay well. Open it by using one or more of the techniques for writing introductions explained in Chapter 3. Then, devote one or two detailed paragraphs to each of the examples you have chosen to prove your thesis. Close by using a conclusion like the type you read about in Chapter 3. Write multiple drafts; then, edit and proofread carefully.

4. Write a letter to the editor of a local or college newspaper complaining about a law, regulation, policy, or practice in your community or on campus. Using examples from personal experience, explain why you are against it; show how negatively it affects you and others in your town or school.

Let's say your college library closes on Saturdays and Sundays. You decide to explain that this policy is hard on students who can't go to the library at other times. To develop your central idea, you might

• Talk about the long trips to other libraries you and other students are forced to make on weekends.

• Discuss your many attempts to find a quiet place to study on Sunday afternoons.

• Explain that 10 of the 20 students in your history class didn't finish their midterm essays on time because they could not get the information they needed.

You are trying to convince your readers of a particular opinion. So pack your letter with examples, but remember that each example should relate directly to that opinion,. As always, state your point clearly in a thesis.

Begin this assignment by looking at the journal responses you made after reading Howard's "The Death of Common Sense." That information might help you complete the first draft of your letter. Once again, be thorough and careful when revising and editing your work.

5. Do some of the rules and regulations enforced by your college, community, or state offend common sense? Or do most laws that govern you seem reasonable? Take one or the other side of this issue or argue that some laws make sense while others are ridiculous. Either way, prove your point by discussing three or four laws, rules, or regulations as examples.

In any case, make your central idea clear from the very beginning. For example, argue that common sense, practicality, and the people's best interest should determine law—not some abstract theory or impractical principle. Then, in the body of the essay, show how the rules and regulations you are discussing meet or fail to meet this standard. If you are arguing both sides of the issue, make sure you discuss examples of both reasonable and unreasonable laws.

Before you begin, check the notes you made in your journal after reading "The Death of Common Sense." They should provide useful facts, insights, and examples with which to develop your paper. As always, apply common sense to your writing: revise, edit, and proofread.

Writing to Learn: A Group Activity

In "English Is a Crazy Language," Richard Lederer comments on the complexities, inconsistencies, and contradictions of the English language. Yet, English is a rich and powerful tongue, with a vocabulary larger than that of any other world language. One reason for this is that, through the ages, English speakers have borrowed words and phrases frequently and freely from other languages and have made them their own. The roots of English are Germanic, but many elements from Greek, Latin, French, Italian, Spanish, Arabic, and even Chinese have now been incorporated into English.

THE FIRST MEETING

Ask each member of the group to research the origins of technical or specialized words that are used in a particular discipline, activity, or pursuit. For example, fine arts such as music and painting contain many words and expressions from Italian and French. Latin and Greek words can be found in medicine and biology. French, Greek, and Latin have contributed to the vocabulary of government and diplomacy. Arabic has given us many words relating to food, clothing, and mathematics, among many other fields. Many Spanish words were adopted by Americans as they pushed into the West; some of these relate to food, others to the natural environment. Ask each student in your group to research the contribution of a particular foreign language to English by providing 10 or 12 examples of words that are used in the same or a related discipline or activity.

RESEARCH

Perhaps the best place to find information quickly is on the Internet. But your library's print sources as well as its online databases can help too. You might also want to interview professors of foreign languages on your campus. After you collect your 10 or 12 examples, make sure that they relate to the same discipline or activity. If one or two do not, find replacements. Then, in two or three paragraphs, explain what these words or phrases mean in the original language and how they came to be incorporated into English. Also explain whether the original meaning of the word or phrase has changed with time. (By the way, the *Oxford English Dictionary*—in print or online—contains a great deal of information about the source of words and the changes they have gone through.) Bring copies of your work to the next group meeting.

THE SECOND MEETING

Discuss the work each member has brought. Has he or she researched a sufficient number of words to demonstrate that the assigned language has contributed significantly to the English vocabulary of a particular discipline, activity, or pursuit? Has he or she explained the origins of each word and the way it got incorporated into English clearly and completely? If appropriate, has he or she traced changes in the meaning of this word or phrase over time? Assign further research if necessary. Then, ask everyone to bring a revised version of his or her work to the next meeting providing enough copies for each group member. This material should also be saved in computer files that everyone can access. Finally, assign one person to write an effective introduction and conclusion for an essay that might contain all of this information. Assign another person to write a works-cited list (you can find the MLA format for writing such lists on this book's website www.mhhe.com/rcw) or other type of bibliography for the sources used by each member of the group.

THE THIRD MEETING

Discuss the final draft of everyone's paragraphs, and make last-minute editing and proofreading corrections. Turn the written copies and the computer files over to the group leader, whose responsibility it will be to combine all of this work into a coherent essay complete with the introduction, the conclusion, and the bibliography supplied him or her by other group members during the second meeting.

CHAPTER 9

Comparison
and Contrast

Comparison and contrast are methods of organizing and developing ideas by pointing out similarities and differences between subjects.

A comparison essay identifies similarities—even between subjects that seem different. For example, you might compare the government of the United States with that of Great Britain; a newly patented drug with an age-old herbal treatment; the methods of building the Egyptian and Mayan pyramids with modern construction methods. A contrast essay identifies differences—even between subjects that seem alike; usually these subjects belong to the same general class or are of the same type. Such is the case in Cowley's "Temptations of Old Age," a selection in this chapter that discusses how two different types of people face the challenges of aging.

Comparison and contrast can also be used to argue for one or both sides of a question. For example, you might discuss the advantages and disadvantages of living in a particular city, the pros and cons of human cloning, or the strengths and weaknesses of a particular political ideology. In "High Anxiety: It Never Ends," student Nancy Terranova argues that although the lifestyles of young adults differ from those of their parents and grandparents, they experience the same levels of fear and anxiety in their daily lives.

Organizing Comparison/Contrast Papers

One of the greatest advantages of using comparison or contrast is the simplicity with which it allows you to organize information. In fact, putting together a successful comparison or contrast essay doesn't have to be difficult if you follow either of the two standard methods of organization: point by point or subject by subject.

Deciding which method to use depends on your topic and purpose. The subject-by-subject method is often used in short pieces, such as Cowley's "Temptations of Old Age." The point-by-point method works well with essays that compare or contrast several qualities or characteristics of two subjects. This arrangement allows readers to digest large quantities of information bit by bit. As such, it helps eliminate the risk that they will forget what you said in the first half of your essay before they finish the second half. Nancy Terranova's "High Anxiety: It Never Ends" uses this pattern.

Visualizing Methods of Comparison

THE POINT-BY-POINT METHOD

Let's say you wanted to contrast the Senate of ancient Rome with the current United States Senate. If you used the point-by-point method, the outline for your paper might look like this:

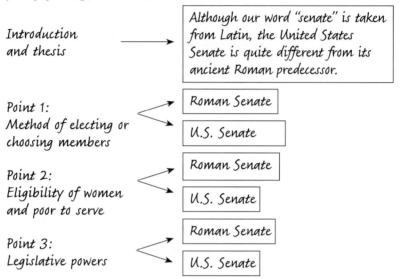

THE SUBJECT-BY-SUBJECT METHOD

Using the subject-by-subject method, you discuss one subject completely before going on to compare or contrast it with another subject in the second half of the essay. Here's how you might outline the essay contrasting the Roman Senate and the U.S. Senate.

Introduction and thesis	Although our word *senate* is taken from Latin, the United States Senate is quite different from its ancient Roman predecessor.
Subject 1: Roman Senate	• Method of electing or choosing members • Eligibility of women and poor to serve • Legislative powers
Subject 2: U.S. Senate	• Method of electing or choosing members • Eligibility of women and poor to serve • Legislative powers

Note that while many comparison/contrast essays use one or the other of these patterns exclusively, some essays make use of both the point-by-point pattern and the subject-by-subject pattern. You can see this in Christopher Daly's "How the Lawyers Stole Winter," which appears near the end of this chapter.

SEEING THE PATTERN IN A COMPARISON/CONTRAST PAPER

Student James Langley's "Watch the Cart!" which appears below, discusses differences between male and female shoppers. It follows the point-by-point pattern, which is often found in longer essays. Notes in the left margin explain how Langley organized his paper. Notes on the right explain how he developed it.

*States
thesis.*

There is nothing similar to the way men and women shop for groceries. Believe me, I know because I work in a major supermarket. After watching scores of people shop for food day in and day out, I have become an expert on the habits of American consumers. I have noticed many things about them, but nothing stands out more clearly than the differences between men and women.

*Establishes
his
expertise.*

*Point 1:
How men
search
for a
product.*

First of all, men never know where anything is. Nine times out of ten, it will be a man who asks an employee to find a product for him. I don't know how many guys come up to me in the course of a night to ask me where something is, but 50% of those who do invariably return to me in five minutes still unaware of the product's location. Men have no sense of direction in a supermarket.

*Begins
with topic
sentence.*

*Includes a
statistic.*

It's as if they're locked up in some life-sized
maze. It has always been my contention
that men who shop should be provided with
specially trained dogs to sniff out the
products they desire. It would certainly
save me valuable time too often wasted as I
explain for the tenth time that soup is in
aisle 9.

Uses a simile.

Point 1:
How women
search for
a product.

Women, on the other hand, rarely ask for
an item's location. When they do, it is
usually for an obscure product only they
have heard of and whose name only they can
pronounce. Whenever a woman asks me where
some such item is, I always tell her to go
to aisle 11—the dog-food aisle. Send a man
there, and he'll forget what he was looking
for and just buy the dog food out of
desperation. Send a woman there, and she'll
be back in five minutes with the product in
hand, thanking me for locating it for her.

Begins with topic sentence.

Uses an example.

Point 2:
How quickly
men and
women shop.

Another difference between men and women
is that women shop at speeds that would get
them tickets on freeways, while men shop
with the speed of a dead snail. A woman can
get her shopping done in the same amount of
time every time she goes. A man who shops
just as often gets worse and worse every
time.

Begins with topic sentence.

Point 3: How well men and women manipulate carts.

The biggest difference between the sexes in regard to shopping, however, involves the manipulation of carts. A woman guides a cart through the store so fluidly and effortlessly that her movements are almost poetic. Men are an entirely different story. A man with a shopping cart is a menace to anyone within two aisles of him. Men bounce their carts off display cases, sideswipe their fellow patrons and create havoc wherever they go. They have no idea of how to control the direction of carts. To a man, a shopping cart is a crazed metal monster designed to embarrass and harass him.

Begins with topic sentence.

Creates a vivid image.

Uses a metaphor.

Conclusion refers to thesis and restates essay's main points.

Overall, then, women are far more proficient shoppers than men. They are efficient, speedy and graceful; men are slow and clumsy. I know these things because I work in a supermarket. I also know these things because I am a man.

Revising Comparison/Contrast Papers

The following essay by Nancy Terranova was written after this student began to reflect upon the daily fears and anxieties faced by her generation, especially in light of the terrorist attacks of 9/11/01. Read the rough draft and an excerpt of the final draft of Terranova's paper. (You can read a full version of her final draft later in this chapter.) As you will see, the author did a thorough revision in which, among other things, she clarified her thesis, made the paper's organization more consistent and logical, and added information to develop her ideas more fully.

Terranova—Rough Draft—High Anxiety

In many ways the lives of young adults in 2002 are different from those of their parents and far different from those of their grandparents. As members of Generation X, we seem to have all the answers and all the toys. Fax machines, email, voice mail, and call-waiting enable us to maintain unbroken strings of communication. Computer software makes us more productive students and business people. Take-home movies, television systems with hundreds of channels, electronic games, and downloads of popular music have allowed us transform ourselves into virtual coach potatoes. Speaking of food, consider the immediate gratification—if not the nutrition—that drive-up hamburger joints, sushi bars, and the makers of microwaveable pizzas provide.

Make tone more formal? Use third-person "they" and "them."

Remove clichés?

But are the important things in our lives really different? According to the French, the more things change the more they stay the same. We might be more technologically advanced than our parents and grandparents, but are our lives any happier and any less stressed-out than theirs?

Use quotation marks?

State thesis explicitly?

Over the last 100 years the longevity of Americans has increased. One reason for that is that, years ago, diseases such as polio, diphtheria, tuberculosis, pneumonia, tetanus, and even influenza took the lives of or crippled so many children and young adults. Back then, they worried about how

Is subject-by-subject method best? Revise to use point-by-point method.

to make a living as well. For example, many men and women of my parents' and grandparents' generations held factory or low-level office jobs. They had to develop skills to get those jobs, which meant finishing high school or learning a trade as an apprentice. In those days, that wasn't so easy. My grandparents remember the Depression, when 1 out of 4 people was out of work. Many of them had to leave high school in order to help support their families, and sometimes finding someone to apprentice with wasn't easy. Besides you could be laid-off easily.

How does this relate to thesis? Strengthen connection.

Finish discussing previous point before starting a new one?

Today, however, the Salk and Sabin vaccines have virtually wiped out polio. Medicine has virtually eliminated diphtheria and tuberculosis as well. And pneumonia and tetanus are easily treated with antibiotics. However, Generation X has other health worries. For example the rates of teenage suicide are much higher today. And young people seem to be more susceptible to drug and alcohol. Sexually transmitted disease including gonorrhea, syphilis and AIDS are also much more prevalent today, because members of my generation are far more sexually active than before. Cases of anorexia and bulimia, virtually unheard of 50 years ago, are commonplace among women in their teens and twenties, and men are getting them too.

Support these ideas with research?

Develop this point more fully?

Today, <u>they tell us</u>, our job opportunities are greater too. But we need more education. Graduating from high school will get you a job at Burger King. The minimum to get started is a community college degree. And the best paying jobs require you to continue studying far beyond your bachelor's. However, even an advanced degree won't keep you from getting laid off, as so many employees

Who is "they"?

of hightech companies have found out in recent years. We may not be having a <u>depression like my grandparents</u>, but we have just come through a recession and that was bad enough. So anxiety about where your next meal is coming from is still around.

Correct illogical comparison.

Develop this point more fully?

And what about war, and national security? I remember my grandmother telling me about worrying so much about my grandfather who had had been shipped out to the Pacific during World War II. Today, we still have war fears, and many of my friends, who are in the reserves, might be called to fight in Iraq. And what about all the terrorism?

Add a formal conclusion?

Terranova—Final Draft—High Anxiety: It Never Ends

In 2002, the lives of people in their late teens and twenties are different in many ways from what they would have been if they had been born half a

Uses a more formal tone.

century earlier. Members of Generation X seem to have advantages their grandparents—and even their parents—never even hoped for. Fax machines, email, voice mail, and call-waiting enable them to maintain unbroken strings of communication even with people across the globe. Computer software makes them more productive students and employees. Take-home movies, television systems offering hundreds of channels, electronic games, and downloads of popular music are, sadly, transforming them into a generation of overweight couch potatoes. And speaking of food, consider the immediate gratification—if not the nutrition—that drive-up hamburger joints, sushi bars, and the makers of microwaveable pizzas provide.

Has removed clichés.

Adds quotation marks.

According to the French, however, "the more things change, the more they stay the same." Today's young adults might live in a technologically advanced

States thesis explicitly.

environment, but are their lives any happier and any less stressful than those of their parents and grandparents? As a matter of fact, they suffer the same kinds of anxieties that their elders experienced.

Switches to point-by-point method of organization.

Take concerns over staying healthy, for example. Through much of the 20th century, diseases such as diphtheria, tuberculosis, pneumonia, tetanus, and even influenza took the lives of many young adults or severely debilitated them. In the 1950's, the world went through a kind of polio hysteria, as bad as that

Condenses what appeared in rough draft.

caused by AIDS in the 1980s. According to
Dr. Edmund Sass, the United States reported 52,000
new cases of polio in 1952 (3). Another 5000 new
cases were reported in Canada (Rutty 1) for that year.

Makes connection with thesis stronger and adds researched material.

Today, medicine has virtually eliminated polio in
the developed world. Diphtheria and tuberculosis,
which plagued earlier generations, are in severe
decline, and pneumonia and tetanus can be treated
with antibiotics. However, Generation X has its own
health worries. For example, according to the Centers
for Disease Control:

Focus of paper now remains steady.

> Many more people die by suicide than by
> homicide in the United States. Suicide rates
> among youth have been increasing steadily
> for the past four decades; suicide is the third
> leading cause of death among children and
> youth between the ages of 10 and 24. (1)

Adds research to support thesis.

Moreover, young people seem to be more susceptible
to drug and alcohol abuse. In a 1997 statement of the
US Senate Judiciary Committee, Senator Orrin Hatch
reported that the use of illicit drugs "among high
school students [had] dramatically increased since
1991—from 11% to 24% in 1996 for 8th graders,
from 21% to 38% for 10th graders, and from 29% to
40% for 12th graders" (1). Sexually transmitted
disease including gonorrhea and syphilis are also
much more prevalent today because members of

Organization is uniform: point-by-point.

Adds research.

Generation X are far more sexually active than their grandparents or even their parents were. AIDS, now at epidemic levels, was unknown fifty years ago. Rates of anorexia and bulimia have also increased in the last two decades especially among women in their teens and twenties. However, even young men are suffering from these ailments.

Practicing Comparison and Contrast

In the spaces provided, write paragraphs that respond to any four of the following items. Remember that comparison explains similarities while contrast explains differences. Before you start writing a paragraph, gather details for it. Then make a rough draft. Before you begin your final draft, make sure the paragraph has a topic sentence.

1. Compare caring for a child and caring for an animal.

   _____

   _____

   _____

   _____

   _____

   _____

   _____

2. Compare writing papers for English class and preparing for a mathematics test.

   _____

   _____

   _____

   _____

   _____

   _____

   _____

3. Compare the cooking of two different cultures. For instance, compare Chinese with Italian, Indian with Mexican, Caribbean with Japanese, or Eastern European with American.

    _____

    _____

    _____

    _____

    _____

    _____

    _____

4. Compare someone you know (perhaps yourself) to an animal. Start by writing " _____ is a snake" or " _____ is a workhorse."

    _____

    _____

    _____

    _____

    _____

    _____

    _____

5. Contrast your work or study habits with those of a friend.

    _____

    _____

    _____

    _____

    _____

    _____

    _____

6. Contrast the ways you and your parents (sister, brother, or other relative) view sex (marriage, education, religion, money, or your friends).

    _____

    _____

    _____

_____

_____

_____

_____

7. Contrast two hobbies you pursue, two sports you play or follow, or two jobs you have held.

_____

_____

_____

_____

_____

_____

_____

8. Contrast two pieces of music, films, paintings, books, or television shows that are about similar subjects or that have similar purposes.

_____

_____

_____

_____

_____

_____

_____

High Anxiety: It Never Ends

Nancy Terranova

The student who wrote this essay majored in English and is now working part-time as an editor for a large publishing house. When asked to write a comparison/contrast essay, she reflected on the kinds of anxieties young American adults were experiencing, especially in the aftermath of the terrorist attacks of 9/11/01. "Nancy Terranova" is a pen name.

Preparing to Read

1. "Generation X" is a term that defines the current generation of young adults, roughly from their mid-teens to about thirty.

2. Note that Terranova uses a two-paragraph introduction and that she follows the point-by-point pattern to organize her essay. However, in the rough draft of this essay, which appears in the chapter's introduction, Terranova began with the subject-by-subject method, then switched to point-by point. Her final draft is far more consistent and logical.

3. Several bits of researched information appear in this essay, along with a Works Cited page, arranged in Modern Language Association style. If you want to learn more about MLA style, go to this book's website: www.mhhe.com/rcw. For now, pay particular attention to how researched information is introduced into this essay and how it helps support the thesis.

Vocabulary

abounds (verb)	Is plentiful.
anxiety (noun)	Worry, uneasiness.
debilitated (adjective)	Weakened.
despots (noun)	Tyrants.
gratification (noun)	Satisfaction.
hysteria (noun)	Extreme agitation, mass fear.
illicit (adjective)	Illegal.
prevalent (adjective)	Common.
susceptible (adjective)	Vulnerable, exposed to.
virtually (adverb)	Nearly, almost totally.

High Anxiety: It Never Ends

Nancy Terranova

IN 2002, THE lives of people in their late teens and twenties are different 1
in many ways from what they would have been if they had been born
half a century earlier. Members of Generation X seem to have advantages
their grandparents—and even their parents—never even hoped for. Fax
machines, email, voice mail, and call-waiting enable them to maintain
unbroken strings of communication even with people across the globe.
Computer software makes them more productive students and employees. Take-home movies, television systems offering hundreds of channels,
electronic games, and downloads of popular music are, sadly, transforming them into a generation of overweight couch potatoes. And speaking
of food, consider the immediate gratification—if not the nutrition—that
drive-up hamburger joints, sushi bars, and the makers of microwaveable
pizzas provide.

According to the French, however, "the more things change, the more they 2
stay the same." Today's young adults might live in a technologically advanced
environment, but are their lives any happier and any less stressful than those of
their parents and grandparents? As a matter of fact, they suffer the same kinds
of anxieties that their elders experienced.

Take concerns over staying healthy, for example. Through much of the 3
20th century, diseases such as diphtheria, tuberculosis, pneumonia, tetanus,
and even influenza took the lives of many young adults or severely debilitated
them. In the 1950's, the world went through a kind of polio hysteria, as bad as
that caused by AIDS in the 1980s. According to Dr. Edmund Sass, the United
States reported 52,000 new cases of polio in 1952 (3). Another 5000 new cases
were reported in Canada (Rutty 1) for that year.

Today, medicine has virtually eliminated polio in the developed world. 4
Diphtheria and tuberculosis, which plagued earlier generations, are in severe
decline, and pneumonia and tetanus can be treated with antibiotics. However,
Generation X has its own health worries. For example, according to the Centers
for Disease Control:

> Many more people die by suicide than by homicide in the United
> States. Suicide rates among youth have been increasing steadily for
> the past four decades; suicide is the third leading cause of death
> among children and youth between the ages of 10 and 24. (1)

Moreover, young people seem to be more susceptible to drug and alcohol
abuse. In a 1997 statement of the US Senate Judiciary Committee, Senator
Orrin Hatch reported that the use of illicit drugs among adolescents had "dramatically increased since 1991—from 11% to 24% in 1996 for 8th graders,

from 21% to 38% for 10th graders, and from 29% to 40% for 12th graders" (1). Sexually transmitted diseases including gonorrhea and syphilis are also much more prevalent today because members of Generation X are far more sexually active than their grandparents or even their parents were. AIDS, now at epidemic levels, was unknown fifty years ago. Rates of anorexia and bulimia have also increased in the last two decades especially among women in their teens and twenties. However, even young men are suffering from these ailments.

People who came of age in the 40's, 50's, and 60's worried about how to 5 make a living. For example, many men and women of our parents' and grandparents' generations held factory or low-level office jobs. They had to develop skills to get those jobs, which meant finishing high school or learning a trade as an apprentice. In those days, that wasn't so easy. My grandparents remember the Great Depression, when 1 out of 4 people was out of work. Many of them had to leave high school in order to help support their families, and sometimes finding someone with whom to apprentice was difficult. In addition, factory lay-offs were common.

Today, a college education is a necessity. Graduating from high school 6 qualifies one for an entry-level job at Burger King. The minimum to launch any worthwhile career is a community college degree. And the best-paying jobs require continued study far beyond the bachelor's. However, even an advanced degree won't prevent the possibility of being laid off, as so many employees of high-tech companies have found out in recent years. This generation may not be experiencing a depression as our grandparents did, but we have just come through a recession, and that was bad enough! So anxiety about keeping a steady job and building a rewarding career still abounds.

Then there are the questions of war and national security. The previous 7 two generations lived through the horrors of World War II and the Korean War, not to mention the Cold War, which is now, we are told, far behind us. But this generation has to deal with its fear of terrorism, which became all too real on 9/11/01. We are leery about boarding airplanes, and we have accustomed ourselves to listening for warnings from the newly created Department of Homeland Security. Some of us might soon be called to fight in the Middle East as did our older brothers and sisters in the 1990 Persian Gulf War or in Kosovo.

No one knows what tomorrow will bring. Perhaps being human means 8 living with anxiety and even fear. If the past is any indication of what the future holds, this generation will follow the example of its predecessors and come through. The American people have distinguished themselves during the past fifty years. After all, they have conquered major diseases, ended the Cold War, invented the computer, helped establish democracies in countries once ruled by despots, strengthened the rights of women and minorities in their own land, and, through it all, managed to maintain the highest standard of living

the world has ever known. If the current generation can do half that much, it
will be just fine.

Works Cited

Centers for Disease Control and Prevention. *Suicide among Youth.*
12 July 2002. 15 July 2002. http://www.cdc:gov/communica-
tion/tips/suicide.htm

Rutty, Christopher J. *Do Something . . . Do Anything! Poliomyelitis
in Canada, 1927–1962.* Apr. 1995. Health Heritage Research
Services. 12 July 2002. http://www.healthheritageresearch.
com/PolioPHD.html

Sass, Edmund. "A Polio History Quest." *Polio History Pages.* 22
Apr. 2002. 12 July 2002. http://www.cloudnet.com/~edrbsass/
poliohistoryquest.htm

United States Senate Judiciary Committee. *Drug Abuse among
Our Children: A Growing National Crisis.* By Senator Orrin
Hatch, Chairman. June 1998. 15 July 2002. http://www.
senate.gov/~judiciary/oldsite/ogh61798.htm

> **MARGINAL NOTE**
>
> Learn how to use MLA format at www.mhhe.com/rcw

Read More on the Web

Essay written by a Case Western Reserve University professor who claims
that young adults are living in an age of anxiety: http://www.cwru.
edu/pubaff/univcomm/anxiety.htm

Ohio State University site on dealing with anxiety in young adults:
http://anxiety.psy.ohio-state.edu/Adolescents.htm

Questions for Discussion

1. The author discusses three major areas of similarity. What are they?
2. Explain why the subject-by-subject method of organization would
    not have been as appropriate to Terranova's purpose as the
    point-by-point method?
3. This essay makes many comparisons; it points out similarities. What
    differences between the sources of anxiety for one generation and
    those for another does Terranova point out? In other words, where
    and why does she use contrast?
4. What does the author's subtitle add to the essay? How does it help
    the reader?
5. What methods of development, other than comparison and contrast,
    does this essay use?

6. Much of this essay's success is due to its use of concrete detail. Analyze one paragraph you think is particularly illustrative of Terranova's ability to use such detail.

Thinking Critically

1. Terranova spends a great deal of time explaining the anxieties young people feel over their health. Do you agree with her assessment? Are you worried about the kinds of problems she mentions? Are you worried about other problems? Are you not worried at all about health problems?

2. Terranova argues that today's young adults have as much to worry about as their parents and grandparents did. If this is so, in what ways are their lives better than those of their predecessors? In what ways are they worse?

Suggestions for Journal Entries

1. Terranova spends more time on questions of health and employment than on national security. Perhaps, for her, the first two are simply more relevant and more immediate. Which one of the concerns that she mentions has the most relevance for you? Use focused freewriting to add details of your own to Terranova's discussion, but focus on only one of the three areas she discusses. If you have no interest in any of the areas that Terranova covers, write about another source of anxiety that is especially important for you.

2. Interview at least two parents, grandparents, or any members of an earlier generation. Begin by talking about the prevailing views of your generation on a certain subject such as sex, war, getting married, religion, or any other issue or concern that affects the lives of people your age. Then, ask the people you are interviewing to identify both similarities and differences in the ways their generation viewed such questions. Like Terranova, you might want to discuss various types of anxieties suffered by your generation and theirs. Or you might ask them about their generations' views on race relations, education, war, the government, patriotism, religion, dating, or drinking.

Temptations of Old Age*

Malcolm Cowley

Malcolm Cowley (1898–1989) was a writer, editor, literary critic, and historian noted for his energy and productivity up until his death at 90. In the last decade of his life, Cowley wrote The View from 80, *a book that explains his very positive attitude toward aging and that offers excellent advice about the latter stages of life.*

Preparing to Read

1. This selection is from a chapter of Cowley's book that discusses several temptations of old age and explains ways to avoid them. Among these temptations are greed, vanity, and a desire to escape life's problems through alcohol. But the greatest temptation, as shown in the following paragraphs, is "simply giving up."

2. Renoir, mentioned in paragraph 4, was a French painter of the nineteenth and twentieth centuries. Goya was a Spanish painter of the eighteenth and nineteenth centuries.

3. What hint about the selection's contents does the word "temptations" provide?

Vocabulary

ailments (noun)	Illnesses, disorders, diseases.
compelling (adjective)	Convincing, strong, valid.
distinguished (adjective)	Well-respected.
distraction (noun)	Amusement, diversion.
infirmities (noun)	Illnesses, weaknesses, ailments.
lithographs (noun)	Prints.
outwitted (verb)	Outsmarted, outmaneuvered.
Rolls-Royce (noun)	Expensive British automobile.
senility (noun)	Forgetfulness and decrease in mental powers affecting some elderly people.
stoical (adjective)	Brave, uncomplaining.
unvanquished (adjective)	Undefeated.

---

*Editor's title.

Temptations of Old Age

Malcolm Cowley

NOT WHISKEY or cooking sherry but simply giving up is the greatest tempta- 1
tion of age. It is something different from a stoical acceptance of infirmi-
ties, which is something to be admired.

The givers-up see no reason for working. Sometimes they lie in bed all 2
day when moving about would still be possible, if difficult. I had a friend, a
distinguished poet, who surrendered in that fashion. The doctors tried to stir
him to action, but he refused to leave his room. Another friend, once a successful artist, stopped painting when his eyes began to fail. His doctor made the
mistake of telling him that he suffered from a fatal disease. He then lost interest
in everything except the splendid Rolls-Royce, acquired in his prosperous days,
that stood in the garage. Daily he wiped the dust from its hood. He couldn't
drive it on the road any longer, but he used to sit in the driver's seat, start the
motor, then back the Rolls out of the garage and drive it in again, back twenty
feet and forward twenty feet; that was his only distraction.

I haven't the right to blame those who surrender, not being able to put myself 3
inside their minds or bodies. Often they must have compelling reasons, physical
or moral. Not only do they suffer from a variety of ailments, but also they are
made to feel that they no longer have a function in the community. Their families
and neighbors don't ask them for advice, don't really listen when they speak,
don't call on them for efforts. One notes that there are not a few recoveries from
apparent senility when that situation changes. If it doesn't change, old persons
may decide that efforts are useless. I sympathize with their problems, but the
men and women I envy are those who accept old age as a series of challenges.

For such persons, every new infirmity is an enemy to be outwitted, an 4
obstacle to be overcome by force of will. They enjoy each little victory over
themselves, and sometimes they win a major success. Renoir was one of them.
He continued painting, and magnificently, for years after he was crippled by
arthritis; the brush had to be strapped to his arm. "You don't need your hand
to paint," he said. Goya was another of the unvanquished. At 72 he retired as
an official painter of the Spanish court and decided to work only for himself.
His later years were those of the famous "black paintings" in which he let his
imagination run (and also of the lithographs, then a new technique). At 78 he
escaped a reign of terror in Spain by fleeing to Bordeaux. He was deaf and his
eyes were failing; in order to work he had to wear several pairs of spectacles,
one over another, and then use a magnifying glass; but he was producing
splendid work in a totally new style. At 80 he drew an ancient man propped
on two sticks, with a mass of white hair and beard hiding his face and with the
inscription "I am still learning."

"Eighty years old!" the great Catholic poet Paul Claudel wrote in his jour- 5
nal. "No eyes left, no ears, no teeth, no legs, no wind! And when all is said and
done, how astonishingly well one does without them!"

Read More on the Web

Washington Post obituary and an interview with Cowley's son: http://www.
geocities.com/Heartland/Hollow/5913/interests/cowley.html

Short biography of Cowley with excerpts from his major works:
http://www.spartacus.schoolnet.co.uk/USAcowleyM.htm

Questions for Discussion

1. Pick out particularly vivid verbs and adjectives in this selection.
2. Where does Cowley signal a transition from one subject to another?
3. Various methods can be combined to develop one idea. Where in this
    piece does Cowley use examples?
4. Do you think the conclusion of this selection is effective? Why or
    why not? If necessary, review ways to write conclusions in Chapter 3.
5. Why, according to the author, do some elderly people simply give up?
6. What does he mean when he says that others see "every new infirmity"
    as "an obstacle to be overcome by force of will" (paragraph 4)?

Thinking Critically

1. Cowley quotes directly from the "unvanquished." Why doesn't he
    also quote from "those who surrender"?
2. This selection uses the subject-by-subject pattern. Why does the
    author begin with the "givers-up" and not end with them? Should he
    have discussed Renoir, Goya, and Claudel first?
3. Would "Temptations of Old Age" have been better organized point by
    point? Why or why not?

Suggestions for Journal Entries

1. What Cowley says might apply to folks of all ages. Do you know
    someone who seems to face all the challenges life has to offer?
    Spend five minutes freewriting about the way this person reacts to
    such challenges. Then do the same for someone you might call a
    "giver-up." Try to include facts about their lives that will describe their
    personalities.
2. In what way are you like the people in your family who have come
    before you? Think about a parent, grandparent, great-aunt, or
    other older relative. Use listing or focused freewriting to explain
    what is similar about your personalities, interests, lifestyles, or your
    opinions about music, politics, other people, or anything else you
    can think of.

They Shoot Helicopters Don't They?
How Journalists Spread Rumors
during Katrina

Matt Welch

Matt Welch (b. 1968) is the assistant editor of the Los Angeles Times *editorial page. This essay first appeared in* Reason *magazine, published monthly by the Reason Foundation based in southern California. According to its website, the Reason Foundation promotes libertarian principles "advancing the values of individual freedom and choice, limited government, and market-friendly policies." Welsh has written for the* Los Angeles Times, *the* Daily Star of Beirut, *the* Columbia Journalism Review, ESPN.com., *and* Salon, *among many other publications. He was also a correspondent for United Press International in Bratislava, Slovakia, and spent several years as a reporter and editor in Eastern Europe.*

Preparing to Read

1. Welch's purpose is to clear away several myths—reported as fact by many newspapers, magazines, and radio and television stations—about the way the citizens of New Orleans reacted to the ravages of Hurricane Katrina, which struck Louisiana, Mississippi, and Alabama at the end of August 2005. The effectiveness of this essay shows that comparison/contrast can be put to many uses.

2. The Associated Press (paragraph 1) is a news service that provides stories to thousands of newspapers, magazines, and other media outlets.

3. Victims of Hurricane Katrina were taken to the Superdome (paragraph 4), a professional football stadium, and to the New Orleans Convention Center (paragraph 10).

4. In paragraph 16, Welch calls the report of people shooting at helicopters an "urban legend." Urban legends are a type of contemporary folklore—wildly exaggerated tales—which often have little basis in fact. Often, however, the people who spread these legends actually believe them to be true. Because of the Internet, email, and other forms of electronic communication, they can spread quickly.

Vocabulary

abounded (adjective)	Were plentiful.
apocalyptic (adjective)	Relating to the end of the world.

atrocity (noun)	Horrible act of violence.
bogus (adjective)	False.
debunked (adjective)	Proven false.
depraved (adjective)	Degenerate, immoral, decadent.
disseminated (adjective)	Spread.
dysfunctional (adjective)	Not acting or operating properly.
far-flung (adjective)	Spread widely.
mea culpas (noun)	Latin phrase meaning "apologies."
premise (noun)	Basis, underlying principle.
protracted (adjective)	Extended, drawn out.
rampant (adjective)	Widespread.
ulterior (adjective)	Secret, underhanded.
urbanites (noun)	City dwellers.
whoppers (noun)	Colloquial term for "huge lies."

They Shoot Helicopters Don't They?
How Journalists Spread Rumors
during Katrina

Matt Welch

ON SEPTEMBER 1, 72 hours after Hurricane Katrina ripped through New 1
Orleans, the Associated Press news wire flashed a nightmare of a story:
"Katrina Evacuation Halted Amid Gunfire. . . . Shots Are Fired at Military
Helicopter."

The article flew across the globe via at least 150 news outlets, from India 2
to Turkey to Spain. Within 24 hours commentators on every major American
television news network had helped turn the helicopter sniper image into the disaster's enduring symbol of dysfunctional urbanites too depraved to be saved.

Golfer Tiger Woods spoke for many of us on September 2 when he re- 3
marked, during a tournament in Boston, that "it's just unbelievable . . . how
people are behaving, with the shootings and now the gang rapes and the gang
violence and shooting at helicopters who are trying to help out and rescue
people."

Like many early horror stories about ultra-violent New Orleans natives, 4
whether in their home city or in far-flung temporary shelters, the A.P. article
turned out to be false. Evacuation from the city of New Orleans was never
"halted," according to officials from the Coast Guard, the Federal Emergency
Management Agency (FEMA), and the Louisiana National Guard. The only
helicopter airlifts stopped were those by a single private company, Acadian
Ambulance, from a single location: the Superdome. And Acadian officials, who
had one of the only functional communications systems in all of New Orleans

during those first days, were taking every opportunity to lobby for a massive military response.

More important, there has been no official confirmation that a single mili- 5
tary helicopter over New Orleans—let alone a National Guard Chinook in the pre-dawn hours of September I—was fired upon. "I was at the Superdome for eight days, and I don't remember hearing anything about a helicopter getting shot at," says Maj. Ed Bush, public affairs officer for the Louisiana Air National Guard. With hundreds of Guard troops always on duty inside and outside the Superdome before, during, and after Hurricane Katrina, if there had been gunfire, "we would have heard it," Bush maintains. "The instant reaction over the radio would have been overwhelming."

The Air Force, to which the Air National Guard reports, also has zero re- 6
cord of helicopter sniping. "We investigated one incident and it turned out to have been shooting on the ground, not at the helicopter," Air Force Maj. Mike Young told *The New York Times* on September 29.

Aside from the local National Guard, the other government agency with 7
scores of helicopters over New Orleans was the U.S. Coast Guard, which rescued more than 33,000 people. "Coast Guard helicopters," says spokeswoman Jolie Shifflet, "were not fired on during Hurricane Katrina rescue operations."

How about the Civil Air Patrol (CAP), the all-volunteer, Air Force-assisting 8
network of around 58,000 private Cessna pilots, 68 of whom flew a total of 833 aid missions after the hurricane? "To my knowledge," says CAP Public Affairs Manager Jim Tynan, "none of our pilots on any Katrina-related mission were taking ground fire."

That doesn't mean that people weren't shooting at helicopters. As Lt. Comdr. 9
Tim Tobiasz, the Coast Guard's operations officer for New Orleans airspace, told me, "It's tough to hear in a helicopter. You have two turbine engines. . . . I don't know if you could hear a gunshot below." And the Bureau of Alcohol, Tobacco, and Firearms arrested a 21-year-old man in the Algiers neighborhood of New Orleans on September 6 for firing a handgun out his window while helicopters flew nearby.

But the basic premise of the article that introduced the New Orleans he- 10
licopter sniper to a global audience was dead wrong, just like so many other widely disseminated Katrina nightmares. No 7-year-old rape victim with a slit throat was ever found, even though the atrocity was reported in scores of newspapers. The Convention Center freezer was not stacked with 30 or 40 dead bodies, nor was the Superdome a live-in morgue. (An estimated 10 people died inside the two buildings combined, and only one was slain, according to the best data from National Guard officials at press time.)

Tales of rapes, carjackings, and gang violence by Katrina refugees quickly 11
circulated in such evacuee centers as Baton Rouge, Houston, and Leesville, Louisiana—and were almost as quickly debunked.

From a journalistic point of view, the root causes of the bogus re- 12
ports were largely the same: The communication breakdown without and

especially within New Orleans created an information vacuum in which wild oral rumor thrived. Reporters failed to exercise enough skepticism in passing along secondhand testimony from victims (who often just parroted what they picked up from the rumor mill), and they were far too eager to broadcast as fact apocalyptic statements from government officials—such as Mayor Ray Nagin's prediction of 10,000 Katrina-related deaths (there were less than 900 in New Orleans at press time) and Police Superintendent Edwin Compass' reference on *The Oprah Winfrey Show* to "little babies getting raped"—without factoring in discounts for incompetence and ulterior motives.

Just about every local official and emergency responder with access to the 13 media in those first heartbreaking days basically screamed, and understandably so, for federal assistance. With their citizens stranded, desperate, and even dying, with their own response a shambles, and with their families and employees in mortal jeopardy, they had ample temptation to exaggerate the wretchedness of local conditions and ample fatigue to let some whoppers fly.

"I think that's exactly what it was," says Maj. Bush. "But the problem is they 14 were doing it on the radio, and then the people in the dome would hear it."

The information vacuum in the Superdome was especially dangerous. 15 Cell phones didn't work, the arena's public address system wouldn't run on generator power, and the law enforcement on hand was reduced to talking to the 20,000 evacuees using bullhorns and a lot of legwork. "A lot of them had AM radios, and they would listen to news reports that talked about the dead bodies at the Superdome, and the murders in the bathrooms of the Superdome, and the babies being raped at the Superdome," Bush says, "and it would create terrible panic. I would have to try and convince them that no, it wasn't happening."

The reports of rampant lawlessness, especially the persistent urban legend 16 of shooting at helicopters, definitely delayed some emergency and law enforcement responses. Reports abounded, from places like Andover, Massachusetts, of localities refusing to send their firefighters because of "people shooting at helicopters." The National Guard refused to approach the Convention Center until September 2, 100 hours after the hurricane, because "we waited until we had enough force in place to do an overwhelming force," Lt. Gen. H. Steven Blum told reporters on September 3.

"One of my good friends, Col. Jacques Thibodeaux, led that security 17 effort," Bush says. "They said, 'Jacques, you gotta get down here and sweep this thing.' He said he was braced for anything. And he encountered nothing—other than a whole lot of people clapping and cheering and so glad that they were here."

At the same time, it is plausible that the exaggerations helped make the 18 outside response quicker than it otherwise would have been, potentially saving lives. As with many details of this natural and manmade disaster, we may never know.

But in the meantime, truth became a casualty, news organizations that were 19 patting their own backs in early September were publishing protracted mea culpas by the end of the month, and the reputation of a great American city has been, at least to some degree, unfairly tarnished.

"New Orleanians have been kind of cheated, because now everybody 20 thinks that they just turned to animals, and that there was complete lawlessness and utter abandon," says Maj. Bush. "And that wasn't the case. . . . There's a whole bunch of stuff out there that never happened at the dome, as I think America's beginning to find out, slowly."

Read More on the Web

Hurricane Katrina

Los Angeles Times report on Katrina rumors: http://www.latimes.com/news/nationworld/nation/la-na-rumors27sep27,0,5492806,full.story?coll=la-home-headlines

University of Southern California's *Online Coverage of Hurricane Katrina.* Detailed reporting with many valuable links: http://www.ojr.org/ojr/wiki/katrina/

Wikipedia site on Hurricane Katrina: http://en.wikipedia.org/wiki/Hurricane_Katrina

Urban Legends

About.com site on urban legends and folklore: http://urbanlegends.about.com/cs/urbanlegends/f/urbanlegends1.htm

Wikipedia site on urban legends with several useful links: http://en.wikipedia.org/wiki/Urban_legend

Questions for Discussion

1. What is Welch's central idea? Is it stated in a formal thesis? Where?
2. As you learned in Preparing to Read, Welch uses contrast to clear up some myths that popped up shortly after the hurricane struck. What might be another purpose the author accomplishes in this essay?
3. This essay contrasts myths with realities. What pattern of organization does the author use to do this: point-by-point or subject-by-subject?
4. Is this pattern effective? Explain why.
5. Few essays use one method of development exclusively. Where in this essay does the author explain causes and effects?

6. Comment on Welch's introduction (the first three paragraphs). What techniques does he use to open this essay? (Review methods for writing introductions in Chapter 3.)

7. In paragraph 1, Welch uses verbs like "ripped" and "flashed." Find other examples of vocabulary that make this essay exciting to read. As you do this, identify at least one figure of speech.

Thinking Critically

1. Who is Tiger Woods? Why does Welch quote him in paragraph 3?

2. In paragraph 12, Welsh explains the "root causes of the bogus reports." Write a summary of that paragraph to prove that you understand Welch's argument.

3. Read or reread "What the Gossips Saw," a poem by Leo Romero in Chapter 4. What does that poem contain to help us appreciate Welch's essay better?

Suggestions for Journal Entries

1. Stories that appeared in the media shortly after Katrina struck portrayed some of the citizens of New Orleans as violent and depraved. Think of a group of people whom you believe are unfairly portrayed by the media—perhaps your own ethnic, religious, or age group. List three or four examples from movies, television, newspapers, and other media outlets to support your view.

2. Can all news stories be trusted? Have there been other incidents in which what the news media reported actually turned out to be false? If you decide to write on this topic, do some research on the Internet to find out more about the incident or incidents you are thinking of.

How the Lawyers Stole Winter

Christopher B. Daly

Christopher Daly (b. 1954) has written for the Washington Post *and has taught journalism at several universities including Harvard and Brandeis. He has published in several major magazines. This essay first appeared in the* Atlantic *in 1995. It is a good example of the versatility of comparison/contrast, for it allows Daly to make a convincing argument that an increase in lawsuits in the United States over the last quarter century has diminished the freedom, joy, and spontaneity of growing up!*

Preparing to Read

1. Pay special attention to the essay's title. It expresses the author's purpose.
2. The thesis does not appear in the first paragraph—look for it elsewhere.

Vocabulary

connoisseurs (noun)	Expert judges of, specialists.
henceforth (adverb)	From then on.
liability (noun)	Legal responsibility.
obverse (noun)	Counterpart.
savvier (adjective)	More knowledgeable.

How the Lawyers Stole Winter

Christopher B. Daly

W HEN I was a boy, my friends and I would come home from school each 1
day, change our clothes (because we were not allowed to wear "play clothes" to school), and go outside until dinnertime. In the early 1960s in Medford, a city on the outskirts of Boston, that was pretty much what everybody did. Sometimes there might be flute lessons, or an organized Little League game, but usually not. Usually we kids went out and played.

In winter, on our way home from the Gleason School, we would go past 2
Brooks Pond to check the ice. By throwing heavy stones on it, hammering it with downed branches, and, finally, jumping on it, we could figure out if the ice was ready for skating. If it was, we would hurry home to grab our skates,

our sticks, and whatever other gear we had, and then return to play hockey for the rest of the day. When the streetlights came on, we knew it was time to jam our cold, stiff feet back into our green rubber snow boots and get home for dinner.

I had these memories in mind recently when I moved, with my wife and 3 two young boys, into a house near a lake even closer to Boston, in the city of Newton. As soon as Crystal Lake froze over, I grabbed my skates and headed out. I was not the first one there, though: the lawyers had beaten me to the lake. They had warned the town recreation department to put it off limits. So I found a sign that said DANGER, THIN ICE. NO SKATING.

Knowing a thing or two about words myself, I put my own gloss on the 4 sign. I took it to mean *When the ice is thin, there is danger and there should be no skating.* Fair enough, I thought, but I knew that the obverse was also true: *When the ice is thick, it is safe and there should be skating.* Finding the ice plenty thick, I laced up my skates and glided out onto the miraculous glassy surface of the frozen lake. My wife, a native of Manhattan, would not let me take our two boys with me. But for as long as I could, I enjoyed the free, open-air delight of skating as it should be. After a few days others joined me, and we became an outlaw band of skaters.

What we were doing was once the heart of winter in New England—and a 5 lot of other places, too. It was clean, free exercise that needed no StairMasters, no health clubs, no appointments, and hardly any gear. Sadly, it is in danger of passing away. Nowadays it seems that every city and town and almost all property holders are so worried about liability and lawsuits that they simply throw up a sign or a fence and declare that henceforth there shall be no skating, and that's the end of it.

As a result, kids today live in a world of leagues, rinks, rules, uniforms, 6 adults, and rides—rides here, rides there, rides everywhere. It is not clear that they are better off; in some ways they are clearly *not* better off.

When I was a boy skating on Brooks Pond, there were no grown-ups 7 around. Once or twice a year, on a weekend day or a holiday, some parents might come by with a thermos of hot cocoa. Maybe they would build a fire (which we were forbidden to do), and we would gather round.

But for the most part the pond was the domain of children. In the absence 8 of adults, we made and enforced our own rules. We had hardly any gear—just some borrowed hockey gloves, some hand-me-down skates, maybe an elbow pad or two—so we played a clean form of hockey, with no high-sticking, no punching, and almost no checking. A single fight could ruin the whole afternoon. Indeed, as I remember it, thirty years later, it was the purest form of hockey I ever saw—until I got to see the Russian national team play the game.

But before we could play, we had to check the ice. We became serious jun- 9 ior meteorologists, true connoisseurs of cold. We learned that the best weather for pond skating is plain, clear cold, with starry nights and no snow. (Snow not only mucks up the skating surface but also insulates the ice from the colder air above.) And we learned that moving water, even the gently flowing Mystic River, is a lot less likely to freeze than standing water. So we skated only on the pond. We learned all the weird whooping and cracking sounds that ice makes as it expands and contracts, and thus when to leave the ice.

Do kids learn these things today? I don't know. How would they? We don't 10 let them. Instead we post signs. Ruled by lawyers, cities and towns everywhere try to eliminate their legal liability. But try as they might, they cannot eliminate the underlying risk. Liability is a social construct; risk is a natural fact. When it is cold enough, ponds freeze. No sign or fence or ordinance can change that.

In fact, by focusing on liability and not teaching our kids how to take risks, 11 we are making their world more dangerous. When we were children, we had to learn to evaluate risks and handle them on our own. We had to learn, quite literally, to test the waters. As a result, we grew up to be savvier about ice and ponds than any kid could be who has skated only under adult supervision on a rink.

When I was a boy, despite the risks we took on the ice no one I knew ever 12 drowned. The only people I heard about who drowned were graduate students at Harvard or MIT who came from the tropics and were living through their first winters. Not knowing (after all, how could they?) about ice on moving water, they would innocently venture out onto the half-frozen Charles River, fall through, and die. They were literally out of their element.

Are we raising a generation of children who will be out of their element? 13 And if so, what can we do about it? We cannot just roll back the calendar. I cannot tell my six-year-old to head down to the lake by himself to play all afternoon—if for no other reason than that he would not find twenty or thirty other kids there, full of the collective wisdom about cold and ice that they had inherited, along with hockey equipment, from their older brothers and sisters. Somewhere along the line that link got broken.

The *whole setting of childhood has changed*. We cannot change it again over- 14 night. I cannot send my children out by themselves yet, but at least some of the time I can go out there with them. Maybe that is a start.

As for us, last winter was a very unusual one. We had ferocious cold 15 (near-zero temperatures on many nights) and tremendous snows (about a hundred inches in all). Eventually a strange thing happened. The town gave in—sort of. Sometime in January the recreation department "opened" a sec-tion of the lake, and even dispatched a snowplow truck to clear a good-sized patch of ice. The boys and I skated during the rest of winter. Ever vigilant, the town officials kept the THIN ICE signs up, even though their own truck could safely drive on the frozen surface. And they brought in "lifeguards" and all sorts of rules about the hours during which we could skate and where we had to stay.

But at least we were able to skate in the open air, on real ice.   16

And it was still free.   17

Read More on the Web

Power of Attorneys' *Stupid Lawsuits and Other Funny Stuff:* http://www.
power-of-attorneys.com/StupidLawsuit.htm

Citizens against Lawsuit Abuse site, *Sick of Lawsuits? You Should Be:* http://
www.sickoflawsuits.org/content/mission/whoweare.cfm

Questions for Discussion

1. Where does Daly state his thesis?
2. Reread paragraphs 1–6. How is this section organized: point by point or subject by subject?
3. What pattern do paragraphs 7–14 follow?
4. What technique does Daly use to conclude this essay? Think back to the methods for ending an essay that you learned in Chapter 3.
5. What, according to Daly, have the lawyers done to steal winter?
6. Where else in this essay does Daly draw conclusions using the cause/effect method?
7. What does Daly mean by "collective wisdom" (paragraph 13)?

Thinking Critically

1. Read Barry Glazer's "The Right to Be Let Alone" in Chapter 12. In what ways is Glazer's argument similar to Daly's position?
2. In what way, according to Daly, has the change he discusses affected children negatively? Can you think of how this change might have affected them positively?

Suggestions for Journal Entries

1. Think of an activity or sport that children used to engage in without the kind of protection required today. For example, they were once allowed to ride bicycles without crash helmets; to swim in ponds, lakes, and rivers that had no lifeguards; and to go skating without wearing protective gear. Gather as much information as you can to explain how children once pursued this sport or activity and how they engage in it today.
2. Think of a sport, activity, or practice that is pursued by members of your generation and that you believe to be dangerous. Use listing or clustering to gather details that might explain why it is so risky. Then gather more information on ways you would recommend to

make it safer. If the sport, activity, or practice cannot be made safer, list reasons that could be used to discourage or prevent people from pursuing it.

3.   Interview your parents, grandparents, or other older people. Ask them for examples of the activities that children of their generation engaged in during their spare time. Then, list ways in which you and your friends spent your spare time when you were children.

Suggestions for Sustained Writing

1.   If you responded to the second journal entry after "High Anxiety: It Never Ends," you interviewed two members of an earlier generation to get their views on how people in their day viewed a particular problem, question, or concern that is also affecting people of your generation. Write an essay that both compares and contrasts the ways that members of your generation and of their generation view this problem. Like Terranova, you might want to do some research—on the Internet or in the library—that will support your thesis. If so, remember to follow principles for including and citing such information as explained in this textbook's website (www.mhhe.com/rcw), which discusses writing a research paper using the Modern Language Association style.

2.   In talking about people who are 80, Malcolm Cowley describes two different types: those who fight on and those who give up. But we see these types in every generation, even our own. In fact, you may have begun discussing such people in your journal. Use these notes in an essay about people you know who fit Cowley's personality types: those who face life bravely and those who just give up.

  On the other hand, if you don't like this topic, you can start from scratch and choose your own basis for contrast. For example, discuss two very different types of students: those who are serious about getting an education and those who are not. Here's an example of a thesis for such a paper:

  > While serious students study hard, do extra reading, and compare notes with classmates, those who just want to get by spend much of their time playing cards or watching television.

  Cowley uses the subject-by-subject method; you might want to do the same. However you decide to organize your essay, discuss two or three people you know as examples of *each* personality type. Begin with a rough draft, adding details with each revision to make your paper clearer and more convincing. In the process, include an effective introduction and conclusion.

Then, rewrite your paper once more. Make sure it has a clear thesis, is easy to follow, and is free of mistakes in grammar, punctuation, spelling, and the like.

3. Write an essay in which you argue against the portrayal of a specific group of people in the media based on ethnicity, nationality, religion, sexual preference, or any other reason. Discuss three or four characteristics of this group put forth by the media. After each one, offer a contrasting opinion and explain why you think the media's view is bogus. By following these instructions, you should end up with an essay whose body paragraphs are organized point by point. However, don't forget to write an effective introduction that entices the reader and states your thesis clearly. If you responded to the first journal prompt after Welch's "They Shoot Helicopters Don't They?" reread your notes. They should provide you with some information you can use to begin your essay.

    As you revise your work, think about adding the kind of concrete and vivid vocabulary that made Welch's essay so interesting, convincing, and memorable. If you need to review what you have learned about effective language, see Chapter 4.

4. If you responded to the second journal assignment after Welch's essay, you may have already begun gathering information about a notorious urban legend. You may also have begun explaining why this legend is, in fact, totally fictitious. Add to this information with material about at least two other urban legends. If you want to research this subject, you can use the library or the Internet (two interesting sites are listed under the Read-More-on-the-Web section that accompanies "They Shoot Helicopters Don't They?"). Then, turn all of this into an essay that uses contrast to show how absurd urban legends can be. Remember that if you take material from another source, you must cite it, that is, give the author credit, whether you quote directly, paraphrase, or summarize. Citing sources using the Modern Language Association style is explained on the website for this book: www.mhhe.com/rcw.

5. If you responded to the first journal entry after Daly's "How the Lawyers Stole Winter," use your notes as the basis for an essay that contrasts the dangerous way a children's sport or activity used to be pursued versus the safer way it is pursued today. Use the subject-by-subject method to organize your essay, but include an introduction that explains the basic elements, rules, or procedures involved in the activity.

    If you responded to the second journal entry, turn your notes into an essay that begins by briefly explaining the reasons you believe a certain sport or activity pursued by members of your generation is dangerous. Then, using the point-by-point method, discuss each of those risks in

detail and offer ways in which to decrease or eliminate its effects. If you
don't like either of these assignments, write an essay that explains in the
first half why a certain contemporary sport, activity, or popular practice
is so dangerous that it should be banned. How about skydiving, bungee-
diving, boxing, body-piercing, or collegiate football? In the second half of
your paper, recommend some ways in which people might be discouraged
or prevented from engaging in it.

Whichever option you choose, fill your essay with details that will
make it convincing. Write at least three drafts; then, edit and proofread
the final draft carefully.

6. Think back to your childhood. How did you and your friends spend your
spare time? Were you couch potatoes who spent all day watching television
or listening to music? Did you collect stamps, coins, or baseball cards? Did
you play baseball, basketball, field hockey, or other sports? Did you go
hiking and camping? Or did you practice playing in your own rock band?

Write an essay in which you compare and/or contrast the way in
which you spent your spare childhood moments with the way people
of earlier generations did. If you responded to the third journal suggestion after Daly's "How the Lawyers Stole Winter," you may have already
interviewed people older than you to gather useful information on this
question. As indicated earlier, you can point out similarities, differences,
or both. The subject-by-subject method is well suited to this assignment,
but if you plan to write a long essay, the point-by-point method might
work as well. As always, revise the rough draft of your essay several
times. Then edit and proofread before submitting your essay to your
instructor.

Writing to Learn: A Group Activity

In "They Shoot Helicopters Don't They: How Journalists Spread Rumors
during Katrina," Matt Welch mentions "urban legends." What are the
most common American urban legends? How do they get started? What
do they say about our culture?

THE FIRST MEETING

Brainstorm to identify a few contemporary American urban legends. If
you have trouble getting started, use the Internet sites listed after Welch's
essay to find 10 or 12 legends that seem to be popular. Discuss these
in your group; then narrow your list down to three or four of the most
intriguing, those that would make good subjects for a group-paper on
what urban legends reveal about us and our culture.

RESEARCH

Assign one legend to each member of the group. In addition to the Internet, use the college library's print collection and online databases to gather important information. For example, try databases such as Academic Search Premier, LEXIS/NEXIS, or JSTOR. But also try the *New York Times Index* and the print version of the *Readers' Guide to Periodical Literature*. Gather enough information to be able to discuss (1) the nature and (2) the origins of each legend as well as to explain (3) how the origins and content of the legend reflect contemporary cultural trends, customs, traditions, and/or modes of thinking.

THE SECOND MEETING

Make sure that everyone in the group has gathered enough information to explain the origins, the content, and the cultural significance of the legend he or she was assigned. Critique each person's notes carefully. Make sure that in each case, enough has been said about each of the three research topics: (1) the content, (2) the origins and (3) the cultural significance of the legend. Assign further research if necessary. Then, ask everyone to bring a fully developed, well written discussion of his or her legend to the next meeting, providing enough copies for each group member. Also, make sure this material has been saved in computer files using word processing software to which everyone has access.

THE THIRD MEETING

Edit each other's work for content and correctness. Then give all of the computer files to one student and ask him or her to combine the discussion of all three or four legends into a coherent research essay with an effective introduction and conclusion. Assign another student to compose a works-cited list (you can find the MLA format for writing such lists on this book's website www.mhhe.com/rcw) or some other style of bibliography. Make sure this material has been saved in a computer file.

THE FOURTH MEETING

Distribute and read this draft of the paper. Make last-minute editing and proofreading revisions, which will be incorporated into the final version of the paper.

CHAPTER 10

Process Analysis

Like illustration and comparison and contrast, process analysis is a way to explain complex ideas and abstract concepts. It can be used to show how something works or how something happens. It also comes in handy when you want to give readers instructions.

Organization, Purpose, and Thesis

Process explanations are organized in chronological order, much like narrative essays and short stories. In narration, however, the writer's purpose is to tell *what* happens. In process analysis, it is to explain *how* something happens (or happened) or *how* it is done.

You would be explaining a process if you wrote an essay discussing how the body uses oxygen, how electric lightbulbs work, how a CD player produces sound, or how the Grand Canyon was formed. An example of such an essay in this chapter is Larry Brown's "On Fire," which explains what happens to a person in the process of becoming a firefighter.

As you can see, process analysis is an important tool in scientific writing. But it can also be applied to topics in history, sociology, economics, the arts, and other subjects. For example, a process paper might be a good way to explain how the U.S. Constitution was ratified, how the stock market works, how people celebrate a holiday or tradition, or how a particular type of music developed. In fact, Dave Barry's "Florida's Fire Ants Headed for Trouble" proves that process analysis can even be used to create humor.

Process analysis is also used in writing instructions. Scientists, doctors, engineers, and computer experts, for example, must often write careful directions to show their readers how to use a tool or machine, how to complete a procedure safely, how to conduct a test to achieve accurate results, or how to run complicated computer software. As a beginning writer, you might want to discuss a more limited subject by showing your readers how to change a tire, hang wallpaper, stop smoking, lose weight, study for a math exam, or accomplish another important task or goal. In this chapter, selections that instruct readers are Adam Goodheart's "How to Fight a Duel," and Triena Milden's "So You Want to Flunk Out of College," which appears in the introduction.

The thesis in a process analysis essay is usually a statement of purpose; it explains why a process is important, why it occurs or occurred, or why it should be completed. For example, if you want to explain how to change the oil in a car, you might begin by saying that changing oil regularly can extend the engine's life. In addition to a statement of purpose, writers often begin with a broad summary or overview of the process so that readers can understand how each step relates to the whole procedure and to its purpose.

Clarity and Directness

As with all types of writing, clarity and directness are important in process writing. You must explain the various steps in your process specifically and carefully enough that even readers who are unfamiliar with the subject will be able to follow each step easily. To be clear and to maintain your reader's interest, keep the following in mind:

1. *Use clear, simple language:* Use words that your readers will have no trouble understanding. If you *must* use terms your readers are not familiar with, provide a brief definition or description. Depending on how much your readers know about how to change a tire, for example, you might have to describe what a lug wrench looks like before you explain how to use it.

2. *Use the clearest, simplest organization:* Whenever possible, arrange the steps of your process in chronological order. In addition, use plenty of connective words and phrases between paragraphs (especially to show the passage of time); this will keep your writing coherent and easy to follow.

3. *Mention equipment and supplies:* Let readers know what equipment, tools, supplies, and other materials are involved in the process. Define or describe items that might be unfamiliar to them. If you are giving instructions, list these materials *before* you start explaining the steps in your process. Otherwise, the reader will have to stop in mid-process to find a needed item. This can be frustrating and time consuming.

4. *Discuss each step separately:* Reserve an entire paragraph for each step in the process; this is especially important when giving instructions. Explaining more than one step at a time can confuse readers and cause you to leave out important information.

5. *Discuss simultaneous steps separately:* If you need to explain two or more steps that occur at the same time, write about these steps in separate paragraphs. To maintain coherence between paragraphs, use connective elements such as "At the same time," "Meanwhile," and "During this stage of the process."

6. *Give all the necessary information:* Always provide enough information to develop each step in the process adequately, and don't forget the small, important details. For instance, if you're explaining how to change the oil in a car, remember to tell your readers to wait for the engine to cool off before loosening the oil-pan bolt; otherwise, the oil could severely burn

their hands. On the other hand, the oil should be warm enough that it all drains off.

7. *Use the right verb tense:* If you're explaining a recurring process (one that happens over and over again), use the present tense. In writing about how your student government works, for instance, say that "the representatives *are elected* by fellow students and *meet* together every Friday afternoon." But if you're writing about a process that is over and done with, such as how one individual ran for election, use the past tense.

8. *Use direct commands:* When giving instructions, make each step clear and brief by simply telling the reader to do it (that is, by using the imperative mood). For example, don't say, "The first thing to do is to apply the handbrake." Instead, be more direct: "First, apply the handbrake."

Visualizing Process Analysis

The following diagram illustrates how you might organize the instructions on removing a flat tire. Transitions are underlined.

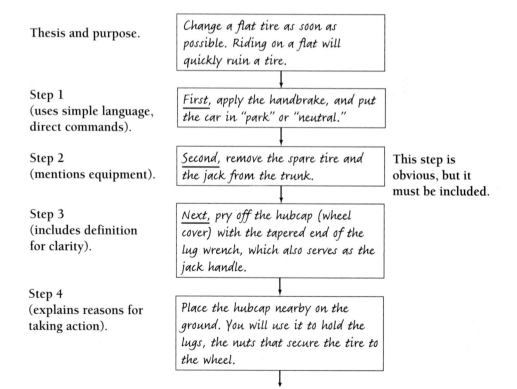

Thesis and purpose.	*Change a flat tire as soon as possible. Riding on a flat will quickly ruin a tire.*
Step 1 (uses simple language, direct commands).	*First, apply the handbrake, and put the car in "park" or "neutral."*
Step 2 (mentions equipment).	*Second, remove the spare tire and the jack from the trunk.* — This step is obvious, but it must be included.
Step 3 (includes definition for clarity).	*Next, pry off the hubcap (wheel cover) with the tapered end of the lug wrench, which also serves as the jack handle.*
Step 4 (explains reasons for taking action).	*Place the hubcap nearby on the ground. You will use it to hold the lugs, the nuts that secure the tire to the wheel.*

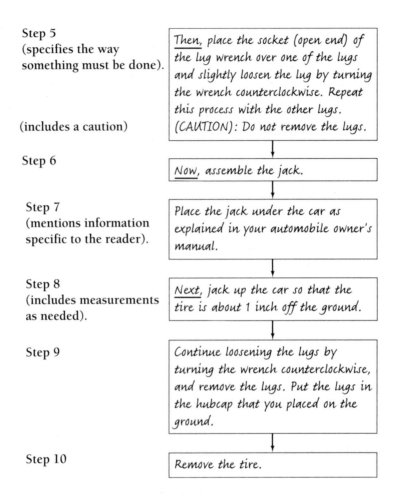

Step 5
(specifies the way
something must be done).

Then, place the socket (open end) of the lug wrench over one of the lugs and slightly loosen the lug by turning the wrench counterclockwise. Repeat this process with the other lugs.

(includes a caution)

(CAUTION): Do not remove the lugs.

Step 6

Now, assemble the jack.

Step 7
(mentions information
specific to the reader).

Place the jack under the car as explained in your automobile owner's manual.

Step 8
(includes measurements
as needed).

Next, jack up the car so that the tire is about 1 inch off the ground.

Step 9

Continue loosening the lugs by turning the wrench counterclockwise, and remove the lugs. Put the lugs in the hubcap that you placed on the ground.

Step 10

Remove the tire.

SEEING THE PATTERN IN A PROCESS ANALYSIS PAPER

The following essay, "So You Want to Flunk Out of College," takes a humorous approach to a serious issue. Student author Triena Milden uses irony by arguing the opposite of what she believes. Nonetheless, her tongue-in-cheek essay illustrates several techniques important to process analysis.

Flunking out of college is a relatively easy task.   It requires little effort and might even be considered fun. Though it is hard to imagine why anyone would purposely try to flunk out of college, many people accomplish

States thesis.

this task easily. In fact, whatever the
reason one might want to flunk out of
college, the process is quite simple.

Uses present tense.

First, <u>do not show up</u> for classes very
often. It is important, however, to show up
occasionally to find out when tests will be
scheduled; the importance of this will
become apparent later in this essay.

Uses transitions for clear, simple organization.

Uses direct commands.

When in class, <u>never raise your hand</u> to
ask questions and never volunteer any answers
to the teacher's questions. If the teacher
calls on you, either answer incorrectly or
say "I don't know." Be sure your tone of
voice conveys your lack of interest.

Discusses each step separately.

Another thing to avoid is homework. There
are two reasons for this. First and most
important, completing homework assignments
only reinforces information learned earlier,
thereby contributing to higher test scores.
Second, although teachers credit homework as
only part of the total grade, every little
bit of credit hurts. Therefore, make sure
that the teacher is aware that you are not
doing your homework. You can do so by making
certain that the teacher sees you writing
down the answers as the homework is
discussed in class.

Provides all necessary information.

Uses simple language.

The next area, tests, can be handled in two ways. They can either not be taken or be failed. If you do not take them, you run the risk of receiving an "incomplete" rather than a failing grade. In order to flunk out of college, failing grades are preferable.

Continues to use direct commands.

Therefore, make sure to take and fail all exams. Incidentally, this is where attendance and homework can really affect performance. Attending class and doing homework regularly can be detrimental to obtaining poor test scores.

Since you won't know the correct answers to test questions, make sure to choose those that are as absurd as possible without being obvious. Even if you guess a few correctly, your overall grade will be an *F* as long as the majority of your answers are wrong. By

Keeps to the present tense.

the way, one sure way to receive that cherished zero is to be caught cheating: all teachers promise a zero for this.

The same ideas pertain to any reports or term papers that you are assigned. If you

Provides all necessary information.

fail to turn them in, you might get an "incomplete." Therefore, hand in all papers, especially if they're poorly written. Make sure to use poor organization, to present information in a confused manner, and to

write on the wrong topic whenever you can.
The paper should be handwritten, not typed,
and barely legible. Misspellings should be
plentiful and as noticeable as possible.
Smudged ink or dirty pages add a nice touch
to the finished product. Finally, try to get
caught plagiarizing.

By following these few simple
suggestions, you will be assured of a
failing grade. Try not to make it too
obvious that your purpose is to fail.

*Ends with
a memorable
conclusion.*

However, if a teacher shows concern and
offers help, be sure to exhibit a poor
attitude as you refuse. Should you decide to
put extra effort into failing, you may even
finish at the bottom of the class. Someone
has to finish last. Why not you?

Revising Process Analysis Papers

After Chuck Russo wrote the first draft of "Do You Want to Be a Millionaire?"
he realized that he needed to make several changes that would help him submit
a successful process analysis paper. Compare the first three paragraphs of his
first and final drafts.

Russo—First Draft

*Write a more
inviting
introduction?*

Everyone wants to be rich, but few ever make
it. You're going to have to have a plan. That's
the bad news. The good news is that many
ordinary people have a net worth over a
million dollars.

Is all of this necessary? Eliminate or condense?

<u>You shouldn't try</u> to get rich while you're still in college. You've got enough worries maintaining your grades, earning some spending money by working part-time (or full-time), and having a social life. For now, <u>you should just make sure</u> that you're making good

Use the imperative (command) here?

Again, use imperative?

Use imperative (command)?

academic progress. However, <u>one ought to consider his or her major.</u> Most of the kinds of millionaires we're talking about held or hold ordinary jobs that do not pay high salaries.

Condense and combine?

In fact, most of them earn or have earned well under $100,000 per year during their entire working lives. In other words, they were middle-income earners. They worked fairly steadily, in fields where layoffs and furloughs were <u>fairly</u> uncommon. Among these <u>fields</u>

Get to the thesis more quickly? State the thesis clearly?

Eliminate wordiness and illogicality? "teachers" and "social workers" aren't "fields."

<u>were public school teachers and civil servants such as police officers, fire fighters, and social workers. Others worked in fields such as accounting and nursing,</u> in which, historically, the demand for employees has been great. <u>You don't need</u> to major in finance, get an MBA from Harvard, and find a job on Wall Street in order to be financially secure. Slow and steady wins the race.

Use a transition? Place this earlier in paragraph?

Clarify? Use transition?

Don't thumb your nose at a job just because it doesn't offer a corner office and a six-figure starting salary. Few starting

Condense this information? jobs offer six-figure salaries. Look at your first, second, and even your third job as opportunities. Enroll in a private pension program. Start contributing to it immediately. Put in as much as you can afford. If your employer matches your contribution, all

Insert a transition for clarity?

Define technical terms? the better. Pretend that the money you are contributing to your <u>401K or your IRA</u> is not

Repetitious and wordy; condense? yours to spend. Contribute some percentage of your salary every pay period. Pretend that the money you put into a private pension fund was never even paid to you. That way, you won't miss it. Live on your take-home pay, minus this contribution.

Russo—Final Draft

Rewrites and expands introductory paragraph. Everybody wants to be rich, but few ever make it. You can certainly try to become a contestant on television's *Who Wants to Be a Millionaire?* but your chances of getting on the show and actually winning are slim. You can buy a ticket for a mega-lottery, but the odds of winning are

Uses a startling remark. more than 10 million to one. You can even try your luck in Las Vegas, but what happens in Vegas stays in Vegas, and that includes your money!

No, you're going to have to plan and work hard to get into the millionaire's club. That's the bad news. The good news is that many people have a net worth over a million dollars, and we're not talking about people like

Eliminates some irrelevant material.

Donald Trump. Many ordinary people—police officers, dental hygienists, and owners of small businesses—have assets in excess of a million dollars. How did such people become wealthy? According to Thomas Stanley, author of *The Millionaire Next Door*, they did it "the dull way—through hard work, perseverance, planning, and self-discipline" (qtd. in Kristof).

Increases interest by adding a question and using quotation from financial expert.

Consider following their example.

States thesis clearly.

Restructures paragraph; adds transition.

First, you don't need an MBA from Harvard to be successful. Many of today's millionaires are middle-income earners in

Corrects illogical construction in the original.

fields where demand for workers is high or layoffs and furloughs are fairly uncommon. So, think about fields like nursing, police work, or government service as career choices.

Paragraph now uses imperative.

Uses a transition to create clarity and to introduce first step in process.

When you start looking for your first job, don't thumb your nose at those that don't offer a corner office and a six-figure salary. Look at your first few jobs as learning opportunities.

Inserts another transition.

From the very beginning, however, start contributing to a pension program. Put in

Condenses.

⎡ as much as you can afford. If your employer
⎣ matches your contribution, all the better.

Defines
technical
terms.

⎡ Pretend that the money you are contributing
⎢ to your 401K or your IRA (investment
⎣ instruments commonly used in pension

plans) is not yours to spend, and contribute

a percentage of your salary every pay period.

Most of these instruments return five to ten

times of the initial investment over 40 years ⎤

of an active work life, and they go a long way   *Adds specific*
                                                  information.
to ensuring a comfortable retirement! By the ⎦

way, don't look to Social Security alone to fund ⎤ *Adds a*
                                                   caution.
your retirement unless you plan to eat pet food ⎦

during your sunset years.

Practicing Process Analysis

Reread Visualizing Process Analysis and the diagram of it on pages 387–388.
Use the method you see there to list instructions on doing a simple task. Write
these steps in the boxes below, one step per box. Be complete; if you need more
boxes, draw them on a piece of paper. As always, make a rough draft first. Here
are examples of the task you might write about.

How to brush your teeth.
How to make a pot of coffee.
How to address an envelope.
How to make out a check.
How to start a car.
How to take a two-minute shower.
How to do laundry in a washing machine.
How to heat leftovers in a microwave.

State task's
purpose

Step 1

Step 2

Step 3

Step 4

Step 5

Step 6

Step 7

Step 8

Do You Want to Be a Millionaire?

Chuck Russo

Charles (Chuck) Russo has a bachelor's degree in English and has been working full-time for several years. When he was asked to offer college freshmen advice based on what he had learned since he left college, he decided to write a process analysis essay stressing the importance of planning ahead—and planning early—for one's future financial security.

Vocabulary

boutique (noun)	Specialty store selling high-priced items.
equity (noun)	Money earned after selling house minus remaining mortgage and realty fees; the percentage of a home actually owned, not mortgaged.
furloughs (noun)	Temporary layoff from work; unpaid, forced leave.
gourmet (adjective)	Specially prepared, sometimes exotic, and always expensive dishes.
initial (adjective)	Beginning, first.

Preparing to Read

1. A mega-lottery (paragraph 1) is sponsored by several states that pool their resources and share the profits. Donald Trump (paragraph 2) is a real estate entrepreneur who hosts *The Apprentice,* a television reality show. An MBA (paragraph 3) is a master's (degree) in business administration.

2. Russo includes information from outside sources, which he cites using the Modern Language Association (MLA) documentation style. To find out more about this style go to www.mhhe.com/rcw.

Do You Want to Be a Millionaire?

Chuck Russo

EVERYBODY WANTS to be rich, but few ever make it. You can certainly try to become a contestant on television's *Who Wants to Be a Millionaire?* but your chances of getting on the show and actually winning are slim. You can buy a ticket for a mega-lottery, but the odds of winning are 10 million to one. You   1 can even try your luck in Las Vegas, but what happens in Vegas stays in Vegas, and that includes your money!

No, you're going to have to plan and work hard to get into the millionaire's 2 club. That's the bad news. The good news is that many people have a net worth over a million dollars, and we're not talking about people like Donald Trump. Many ordinary people—police officers, dental hygienists, and owners of small businesses—have assets over a million dollars. How did such people become wealthy? According to Thomas Stanley, author of *The Millionaire Next Door,* they did it "the dull way—through hard work, perseverance, planning, and self-discipline" (qtd. in Kristof). *Consider following their example.*

First, you don't need an MBA from Harvard to be successful. Many of 3 today's millionaires are middle-income earners in fields where demand for workers is high or layoffs and furloughs are fairly uncommon. So, think about fields like nursing, police work, or government service as career choices.

When you start looking for your first job, don't thumb your nose at those 4 that don't offer a corner office and a six-figure salary. Look at your first few jobs as learning opportunities. From the very beginning, however, start contributing to a pension program. Put in as much as you can afford. If your employer matches your contribution, all the better. Pretend that the money you are contributing to your 401K or your IRA (investment instruments commonly used in pension plans) is not yours to spend, and contribute a percentage of your salary every pay period. Most of these instruments return five to ten times of the initial investment over 40 years of an active work life, and they go a long way to ensuring a comfortable retirement! By the way, don't look to Social Security alone to fund your retirement unless you plan to eat pet food during your sunset years.

During your first years in the workforce, live modestly, and save as much 5 money as you can. Why? You will want to accumulate a down payment on a house. Over the years, real estate has been a great investment, and the earlier you get into the market the better. After all, you have to live somewhere, and owning is wiser than renting. Owning a home lets you build equity; renting gets you rent receipts.

Once you have learned to live modestly, make it a habit. According to 6 Laura Bruce, a financial reporter for *Bankrate.com,* most millionaires "live below their means." That doesn't mean that you must deprive yourself of all life's pleasures; it means being reasonable. You don't need to have a new Cadillac or Land Rover every three years. Buy a Saturn or a Honda and keep it for a while. Today, a decent car that is well maintained can last 8 to 10 years or even longer. Also, purchase only what you need. If you have a large family or own a small business that requires you to transport cargo frequently, the Ford Explorer or even the Expedition might be necessary. But if you use your car only for commuting and your family consists of 3 or 4, the smaller, less costly, more efficient Ford Escort is just fine. Jonathan Wegner of the *Omaha-World Herald* put it well: "Making a million is as much about making choices as it is about making money. Time and self-control can have a bigger impact on your net worth than what you earn each month."

Of course, there are certain expenses that you just can't avoid or even minimize. You have to pay off your mortgage and taxes, buy groceries, pay for utilities, and maintain you home. But you don't have to go on fancy vacations twice a year or own the largest television on the block. You don't have to shop for clothes at an expensive fashion boutique; you don't even have to go to the movies often or eat at gourmet restaurants. In fact, one of the biggest drags on a family budget is entertainment, and that includes eating out. Today a dinner at a family restaurant costs—at the least—between 40 and 50 dollars for a family of four. If you can cut out one of those meals a week, you can save about $2000 per year, which makes a nifty contribution to your Individual Retirement Account (IRA). 7

Finally, avoid debt. According to financial analyst Dave Cole, debt is one of the biggest obstacles to the attainment of wealth. So, if the interest rate on your mortgage is high when you first take it out, think about refinancing later on when interest rates go down. Many people who were paying 9% interest on their mortgages in the mid-1990s refinanced at 5% in 2002–2006, when rates dropped to as low as 4.25%. The best advice, of course, is to get rid of all credit card debt. Limit yourself to one or two major credit cards such as MasterCard, Visa, or American Express, and pay off the balance every month so that you don't get hit with late fees and astronomical interest rates. By the way, not all credit cards are equal. Some charge lower interest than others. Check out current rates in the business section of a national newspaper, in magazines such as *Money* or *BusinessWeek,* or online. 8

Becoming a millionaire takes hard work, steady application, and careful planning. You will probably never own your own Trump Tower but, along the way, you will get to live a secure and comfortable life—financially at least. And you might even manage to leave your heirs something to get them started on once you have left this planet. 9

Works Cited

Bruce, Laura. "Wealth Personalities: Six Types of Millionaires." *Bankrate. com* 2006. 17 June 2006. http://www.bankrate.com/brm/news/advice/wealth/wealth-home.asp

Cole, Dave. "How to Become a Millionaire in Seven Easy Steps." *SelfGrowth.com.* 2001. 15 June 2006. http://www.selfgrowth.com/articles/Cole3.html

Kristof, Kathy. "To Be Wealthy Don't Get Trapped in Trappings." *Los Angeles Times.* 16 June 2006. http://www.latimes.com/business/investing/laspendsave-story-17,1,2328685.story

MARGINAL NOTE

Learn how to use MLA format at www.mhhe.com/rcw.

Wegner, Jonathan. "Becoming a Millionaire Is within Reach
for Many Americans." *Omaha World-Herald.* 11 June 2006.
Lexis-Nexis. Middlesex County College Library, Edison,
NJ. 17 June 2006. http://192.150.150.5:2052/universe/
document?_m=a45dedaflelelc4

Read More on the Web

Ric Edelman: "Becoming a Millionaire: The Story behind Ordinary
People and Wealth." *Inside Personal Finance* writer's advice for
accumulating wealth:http://www.ricedelman.com/planning/
retirement/millionaire.asp

"Dollar Signs: How to Become a Millionaire." CNN Live television show
hosted by Kelly Wallace and featuring David Hinson, founder
of Wealth Management Network, and Russell Pearlman, senior
writer for *Smart Money* magazine:http://transcripts.cnn.com/
TRANSCRIPTS/0409/11/cst.02.html

Questions for Discussion

1. What transitions does Russo use at the beginning of paragraphs
to introduce different steps he recommends in the process of
accumulating wealth?
2. Summarize the reasons Russo provides for each bit of advice he
offers?
3. In paragraph 3, the author tells us that we don't need an MBA from
Harvard. Why does he include this statement?
4. In many process papers written by scientists and technicians, we
are warned or cautioned about certain consequences, actions, or
procedures. Where does Russo caution us?
5. What is the effect of Russo's asking a question in paragraph 5?

Thinking Critically

1. Is this essay well organized? Explain the structure the author has
followed; write an informal outline for it. You can learn more about
informal outlines in Getting Started.
2. Reread this essay. Make marginal comments that reveal if and how
Russo's advice or comments might apply to you right now. For
example, do you carry a heavy credit card debt?

Suggestions for Journal Entries

1. Russo relied on personal experience for the advice he provided you in this essay. Rely on your own experiences for tips you might pass along to a younger sibling or friend about how to accomplish something important. For example, perhaps your brother has Mr. Harrington, the same high school chemistry teacher from whom you earned D's in the first two marking periods, but A's during the rest of the year. What advice would you give your brother to help him succeed? Or perhaps you might offer your sister advice on dating, dealing with your parents, or joining an athletic team.

2. Do your own research on how to accumulate wealth. Start by visiting the sites listed under Read More on the Web. However, also visit the library to find print sources on this subject. List in your journal any advice that Russo doesn't mention.

How to Fight a Duel

Adam Goodheart

Adam Goodheart was an associate editor with Civilization *magazine, published by the Library of Congress in Washington, DC. Goodheart wrote a column called "Lost Arts" in which he explained how to master arts, skills, or activities from the past. Among these intriguing articles are "How to Host a Roman Orgy" and "How to Fly a Zeppelin." "How to Fight a Duel" appeared in 1996.*

Preparing to Read

1. Tort reform (paragraph 1) is a movement to change laws governing suits brought to gain compensation for injury to one's person, property, or reputation.
2. In paragraph 4, Goodheart mentions a "second." This is a person who accompanied and assisted the duelist and even took his or her place if necessary.
3. As with the other articles in his column, Goodheart explains a serious subject humorously. One way he does this is to mix formal, even exotic, language with everyday vocabulary, including slang.

Vocabulary

à la terre (adverb)	To the ground (French).
blunderbuss (noun)	A gun with a wide muzzle used at close range.
calumniating (adjective)	Slandering, making malicious and untrue statements about.
frock coat (noun)	Close-fitting, knee-length coat.
impertinent (adjective)	Arrogant, rude, presumptuous.
languid (adjective)	Listless, lacking in energy or spirit.
lanky (adjective)	Tall and thin.
latitude (noun)	Degree of freedom.
litigious (adjective)	Given to lawsuits, argumentative.
prescribed (verb)	Directed, specified.
prevaricating (adjective)	Speaking falsely or in a misleading way.
provoke (verb)	Incite, anger.
sangfroid (noun)	Cold-bloodedness, cool-headedness (French).
trifle (noun)	Something of no importance.

How to Fight a Duel

Adam Goodheart

TORT REFORM IS for wimps. If we really want to fix our litigious society, how   1
about reviving the old-fashioned pistol duel? As the author of *The Art of Duelling* wrote in 1836, "It is certainly both awful and distressing, to see a young person cut off suddenly in a duel . . . but the loss of a few lives is a mere trifle, when compared with the benefits resulting to Society at large"—such as enforcing good manners. Though you may protest that you don't know a flintlock from a fife cleaner, the rules for duels are really quite simple.

Equipment

Two (2) smoothbore flintlock pistols.

Gunpowder.

Some round lead bullets and linen patches.

A surgeon's kit.

A frock coat.

A handkerchief.

A mortal enemy.

1. The Challenge. In the 18th and 19th centuries, elaborate manuals pre-   2
scribed the exact circumstances under which duels were fought. A slur against one's wife or mistress was a common motive, though the Irish dueling code of 1777 ruled such insults justified if they had "the support of ladies' reputations." (But ladies dueled too; in 1721 the Countess de Polignac plugged Lady de Nestle over the handsome Duc de Richelieu.)

Still, if the offense has not been obvious, you'll often find it necessary to   3
provoke a challenge by insulting your would-be enemy. Here, more creative latitude is permitted. Some insults for you to choose from: "impertinent puppy" (Major Oneby to a Mr. Gower, 1720); "prevaricating, base, calumniating scoundrel, poltroon and coward" (Gen. James Wilkinson to Rep. John Randolph, 1807); "Baron—of Intellect" (Harry Maury to Baron Henri Arnous de Riviere, 1858). Or you can bypass such formalities like Lord Cobham who, in 1750, simply seized Lord Hervey's hat and spat into it.

2. Preliminaries and Precautions. Once a duel has been agreed upon, it is   4
customary simply to exchange cards and then leave all further arrangement to your seconds. The challenger's second then calls upon the challenged party to arrange the confrontation. Such a visit should be cordial if not exactly friendly; sangfroid, at least, is essential. In an 1870 duel, Prince Pierre Bonaparte grew flustered and fired a bit prematurely—killing, that is to say, the unfortunate second who had come to deliver a challenge.

Traditionally, the duel must take place within the next 48 hours—to re-   5
duce practice time—and preferably at dawn. Pick a secluded spot; if there's a state or national boundary handy, fight near enough to it so you can escape

across if you prove victorious. And be discreet, even with friends and family. In 1898, a Berlin duel was cut short when the opponents' fathers burst out of the shrubbery and began thrashing the young men with canes.

3. Taking the Field. Arrive properly attired in a dark frock coat—one without gilt buttons and with lapels to hide your white collar, since these make easy targets. (In 1806, Andrew Jackson scandalized Kentucky—a tough feat in those days—by fighting Charles Dickinson wearing a loose dressing gown draped over his lanky frame.) Greet your antagonist and take your place. The more serious the dispute, generally, the closer you will stand. Anywhere from 10 to 50 paces is customary, although in 1819 Armistead Mason and John McCarty—they were rival politicians—blasted holes in each other with shotguns at four paces. Before shots are exchanged, the seconds can try to effect a reconciliation. If your thirst for vengeance is implacable, proceed to Step 4. 6

4. Ready, Aim, Fire. You and your antagonist will fire simultaneously on cue, usually the dropping of a handkerchief. You should be standing sideways to offer as narrow a target as possible—though not if you're built like British politician Charles James Fox, who exclaimed at a 1779 duel, "Why, man, I'm as thick one way as the other!" If you're considering firing into the air, inform yourself as to local custom. While the languid Brits thought it unsporting under any circumstances to take careful aim, the Germans were deeply offended if you didn't shoot to kill. 7

If both bullets miss, you can either declare the affair settled or go for another round. If you hit your foe, advises *The Art of Duelling*, "An expression of regret should always precede [your] quitting the field." If you're hit, the handbook continues, "treat the matter coolly"; if you happen to die, "go off with as good a grace as possible." 8

Warning Don't try any fancy stuff. In 1808, two Frenchmen fought a duel with blunderbusses in balloons; M. Grandprée sent M. le Pique plummeting *à la terre*. Late in the century, the "dynamite duel" came into vogue—participants would hurl sticks of TNT at each other. But gentlemen prefer pistols at 10 paces. 9

Read More on the Web

Original essay by Adam Goodheart on one of Thomas Edison's worst inventions: http://flyingmoose.org/truthfic/edison.htm

Original essay by Goodheart on how to mummify a pharaoh: http://lancefuhrer.com/mummify_a_pharaoh.htm

Questions for Discussion

1. Earlier in this chapter you read about techniques writers of process analysis use to keep their work interesting and clear. Find examples of such techniques.

2. As you would expect, Goodheart lists steps involved in a duel in chronological order. Why does he arrange these steps into four separate categories?

3. What does the author propose as the purpose for dueling?

4. What method or methods of development that you learned about in Chapter 2, other than process analysis, does this essay use?

5. Why does the author include a separate list of equipment? Why didn't he just include these items in the text as he went along?

6. You learned in Preparing to Read that Goodheart creates humor by mixing informal and formal language. You can find one such example in paragraph 1. Look for at least one other and explain why it is funny.

Thinking Critically

1. Considering what you have learned about dueling, what can you add to the warning given at the end of the essay?

2. Paragraph 3 reports that Harry Maury called Henri Arnous de Riviere the "Baron—of Intellect." How do you interpret his insult?

3. What does paragraph 5 say about the image of dueling even in the past?

Suggestions for Journal Entries

1. What is worth fighting for? Make a list of people, beliefs, or ideas for which you might risk your well-being or even your life.

2. Defined broadly, a duel could be any confrontation, contest, or encounter between two people. Consider the following:

> Bargaining when buying a car.
>
> Convincing a child to do something he or she does not want to do.
>
> Asking for a raise or time off at your job.
>
> Talking your way out of a traffic ticket.
>
> Convincing someone you dislike to stop calling or annoying you.

These are only a few examples. You can probably think of many more. Focus on one such "duel"; use clustering, freewriting, or brainstorming with a friend to gather information that might explain how to prepare for and fight your particular duel successfully.

On Fire

Larry Brown

Larry Brown (1951–2004) lived in Oxford, Mississippi, attended the University of Mississippi, and served in the Marine Corps during the Vietnam War. Brown joined the Oxford fire department in 1973 and was promoted to captain in 1986. At the same time, he began writing part-time, publishing his first short stories in magazines such as Easy Rider. *Eventually, he published two collections of short stories:* Facing the Music *(1998) and* Big Bad Love *(1990).*

In 1990, Brown decided to retire from the fire department and pursue writing full-time. He was quite successful, winning the Southern Book Award for Fiction, among others, and serving as writer-in-residence at the University of Mississippi. Brown published five novels and two works of nonfiction, including On Fire *(1995), which covers his 17 years as a firefighter. The essay that follows is taken from that book.*

Preparing to Read

1. This is not an essay that teaches the reader to do something, but it does address the reader directly to trace the process by which someone evolves into a firefighter.
2. "On Fire" explains both the technological and the human aspects of firefighting. As you read this essay, look for and mark references to both these important considerations.

Vocabulary

advent (noun)	Coming.
culverts (noun)	A drain or channel that goes under a road or sidewalk.
gauntlets (noun)	Extended cuffs on a glove.
Imron (adjective)	A brand of industrial paint made by Dupont.
psi (noun)	Pounds per square inch.
turnouts (noun)	Apparel used while fighting a fire.

On Fire

Larry Brown

Y OU LEARN EARLY to go in low, that heat and smoke rise into the ceiling, that 1
cooler air is near the floor. You learn to button your collar tightly around
your neck, to pull the gauntlets of your gloves up over the cuffs of your coat,
that embers can go anywhere skin is exposed. You learn that you are only human flesh, not Superman, and that you can burn like a candle.

You try to go easy on the air that's inside the tank on your back, try to be 2
calm and not overly exert yourself, try and save some of your strength. You
learn about exhaustion and giving it all you've got, then having to reach back
and pull up some more. Suck it up and go.

You learn eventually not to let your legs tremble when you're pressing 3
hard on the gas or the diesel pedal, when you're driving into something that
is unknown.

One day if you make rank you will be promoted to driver or pump opera- 4
tor or lieutenant and you will discover what it feels like to roll up to a burning
structure, a house that somebody lives in, or a university dormitory where
hundreds of people live, or a business upon whose commerce somebody's
livelihood depends. You will change in that moment, stop being a nozzleman
and become instead the operator of the apparatus the nozzlemen are pulling
lines from, and you will know then that the knowledge pushed into your head
at dry training sessions in the fire station must now be applied to practical use,
quickly, with no mistakes, because there are men you know whose lives are
going to depend on a steady supply of water, at the right pressure, for as long
as it takes to put the fire out.

And on that first time you'll probably be like I was, scared shitless. But you 5
can't let that stop you from doing your job.

You learn the difficulty of raising a ladder and pulling the rope and raising 6
the extensions up to a second-floor window, and the difficulty of climbing that
ladder with a charged inch-and-a-half line and then opening it and staying on
the ladder without falling.

You learn of ropes and safety belts, insulated gloves to move downed high- 7
voltage lines, nozzle pressure and friction loss and the rule of thumb for a
two-and-a-half-inch nozzle. You learn to check the flow pressure on a fire
hydrant and what burning plastic tastes like, the way it will make you gag and
cough and puke when those fumes get into your lungs and you know that
something very bad has come inside your body. You see death and hear the
sounds of the injured. Some days you look at the fire phone and have a bad
feeling, smoke more cigarettes, glance at the phone, and sometimes it rings.
Sometimes you're wrong and the night passes without trouble.

You learn to love a job that is not like sacking groceries or working in a 8
factory or painting houses, because everybody watches you when you come

down the street. You wear a blue uniform with silver or brass or gold, and you get free day-old doughnuts from the bakery shop down the street. At Christmas people bring in pies, cakes, cookies, ham, smoked sausage, cheese, half-pints of whiskey. They thank you for your work in a season of good cheer. One freezing December night the whole department gathers with eighty steaks and Wally parks his wheeled cooker and dumps in sixty or seventy pounds of charcoal to cook them and you have drinks and play Bingo for prizes that businesses in your town have donated, a rechargeable flashlight from the auto supply, a hot-air popcorn popper from a department store, a case of beer from the grocery down the street.

You lay out hose in the deadly summer heat on a street with no shade, 9 hook it all up, hundreds and hundreds of feet of it, put closed nozzles on the end of the hose, and run the pressure up to three hundred psi and hold it for five minutes. If a piece bursts and creates a waterstorm on the street, you remove that section from the line and throw it away. Then you shut it down and drain it and write down the identification number of every piece of hose that survived the test and put it all back on the truck, thirteen hundred feet of it, and you make new bends and turns so the rubber coating inside it won't kink and start to dry-rot.

You learn the major arteries of the body and the names of the bones and 10 how to splint a leg or an arm, how to tie off and cut an umbilical cord. You learn to read blood pressure, administer oxygen. You see amounts of blood that are unbelievable, not realizing until it's actually spilled how much the human body holds. You crawl up under taxpayers' houses for their dogs, go inside culverts where snakes may be hiding for their cats. You learn to do whatever is called for.

No two days are ever the same and you're thankful for that. You dread 11 the winter and the advent of ice. On an August day you pray that the city will behave and let you lie under the air conditioner and read a good book, draw easy money.

You learn that your muscles and bones and tendons get older and that 12 you cannot remain young forever. You test the pump on the truck every day when you come on duty, make sure it's full of fuel, clean, full of water, that the extinguishers are up. You check that your turnouts are all together, hanging on the hook that has your name written above it, and that both your gloves are in your coat pocket. You make sure your flashlight works. You test the siren and the lights because everything has to be in readiness. You shut it all down and stand back and look at the deep red Imron paint, the gold leafing and lettering, the chrome valves and caps, the shiny chains and levers, the fluid-filled pressure gauges, the beds filled with woven nylon, the nozzles folded back into layers of hose, the hydrant wrenches snug in their holders, everything on this magnificent machine. You learn every inch of your truck and you know which compartments hold the forcible entry tools, the exhaust fans for removing smoke from a house, the power saws, the portable generator, the pike poles, the scoops, the salvage covers, the boltcutters, the axes, the ropes, the rappelling gear. You look at all of it over and over again and then you go inside the fire station and get a cup of coffee, sit down with a magazine or a newspaper, and once more, you wait for whatever comes your way.

Read More on the Web

Book Page interview with Larry Brown: http://www.bookpage.com/ 0004bp/larry_brown.html

Hall of Flame Fire Museum site: http://www.hallofflame.org/

Southern Register obituary of Larry Brown: http://www.olemiss.edu/depts/ south/register/two.htm

U.S. Bureau of Labor Statistics site on firefighting occupations: http://www.bls.gov/oco/ocos158.htm#conditions

Questions for Discussion

1. What is Brown's purpose? How would you describe his audience?
2. If Brown had stated his central idea explicitly in a thesis, what might it be?
3. Analyze the author's language. Aside from being simple and straightforward, how does Brown's choice of words contribute to the essay's effectiveness?
4. This essay is well organized even though it is not a series of steps. Explain the principle behind its organization.
5. Many process papers include lists of equipment and supplies. Where does Brown include such information?
6. There is much that is technical here, such as what we read in paragraph 9. But where does Brown appeal to the emotions? To what end does he include this kind of material?
7. Why does Brown address the reader directly, by using the second person?
8. What evidence do you find in this essay to indicate that Brown was a dedicated firefighter?

Thinking Critically

1. In paragraph 10, the author tells us that he did "whatever [was] called for," providing us with an entirely new perspective on the duties of firefighters. What were some of these unusual tasks? Can you imagine others?

2. Summarize what for Brown were the worst aspects of being a firefighter. Then explain what he liked about the job.

3. Several selections in this book discuss people's working lives: "The Dago Shovelman" (Getting Started), "Burger Queen" (Chapter 2), and "Watching the Reapers" (Chapter 6). Identify a few ways in which "On Fire" is similar to at least two of these selections.

Suggestions for Journal Entries

1. In preparation for writing a full-length essay, focus on a job you have held and list some skills, talents, and qualities one must have or acquire to become proficient at it. For example, what makes an effective police officer, customer service representative, sales clerk, landscaper, fast-food cook, construction worker, soldier, practical nurse, or supermarket checker? Begin by listing technical or manual skills, but don't forget to mention important personal characteristics. For example, are physical strength and courage important? Are patience and forbearance necessary? Must one have a strong stomach and nerves of steel?

2. Paragraph 2 of "On Fire" ends with "Suck it up and go," an idea that reveals much about the attitude required of firefighters. Have you ever been forced to deal with a situation or person you found distasteful or repugnant at work, at school, or at another place? Write a short paragraph that recalls the problem. Then, make a list of steps or actions that, if expanded into a full-length essay, would explain the process by which you learned to "suck it up."

Florida's Fire Ants Headed for Trouble

Dave Barry

Dave Barry is a humor columnist for the Miami Herald, *but his work appears regularly in hundreds of newspapers around the world. Among the twenty-four books that Barry has published are* Dave Barry Hits Below the Beltway *(political satire),* Dave Barry Is Not Taking This Sitting Down *(collected columns),* Dave Barry Is from Mars and Venus, *and* Dave Barry's Book of Bad Songs. *Two of his books have been used as the basis for the television sitcom* Dave's World. *"Florida's Fire Ants Headed for Trouble," published in 2003, is one of his syndicated columns.*

Preparing to Read

1. This essay explains a natural process. Because it is so humorous, it is not typical of scientific writing. Yet, it does contain ingredients important to pieces of process analysis found in the world of science. For example, Barry explains the purpose of the process when, early in the essay, he says the "phorid fly" has been introduced to control fire ants.

2. One characteristic common to many of Barry's columns is that they poke as much fun at their author as at the subjects they discuss. Make sure to mark places in this essay where the author turns the comedy on himself.

3. To create humor, writers often manipulate language in several ways. Here are only a few tools that Barry uses:

   - **Hyperbole** (exaggeration). For example, Barry claims that fire ants have 5,684 eyes.

   - **Irony,** saying the very opposite of what is meant. According to Barry, being attacked by a fire ant "was my own stupid fault: I sat on my lawn."

   - **Sarcasm,** a type of irony with an edge. The author pokes fun at a late-night television personality when he compares the thickness of a snake to a "thigh of Anna Nicole Smith."

   - **Figurative language.** Barry compares being bit by a fire ant to sticking his hand into "a toaster-oven set on 'pizza' " (simile). He also personifies the fire ant "Arnie."

   - **Unusual or unconventional wording.** Notice the phrase "Special Recipe fire-ant venom."

Vocabulary

carnivorous (adjective) Meat-eating.

crabgrass (noun) An unsightly weed that often appears in lawns.

ecosystems (noun) Natural groupings of organisms living together.

maggot (noun) Insect larva or offspring.

pheromones (noun) Hormones secreted by animals to get a response from others of their species.

predatory (adjective) Associated with animals that hunt.

seething (adjective) Fuming, boiling, overflowing.

Florida's Fire Ants Headed for Trouble

Dave Barry

ALMOST THE first thing that happened to me when I moved to South Florida 1 was that I got attacked by a fire ant. This was my own stupid fault: I sat on my lawn.

I thought this was safe because I had come from Pennsylvania, where 2 lawns are harmless ecosystems consisting of 93 percent crabgrass (my lawn was, anyway); 6 percent real grass; and 1 percent cute little critters such as worms, ladybugs and industrious worker ants who scurry around carrying objects that are 800 times their own weight. (They don't USE these objects; they just carry them around. That's how industrious they are.)

Your South Florida lawn, on the other hand, is a *seething* mass of preda- 3 tory carnivorous organisms, including land crabs, alligators, snakes ranging in thickness from "knitting needle" to "thigh of Anna Nicole Smith," lizards the size of small dogs, and giant hairy spiders that appear to have recently *eaten* small dogs, and are now wearing their pelts as trophies.

But the scariest South Florida lawn-dweller is the fire ant, a quarter-inch- 4 long insect that can easily defeat a full-grown human in hand-to-hand combat. That's what happened to me. I sat on my lawn, put my hands down and YOW a fire ant—let's call him Arnie—injected me with his Special Recipe fire-ant venom, and then watched, with a merry twinkle in each of his 5,684 eyes, as I leaped up and danced wildly around, brushing uselessly at my hand, which felt as though I had stuck it into a toaster-oven set on "pizza." I'm sure the other ants had a hearty laugh when Arnie got back to the colony and communicated this story by releasing humor pheromones. ("Then this MORON puts his HAND down! Yes! On the LAWN! Ha ha! Must be from Pennsylvania.")

That happened 17 years ago, and my hand just recently finished healing. 5
So I am not a fan of fire ants. This is why I was excited when I read a story by
Jennifer Maloney in the *Miami Herald* about a U.S. Department of Agriculture
program, right in my neighborhood, to control fire ants by releasing a won-
drous little creature called the decapitating phorid fly. This is an amazing fly
that kills fire ants via a method that, if insects wrote horror novels, would have
been dreamed up by the fire-ant Stephen King.

What happens is, the female phorid fly swoops in on a fire ant and, in less 6
than a tenth of a second, injects an egg into the ant's midsection. When the egg
hatches, the *maggot* crawls up inside the ant, and—here is the good part—*eats
the entire contents of the ant's head.* This poses a serious medical problem for the
ant, which, after walking around for a couple of weeks with its insides being
eaten, has its head actually fall off. At that point it becomes a contestant on *The
Bachelorette.*

No, seriously, at that point the ant is deceased. Meanwhile, inside the de- 7
tached head, the maggot turns into a fly, and, when it's ready crawls out and
goes looking for more ants.

You can see an amazing video of phorid flies in action at <u>www.cmave.saa.</u> 8
<u>ars.usda.gov/fireant/news1.htm</u>. The video, which has a soundtrack of wild,
jungle-style drum music, shows female flies zipping around fire ants like tiny
fighter planes, giving the ants FITS. The video also shows how, when a fly isn't
fast enough, it gets turned into Purina Ant Chow.

On a recent Friday I went to watch University of Florida Extension Agent 9
Adrian Hunsberger, and Miami-Dade County biologist Ruben Regalado, release
phorid flies on the grounds of Baptist Hospital in Kendall. To start the procedure, Ruben stuck a shovel into a fire-ant mound and turned over a bunch of
dirt. Immediately, fire ants charged out and began scurrying angrily around.

"They're looking for whoever disturbed their mound," said Adrian.   10

"I HAD NOTHING TO DO WITH DISTURBING YOUR MOUND," I 11
shouted at the ants. "RUBEN DISTURBED YOUR MOUND. I AM HERE AS A
JOURNALIST."

It's important to maintain your objectivity.   12

While the mound was swarming, Adrian opened a vial and released a 13
bunch of phorid flies. The flies, which are almost invisible—little swoop-
ing specks—immediately went after the ants. At least the female flies did.
Presumably the males, observing the Universal Guy Top Priority, tried to mate
with the females.

Anyway, I think it's a terrific idea, using natural enemies to attack fire ants.
To the Department of Agriculture, I say: Good work! To the female phorid flies,
I say: You go, girls! And to any fire ants that happen to be crawling on this col-
umn, I say: REMEMBER, I DID NOT DISTURB YOUR MOUND.

Read More on the Web

Links to some of Barry's other columns: http://www.miami.com/mld/miamiherald/living/columnists/dave_barry/

Dave Barry's Official Website: http://www.davebarry.com/

Questions for Discussion

1. What is the purpose of this essay?
2. Where does Barry explain the process itself? Express each of the steps of that process in your own words.
3. Process analysis pieces often contain statements cautioning or warning readers about dangers to life and property. Can you find anything resembling a caution or warning in Barry's essay?
4. Where in Barry's essay do you find examples of hyperbole, irony, or any of the other methods for creating humor?
5. Find examples of transitions in and between paragraphs.
6. What does "decapitating" mean? Where does Barry define this term? What methods of development—other than process analysis—does this essay use?
7. What is the purpose of Barry's including a reference to a website in paragraph 8?

Thinking Critically

1. Find examples of Barry's making fun of himself. Why does he do this? What can you tell about the speaker of this essay?
2. Read Adam Goodheart's "How to Fight a Duel," which also appears in this chapter. What does it have in common with "Florida's Fire Ants Headed for Trouble"?

Suggestions for Journal Entries

1. Access the website that Barry mentions in paragraph 8 or look up information on using phorid flies to control fire ants on any other website or in any printed source. In your own words, explain how these flies kill fire ants.

2. Use freewriting or clustering to make notes on how to deal with pests. You might explain how to control ants or cockroaches, how to rid your house of mice, or how to eliminate mildew in a bathroom. Then again, you might explain how to deal with an annoying "friend" or a former sweetheart who just won't let go. Other possibilities include handling telemarketers or blocking computer SPAM.

Suggestions for Sustained Writing

1. Triena Milden takes an ironic or tongue-in-cheek approach to academic studies in "So You Want to Flunk Out of College," which appears in the chapter's introduction (pages 388–391). Using this approach, write a complete set of instructions on how to fail at something important. Put these instructions into a letter addressed to someone you know well.

   Begin by explaining how hard or easy it is to fail at the task at hand. In your introduction, explain why someone might want to fail at it in the first place. Revise and edit your letter to make sure it is easy to follow and fun to read.

2. If Suggestion 1 does not appeal to you, write an essay that explains how not to do something. Here are some topics you might choose from:

   > How not to study for an exam.
   > How not to do laundry.
   > How not to start exercising.
   > How not to lie to your parents, children, spouse, or sweetheart.
   > How not to drive a car if you want it to last.
   > How not to get depressed when life gets difficult.
   > How not to become addicted to tobacco, drugs, alcohol, or other substances.
   > How not to get hooked on watching television, playing video games, surfing the Web, or any other activity.

3. If you responded to the first journal entry after Charles Russo's "Do You Want to Be a Millionaire?" you have already begun recording bits of advice that you might give to a younger sibling or friend about accomplishing something important, something with which you have had experience. For example, you might have put down advice about what your reader should do to succeed in a particular high school class, to weather a breakup with a sweetheart, or to survive the first day at a new job.

Reread your journal entry and insert as much additional information as you can. Then, try interviewing other people who have had experience with your topic. Record whatever advice they might add. Next, look over all of your notes, and construct an informal outline for a letter or essay in which to place your advice. In either case, make sure to include a thesis statement and/or a statement of purpose.

As always, don't be satisfied with a rough draft. As you revise your document, make sure you have included enough transitions to make it easy to follow. Also, check to see that you have addressed the reader directly throughout, and that you have used the imperative (command) mood. Be as detailed as you can when it comes to explaining why you believe a particular bit of advice will be effective. Before you begin editing and proofreading, read your final draft to make sure that your advice is clear and presented logically. If it isn't, continue revising.

4. The word *duel* can have many meanings. If you responded to the second journal suggestion after Adam Goodheart's essay, you have probably gathered some pointers on how to prepare for and fight a modern duel (contest, confrontation, or encounter) such as the kind people face every day. Read your notes, and use them as the basis of a paper that provides complete instructions.

    Begin with an outline that, as in Goodheart's essay, divides the process chronologically into major components. Let's say you want to teach your reader how to bargain over the price of a car. You might list headings such as Adopting the Right Attitude, Researching Dealer Costs, Visiting Several Dealerships, Making an Offer, and Closing the Deal. As you write your first draft, list and explain in detail particular steps under each of these headings.

    When you revise your first draft, make sure you have explained each step separately and clearly, used direct commands, and provided all needed information. If necessary, include a list of supplies/equipment in your introduction and a warning in your conclusion. Now, ask a fellow student to read and comment on your work. Revise it once more. Then edit and proofread.

5. If you responded to the first of the journal entries after Larry Brown's "On Fire," use the notes you made in an essay that explains the process by which a person becomes proficient at a certain job. As suggested in the journal prompt, try writing about a job you have held. As you outline your paper, make sure to include sections that discuss both the technical or practical skills required as well as the personal attributes—intellectual, physical, and emotional—that a successful job holder needs to have or to develop.

    If this assignment doesn't interest you, review the notes you made in response to the second journal prompt after Brown's essay. You have probably gathered information on how you once dealt with a person or problem you found distasteful or repugnant at work, at home, or at some other place. Use these notes in an essay that begins by recalling the situation and explaining why you found it so negative. Then, spend the bulk of your essay explaining how you learned to deal with it. There is no need to provide a step-by-step list of the actions you took, but remember that you are writing a process, not a narrative. As you revise your rough draft, take your lead from Brown and make sure that you have discussed the technical or material aspects of the situation, if any. Then, make sure you have explained how you were able to control your emotions and to "suck it up." Before you start editing and proofreading, ask yourself if there is information you might add to make your essay even more convincing and interesting. If so, go back to the prewriting to gather some more details.

6. If you responded to the second of the journal prompts after Barry's "Florida's Fire Ants Headed for Trouble," turn the notes you made into a fully developed essay that explains how you got rid of a pest or that provides instructions on how to get rid of one. Remember that the pest you choose to discuss can be an insect or other animal, a plant, a mold or fungus, a human being, or even an electronic pest such as computer SPAM.

   Your essay can be straightforward and serious. However, you will have more fun if, like Barry, you take a humorous approach. In fact, you might use some of the devices for making readers laugh that Barry used: hyperbole, irony, sarcasm, figurative language, and interesting phrasing. However, this is a process paper; you must explain things clearly. As always, remember that writing itself is a process, so revise, edit, and proofread your work carefully.

Writing to Learn: A Group Activity

In his column in *Civilization,* Adam Goodheart gave instructions on "lost arts." Have some fun by writing instructions on how to perform an art, skill, or other activity that today is rarely or no longer practiced.

THE FIRST MEETING
Choose a lost art to research. Here are some suggestions. How to

> Plan and prepare a Christmas dinner for George and Martha Washington.
> Make a stained glass window for a church or cathedral.
> Build an ancient pyramid (Egyptian, Aztec, or Mayan).
> Plan and build a Buddhist pagoda.

Lead a camel caravan across desert trade routes.

Construct an Iroquois long house.

Make and bury a mummy.

Use leeches to treat a patient suffering from a fever or other illness.

After you have decided on a subject, brainstorm to identify questions to research. Let's say your group decides to explain how to construct and use a Roman catapult. One of you might investigate the purpose for which this war machine was developed. Another could find information classifying various types of Roman catapults. Still another could learn about their construction and operation. Someone else might research the dangers of operating a catapult.

RESEARCH

Research the Internet, specialized encyclopedias and other works in your library's reference section or books listed in the card or online catalog. Bring the notes you take and photocopies of pages from your sources to the next meeting.

THE SECOND MEETING

Make sure the group has gathered enough information to compose a paper that (1) explains the purpose of the process, (2) lists and explains all necessary materials, and (3) provides step-by-step instructions for carrying out the process. Then, write an outline of a paper that addresses each of these items in a separate section. Have each student write two or three paragraphs for one of these sections. You might also ask someone to write an attention-grabbing introduction and a warning paragraph that identifies hazards or dangers involved in the process. Bring photocopies of your work to the next meeting.

THE THIRD MEETING

Critique each other's contributions; offer suggestions for revision. Make sure your work is clear and easy to follow. Assign one student to collect the final versions of everyone's work and create a draft of a complete paper to be distributed at the next meeting.

THE FOURTH MEETING

Distribute and read the draft of the paper. Make last-minute suggestions for revision. Ask one student to edit the paper and another to type and proofread it.

CHAPTER 11

Definition

As explained in Chapter 2, definition is a way to explain a new, complicated, or sophisticated term or concept. Description is akin to definition, but description usually deals with subjects that are concrete—often those that can be explained with information from the five physical senses. Definition goes beyond description to explain the nature of the thing discussed. For example, Claudia Glen Dowling's "Fire in the Sky" describes what an aurora (the Northern Lights, for example) looks like, but it also explains its causes, effects, and significance. Indeed, definition is often used to explain natural phenomena beyond what pure description says about them.

Definition can also explain abstractions, which are as real and as important as anything we can see and touch, but they are conceptual rather than physical. Therefore, while you might write a descriptive essay to introduce your readers to the new "hybrid" car you bought, you would probably write a definition essay to explain what the word "hybrid" means when it comes to automobiles. While you might describe the dimensions and appearance of an execution chamber, you would write a definition paper on the moral implications, causes, and effects of capital punishment.

Types of Definition

Broadly speaking, there are three types of definition: lexical, stipulative, and extended. Lexical definitions are of the type found in the dictionary. Such definitions are valuable as a first step in understanding concepts that may be new and strange to us. But their usefulness is limited, for dictionary definitions are, by necessity, short, general, and abstract. In most cases, they explain concepts without reference to particular contexts. Dictionaries provide the **denotative** or specific meaning of a word or phrase. This is usually the definition as understood and accepted by the vast majority of people. What dictionaries don't explain is the **connotative** definition, which often includes associations the word takes on in particular contexts as well as the ideas and the emotions it elicits among particular people. Some words—especially slang terms or colloquialisms—have easily recognized connotations. "Geezer," for example, is an unflattering term for an elderly person. However, more formal language can also carry connotations. "Miserly," for example, differs markedly in connotation from its synonym "frugal." At any rate, connotation plays an important role in the writing of extended definitions, which is explained below.

Stipulative definitions are determined by the writer, who assigns a specific meaning to a word or phrase as determined by his or her purpose. While practical, such definitions are also limited to special purposes. For example, let's say you were writing an essay on the pros and cons of working part-time as a supermarket checker while attending college full-time. For the purposes of your essay, you might have to *stipulate* that working "part-time" means working 20 hours or less per week, and that attending college "full-time" means carrying at least 12 credits per term.

Extended Definitions

As you can see, lexical and stipulative definitions have their applications, but extended definitions are far more useful when it comes to developing a detailed and complete explanation of a topic that is abstract and often complex. Indeed, writing an essay-length definition is a systematic way to grapple with important social, psychological, ethical, and even scientific questions. It can help us understand human motivations, character types, and social movements. It can even, as in the case of Noonan's "The D-Day Generation," help us understand a specific kind of heroism and pay homage to those who practiced it.

Having to define a concept, principle, or belief **in detail** also forces you to think critically and deeply. It is a way to discover and correct often dangerous misconceptions about people, places, and ideas, and, thereby, to see them in a clearer and more objective way. For example, you may have preconceived notions about terms such as *environmentalism, libertarianism, gay marriage, illegal alien, poverty, glass ceiling, born-again Christian,* or *stem-cell research.* But are those notions correct and fair? In fact, how much do you really know about such topics? Have you read and thought about them much, or is your understanding only superficial, simplistic, and vague? Did you form your opinion after carefully and sincerely considering the evidence, expert testimony, and values you live by, or are you simply adopting the views held by classmates, friends, and family?

Earlier you read that exploring the connotation of a term is an important part of writing an extended definition. Remember that the same term might have a different connotation for different people. In short, an extended definition can be colored by your personal perspective—your knowledge, your emotions, your values. For example, if a typical American college student were writing an extended definition of the term "affluent," she might discuss people who live in 5,000-square-foot homes, own at least three cars, send their children to expensive private schools, vacation in Europe or expensive Caribbean resorts at least twice a year, employ a gardener and a housekeeper, and wear only designer clothes. But what if the same essay were written by a student who had grown up in a country with a standard of living far below that of the United States or Canada—say Haiti or Cambodia, for example? This student might define "affluence" as eating three healthy meals a day; living in a clean, peaceful neighborhood; owning a used car; and being able to go to the movies or to a sporting event two or three times a year. Which definition is valid? Of course, they both are.

Quite often, then, definition essays present us with the author's unique perspective on a subject. Such is the case with Anju Jha's essay, "The Ordinariness of Evil," in which the student argues that contrary to popular belief, the most heinous crimes can be, and often are, committed by the most normal and ordinary of people.

Purpose and Audience

Writing a definition essay requires that you have a clear notion of your purpose. Though classified as one of the methods of development, definition has more to do with the notion of purpose than with a special set of techniques and practices. Look ahead to Visualizing Definition on page 427. Note that "Fire in the Sky" begins by stating the significance of the natural phenomenon it discusses as well as the author's purpose.

A writer can choose from a variety of approaches depending upon the purpose and topic of an extended definition. For example, an essay like Joseph Epstein's "The Perpetual Adolescent," which critiques the "youth culture," would have a far different purpose and take a very different approach from one that simply explains why the two decades before World War I were termed the *belle époque*. In either case, however, the writer must be clear about the significance of the topic and the purpose he or she wants to accomplish.

As with any piece of writing, it is important to consider your readers and to ask yourself the kinds of questions important to audience evaluation, such as

- How much do they already know about the subject?
- Do they already hold strong opinions about it?
- What aspects of the subject are they most interested in?
- What special or technical terms will I have to define or clarify for them?

Let's say you were trying to explain what it means to live with an obsessive-compulsive disorder (OCD). If you begin by telling your readers that OCD is a *neurosis* that is classified as an *anxiety disorder,* you might also have to explain how *neurosis* differs from *psychosis* and how *anxiety* differs from *fear.*

In some cases, you might even have to change your readers' minds. Pretend you are writing an essay on patriotism for *the American Legion* magazine, whose typical reader is a war veteran. If you claim that marching on Washington to protest American foreign policy is as patriotic as taking up arms against foreign enemies, you will have to explain your reasoning in a way that appeals to your readers' more conventional notion of patriotism and to their love of American democracy. You might remind them that the right to assemble and to protest has been guaranteed by the Bill of Rights since the nation's founding—indeed, that the need to protest gave impetus to the Revolution. You might add that it was for that and similar basic human rights that heroic Americans, including many of your readers themselves, have fought wars.

Thesis

As with any other essay, you should try to include an explicit statement of your central idea. In most cases, students are encouraged to place their thesis early in the essay and certainly within their introductions. This is the kind of advice that serves beginning college writers well. In "The D-Day Generation," for example, Peggy Noonan states her thesis in the first paragraph: "They are an impenetrable inspiration." This brilliant summation gives direction and purpose to the rest of her essay.

However, professional writers often put their thesis statements in places that serve their own purposes best. In "The Perpetual Adolescent," Joseph Epstein waits until paragraph 7 to announce that "the ideal . . . is to seem young for as long as possible," an idea for which he has prepared us in the first six paragraphs.

Of course, sometimes, professional writers choose not to state the central idea in a thesis. Instead, they leave it implied. In any event, to exploit the strengths of an extended definition fully, the central idea of a definition essay should express the writer's unique view. Central ideas that do this often lead to the creation of essays that are both meaningful and interesting. Your thesis need not be sophisticated or complicated. In fact the simple and the more sincere, the better. Just make sure that you put the stamp of your own thinking on what you write, as David Blankenhorn did in "Life without Father": "Fatherlessness is the most harmful demographic trend of this generation."

Organization and Development

As you probably know, zoologists classify animals into various categories including order, family, and genus, with each category becoming more and more specific. They then provide distinguishing characteristics to indicate an animal's species (specific class). For example, the African elephant is distinguished from the Asian elephant by its physical characteristics: (1) small ears in the shape of the Indian subcontinent, (2) wrinkled skin, (3) a protruding forehead, and (4) a head with two bumps.

This system can also be used to begin to define ideas, concepts, processes, and other abstract terms:

Term	General Class	Distingushing Characteristics
Socialism	A political and economic system	in which the government controls the major means of production and distribution.
Satire	A genre of literature and other art forms	that criticizes people, practices, and institutions by poking fun at them in order to correct wrongs and abuses.
Photosynthesis	A biological process	by which green plants use sunlight and water to create glucose, which they then store as food.
Phychosis	A mental illness	whose symptoms include delusions, hallucinations, dangerous lapses in judgment, and inappropriate, sometimes violent, reactions to everyday problems and situations.

Of course, these definitions resemble the kinds you will find in a dictionary, and using a dictionary definition is, as explained later, rarely appropriate to an extended definition. However, using this pattern can at least provide you with an outline for an extended definition. To develop a paper adequately, however, you will have to apply your own unique perspective to it. You will have to focus your essay on a particular point and use a variety of rhetorical methods and strategies appropriate to your purpose and subject.

You read earlier that writers use a variety of methods—from narration to cause/effect—to develop extended definitions. Their choice of methods depends, again, on their topic and their purpose. For example, in "The D-Day Generation," Peggy Noonan combines illustration, anecdote, and description to probe the character of the Americans who ensured the survival of liberty in World War II. Joseph Epstein relies on comparison/contrast and illustration to explain what he means by "the triumph of the youth culture."

In short, approaches to the process of defining vary from author to author and from purpose to purpose. Keep this idea in mind as you develop your own essays. For now, read the following items, which explain projects typical of those that college students face when completing essay exams in or writing papers for a variety of classes.

1. You are asked to define *Marxism-Leninism:* You write that one of its major tenets is the violent overthrow of capitalism and the spread of communism through armed conflict. You develop this idea through

illustration, discussing the Russian, Chinese, and Cuban revolutions and their effects in Europe, Asia, and Latin America as primary examples.

2. You are asked to define *psychosis:* You begin by classifying psychosis into its major subcategories, then you use description and illustration to discuss the most typical behaviors associated with this illness. You even mention the most common causes of each type of psychosis.

3. You are asked to define the philosophical movement known as existentialism: You use comparison by claiming that all existentialists focus on the individual and on his or her relationship with the world, perhaps even citing the work of writers like Kierkegaard and Sartre, as examples of this commonality. However, you then contrast the ideas of Kierkegaard, who wrote about the ethical claims made upon the individual by a God-created universe, with those of Sartre, who believed that there is neither a God nor a fixed moral order.

In addition to using traditional methods of development like comparison, illustration, and anecdote, you should keep in mind several other important strategies when writing extended definitions.

1. Begin your essay with an introduction that catches the readers' attention and gets them to read on. Several methods for writing such introductions appear in Chapter 3. However, never begin your essay with a dictionary definition. Doing so will lead your readers to assume—correctly or not—that the rest of your essay also lacks creativity and energy.

2. If possible, distinguish your subject from what it is not. This is called defining by negation. For example, if you are defining the term "patriot," you might make it clear that a patriot need not be a zealot, a chauvinist, or a fanatic. You might also explain that unthinking and unquestioning loyalty to government policies and practices is more akin to fascism than to genuine patriotism.

3. When appropriate, trace the etymology or evolution of a word to show how its meaning developed and perhaps changed over the years. For example, if you were defining the term *gestalt psychology,* you might mention that the German word *gestalt* means "shape" or "form," and that this school of analysis teaches that emotional phenomena should be viewed as whole constructs rather than simply the sum of individual actions or behaviors. If you were defining *glasnost,* a term that Mikhail Gorbachev used in the 1980s to describe a more open Soviet government, you might explain that *glas* in Russian means "voice." Finally, you might also explain that the ancient Greek *hoi polloi,* which literally means "the many," hence "the common folk," is often perverted and used to mean just the opposite—"the elite."

4. List the characteristics or practices of an intellectual, artistic, or political movement. For example, if you were defining the ideology of

Marxist-Leninists you might say that they believe in (1) the violent overthrow of capitalism, (2) the creation of a government ruled by the proletariat (the workers), (3) state control of the means of production, and (4) the spread of the communist revolution throughout the world. If you were defining the nineteenth-century art movement known as Impressionism, you might say that the impressionists (1) emphasized the changing qualities of light and the passage of time; (2) used light colors; (3) painted outdoors, preferring natural light to studio light; and (4) used subjects from nature and everyday life.

5. Ask and answer a question important to understanding the term you are defining. David Blankenhorn does just this when, in "Life without Father," he asks "Does every child need a father?"

6. Make a literary, cultural, or historical reference or allusion. Peggy Noonan does this in "The D-Day Generation," the title of which is itself a historical allusion. But she also mentions former New York governor Mario Cuomo, and she alludes to General George Patton, the American general nicknamed "Blood 'n Guts," who fought in Italy, North Africa, and Europe during World War II.

Visualizing Definition

Fire in the Sky

Claudia Glen Dowling

Nights are long and bitter in the polar winters, but

the compensations can be spectacular: The skies

Uses description to explain the significance of the thing defined.

blaze in a display of energy called the aurora borealis

in the Arctic, aurora australis in the Antarctic.

Ancient tribes who saw the lights believed that

they were caused by the bonfires of spirits; today we

know that awe-inspiring physical forces create the

heavenly arrays. And we're about to know more. A

First paragraph states the author's purpose.

hardy breed of scientists—who don't mind odd hours

or sub-zero temperatures—are investigating the

powerful magnetic storms hidden within the aurora's

glory. A few years ago, some of these researchers put
up a sign outside their University of Alaska lab near
the tiny village of Poker Flats. It said it all: "Center
for the Study of Something which, on the face of it,
might seem trivial, but on closer examination takes
on Global Significance."

Uses direct quotation.

Makes another reference to the essay's purpose.

Uses process analysis to explain how auroras form.

Auroras are born on the sun, where
thermonuclear storms tear apart hydrogen atoms,
blasting protons and electrons toward earth at
up to 1,000 miles per second. As this solar wind
approaches Earth's magnetic field, particles are
drawn to the poles like iron filings to the ends of a
bar magnet. When the particles collide with gases
in the Earth's atmosphere, they create electrical
discharges that glow purple, green, red and white.
The effect is similar to the collision of electrons and
gases inside a color television tube.

Makes comparisons.

Describes auroras' chief characteristics: their violence, release of energy, and substorms.

The beauty of an auroral storm hides its
violence—the release of millions of amperes
of electricity, 20 times that found in a bolt of
lightning. Surges within auroras, called substorms,
tap energy trapped by the Earth's magnetic field
on the side of the planet away from the sun. One
physicist poetically calls this energy pool Earth's
"electromagnetic soul."

Uses a metaphor in a direct quotation.

A series of such storms knocked out power
in all of Quebec as well as several U.S. states
in 1989. Earlier this year surges damaged two

Explains auroras' effects on the civilized and natural worlds.

communications satellites. NASA researchers theorize that the substorms, which produce nitrogen oxides, may also damage the ozone layer above the poles. No one knows what effect the electrical charge may have on human beings, although Japanese travel agencies book tours to the Arctic specifically for couples who believe that their chances of conceiving a child are better under the aurora.

Lately, interest in mapping and predicting substorms has led to increased government spending. (That may be why, not long ago, the sign at Poker Flats was changed to read: "This facility is uniquely dedicated to studies of the aurora borealis and other atmospheric research studies for the paying customer such as the National Aeronautics and Space Administration, the United States Air Force . . . ") Last month, NASA launched a satellite—dubbed Wind—to monitor the solar wind as it howls toward Earth. Another, called *Polar*, the size of a school bus, is planned to orbit closer to the planet, photographing auroras with sensitive cameras. Next year, Russia will launch two similar probes. And in November a consortium of European nations will open a radar installation in Spitsbergen, Norway, with high-powered dishes that will collect information about the velocity, density, and temperature of solar particles. A European satellite that is designed to circle the Arctic will collect similar data from above.

Uses direct quotation.

Explains what we are doing to learn more about auroras.

Uses examples and explains effects of increased interest in auroras.

Still, a nonscientific observer need only be in the right place at the right time to study this natural wonder. A jargon-filled recorded message from the National Oceanic and Atmospheric Administration in Boulder, Colo. (303-497-3235), tells aficionados when conditions are favorable for a good show.

Tells readers when and where to look for auroras.

Although the aurora can be seen year-round—the atmosphere is always being bombarded by the solar wind—and is sometimes visible as far away as the equator, it occurs most often in the extreme north and south and is easiest to see on a clear, dark winter night. Photographer Norbert Rosing's favorite site is Churchill, Manitoba, where winter skies are cloudless 80 percent of the time. There, every February and March, he waits in the cold, warming his film with his car heater so it won't crack. "When you see the northern lights," he says, "you're in love."

Uses hyperbole (exaggeration) to capture the emotions associated with witnessing an aurora.

Revising Definition Essays

Student Anju Jha's "The Ordinariness of Evil" appears later in this chapter. After completing some prewriting, an outline, and a rough draft for a research assignment made in her freshman writing course, Jha believed that she could develop her ideas in greater detail and make clearer and more convincing her thesis that the worst evil can be perpetrated by ordinary people. The result was a first-class definition essay. Several body paragraphs from Jha's rough draft and final draft appear below.

Jha—Rough Draft

8. Many experts think that socialization has a big role in the formation of an evil society. Socialization is the fundamental step which creates what the

Relate this more closely to thesis: "The worst evil can be perpetrated by ordinary people"?

philosopher Eric Fromm would call "authoritarian conscience." According to Eric Fromm, our conscience, or our inner voice, has two distinct parts, the "humanistic conscience, which guides us to our humanity, and the "authoritarian conscience," which is similar to Freud's super-ego and develops as a result of social conditioning based on reward and punishment. Our "authoritarian conscience," and

Clarify?

Develop and clarify?

"humanistic conscience" are so much harmonized that most of the time we are completely unable to make the distinction between the two (Fromm). In the case of mass murderers an "authoritarian conscience" is created either by propaganda or by "professionally socializing them and that produces hatred for the victims in their minds."

Is paragraph 9 necessary?

9. Today the world is facing one of the cruelest forms of mass murder—terrorism. Terrorism works a little differently from other forms of mass murder.

Why not continue discussing how socialization can create mass murderers?

The terrorist organizations are not structured in the form of hierarchical organizations, but they share other aspects of a typical organization involved in genocide such as feelings of hatred, alienation, and anger toward the victims. Terrorist organizations use the concept of "authoritarian conscience" very effectively, in fact much better than other groups.

Combine ideas here with those in paragraph 8?

10. Every society and culture creates the "authoritarian conscience" that suits it the most. It makes unjust and cruel practices prevalent in

the society normal and rational. People do not ask questions even when they see injustice and cruelty around them. They just accept everyone else's actions and start to behave the same way themselves. And that creates problems such as terrorism, racism, slavery, and various other social maladies. Edward Herman in his article "The Banality of Evil" writes, "That was the way it was; racism was so routine that it took years of incidents, movement actions, reading and real-world traumas to overturn my own deeply imbedded bias." Once an unjust and biased social order is in place, people resist any change. Unfortunately, most of the time, the change only comes through violent and destructive movements.

> *The way __what__ was? Provide a context and clarify?*

Jha—Final Draft

> *Paragraph now relates directly to thesis—"the worst evil can be perpetrated by ordinary people."*

8. Socialization, which plays an important role in determining the moral character of any group, can be manipulated to create Eichmanns.* According to philosopher Erich Fromm, our conscience has two parts. The first is our "humanistic conscience," an inborn knowledge in every human being of what is good and evil—what is human and what is not. The second is our "authoritarian conscience," which develops as a result of social conditioning based on reward and punishment (Fromm). Every culture develops an "authoritarian conscience" that best

> *Clarifies distinction between "humanistic" and "authoritarian" conscience.*

---

*Adolf Eichmann engineered and carried out the Holocaust for Hitler.

Inserts information from rough draft's paragraph 10.

suits its values. Sometimes, injustice and cruelty are portrayed as normal, rational activities, to the extent that many people fail to recognize evil; instead, they simply accept everyone else's actions and behave the same way. In this atmosphere, various social maladies, such as racism, slavery, and terrorism can flourish, and ordinary people can become agents of terror and genocide.

Removes old paragraph 9; continues to discuss role of socialization in creating mass murderers.

9. In "A Duplex Theory of Hate," Robert J. Steinberg argues that the process by which ordinary people can be turned into mass killers has three components. First they are systematically distanced from their victims and, through propaganda, are instilled with disgust and hatred for them. Second, again through propaganda, they are convinced that the victims pose an imminent threat to their safety. Third, the victims are constantly devalued, belittled, and dehumanized. As Steinberg shows, Hitler used all three components in a process of socialization that turned ordinary citizens into agents of genocide.

10. Unfortunately, once an unjust and biased social order is in place people resist changing it. In "The Banality of Evil," Edward Herman writes: "When I was a boy, and an ardent baseball fan, I never questioned, or even noticed, that there were no Black baseball players in the big leagues. That was the way it was; racism was so routine that it took years of incidents, movement actions, reading, and real-world traumas to overturn my own deeply imbedded bias."

Adds material that provides a context and clarifies.

Practicing Definition

Earlier you learned that a term can be defined by discussing its general class and its distinguishing characteristics. Write a paragraph-length definition (50 to 100 words) for each of the following terms. Begin by identifying the general class into which each term falls. For example, you might write that "a single parent is a mother or father who has the sole responsibility for managing a family." Then provide distinguishing characteristics according to the directions given for developing each paragraph.

1. *Single parent*

   Directions: Use contrast and/or illustration. For example, contrast the workload of a single parent with that of a married parent. Then discuss the difficulties a particular single parent you know must face as she or he tries to manage a family.

2. *Egotist*

   Directions: Describe the personalities of one or two egotists you have known. Discuss their behavior, and/or quote them directly. Also, explain the causes and the effects of having an inflated ego.

3. *Sports Utility Vehicle (SUV)*

   Directions: Contrast SUVs and more traditional cars by discussing their capabilities, purchase price, and gas mileage versus traditional cars. Then, try classifying five or six different SUVs according to size, reliability, and/or standard features. Make sure to name specific SUV models.

4. *Envy*

   Directions: Explain various causes for envy. For example, you might mention that some people become envious because of their own lack of self-esteem. Also, mention some of the negative effects of envy, and try to suggest ways in which one might control or overcome the tendency to be envious.

5. *Racism*

   Directions: Include examples of racist remarks. Narrate one or two anecdotes from your own experience to show how harmful racist remarks can be. Finally, speculate on what causes people to be racist.

The Ordinariness of Evil

Anju Jha

Anju Jha has a bachelor's degree in engineering from Ranchi University in Jahrhand, India. In 1993, she immigrated to the United States, where she worked as a consultant for the Chase Manhattan Bank. A few years later, Jha began taking additional college courses with the intention of becoming a certified public accountant, a goal she has nearly accomplished. The "Ordinariness of Evil" was written in response to a freshman research assignment.

Preparing to Read

1. The Holocaust was the attempt by the Nazis to exterminate the Jews of Europe; it resulted in the systematic murder of over six million people. In their concentration camps, the Nazis also murdered millions of Poles, Czechs, Gypsies, and members of other ethnic groups as well as political prisoners, homosexuals, and people with mental or physical maladies.

2. Jha includes examples of otherwise ordinary people who were capable of great evil. From this number, however, she excludes monsters such as Adolf Hitler and Pol Pot (the madman who led the Cambodian genocide in the 1980s), who were the very embodiment of evil. Doing this allows her to define by negation.

3. Look for places in which Jha uses cause/effect and contrast.

4. Iago, who is mentioned with Macbeth in paragraph 1, is the embodiment of deception and evil in Shakespeare's play *Othello*.

5. Note that Jha makes excellent use of the Modern Language Association (MLA) style of documentation. To learn more about MLA style, go to www.mhhe.com/rcw.

Vocabulary

animus (noun)	Hatred.
ardent (adjective)	Enthusiastic, zealous.
atrocities (noun)	Horrors, crimes against humanity.
banal (adjective)	Ordinary, commonplace, boring.
genocide (noun)	Mass murder, the attempt to kill an entire race.
hierarchical (adjective)	Relating to an order by which items are arranged by importance.
ideological (adjective)	Relating to a belief, philosophy, or creed.
imminent (adjective)	Pending, about to happen.

lethal (adjective)   Deadly.
nonchalantly (adverb)   Casually, indifferently, without emotion.
perverse (adjective)   Evil, vicious, twisted.
sadistic (adjective)   Taking pleasure in inflicting pain.

The Ordinariness of Evil

Anju Jha

THE PHRASE "banality of evil" was used by Hannah Arendt in *Eichmann in* 1
Jerusalem, a book on the trial of Adolf Eichmann, the infamous bureaucrat
responsible for countless atrocities against Jews during the Holocaust. Arendt
was struck by the ordinariness, mediocrity, and utter lack of imagination of the
man who was responsible for the torture and extermination of millions of Jews.
To her, nothing about him appeared extraordinary. "Eichmann was not Iago
and not Macbeth. . . . Except for an extraordinary diligence in looking out for
his personal advancement, he had no motive at all" (Arendt 287). Indeed, the
most striking thing about Eichmann was that he did not have any particular
hatred for Jews. He considered Hitler's orders to be the laws of the land and
dutifully followed them like any other law-abiding citizen. Neither was he deranged, for half a dozen psychiatrists had certified him to be absolutely normal
(Arendt 24–25).

Arendt's suggestion that evil can be "banal" created a furor among her 2
critics. Even the suggestion that Eichmann was a normal and ordinary individual seemed preposterous. As Arendt explains, "it would have been very
comforting indeed to believe that Eichmann was a monster." However, "the
trouble with Eichmann was precisely that so many were like him, and that the
many were neither perverted nor sadistic, that they were, and still are, terribly
and terrifyingly normal" (276). In short, the worst evil can be perpetrated by
ordinary people.

At the time of Eichmann's trial in 1961, Stanley Milgram, a social psy- 3
chologist at Yale University, was working on an obedience experiment. Milgram
recruited volunteers, selecting people from different backgrounds and professions, to participate in what he described as a study in learning. The subjects of
the experiment were the "teachers." The other participants were the "learners"—
who actually were actors—and the experimenter. The subjects were made
to believe that the "learners" were wired to an electric chair. Each time a
learner gave an incorrect answer to a question, the "teacher" was told by the
experimenter to administer an electric shock, increasing the voltage for each
subsequent mistake. Sixty-five percent of the subjects administered the level of
voltage that would have been lethal in real life. In each case, the actors sitting
on the chair kept protesting, screaming, exhibiting excruciating pain. But the
subject went ahead on the insistence of the experimenter (Milgram).

The results of Milgram's experiment astounded the world. When he had 4 consulted behavior experts before the experiment, they had unanimously predicted that "all the subjects would refuse to obey the experimenter. The psychiatrist, specifically, predicted that most subjects would not go beyond 150 volts, when the victim makes his first explicit demand to be freed" (Milgram). Obviously, the results proved them wrong. The experiment was repeated many times at various locations throughout the world, but the results were consistent. They proved that obedience—a virtue needed for the functioning of any society—could also be used by the establishment to make people commit the worst crimes against humanity. The subjects of the experiment were ordinary people belonging to the most normal strata of society, not the sadistic fringe. "Milgram's subjects—with no obligatory, cultural, or ideological commitments and without prior training or conditioning—were willing to inflict excruciating pain on someone just like themselves, against whom they had no animus at all" (Waller 108). It is true that most of them got extremely uncomfortable as the experiment progressed, but they kept complying with the experimenter. Also, at no time during the experiment were they under any threat of losing their lives, of risking the safety of their loved ones, or of jeopardizing their social status, nor were they offered monetary gains. Thus, the only motivation for them to go ahead with the experiment was to please the experimenters.

Although Milgram's experiment is compelling, it would be simplistic 5 to compare the compliance shown by Milgram's subjects with that of mass murderers. There are many aspects of his experiment that do not correspond with mass killings. In *Becoming Evil*, James Waller discusses significant distinctions between Milgram's subjects and mass murderers. First, unlike what occurred in the experiment, no one reassures people committing genocide that the victims will not suffer permanent physical damage. Second, given the slightest excuse to avoid obedience, Milgram's subjects did so, which is not characteristic of mass murderers. Third, mass murderers do not exhibit great anguish when torturing their victims as Milgram's subjects did. Fourth, it would have been extremely difficulty for Milgram to continue his experiment for more than an hour, while genocidal activities last for months or years (107–108).

Despite these valid observations, Milgram "focuses our attention to social 6 and situational pressures that can lead ordinary people to commit evil" (Waller 108). Moreover, according to Milgram, the fact that hundreds of subjects of his experiments submitted to authority, lends credibility to Arendt's concept of the "banality of evil." Milgram believes that the most fundamental lesson of his study is that "ordinary people, simply doing their jobs, and without any particular hostility on their part, can become agents in a terrible destructive process." For Milgram, this "agentic state" makes possible the psychological connection between his subjects and the perpetrators of genocide. Significantly, in the agentic state, individuals cease to be autonomous and refuse to accept responsibility for their actions (Waller 109).

Of course, acting as an agent does not explain the conduct of everyone 7
who perpetrates genocide. Obviously, criminals like Hitler and Pol Pot do not
operate in the "agentic state." They are genuinely evil, and neither Arendt or
Milgram includes them in the scope of their studies. Their focus is the millions of ordinary people who make genocide possible just by doing what they
perceive to be their duty. For them, working for dictators is no different from
working for a corporation.

Socialization, which plays an important role in determining the moral 8
character of any group, can be manipulated to create Eichmanns. According
to philosopher Erich Fromm, our conscience has two parts. The first is our
"humanistic conscience," an inborn knowledge in every human being of what
is good and evil—what is human and what is not. The second is our "authoritarian conscience," which develops as a result of social conditioning based on
reward and punishment. Every culture develops an "authoritarian conscience"
that best suits its values. Sometimes, injustice and cruelty are portrayed as
normal, rational activities, to the extent that many people fail to recognize
evil; instead, they simply accept everyone else's actions and behave the same
way. In this atmosphere various social maladies, such as racism, slavery, and
terrorism can flourish, and ordinary people can become agents of terror and
genocide.

In "A Duplex Theory of Hate," Robert J. Steinberg argues that the process 9
by which ordinary people can be turned into mass killers has three components. First they are systematically distanced from their victims, and through
propaganda, are instilled with disgust and hatred for them. Second, again
through propaganda, they are convinced that the victims pose an imminent
threat to their safety. Third, the victims are constantly devalued, belittled,
and dehumanized. As Steinberg shows, Hitler used all three components
in a process of socialization that turned ordinary citizens into agents of
genocide.

Unfortunately, once an unjust and biased social order is in place, people 10
resist changing it. In "The Banality of Evil," Edward Herman writes: "When I
was a boy, and an ardent baseball fan, I never questioned, or even noticed, that
there were no Black baseball players in the big leagues. That was the way it was;
racism was so routine that it took years of incidents, movement actions, reading, and real-world traumas to overturn my own deeply imbedded bias."

Another important aspect of the "banality of evil" is that in a hierarchical 11
system, ordinary people are usually concerned only about doing their own
part and are unaware of the consequences of the final act. Milgram described
this as the shortsightedness of the "intermediate link." The problem is that
often, because of a division of labor, a single person is unable to see the whole
picture. During the Holocaust, while one person was just doing paperwork,
others prepared the gas chambers. All were performing their assigned jobs and
following orders from above. And since nobody was there to take responsibility

for the whole act—killing and torturing Jews—all kept playing their parts nonchalantly (Milgram).

People who take part in genocide can be and often are the most ordinary of 12 human beings, simply fulfilling their responsibilities as the situation demands. They are not born with evil or sadistic characters. Generally, obedience to authority, conformity to the group or community, perverse societal values and ideologies, fear and hatred of people of different ethnic or religious groups, and, above all, corrupt and twisted leaders motivate ordinary people to commit extraordinary evil. Although experts may disagree over the extent to which each of these factors contributes to the commission of evil by ordinary people, they cannot dismiss the "banality of evil" altogether.

Works Cited

Arendt, Hannah. *Eichmann in Jerusalem.* New York: Penguin, 1977.

Fromm, Erich. "Disobedience as a Psychological and Moral Problem." *On Disobedience and Other Essays.* London: Routledge & Kegan Paul, 1984. 1–8.

Herman, Edward. "The Banality of Evil." *The Triumph of the Market.* Cambridge: South End Press, 1995. Information Clearing House. 29 June 2005. http://www.informationclearinghouse.info/article7278.htm

Milgram., Stanley. "The Perils of Obedience." Abridged and adopted from *Obedience to Authority* by Stanley Milgram. *Harper's Magazine* 1974. 13 July 2005. http://home.swbell.net/revscat/perilsOfObedience.html

Steinberg, Robert. "A Duplex Theory of Hate: Development and Application to Terrorism, Massacres, and Genocide." *Review of General Psychology* Sept. 2003: 299–328. PsychArticles EBSCOhost. Middlesex County College Library. 1 July 2005. http://search.epnet.com

Waller, James. *Becoming Evil.* New York: Oxford, 2002.

> **MARGINAL NOTE**
>
> Learn how to use MLA format at www.mhhe.com/rcw

Read More on the Web

"Eichmann, the Banality of Evil, and Thinking in Arendt's Thought" by *Bethania Assy:* http://www.bu.edu/wcp/Papers/Cont/ContAssy.htm

University of Dayton site on Stanley Milgram: http://elvers.stjoe.udayton.edu/history/people/Milgram.html

Wikipedia site on Adolf Eichmann: http://en.wikipedia.org/wiki/Adolf_Eichmann

Questions for Discussion

1. Find at least two places where Jha states her thesis.

2. What is the "agentic state" first mentioned in paragraph 6? Why does Jha bother to define this term? How does her explanation relate to her thesis?

3. What other special terms does she make sure to define in this extended definition of "the banality of evil"?

4. What is socialization? What role does it play in the transformation of an ordinary person into a mass murderer?

5. You learned earlier that the discussion of distinguishing characteristics can make for an effective definition. Make a list of the distinguishing characteristics that Jha uses.

6. Why does the author include the quotation by Edward Herman in paragraph 10? How does this quotation advance Jha's thesis?

7. Where and for what reason does Jha use contrast? How about cause/effect?

8. Earlier you learned that by excluding Hitler and Pol Pot from the list of ordinary people who became mass murderers (paragraph 7), Jha is defining by negation. Where else does she define by negation?

Thinking Critically

1. Write a paragraph that explains the distinction between the "humanistic conscience" and the "authoritarian conscience" (paragraph 8). In the process, explain how the "authoritarian conscience" can be used to create mass murderers.

2. In your own words explain what Jha means by the term "hierarchical system" as it relates to "the banality of evil" (paragraph 11).

Suggestions for Journal Entries

1. Have you ever been told by a teacher, employer, or other authority figure to do something you believed was wrong? Have you been pressured by peers to do something you didn't want to do? Use focused freewriting to gather information about this incident.

2. Do you know of another example of a seemingly ordinary person who committed an unspeakable wrong? You may have read or heard about such a person—or even known one personally. Use listing to gather details that might describe this person's character; then use focused freewriting to explain his or her wrongdoing.

The D-Day Generation

Peggy Noonan

Peggy Noonan (b. 1950) is a contributing editor to the Wall Street Journal *and has written for* Forbes, Newsweek, *the* Washington Post, *and the* New York Times, *among other magazines and newspapers. The author of several books on politics and culture, Noonan served as special assistant to President Ronald Reagan and as a speechwriter for George H. W. Bush, when he ran for president in 1988.*

Among her books are John Paul the Great: Remembering a Spiritual Father *(2005);* A Heart, a Cross, and a Flag *(2003), a collection of her newspaper columns written after 9/11;* When Character Was King: A Story of Ronald Reagan *(2001);* The Case against Hillary Clinton *(2000); and* What I Saw at the Revolution *(1990). "The D-Day Generation" first appeared in* Washington Monthly *(1994). D-Day was June 6, 1944, the day the Allies landed on the beaches of Normandy, France. Known as Operation Overlord, the battle cost the lives of thousands of soldiers—most of them American, British, and Canadian—who sacrificed themselves to liberate Europe from the Nazis. This essay is a testament to the bravery and forbearance of those who served in World War II and of the people back home who waited for and helped sustain those heroes.*

Preparing to Read

1. The effectiveness of this essay derives, in part, from the appreciation that Noonan freely expresses for the D-Day generation. She could have defined this generation by using facts and statistics and coldly recounting events. Instead, she explains the term's connotation by expressing the very personal emotions it elicits in her and, thereby, she creates a far more meaningful essay.

2. Make sure you are familiar with the (Great) Depression and the fall of Communism (paragraph 1).

3. *The Graduate,* a 1970s film mentioned in paragraph 3, satirizes the artificiality and materialism of contemporary American life.

4. Mario Cuomo (paragraph 5) was governor of New York from 1983 to 1995. "Loose lips sink ships" (paragraph 7) admonished defense workers to keep the specifics of their work secret to ensure national security. "Blood 'n' Guts" (paragraph 9) was the nickname of General George Patton, who led American troops in Africa, Italy, and France.

Vocabulary

affluence (noun)	Wealth.
impenetrable (adjective)	Impassable, unable to be entered.
integrator (noun)	Something that brings different people or things together.
memorabilia (noun)	Mementos, objects that elicit memories.
reticent (adjective)	Quiet, reserved.
shrapnel (noun)	Bomb or shell fragments.
trauma (noun)	Shock, suffering.

The D-Day Generation

Peggy Noonan

1 I KEEP WONDERING about who we are these days, all of us. I keep wondering if we're way ahead of our parents—more learned, more tolerant, and engaged in the world—or way behind them. They touch my soul, that generation. They are an impenetrable inspiration. They got through the Depression and the war—they got drafted for five years and said Okay, Uncle Sam! and left, and wrote home. They expected so little, their assumptions were so modest. A lot of them, anyway. The women shared the common trauma of a childhood in hard times and the men had the common integrator of the barracks, and I feel that they understood each other. They knew what they shared. When Communism fell we should have had a parade for them, for it meant their war was finally over. We should have one for them anyway, before they leave.

2 They weren't farmers, or the ones I knew weren't farmers, but they were somehow—closer to the soil, closer to the ground. The ones in Brooklyn, Rochester, wherever, they were closer to the ground.

3 Affluence detaches. It removes you from the old and eternal, it gets you out of the rain. Affluence and technology detach absolutely. Among other things, they get you playing with thin plastic things like Super Nintendo and not solid things like—I don't know—wood, and water. Anyway, the guy who said "Plastics" to Benjamin 25 years ago in *The Graduate* was speaking more truth than we knew.

4 Also, our parents were ethnic in a way I understood. Back in that old world the Irish knew they were better than the Italians and the Italians knew they were better than the Irish and we all knew we were better than the Jews and they knew they were better than us. Everyone knew they were superior, so everyone got along. I think the prevailing feeling was, everyone's human. Actually, that used to be a saying in America: Everyone's human.

5 They all knew they were Americans and they all knew they weren't, and their kids knew it too, and understood it was their job to become the Americans.

Which we certainly have. A while ago a reporter told me how an old Boston pol summed up Mario Cuomo. The pol said, "He's not a real ethnic. He's never been ashamed of his father." The reporter—45, New York, Jewish—laughed with a delighted grunt. The ordeal of ethnicity. I Remember Papa.

There were ethnic, religious, and racial resentments, but you didn't hear   6 about them all the time. It was a more reticent country. Imagine chatty America being reticent. But it was.

I often want to say to them, to my parents and the parents of my friends,   7 "Share your wisdom, tell me what you've learned, tell me what we're doing wrong and right." But, you know, they're still reticent. Loose lips sink ships. Also, they tend not to have big abstract things to say about life because they were actually busy living it, and forgot to take notes. They didn't have time, or take time, to reflect. They were not so inclined.

They're like an old guy I met a few years ago when I was looking for a house   8 in Washington. He had gray hair and was stooped in a crouched, still-muscular way and had just one good eye, the other was scarred and blind. He had an old brick house off George Washington Parkway and I had walked through it; it was perfect but too near the highway for a woman with a two-year-old. When I was in the basement I saw his World War II memorabilia—he still had framed citations on the wall, and I could see he'd seen action island-hopping in the South Pacific. And one of the old framed papers said Guadalcanal, and this was exciting, so I said to him, for the most interesting things you hear in life come by accident, "Did you know Richard Tregaskis?" And his good eye squinted. I thought he might not recognize the reference, so I said to him, "He was the one who wrote *Guadalcanal Diary*." And the squint gets deeper and he says, "Yeah, well, I was a grunt. We'd already done the work and left by the time the writers came." I sort of smiled and asked if I could use the bathroom, where I plucked a piece of shrapnel from my heart.

Now they're all retired, and most of the ones I know are in pretty good   9 shape. My friend Susan's parents go to Atlantic City and catch a few shows, play the slots. They own their house. My father—army infantry, Italy under Blood 'n' Guts—has a small apartment in Santo Domingo and swims and says he can feel the sun to his bones. My mother lives here in town and flies off when one of her children is having a baby, to be a continuity, to say by her presence, "We did this too, years ago, so don't worry." Lisa's parents just got back from Europe. George's father, who for 25 years worked in a Newark welfare office, married a woman with a farm in Pennsylvania. Now he walks in the mud in big rubber boots, holding a piece of corn. He's happy. There was more divorce than I think we've noted in our parents' generation, and a lot of them did it in a funny way, not after a year or 10 years but after 25, 35 years. After a life. There are always serious and individual reasons for such things, but I would include the seventies, the decade when America went crazy, the decade when, as John Updike said, the sixties had finally percolated down to everybody.

Read More on the Web

Encyclopedia Britannica's Guide to Normandy 1944:
 www.britannica.com/dday

U.S. Department of Labor electronic bibliography on the Greatest
 Generation: http://www.dol.gov/oasam/ library/bib/world_war2.htm

Wikipedia site on the G.I. Generation:
 http://en.wikipedia.org/wiki/G.I._Generation

Questions for Discussion

1. As you learned earlier, the thesis for this essay appears in paragraph 1:
 "They are an impenetrable inspiration." Explain what Noonan means
 by this? Then, explain how the ideas and details in the rest of the essay
 support the thesis.

2. In paragraphs 1 and 2, Noonan comments upon the character of
 members of the D-Day generation. What does she say about their
 values and priorities?

3. Where does Noonan use negation to define the D-Day generation? In
 other words, where does she explain what that generation is not?

4. What does Noonan's anecdote about the "old guy" in paragraph 8 add
 to her definition?

5. In paragraph 9, Noonan tells us about members of the D-Day
 generation who are in "pretty good shape." Why does she do this?

6. Why does she discuss noncombatants—like her mother, for example?
 Given the title of her essay, should she have discussed combat
 veterans exclusively?

7. Consider the last three sentences. How do her comments about
 divorce among the D-Day generation help define this group?

Thinking Critically

1. Explain Noonan's comment at the end of paragraph 8. What does this
 metaphor add to her definition?

2. Explain the allusion to *The Graduate.* How might the generations
 portrayed in that movie differ from the D-Day generation? What
 contrast does Noonan imply between today's youth and the young
 people who lived through and fought in World War II?

Suggestions for Journal Entries

1. In preparation for writing an essay in which you define a particular
 generation—perhaps your own or that of your parents—make a

list of the strengths, values, and positive qualities you see in that generation. Then, make a list of its negative qualities.

2. Noonan mentions the film *The Graduate*. Think of a book, movie, or television show that you think portrays your generation. Using focused freewriting, listing, or brainstorming with one or two friends, record what you think it says about you and others in your age group.

Life without Father

David Blankenhorn

*David Blankenhorn, who was born in 1955 in Jackson, Mississippi, has de-
voted his career to writing about the importance of the family and its place
in a healthy society. He is the founder of the Institute for American Values, a
nonpartisan organization devoted to researching and publishing on issues that
affect the family. In 1994, he helped found the National Fatherhood Initiative.
He has written for the* New Republic, *the* Washington Post, *the* New York
Times, *and the* Public Interest, *among others. He has also appeared on numerous television programs to discuss public policy and the family. This essay is
from Blankenhorn's book* Fatherless America: Confronting Our Most Urgent
Social Problem *(1995).*

Preparing to Read

1. Blankenhorn's introduction is six paragraphs long. Read these
   paragraphs twice and look for methods for writing introductions that
   you learned about in Chapter 3.
2. Earlier you learned that writing an effective definition requires a clear
   purpose. Blankenhorn makes his purpose clear in several places.
   Mark those places as you read his essay.

Vocabulary

atomized (adjective)	Isolated, not part of a community.
conscripted (adjective)	Drafted, made to serve.
demographic (adjective)	Relating to population.
equanimity (noun)	Calmness, resignation.
extralegal (adjective)	Not related to the law.
parity (noun)	Equivalence, equality.
puerile (adjective)	Childish, immature.
superfluous (adjective)	Unimportant, unnecessary.
waywardness (noun)	Lack of moral responsibility.

Life without Father

David Blankenhorn

THE UNITED STATES is becoming an increasingly fatherless society. A genera- 1
tion ago, a child could reasonably expect to grow up with his or her father.

Today, a child can reasonably expect not to. Fatherlessness is approaching a rough parity with fatherhood as a defining feature of childhood.

This astonishing fact is reflected in many statistics, but here are the two 2 most important: Tonight, about 40 percent of U.S. children will go to sleep in homes in which their fathers do not live [see the accompanying chart]. More than half of our children are likely to spend a significant portion of childhood living apart from their fathers. Never before in this country have so many children been voluntarily abandoned by their fathers. Never before have so many children grown up without knowing what it means to have a father.

Fatherlessness is the most harmful demographic trend of this generation. 3 It is the leading cause of the decline in the well-being of children. It is also the engine driving our most urgent social problems, from crime to adolescent pregnancy to domestic violence. Yet, despite its scale and social consequences, fatherlessness is frequently ignored or denied. Especially within our elite discourse, it remains a problem with no name.

Surely a crisis of this scale merits a name—and a response. At a minimum, 4 it requires a serious debate: Why is fatherhood declining? What can be done about it? Can our society find ways to invigorate effective fatherhood as a norm of male behavior? Yet, to date, our public discussion has been remarkably weak and defeatist. There is a prevailing belief that not much can or even should be done to reverse the trend.

As a society, we are changing our minds about men's role in family life. 5 Our inherited understanding of fatherhood is under siege. Men are increasingly viewed as superfluous to family life: either expendable or part of the problem. Masculinity itself often is treated with suspicion, and even hostility, in our cultural discourse. Consequently, our society is unable to sustain fatherhood as a distinctive domain of male activity.

DISAPPEARING DADS

U.S. KIDS LIVING WITH . . .	1960	1980	1990
Father and mother	80.6%	62.3%	57.7%
Mother only	7.7	18	21.6
Father only	1	1.7	3.1
Father and stepmother	0.8	1.1	0.9
Mother and stepfather	5.9	8.4	10.4
Neither parent	3.9	5.8	4.3

Sources: *America's Children* by Donald Hernandez, U.S. Census Bureau. Because the statistics are from separate sources, they don't total 100%.

The core question is simple: Does every child need a father? increasingly, 6
our society's answer is "no." Few idea shifts in this century are as consequential
as this one. At stake is nothing less than what it means to be a man, who our
children will be and what kind of society we will become.

My . . . criticism [is] not simply of fatherlessness but of a *culture* of father- 7
lessness. For, in addition to fathers, we are losing something larger: our idea
of fatherhood. Unlike earlier periods of father absence in our history, such as
wartime, we now face more than a physical loss affecting some homes. The
1940s child could say: My father had to leave for a while to do something
important. The '90s child must say: My father left me permanently because he
wanted to.

This is a cultural criticism because fatherhood, much more than mother- 8
hood, is a cultural invention. Its meaning is shaped less by biology than by a
cultural script, a societal code that guides—and at times pressures—a man into
certain ways of acting and understanding himself.

Like motherhood, fatherhood is made up of both a biological and a social 9
dimension. Yet, across the world, mothers are far more successful than fathers
at fusing these dimensions into a coherent identity. Is the nursing mother
playing a biological or a social role? Feeding or bonding? We can hardly separate the two, so seamlessly are they woven together. But fatherhood is a different matter. A father makes his sole biological contribution at the moment
of conception, nine months before the infant enters the world. Because social
paternity is linked only indirectly to biological paternity, a connection cannot
be assumed. The phrase "to father a child" usually refers only to the act of in-
semination, not the responsibility for raising the child. What fathers contribute
after conception is largely a matter of cultural devising.

Moreover, despite their other virtues, men are not ideally suited to re- 10
sponsible fatherhood. Men are inclined to sexual promiscuity and paternal
waywardness. Anthropologically, fatherhood constitutes what might be termed
a necessary problem. It is necessary because a child's well-being and societal
success hinge largely on a high level of paternal investment: men's willingness
to devote energy and resources to the care of their offspring. It is a problem because men frequently are unwilling or unable to make that vital investment.

Because fatherhood is universally problematic, cultures must mobilize to 11
enforce the father role, guiding men with legal and extralegal pressures that
require them to maintain a close alliance with their children's mother and in-
vest in their children. Because men don't volunteer for fatherhood as much as
they are conscripted into it by the surrounding culture, only an authoritative
cultural commitment to fatherhood can fuse biological and social paternity into
a coherent male identity. For exactly this reason, anthropologist Margaret Mead
and others have observed that the supreme test of any civilization is whether it
can socialize men by teaching them to nurture their offspring.

The stakes could hardly be higher. Our society's conspicuous failure 12
to sustain norms of fatherhood reveals a failure of collective memory and a

collapse of moral imagination. It undermines families, neglects children, causes or aggravates our worst social problems and makes individual adult happiness, both female and male, harder to achieve.

Ultimately, this failure reflects nothing less than a culture gone awry, un- 13 able to establish the boundaries and erect the signposts that can harmonize individual happiness with collective well-being. In short, it reflects a culture that fails to "enculture" individual men and women, mothers and fathers.

In personal terms, the main result of this failure is the spread of a me-first 14 egotism hostile to all except the most puerile understandings of personal happiness. In social terms, the results are a decline in children's well-being and a rise in male violence, especially against women. The most significant result is our society's steady fragmentation into atomized individuals, isolated from one another and estranged from the aspirations and realities of common membership in a family, a community, a nation, bound by mutual commitment and shared memory.

Many voices today, including many expert voices, urge us to accept the 15 decline of fatherhood with equanimity. Be realistic, they tell us. Divorce and out-of-wedlock childbearing are here to stay. Growing numbers of children will not have fathers. Nothing can be done to reverse the trend itself. The only solution is to remedy some of its consequences: More help for poor children. More sympathy for single mothers. Better divorce. More child-support payments. More prisons. More programs aimed at substituting for fathers.

Yet what Abraham Lincoln called the better angels of our nature always 16 have guided us in the opposite direction. Passivity in the face of crisis is inconsistent with the American tradition. Managing decline never has been the hallmark of American expertise. In the inevitable and valuable tension between conditions and aspirations—between the social "is" and the moral "ought"—our birthright as Americans always has been our confidence that we can change for the better.

Does every child need a father? Our current answer hovers between "not 17 necessarily" and "no." But we need not make permanent the lowering of our standards. We can change our minds. We can change our minds without passing new laws, spending more tax dollars or empaneling more expert commissions. Once we change our philosophy, we might well decide to pass laws, create programs or commission research. But the first and most important thing to change is not policies, *but ideas.*

Our essential goal must be the rediscovery of the fatherhood idea: For 18 every child, a legally and morally responsible man.

If my goal could be distilled into one sentence, it would be this: A good 19 society celebrates the ideal of the man who puts his family first. Because our society is lurching in the opposite direction, I see the Good Family Man as the principal casualty of today's weakening focus on fatherhood. Yet I cannot imagine a good society without him.

Read More on the Web

U.S. Department of Health and Human Services site—"Building Blocks for Father Involvement": http://www.acf.hhs.gov/programs/region3/docs/Fatherhood/building_blocks1.pd

U.S. Department of Health and Human Services site—"Fighting the Fatherlessness Epidemic": http://www.omhrc.gov/assets/pdf/checked/Fighting%20the%20Fatherlessness%20Epidemic.pdf

Questions for Discussion

1. What is Blankenhorn's thesis?
2. What is the purpose of this essay?
3. What methods explained in Chapter 3 does Blankenhorn use in this essay?
4. What does the author want his introduction to accomplish?
5. According to Blankenhorn, what are the root causes of fatherlessness? What are its effects?
6. Where in this essay does Blankenhorn use comparison?
7. Where does he use contrast? Explain the contrast between the causes of fatherlessness in the 1940s and the causes of fatherlessness today.
8. What does Blankenhorn mean when, in paragraph 8, he calls fatherhood a cultural invention?
9. What does he mean when, in paragraph 13, he claims that we fail to "*enculture* individual men and women, mothers and fathers"?
10. What does the author think about our present efforts to address fatherlessness? What does he suggest we do to change our approach?
11. Comment on Blankenhorn's conclusion. What is its purpose?

Thinking Critically

1. In paragraph 16, the author refers to "what Abraham Lincoln called "the better angels of our nature." Explain what this term means. Then write a short paragraph explaining why this paragraph is crucial to Blankenhorn's purpose.
2. In paragraph 17, Blankenhorn tells us that "the first and most important thing to change is not policies *but ideas.*" Write a paragraph that explains what that idea means in light of what the author says in the rest of the essay.

Suggestions for Journal Entries

1. Reread paragraph 9. Then, summarize the characteristics of fatherhood that the author explains there. Next, make a list of other characteristics you might add.

2. In preparation for the writing of an essay that defines the ideal parent, grandparent, sibling, aunt, *or* uncle, make a list of people you know who are your role models. Then, make a list of the people you know who fall far short of the ideal. In order to preserve the anonymity of those who are not role models, don't use their real names.

3. In preparation for writing an essay that defines the public image of parenthood, make a list of four or five television programs or movies in which a parent is one of the major characters. Next, make a list of the personal characteristics associated with each of these people. Finally decide if the media's portrayal of parents is positive, negative, or mixed.

The Perpetual Adolescent

Joseph Epstein

Joseph Epstein (b. 1937) is an essayist whose latest books include Narcissus Leaves the Pool: Familiar Essays *(1999),* Snobbery: The American Version *(2002), and* Envy *(2003). He has also authored two short-story collections including* Fabulous Small Jews *(2003). His essays have been published in* Commentary, the New Yorker *and* Harper's, *among other periodicals. From 1974 to 2002, Epstein taught at Northwestern University in Chicago, and he served as editor of the* American Scholar, *the magazine of the Phi Beta Kappa honor society. "The Perpetual Adolescent," an excerpt of which appears here, was published in the* Weekly Standard *in 2004.*

Preparing to Read

1. Epstein makes references to numerous important historical and contemporary figures. Among those you might want to read more about (in print or on the Internet) are Joe DiMaggio (paragraph 1); H. L. Mencken (paragraph 3); Aristotle (paragraph 6); and Alan Greenspan, Jeane Kirkpatrick, Robert Rubin, Warren Buffett, and Sol Linowitz (paragraph 8); and Soren kierkegaard (paragraph 10).

2. The Wordsworth, mentioned in paragraph 10, was William Wordsworth, one of the founders of British Romanticism, an artistic and intellectual movement that flowered during the early part of the nineteenth century. William Butler Yeats (paragraph 11) was a nineteenth-century Irish writer, whose poem "Sailing to Byzantium" begins "This is no country for old men."

3. Holden Caulfield (paragraph 9) is the name of the main character of *The Catcher in the Rye,* an extremely popular coming-of-age novel. Enron (paragraph 17) is an energy company, which filed for bankruptcy in 2001 after it was alleged—and later proven—that several top executives had committed stock fraud. As a result, more than 4,000 Enron employees lost their jobs, and the Enron scandal became a symbol for corporate corruption.

Vocabulary

advent (noun)	Arrival, introduction, coming.
anomalous (adjective)	Uncharacteristic, out of the ordinary, abnormal.
benign (adjective)	Harmless.

cataclysmic (adjective)	Catastrophic, disastrous.
crucibles (noun)	Difficult experiences or tests that result in significant changes or new phenomena.
de riguer (adjective)	French for ordinary, common.
ephemeral (adjective)	Fleeting, not permanent, of no lasting value.
grotesque (adjective)	Extremely ugly or distasteful.
hierarchy (noun)	Order, ranking.
inexorably (adverb)	Inevitably, inescapably.
injunction (noun)	Order, command.
transcendent (adjective)	Extraordinary.
utopia (noun)	An imaginary place that offers the ideal government, society, and living conditions.
vaunted (adjective)	Highly praised.

The Perpetual Adolescent

Joseph Epstein

WHENEVER ANYONE under the age of 50 sees old newsreel film of Joe 1
DiMaggio's 56-game hitting streak of 1941, he is almost certain to be
brought up by the fact that nearly everyone in the male-dominated crowds—in
New York, Boston, Chicago, Detroit, Cleveland—seems to be wearing a suit
and a fedora or other serious adult hat. The people in those earlier baseball
crowds, though watching a boyish game, nonetheless had a radically different
conception of themselves than most Americans do now. A major depression
was ending, a world war was on. Even though they were watching an entertainment that took most of them back to their boyhoods, they thought of themselves as adults, no longer kids, but grown-ups, adults, men.

How different from today, when a good part of the crowd at any ballgame, 2
no matter what the age, is wearing jeans and team caps and T-shirts; and let us
not neglect those (one hopes) benign maniacs who paint their faces in home-
team colors or spell out, on their bare chests, the letters of the names of star
players: S-O-S-A.

Part of the explanation for the suits at the ballpark in DiMaggio's day 3
is that in the 1940s and even '50s there weren't a lot of sport, or leisure, or
casual clothes around. Unless one lived at what H. L. Mencken called "the
country-club stage of culture"—unless, that is, one golfed, played tennis, or
sailed—one was likely to own only the clothes one worked in or better. Far
from casual Fridays, in those years there weren't even casual Sundays. Wearing
one's "Sunday best," a cliché of the time, meant wearing the good clothes one
reserved for church.

Dressing down may first have set in on the West Coast, where a certain 4
informality was thought to be a new way of life. In the 1960s, in universities

casual dress became absolutely *de rigueur* among younger faculty, who, in their ardor to destroy any evidence of their being implicated in evil hierarchy, wished not merely to seem in no wise different from their students but, more important, to seem always young; and the quickest path to youthfulness was teaching in jeans, T-shirts, and the rest of it.

This informality has now been institutionalized. Few are the restaurants   5
that could any longer hope to stay in business if they required men to wear a jacket and tie. Today one sees men wearing baseball caps—some worn backwards—while eating indoors in quite good restaurants. In an episode of "The Sopranos," Tony Soprano, the mafia don, representing life of a different day, finds this so outrages his sense of decorum that, in a restaurant he frequents, he asks a man, in a quiet but entirely menacing way, to remove his goddamn hat.

Life in that different day was felt to observe the human equivalent of the   6
Aristotelian unities: to have, like a good drama, a beginning, middle, and end. Each part, it was understood, had its own advantages and detractions, but the middle—adulthood—was the lengthiest and most earnest part, where everything serious happened and much was at stake. To violate the boundaries of any of the three divisions of life was to go against what was natural and thereby to appear unseemly, to put one's world somehow out of joint, to be, let us face it, a touch, and perhaps more than a touch, grotesque.

Today, of course, all this has been shattered. The ideal almost everywhere   7
is to seem young for as long as possible. The health clubs and endemic workout clothes, the enormous increase in cosmetic surgery (for women and men), the special youth-oriented television programming and moviemaking, all these are merely the more obvious signs of the triumph of youth culture. When I say youth culture, I do not mean merely that the young today are transcendent, the group most admired among the various age groups in American society, but that youth is no longer viewed as a transitory state, through which one passes on the way from childhood to adulthood, but an aspiration, a vaunted condition in which, if one can only arrange it, to settle in perpetuity.

This phenomenon is not something that happened just last night; it has   8
been under way for decades. Nor is it something that can be changed even by an event as cataclysmic as that of September 11, which at first was thought to be so sobering as to tear away all shreds of American innocence. As a generalization, it allows for a wide variety of exceptions. There still are adults in America; if names are wanted, I would set out those of Alan Greenspan, Jeane Kirkpatrick, Robert Rubin, Warren Buffett, Sol Linowitz, and many more. But such men and women, actual grown-ups, now begin to appear a bit anomalous; they no longer seem representative of the larger culture.

The shift into youth culture began in earnest, I suspect, during the 10   9
or so years following 1951, the year of the publication of *Catcher in the Rye*. Salinger's novel exalts the purity of youth and locates the enemy—a clear case

of Us versus Them—in those who committed the sin of having grown older, which includes Holden Caulfield's pain-in-the-neck parents, his brother (the sellout screenwriter), and just about everyone else who has passed beyond adolescence and had the rather poor taste to remain alive.

The case for the exaltation of the young is made in Wordsworth's "Intima- 10 tion of Immortality," with its idea that human beings are born with great wisdom from which life in society weans them slowly but inexorably. Plato promulgated this same idea long before: For him we all had wisdom in the womb, but it was torn from us at the exact point that we came into the world. Rousseau gave it a French twist, arguing that human beings are splendid all-round specimens— noble savages, really—with life out in society turning us mean and loutish, which is another way of saying that the older we are, the worse we get. We are talking about romanticism here, friend, which never favors the mature, let alone the aged.

The triumph of youth culture has conquered perhaps nowhere more com- 11 pletely than in the United States. The John F. Kennedy administration, with its emphasis on youthfulness, beginning with its young president—the first presi- dent routinely not to wear a serious hat—gave it its first public prominence. Soon after the assassination of Kennedy, the Free Speech Movement, which spearheaded the student revolution, positively enshrined the young. Like Yeats's Byzantium, the sixties utopia posited by the student radicals was "no country for old men" or women. One of the many tenets in its credo—soon to become a cliché, but no less significant for that—was that no one over 30 was to be trusted. (If you were part of that movement and 21 years old in 1965, you are 60 today. Good morning, Sunshine.)

Music was a key element in the advance of youth culture. The dividing 12 moment here is the advent of Elvis. On one side were those who thought Elvis an amusing and largely freakish phenomenon—a bit of a joke—and on the other, those who took him dead seriously as a figure of youthful rebellion, the musical equivalent of James Dean in the movie *Rebel Without a Cause,* another early winning entry in the glorification-of-youth sweepstakes then forming. Rock 'n' roll presented a vinyl curtain, with those committed to retaining their youth on one side, those wanting to claim adulthood on the other. The Beatles, despite the very real charms of their non-druggie music, solidified things. So much of hard rock 'n' roll came down to nothing more than a way of saying bugger off to adult culture.

Reinforcement for these notions—they were not yet so coherent as to 13 qualify as ideas—was to be found in the movies. Movies for some years now have been made not only increasingly for the young but by the young. I once worked on a movie script with a producer who one day announced to me that it was his birthday. When I wished him happy returns of the day, he replied that it wasn't so happy for him; he was turning 41, an uncomfortably old age in Hollywood for someone who hadn't many big success-scalps on his belt.

Robert Redford, though now in his mid-sixties, remains essentially a guy 14 in jeans, a handsome graduate student with wrinkles. Paul Newman, now in his late seventies, seems uncomfortable in a suit. Hugh Grant, the English actor, may be said to be professionally boyish, and in a recent role, in the movie *About a Boy,* is described in the *New York Times* as a character who "surrounds himself with gadgets, videos, CDs, and other toys" and who "is doing everything in his power to avoid growing up." The actor Jim Carrey, who is 42, not long ago said of the movie *The Majestic,* in which he stars, "It's about manhood. It's about adulthood," as if italicizing the rarity of such movies. He then went on to speak about himself in standard self-absorbed adolescent fashion: "You've got that hole you're left with by whatever your parents couldn't give you." Poor baby.

Jim Carrey's roles in movies resemble nothing so much as comic-book 15 characters come to life. And why, just now, does so much of contemporary entertainment come in the form of animation or comic-book cartooning? Such television shows as *The Simpsons* and *King of the Hill,* the occasional back page in the *New York Times Book Review* or the *New Yorker* and the comic-book novel, all seem to feel that the animated cartoon and comic-book formats are very much of the moment. They are of course right, at least if you think of your audience as adolescent, or, more precisely, as being unwilling quite to detach themselves from their adolescence.

Recent history has seemed to be on the side of keeping people from growing 16 up by supplying only a paucity of stern tests of the kind out of which adulthood is usually formed. We shall never have another presidential candidate tested by the Depression or by his experience in World War II. These were events that proved crucibles for the formation of adult character, not to say manliness. Henceforth all future presidential—and congressional—candidates will come with a shortage of what used to pass for significant experience. Crises for future politicians will doubtless be about having to rethink their lives when they didn't get into Brown or found themselves unequipped emotionally for Stanford Business School.

Corporate talent these days feels no weightier. Pictures of heads of corpora- 17 tions in polo shirts with designer logos in the business section of the *New York Times,* fresh from yet another ephemeral merger, or acquiring an enormous raise after their company has recorded another losing year, do not inspire confidence. "The trouble with Enron," said an employee of the company in the aftermath of that corporation's appalling debacle, "is that there weren't any grown-ups."

The increasing affluence the United States enjoyed after World War II, ex- 18 tending into the current day, also contributed heavily to forming the character I've come to think of as the perpetual American adolescent. Earlier, with less money around, people were forced to get serious, to grow up—and fast. How quickly the Depression generation was required to mature! How many stories one used to hear about older brothers going to work at 18 or earlier, so that a younger brother might be allowed to go to college, or simply to help keep the family afloat! With lots of money around, certain kinds of pressure were removed. More and more people nowadays are working, as earlier generations were not, with a strong safety net of money under them. All options opened, they now swim in what Kierkegaard called "a sea of possibilities," and one of these possibilities in America is to refuse to grow up for a longer period than has been permitted any other people in history.

All this is reinforced by the play of market forces, which strongly encour- 19 age the mythical dream of perpetual youthfulness. The promise behind 95 percent of all advertising is that of recaptured youth, whose deeper promise is lots more sex yet to go. The ads for the $5,000 wristwatch, the $80,000 car, the khakis, the vodka, the pharmaceuticals to regrow hair and recapture ardor, all whisper display me, drive me, wear me, drink me, swallow me, and you stop the clock—youth, Baby, is yours.

The whole sweep of advertising, which is to say of market culture, 20 since soon after World War II has been continuously to lower the criteria of youthfulness while extending the possibility for seeming youthful to older and older people. To make the very young seem older—all those 10- and 12-year-old Britney Spears and Jennifer Lopez imitators, who already know more about brand-name logos than I do about English literature—is another part of the job. It's not a conspiracy, mind you, not six or eight international ad agencies meeting in secret to call the shots, but the dynamics of market-ing itself, finding a way to make it more profitable all around by convincing the young that they can seem older and the old that they can seem a lot younger. Never before has it been more difficult to obey the injunction to act one's age.

Read More on the Web

CBS News site that contains Epstein's complete essay as well as links to related articles: http://www.cbsnews.com/stories/2004/03/10/opinion/main605169.shtml

Epstein's "The Green-Eyed Monster: Envy Is Nothing to Be Jealous Of": http://www.washingtonmonthly.com/features/2003/0307.epstein.html

Questions for Discussion

1. The clearest statement of Epstein's central idea appears in paragraph 7. What is it? Should it have appeared earlier?
2. How would you describe Epstein's tone (see especially paragraph14)?
3. What is the essay's purpose?
4. How does Epstein characterize adulthood as seen through the eyes of people living in the 1950s (paragraph 6)?

5. What does he mean when, in paragraph 7, he says that, today, youth is seen as "an aspiration"?

6. Where in this essay does Epstein use illustration?

7. Where does he use comparison? Contrast?

8. What methods of development does Epstein use in paragraphs 9 and 10?

9. What role did the publication of *A Catcher in the Rye* play in our society's embracing the "youth culture"? What role did the Kennedy administration play?

10. Why does the author mention Jim Carrey, Paul Newman, Robert Redford, and other popular entertainers?

11. What influence have *The Simpsons* and other television cartoon shows had on what we might assume to be serious writing?

Thinking Critically

1. Write a paragraph in which you agree or disagree with Epstein's statement in paragraph 16 that "henceforth all future presidential— and congressional—candidates will come with a shortage of what used to pass for significant experience." Make reference to politicians whom you know about or who are often in the news.

2. Summarize the "triumph of youth culture" as explained in paragraphs 9–15.

Suggestions for Journal Entries

1. Do you agree with Epstein? Is our society fostering the creation of perpetual adolescents? If so, make a list of examples from what you see in the media or what you experience or observe in daily life to prove your point. If not, list examples that might be used to convince people that our society places emphasis on the importance of being an adult and on the responsibilities adults must assume. You might also list evidence to prove that our society is as much concerned with its elderly as with any other generation.

2. A television commercial once described the youth of America as the "Pepsi Generation." What term might you use to define your generation? The jean-and-tee-shirt generation? The Internet generation? The I-Pod generation? The cell-phone generation? Use focused freewriting to produce a paragraph in which you fully define this term by using illustrations taken from your own experiences and observations.

Suggestions for Sustained Writing

1. In "The Ordinariness of Evil," Jha explains that, given the right circumstances, people who seem ordinary and moral can be made to do wrong. To continue the discussion, write an essay in which you recall an incident in which you were pressured—by an authority figure or by a peer—to do something you believed was wrong. If you responded to the first journal suggestion after Jha's essay, you may have already begun gathering information for this project.

   Read your journal notes. Then, add to them. In addition to telling what happened, explain why you chose to comply or how you withstood the pressure. In the process, describe the emotions you felt during this process. Put this information into your rough draft. When you revise this draft, use information and insights from Jha's essay to show in what ways your situation parallels the kinds of situations she uses to explain "the ordinariness of evil." If you want, turn this assignment into a research paper by taking material from other secondary sources found in the library or online. As always, use an appropriate citation system, such as Modern Language Association (MLA) style, which can be accessed at www.mhhe. com/rcw.

   In your conclusion, make a statement that explains the extent to which you agree with Jha's thesis. As always, edit and proofread your paper carefully, and make sure you have cited any information taken from secondary sources including "The Ordinariness of Evil."

2. If you responded to the first journal entry after Peggy Noonan's "The D-Day Generation," use the information you recorded in an essay that defines a particular generation—yours or an earlier generation—by discussing its positive qualities. Mention its values, its strengths, its accomplishments, and its other merits, but also discuss its shortcomings. (Also check the notes you made if you responded to the second journal suggestion after Epstein's "The Perpetual Adolescent.")

   Use contrast to organize your paper. Discuss the positive qualities in the first half of your rough draft, the negative qualities in the second. Include examples of the strengths and weaknesses you are discussing. Reference specific events and people—those you have heard/read about or those you have experienced/observed personally—to convince readers that your claims are valid.

   If this assignment doesn't interest you, write an essay in which you predict what a future generation might be like, say a group of 20+-year-olds living in the year 2250. In either case, outline, draft, and revise your paper carefully. Provide enough detail to make it convincing. Finally, take pains to edit and proofread.

3. If you responded to the second journal entry after Noonan's "The D-Day Generation," you may have gathered information about a book, movie, or television show that portrays your generation. Find two more such books, movies, or shows, and take notes that will explain how these works portray your generation.

    Next, write an outline and a rough draft for a paper that explains the image of your generation in the media. When you revise, make sure you have provided a clear thesis statement and enough detail to prove your point. Make direct reference to what you have read or seen. As appropriate, include internal (parenthetical) citations and a works cited list according to Modern Language Association (MLA) documentation style (or another style recommended by your instructor). To learn more about MLA documentation, go to www.mhhe.com/rcw.

4. If you were inspired by David Blankenhorn's "Life without Father," write an essay in which you define what, for you, is the ideal father, mother, sibling, or other relative. Begin by checking the journal notes you made after reading Blankenhorn's essay. Add to these notes, if necessary. Just make sure you have compiled a list of people who could serve as role models for fathers, mothers, and so on. Also make sure that you have a list of other people who are ill-suited to this role.

    Each of your lists need contain no more than three or four people. As you review each group, make another list of personal characteristics—positive or negative—that each person exhibits. Use this information to develop an essay that, on one hand, explains what an ideal father, mother, or other person is and, on the other, explains what the ideal is not. As you revise, make sure to have included sufficient detail. For example, have you discussed the kinds of sacrifices the ideal parent must make? Have you talked about the hardships he or she must overcome or the patience he or she must possess? Have you mentioned the integrity, honesty, and strength—both emotional and physical—needed to fulfill this role?

5. Do you agree with Joseph Epstein that our society seems to foster perpetual adolescence? Read the notes you may have made in response to the first suggestion for journal entries following "The Perpetual Adolescent." Then write an essay that supports or rejects Epstein's position. The information you have already gathered will probably have come from what you have read, seen, and heard in the media as well as what you have experienced firsthand. Now add even more information by researching this subject in books and articles on the Internet, in your college library's electronic databases, or, of course, in print. As you draft and revise your paper, make sure to include internal (parenthetical) citations and a works-cited list using the Modern Language Association (MLA) documentation style or another style recommended by your instructor. You can learn more about MLA style at www.mhhe.com/rcw.

Writing to Learn: A Group Activity

Sometimes concepts can be defined efficiently by using classification, a method that divides a subject into its component categories, then explains each category in depth. Another method is comparison and contrast.

First Meeting

Decide on a topic for writing. Topics that lend themselves to definition through classification and comparison/contrast can be drawn from a variety of academic disciplines including medicine, earth science, biology, archaeology, geology, environmental science, political science, sociology, psychology, religious studies, music, and language and literature.

For example, say you wished to define the term "creationism." You might put together a paper that discusses the way that several major cultures or religions have explained the creation of the universe. In the process, you can point out both similarities and differences between these systems. On the other hand, you might want to define the term "evolution" by using classification to discuss various theories of evolution put forth by scientists like Darwin, Lamarck, and others. Pointing out contrasts and similarities among these theories would also be helpful.

Another option is to discuss one of the world's great religions such as Christianity, Judaism, or Islam. You might begin by discussing fundamental beliefs, those tenets that are common to and respected by all members of that faith. You can then identify the major sects or groups that make up the religion, pointing out variations in belief ritual, and/or moral law. Then again, you might want to discuss various styles of modern painting, various types of jazz, or even various types of rock music.

Preliminary Research

Each group member should become familiar with the topic by researching it in the library or on the Internet with an eye toward helping the group arrive at a general and preliminary definition during your second meeting. For example, let's say you are trying to define the term "jazz." After doing some preliminary research, you all agree that it is a type of popular music that originated in New Orleans at the beginning of the twentieth century, that it is both intensely rhythmical and energetic, and that it is often played in small groups featuring woodwinds, such as clarinets and saxophones; brass instruments, such as trombones and trumpets; guitars, banjos, and other strings; and drums and other percussion instruments.

(continued)

SECOND MEETING

MARGINAL
NOTE

Learn how to use
MLA format at
www.mhhe.com/rcw

After having decided on a general, preliminary statement, assign each member of your group to research a major category of your topic. Following the above example, you might ask one member to research Dixieland jazz, another to read up on progressive jazz, and so on. In preparation for the next meeting, have each student prepare a written discussion of his or her assigned subtopic, ranging between 100 and 200 words, with photocopies that can be distributed at the next meeting. This work should be accompanied by a bibliography in the form of a works-cited list (Modern Language Association style) or a references list (American Psychological Association style).

THIRD MEETING

Evaluate the work that each student has submitted and make suggestions for revision. Pay special attention to the accompanying bibliographies to make sure that the sources used are sufficient in number and adequate in quality. Ask each student to rewrite his or her work and to submit it to the group leader before the next meeting.

FINAL MEETING

Discuss and revise the work that has been submitted to the group leader. Ask one student to write an introduction and conclusion for the paper. Ask another to rewrite the complete paper with an eye toward creating a consistent style. Then ask him or her to deliver it to yet another student, who will edit and proofread.

Argumentation and Persuasion

Argumentation and persuasion are similar, and they often work together. In fact it is rare to find an essay that is pure argumentation without the slightest hint that the author is trying to persuade the readers. It is even rarer to find an effective persuasive essay that is not based on a logical argument. However, argument and persuasion are not identical.

Establishing Purpose: Choosing to Argue or Persuade

To begin with, a formal "argument" is not a fight, altercation, or heated discussion with tempers flaring and threats being exchanged. *Argument* is the defense of an opinion or of a position on an issue that is supported by concrete evidence and that is presented logically. The purpose of a written argument is limited: to prove a point, a thesis—sometimes referred to as a proposition. Scientists use argument to prove a theory or hypothesis. Historians engage in argumentation when they dispute theories about the causes of a war or of an economic depression. A psychologist might argue that genetic factors caused someone to become a serial killer, and an economist could use argumentation to present theories about the business cycle or the effects of taxation.

Persuasion begins with logical argument. It too uses logic and concrete evidence to make a point, to prove a thesis. However, *persuasion* goes beyond argument and also appeals to the reader's emotions, values, and self-interest. The Declaration of Independence, a classic piece of persuasion, even attempts to inflame our passions. Finally, the purpose of persuasion is not simply to prove a point; it is to get readers to act. Lawyers use persuasion to get judges and juries to rule in favor of their clients. Politicians use persuasion to get voters to support them.

So first of all, you need to decide if your purpose is to argue or to persuade. Your decision will affect the word choices you make, the tone of your paper, and even its content. You would be writing an argument if you tried to convince your readers that the Internet and other electronic means of publishing information will someday replace the printed books and paper journals now on college library shelves. You would also be arguing if you proved that devoting

463

too much time to a job while attending college full-time reduces the chances for academic success. On the other hand, you would be writing persuasively if you tried to convince your college president to reduce the library's book budget and allocate the money to the purchase of CD ROMs or subscriptions to periodical databases. You would also be trying to persuade if you wrote a letter to your college newspaper so as to convince students to reduce their work hours and spend more time on their studies.

Appealing to Your Audience

The kind of audience you are writing to will often have as much influence on whether to argue or to persuade as your purpose does. For example, let's say you have been assigned to write a paper on the effects of regular aerobic exercise on the emotional health of people over 65. Your paper will be duplicated and read by all of the members of your class, none of whom happens to be over 65. So you decide to stick to pure argument and simply lay out the facts in support of an opinion. You cite statistics from journal articles published by senior-citizen groups and insurance associations, draw on studies in the *New England Journal of Medicine,* and quote a cardiologist you have interviewed to support the idea that aerobics promote emotional health in seniors. In short you write an essay that argues.

Now, take another scenario. You have been asked to write a similar article for a magazine read primarily by senior citizens. Your purpose this time is not simply to prove a point. You also want to get your readers to follow your advice—to get them on that treadmill or into that jazzercize class. So, in addition to doing research on your subject, you spend time evaluating your readers' goals, interests, and values and even their preconceived notions about aerobic exercise so that you can address these "motivational" factors when you write your essay. For example, your paper might appeal to your readers' desire to maintain their emotional health in order to enjoy their children and grandchildren better. It might even suggest that regular aerobic exercise improves sex, regardless of age. Now that's motivation!.

NOTE: As you consider your audience, keep the following in mind:

- If you are trying to persuade your readers, make sure you are familiar with their needs, their interests, and their opinions.
- Assess the readers' familiarity with the issue. Include background information as necessary to help readers new to the issue understand it fully. However, include only enough explanatory information and data to make your claims clear and convincing. Don't include three illustrations and six sets of statistics when one will do.
- Express yourself clearly and simply. Don't use highly sophisticated or technical vocabulary unless you are sure your readers will understand it. Otherwise, they might suspect you are trying to confuse them or to cloud the issue.

Choosing a Thesis (Claim) That Is Debatable, Supportable, and Focused

The thesis for an argumentative paper is often referred to as the claim—the opinion the writer wishes to prove, defend, or support. Start with a preliminary thesis, but remember that writing is a process of discovery. So, as you become more knowledgeable about your thesis by gathering information for, outlining, and drafting your paper, you might see the need to rewrite the thesis by revising your stand on the issue or even changing it completely.

Unless your instructor assigns a specific topic, write on a question you already know something about or are concerned about, such as health care, animal rights, the homeless, affirmative action, school choice, the criminal justice system, or the environment, for example. Those ideas can lead to the framing of a thesis—at least a preliminary thesis. Writing about something you believe is important provides the intellectual energy and commitment to complete an effective argumentative or persuasive essay.

At the same time, keep the following three criteria in mind as you frame your preliminary claim or thesis:

1. **An effective claim is debatable.** It is more than a simple statement of fact or of personal opinion, which will not lead to a sustained discussion.

   > **Statement of Fact:** My college major requires that I complete 28 hours of laboratory science.
   >
   > **Debatable Thesis:** My college needs to install more up-to-date equipment in the chemistry labs.

   The first item cannot be debated. Either your major requires 28 hours of laboratory science or it doesn't. The second item, on the other hand, can yield sustained discussion through evidence that the current lab equipment does not enable students to keep up with advances in the chemical industry.

   > **Personal Opinion or Preference:** A vegetarian diet is as satisfying as one that includes meat and fish.
   >
   > **Debatable Thesis:** Following a vegetarian diet can help lower cholesterol and prevent heart disease.

   The first item is based on personal taste, an invalid criterion for argument. The second can be discussed in light of objective medical research.

NOTE: You don't have to take one side of an issue exclusively. For example, you can argue against illegal immigration while expressing your understanding for the reasons that people from poor countries try to enter the United States illegally.

2. **An effective claim is defensible**. Before taking a position, think it through and decide if you can collect enough evidence to argue it effectively.

> **Indefensible:** People who wear leather and fur are cruel to animals.

> **Defensible:** People who wear leather and fur support industries whose harvesting methods are cruel to animals.

The first claim requires the writer to prove an impossibility: that the wearing of fur or leather itself is cruel. The second can be argued by calling upon evidence from government or industry sources, eyewitness testimony, or scientific research.

3. **An effective claim is focused**. For most college assignments, your thesis must be focused enough to be argued effectively in a short essay.

> **Too General:** Policies at two public colleges in my state violate students' rights.

> **Focused:** Policies governing speech at two public colleges in my state violate rights guaranteed to students by the First Amendment to the Constitution.

The first item would result in an essay whose length might exceed what was assigned. It covers too wide a range of policies. Moreover it does not focus on particular "student rights," as does the second item. Writing an essay on the second item would be much easier.

Read More on the Web

Here are three websites on writing thesis statements for argument/persuasion papers:

Humboldt University Argumentation and Critical Thinking Tutorial: http://www.humboldt.edu/~act/html

University of Nebraska Communications 109 Home Page: http://www.
unl.edu/speech/comm109

Purdue University Online Writing Center: http://owl.english.purdue.edu/
handouts/general/gl_argpers.html

Gathering Evidence to Support Your Thesis

Many ways to develop any essay, as explained in Chapter 2, can also be used
to approach an argument. For example, to argue that your college's policies
restrict students' freedom of speech, you might first define the right of free
speech and reveal the source of that right. If you argue that the college's lab
equipment needs to be replaced, you might use cause-and-effect to explain the
difficulties new chemistry graduates are having when they get jobs in industry.
Whatever your approach, communicate your position through sufficient concrete evidence to be convincing.

The most effective types of supportive evidence are documented facts and
statistics, expert testimony, and illustrations.

DOCUMENTED FACTS AND STATISTICS

To argue that being overweight contributes to heart disease and stroke, you can
quote data published in scientific journals. You might also use statistics taken
from medical studies or insurance sources to show that obese people suffer
higher mortality rates from coronary disease and stroke than others do.

NOTE: Too many statistics can overwhelm or bore some readers, especially
those who are not used to analyses of issues based on mathematical evidence.

EXPERT TESTIMONY

Including what experts in a particular field say or have written strengthens your
argument. When you introduce such material, however, state your source's credentials. In other words, explain why your expert is in fact an expert. Mention
academic degrees, professional experience, publications, awards, and other
information that will convince readers of your source's value.

You might use expert testimony in the form of statements from college
faculty, staff, and students to prove that the college's laboratories are outdated.
You might quote constitutional lawyers, judges, or government experts to support your claim that the college's policies restrict free speech.

Read More on the Web

Cite sources of facts, statistics, and expert testimony by using MLA, APA,
or other acceptable formats:

http://www.liu.edu/ewis/CWP/library/workshop/citmla.htm

http://owl.english.purdue.edu/handouts/research/
http://www.psywww.com/resource/apacrib.htm

ILLUSTRATIONS

As you learned earlier in this book, illustrations are factual examples or instances of the idea you are trying to support. You would be using illustrations if you wrote about specific cases in which college policy was invoked to punish or silence students who had expressed unpopular opinions on controversial campus issues. Always make sure these examples are concrete and well developed. Mention names of the people involved, include statements of the charges and punishments, explain the "offense," summarize arguments, quote testimony from hearings, and reference specific parts of the college policy. Finally choose examples that are directly relevant to your claim and that appeal to your audience. For example, in discussing an alleged violation of the college policy, you would do more than claim that Oscar Outspoken criticized the History Department. You might add that he did so in a polite, well-reasoned letter to the college newspaper, which calls itself "the student's voice." You might even quote directly from that letter.

Of course, most argumentative essays use a combination of these kinds of evidence. For example, to strengthen your claim that college policy violates students' rights of free speech, you might include the testimony of legal experts when you cite examples. Again, the important thing is that you use enough concrete evidence to be convincing.

Determining Tone and Content

The tone and language of an argument are usually objective, neutral, specific, and rational. The argument might draw on the testimony of experts, on statistics, or on historical or scientific studies. Experts and authorities in a particular field who have a reputation for evaluating issues fairly are often cited by writers of argument. Argument depends on logic. In persuasive essays, writers also use language that is more personal and emotionally charged. They sometimes involve themselves in the essay by viewing things subjectively; they focus on particular people and incidents more than on abstract studies and statistics; and they usually defend their positions vigorously and even passionately.

Let's say you are writing an argument that victims of violent crime ought to be compensated by the government. You might include Department of Justice statistics on the annual medical bills for victims of crime nationwide. You might remind readers that the government often helps victims of natural disasters and cite specific instances or programs in which such aid has been distributed. You might even describe a program used in another country that forces convicted criminals to work so as to fund a compensation program for crime victims. The tone of your argument would be dispassionate, and your presentation logical.

On the other hand, if you are writing an article to gather support for a rally to get Congress to pass a crime-victims bill, you might describe the long-term emotional and physical effects that specific crime victims are suffering. You might create vivid images of people no longer able to walk, to work, or to live pain-free lives. You might also appeal to the readers' self-interest by asking them to predict the horrors they might endure if ever victimized by some thug. Your language will probably be emotionally charged, and the images you paint will be startling. This is what we see in Angela Brandli's research essay, which appears on this book's website: www.mhhe.com/rcw. So persuasive was the author that she convinced state legislators to pass a bill that increased compensation for victims of violent crime.

Expressing a Voice

Although argument relies on logic and although persuasion can appeal to the reader's emotions as well, the line between pure argument and pure persuasion sometimes gets blurred. In fact, writers of argument frequently reveal their feelings about a topic, if ever so subtly. In "The Right to Be Let Alone" (Chapter 12), Barry Glazer uses emotionally charged language when he asserts that if he were "in the throes of terminal cancer or facing the horror of Alzheimer's disease" he should be allowed to commit suicide. Thus, while his purpose is not to move his readers to action, Glazer does touch our emotions, and we are the more convinced. An effective argument needs to be logical and well supported, but no writer should ever refrain from expressing his or her personal voice in a piece of formal writing, as long as it remains reasonable and restrained.

Being Fair, Accurate, and Logical

You will learn more about specific techniques you can use when writing either argumentation or persuasion essays in the next two chapters. However, whether you are writing argument or persuasion, remember to be accurate and fair. Being persuasive is not a license to mislead your readers. Unfortunately, sometimes both argument and persuasion suffer from logical fallacies. In many cases, writers commit such fallacies unknowingly. Dishonest writers do so intentionally.

TEN LOGICAL FALLACIES
Errors in logic, though sometimes subtle and hard to detect, appear in political speeches and advertisements, in television commercials, in newspaper editorials, and even in well-written and sincere arguments of bright college students. Here is a list of ten logical fallacies that you should look for when reading or listening to argumentation or persuasion and that you should avoid in your own writing.

Generalizations Supported by Insufficient Evidence   Writers sometimes draw conclusions not justified by the amount or kind of information they
have gathered. Failing to consider enough or the right kind of evidence can lead
to faulty generalizations. Here are a few examples of insufficient evidence:

1. My neighbors never finished high school, but they have built a very
    lucrative plumbing company. Therefore, the claim that education
    improves one's chances for success is false.

2. The president will veto a bill lowering tax rates for married couples.
    Obviously, he doesn't want to help families.

3. The directory assistance operator could not find the name or number of
    a company that I know is listed. The telephone company should train
    their employees better.

4. The Supreme Court refused to review a lower court's judgment against
    the tobacco industry. Obviously, the Supreme Court is antibusiness.

The Straw Man   As the name implies, the straw man is an argument that is
weak and easy to knock down. The straw man comes into play when a writer
falsely claims that the opposing side supports an idea that is indefensible. The
writer then refutes this obviously bad idea and, in the process, casts the opposition in a bad light. The straw man is a pretense; it has little to do with the
point being debated, nor does it represent the opponent's views fairly and accurately. In fact, it is often used only to distract readers from valid arguments
of the opposition.

> **Your position:** You argue that we should create a plan to force
> those convicted of violent crime to compensate their victims and
> their victims' families. You propose that prisons establish small fac-
> tories in which prisoners must work so as to earn the money to com-
> pensate their victims.
> **Your opponent's position:** Using the "straw man," your opponent
> argues that you are suggesting a return to the chain-gang system of
> punishment and that you are in favor of slave labor.
>
> **Your position:** You argue that people who have no children in the
> public school system should pay less school tax than those who do.
> **Your opponent's position:** You are an elitist who cares little for pub-
> lic education and is concerned only with educating the children of
> the rich, most of whom attend private schools.
>
> **Your position:** You argue that the government should preserve
> thousands of acres of untouched wilderness that happens to be
> located upon huge oil reserves.
> **Your opponent's position:** You care more about trees and wildlife
> than you do about the consumers who would benefit from cheaper
> heating oil and gasoline prices.

The Ad Hominem Argument   *Ad hominem* is Latin for "to the person."
When writers indulge in this unethical tactic, they attack the person's character
rather than his or her position, logic, opinions, or history.

For example, when John F. Kennedy ran for president in 1962, some
unscrupulous people attacked him because he was a Roman Catholic. They
ignored the fact that Kennedy had on numerous occasions affirmed his commitment to the separation of church and state. When Ronald Reagan ran for
governor in California in the 1970s and, again, when he ran for president,
some opponents attacked him because he had been an actor, not because of
the issues he supported.

You would be arguing *ad hominem* if you claimed that Senator Alvarez cannot represent the interests of families because she is single, or that Representative
Kelly will not fight to increase community-college funding because he attended
a private university. On the other hand, you would be arguing fairly if you mentioned that Senator Alvarez has consistently opposed pro-family legislation or
that Representative Kelly has made several speeches arguing for an increase in
community-college tuition so as to decrease state funding for such schools.

Begging the Question   This fallacy occurs when a writer draws an invalid
conclusion from a false assumption or an assumption that cannot be proven.
Thus, the writer avoids addressing the real issue or question.

For example, you would be begging the question if you argued that,
because Angela is a member of Alcoholics Anonymous, she could not have
been the one you saw having a beer at Calhoun's Saloon last night. The false
assumption here is that members of Alcoholics Anonymous never fall back
into their old habits. The argument begs the question: *Did Angela drink a beer
at Calhoun's Saloon last night?*

The Red Herring   The red herring distracts the audience from the real issue
at hand. It gets its name from a practice used by farmers to protect their newly
planted fields from fox hunters and their dogs. Farmers often dragged a red herring along the edge of their fields where it would leave a strong scent. This scent
distracted the dogs and kept them and the hunters from trampling the crops.

Most visibly, red herrings can be found in commercials and advertisements. Automobile commercials picture cars and their drivers winding through
beautiful mountain passes as they head toward stunning sunsets; exercise
machines are pictured against exotic, tropical landscapes populated by people
with perfect bodies; soft drinks are promoted through television spots that
picture athletic young people engaged in exciting sports such as rock climbing,
hang gliding, or surfing. None of these tells us much about the product. They
are selling an image that, like the farmer's red herring, is supposed to draw our
attention away from what is really being sold.

One commercial goes so far as to portray a four-wheel-drive vehicle as an
adult toy. It suppresses the fact that most people really buy cars for one practical

reason—safe and reliable transportation. It encourages the notion of "fun" and, red-herring fashion, distracts us from the reality that, in order to pay for this "toy," we will have to work extra hard and, in most cases, tie ourselves to an all-too-real auto loan that takes three, four, or five years to pay off!

Non-Sequitur   A Latin term, *non sequitur* translates roughly to "does not follow." It occurs when a statement does not proceed logically from the previous statement. Here are two examples.

> My 90 year-old grandfather smokes a pack of
>
> cigarettes a day. Therefore, smoking can't be bad for
>
> one's health.

> Gina finds accounting a challenging course. She will
>
> never succeed in business.

Neither of these statements follows directly from the other. The fact that one man who smokes heavily has reached the age of ninety in no way contradicts the massive research proving that, for the vast majority of people, smoking is a health hazard. Similarly, although Gina finds accounting challenging, the time and effort she puts into studying this subject may enable her to master it eventually. On the other hand, a mastery of sophisticated accounting principles may not be necessary to success in the kind of business she plans to pursue.

False Analogy   An argument based on a false analogy incorrectly assumes that because situations may be alike in some respects, the same rules, principles, or approaches apply to both or the same conclusions can be drawn about both. You would be guilty of false analogy if you wrote:

> Jason's father had a heart attack at fifty; Jason will
>
> suffer from heart disease too.

The analogy presumes that the only cause for heart disease is heredity. But what if Jason has a healthy lifestyle, while his father smokes heavily, fails to exercise, and eats a high-fat diet?

Either . . . Or Fallacy   Failing to see all the aspects or all the choices associated with a problem or situation can result in an "either . . . or" fallacy. You would create such a fallacy if you wrote:

> The only way students get through Prof. Wilson's
>
> history class is to cheat on her exams or resign
>
> themselves to a D.

Of course, no matter how demanding the instructors, there is a third alternative: to study hard.

Erroneous Cause   In Latin, this is called the *post hoc, ergo propter hoc (after this; therefore, because of this)* fallacy. It occurs when the writer assumes that because one thing follows another it must necessarily have resulted from (been caused by) the other. Here's an example:

> The College restricted student parking to Lots A and
>
> B last semester, so Rachel got more parking tickets
>
> than ever.

The reason Rachel got more parking tickets was not directly caused by the college's decision to restrict student parking. After all, Lots A and B might be sufficient to hold all student cars. Rachel's getting more tickets is a direct result of her choosing to park where she shouldn't.

Going-Along or Bandwagon Fallacy   This fallacy assumes that an idea, action, or proposal must be valid if a great many people support or believe in it. Recall that in some primitive cultures the vast majority of people believed in the practice of human sacrifice to appease their gods. You would be falling into this logical error if you wrote:

> Overwhelming popular support for the new mayor
>
> shows she can achieve greatness.

Read More on the Web

Web Site on Justice Louis Brandeis: http://faculty.pnc.edu/bbk/brandeis.htm

Cornell Law School Web Site on Privacy: http://www.law.cornell.edu/wex/index.php/Privacy

CHAPTER 12

Argumentation

As you have learned in the introduction to Section Five, a formal, written argument is very different from a loud or excited discussion about a point of controversy! In fact, when it comes to writing, *argumentation* is an attempt to prove a point—also known as a thesis or proposition—or to support an opinion through calm if vigorous logic and the presentation of evidence.

Mastering Deduction and Induction

Traditionally, two types of thinking have been used in argumentation: induction and deduction. Both support an opinion or belief the writer expresses in a conclusion. Of course, since all persuasive essays begin with logical arguments, as you will see in Chapter 13, induction and deduction are also important components of persuasion. Deduction moves from general premises to a limited conclusion; induction moves from specific evidence to a general conclusion.

DEDUCTION: FROM GENERAL TO SPECIFIC

Deduction draws a limited conclusion from premises, ideas upon which that conclusion is based. Using deduction, writers start with a general statement or idea they believe their readers agree with. Next, they apply a specific case or example to that statement. Finally, they draw a limited conclusion from the two. The logical structure through which this is done is called a syllogism. You would be using deduction if you argued:

> **General statement:** All full-time students can use the college exercise room free of charge.
> **Specific case:** I am a full-time student.
> **Conclusion:** Therefore, I can use the college exercise room free of charge.

Alice Callaghan uses deductive reasoning in "Desperate to Learn English," an essay that appears later in this chapter. Her argument goes something like this:

> **General statement:** Mastering English is essential to success in school.
> **Specific case:** Bilingual education makes it harder for non-native speakers to learn English.
> **Conclusion:** Bilingual education should be abolished.

INDUCTION: FROM SPECIFIC TO GENERAL

Inductive thinking involves collecting separate facts, reasons, or other pieces of evidence and then drawing a conclusion from that information. Say you come down with a case of food poisoning—cramps, vomiting, a headache, the works. When you call the other five people with whom you shared a pot of stew the night before, each tells the same horrible story about cramps, vomiting, and so on. It's safe to say the stew made you sick. That's your conclusion. Support for that conclusion comes in the form of six separate tales of woe.

As a matter of fact, induction is the kind of thinking behind conclusion and support, one of the methods of developing paragraphs and essays explained in Chapter 2. Papers developed through this method express a conclusion or opinion in a formal thesis statement. A good example is Philip K. Howard's "The Death of Common Sense" in Chapter 8. Howard claims that America is being overregulated. This is his *conclusion,* which he expresses in his thesis. He then goes on to discuss *supportive evidence* from which he drew that conclusion.

Here's an example of a paragraph developed using the conclusion-and-support method. It is based upon information from an essay by Lester Brown:

> In the next century, increases in the levels of air pollution caused by the burning of fossil fuels will force us to seek alternative sources of energy. *Thankfully, such alternatives are plentiful.* Around the equator and in deserts, homeowners and industries will install solar panels on rooftops and on the summits of hills to collect energy that will generate electricity or heat water directly. People living on windswept prairies will create their own power by using windmills. Geothermal energy may be tapped by those living in countries around the Mediterranean Sea. Finally, governments might once again fund large-scale hydroelectric projects, such as those created by the Tennessee Valley Authority during the Great Depression.

The second sentence (in italics) in this paragraph is the *conclusion,* which is expressed as the paragraph's topic sentence: "Thankfully, such alternatives are plentiful." This is the point the writer wishes to make, the proposition he wishes to prove. The rest of the paragraph provides evidence to *support that conclusion.*

Induction and deduction are two different ways of reasoning, but they almost always complement each other. In fact, logical and well-supported arguments often reflect both types of thinking.

Reasoning through the Use of Claims and Warrants

British rhetorician Steven Toulmin designed a technique for argumentation and persuasion, which he believed is close to the way people actually debate. Resembling the inductive method in some ways, Toulmin's "Layout of

Argumentation" is applicable to any discipline, issue, or question. As you read about his method, you may decide to incorporate parts of it into your own brand of argumentation or persuasion. It contains six major components:

1. **Data:** Information that leads the writer/speaker to take a position on a question or issue.

2. **Claim:** A statement of the position being defended: the thesis.

3. **Warrants:** Major ideas used to support a claim. There are three types of warrants: authoritative, substantive, motivational. Warrants must relate directly and logically to the claim.

4. **Backing:** Evidence used to support or prove a warrant. It comes in three forms: expert testimony, data and statistics, and concrete illustrations.

5. **Reservation:** Statement anticipating an opposing argument before it decreases your argument's credibility.

6. **Qualifier:** Statement or phrase that restricts the scope of the claim.

As you read above, Toulmin's "claim" is another word for the thesis, the point you are trying to prove. However, he also uses "warrants" in his "Layout of Argumentation." These are major ideas that relate directly to and support the claim. In some ways, they resemble topic sentences, ideas that support a thesis. They, in turn, are developed via concrete evidence, which Toulmin calls "backing." There are three types of warrants:

> **The authoritative warrant** relies on theories, opinions, and studies put forth by experts. Such information may be paraphrased, summarized, or quoted directly. For example, if you claimed that listening regularly to classical music increases IQ in children, you might quote experts in child development, psychologists, and testing specialists. You might also make reference to scientific studies conducted by universities, professional organizations, or government agencies.

> **The substantive warrant** uses a variety of rhetorical modes—especially the conclusion-and-support, comparison/contrast, cause-and-effect, and process analysis methods—to present concrete facts, data, and illustrations that support the claim. For example, you might explain how (process analysis) listening to classical music affects the human brain in the formative stages. You might compare (comparison/contrast) those effects to the effects of listening to other kinds of music or of being exposed to no musical stimulation. In addition, you can cite hard statistics found in professional studies (conclusion and support) to help develop this warrant. Or you can describe the effects of classical music documented in case studies (illustration) of children who were exposed to the works of Mozart and Beethoven on a regular basis.

The motivational warrant can be used if the writer feels knowledgeable about the nature of the audience, their needs, and their opinions. In such cases, he or she might appeal to their personal and professional beliefs, their values, their pride, or even their self-interest. As you might assume, the motivational warrant is particularly **useful when writing persuasion,** which is discussed in the next chapter. For example, if you know that you are writing to the parents of school-age children, you will want to link exposure to classical music to the child's performance on standardized mathematics tests in elementary and high school. You might also point out that, later on, such scores will surely help the student's chances of being admitted to a prestigious college and even of being awarded an academic scholarship.

Read More on the Web

For more on the Toulmin method, refer to these websites:

http://www.unl.edu.speech/comm109/Toulmin/
http://writing.colostate.edu/references/reading/Toulmin/

Developing Ideas in an Argument

In Chapter 2, you learned that there are several ways to develop a paragraph or essay whether your purpose is to explain or to argue or persuade. One of the most popular is conclusion and support, the method you just learned about. As the selections in this chapter show, however, writers of argument often use a combination of methods to provide evidence that proves a point or supports a proposition (thesis). For example, in "Free Speech on Campus," Nat Hentoff uses comparison, mentions the opinions of others via direct quotations, and includes examples to make his point. Student Barry Glazer appeals to authority in "The Right to Be Let Alone" when he makes specific reference to the U.S. Constitution and quotes Supreme Court Justice Louis Brandeis. Alice Callaghan uses narration and statistics effectively in "Desperate to Learn English."

The most important thing to remember about an effective argument is that it is both *logical* and *well supported.* You can use inductive reasoning, deductive reasoning, or both, but your arguments must be reasonable and easy to follow. You can support ideas with examples, facts, statistics, the knowledge or opinions of experts, analogies, comparisons, definitions, firsthand observations, and the like. But your writing must contain enough supportive information to be clear, convincing, and easily understood.

Establishing Your Authority

Of course, the best way to establish your authority—to show that you are knowledgeable about a subject and that you should be believed—is to amass relevant facts and opinions that show you know what you are talking about. In some cases, there is no need for the author to establish his or her credentials. Nat Hentoff, whose essay "Free Speech on Campus" appears in this chapter, doesn't need to tell us he is an expert on this topic because his reputation as a defender of the First Amendment is widespread. On the other hand, it sometimes helps to remind readers of your credentials and experience. That's what Dudley Barlow does in the beginning of his essay on bilingual education, which appears in this chapter, when he alludes to the fact that he is an experienced teacher.

Anticipating and Addressing Opposing Opinions

It is always a good idea to think about points of view in opposition to your own. Doing so shows that you are open-minded, that you have considered more than one side, that you have thought out your position and others' as well, and that you are knowledgeable about your subject. In short, it lends authority to your writing. This is very important when writing persuasion, but it also plays a part in argument. One way to address an opposing opinion is simply to show that it lacks validity, when this is the case. Another effective way is to recognize the validity of your opponent's argument while offering your own as the more realistic or logical alternative. To succeed, each of these tactics requires you to demonstrate to your reader your fair and accurate understanding of the opposing view. Barry Glazer's "The Right to Be Let Alone" and the two essays discussing bilingual education in this chapter illustrate ways in which to deal with opposing arguments.

Visualizing Strategies for Argument

Read the following editorial, published in *USA Today*. Then, read the two discussions that follow it, which show how it uses both deduction and induction.

Drug Tests Fail Schools

USA Today *Editorial*

IMAGINE YOU wanted to go out for your company's softball team and your boss 1
told you: "Pee in this cup—in front of me."

Most adults would consider such a demand outrageous. Yet, that's what 2
some public schools were demanding from student athletes in the war against drugs when 12-year-old James Acton came along in 1991.

The would-be seventh-grade football player put a damper on such demands. 3
First, he told Vernonia, OR, public school officials that he wouldn't go along.
Then he went to court. His claim: The district's drug tests—required of all those
trying out for sports—violate Fourth Amendment rights to privacy.

Last year, a federal appeals court in San Francisco agreed. In doing so, 4
it made such testing illegal in nine Western states under its jurisdiction. And
it discouraged schools elsewhere from starting testing programs until the
Supreme Court rules on the case.

Today, the high court hears arguments. And if students, schools and tax- 5
payers are lucky, it will kill all such required drug tests for student athletes by
next fall.

Drug testing can be smart, when it's conducted to protect public safety and 6
security, as with transportation workers and drug enforcement agents. And it
may even be sensible when it's done to ensure role models, such as professional
and college athletes, don't abuse narcotics.

But it wastes money and violates rights when forced upon thousands of 7
youngsters.

Vernonia began its program mostly because of increased disciplinary 8
problems.

But school officials chose not to focus on the problem kids. They lassoed 9
mostly innocent ones. Of 500 students tested in 4 1/2 years, a mere 12 tested
positive, not many for a district claiming huge problems.

And who paid for the willy-nilly testing? Not local folks, but deficit-riddled 10
Uncle Sam through the federal drug-free schools program. Vernonia's cut:
$7,500 a year.

History shows there's a fairer way. Teen drug use was cut substantially 11
during the 1980s, not because a few schools tested students for drugs but because most taught students the dangers of abuse and involved parents in their
programs.

Schools should do the same today. They should call parents of kids sus- 12
pected of drug use and get permission for any testing.

That would save money, focus the drug fight on those causing problems 13
and not invade the privacy of innocent kids whose only crime is trying out for
a sport.

Deduction in "Drug Tests Fail Schools"   As you have learned, deduction moves from general to specific. The process starts with a general statement, to which a specific case or example is applied. Then, a conclusion
is drawn from these two. Here's how deduction works in "Drug Tests Fail
Schools":

> **General statement:** Drug testing should be permitted only to pro-
> tect public safety or to ensure that role models don't abuse drugs
> (paragraph 6).

Specific case or example: Forcing students to test for drugs only wastes money and violates rights; it does not protect public safety (paragraph 7).
Conclusion: Therefore, forcing students to take drug tests should be stopped.

Induction in "Drug Tests Fail Schools" Earlier you read that induction is the basis of the conclusion-and-support method for developing a paper. Support for a conclusion comes in the form of evidence or reasons behind it. Here's how induction works in "Drug Tests Fail Schools":

> *Support*
> A federal appeals court ruled that forcing students to take drug tests violates the Fourth Amendment (paragraph 4).

> *Support*
> Of 500 students tested for drugs in Vernonia, Oregon, only 12 tested positive (paragraph 9).

> *Support*
> Testing for drugs in Vernonia cost taxpayers $7,500 (paragraph 10).

> *Support*
> Studies show teen drug use can be cut through education and parental involvement (paragraph 11).

> *Conclusion*
> Forcing students to take drug tests should be stopped.

Revising Argument Papers

An argument requires logical and clear writing, and such writing takes hard work. Barry Glazer, a student whose essay appears in this chapter, wrote several drafts of a paper on individual rights before he arrived at a version with which he was satisfied. His rough draft contained the germ of an idea and several good examples but by the time Glazer wrote his final draft, the paper had been transformed into a first-rate argument paper. Even the title had changed.

Glazer—Rough Draft

It Ain't Nobody's Business but My Own

Help? In what way? Government is supposed to help people, not hurt them. Those we elect to public office are there to make things better for everyone. However, many of them are doing

What kinds of things? things that annoy and frighten me. If I am

Expand? Clarify? not hurting anybody, the government should stay out of my private affairs. What I do, if it isn't causing anyone else harm, is no one's business but my own.

Support this claim. If I have a terminal disease, I should be allowed to kill myself or get a doctor to help me do so.

They don't? Support this claim. If I am driving home late at night the police have no right to stop me just because I am young and look suspicious. Recently, I was walking around the block at three in the morning and the police stopped and questioned me. Yet, all I was doing was taking a late-night stroll.

. . .

What kinds of things? Yes, we need government to take care of important things. But the government and the police should stay out of people's lives when it is none of their business. They should just leave us alone.

Glazer—Final Draft

The Right to Be Let Alone.] *Revises title.*

Government is the instrument of the people,

Appeals to authority. [says the <u>United States Constitution</u>. Those

to whom the people entrust power are charged

with <u>maintaining justice</u>, <u>promoting the</u>] *Explains how government "is supposed to help people."*

<u>general welfare</u>, and <u>securing the blessings</u>

<u>of liberty for us all</u>. Recent newspaper

Explains what he meant by "things that annoy and frighten me." [opinion polls, however, suggest that many

Americans are dissatisfied with the men and

women running our communities, our states,

and our nation. More and more of us have

come to believe that our leaders are

isolated from the realities ordinary people

face. We fear we are losing control.

Instead of helping to alleviate this

feeling of impotence, however, politicians

and bureaucrats continue to make and enforce

regulations that constrain our lives and

constrict our freedoms. To help people

regain a rightful measure of control,

government—whether national, state, or

local—should stay out of our private lives

Appeals to authority. [whenever possible. As Supreme Court Justice

Louis Brandeis noted, Americans treasure

their "right to be let alone."

There is no reason for the government to

interfere in our lives if our behavior does

Supports claim with convincing details.

not adversely affect others or if there is no immediate necessity for such interference. Were I in the <u>throes</u> of terminal <u>cancer</u> or <u>facing the horror of</u> <u>Alzheimer's disease</u>, I should be allowed to kill myself. Faced with the <u>agonizing</u> <u>degeneration</u> of my memory and personality, I would probably want to end my life in my own way. But the government says this is illegal. Indeed, were I to call upon a doctor to assist me on this final quest, she would stand a good chance of being charged with murder.

Appeals to emotions.

Supports claim by appealing to authority.

    The government should also stay out of an individual's life if there is no reason to believe he is doing wrong. <u>The Bill of</u> <u>Rights protects us from unlawful searches</u> <u>and seizures</u>. Yet, if I drive home from work in the early morning, I stand a reasonable chance of being stopped without cause at a police roadblock. While armed, uniformed officers shine flashlights in my face, I can be subjected to questions about my destination and point of origin. I can be told to produce my papers and to step out of my car. I can be made to endure the <u>embarrassment of performing tricks to prove</u> <u>my sobriety</u>. Allowing the police such powers is hardly in keeping with our

Appeals to reader's self-interest and personal values.

*Defines
government's
true roll.* | government's mission to promote justice,
security, and liberty.

. . .

*Supports
preceding
statement.* | Clearly, government is a necessity.
Without it, we would face anarchy. Yet,
those who roam the halls of power should
remember from where their power originates
and should find ways to reduce the burden of
unnecessary regulations heaped on the backs
of the American people.

*Closes with
a memorable
statement.*

Practicing Strategies for Argument

Practice Deduction   Read the following general statements. Think of a
specific case or example that applies to each. Then draw a conclusion. Write
your responses in the spaces provided.

1. **General statement:** Students who have had three years of high school
mathematics can enroll in Math 101.

   Specific case: _____

   _____

   _____

   _____

   Conclusion: _____

   _____

   _____

2. **General statement:** Students who commute to the college by car must
buy parking decals.

   Specific case: _____

   _____

   _____

   Conclusion: _____

   _____

3. **General statement:** Cars more than five years old must be inspected once per year.

    Specific case: _____

    _____

    _____

    _____

    Conclusion: _____

    _____

4. **General statement:** People whose families have a history of heart disease should have annual coronary examinations.

    Specific case: _____

    _____

    _____

    _____

    Conclusion: _____

    _____

5. **General statement:** People who don't vote should not complain about the way government is run.

    Specific case: _____

    _____

    _____

    _____

    Conclusion: _____

    _____

Practice Induction Read each group of supportive statements below. Then, using induction, draw a general conclusion from each group. Write the conclusion in the space provided.

1. **Support:** None of the restaurants on the east side of town offers meals for under $30.

    Support: The east side is full of luxury high-rise apartment buildings.

    Support: The east side has no discount clothing, drug, or grocery stores.

    Conclusion: _____

    _____

2. **Support:** Students who attend Professor Villa's class regularly have a good chance of passing her tests.

    Support: Professor Villa encourages students to come to her office for extra help.

    Support: Professor Villa's assignments are clear and practical.

    Conclusion: _____

    _____

3. **Support:** The lock on the door had been broken.

    Support: I couldn't find my jewelry.

    Support: Furniture, pictures, and pillows had been moved.

    Conclusion: _____

    _____

4. **Support:** Serena dragged herself into the apartment and turned on the light.

    Support: There were circles under her eyes.

    Support: In about five minutes, the apartment was dark again.

    Conclusion: _____

    _____

5. **Support:** Miguel Hernandez plans to attend medical school after getting his bachelor's degree in biology.

    Support: His sister wants to become a dentist.

    Support: His brother is enrolled in a five-year program in architecture.

    Conclusion: _____

    _____

The Right to Be Let Alone

Barry Glazer

Barry Glazer became interested in writing when he enrolled in a basic-skills composition class during his first semester in college. He went on to major in history and English, to become editor of his college newspaper, and to take a bachelor's and a master's degree.

Preparing to Read

1. This essay is logical, clear, and well developed, but it goes beyond pure argument and often appeals to the emotions.
2. Glazer organizes his work around three principles by which he would restrict the government's ability to interfere with our lives. Identify these principles as you read "The Right to Be Let Alone."
3. Louis Brandeis, mentioned in paragraph 2, was associate justice of the United States Supreme Court (1916–1939). He was a champion of individual rights.

Vocabulary

adversely (adverb)	Negatively.
alleviate (verb)	Reduce, lessen, relieve.
anarchy (noun)	Chaos, disorder, lawlessness.
bureaucrats (noun)	Government officials.
constrain (verb)	Restrain, hold in check, bind.
constrict (verb)	Bind, choke, squeeze.
endure (verb)	Suffer, bear, submit to.
entrust (verb)	Give to for safekeeping.
impotence (noun)	Lack of power.
reflect (verb)	Think.
refrain from (verb)	Stop, cease, avoid.
throes (noun)	Agony, pain.

The Right to Be Let Alone

Barry Glazer

GOVERNMENT IS THE instrument of the people, says the United States   1
Constitution. Those to whom the people entrust power are charged with maintaining justice, promoting the general welfare, and securing the blessings

of liberty for us all. Recent newspaper opinion polls, however, suggest that many Americans are dissatisfied with the men and women running our communities, our states, and our nation. More and more of us have come to believe that our leaders are isolated from the realities ordinary people face. We fear we are losing control.

Instead of helping to alleviate this feeling of impotence, however, politicians and bureaucrats continue to make and enforce regulations that constrain our lives and constrict our freedoms. To help people regain a rightful measure of control, government—whether national, state, or local—should stay out of our private lives whenever possible. As Supreme Court Justice Louis Brandeis noted, Americans treasure their "right to be let alone."   2

There is no reason for the government to interfere in our lives if our behavior does not adversely affect others or if there is no immediate necessity for such interference. Were I in the throes of terminal cancer or facing the horror of Alzheimer's disease, I should be allowed to kill myself. Faced with the agonizing degeneration of my memory and personality, I would probably want to end my life in my own way. But the government says this is illegal. Indeed, were I to call upon a doctor to assist me on this final quest, she would stand a good chance of being charged with murder.   3

The government should also stay out of an individual's life if there is no reason to believe he is doing wrong. The Bill of Rights protects us from unlawful searches and seizures. Yet if I drive home from work in the early morning, I stand a reasonable chance of being stopped without cause at a police roadblock. While armed, uniformed officers shine flashlights in my face, I can be subjected to questions about my destination and point of origin. I can be told to produce my papers and to step out of my car. I can be made to endure the embarrassment of performing tricks to prove my sobriety. Allowing the police such powers is hardly in keeping with our government's mission to promote justice, security, and liberty.   4

Finally, the government should refrain from creating unnecessary burdens for the American people. It should stay out of a person's private business if such involvement burdens the individual unnecessarily or unfairly. Recently, my faithful dog Linda was dying. Because of years of abuse at the hands of her previous owner, she was no longer able to walk and had to be carried in my arms. At that time, the dog warden knocked on my door and threatened me with fines for my continued refusal to license the animal. When I told him that Linda was unable to walk, let alone leave my property, he threatened to return with the police.   5

Similarly, when I wanted to convert my garage into a den, I was overwhelmed by official red tape. The cost of construction permits and of measures to meet complex building codes cost more than the lumber, wall board, and other supplies for the project. Another example of governmental red tape became evident when I attempted to enroll in a Japanese language course at a community college. I was told the state required that I take a mathematics placement test or pass a course in elementary algebra first!   6

Clearly, government is a necessity. Without it, we would face anarchy. Yet   7
those who roam the halls of power should remember from where their power
originates and should find ways to reduce the burden of unnecessary regulations heaped on the backs of the American people.

Read More on the Web

Website on Justice Louis Brandeis:
   http://faculty.purduenc.edu/bbk/brandeis.htm
Purdue University site on right to privacy:
   http://faculty.purduenc.edu/bbk/privacy.html
Privacy Rights Clearinghouse site with links to other sources:
   http://www.privacyrights.org/
Article by George Mason University professor Walter Williams, a noted
   social critic: http://www.gmu.edu/departments/economics/wew/
   articles/99/Left-Alone.htm

Questions for Discussion

1. What one sentence in this essay best expresses Glazer's purpose and
    central idea?
2. In Preparing to Read, you learned that the author defends three
    principles by which he would limit government interference. What
    are these principles?
3. What method of development does Glazer rely on most?
4. Pick out vocabulary that appeals to the reader's emotions.
5. Why does Glazer bother to tell us that Justice Brandeis is the source
    of the quotation in paragraph 2 (and of the essay's title)?
6. Find examples of deductive reasoning in this essay. In your own
    words, construct a syllogism that explains each example.
7. Where does the author address an argument that an opponent might
    use to dispute his?

Thinking Critically

1. What side would Barry Glazer take in the debate over mandatory
    testing of school-age athletes as expressed in the selection earlier in
    the chapter, "Drug Tests Fail Schools"? Support your answer with
    reference to both reading selections.
2. If you haven't done so already, read Howard's "The Death of Common
    Sense," an essay in Chapter 8. On what points might Glazer agree
    and disagree with Howard?

Suggestions for Journal Entries

1. Glazer calls up several examples from experiences similar to those you or people like you might have had. Use focused freewriting to narrate an incident that explains how a government rule or regulation interferes with the right of privacy. Interpret the word *government* broadly; write about the federal, state, local, or college regulation you most disagree with. You might even address a rule followed by your family, your athletic team, or other group to which you belong.

2. Play the role of Glazer's opponent by responding to at least one of the examples he uses to support his thesis. Explain why requiring licenses for all dogs is reasonable; why strict building codes are important; why the police should have the right to stop and question drivers; why doctors should not be allowed to help terminally ill patients commit suicide; or why states should set academic standards in public colleges.

3. Even if you agree with Glazer, you may know of instances in which people welcome government "interference." List as many examples of such beneficial interference as you can.

A Cool and Logical Analysis of the Bicycle Menace

P. J. O'Rourke

A satirist whose targets are politics and social mores, P. J. O'Rourke graduated from Miami University of Ohio. In 1978, he was appointed editor-in-chief of The National Lampoon. *His articles have appeared in* American Spectator, Esquire, Vanity Fair, Harper's, *and many other well-known magazines.* O'Rourke *is now on staff with* Rolling Stone *and frequently contributes to the* Atlantic Monthly. *He is the author of ten books including* Parliament of Whores *(1991),* All the Trouble in the World *(1994),* Age and Guile Beat Youth, Innocence, and a Bad Haircut *(1996), and* The Bachelor Home Companion *(1997). "A Cool and Logical Analysis of the Bicycle Menace," which appears in* Republican Party Reptile *(1987), reveals O'Rourke as the master of the ironic.*

Preparing to Read

1. This essay is an example of irony, a technique used by writers to create humor by saying something that is different from—often the very opposite of—what they really mean. Often referred to as the tongue-in-cheek method, verbal irony can be used to produce biting satire or simply to create humor. In this essay, O'Rourke is obviously using the latter.

2. Among the products of O'Rourke's irony are several examples of the kinds of logical fallacies explained in the introduction to Section Five: Argumentation and Persuasion. After you read this essay for the first time, reread it and try to find examples of some of those fallacies.

3. Paragraph 16 mentions UNICEF, the United Nations Children's Fund. Paragraph 18 mentions the DOT, the Department of Transportation; CAFE, Corporate Average Fuel Economy standards; and NHTSA, the National Highway Traffic Safety Administration.

Vocabulary

eons (noun)	Ages.
faddist (noun)	Someone who follows a fashion or trend.
ferrules (noun)	Metal sleeves.
haplessly (adverb)	Unluckily, unfortunately.
impuissant (adjective)	Powerless, ineffective.
phalanx (noun)	A body of troops in close formation.
Pleistocene (noun)	An early geological period.
savanna (noun)	Flat grassland.

A Cool and Logical Analysis of the Bicycle Menace

P. J. O'Rourke

OUR NATION IS afflicted with a plague of bicycles. Everywhere the public 1
right-of-way is glutted with whirring, unbalanced contraptions of rubber,
wire, and cheap steel pipe. Riders of these flimsy appliances pay no heed to
stop signs or red lights. They dart from between parked cars, dash along double
yellow lines, and whiz through crosswalks right over the toes of law-abiding
citizens like me.

In the cities, every lamppost, tree, and street sign is disfigured by a bicycle 2
slathered in chains and locks. And elevators must be shared with the cycling
faddist so attached to his "moron's bathchair" that he has to take it with him
everywhere he goes.

In the country, one cannot drive around a curve or over the crest of a hill 3
without encountering a gaggle of huffing bicyclers spread across the road in
suicidal phalanx.

Even the wilderness is not safe from infestation, as there is now such a 4
thing as an off-road bicycle and a horrible sport called "bicycle-cross."

The ungainly geometry and primitive mechanicals of the bicycle are an 5
offense to the eye. The grimy and perspiring riders of the bicycle are an offense
to the nose. And the very existence of the bicycle is an offense to reason and
wisdom.

Principal Arguments Which May Be Marshaled against Bicycles

1. BICYCLES ARE CHILDISH.

Bicycles have their proper place, and that place is under small boys delivering 6
evening papers. Insofar as children are too short to see over the dashboards of
cars and too small to keep motorcycles upright at intersections, bicycles are
suitable vehicles for them. But what are we to make of an adult in a suit and
tie pedaling his way to work? Are we to assume he still delivers newspapers for
a living? If not, do we want a doctor, lawyer, or business executive who plays
with toys? St. Paul, in his First Epistle to the Corinthians, 13:11, said, "When
I became a man, I put away childish things." He did *not* say, "When I became a
man, I put away childish things and got more elaborate and expensive childish
things from France and Japan."

Considering the image projected, bicycling commuters might as well pro- 7
pel themselves to the office with one knee in a red Radio Flyer wagon.

2. BICYCLES ARE UNDIGNIFIED.

A certain childishness is, no doubt, excusable. But going about in public with 8
one's head between one's knees and one's rump protruding in the air is nobody's
idea of acceptable behavior.

It is impossible for an adult to sit on a bicycle without looking the fool. 9
There is a type of woman, in particular, who should never assume the bicycling
posture. This is the woman of ample proportions. Standing on her own feet
she is a figure to admire—classical in her beauty and a symbol, throughout
history, of sensuality, maternal virtue, and plenty. Mounted on a bicycle, she is
a laughingstock.

In a world where loss of human dignity is such a grave and all-pervading 10
issue, what can we say about people who voluntarily relinquish all of theirs and
go around looking at best like Quixote on Rosinante and more often like something in the Macy's Thanksgiving Day parade? Can such people be trusted? Is a
person with so little self-respect likely to have any respect for you?

3. Bicycles Are Unsafe.

Bicycles are topheavy, have poor brakes, and provide no protection to their rid- 11
ers. Bicycles are also made up of many hard and sharp components which, in
collision, can do grave damage to people and the paint finish on automobiles.
Bicycles are dangerous things.

Of course, there's nothing wrong, *per se,* with dangerous things. Speedboats, 12
racecars, fine shotguns, whiskey, and love are all very dangerous. Bicycles, however, are dangerous without being any fun. You can't shoot pheasants with a
bicycle or water-ski behind it or go 150 miles an hour or even mix it with soda
and ice. And the idea of getting romantic on top of a bicycle is alarming. All
you can do with one of these ten-speed sink traps is grow tired and sore and
fall off it.

Being dangerous without being fun puts bicycles in a category with open- 13
heart surgery, the war in Vietnam, the South Bronx, and divorce. Sensible
people do all that they can to avoid such things as these.

4. Bicycles Are Un-American.

We are a nation that worships speed and power. And for good reason. Without 14
power we would still be part of England and everybody would be out of work.
And if it weren't for speed, it would take us all months to fly to L.A., get involved in the movie business, and become rich and famous.

Bicycles are too slow and impuissant for a country like ours. They belong 15
in Czechoslovakia.

5. I Don't Like the Kind of People Who Ride Bicycles.

At least I think I don't. I don't actually know anyone who rides a bicycle. But 16
the people I see on bicycles look like organic-gardening zealots who advocate
federal regulation of bedtime and want American foreign policy to be dictated
by UNICEF. These people should be confined.

I apologize if I have the wrong impression. It may be that bicycle riders 17
are all members of the New York Stock Exchange, Methodist bishops, retired
Marine Corps drill instructors, and other solid citizens. However, the fact that

they cycle around in broad daylight making themselves look like idiots indicates that they're crazy anyway and should be confined just the same.

6. BICYCLES ARE UNFAIR.

Bicycles use the same roads as cars and trucks yet they pay no gasoline tax, 18 carry no license plates, are not required to have insurance, and are not subject to DOT, CAFE, or NHTSA regulations. Furthermore, bicyclists do not have to take driver's examinations, have eye tests when they're over sixty-five, carry registration papers with them, or submit to breathalyzer tests under the threat of law. And they never get caught in radar traps.

The fact (see No. 5, above) that bicycles are ridden by the very people who 19 most favor government interference in life makes the bicycle's special status not only unfair but an outright incitement to riot.

Equality before the law is the cornerstone of democracy. Bicycles should be 20 made to carry twenty-gallon tanks of gasoline. They should be equipped with twelve-volt batteries and a full complement of taillights, headlamps, and turn signals. They should have seat belts, air bags, and safety-glass windows too. And every bicycle rider should be inspected once a year for hazardous defects and be made to wear a number plate hanging around his neck and another on the seat of his pants.

7. BICYCLES ARE GOOD EXERCISE.

And so is swinging through trees on your tail. Mankind has invested more 21 than four million years of evolution in the attempt to avoid physical exertion. Now a group of backward-thinking atavists mounted on foot-powered pairs of Hula-Hoops would have us pumping our legs, gritting our teeth, and searing our lungs as though we were being chased across the Pleistocene savanna by sabertoothed tigers. Think of the hopes, the dreams, the effort, the brilliance, the pure force of will that, over the eons, have gone into the creation of the Cadillac Coupe de Ville. Bicycle riders would have us throw all this on the ash heap of history.

What Must Be Done about the Bicycle Threat?

Fortunately, nothing. Frustrated truck drivers and irate cabbies make a point 22 of running bicycles off the road. Terrified old ladies jam umbrella ferrules into wheel spokes as bicycles rush by them on sidewalks. And all of us have occasion to back over bicycles that are haplessly parked.

Bicycles are quiet and slight, difficult for normal motorized humans to see 23 and hear. People pull out in front of bicycles, open car doors in their path, and drive through intersections filled with the things. The insubstantial bicycle and its unshielded rider are defenseless against these actions. It's a simple matter of natural selection. The bicycle will be extinct within the decade. And what a relief that will be.

Read More on the Web

O'Rourke's "Liberty Manifesto": www.libertarian.org/cato/manifesto.html
"All People Are Crazy": An *Atlantic* online interview with O'Rourke:
   http://www.theatlantic.com/unbound/interviews/int2002-08-08.htm

Questions for Discussion

1. What is O'Rourke's thesis? Where does he state it? What does this thesis tell you—ironically at least—about the way he will defend it?

2. In which paragraphs does O'Rourke use induction? What conclusions does he draw using this process?

3. Paragraphs 6, 18, and 20, among others, use deduction. Create syllogisms that trace O'Rourke's logic in at least two such paragraphs.

4. Where does O'Rourke anticipate opposing arguments? How does he respond to such arguments? Does he ever acknowledge the validity of such arguments?

5. How does the author defend his not knowing anyone who rides a bicycle (paragraph 16)?

6. Find an example in this essay of what Toulmin would call "data," information that leads the writer to take a position on an issue.

7. Find an example of what Toulmin would call a "substantive warrant." Why doesn't O'Rourke include authoritative warrants?

8. Find examples of at least five of the logical fallacies discussed in the introduction to Section Five: Argumentation and Persuasion.

Thinking Critically

1. The nation of Czechoslovakia, which O'Rourke mentions in paragraph 15, no longer exists. (In the early 1990s, it was divided into two separate countries: Slovakia and the Czech Republic.) Explain O'Rourke's reference to Czechoslovakia. You might have to read more about this country on the Internet or in your library.

2. In item 8 under Questions for Discussion, you were asked to find examples of five logical fallacies in this essay. Now, explain how each of those examples illustrates the fallacy you think it represents.

Suggestions for Journal Entries

1. Using clustering or any other prewriting technique you read about in "Getting Started," gather information to include in your own humorous "analysis" of a particular activity. Remember, your purpose

here is to collect reasons that might be used in an ironic, tongue-in-cheek, essay. Like O'Rourke, you will want to show—ironically, of course—why the activity is "a menace" or why it should be stopped. Here are a few suggestions to choose from, but you can probably think of a better one yourself:

- Exercising on a regular basis.
- Shopping in a supermarket or other kind of store.
- Going shopping with a spouse or member of the opposite sex.
- Going camping, hiking, boating, skiing, etc.
- Reading the daily newspapers.
- Driving an SUV, a pickup truck, or any other kind of car or truck.
- Majoring in (you pick it).
- Following a low-fat or any other type of diet.
- Beginning work on a research paper more than one day before it's due.

2. Use clustering or any other prewriting technique you read about in "Getting Started" to gather information that you might use in a serious essay endorsing or criticizing a particular activity. In other words, your purpose here is to gather reasons that might get people to adopt or reject this activity.

Free Speech on Campus

Nat Hentoff

Nat Hentoff (1925–) is one of the most important defenders of free speech in America. He writes a regular column for the Village Voice, *a New York weekly, and he contributes regularly to prestigious newspapers, magazines, and journals across the country. A native of Boston, Hentoff attended Northeastern and Harvard Universities as well as the Sorbonne in Paris, where he studied on a Fulbright fellowship. Although he writes on many subjects, his reputation rests chiefly on his defense of the First Amendment of the U.S. Constitution and his consistent opposition to censorship. Among his books is* The First Freedom: The Tumultuous History of Free Speech in America *(1989).*

Hentoff is generally considered a liberal in politics, but when it comes to free speech he is nonpartisan. In recent years, he has found fault with the Left for its attempts to silence those whose opinions it finds offensive or distasteful. This essay is excerpted from a longer piece, which first appeared in The Progressive *(1989).*

Preparing to Read

1. The First Amendment to the U.S. Constitution states that "Congress shall make no law respecting the establishment of religion, or prohibiting the free exercise thereof; or abridging the freedom of speech, or of the press; or the right of the people peaceably to assemble, and to petition the Government for a redress of grievances."

2. The Fourteenth Amendment (paragraph 21) guarantees due process and equal protection under the law. Due process (paragraph 13) allows citizens to defend themselves in both criminal and civil actions against accusations that can have legal, financial, or other serious consequences.

3. Lenny Bruce, Richard Pryor, and Sam Kinison, who are mentioned in paragraph 13, have used language that some might find offensive or even obscene in their comedy acts.

4. Affirmative action (paragraph 16) is the name given to government regulations that set goals for the admission of minorities to educational institutions and for the hiring of minorities in both the private and public sectors.

5. "Politically correct" is a term used by critics of the Left. They accuse liberals of insisting that only certain beliefs and behaviors are legitimate despite constitutional and other legal guarantees.

6. Oliver Wendell Holmes was a U.S. Supreme Court Justice famous for his writings on the First Amendment.

Vocabulary

aggravated (adjective)	Heightened, made worse.
condemnation (noun)	Blame, censure.
constitute (verb)	Make up or equate to.
derogatory (adjective)	Degrading, disdainful.
dissented (verb)	Refused to conform or obey.
inquiry (noun)	Questioning, exploration, debate.
knownothingism (noun)	A term that has come to mean intolerance and bigotry. The Knownothing Party of the nineteenth century wished to close U.S. borders to further immigration.
malignancies (noun)	Cancers.
orthodoxy (noun)	Strict adherence to a doctrine or set of beliefs.
pall (noun)	Gloom, sadness.
pariah (noun)	Social outcast, renegade.
perpetuate (verb)	Continue, keep alive.
pietistic (adjective)	Solemn, but in an affected or false way.
resurgence (noun)	Rebirth.
sanctions (noun)	Punishments.
scant (adjective)	Little.
secular (adjective)	Worldly.
short shrift (noun)	Little attention.
stifling (adjective)	Suffocating.
tempered (adjective)	Balanced, controlled.
ukase (noun)	Proclamation, decree, order.

Free Speech on Campus

Nat Hentoff

A FLIER DISTRIBUTED at the University of Michigan some months ago proclaimed that blacks "don't belong in classrooms, they belong hanging from trees."   1

At other campuses around the country, manifestations of racism are becoming commonplace. At Yale, a swastika and the words WHITE POWER! were painted on the building housing the University's Afro-American Cultural Center. At Temple University, a White Students Union has been formed with some 130 members.   2

Swastikas are not directed only at black students. The Nazi symbol has been spray-painted on the Jewish Student Union at Memphis State University. And on a number of campuses, women have been singled out as targets of   3 wounding and sometimes frightening speech. At the law school of the State University of New York at Buffalo, several women students have received anonymous letters characterized by one professor as venomously sexist.

These and many more such signs of the resurgence of bigotry and 4 knownothingism throughout the society—as well as on campus—have to do solely with speech, including symbolic speech. There have also been physical assaults on black students and on black, white, and Asian women students, but the way to deal with physical attacks is clear: call the police and file a criminal complaint. What is to be done, however, about speech alone—however disgusting, inflammatory, and rawly divisive that speech may be?

At more and more colleges, administrators—with the enthusiastic support of 5 black students, women students, and liberal students—have been answering that question by preventing or punishing speech. In public universities, this is a clear violation of the First Amendment. In private colleges and universities, suppression of speech mocks the secular religion of academic freedom and free inquiry.

The Student Press Law Center in Washington, D.C.—a vital source of 6 legal support for student editors around the country—reports, for example, that at the University of Kansas, the student host and producer of a radio news program was forbidden by school officials from interviewing a leader of the Ku Klux Klan. So much for free inquiry on that campus.

In Madison, Wisconsin, the *Capital Times* ran a story in January about 7 Chancellor Sheila Kaplan of the University of Wisconsin branch at Parkside, who ordered her campus to be scoured of "some anonymously placed white supremacist hate literature." Sounding like the legendary Mayor Frank ("I am the law") Hague of Jersey City, who booted "bad speech" out of town, Chancellor Kaplan said, "This institution is not a lamppost standing on the street corner. It doesn't belong to everyone."

Who decides what speech can be heard or read by everyone? Why, the 8 Chancellor, of course. That's what George III used to say, too.

University of Wisconsin political science professor Carol Tebben thinks 9 otherwise. She believes university administrators "are getting confused when they are acting as censors and trying to protect students from bad ideas. I don't think students need to be protected from bad ideas. I think they can determine for themselves what ideas are bad."

After all, if students are to be "protected" from bad ideas, how are they go- 10 ing to learn to identify and cope with them? Sending such ideas underground simply makes them stronger and more dangerous.

Professor Tebben's conviction that free speech means just that has become 11 a decidedly minority view on many campuses. At the University of Buffalo Law School, the faculty unanimously adopted a "Statement Regarding Intellectual Freedom, Tolerance, and Political Harassment." Its title implies support of intellectual freedom, but the statement warned students that once they enter "this legal community," their right to free speech must become tempered "by the responsibility to promote equality and justice."

Accordingly, swift condemnation will befall anyone who engages in 12 "remarks directed at another's race, sex, religion, national origin, age, or sex preference." Also forbidden are "other remarks based on prejudice and group stereotype."

This ukase is so broad that enforcement has to be alarmingly subjective. 13 Yet the University of Buffalo Law School provides no due-process procedures for a student booked for making any of these prohibited remarks. Conceivably, a student caught playing a Lenny Bruce, Richard Pryor, or Sam Kinison album in his room could be tried for aggravated insensitivity by association.

When I looked into this wholesale cleansing of bad speech at Buffalo, I 14 found it had encountered scant opposition. One protester was David Gerald Jay, a graduate of the law school and a cooperating attorney for the New York Civil Liberties Union. Said the appalled graduate: "Content-based prohibitions constitute prior restraint and should not be tolerated."

You would think that the law professors and administration at this public 15 university might have known that. But hardly any professors dissented, and among the students only members of the conservative Federalist Society spoke up for free speech. The fifty-strong chapter of the National Lawyers Guild was on the other side. After all, it was more important to go on record as vigorously opposing racism and sexism than to expose oneself to charges of insensitivity to these malignancies.

The pressures to have the "right" attitude—as proved by having the "right" 16 language in and out of class—can be stifling. A student who opposes affirmative action, for instance, can be branded a racist.

At the University of California at Los Angeles, the student newspaper ran 17 an editorial cartoon satirizing affirmative action. (A student stops a rooster on campus and asks how the rooster got into UCLA. "Affirmative action," is the answer.) After outraged complaints from various minority groups, the editor was suspended for violating a publication policy against running "articles that perpetuate derogatory or cultural stereotypes." The art director was also suspended.

When the opinion editor of the student newspaper at California State 18 University at Northridge wrote an article asserting that the sanctions against the editor and art director at UCLA amounted to censorship, he was suspended too.

At New York University Law School, a student was so disturbed by the 19 pall of orthodoxy at that prestigious institution that he wrote to the school newspaper even though, as he said, he expected his letter to make him a pariah among his fellow students.

Barry Endick described the atmosphere at NYU created by "a host of 20 watchdog committees and a generally hostile classroom reception regarding any student comment right of center." This "can be arguably viewed as symptomatic of a prevailing spirit of academic and social intolerance of . . . any idea which is not 'politically correct.' "

He went on to say something that might well be posted on campus bulletin 21
boards around the country, though it would probably be torn down at many of
them: "We ought to examine why students, so anxious to wield the Fourteenth
Amendment, give short shrift to the First. Yes, Virginia, there are racist assholes.
And you know what, the Constitution protects them, too."

Not when they engage in violence or vandalism. But when they speak or 22
write, racist assholes fall right into this Oliver Wendell Holmes definition—
highly unpopular among bigots, liberals, radicals, feminists, sexists, and college administrators: "If there is any principle of the Constitution that more
imperatively calls for attachment than any other, it is the principle of free
thought—not free only for those who agree with us, but freedom for the
thought we hate."

The language sounds like a pietistic Sunday sermon, but if it ever falls 23
wholly into disuse, neither this publication nor any other journal of opinion—
right or left—will survive.

Read More on the Web

Site explores university responses to censoring the Internet. Includes
    useful bibliography: http://hsb.baylor.edu/ramsower/ais.ac.97/
    papers/peace.htm
Nat Hentoff Archives: Three years of Hentoff columns on the Web:
    http://www.jewishworldreview.com/cols/hentoff.archives.asp
American Civil Liberties Union online essay: "Racist Speech on College
    Campuses": http://archive.aclu.org/library/aahate.html

Questions for Discussion

1. What use of expert testimony and opinion does Hentoff make?
2. What use of anecdotes does he make? Of contrast?
3. Analyze the essay's introduction. What techniques are used here to
    draw our attention?
4. What is the question Hentoff asks in paragraph 4? How does this
    question help him introduce his essay?
5. In what way is symbolic speech similar to speech? Why does Hentoff
    bother to mention symbolic speech?
6. What distinction does the author draw between speech and action?
    Why is this distinction important to his thesis? What is his thesis?
7. Why does Hentoff quote Professor Carol Tebben (paragraph 9) and
    David Gerald Jay (paragraph 14)? What do their words add to the
    author's argument?
8. Where does Hentoff address opposing opinions?

9. Describe Hentoff's tone? Does he ever reveal his personal feelings about this issue?
10. Describe the essay's intended audience.

Thinking Critically

1. Reread Barry Glazer's essay, which appears earlier in this chapter. How might Hentoff respond to Glazer's arguments?
2. Reread Hentoff's essay. Then, using deduction, summarize it into a syllogism. In your own words, state its major premise, its minor premise, and its conclusion.

Suggestions for Journal Entries

1. Can you think of any circumstances when you might agree that speech should be censored? Make a list of such circumstances; then, explain why each might warrant limitations on free speech.
2. Are you in favor of unlimited free speech under all circumstances? If so, explain your reasons. As a way to anticipate arguments opposed to your own, explain how and why you would defend the rights of people to speak—verbally or symbolically—in ways that you might find distasteful, immoral, abhorrent, or even dangerous.
3. Consider an issue on your campus that you feel strongly about. It doesn't have to have earth-shaking consequences. The benefits of keeping the library open all night, the need for more parking spaces, or the advantages of majoring in a particular subject area might make fine topics for argumentation. Use freewriting or clustering to gather information you might later use to argue your position and to anticipate opposing arguments in a formal, full-length essay.

Bilingual Education: Opposing Views

"Desperate to Learn English" by Alice Callaghan
"Melting Pot or Tossed Salad" by Dudley Barlow

A priest in the Episcopal Church, Alice Callaghan directs Los Familias del Pueblo Community Center in Los Angeles, California. "Desperate to Learn English" first appeared on August 15, 1997, on the New York Times op-ed page.

Dudley Barlow is a high-school teacher in Canton, Michigan. He writes "The Teachers Lounge" and "Education Resources" for Education Digest, a research journal in education. "Melting Pot or Tossed Salad" appeared in the March 1996 issue of that journal.

Preparing to Read

1. In November 1997, *U.S. News & World Report* magazine claimed that a "measure that would virtually eliminate bilingual education in California" would most certainly appear on the ballot in 1998. A referendum limiting state funding for bilingual education was passed by the voters in that year.

2. Analyze each of the titles of the essays presented here. What do the titles tell us about the contents of the essays to which they belong?

Vocabulary

acknowledge (verb)	Admit, recognize.
adios, amigo (verb/noun)	Spanish for "goodbye, friend." Used sarcastically.
advocates (noun)	Supporters.
assimilation (noun)	Absorption.
ballot initiative (noun)	Referendum putting a question to a public vote.
compatriots (noun)	Colleagues, co-workers.
confines (noun)	Borders.
critical mass (noun)	Extremely large number, breaking point.
denounced (verb)	Severely criticized, condemned.
entrenched (adjective)	Dug in, securely established.
ethnic (adjective)	Relating to a race or nationality.
havens (noun)	Safe places.
languish (verb)	Lose strength or energy, fade.
lectern (noun)	A podium or platform from which a speaker addresses listeners.

linguistic (adjective)   Relating to language and the study of language.
monoglots (noun)   Speakers of only one language.
proficiency (noun)   Skill, ability.
relinquished (verb)   Gave up, surrendered.

Desperate to Learn English

Alice Callaghan

JUANA AND FLORENCIO left the poverty of their rural Mexican village in 1985   1
and came to Los Angeles to work in the garment district's sweatshops. In
1996, they pulled their three children—all born in Los Angeles—out of school
for nearly two weeks until the school agreed to let them take classes in English
rather than Spanish.

Seventy other poor immigrant families joined this school boycott in   2
February 1996, insisting that their children be allowed out of the city's bilingual
program, which would not teach English to children from Spanish-speaking
homes until they learned how to read and write in Spanish. In the end, the
parents prevailed.

Yet, throughout California and elsewhere in the country, many Hispanic   3
parents are worried that bilingual education programs are keeping their children from learning English.

These children live in Spanish-speaking homes, play in Spanish-speaking   4
neighborhoods and study in Spanish-speaking classrooms. With little exposure
to English in the primary grades, few successfully learn it later.

This is why many Latino parents are backing a California ballot initiative   5
that would end bilingual education for most children in the state. The measure
will be put to a vote in June if enough signatures are gathered to put it on the
ballot.

School administrators, Latino politicians and other advocates of bilingual   6
education have denounced the measure. Though they acknowledge the failings
of the system, they insist they can fix it with time.

Yet after 25 years, bilingual education has few defenders among Latino   7
parents. In a *Los Angeles Times* poll this year, 83 percent of Latino parents in
Orange County said they wanted their children to be taught in English as soon
as they started school. Only 17 percent of those surveyed said they favored
having their children taught in their native language.

One reason bilingual education is so entrenched is money. Bilingual   8
teachers in Los Angeles are paid extra, up to $5,000 a year; schools and school
districts receive hundreds of dollars for each child who is designated as having
limited proficiency in English. About $400 million in state and Federal money
supports bilingual educational programs in California. Because such money is
not readily relinquished, students languish in Spanish-language classes.

Moreover, there are not enough bilingual teachers. In Los Angeles, the   9
shortfall has been so severe that the city has granted emergency credentials
to people whose only claim to a classroom lectern is their ability to speak
Spanish.

Latino parents know that placing their children in English-language classes 10
will not cure the many problems plaguing California schools, where the Latino
dropout rate is 40 percent and Latino students have consistently low achievement test scores. Unless these students can learn in English, future school
reform efforts will not help them.

Most parents who participated in the school boycott last year labor in   11
garment district sweatshops. Others wait on tables, clean downtown offices or
sell fruit or tamales on street corners. All struggle on average monthly incomes
of $800.

Education is their only hope for a better future for their children. The first 12
step is learning English.

Melting Pot or Tossed Salad

Dudley Barlow

IT WAS a student named Brian, during my first year of teaching, who intro- 1
duced me to Hyman Kaplan, the main character in Leonard Q. Ross's wonderful little book, *The Education of H*y*m*a*nK*a*p*l*a*n*. The character
is a German Jewish immigrant in his forties, and he is in Mr. Parkhill's class
entitled "American Night Preparatory School for Adults." Kaplan first came
to Parkhill's attention when the class turned in an assignment on common
nouns and their plural forms. Kaplan's paper read: "house . . . makes . . .
houses, dog . . . makes . . . doggies, library . . . makes Public library, cat . . .
makes . . . Katz."

Throughout the book, we watch as Kaplan plunges enthusiastically into 2
this puzzle of a new and difficult language. On the final exam, he writes Parkhill
a note because, "In the recass was som students asking if is right to say Its Me
or Its I . . . a planty hard question, no? Yes."

Kaplan has the whole puzzle neatly solved. "If I am in hall and knok, knok, 3
knok; and I hear insite (insite the room) somebody hollers 'Whose there'—I
anser strong '*Its Kaplan*'!!

"Now is fine! Plain, clear like gold, no chance mixing up Me, I, Ect.   4

"By *Thinking* is Humans making big edvences on Enimals. This we call 5
Progriss."

Kaplan came to my mind as I started writing this column. He was fortu- 6
nate to be able to struggle with this new language in the company of the long-
suffering Parkhill. A few weeks ago, I saw a news story on television about two
non-English speakers who were not so fortunate.

The story concerned a bar owner somewhere in the state of Washington 7
who refused to serve two Mexican patrons because they did not speak English.
I believe she even went so far as to have the two men thrown out of the establishment. On the wall of the bar was a sign that said something like, "If you
don't speak English, adios, amigo." When the TV reporter covering the story
asked the woman about the incident, she said, "I thought this was America. In
America, we speak English."

This woman reminded me of something my wife's uncle, Joe Zadzora, 8
once told me. Joe was born in a coal town in Pennsylvania in the early 1920s,
and he worked in the mines before joining the army during World War II. He
told me about the ethnic groups—including Poles, Slavs, Russians, Irish, and
Hungarians —who mined the coal and lived in the company town above the
shafts. They had come to this country for the same reasons that immigrants
have always come here: There was work to be had in America, and if they
worked hard at difficult and sometimes dangerous jobs, maybe they could
make it possible for their children to have better jobs and better lives.

Many, perhaps most, of them did not speak English. They did not need it. 9
They could cut, blast, and shovel coal below ground with their compatriots,
and above ground they lived in ethnic neighborhoods where the languages of
their homelands worked just fine. But for their children, it was a different story.
They went to school to learn, among other things, how to speak English to fit
into this new land. English was the first key to assimilation into the broader
culture beyond the company town.

The first generation born here would speak two languages with ease: the 10
old world language used at home and English in the larger world. The next generation would have a new mother tongue, but would still be able to understand
their grandparents. By the third generation, though, they would be monoglots
again, and their ancestral languages would be lost.

This has been pretty much the normal course of events for immigrant 11
families here. Big cities with their ethnic neighborhoods sometimes provided
linguistic havens where the old languages could hang on for generations.
Foreign-born folks less adventuresome than Hyman Kaplan could find everything they needed within the confines of a few blocks and within the familiar
tongues of their former homes.

Ultimately, though, assimilation was what everyone wanted. Immigrants 12
wanted to acquire our language to be able to partake of the American Dream,
and we knew that they were right in wanting to be like us.

Now, though, things are changing. In some parts of our country, in the 13
Southwest in particular, non-native English speakers are reaching a critical
mass which has weakened the arguments for learning English.

The melting pot is becoming a tossed salad in which the various elements 14
are mixed together but retain their individual identities. So, how do we respond to this new situation? What do government printing offices do? Does
the Internal Revenue Service print forms in Spanish as well as English? What

about road signs: Do cities in California, Arizona, and Texas print directions in both languages?

And how do those of us in the education business respond to this new situ- 15 ation? What are schools where Spanish-speaking students outnumber English-speaking students to do?

Some policymakers would respond the way the owner of that Washington 16 pub did, and insist that "in America, we speak English." This "English only" approach would have all lessons taught only in English to force non-English speakers to learn our language.

Others would have us offer bilingual instruction designed to communicate 17 with students in the language with which they are most familiar while trying to equip them with the language that would carry them beyond the confines of their own ethnic group.

There must also be a third group that would argue that, if a class is made 18 up entirely or even predominantly of Spanish speakers, the lessons should be taught entirely in Spanish. To force these students to abandon Spanish for English, this group would argue, is a form of linguistic racism.

My sympathies are with the second group. If a school has a student popula- 19 tion made up primarily of Spanish speakers, I think it would be foolhardy not to communicate with them in the language they understand best. At the same time, we need to recognize (and these students need to understand) that the language of commerce—the language of the widest range of opportunities in our country—is English. For this reason, these students also need to acquire English language skills.

And what about the road signs and IRS forms? We need to take a cue from 20 business here. The instructions telling me how to set up my computer came in English and Spanish, and the instructions in a box of film or cough syrup come in several languages. As Kaplan would say, "This we call Progriss."

As a footnote, one final comment about the Washington bar owner who 21 refused to serve the patrons who did not speak English. I believe her name was Orlander. Something tells me that her first ancestors to reach American soil didn't speak English, either. Someone must have served them.

Read More on the Web

Links to sites for and against bilingual education: http://www.wellesley. edu/Spanish/NEWEduc308/bilingual1.html

Site which explains California's Proposition 227 with links to full text: http://primary98.ss.ca.gov/VoterGuide/Propositions/227.htm

Questions for Discussion

1. Where in her essay does Callaghan use statistics?
2. Does Callaghan rely on authority to support her opinions? Where?

3. How does she anticipate arguments of the opposition?
4. Comment on Callaghan's introduction. What purpose does it serve?
5. Find examples of deductive reasoning in Callaghan's essay. Create syllogisms that trace her logic in these examples.
6. Explain how Callaghan tries to appeal to our emotions.
7. What methods of development does Barlow use in "Melting Pot or Tossed Salad"?
8. Where does Barlow address opposing arguments?
9. Why is Barlow's introduction so long?
10. Why does he quote Hyman Kaplan so extensively?
11. What is the thesis of "Melting Pot or Tossed Salad"?
12. How does the author's contrasting the metaphors of the "melting pot" and the "tossed salad" describe the current U.S. population?
13. Why does Barlow mention three different positions on bilingual education (paragraphs 16, 17, and 18)? Why doesn't he limit himself to the two opinions in paragraphs 16 and 17?

Thinking Critically

1. Is Callaghan being fair in her criticisms of the bilingual-education establishment (paragraphs 8 and 9)? Why or why not?
2. Early in "Desperate to Learn English," we learn that 71 families joined in the school boycott. Is this statistic convincing? Why or why not?
3. What does Barlow mean when he claims that "non-native speakers are reaching a critical mass, which has weakened the arguments for learning English"? Do you agree with this statement?
4. If these two authors met in a debate, on what points would they definitely disagree? Are there any points on which they might agree?

Suggestions for Journal Entries

1. What's your opinion? Should we abolish bilingual education, keep it as it is, or change it in some way? Interview educators (including those who teach in bilingual programs, if possible) to gather insights.
2. Think of a particular change we should make in public education and list arguments that would support that change. Here are some examples of changes one might advocate:

> Increase services for learning-disabled students.
>
> Increase or decrease the number of electives high school students can take.

Grant tax credits to parents whose children attend private or parochial schools.

Require foreign-language study from first through twelfth grade.

Fund all public schools in America by allocating the same amount of tax money for every student regardless of the community or state in which he or she lives.

Suggestions for Sustained Writing

1. Like Barry Glazer, many of us have strong opinions about the right of privacy. Perhaps you discussed some of your own in your journal after reading "The Right to Be Let Alone."

    Write an essay arguing that some government regulations interfere unnecessarily with the way we live. Use examples of federal, state, or local laws you think limit our freedom. If you interpret the word *government* broadly, you can even focus on rules enforced by your college, your family, or another group to which you belong.

    One way to introduce this essay is to show readers that you are reasonable. Begin by admitting that some rules are necessary and should be fully enforced. For example, voice your support for tough laws against child abuse, rape, and drunk driving. At the end of your introduction, however, state your thesis forcefully: explain that some rules enforced by the government, by your family, or by another group are inappropriate and should be abolished. Then, like Glazer, develop your essay with examples from your experiences or from those of people you know or have read about.

    Read your first draft carefully, adding details as you go along to make your opinions clear and convincing. Then, edit your work thoroughly.

2. Read "The Right to Be Let Alone" again. Then, write an essay in which you play Glazer's opponent. Argue that, although some government regulations are inappropriate, the ones he criticizes should be strictly enforced.

    One way to organize your paper is to defend the regulations Glazer attacks in the same order he presented them. As such, you might outline the body of your essay like this:

    Terminally ill patients should not have the right to commit suicide.

    Police have the right to stop and question motorists at random.

    Pets should be licensed.

Strict building codes are necessary.

Colleges should enforce academic requirements.

Develop each of these points in concrete and convincing detail using any of the methods mentioned earlier in this chapter. After completing several drafts, write a conclusion that restates your thesis or that uses one of the methods for closing explained in Chapter 3. As always, be sure your final draft is organized and edited well.

3. If you responded to either of the Suggestions for Journal Entries after O'Rourke's "A Cool and Logical Analysis of the Bicycle Menace," use these notes as the basis for an essay in which you present reasons to adopt or to reject a particular activity. If you responded to the first journal suggestion, you have probably gathered information that will help you write a humorous essay. If you responded to the second journal prompt, you will most likely write a serious argument.

In either case, state a thesis clearly and defend that thesis by explaining numerous reasons for it. In fact, you might want to develop your essay by including what Toulmin calls "substantive warrants," as well as "authoritative warrants," if appropriate. If you include "authoritative warrants"—researched information and ideas—make sure to cite your sources. (The website for this textbook—www.mhhe.com/rcw—explains how to do so using Modern Language Association style.) When it comes time to edit and proofread your paper, make sure to double check quotations and correct any mistakes with in-text citations or with the items in your list of sources.

4. Reread the notes that you made in response to the first two Suggestions for Journal Entries after Nat Hentoff's "Free Speech on Campus." Turn these notes into a full-length essay in which you argue one of the following:

Some circumstances allow for limiting free speech.

Free speech should be limited under no circumstances.

If this assignment doesn't interest you, write an essay based on the notes you made in response to Suggestion 3 after Hentoff's essay.

Whichever option you choose, be as complete and convincing as you can by gathering sufficient information to support your proposition. You might want to gather additional details, ideas, and opinions by brainstorming with fellow students or interviewing professors who can offer expert testimony. Also, try looking for more information on the Internet. If possible, use direct quotations.

Whether you organize your essay primarily around deduction or induction, check to be sure that you have not committed any of the logical fallacies discussed in the introduction to Section Five. You can do this when you revise your first draft. Also, make sure that your thesis is clearly stated and that your paper is well organized and easy to follow. As with other papers, edit and proofread carefully. Grammar, mechanical, spelling, and other such errors weaken an argument's effectiveness and lose your reader's trust.

5. Read the notes you made in response to the second of the Suggestions for Journal Entries after the essays by Callaghan and Barlow. (If you have not responded; do so now.)

Add to your notes, and write a preliminary thesis statement for an essay that would argue for a particular change in public education. Make sure you limit yourself to a specific question. For example, don't argue that all students should learn more about the fine arts. Instead, argue that a year of art appreciation and a year of music appreciation be required of all high school graduates.

As you draft your paper, make sure to anticipate and address opposing arguments. You can do this by exposing those arguments as unsupported, illogical, or untrue; or you can admit that they have value while arguing that yours make even better sense. If you wish, use your introduction to accomplish this. Then, devote the body of your paper to supporting your own point of view.

Revise your paper several times, adding information as needed, and make sure your opinion is clear, logical, and well supported. Conclude your work on this project with meticulous editing and proofreading.

Writing to Learn: A Group Activity

Should institutions of higher learning regulate speech? If so, to what extent should they regulate it? What kinds of speech should be prohibited, if any, and for what reasons? And who should do the regulating? As a group, review and critique at least two college or university speech policies. (Note: a *critique* is not necessarily a criticism of a document; it is an evaluation.) Begin by finding and photocopying your own school's speech code if it has one. If it doesn't, find the policies of two other schools that are similar to yours or that are located in your county or state. You can do this by searching for these institutions' websites on the Internet. Make copies of both policies for everyone.

THE FIRST MEETING

Distribute copies of the policies. Read and discuss them as a group. Most speech policies are not long, so you might be able to do this during your meeting. Then, come to a consensus about the contents of each policy, item by item or point by point. Does the group agree or disagree with each of the points? (If you can't reach a consensus, rely on a majority vote.) Then, decide if you agree or disagree with the overall philosophy and purpose of the documents under discussion.

RESEARCH

Ask each group member to search the Internet and/or the library's periodical indexes for articles (online or on paper) that discuss free speech on college campuses. One source you might find effective is the American Civil Liberties Union's website (http://www.aclu.org). Take notes on and bring copies of informative articles to the next meeting.

THE SECOND MEETING

Invite each group member to share his or her research by distributing copies of the materials found and by summarizing important points and ideas orally. After discussing these points and reading from relevant portions of useful articles, start discussing the speech policies you began to consider at your last meeting. Have your views on these policies changed in light of the research?

Whatever your answer, use both the group's reactions to the policies and the insights gained through research to list major points you might develop in a critique of the policies. Ask one student to write a draft of an essay that critiques the first policy and another to write a draft of an essay that critiques the second. Remind them to

- Address the points the group has agreed to develop.
- Make frequent reference to their primary sources (the policies themselves).
- Include information and insights gathered through research.

Finally, ask them to bring photocopies of the completed drafts to the next meeting, enough for each group member.

THE THIRD MEETING

Distribute copies of the drafts. Then, revise the critiques by adding or deleting information, clarifying ideas, and making the structure of the essays easier to follow. When you have finished, assign a third student to combine all of this into a single essay and to write an appropriate introduction and conclusion. Also, ask this person to write a thesis statement that expresses the group's opinion of the speech codes or of speech codes in general. As before, remind the writer to photocopy this draft.

(continued)

THE FOURTH MEETING

Distribute copies of the draft mentioned above and, together, revise it for logic, clarity, and development. Next, edit it for grammar, sentence structure, punctuation, and other language considerations. After the group has agreed to all changes, assign a fourth student to type, proofread, and photocopy a final draft. Submit the original to the instructor and distribute copies to the group members. (You might even want to send a copy to the editor of your college paper for publication.)

CHAPTER 13

Persuasion

As you learned in the introduction to Section Five, effective persuasion always begins with a solid argument based on evidence that is presented logically. However, persuasion goes beyond pure argument. Writers engage in persuasion not only to prove a point but also to convince readers to adopt their point of view and to act on it.

So, if you want to convince readers that your stand on a controversial issue has merit or that a conclusion you have drawn about a complex issue is correct, a strong argument is probably enough. If you need to change people's attitudes or urge them to action, on the other hand, logic and evidence might not be enough to get the job done. You will need to be persuasive. Thus, while remaining clear-headed and fair, you might also want to appeal to the reader's values, pride, emotions, and even self-interest. Before doing so, you will have to consider the attitudes and opinions of your audience.

Appealing to the Readers' Values and Pride

Let's say your college is having a problem with litter, which makes the campus unsightly and even causes minor sanitation problems. As a member of the Student Senate, you are asked to write an open letter to the student body. Your letter will appear on the front page of the college newspaper accompanied by pictures of a parking lot where people have emptied ashtrays or left empty bottles, of a lunchroom table covered with trash, and of classrooms in which papers, used pens, a stray sneaker, and other refuse have been left behind.

Your job is to persuade students to clean up after themselves and to stop trashing the campus. You begin by explaining that common courtesy and concerns over health and sanitation demand that people deposit their garbage properly. The campus is a public place, you argue, and as such it demands that those who use it respect it and keep it clean for others. You also explain that keeping the grounds clean is easy if only everyone participates.

After reading your letter, you decide that your opinions are reasonable and fair. No one would disagree with them. In fact, your letter might be the very model of an effective written argument. However, you realize that it will not convince people to act on your recommendations—it simply does not go far enough.

The next step is to appeal to your readers' values and pride. You start by addressing their sense of fellowship, their pride in being members of an academic community. Remind them that they are college students, not adolescents who need to be taught table manners. You can also appeal to their self-image by explaining that the way students behave reflects their respect—or lack of respect—for the college, for professors, for classmates, and for themselves.

Appealing to the Readers' Emotions

If you are dealing with an especially hard-to-convince group, ask them to put themselves into the shoes of other students, of faculty, and of visitors—not to mention the janitorial staff—who enter the cafeteria to find tables and floors covered with soiled plates and napkins, half-eaten sandwiches, and dirty coffee cups. Express your disgust over the cigarette butts, empty bottles, and paper bags dumped in the parking lots. Complain about yogurt containers, aluminum cans, and other debris left in student lounges. In the process, use colorful images, concrete nouns, and strong verbs, adjectives, and adverbs to get your point across and shake up your audience. Use figures of speech: ask your readers not to turn the place into an academic "pigsty"; or compare the cafeteria at day's end to a "small village that has been looted and trashed by invading barbarians." You will see several excellent examples of speech that appeals to the emotions in Wilfred Owen's "Dulce et Decorum Est," a poem that appears in this introduction.

Appealing to the Readers' Self-Interest

Often this is the only way to move an especially obstinate audience. Try arguing that the dirtier the campus, the more unpleasant it is to be there, and remind your fellow students of the amount of time each of them spends on campus. You might even suggest that it is easier to study and to learn in a clean, attractive setting than in a dump! More important, explain that a dirty campus must be cleaned up and that this increases the cost of janitorial services. Of course, higher operating costs translate into higher tuition levels, so students might have to work longer hours to pay for college, or their parents might have to sacrifice a bit more to send them there.

Anticipating and Addressing Opposing Opinions

You learned in Chapter 12 that anticipating and responding to an opposing argument is important to making your point. Doing this is even more important when engaging in persuasive writing. When you argue, you need show only that while other opinions have merit, your case is the strongest. When it comes to persuasion, on the other hand, you are asking readers to make a choice and to act on that choice. If they have any doubt that your opinion stands out as the strongest and wisest, they will not follow your lead, and they may, in fact, decide to do nothing. As you read the selections that follow, try to find places where writers address and respond to opposing arguments. More important, make use of this practice whenever you write to persuade.

Establishing Your Authority

Again, you read in Chapter 12 that when writing argument papers, it is important to gain the confidence of your readers by convincing them you know what you are talking about. This is even more important when writing persuasively. If readers are going to follow your lead and act as you suggest, they will have to trust in your knowledge. As with all writing, the best way to show you are knowledgeable is to use concrete facts—hard evidence—to support your opinions. In addition, however, you might want to explain the source of your knowledge of a particular topic or problem. In "Education Is the Priority," student Nicholle Palmieri persuades her readers that working too many hours can often interfere with one's studies. She establishes her authority by explaining that while working in the dean's office, she encountered too many students who had failed to make academics their priority and, as a result, were about to flunk out!

Using Conciliation—The Rogerian Approach

As you learned earlier, it is always appropriate to anticipate opposing arguments and to recognize their validity when possible. Sometimes, however, you will have to go even further. In some cases, you will be writing or speaking to an audience whose positions on a particular issue are so solidified that nothing you say will change minds. Think about writing to or addressing an audience whose views on subjects such as abortion, gun control, the 9/11 attacks, the Iraq War, or homosexuality are diametrically opposed to yours. In such cases, an approach developed by psychologist Carl Rogers might be helpful. Rogers believed that before people who hold entrenched positions can begin to discuss issues productively, some conciliation must be made. His method involves the following:

Establish Common Ground You will first need to prove to your audience not simply that you understand and appreciate their position but that you accept it as viable. One way to do this is to establish common ground by identifying points on which you can agree. For example, say you were to write a letter to your college newspaper arguing for the creation of a foreign-language graduation requirement for students in all majors. It's a good bet that most of your readers oppose adding new graduation requirements. So, you might first explain that:

- Like your readers, you are enrolled in a curriculum already packed with requirements and that adding more requirements will make it even more demanding.
- Adding requirements might prevent both you and your readers from taking a few electives particularly relevant to your individual career plans.
- Adding requirements might delay graduation and add tuition costs for you and your readers.
- Taking a foreign language will yield no immediately measurable benefit for either you or them.

You can then start to present arguments in favor of requiring foreign languages by explaining the importance of learning about other cultures, the emergence of a global economy, the advantages of using a foreign language when traveling, and the need to communicate with people of other cultures both in English and in their languages in order to promote international understanding.

Use Nonthreatening Language   It's one thing to tell an audience of gun-control opponents that their right to own guns is the thing that is causing so much crime. It's another to explain that limiting the right to own guns will decrease violent crime and make their lives safer. The first statement is negative, the second far more positive. The same is true of this pair:

Threatening: If we do not improve homeland security and impose stricter security regulations at airports, in bus and train terminals, and in public buildings, the events of 9/11 will be repeated.

Nonthreatening: Strengthening homeland security and instituting careful screening procedures at airports, in bus and train terminals, and in public buildings will make the country safer.

Express Opposing Views Accurately and Fairly   Let's say that you are opposed to the enactment of an on-campus speech policy that the college administration is introducing in order to enforce professional decorum in academic discussions, to protect the institution from the legal repercussions of slanderous and libelous statements made by employees or students, and to make the library a quieter place to study. You could certainly argue that any speech policy, albeit benign in purpose and design, would limit the students' constitutional right to free speech. However, it would probably be unfair and inaccurate to characterize this policy as an attempt to limit student participation in class, to prevent people from speaking out against college policies and regulations, or to treat the students as if they were high school adolescents.

Visualizing Strategies for Persuasion

The following antiwar poem was written by Wilfred Owen (1893–1918), a British soldier who witnessed the horror of trench warfare in World War 1. The title is Latin for "It is sweet and fitting." The last lines, taken from the Latin poet Horace, translate to "It is sweet and fitting to die for one's country."

Dulce et Decorum Est *Uses an ironic title.*

Bent double, like old beggars under sacks,

Knock-kneed, coughing like hags, we cursed through
sludge,

Till on the haunting flares we turned our backs

And towards our distant rest began to trudge.

Opens with a startling image; uses figures of speech.

Men marched asleep. Many had lost their boots

But limped on, blood-shod [shoed in blood]. All
went lame; all blind;

Drunk with fatigue; deaf even to the hoots

Of tired, outstripped Five-Nines that dropped behind.

Includes vivid verbs and adjectives.

Gas! Gas! Quick, boys!—An ecstasy of fumbling,

Fitting the clumsy helmets just in time;

Startles readers with the soldiers' cries.

Narrates action vividly. But someone still was yelling out and stumbling,

And flound'ring like a man in fire or lime.

Dim, through the misty panes and thick green light,

As under a green sea, I saw him drowning.

Creates an extended metaphor to describe the horror of a gas attack.

In all my dreams, before my helpless sight,

He plunges at me, guttering, choking, drowning.

Uses adjectives to evoke an emotional response.

Addresses readers directly to get them to change their minds.

> If in some smothering dreams you too could pace
>
> Behind the wagon that we flung him in,
>
> And watch the white eyes writhing in his face,
>
> His hanging face, like a devil's sick of sin;
>
> If you could hear, at every jolt, the blood

Come gargling from the froth-corrupted lungs

Obscene as cancer, bitter as the cud

Of vile, incurable sores on innocent tongues,—

My friend, you would not tell with such high zest

To children ardent [eager] for some desperate glory,

The old Lie: Dulce et decorum est

Pro patria mori.

Continues direct address; persuades readers to stop glorifying war.

Obviously, this is a message to stir our passions. Startling words, images, and figures of speech appeal to the emotions and create in us the sense of the horror that Owen experienced. The poem's central idea is, of course, that war is *not* sweet and fitting and that we must stop lying about it to children. In the last stanza (verse paragraph), the poet addresses his readers directly. He does this first in order to make his argument strike home more directly, to make it more compelling. He appeals to the readers' self-interest; after all they too might be asked to send their children to war. He also does this so as to answer an opposing argument offered by people who have not seen war close up. We lie to children—"ardent for some desperate glory"—when we romanticize war. In no way is it sweet and fitting to die for one's country, and the poet demands that we stop telling them it is.

Considering Visuals That Persuade

Commercial advertisements and editorial cartoons often combine words and pictures that persuade. Consider the following examples. As you do, identify the intended audiences and determine which tools ordinarily found in written persuasion each item uses. Then, write a paragraph or two that responds to the exercise prompt following each visual.

1. SOME PRESENTATIONS YOU DON'T WANT MESSED WITH

This advertisement for Adobe Acrobat 5.0 pictures Moses holding three tablets with fifteen commandments. It appeals to the readers' need for electronic document security and maintenance.

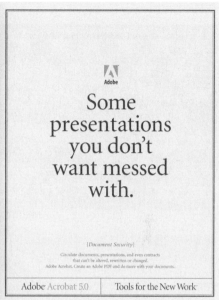

© 2002 Adobe Systems, Inc., Courtesy of Goodby, Silverstein & Partners.

Exercise: Make sure you know the biblical story of Moses. You can find it in the Bible, in an encyclopedia, or on the Internet (a helpful site is http://www. newadvent.org/cathen/10596a.htm). Write a paragraph or two that identifies the message the ad conveys, and explain how Moses' holding three tablets helps the manufacturers of Adobe Acrobat 5.0 make their point.

2. HELP EDITORIAL CARTOON

This cartoon, originally appearing in the *Chicago Tribune,* was reprinted in the July 29, 2002, issue of *National Review,* a magazine whose editorial policy is politically conservative. It addresses a lawsuit to prohibit the reciting of the Pledge of Allegiance in public schools. The suit was brought by people who believe that the presence of the word "God" in the pledge violates the First Amendment to the Constitution: "Congress shall make no law respecting an establishment of religion." It also references a Supreme Court decision that, several years ago, struck down a state law prohibiting the burning of the American flag.

Exercise: Write a paragraph that explains the sources of this cartoon's appeal to readers. How would you describe those readers? How does the cartoon appeal to their pride, emotions, and values?

HELP!!!!

Dick Locher. © 2002 Tribune Media Services, Inc. All rights reserved. Reprinted with permission.

3. PREVENT CHILD ABUSE AMERICA PUBLIC SERVICE ANNOUNCEMENT (PRINT AD)

This advertisement dramatizes the horrors and pain of child abuse. At the same time, it urges the reader to take specific action to help prevent the abuse of children, including finding out more about this problem.

Exercise: Analyze this ad. Discuss the images created by the reference to macaroni and cheese. What images are suggested by the stove top? Why are the words "sorry for what he did" so much larger than those in the rest of the sentence? How would you characterize the advice offered under the picture? Is it effective? Why or why not?

© Reprinted courtesy of Prevent Child Abuse America, the Advertising Council and Lowe.

4. WHICH ONE REALLY NEEDS A HEART?

A Steve Benson creation, this cartoon, published on February 25, 2003, addresses a controversy over an illegal alien's receiving an organ transplant at the expense of U.S. taxpayers.

Exercise: Analyze the two characters in this cartoon. What kinds of emotions do these two portraits tap in you?

By permission of Steve Benson and Creators Syndicate, Inc.

Revising Persuasion Papers

Revising any kind of paper takes hard work, but persuasion papers often ask the reader to accomplish tasks or goals or to change deeply held views, so it is important that they be as clear, logical, well supported, and strong as possible. Student Nicholle Palmieri rewrote "Education Is the Priority," which appears in this chapter, to make it the kind of paper she thought would get her fellow students to decrease the emphasis they placed on work in favor of their real goal— to get a college education.

Palmieri—Early Draft

Education Is the <u>First</u> Priority] *Redundant.*

About a year ago, I quit my full-time job to

return to college. Despite all of the

Wordy. [obstacles <u>that stood</u> in my way, I was lucky

enough to find <u>a job in the office of Dean

Russell. I say "lucky" for many reasons.</u>] *More information needed.*

The dean and her administrative assistant,

Karen Gormish, are two of the <u>nicest people

on the face of the earth</u>, not to mention the] *Cliché.*

fact that I don't have to worry about my job

interfering with my studies. I am able to

fit my work hours around my class schedule,

and I still manage to get in enough hours to

sufficiently cover my bills.

Vague. [Working there, though, <u>has been quite a

learning experience</u>. Almost every day, at

least one student comes into the <u>office</u>,] *Language seems flat, unappealing.*

<u>their eyes scared, pleading</u> to be taken off] *Wrong pronoun agreement.*

academic probation. I am often the first

Wordy. [person that greets them and, therefore, <u>I

have the privilege of seeing their appeals

firsthand</u>. Most of these students have

failed to make their educations their <u>top</u>] *Redundant.*

priority, and they are paying for it dearly,

and there is one claim that almost all have

in common <u>their</u> hours at work have taken] *Fused sentence.*

precious time away from their college

studies. Mind you, most of these kids (I

*Develop
the notion
of their
being "kids"?*

say "kids" because that is what the majority

of them are) are living at home and taking

about 15 credits per semester. Most of them

occupy menial positions at fast-food

*Use language
that appeals
to emotions.*

restaurants or retail stores. They take

orders from tough supervisors and work long

hours toward their future in hopes of

*Add details
about their
situations?
Appeal to
the emotions?*

someday having a real job. From what I

understand, most of these students work such

hours under threat by their managers of

being fired if they refuse.

I find fault with this whole scenario.

*Smooth
out
syntax.*

Fifty years ago, it was unheard of that

full-time college students should even work

two hours a week let alone forty, and that

*Support
this with
research?*

was for a good reason.

Palmieri—Final Draft

Education is the Priority   *Removes redundancy.*

About a year ago, I quit my full-time job to

*Eliminates
wordiness.*

return to college. Despite all of the

obstacles in my way, I was lucky enough to

find a job as a work-study assistant in the

office of Dean Bernadette Russell. I say

"lucky" for many reasons. The Dean and her

*Adds
information
about her
job.*

administrative assistant, Karen Gormish, are
supportive of students and are willing to
accommodate their needs. Because of their

Replaces cliché with fresher language.

support and flexibility, I don't have to
worry about my job interfering with my
studies. I am able to fit my work hours
around my class schedule—not the other way
around—and still manage to work enough hours

Adds emphasis.

to pay my bills.

Working in the Dean's office has taught
me a great deal about college students and
their priorities. Almost every day, at

Uses language that is clearer, more specific.

Uses language that is more evocative.

least one of them comes into the office,
eyes fraught with desperation. They plead
to be taken off academic probation,
restriction, or suspension. Some beg to
have their dismissals lifted and to be

Adds important information.

allowed to re-enroll.

Eliminates wordiness.

I am often the first person who greets
them and, therefore, I see their appeals
first. Most of these students have failed to
make education their priority, and they are
paying for it dearly. In fact, there is one

Removes redundancy.

claim that almost all have in common: their
hours at work have taken precious time away

Inserts colon to correct fused sentence.

from their college studies. Mind you, most
of these kids (I say "kids" because that is

what the majority of them are) are living at home and taking about 15 credits per semester. It is not as if they are seasoned adults who have worked at full-time jobs for fifteen years, have learned to manage their time, and are able to squeeze in a course or two in the evenings and weekends. On the contrary, most of them work at menial positions in fast-food restaurants or retail stores. They take orders from demanding, unreasonable supervisors, and they work asinine, exhausting hours that no human being should have to work—certainly not someone who is attending college classes full-time and devoting hours of endless study toward earning an education and entering a rewarding career. From what I understand, most of these students work such hours under threat of being fired by their managers if they refuse.

Defines notion of "kids" by contrasting them to "seasoned adults."

Adds words and information that appeal to emotions.

I find the whole scenario appalling. Fifty years ago, it was unheard of that full-time college students should even work two hours a week, let alone forty, and that was for a good reason. According to the website of the Division of Student Affairs at Virginia Polytechnic Institute and State

Smooths out syntax.

University, being a successful college student requires "about two hours of preparation for each hour in the classroom. This means that [a student carrying fifteen credits] has at least a forty-five hour work week, and is consequently involved in a full-time occupation"(1). At Newbury College, incoming freshmen are advised to attend classes regularly ("This is a must!"), seek help at the Academic Resources Center, visit their professors regularly during office hours, enroll in "the Academic Enrichment Program," and join a student study group (1). These activities take time—the bulk of your time—but in order to be successful in college you must commit to them. That also means that you will have little time for work outside your studies. For a full-time student, most college counselors recommend no more than 15 hours of work per week. Consider this: If you fail to nurture your education, you will find yourself on academic probation, restriction, or suspension. Even worse, you might get yourself dismissed, a blow from which it is hard to recover even if you manage to transfer to another college.

Finds supportive information through research.

Adds direct quotations from authorities on succeeding in college.

Practicing Strategies for Persuasion

Reread Wilfred Owen's poem, "Dulce et Decorum Est," on pages 519–520. Pay close attention to the language Owen uses to stir our emotions and appeal to our self-interest. Now use vivid, moving language in a *persuasive* paragraph or two responding to each of the following:

1. Describe the effects of cigarette smoking to persuade someone to kick the habit.

   _____

   _____

   _____

   _____

2. Explain the dangers of drinking and driving to a group of teenagers so as to get them to choose a designated driver whenever they attend parties where alcohol is served.

   _____

   _____

   _____

   _____

3. Discuss the serious, even dangerous effects of promiscuous and/or unprotected sex to a group of 18-year-old males. Your ultimate purpose is to persuade them to abstain from sex until marriage.

   _____

   _____

   _____

   _____

4. Explain the effects of a high-fat diet and a lack of physical exercise to convince a friend to change his or her lifestyle.

   _____

   _____

   _____

   _____

5. Allow readers to visualize the long-term consequences of marrying a particular person, entering a particular career, or making another important life decision. You can either defend or attack this decision.

_____

_____

_____

_____

Review your responses to the five items above. Then, in each case, write a paragraph that addresses an appropriate opposing argument.

In addition to the selections that follow, you can find another persuasive essay in this book's website (www.mhhe.com/rcw). Student Angela Brandli's "Victims of Violent Crime: Equal Treatment" was first written as a letter to New Jersey legislators. It was so persuasive that it became the basis for a law passed in 1999, and it has come to be known as the "Brandli Bill."

Education Is the Priority

Nicholle Palmieri

Nicholle Palmieri wrote this essay as a letter to the editor of her college newspaper. As a work-study assistant in the office of the Dean of Liberal Arts, Palmieri came into contact with many full-time students who were doing poorly in their studies because they had not made education a priority. The vast majority of these had underestimated the amount of time a successful college career demands, and they were spending too many hours at their jobs. Some of them even held full-time jobs while attending college full-time.

Much of what Palmieri discusses here was inspired by her own experiences. As a junior in high school, she held a job as a sales clerk at a store in a large shopping mall. When she told her boss that she could not work overtime because she had to study for an exam the next day, he threatened to fire her. But this student knew her priorities, and she quit before he could do so. Palmieri graduated from Douglass College with a major in English. She is now pursuing a career in publishing.

Preparing to Read

1. Palmieri's title is, essentially, her thesis. As you learned above, she wrote this selection as a letter to her college newspaper. What does this tell you about her purpose and her audience?

2. The biographical note on this student author reveals something about her personality. What might that be? How will this character trait be reflected in the selection that follows?

3. Palmieri appeals to the reader's emotions, values, and self-interest. Underline places where she does this as you read her essay.

4. The author uses the terms academic "probation," "restriction," and "suspension" to designate the statuses of students whose grades need immediate improvement. "Dismissal" occurs when a student's grades are so low that he or she is asked to leave the college.

Vocabulary

accommodate (verb)	Meet or serve.
appalling (adjective)	Shocking.
asinine (adjective)	Foolish, idiotic.
fraught with (adjective)	Accompanied by, filled with.
menial (adjective)	Low level.
nurture (verb)	Care for, provide for, nourish.

priority (noun)   Item of greatest importance.
scenario (noun)   Situation.
seasoned (adjective)   Experienced.
serf (noun)   Slave, someone bound to the land or to a
                              master.

Education Is the Priority

Nicholle Palmieri

ABOUT A YEAR ago, I quit my full-time job to return to college. Despite all of   1
the obstacles in my way, I was lucky enough to find a job as a work-study
assistant in the office of Dr. Bernadette Russell, Dean of Liberal Arts at my college. I say "lucky" for many reasons. The Dean and her administrative assistant,
Karen Gormish, are supportive of students and are willing to accommodate
their needs. Because of their support and flexibility, I don't have to worry about
my job interfering with my studies. I am able to fit my work hours around my
class schedule—not the other way around—and still manage to work enough
hours to pay my bills.

Working in the Dean's office has taught me a great deal about college stu-   2
dents and their priorities. Almost every day, at least one of them comes into
the office, eyes fraught with desperation. They plead to be taken off academic
probation, restriction, or suspension. Some beg to have their dismissals lifted
and to be allowed to re-enroll.

I am often the first person who greets them and, therefore, I see their   3
appeals first. Most of these students have failed to make education their priority, and they are paying for it dearly. In fact, there is one claim that almost all
have in common: their hours at work have taken precious time away from
their college studies. Mind you, most of these kids (I say "kids" because that is
what the majority of them are) are living at home and taking about 15 credits
per semester. It is not as if they are seasoned adults who have worked at full-
time jobs for fifteen years, have learned to manage their time, and are able to
squeeze in a course or two in the evenings and weekends. On the contrary,
most of them work at menial positions in fast-food restaurants or retail stores.
They take orders from demanding, unreasonable supervisors, and they work
asinine, exhausting hours that no human being should have to work—certainly
not someone who is attending college classes full-time and devoting hours of
endless study toward earning an education and entering a rewarding career.
From what I understand, most of these students work such hours under threat
of being fired by their managers if they refuse.

I find the whole scenario appalling. Fifty years ago, it was unheard of that   4
full-time college students should even work two hours a week, let alone forty,
and that was for a good reason. According to the website of the Division of

Student Affairs at Virginia Polytechnic Institute and State University, being a successful college student requires "about two hours of preparation for each hour in the classroom. This means that [a student carrying fifteen credits] has at least a forty-five hour work week, and is consequently involved in a full-time occupation" (1). At Newbury College, incoming freshmen are advised to attend classes regularly ("This is a must!"), seek help at the Academic Resources Center, visit their professors regularly during office hours, enroll in "the Academic Enrichment Program," and join a student study group (1). These activities take time—the bulk of your time—but in order to be successful in college you must commit to them. That also means that you will have little time for work outside your studies. For a full-time student, most college counselors recommend no more than 15 hours of work per week. Consider this: If you fail to nurture your education, you will find yourself on academic probation, restriction, or suspension. Even worse, you might get yourself dismissed, a blow from which it is hard to recover even if you manage to transfer to another college.

Why would anyone want to do that to herself for the sake of some no- 5 brainer, dead-end job that pays $5.05 per hour? I understand that many students need money because they have bills to pay, not the least of which might be tuition. However, there comes a point when enough is enough. I too have bills to pay, and I manage to pay them by working 15 hours a week or less. I could not possibly devote sufficient time to my studies if I worked a minute more, and my supervisor understands this. Managers who don't understand this aren't worth working for, and they would do students in their employ a favor by firing them.

No words can overemphasize the importance of education. Without one, 6 the "kids" I mentioned earlier might be condemned to work as under-paid, under-appreciated, under-respected cashiers and stock clerks for the rest of their lives. It is time college students put their educations first and told their supervisors at McDonald's or Burger King to find another serf if they don't like it. This is a free country. There is nothing—least of all a dead-end job or a cranky fast-food manager—that can deprive you of your right to a quality education and to a successful future.

wWorks Cited

Division of Student Affairs Home Page. Division of Student Affairs, Virginia
   Polytechnic Institute and State University. 4 Mar. 2000.
   http://www.ucc.vt.edu/stdysk/htimesch.html

How to Be a More Active Learner at Newbury College. Newbury College.
   4 Mar. 2000. http://www.newbury.edu/support/active.htm

MARGINAL
NOTE

Learn how to use
MLA format at
www.mhhe.com/rcw

Read More on the Web

SUNY Brockport site on working while in college: http://www.brockport.
   edu/career01/upromise.htm

University of Michigan college survival tips: http://www.flint.umich.edu/
   departments/advising/SurvTips.htm

Wisconsin Student Public Interest Research Group report on working
   while in college: http://www.wispirg.org/student/wicampus.
   asp?id2=6478

Questions for Discussion

1. What is Palmieri's thesis? Where does she state it most clearly?

2. Does this selection illustrate the uses of deduction, which you learned
    about in Chapter 12? Explain Palmieri's thinking by creating a
    syllogism in your own words: start with a general statement, apply a
    specific case to that statement, and then draw a conclusion.

3. Where does Palmieri use induction? What conclusions does she draw
    using this process?

4. Where does the author appeal to her audience's values? To their
    self-interest?

5. What use does she make of the testimony of experts on her subject?
    Why did she choose these sources to quote directly? Why not include
    direct quotations from students "fraught with desperation," whom
    she met in the dean's office?

6. Palmieri chooses her persuasive vocabulary well. Identify and analyze
    a paragraph or two in which her language appeals to our emotions.

7. Does the author anticipate and answer opposing arguments? Where?

8. Why does Palmieri tell us so much about herself in this essay,
    especially in her introduction?

Thinking Critically

1. Reread "Study Calculus!" by William J. Bennett and "Burger Queen"
    by Erin Sharp in Chapter 2. How might each of them react to
    Palmieri's essay?

2. Palmieri criticizes employers who do not accommodate students who
    work for them. How might an employer respond to her comments?

Suggestions for Journal Entries

1. Think about the opposing argument Palmieri addressed in paragraph 5. Can you make a case for this argument? Are there other reasons for working more than 15 hours per week while carrying a full academic load? Brainstorm with two or three classmates to gather relevant information you might use later on to write a rebuttal to Palmieri's essay.

2. Think about an issue that is crucial to student success in college and that you might write about in a letter to the editor of your student newspaper. Palmieri's essay focuses on making education, not work, the priority. Yours might discuss study habits, time management, stress management, participation in community service projects, the dangers of alcohol or drug abuse among students, or any other issue you believe is important to your fellow students. If you need inspiration picking a topic, visit either of the two Internet sites Palmieri mentions in her works-cited list, or go to the websites of other colleges and universities.

I Have a Dream

Dr. Martin Luther King, Jr.

After graduating from Morehouse College at nineteen, Martin Luther King, Jr. (1929–1968), entered the seminary and later became a minister in Atlanta's Ebenezer Baptist Church, where his father was pastor. In 1957, he founded the Southern Christian Leadership Conference, a civil-rights organization. Influenced by the philosophy of human-rights activist and pacifist Mahatma Gandhi, King led several important demonstrations against racial segregation in the South and in the North. Among the most famous was the march in Birmingham, Alabama, in 1963, for which King was arrested. It was during this imprisonment that he wrote "Letter from Birmingham Jail," a landmark in the literature of American human rights. In that same year, King made a stirring speech during the great March on Washington. Delivered before 200,000 people assembled at the Lincoln Memorial, the text of this speech has come to be known as "I Have a Dream." King won several awards for his work in support of human rights, including the Nobel Prize for Peace in 1964. On April 4, 1968, Dr. King was assassinated while he spoke with other civil-rights leaders on a motel balcony in Memphis, Tennessee.

Preparing to Read

1. King refers to the Declaration of Independence and the U.S. Constitution as a "promissory note to which every American was to fall heir." If you haven't done so already, read these documents. You can find them in any college or public library or on the Internet.

2. Look up Martin Luther King, Jr., and/or the American civil rights movement in a library reference book or on the Internet to familiarize yourself with some of the issues and events that King refers to in this speech.

3. Given the fact that King was a Christian minister, what allusions and references might he use in this speech to support his advocacy of civil rights and to move his audience?

Vocabulary

defaulted (verb)	Failed to pay a debt.
devotees (noun)	Disciples, those who believe in.
hallowed (adjective)	Holy, sacred.
inextricably (adverb)	Permanently, unable to be removed.
interposition (noun)	Attempts to stop the enforcement of laws, in this case those guaranteeing civil rights.

jangling (adjective)	Clanking, clattering.
languishing (adjective)	Lying weak and ill.
manacles (noun)	Handcuffs.
militancy (noun)	Aggressiveness, willingness to do battle.
momentous (adjective)	Extremely important, weighty.
nullification (noun)	Refusal to enforce or recognize laws, in this case those guaranteeing civil rights.
redemptive (adjective)	Redeeming, saving.
unalienable (adjective)	Natural, undeniable.
withering (adjective)	Decaying, dying.

I Have a Dream

Dr. Martin Luther King, Jr.

FIVE SCORE YEARS ago, a great American, in whose symbolic shadow we stand, 1
signed the Emancipation Proclamation. This momentous decree came as a
great beacon light of hope to millions of Negro slaves who had been seared in
the flames of withering injustice. It came as a joyous daybreak to end the long
night of captivity.

But one hundred years later, we must face the tragic fact that the Negro 2
is still not free. One hundred years later, the life of the Negro is still sadly
crippled by the manacles of segregation and the chains of discrimination. One
hundred years later, the Negro lives on a lonely island of poverty in the midst
of a vast ocean of material prosperity. One hundred years later, the Negro is still
languishing in the corners of American society and finds himself an exile in his
own land. So we have come here today to dramatize an appalling condition.

In a sense we have come to our nation's capital to cash a check. When the 3
architects of our republic wrote the magnificent words of the Constitution and
the Declaration of Independence, they were signing a promissory note to which
every American was to fall heir. This note was a promise that all men would be
guaranteed the unalienable rights of life, liberty, and the pursuit of happiness.

It is obvious today that America has defaulted on this promissory note 4
insofar as her citizens of color are concerned. Instead of honoring this sacred
obligation, America has given the Negro people a bad check; a check which
has come back marked "insufficient funds." But we refuse to believe that the
bank of justice is bankrupt. We refuse to believe that there are insufficient
funds in the great vaults of opportunity of this nation. So we have come to
cash this check—a check that will give us upon demand the riches of freedom
and the security of justice. We have also come to this hallowed spot to remind
America of the fierce urgency of *now*. This is no time to engage in the luxury
of cooling off or to take the tranquilizing drugs of gradualism. *Now* is the time
to make real the promises of Democracy. *Now* is the time to rise from the dark

and desolate valley of segregation to the sunlit path of racial justice. *Now* is the time to open the doors of opportunity to all of God's children. *Now* is the time to lift our nation from the quicksands of racial injustice to the solid rock of brotherhood.

It would be fatal for the nation to overlook the urgency of the moment 5 and to underestimate the determination of the Negro. This sweltering summer of the Negro's legitimate discontent will not pass until there is an invigorating autumn of freedom and equality. Nineteen sixty-three is not an end, but a beginning. Those who hope that the Negro needed to blow off steam and will now be content will have a rude awakening if the nation returns to business as usual. There will be neither rest nor tranquility in America until the Negro is granted his citizenship rights. The whirlwinds of revolt will continue to shake the foundations of our nation until the bright day of justice emerges.

But there is something that I must say to my people who stand on the warm 6 threshold which leads into the palace of justice. In the process of gaining our rightful place we must not be guilty of wrongful deeds. Let us not seek to satisfy our thirst for freedom by drinking from the cup of bitterness and hatred. We must forever conduct our struggle on the high plane of dignity and discipline. We must not allow our creative protest to degenerate into physical violence. Again and again we must rise to the majestic heights of meeting physical force with soul force. The marvelous new militancy which has engulfed the Negro community must not lead us to a distrust of all white people, for many of our white brothers, as evidenced by their presence here today, have come to realize that their destiny is tied up with our destiny and their freedom is inextricably bound to our freedom. We cannot walk alone.

And as we walk, we must make the pledge that we shall march ahead. We 7 cannot turn back. There are those who are asking the devotees of civil rights, "When will you be satisfied?" We can never be satisfied as long as the Negro is the victim of the unspeakable horrors of police brutality. We can never be satisfied as long as our bodies, heavy with the fatigue of travel, cannot gain lodging in the motels of the highways and the hotels of the cities. We cannot be satisfied as long as the Negro's basic mobility is from a smaller ghetto to a larger one. We can never be satisfied as long as a Negro in Mississippi cannot vote and a Negro in New York believes he has nothing for which to vote. No, no, we are not satisfied, and we will not be satisfied until justice rolls down like waters and righteousness like a mighty stream.

I am not unmindful that some of you have come here out of great trials 8 and tribulations. Some of you have come fresh from narrow jail cells. Some of you have come from areas where your quest for freedom left you battered by the storms of persecution and staggered by the winds of police brutality. You have been the veterans of creative suffering. Continue to work with the faith that unearned suffering is redemptive.

Go back to Mississippi, go back to Alabama, go back to South Carolina, go 9 back to Georgia, go back to Louisiana, go back to the slums and ghettos of our northern cities, knowing that somehow this situation can and will be changed. Let us not wallow in the valley of despair.

I say to you today, my friends, that in spite of the difficulties and frustra- 10 tions of the moment I still have a dream. It is a dream deeply rooted in the American dream.

I have a dream that one day this nation will rise up and live out the true 11 meaning of its creed: "We hold these truths to be self-evident; that all men are created equal."

I have a dream that one day on the red hills of Georgia the sons of former 12 slaves and the sons of former slaveowners will be able to sit down together at the table of brotherhood.

I have a dream that one day even the state of Mississippi, a desert state 13 sweltering with the heat of injustice and oppression, will be transformed into an oasis of freedom and justice.

I have a dream that my four little children will one day live in a nation 14 where they will not be judged by the color of their skin but by the content of their character.

I have a dream today.   15

I have a dream that one day the state of Alabama, whose governor's lips 16 are presently dripping with the words of interposition and nullification, will be transformed into a situation where little black boys and black girls will be able to join hands with little white boys and white girls and walk together as sisters and brothers.

I have a dream today.   17

I have a dream that one day every valley shall be exalted, every hill and 18 mountain shall be made low, the rough places will be made plain, and the crooked places will be made straight, and the glory of the Lord shall be revealed, and all flesh shall see it together.

This is our hope. This is the faith with which I return to the South. With 19 this faith we will be able to hew out of the mountain of despair a stone of hope. With this faith we will be able to transform the jangling discords of our nation into a beautiful symphony of brotherhood. With this faith we will be able to work together, to pray together, to struggle together, to go to jail together, to stand up for freedom together, knowing that we will be free one day.

This will be the day when all of God's children will be able to sing with 20 new meaning

> My country, 'tis of thee,
> Sweet land of liberty,
>> Of thee I sing:
> Land where my fathers died,
> Land of the pilgrims' pride,
> From every mountain-side
>> Let freedom ring.

And if America is to be a great nation this must become true. So let freedom 21 ring from the prodigious hilltops of New Hampshire. Let freedom ring from the mighty mountains of New York. Let freedom ring from the heightening Alleghenies of Pennsylvania!

Let freedom ring from the snowcapped Rockies of Colorado! 22

Let freedom ring from the curvaceous peaks of California! 23

But not only that; let freedom ring from Stone Mountain of Georgia! 24

Let freedom ring from Lookout Mountain of Tennessee! 25

Let freedom ring from every hill and molehill of Mississippi. From every 26 mountainside, let freedom ring.

When we let freedom ring, when we let it ring from every village and 27 every hamlet, from every state and every city, we will be able to speed up that day when all of God's children, black men and white men, Jews and Gentiles, Protestants and Catholics, will be able to join hands and sing in the words of the old Negro spiritual, "Free at last! free at last! thank God almighty, we are free at last!"

Read More on the Web

The Martin Luther King, Jr. Papers Project at Stanford University: http://www.stanford.edu/group/King/

National Civil Rights Museum site: http://www.mecca.org/~crights/mlk.html

Questions for Discussion

1. King's central idea is expressed most forcefully in the sentences that begin "I have a dream ..." Of these, which has the greatest effect on you?

2. Where does King appeal to authority? How does such an appeal strengthen his argument?

3. Where does he use facts to support his point of view?

4. Why does King mention so many southern states by name?

5. In what parts of this address does the speaker appeal to his audience's values?

6. Where does he appeal to the self-interest of the African-Americans in his audience?

7. Where does he appeal to the self-interest of whites?

8. The speaker uses parallelism to evoke our emotions. Find examples of this rhetorical technique. If necessary, review what you learned about parallelism in Chapter 5.

9. Find several figures of speech, and explain how they help King achieve his purpose.
10. King addresses two sets of opposing arguments in this speech. Explain how he does this.

Thinking Critically

1. Reread paragraphs 2 and 3. Explain the extended metaphors used in them.
2. Turn back to Chapter 5 in this book, and read Lincoln's Gettysburg Address. Pay particular attention to the word "hallowed," used in paragraph 2 of that document. This is the same word King uses in paragraph 4 here. What other similarities can you identify in these two addresses?
3. Who is King's audience? Is it only the 200,000 people assembled at the Lincoln Memorial?

Suggestions for Journal Entries

1. Have we made progress in guaranteeing the civil rights of minorities since Dr. King spoke these words? Make a list of the most important advances. Start by reviewing "I Have a Dream" and deciding if the wrongs mentioned there have been dealt with. You might want to do some Internet research on the history of the American civil rights movement—as already suggested in Preparing to Read—to gather facts. You might also want to interview a professor of history, literature, or government at your college to find out more about this question.
2. Do you have your own dream for the world? What major problem affecting the United States or another country would you like to see solved in the next few decades? Perhaps you might address poverty, illiteracy, drug abuse, or teenage pregnancy in America, the AIDS epidemic in Africa, or famine in any of several parts of the world.

   Again you might have to do some library or Internet research or interview a professor who is knowledgeable about the issue you are addressing.

In-State College Tuition for Illegal Immigrants: Opposing Views

"In-State Tuition for Children of Illegal Migrants?" by the Editors of Utah's Daily Herald

"An Unfair Reward for Illegal Immigrants" by Kerry Healey

"Educating Illegal Immigrants" by Todd Rosenbaum

Offering in-state tuition rates to illegal immigrants has become a major point of controversy in the larger debate over illegal immigration. The three essays that follow represent three different opinions: The editors of the Daily Herald, *which serves central Utah, believe that in-state tuition should be available to illegal immigrants. Kerry Healey, formen lieutenant governor of Massachusetts, disagrees. Todd Rosenbaum, a student who writes an opinion column for the University of Virginia's* Cavalier Daily, *offers a compromise.*

Preparing to Read

1. Section 505 of the U.S. Immigration Reform Act of 1996 prohibits the extension of in-state tuition rates to illegal immigrants attending public colleges and universities. Nonetheless, several states, including California, Texas, New York, and Utah, now offer illegal aliens in-state tuition, with many more considering their own bills to subsidize tuitions for illegal immigrants, despite the federal law against it. In fact, in 2003, two U.S. senators introduced the Development, Relief, and Education for Alien Minors (DREAM) Act, which would, in essence, overturn Section 505 and allow states to offer in-state tuition to students regardless of their immigration status.

2. All three essays appeal to the reader by establishing common ground, as recommended in Rogerian model. Identify places where they do this as you read each essay.

3. The essay originally published in the *Daily Herald* was an editorial; editorials often use short—even one-sentence—paragraphs.

Vocabulary

counterintuitive (adjective)	Illogical, unreasonable.
exposures (noun)	Risks.
impeccable (adjective)	Without a flaw.
plaintiffs (noun)	People who file a lawsuit.
prerogative (noun)	Privilege.
spurious (adjective)	False, counterfeit.
starkly (adverb)	Extremely.
ubiquitous (adjective)	Found everywhere, omnipresent.
viable (adjective)	Useful, effective, practical.

In-State Tuition for Children of Illegal Migrants?

Editors of Utah's Daily Herald

IN 2002, the Utah State Legislature agreed to charge in-state tuition to the 1
children of some illegal immigrants. Utah was one of four states that had the
rule, and Congress was considering it under the Dream Act.

Now, a Utah lawmaker is seeking to undo that and raise the cost of educa- 2
tion for the immigrants' children.

Rep. Glenn Donnelson, R-North Ogden, claims the tuition policy violates 3
federal law by giving illegal immigrants an educational benefit that is not available to all U.S. citizens. A group of out-of-state students at the University of
Utah are threatening to sue the state because they are charged non-resident
rates while illegal immigrants in Utah pay the lower in-state rate.

House Bill 7 awaits a vote in the full House of Representatives. The House 4
should scrap the bill as an unjust act against innocent people.

Allowing illegal immigrants to get in-state tuition was not the idea of a 5
wild-eyed liberal. The original legislation was sponsored by Rep. David Ure,
R-Kamas, a man with impeccable conservative credentials. Ure argued at the
time it was a matter of fairness. He said there were some Utahns who could not
go to college because they happened to be the children of illegal immigrants.
In some cases, the children were unaware of their parents' immigration status.

Our legal system does not believe in punishing children for the crimes of 6
their fathers or mothers. Many of the students affected by the law were brought
into the country as small children or infants who had no say in whether they
wanted to make the trip. But they ended up being residents of Utah.

If not for their parents' status as illegal immigrants, these children would 7
be entitled to in-state tuition. They've gone through Utah's public education
system, worked at Utah jobs and paid Utah taxes.

The tuition law is hardly a perk that would encourage more illegal im- 8
migrants to come to Utah. The students seeking to take advantage of it must

go to school in Utah for three years, graduate from a Utah high school and be actively working toward U.S. citizenship.

Anyone who thinks becoming a U.S citizen is easy is not an immigrant. 9 Aside from having five years' residency, potential U.S. citizens must show good character, submit to being photographed, fingerprinted and interviewed, as well as take a test on the English language and U.S. civics. The civics test, those who have taken it say, would challenge many native-born Americans' knowledge of U.S. history, of how their government works and of what's contained in the Constitution.

To get a taste of what the test is like, go to http://uscis.gov/graphics/exec/ 10 natz/natztest.asp and try some sample questions. It's no freebie, as H.B. 7's proponents claim.

The bars have been plenty high enough to limit the number of people who 11 actually take advantage of the discounted tuition rule. In the 2004–05 school year, only 169 children of immigrants applied for in-state tuition, hardly the flood of illegal immigrants that critics suggest.

The argument that the immigrant children are getting a benefit that U.S. 12 citizens are not eligible for is spurious. Utah does not have to give in-state tuition to people who live in Wyoming, California or New York. The immigrants who are applying for this are Utah residents.

The law also helps Utah by allowing a segment of its population to break 13 the poverty cycle and gain higher-paying jobs. People with education are less likely to require welfare services or go to prison.

Utah should not abandon its current policy. It should not punish the 14 innocent.

An Unfair Reward for Illegal Immigrants

By Kerry Healey

AMERICA IS A nation of immigrants, but equally so, America is also a nation 1 of laws.

I support legal immigration. Every year we open our doors to 35,000 legal 2 noncitizens. In Massachusetts, our total foreign-born population is close to 1 million people. Our nation was built by men and women seeking a better life. In America, if you play by the rules, if you work hard, you are limited only by your dreams. But, unfortunately, not everyone comes here legally. There are some foreigners who arrive on our shores without going through the normal channels. As much as we may sympathize with their desire to be here, they are violating federal law.

A bill currently being considered by the Legislature would provide in- 3 state tuition at our public colleges and university to individuals who are in the United States illegally. That is wrong. Because a family breaks the law, that should not entitle them to a taxpayer subsidy. Enactment of this legislation would encourage more illegal immigration and send the wrong message to those immigrants who played by the rules. Governor Romney vetoed a similar provision last June, and he is prepared to do so again.

For the University of Massachusetts, the difference between out-of-state 4 and in-state tuition is about $9,000. If, as some claim, there are 400 illegal immigrants who would attend UMass if this bill became law, the cost to the taxpayers would be $14.4 million over four years. This is money that would be better spent helping our legal immigrant community acquire the English skills they need to be productive members of our workforce. The waiting list is long for people trying to get into English as a second language classes. Clearing that waiting list has been a priority of the Romney-Healey administration.

There are other financial exposures. Kansas, which extended in-state 5 tuition to illegal aliens, is being sued in federal court by out-of-state residents seeking to pay in-state tuition rates. The plaintiffs argue that any state benefit made available to illegal immigrants must be offered to legal residents of the other 49 states. Kansas Attorney General Phil Kline rightly said the granting of benefits to illegal immigrants "rewards illegal activity" and recused himself so he wouldn't have to defend the policy in court. If this same bill were to become law over Governor Romney's veto, we can expect similar litigation here in Massachusetts. The result could be either an end to in-state tuition for all Massachusetts residents or a dramatic increase in the cost of public higher education for the taxpayers.

This bill does not fix a problem; it compounds an existing one. It makes no 6 sense for Massachusetts taxpayers to bear the cost of a college education for an illegal immigrant when that same immigrant cannot legally work in the United States and contribute to our economy after graduation.

America continues to be a beacon of freedom and opportunity, welcoming 7 people from around the world. We are all the sons and daughters of immigrants who came here to realize the American dream, but we must insist that immigrants follow the law and immigrate legally. Similarly, elected officials must be reminded, too, that we all took an oath to protect and uphold the Constitution and the law of the land. To do less would be a violation of that oath.

Educating Illegal Immigrants

Todd Rosenbaum

IMAGINE THAT you're a 20-year-old University student—this should be a rela- 1 tively easy exercise for many of you. You've got the entire world at your feet, a wealth of opportunities which are not afforded to those without a college degree. Now imagine that you're suddenly forced to withdraw from school because you can no longer afford tuition. Suddenly, all of those opportunities you had a split-second ago vanish. If only you were granted in-state tuition, you could afford to stay. But you're not, and here's the clincher: You've lived in Virginia for the past 10 years.

Sadly, this is reality for many students who reside in the Commonwealth. 2 They are the sons and daughters of illegal immigrants, who came to the United States as children with no say in their destinies. And a few Virginia lawmakers are doing all they can to make it difficult for them to enroll in Virginia's public colleges and universities. By not extending in-state tuition to these students, most of them are effectively barred from attending our public institutions of higher education because they cannot afford to. As non-U.S. citizens, they do not qualify for student loans or grants. Chances for them to improve their own situations are starkly limited.

It should not be our lawmakers' prerogative to discriminate against them 3 because of their parents' decisions. Instead, they should focus on helping young illegal immigrants in Virginia to establish legal status. This also means affording them opportunities which will allow them to develop as productive and responsible members of our society.

Comforted by our ubiquitous diversity statements and anti-discrimination 4 clauses, we are often fooled into thinking that discrimination like this no longer exists in the United States. But some Virginia lawmakers have tried unsuccessfully in the past to ban outright the enrollment of illegal immigrants in the Commonwealth's institutions of higher education. Now, they are seeking to keep most illegal immigrants out of our colleges and universities by ensuring that in-state tuition rates are never extended to them. Federal statute backs this discriminatory attitude: states are forbidden to extend higher-education benefits to students who reside here illegally, if the benefits are not extended to all non-U.S. citizens. Any state law that violates this statute would require a successful legal challenge in federal court in order to be upheld.

But why should we extend these benefits to those who have chosen 5 to disregard our immigration laws? Again, young illegal immigrants rarely make the choice to immigrate on their own. More importantly, there is also federal constitutional precedent for affording illegal immigrants educational benefits.

A 1982 Supreme Court case ensured that those residing in the United 6 States are able to attend public primary and secondary schools regardless of their legal statuses. Many of the students who have benefited from that decision are now graduating from our nation's public high schools—fully capable of excelling in college, but unable to afford to do so. Many of them have taken steps towards naturalization and are awaiting approval, which can take years. Others are unable to afford the application costs which accompany the naturalization process. Returning to their countries of origin, after having made so much educational progress, is hardly a viable option.

At the same time, lawmakers must be sensitive to how a law which extends 7 in-state tuition to illegal immigrants residing in the Commonwealth could impact its general policy on who qualifies for in-state rates. Offering reduced tuition for undocumented residents of the state could legally bind Virginia to extend in-state rates to all out-of-state students, hardly a realistic option.

A compromise worthy of attention has been proposed by state Sen. 8 Emmett W. Hanger Jr., R-Mount Solon, which would not extend in-state tuition to illegal immigrants in general, but would make an exception for those who have a history in the Commonwealth. For example, graduating from high school here, belonging to a family that pays taxes and is actively seeking legal residency could together form acceptable criteria. According to the *Washington Post*, this could allow up to a few thousand illegal immigrants who reside in Virginia a chance to attend college here.

For those who worry about illegal immigrants' drain on our state and 9 national resources, it seems counterintuitive to oppose such legislation. In the long-term, allowing these immigrants improved access to higher education is likely to improve their contributions to our society and reduce the burdens they place on it. It will only aid us to help those who are willing and eager to improve their own situations to do so.

Read More on the Web

"An Illegal Advantage" by Peter Kirsanow of the *National Review Online*: http://article.nationalreview.com/?q= OTUyNzg5YWFiZDU5NjU4ZjY0ZTUyMDMwZWM4NTQ5YzY=

"Legally Educate Illegals"—*Palm Beach Post* editorial: http://www. palmbeachpost.com/opinion/content/opinion/epaper/2006/04/29/ a14a_immigtuition_edit_0429.html

"NCLR Applauds the Reintroduction of the Dream Act"—News Release of the National Council of La Raza: http://www.nclr.org/content/ news/detail/2377

Standing Up for Immigrant Students—by the Editors of *Rethinking Schools Online*: http://www.rethinkingschools.org/archive/18_02/ stan182.shtml

"Taxpayers Should Not Subsidize College for Illegal Aliens"—posting of the Federation for American Immigration Reform: http://www.fairus. org/site/PageServer?pagename=iicimmigrationissuecenters6be3

"Why Illegal Immigrants Should Not Receive Tuition Subsidies" by Dan Stein, Executive Director of the Federation for American Immigration Reform: http://www.findarticles.com/p/articles/mi_ m0LSH/is_3_5/ai_95447605

Questions for Discussion

1. Where do the editors of the *Daily Herald* state their thesis? Where does Healey state hers?

2. Why does Rosenbaum put his thesis near the end of his essay?

3. The *Daily Herald* editorial seems to appeal to our sense of fairness, while Healey seems to appeal to our sense of justice. Explain the difference.

4. How would you characterize Rosenbaum's approach? Does he appeal to fairness, to justice, or to both?

5. Find instances in which all three articles use language that appeals to our emotions. Evaluate the fairness with which each of these pieces uses that language.

6. Comment on the success with which all three essays address opposing arguments. Do they treat the opposition fairly? In each case, does the author's dismissal of opposing arguments strengthen or weaken his or her own credibility.

7. Explain how the authors of all three pieces establish their authority to talk about this issue.

8. Healey's article first appeared in the *Boston Globe*, a newspaper read throughout Massachusetts. Does her essay appeal to the readers' self-interest? Where? Do the other two essays do this?

9. In paragraph 4, Healey says that money saved by not extending in-state tuition to illegal immigrants could be better spent on helping immigrants learn English. Does this strengthen or weaken her essay?

10. What method does Rosenbaum use to introduce his essay? What purpose does it serve? How does it differ from what we see in the other two pieces?

Thinking Critically

1. In a short paragraph, summarize the *logical arguments and evidence* that the editors of the *Daily Herald* use to persuade readers that in-state tuition should be granted to illegal immigrants. Now do the same for the positions put forth by Healey and Rosenbaum.

2. The three essays discuss various bills pending in the legislatures of three states: Utah, Massachusetts, and Virginia. Summarize what each law proposes.

Suggestions for Journal Entries

1. In preparation for writing an essay on extending in-state tuition to illegal immigrants, use focused freewriting to explain why you agree or disagree with the compromise put forth in Rosenbaum's essay.

2. Find and read the material listed under Read More on the Web. Take notes on information and ideas that will later help you write an essay expressing your own opinion about extending in-state tuition to illegal immigrants.

Suggestions for Sustained Writing

1. Write an essay that tries to persuade your readers that working more than 15 hours a week while pursuing a full-time academic career is reasonable. You might explain that working longer hours is necessary if you are to pay your expenses. You might also explain that some full-time students are so organized or talented that they can handle more than 15 hours of work. If this idea does not interest you, write an open letter to your fellow students trying to persuade them to adopt a particular behavior or attitude concerning an issue important to them. For example, offer advice on time or stress management, persuade them to change their study habits, encourage their participation in community service, or warn them about the dangers of alcohol abuse. If you responded to either of the journal suggestions after Palmieri's essay, look over the notes you made before you begin this assignment.

   Another alternative is to write an essay in which you try to persuade your fellow students to devote 100 percent of their time to school and to quit even the least demanding part-time job. Of course, you will have to suggest alternative sources of income—such as scholarships, loans, and other types of financial aid—that students might tap to pay tuition and living expenses.

   Like Palmieri, try to support your arguments with the testimony of experts and present your arguments logically. However, remember that this is a persuasive assignment. Use language that will appeal to your fellow students' pride, self-interest, and emotions. Try to rouse them if you can! In addition, however, make sure to raise and to address opposing arguments. If you are using researched materials, credit your sources with internal citations, as Palmieri did, and include a list of works cited. More information on how to do this can be found on the website for this book (www.mhhe.com/rcw). It discusses documentation principles used by the Modern Language Association.

2. Look back to the journal notes you made after reading Dr. King's "I Have a Dream." Whether you responded to item 1 or 2 in the Suggestions for Journal Entries, expand your notes into a persuasive address that you might deliver to a large group of people if you had the opportunity.

    If you responded to item 1, you might be satisfied by relating the progress the United States has made in the decades since Dr. King spoke at the Lincoln Memorial. In the process, you could take the position that we have done enough in this area, and that further measures will simply be redundant and even counterproductive. Then again, you might argue that not enough has been done, and you could persuade your listeners that we need to take additional steps to assure everyone's civil rights. However you approach this question, try to be as specific and detailed as you can, relying on library or Internet research and/or using information you have acquired through interviews with faculty members on your campus.

    If you responded to item 2, write a speech in which you try to persuade your listeners to support measures to solve a serious problem that threatens our people, society, culture, or environment or that affects the people, environment, or society of another part of the world. Again, be as specific and detailed as you can and rely on research.

3. Read the notes you made in response to the two Suggestions for Journal Entries after "In-State College Tuition for Illegal Immigrants." If you haven't completed both items, do so now. Next, write a preliminary thesis statement that expresses your opinion on this issue. You might take a position similar to the one expressed in the *Daily Herald* editorial (pro) or one similar to the views of Lieutenant Governor Kerry Healey (con). Then, again, you might take a middle stance.

    As you begin your essay, address it to intelligent readers who have some knowledge of the topic. However, don't hesitate to provide background material that might make your position clearer. For example, mention that federal law now prohibits the extension of in-state tuition to illegal immigrants but that several states have ignored that statute. In your first draft, draw opinions and information from your own experiences or personal knowledge, but also try to use material from all three of the essays included under "In-State College Tuition for Illegal Immigrants." As you revise your paper, you can even include more material found in sources such as those under Read More on the Web.

    This is not an easy assignment, so take your time. Remember to appeal to the readers' sense of fairness and justice as well as to their self-interest. In addition, make sure to address opposing viewpoints. After you are convinced that you have presented your case as persuasively as you can, make sure to edit and proofread. Mistakes in grammar and the like can severely weaken your credibility.

4. Write an essay in which you try to persuade the people in charge at your college, your place of worship, your workplace, or your town to change a particular policy that is now in effect or to solve a problem. For example, you might ask the college to lower the maximum number of students in a class or to revise the current system by which students evaluate faculty. Then again, you might ask your boss to provide better creature comforts at work, suggesting that free coffee be provided during breaks, that employee restrooms be better cleaned and maintained, and that the workplace be heated, cooled, and ventilated more effectively.

    As you write your rough draft, include information that explains just what needs fixing or changing. For example, if writing to the college president, you might claim that last semester your chemistry lecture was so crowded that some students could not find seats. If writing to your boss, you might explain that employees often opt to use the nearby filling station's restroom rather than to risk contracting a disease in your company's toilet.

    In your second draft, use some of the persuasive techniques you read about earlier. For example, appeal to your boss's self-interest by explaining that a clean restroom means improved employee morale, which then translates into a more efficient workforce. As you revise and edit, make sure you have included language that, while reasonable and fair, might appeal to the reader's emotions and sense of fair play.

Writing to Learn: A Group Activity

In the introduction to this chapter (page 522), you saw a cartoon relating to the controversy over reciting the Pledge of Allegiance in public schools. According to people who have filed suit against reciting the Pledge, the words "under God" added to it in the 1950s violate part of the First Amendment to the U.S. Constitution: "Congress shall make no law respecting an establishment of religion." However, the First Amendment is even better known for its protection of free speech. "Congress shall make no law . . . abridging the freedom of speech or of the press."

Although seemingly simple the First Amendment has been the subject of various interpretations and much debate. What's your opinion? Should we protect freedom of expression no matter what the circumstances, who is involved, or what the consequences?

THE FIRST MEETING
Brainstorm a list of circumstances or situations that might cause you to argue for limiting free speech. The classic example was put forth by

Supreme Court Justice Oliver Wendell Holmes. The First Amendment, he argued, does not protect one from falsely shouting "Fire!" in a crowded theater, for doing so would cause panic and endanger lives. More recently, the courts ruled child pornography illegal. However, other restrictions of the freedom of expression are still being debated. Here are some you might use to start brainstorming a list of your own:

Regulating the content of the Internet.

Censoring or rating radio and television shows.

Regulating or rating films, CDs, or other entertainment products.

Enforcing criteria for what is shown, displayed, or performed in public places such as city museums, train stations, public squares, municipal buildings, or public schools.

Setting criteria for what public libraries put on their shelves.

Writing policies or codes governing speech on college campuses.

After you have brainstormed a list of your own issues (include those above if you like), assign each student the task of researching one particular topic. Ask him or her to find information and opinions on both sides of the issue.

RESEARCH

Search the Internet as well as print and online periodical indexes for articles on your topic published in the last five or six years. Bring your notes and photocopies of pages from sources to the next meeting. For general information on the First Amendment, try the American Civil Liberties Union website on the Internet (http://www.aclu.org).

THE SECOND MEETING

Distribute copies of articles students have read and notes they have taken. Make sure each has gathered information on both sides of his or her topic. After the group has read these materials, debate the pros and cons of each question and, if possible, take a group stand or position on it. (Ask each student to take notes on the group's discussion of the question he or she researched.)

Before closing the meeting, ask everyone to write one or two paragraphs explaining both sides of his or her issue and stating the group's position on it. Encourage him or her to incorporate both researched information and the opinions of fellow group members. Finally, remind everyone to bring copies of this work to the next meeting.

(continued)

THE THIRD MEETING

Distribute, read, and critique each other's writing; offer suggestions for revision. Ask one student to collect the final versions of everyone's work and use them in a draft of a complete paper that takes positions on the free-speech questions members of your group researched. If possible, have a second student write the introduction and the conclusion to this paper.

THE FOURTH MEETING

Distribute and read the draft of the paper. Make last-minute suggestions for revision. Ask a third student to edit the paper and a fourth to type and proofread it.

abstract language   Words that represent ideas rather than things we can see, hear, smell, feel, or taste. The word *love* is abstract, but the word *kiss* is concrete because we can perceive it with one or more of our five senses. (See Chapter 4.)

allusion   A passing reference to a person, place, event, thing, or idea with which the reader may be familiar. Allusions can be used to add detail, clarify important points, or set the tone of an essay, a poem, or a short story.

analogy   A method by which a writer points out similarities between two things that, on the surface, seem quite different. Analogies are most often used to make abstract or unfamiliar ideas clearer and more concrete. Chapters 2 and 3 contain examples of analogy.

anecdote   A brief, sometimes humorous story used to illustrate or develop a specific point. (See Chapter 8.)

argument   A type of writing that relies on logic and concrete evidence to prove a point or support an opinion. (See Chapter 12.)

central idea   The idea that conveys a writer's main point about a subject. It may be stated explicitly or implied. Also known as the *main idea* or *controlling idea,* it determines the kinds and amount of detail needed to develop a piece of writing adequately. (See Chapter 1.)

chronological order   The arrangement of material in order of time. (See Chapter 7.)

coherence   The principle that writers observe in making certain that there are logical connections between the ideas and details in one sentence or paragraph and those in the next. (See Chapter 2.)

conclusion   A paragraph or series of paragraphs that ends an essay. Conclusions often restate the writer's central idea or summarize important points used to develop that idea. (See Chapter 3.) A conclusion can also be defined as a principle, opinion, or belief a writer supports or defends by using convincing information. (See Chapters 2 and 12.)

concrete language   Words that represent material things—things we can perceive with our five senses. (See *abstract language* above, and see Chapter 4.)

coordination   A technique used to express ideas of equal importance in the same sentence. To this end, writers often use compound sentences, which are composed of two independent (main) clauses connected with a coordinating conjunction. "Four students earned scholarships, but only three accepted them" is a compound sentence. (See Chapter 5.)

deduction   A kind of reasoning used to build an argument. Deductive thinking draws conclusions by applying specific cases or examples to general principles, rules, or ideas. You would be thinking deductively if you wrote: "All students must pay tuition. I am a student. Therefore, I must pay tuition." (See Chapter 12.)

details   Specific facts or pieces of information that a writer uses to develop ideas.

emphasis   The placing of stress on important ideas by controlling sentence structure through coordination, subordination, and parallelism. (See Chapter 5.)

figurative language (figures of speech)   Words or phrases that explain abstract ideas by comparing them to concrete realities the reader will recognize easily. Analogy, metaphor, simile, and personification are types of figurative language. (See Chapter 4.)

image   A verbal picture made up of sensory details. It expresses a general idea's meaning clearly and concretely. (See Chapter 4.)

induction   A kind of reasoning used to build an argument. Inductive thinking draws general conclusions from specific facts or pieces of evidence. If you heard the wind howling, saw the sky turning black, and spotted several ominous clouds on the horizon, you might rightly conclude by induction that a storm was on its way. (See Chapter 12.)

introduction   A paragraph or series of paragraphs that begins an essay. It often contains a writer's central idea in the form of a thesis statement. (See Chapter 3.)

irony   A technique used by writers to communicate the very opposite of what their words mean. Irony is often used to create humor. An effective example of irony can be found in Milden's "So You Want to Flunk Out of College," which appears in the introduction to Chapter 10.

linking pronouns   Pronouns that make reference to nouns that have come before (antecedents). They are one of the ways to maintain coherence in and between paragraphs. (See Chapter 2.)

main point   The point that a writer focuses on in a thesis or topic sentence. (See Chapter 1.)

metaphor   A figure of speech that, like a simile, creates a comparison between two things to make the explanation of one of them clearer. Unlike a simile, a metaphor does not use *like* or *as*. "The man is a pig" is a metaphor. (See Chapter 4.)

parallelism   A method to express facts and ideas of equal importance in the same sentence and thereby to give them added emphasis. Sentences that are parallel express items of equal importance in the same grammatical form. (See Chapter 5.)

personification   A figure of speech that writers use to discuss animals, plants, and inanimate objects in terms normally associated with human beings: for example, "Our neighborhoods are the *soul* of the city." (See Chapter 4.)

persuasion   A type of writing that supports an opinion, proves a point, or convinces the reader to act. (See Chapters 2 and 13.)

point of view   The perspective from which a narrative is told. Stories that use the first-person point of view are told by a narrator who is involved in the action and who uses words such as *I, me,* and *we* to explain what happened. Stories that use the third-person point of view are told by a narrator who may or may not be involved in the action and who uses words such as *he, she,* and *they* to explain what happened. (See Chapter 7.)

simile   A figure of speech that, like a metaphor, compares two things for the sake of clarity and emphasis. Unlike a metaphor, however, a simile uses *like* or *as.* "Samantha runs like a deer" is a simile. (See Chapter 4.)

subordination   A technique used to emphasize one idea over another by expressing the more important idea in the sentence's main clause and the other in its subordinate clause. (See Chapter 5.)

syllogism   The logical structure through which a writer uses deduction. To create a syllogism, a writer makes a general statement, then applies a specific case or example to that statement, and then draws a limited conclusion from the two. You would be using deduction in a syllogism if you wrote:

> **general statement:**   All lifeguards must know how to swim.
> **specific case:**   Marvin does not know how to swim.
> **conclusion:**   Marvin cannot be a lifeguard.

thesis statement   A clear and explicit statement of an essay's central idea. It often appears in an introductory paragraph but is sometimes found later in the essay. (See Chapter 1.)

topic sentence   A clear and explicit statement of a paragraph's central idea. (See Chapter 1.)

transitions (connectives)   Words or phrases used to make clear and direct connections between sentences and paragraphs, thereby maintaining coherence. (See Chapter 2.)

unity   The principle that writers observe in making certain that all the information in an essay or paragraph relates directly to the central idea, which is often expressed in a thesis statement or topic sentence. (See Chapter 2.)

ACKNOWLEDGMENTS

Albrecht, Ernest. From "Sawdust" by Ernest Albrecht. Reprinted by permission of the author.

America: The National Catholic Weekly. From editorial, "Innocence and the Death Penalty," *America: The National Catholic Weekly,* Vol. 192, No. 4, February 7, 2005. Copyright © 2005. All rights reserved. Reprinted with permission of America Press.

America: The National Catholic Weekly. From editorial, "Refugees: Darfur and Beyond," *America: The National Catholic Weekly,* Vol. 191, No. 4, August 16, 2004. Copyright © 2004. All rights reserved. Reprinted with permission of America Press.

Aronowitz, Paul. "A Brother's Dreams," *The New York Times Magazine,* January 24, 1988. Copyright © 1988, Paul Aronowitz. Reprinted with permission.

Barlow, Dudley. "Melting Pot or Tossed Salad?" Reprinted from *The Education Digest,* March 1996, Ann Arbor, MI. Reprinted with permission.

Barry, Dave. "Florida's Fire Ants Headed for Trouble," *Miami Herald,* May 4, 2003. Copyright © Tribune Media Services, Inc. All Rights Reserved. Reprinted with permission.

Barry, Dave. From "We Interrupt This Column," *The Miami Herald,* May, 7, 1989. Copyright © Tribune Media Services, Inc. All Rights Reserved. Reprinted with permission.

Bennett, William J. Reprinted with the permission of Simon & Schuster Adult Publishing Group from *The De-Valuing of America* by William J. Bennett. Copyright © 1992 William J. Bennett.

Blankenhorn, David. From *Fatherless America: Confronting Our Most Urgent Social Problems* by David Blankenhorn. Copyright © 1995 by Institute for American Values. Reprinted by permission of Basic Books, a member of Perseus Books Group.

Brown, Larry. From *On Fire* by Larry Brown. Copyright © 1993 by Larry Brown. Reprinted by permission of Algonquin Books of Chapel Hill.

Brownback, Sam. "All Human Cloning Is Wrong." First appeared in *USA Today,* January 3, 2003. Reprinted by permission of Senator Sam Brownback.

Callaghan, Alice. "Desperate to Learn English," *New York Times,* August 15, 1997. Reprinted by permission of the author.

Cannon, Angie. "Jeffrey Dahmer, Cannibal," *U.S. News & World Report,* December 6, 1999. Copyright © 1999 U.S. News & World Report, L.P. Reprinted with permission.

Chelminski, Rudy. "The Curse of Count Dracula" by Rudy Chelminski. Copyright © 2003 by Rudy Chelminski. Originally appeared in *Smithsonian,* April 2003. Reprinted by permission of the author.

Ciardi, John. From "Dawn Watch" from *Manner of Speaking* by John Ciardi. New Brunswick, NJ: Rutgers University Press, 1972. By permission of the Ciardi Family Trust, John L. Ciardi, Trustee.

Cowley, Malcolm. "The View from 80" by Malcolm Cowley as appeared in *Life,* December 1978. Reprinted by permission of the Estate of Malcolm Cowley.

Cutforth, René. From "Padre Blaisdell and the Refugee Children" from *Korean Reporter* by René Cutforth. London: Allan Wingate, 1952. Reprinted by permission of Sheila Cutforth.

Daily Herald. Editorial, "In-State Tuition for Children of Illegal Migrants?" *Daily Herald,* February 10, 2006. Reprinted by permission of the Daily Herald, Provo, Utah.

Daly, Christopher B. "How the Lawyers Stole Winter." Copyright © 1995 Christopher B. Daly, as first published in *The Atlantic Monthly.*

Dowling, Claudia Glenn. "Fire in the Sky," *LIFE Magazine,* December 1994. Copyright 1994 Life Inc. Reprinted with permission. All rights reserved.

Epstein, Joseph. From "The Perpetual Adolescent and the Triumph of the Youth Culture," *The Weekly Standard,* Vol. 9, Issue 26, March 15, 2004. Reprinted by permission of The Weekly Standard.

Ericson, Edward E. From "Gen X Is OK, Part 1," *The American Enterprise,* January/February 1998. Reprinted by permission of the author.

Fox, Stephen. Excepted from Stephen Fox, "The Education of Branch Rickey," *Civilization* Magazine, September/October 1995. Copyright © 1995 Stephen Fox. Reprinted by permission of the author and his agent, Robin Straus Agency, Inc.

Fu, Shen C. Y. Reprinted, with permission, from "A Closer Look at Chinese Calligraphy." Copyright, Freer Gallery of Art and Arthur M. Sackler Gallery, Smithsonian Institution. All rights reserved.

Gansburg, Martin. "37 Who Saw Murder Didn't Call the Police," *New York Times,* March 27, 1964. Copyright © 1964 by The New York Times Co. Reprinted with permission.

Goodheart, Adam. "How to Fight a Duel" by Adam Goodheart. Reprinted by permission from the May/June 1996 issue of *Civilization.*

Hamill, Pete. From *A Drinking Life* by Pete Hamill. Copyright © 1994 by Deidre Enterprises, Inc. By permission of Little, Brown and Co.

Harris, Sydney. "How to Keep Air Clean," from *For the Time Being* by Sydney J. Harris. Copyright © 1972 by Sydney J. Harris. Copyright © 1969, 1970, 1971, 1972 by Publishers-Hall Syndicate. Reprinted by permission of Houghton Mifflin Company. All rights reserved.

Hayden, Robert. "Those Winter Sundays." Copyright © 1966 by Robert Hayden, from *Collected Poems of Robert Hayden* by Robert Hayden, edited by Frederick Glaysher. Used by permission of Liveright Publishing Corporation.

Healy, Bernadine. From "Mother Nature, Terrorist," *U.S. News & World Report,* January 10, 2005. Copyright © 2005 U.S. News & World Report, L.P. Reprinted with permission.

Heaney, Seamus. "Mid-Term Break" from *Opened Ground: Selected Poems 1966-1996* by Seamus Heaney. Copyright © 1998 by Seamus Heaney. Reprinted by permission of Farrar, Straus and Giroux, LLC., and Faber and Faber Ltd.

Hentoff, Nat. "Free Speech on Campus." Copyright © 1989 by Nat Hentoff. Reprinted by permission of the author. Nat Hentoff is a columnist/author for *The Village Voice* and United Media Newspaper Syndicate.

Herman, Marc. From "Searching for El Dorado," *Civilization* magazine, June/July 1997. Reprinted by permission of the author.

Howard, Philip K. From *The Death of Common Sense* by Philip K. Howard. Copyright © 1994 by Philip K. Howard. Used by permission of Random House, Inc.

Howe, Robert F. "Covert Force," *Smithsonian,* October 2002. Copyright © 2002 by Robert F. Howe. Reprinted by permission of the author.

Hughes, Langston. "Harlem (2)," copyright © 1951 by Langston Hughes, from *The Collected Poems of Langston Hughes* by Langston Hughes. Used by permission of Alfred A. Knopf, a division of Random House, Inc.

Ichimaru, Michito. "Nagasaki," August 9, 1945.

King, Jr., Martin Luther. "I Have a Dream." Reprinted by arrangement with The Heirs to the Estate of Martin Luther King Jr., c/o Writers House as agent for the proprietor New York, NY. Copyright © 1963 Martin Luther King Jr., copyright renewed 1991 © Coretta Scott King.

Kozol, Jonathan. From "The Human Cost of an Illiterate Society" from *Illiterate America* by Jonathan Kozol. Copyright © 1985 by Jonathan Kozol. Used by permission of Doubleday, a division of Random House, Inc.

Laurence, Margaret. From "Where the World Began." From *Heart of a Stranger,* University of Alberta Press, 2003, McClelland & Stewart, 1976. Copyright © 1976 Margaret Laurence. With permission.

Lederer, Richard. Reprinted with the permission of Atria Books, an imprint of Simon & Schuster Adult Publishing Group. From *Crazy English: The Ultimate Joy Ride Through Our Language* by Richard Lederer. Copyright © 1989 Richard Lederer.

Louv, Richard. "Skinwalkers," excerpted from *The Web of Life: Weaving the Values That Sustain Us* by Richard Louv, with permission of Conari Press, imprint of Red Wheel/Weiser. To order call 1-800-423-7087.

Wall Street Journal. From editorial, "Affirmative Reaction," *The Wall Street Journal,* April 20, 1995, p. A12. Copyright 1995 by Dow Jones & Company, Inc. Reproduced with permission of Dow Jones & Company, Inc. in the format textbook via Copyright Clearance Center.

Welch, Matt. "They Shoot Helicopters, Don't They?: How Journalists Spread Rumors During Katrina," *Reason,* December 2005. Reprinted by permission of Burr Media Group, LLC.

Wellstone, Paul. From "If Poverty Is the Question..." Reprinted with permission from the April 14, 1997 issue of *The Nation.* For subscription information, call 1-800-333-8536. Portions of each week's *Nation* magazine can be accessed at http://www.thenation.com.

White, Bailey. "Fish Camp" from *Sleeping at the Starlite Motel* by Bailey White. Copyright © 1995 by Bailey White. Reprinted by permission of Da Capo Press, a member of Perseus Books Group.

Wiesel, Elie. "A Prayer for the Days of Awe," *The New York Times,* October 2, 1997. Reprinted by permission of the author.

Wong, Jade Snow. "Uncle Kwok" from *Fifth Chinese Daughter* by Jade Snow Wong. Copyright © 1950/1989 by Jade Snow Wong. Used by permission of the University of Washington Press.